Urban Planning and Real Estate Development

Third Edition

The twin processes of planning and property development are inextricably linked – it's not possible to carry out a development strategy without an understanding of the planning process, and equally planners need to know how real estate developers do their job.

This third edition of *Urban Planning and Real Estate Development* guides students through the procedural and practical aspects of developing land from the point of view of both planner and developer. The planning system is explained, from the increasing emphasis on spatial planning at a regional level down to the detailed perspective of the development control process and the specialist requirements of historic buildings and conservation areas. At the same time the authors explain the entire development process from inception through appraisal, valuation and financing to completion and disposal.

In recent years both planning and real estate development have had to become increasingly aware of their legal and moral obligations. Sustainability and corporate social responsibility and their impact on the planning and development processes are covered in detail.

Written by a team of authors with many years of academic, professional and research experience, and illustrated throughout with practical case studies, *Urban Planning and Real Estate Development* is an invaluable textbook for real estate and planning students, and helps to meet the requirements of the RICS and RTPI Assessment of Professional Competence.

John Ratcliffe is Director of the Faculty of the Built Environment, Dublin Institute of Technology, Honorary Visiting Professor at the University of Salford, and a Chartered Planning and Development Surveyor with over 35 years in practice as a Consultant.

Michael Stubbs is a Member of the Royal Town Planning Institute and Royal Institution of Chartered Surveyors. He specializes in planning work and is an Adviser to the National Trust.

Miles Keeping is a Chartered Surveyor, Research Director and Head of Sustainability at GVA Grimley, International Property Consultants.

The Natural and Built Environment Series
Editor: Professor John Glasson, Oxford Brookes University

Urban Planning and Real Estate Development

Third Edition

John Ratcliffe, Michael Stubbs
and Miles Keeping

Routledge
Taylor & Francis Group

LONDON AND NEW YORK

First edition published 1996
by UCL Press
Second edition published 2004
by Spon Press
This edition published 2009
by Routledge
2 Park Square, Milton Park, Abingdon, Oxon OX14 4RN

Simultaneously published in the USA and Canada
by Routledge
270 Madison Avenue, New York, NY 10016, USA

Routledge is an imprint of the Taylor & Francis Group,
an informa business

Typeset in 10/12pt Goudy by Graphicraft Limited, Hong Kong
Printed and bound in Great Britain by
CPI Antony Rowe, Chippenham, Wiltshire

British Library Cataloguing in Publication Data
A catalogue record for this book is available from the British Library

Library of Congress Cataloging in Publication Data
Ratcliffe, John.
Urban planning and real estate development / John Ratcliffe,
Michael Stubbs & Miles Keeping. – 3rd ed.
p. cm. – (The natural and built environment)
Includes bibliographical references and index.
1. City planning. 2. Real estate development. I. Stubbs, Michael,
1962– II. Keeping, Miles. III. Title.
HT165.5.R37 2009
307.1′216–dc22   2008020964

ISBN10: 0-415-45077-2 (hbk)
ISBN10: 0-415-45078-0 (pbk)
ISBN10: 0-203-93572-1 (ebk)

ISBN13: 978-0-415-45077-5 (hbk)
ISBN13: 978-0-415-45078-2 (pbk)
ISBN13: 978-0-203-93572-9 (ebk)

For our families
(and the staff at Cliveden who saved Mike's manuscript, July 2007)

Contents

Figures

measure of regulation and, increasingly, urban local government took control over matters of water supply, sewerage and urban layout. A series of local regulations (introduced under powers granted by the Public Health Act of 1875) afforded local control over housing layout to rule out the 'very cheap and high-density back-to-back building' typical of the Victorian slum. The grid-iron pattern of late Victorian inner suburbs (at 25 dwellings per hectare) characterized and gave physical form to this newly established regulation. Yet it was not an attempt to 'plan' whole districts and to integrate land uses but rather a further attempt to prevent the disease-ridden slum dwellings of the previous seventy-five years by provision of sanitation within, and space around, individual dwellings.

The notion of planning entire areas is perhaps best traced to the Garden City movement of the turn of the twentieth century. The 'Garden City' was something of an umbrella term, encapsulating many planning and property development principles in the quest for an environment based upon amenity or quality. Further, the Garden City represented a reaction against the squalor of the Victorian city, just as today the planning system strives to create sustainable environments as a reaction against environmental degradation.

> The Garden City idea and the movement it spawned were crucial precursors to the town planning movement in Britain.
>
> (Ward 1994)

Howard published his 'theory' of the Garden City in 1898.[2] This was based on the notion that a planned decentralized network of cities would present an alternative to the prevailing Victorian system of urban concentration. The Garden City was created on the development of four key principles. First was the finite limit to development. Each city would grow by a series of satellites of 30,000 population to a finite limit of around 260,000. A central city of 58,000 would provide specialist land uses like libraries, shops and civic functions. Each satellite would be surrounded by a greenbelt. Second, 'amenity' would be of fundamental importance so that open space and landscaping would provide valuable recreational and aesthetic benefit. Third, this pattern of development would create a topography based on the notion of a 'polycentric' (many-centred) social city with a mix of employment, leisure, residential, and educational uses within close proximity. Finally, all land would be under 'municipal control', so that the appointed Garden City Company would acquire land, allocate leasehold interests and collect rents. Initial capital to create the company would be raised from the issuing of stocks and debentures. In effect a development company would be created that would be managed by trustees, and a prescribed dividend would be paid (a percentage of all rental income to the company). Any surplus accrued would be used to build and maintain communal services like schools, parks and roads. Howard's theory has been encapsulated as a kind of non-Marxist utopian socialism (Miller 1989) seeking at the time a reform of land ownership without class conflict.

Such a theory was itself derived from a combination of sources, in particular the concept of land nationalization in the late nineteenth century. This involved the creation of social change through land ownership. Further, Howard was affected by the aesthetic ideas of socialists such as William Morris and the 'model communities' of Victorian philanthropists such as Sir Titus Salt (Saltaire, Bradford 1848–63), George Cadbury (Bournville 1894), William Lever (Port Sunlight 1888), and Sir Joseph Rowntree (Earswick, York 1905). All these projects conceived the notion of the utopian industrial suburbs to improve the conditions of the workers. Saltaire was noted for its communal buildings (schools, institute and infirmary), Bournville for its extensive landscaping and large plot size, Port Sunlight for its good-quality housing, and Earswick for its spacious layout.

In 1903 Howard embarked on the development of Letchworth in Hertfordshire, with Welwyn Garden City to follow in 1920. A Garden City company was established and remains today. The town plan showed a group of connected villages, linked to a civic centre and separated from an industrial area. The concept of 'planned neighbourhood' was born.

> Letchworth was probably the first English expression of a new town on a large scale.
>
> (Smith-Morris 1997)

Two architects previously employed at Earswick, Raymond Unwin (1863–1940) and Barry Parker (1867–1947) added design to Howard's theory, producing medium-density (30 dwellings per hectare) low-cost cottage housing in tree-lined culs-de-sac (a layout first created at Bournville). The vernacular design exhibited the strong Arts and Crafts influences of William Morris (1834–96), C.F.A.Voysey (1857–1941), Richard Norman Shaw (1831–1912) and Philip Webb (1831–1915). Morris had viewed 'the home as a setting for an enlightened life and projected its virtues outwards to embrace community' (Miller and Gray 1992). Arts and Crafts architecture emphasized the picturesque, using gables and chimneys, and reviving traditional construction, including timber framing. Raymond Unwin developed the 'local greens' (or village greens) and culs-de-sac used in Letchworth and also in Hampstead Garden Suburb (North West London).

Other schemes were to follow, notably Wythenshawe (Manchester) and Hampstead Garden Suburb. Howard had taken the rudimentary public health legislation of 1848 and 1875 and produced the 'master planning' of an entire area, based upon design innovation, affordable housing, mixed use and social ownership. Such principles are of great importance today as government policy sets out to engender an urban renaissance. A summary of developments leading to the establishment of the Garden City movement is set out in Figure 1.1.

The key principles upon which the 'model communities' of the late nineteenth century – and the Garden Cities/suburbs of early twentieth-century – were based

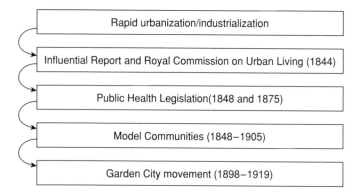

Figure 1.1 Development of the Garden City

are set out in Table 1.1. When considering the density as displayed (dwellings per hectare), it is worth comparing these data with the 1875 by-law figure of 25 dwellings per hectare and the post-war norm of between 15 and 20 dwellings per hectare. Historically, housing densities have fallen progressively over the last 125 years or so. What is perhaps most interesting is that they have fallen from the Victorian city, where overcrowding prevailed, to the low-density post-war suburbs of volume (i.e. mass-market) housebuilders. In other words, they have fallen from the insanitary to the inefficient. Up to 2000, new housing layouts were wasteful in their use of land. By comparison, Letchworth and Welwyn Garden City, as originally built, involved densities in excess of 30 dwellings per hectare yet maintained a leafy environment in which open spaces and amenities pre-dominated. Much can still be learnt from examination of environments like this in the building of pleasant medium- to high-density housing without the need for a return to the high-rise schemes of the 1960s.

So at the beginning of the twentieth century a series of urban planning experiments pointed the way forward. A statutory system lagged very far behind. The first town planning legislation (the Housing, Town Planning, etc. Act 1909)[3] introduced 'town planning schemes', which allowed councils to plan new areas, mostly for future urban extensions or suburbs – although a poor take-up resulted in only fifty-six schemes being drawn up in the first five years (by 1914). Yet in the inter-war years 'the town extension policies which had been embodied in the 1909 Act were now being implemented on a vast scale' (Ward 1994). Further legislation was enacted in 1919 with the Housing, Town Planning, etc. Act. This legislation incorporated a series of design space and density standards recom-mended by a government committee the previous year (the Tudor Walters Report) that importantly endorsed a housing model based upon Garden City densities of 12 houses per acre (30 per hectare). The Act imposed a duty on all towns in excess of 20,000 population to prepare a town planning scheme, albeit that take-up was again poor.

Table 1.1 Principles of early town planning

Place	Years	Size	Housing or population	Density and key features
Bournville	1895–1900	133 hectares	313 houses	• Density: 24 dwellings/hectare • Provision of open space and sunlight to dwellings
New Earswick	1902–1903	61 hectares	24 cottages	• First scheme designed by Parker and Unwin
Letchworth	1903–1933	1546 hectares	5000 population	• Density: 30 dwellings/hectare • Open layout of roads and houses • Cottage design of red tiles and rough cast bricks
Welwyn Garden City	1920–1934	1000 hectares	10,000 population	• Density: 30–35 dwellings/hectare • Distinct neighbourhoods
Hampstead Garden Suburb	1907–1914 and extension of 1920–1930s	96 hectares	120 houses (by 1908)	• Density: 20 dwellings/hectare • Parker and Unwin design • Enclosed spaces to create village atmosphere • Use of closes and culs-de-sac

infrastructure proposals without recourse to local authorities. Part of this procedural streamlining was a consequence of the ambitious targets for house building (in the Housing White Paper 2007) that sought up to 220,000 dwellings annually, of which 70,000 would be affordable, including 45,000 socially rented.

One area which has become the subject of an almost endless round of reviews and consultation papers is the future of planning obligations, sometimes colloquially referred to as 'planning gain'. This refers to the practice of developers contributing (in cash or kind) towards infrastructure necessary to facilitate their development. Traditionally this system has been used to finance roads and other physical infrastructure (such as open spaces, schools and sewerage facilities) as generated by planning applications. More controversially, albeit in the minority of cases, it has been used for matters unrelated to the development in question. The government was perhaps swayed into action by the Nolan Report, which reported the perception that this amounted to 'planning permissions being bought and sold' (*Standards in Public Life* 1997). Even if erroneous, this perception is damaging because it is harmful to public confidence in the system. The (2001) consultation paper argued the case for scrapping this negotiated system in favour of standardized set tariffs. Between 2001 and 2004 the government oscillated between wholesale reform of the system (the introduction of tariffs) and the concept of an upfront payment in lieu of negotiated planning obligations (referred to as the 'planning contribution' or the 'optional planning charge'). The Kate Barker review of housing supply (HM Treasury 2004) examined ways of bringing forward residential development land and arguably galvanized the government into action. In December 2005 the Chancellor of the Exchequer announced a consultation on what would be a radical departure. Tariffs were proposed, to be calculated as a development tax or levy to fund additional infrastructure. This levy on the development industry would be known as the 'Planning Gain Supplement' (PGS). It would apply to all development and would be calculated as a portion of the uplift in land value resulting from the grant of a planning permission. The consultation paper put this as a 'modest' capture of value which would allow the wider community to share in the development gains which a grant of planning permission will create (HM Treasury 2006a). Following a tirade of criticism from the development industry, these ideas were dropped in summer 2007, but replaced with a strangely similar format in the form of the 'Community Infrastructure Levy' which was incorporated into the Planning and Reform Bill (now Act), during its Parliamentary progress.

New systems of plan monitoring and production were introduced with the 2004 Act. New-style portfolios of Local Development Frameworks, comprising up to seven separate document, progressively replaced the previous and somewhat cumbersome system of Structure/Local/Unitary Development Plans. Regional planning policy was given more 'teeth' with the introduction of Regional Spatial Strategies by the Regional Assemblies, providing a spatial vision for the next twenty years and a series of development principles which the lower tier Local Development Frameworks would have to conform to.

Governments have been increasingly concerned about the lack of engagement in the planning system. A series of new participation techniques have been introduced to promote public involvement in the design stage of a planning proposal. One of these, 'Planning for Real', seeks greater community involvement in the design of planning applications (Wates 1999), the principal objective being that people become more engaged in the formulation of projects/development proposals and feel less cut off from the system. Historically, the planning system has involved the public principally in that they are 'consulted' on a planning application, i.e. they are permitted to respond to advertisements about a planning application. This provides them with one solitary avenue for voicing opposition to be considered by the local planning committee. Certain initiatives by bodies like the Prince's Foundation (2000) and a number of local authorities have set out to enable the public to become more proactive in their dealings with the planning system. The 2004 Act introduced 'Statements of Community Involvement' in which each local authority sets out a strategy for public involvement in both policy and applications. The Statement is subject to community consultation and independent scrutiny by a planning inspector. With the rise of electronic media many authorities have sought to harness the Internet to deliver various web portals to allow access to planning permission histories and submission of online consultations. The submission of electronic planning applications is increasingly commonplace and an innovation promoted by the government's impressive online planning resource, the 'Planning Portal' (www.planningportal.gov.uk). From April 2008, all planning applications are to be submitted on the same (standard) format, with increasing numbers of authorities seeking electronic submission of the forms and/or all details. Today, the system is more accessible in that the public have more methods by which to respond to new planning policy and planning applications. It remains to be seen if more people feel truly engaged in the creation of longer-term policy matters as opposed to reacting to the perceived threat of development when an application is proposed which is within or near to their home environment.

To study planning and its relationship to property development presents many challenges. One of the most demanding of these is to remain conversant with the vast amount of documentation cascading from national and local government. Combine this with the volume of proposed reforms to the system and the enormous size of the task soon becomes apparent. The Urban Task Force itself identified the importance of built-environment courses in creating inter-disciplinary graduates:

> The main emphasis should be on broader-based courses that bring the skills together with a strong emphasis on problem-solving and multi-professional teamwork.
>
> (Urban Task Force 1999)

The Task Force listed studies in property finance, urban design, environmental planning and urban management as being key foundations for all built-environment education. The inter-disciplinary and indeed multi-disciplinary nature of planning and development makes for exciting times ahead when applied to the task of achieving sustainable development and/or reviving our urban environments. The launch of the Academy for Urbanism in 2006 to promote inter-disciplinary educational training programmes (under the umbrella 'Univer-cities') will further enhance the delivery of a new syllabus exclusively focused on urban enhancement. The planning system, vested with the responsibility of delivering this change, is itself the subject of much review and reform. While sustainability and climate change remain the key issues for the next generation of professionals, we must not lose sight of the issues of democracy and public participation, which have been the hallmark of the 1947 system. Future reforms must deliver on both sustainable development patterns and reducing carbon emissions by dint of location and design, while the guiding principles that shape the system must maintain public confidence through adequate consultation and participation.

Part Two

Urban planning
organization

2 Policy and implementation of urban planning

The modern-day planning system is a post-war invention, traced to the passing of the 1947 Town and Country Planning Act, which established a comprehensive and universal system of land-use control. Then, as now, the system served the key function of balancing public and private interests. Today, the key policy objective is one of 'sustainable' development in an attempt to both mitigate and adapt to climate change, so that government planning policy seeks (by 2008) that 60 per cent of new housing is constructed on brownfield land (previously developed land), that housing density exceeds 30 dwellings per hectare (unless an exceptional case) and that development plans promote low carbon development with renewable sources accounting for 10 per cent of energy supply. Land-use change statistics have consistently reported, since the early 2000s, an increase, year on year, in the percentage of development on brownfield land and the density of new development. By 2007, and with the issuing of new national planning policy on climate change (in the 'planning and climate change' supplement to PPS1 – 'Planning Policy Statement 1'), attention has turned to achieving zero carbon development.

Government targets are established to reduce greenhouse gas emissions by 12.5 per cent of 1990 levels by 2012 and to increase the proportion of energy generated in the UK from renewable sources to 10 per cent by 2010. Planning policy has a vital role to play in the delivery of these objectives. From 2004 the planning system has a statutory requirement (in section 39 of the Planning and Compulsory Purchase Act 2004) that regionally and locally produced planning policy contributes to the achievements of sustainable development. Further, the government have included a series of detailed national policies on climate change and the planning system as a supplement to PPS1 which, amongst a series of measures, sets out to stabilize carbon emissions from development (mitigation) and take into account the unavoidable consequences of climate change (adaptation).

We turn now to consider the detailed mechanics of the system. The planning system is often viewed as being 'quasi-judicial' or 'quasi-legal'. This can be a confusing starting point to the subject. Lord Nolan, in his 1997 report into Standards in Public Life, dealt with this by stating:

It is true that the process of arriving at a planning decision has similarities to a legal process. Yet, the difference between judges and councillors is obvious. Councillors are leading local political figures who naturally have strong views on development proposals affecting their council: indeed, they might have been elected for precisely that reason.

Members of planning committees perform an essentially administrative task. They balance the two (not always harmonious) roles of determining planning applications and representing the public opinion of their communities. Law defines this decision-making duty. Failure to act within the confines of this law may render the Council open to legal challenge by means of Judicial Review, in which a successful legal challenge would quash a decision and send it back for reconsideration by the decision-making body.

This chapter will, with reference to some case law and examples from practice, detail the current system of both plan making and implementation through decision making on individual planning applications. These decisions are made by laypeople in the form of elected local councillors who are guided by the chief planning officer and his or her team of professional staff. This democratic component is frequently misunderstood.

The foundations of the 1947 system were based upon a fundamental principle which still applies today, notably that private interests would need to be sacrificed for the public good as far as land-use issues were concerned. Any system of land-use protection would need to achieve the democratic goals of public policy, the economic goals of managing scarce resources and a measure of market regulation (Needham 2006). Rights of (private) land ownership would, therefore, not offer a carte blanche for ignoring matters of public law or policy (Needham 2006). This principle ensures that the system seeks wider gains than, say, just matters of land value, accepting of course that planning issues have a very considerable influence on land supply and thus its cost.

Local government is responsible for the day-to-day implementation of this planning function by means of production of local policy and determination of planning applications. National government dictates the overall structure and direction of the system by enacting legislation that dictates just exactly what does need consent and how local policy shall be produced as well as producing national policy guidance to set out more detail on acceptable forms of development. Thus, the national government does enjoy a detailed level of intervention to set up the system (by legislation) and influence its outcomes (by planning policy statements).

Today, national government departments, in particular the Secretary of State for Communities and Local Government[1] (or Scottish Executive and Welsh Assembly (Planning Division)), have responsibility for the policy outcomes of the planning system. The Secretary of State, Scottish Executive and Welsh Assembly issue Planning Policy Statements and Circulars containing the views of the Secretary of State on a wide variety of policy areas. These documents constitute important material considerations and must be taken into account in decisions on planning applications and appeals. Other government departments, notably the Department of Culture, Media and Sport (DCMS) and Department of Environment, Farming and Rural Affairs (DEFRA) also influence the system. From October 2008, the Department of Energy and Climate Change was created to focus on these key policy areas. DEFRA, is the government department responsible for sponsoring the Climate Change Bill during its Parliamentary passage in 2008.

The Town and Country Planning Act 1968 introduced a significant reform to the system of plan preparation, with the introduction of structure plans and local plans. These documents set out both strategic and longer-term planning objectives, such as major housing allocations or green belt identification and short-term allocations for development on individual sites. This system was further consolidated in the Town and Country Planning Act 1971, in the Town and Country Planning Act 1990 and in the Planning and Compensation Act 1991. The only other significant statutory reforms introduced between 1971 and 2000 dealt with the delivery of the planning function in the reform of the local government structure. The Local Government Act 1972 created a new system in England and Wales (which came into force in 1974), except for Greater London, which had been reorganized in the early 1960s under the Local Government Act 1963 (which came into force in 1965). In Scotland similar reforms to local government structure were introduced by the Local Government (Scotland) Act 1973 (which came into force in 1975).

Local government today is a confusing mix of two-tier and single-tier authorities. The system has been the subject of frequent review and revision by central government. What is perhaps key is that the planning function is predominantly performed by the lower tier, in other words the Borough, District or City councils. During the late 1990s the government's appetite for further structural reform of local government remained undiminished. The creation of devolved government within the United Kingdom (the Welsh Assembly, Northern Ireland Legislative Assembly and Scottish Parliament) was followed by non-elected regional assemblies within England. London government was reintroduced in 2000 (fourteen years after the abolition of Greater London Council) with the creation of the Greater London Assembly (GLA) and a mayor for London. The mayor would take a strategic lead in a number of areas (transport, economic development, spatial development, sustainability and the environment), with the Assembly responsible for scrutiny of and comment upon the performance of the mayor's office. The London Development Agency (LDA), as the regional development agency for the capital, became responsible for delivering the mayor's economic development strategy. In 1999 the government created eight other Regional Development Agencies, vested with powers of economic development/ regeneration, promotion of business/employment, skills training, and promotion of sustainable development. If English regional government should become a reality then these bodies will provide powerful institutions directed at achieving inward investment, economic redevelopment and sustainable development. Each regional assembly would be responsible for preparing a pan-regional spatial

Table 2.1 Local government post-2000

England (conurbations)	36 Metropolitan Borough Councils in: Greater Manchester (10), West Midlands (7), Merseyside (5), South Yorkshire (4), West Yorkshire (5), Tyne and Wear (5)
England (London)	Mayor and 33 London Boroughs and Greater London Authority
England (Non-Metropolitan)	47 'Shire' Unitary Authorities 34 County Councils, linking with 238 'shire' District Councils
Wales	22 Unitary Authorities
Scotland	32 Unitary Authorities

Notes
1. Most councils are unitary (i.e. responsible for both strategic and local functions) except in English non-metropolitan areas.
2. In English non-metropolitan areas, powers are geographically divided between Unitary Authorities (mostly cities outside the big conurbations like Nottingham) and the County (Strategic) and District (Local) Councils in rural or 'shire' areas.
3. Town or Parish Councils are omitted. They are optional for District Councils to establish and do not have planning powers.
4. From 2004, County Councils lost strategic planning powers.
5. From 2005 Regional Assemblies have produced Regional Spatial Strategies.
6. The Greater London Authority sets the overall strategic framework for planning in London while Boroughs continue to deal with local planning matters and applications.

framework for the production of development, land use and transport, to be known as the Regional Spatial Strategy (RSS). During 2007 the government dithered over what was called a 'sub-national' review, in which the powers to produce an RSS would pass from the regional assembly to the regional development agency. No formal decision was made but much speculation over the future of the regional assemblies (and their planning powers) led to the Secretary of State revealing that no decision would be taken until 2010, thus permitting some opportunity for the new RSS system to bed down.

In the realm of town planning, the mayor and Assembly enjoy an array of strategic functions as allocated by the Mayor of London Order 2000 (with additional development control and local policy powers granted in 2008) and Spatial Development Strategy Regulations. The mayor produces a Spatial Development Strategy (SDS) to provide a framework for all mayoral responsibilities over land-use matters. This was published as 'The London Plan' in 2004. While the mayor has a broad remit of policy areas, including housing, leisure, natural environment, and urban quality, the London boroughs remain in control of the development control functions and production of their own Unitary Development Plan policies. The mayor enjoys limited, albeit important, powers of intervention over strategic matters and is required to issue a certificate of conformity to establish that any plan produced by a London borough complies with the London Plan. The mayor must be consulted on applications that raise matters of strategic importance, and if he directs refusal and a subsequent appeal is lodged, he will be required to defend that decision. One other significant area covers power over heritage, with the mayor responsible for framing conservation policies (working with English Heritage and London boroughs), although the boroughs retain control over individual Conservation Areas and Listed Building Consent applications. The general powers of mayoral intervention in the planning process were enhanced in 2008, following the Greater London Authority Act 2007 and Town and Country Planning (Mayor of London) Order 2008. Threshold criteria for referral of applications were revised downward, so that the mayor could now comment on residential schemes of 150 homes or above (it was 500 previously). The most significant change was that the boroughs must consult the mayor about their Local Development Schemes (i.e. menu of planning documents to come forward as local planning policy). The mayor also enjoys new powers to become a consultee on planning applications outside London but with an impact on the strategic planning of the capital. In such cases the mayor will be able to make representations but will have no formal planning powers.

After 2005, and following reforms set out in the government's planning Green Paper of 2001 (Planning – delivering a fundamental change, see the paragraph below on these reforms) and bolstered by the creation in 2000 of Regional Development Agencies (to deliver economic regeneration), the government set about reforming the planning system by introducing statutory 'Regional Spatial Strategies' to replace (previously rather weak) regional planning guidance. All new local policy (to create a local development framework) would have to be in general conformity with this guidance. The Regional Spatial Strategy would not simply be planning-based, but would integrate pan-regional development with economic strategies and transport infrastructure developments. Eight regional assemblies would produce these new documents, encapsulated by government as a 'spatial vision'. County councils would cease to have any planning policy powers but would continue to deal with waste and minerals development control.

The development control process: a definition?

> Development control is a process by which society, represented by locally elected councils, regulates changes in the use and appearance of the environment.
>
> (Audit Commission 1992)

The development control function is of itself difficult to define. It has been referred to as 'the Cinderella of the planning system' in that it deals with the day-to-day administration of planning control. In many ways this function operates at the 'sharp end' of the system, as it deals with decision making on planning applications, representations at appeal, and the enforcement of planning control. This all takes place within a political system whereby locally elected politicians make decisions within a planning committee, or delegate such decision-making powers to officials, principally the chief planning officer of a local authority. To understand how this system operates, it is necessary first to examine the historical background of development control, as well as the debate surrounding the quality and service delivery of this function.

The basis of today's planning system can be most easily traced to reforms introduced by the Town and Country Planning Act of 1947. This legislation introduced a system of comprehensive control over development. What constituted development was defined by statute, and would require planning permission by means of an application to a local authority. The system would be overseen by a government department (initially the Ministry of Housing and Local Government and today the Secretary of State for Communities and Local Government) although the emphasis was on local control.

The Dobry Report 1975

The first comprehensive review of the development control system took place in 1973, led by George Dobry QC (Dobry 1975). The review was established to consider the current arrangements for planning appeals as well as appraising whether the development control system adequately met current needs, with a view to advising on areas for improvement. The report was commissioned against a background of dramatic increases in the numbers of planning applications and appeals submitted between 1968 and 1972. By 1972 the number of planning applications submitted had increased by more than 67 per cent over 1968 levels. Dobry concluded that, although the system was very good, its procedures did not adequately meet current needs, and he criticized them for being slow and cumbersome. A series of detailed recommendations were designed to speed the administrative and procedural side of the development control function, rather than the quality of the decisions made (a recurrent theme in subsequent reviews of development control).

The most significant recommendation, which the government considered to be too radical to enact, proposed that all planning applications be split into two categories, with differing procedural requirements. Category (A) would be 'simple' applications of a small-scale nature or non-contentious (i.e. those in accordance with the development plan). Category (B) would be large-scale proposals or contentious proposals (i.e. not in accordance with the development plan). The planning authority would be required to issue a decision on (A) applications within 42 days of submission and on (B) applications within three months of submission. Failure to issue a decision on Category (A) within 42 days would result in a deemed grant of planning permission. No such deemed consent would apply to Category (B).

Although Dobry's major recommendation of Categories (A) and (B) was rejected by the government, several of its minor recommendations were to be incorporated into various administrative reforms, notably the use of a standard application form when applying for permission, greater delegation of decisions to officers, publicity and public consultation for planning applications, and the introduction of a charge for submitting a planning application. The Dobry Report dealt with areas for improvement of efficiency within the system and it is important to distinguish between the desire to improve the efficiency of the development control process and the quality of the decisions made. Dobry dealt almost exclusively with seeking to improve the speed of decisions without affecting their quality.

This philosophy has been followed through more recently with the publication of three reports into the operation of development control, as follows:

The Royal Town Planning Institute (RTPI) Report 1991

In identifying the strengths and weaknesses of the current system, this report dealt with the problems surrounding an examination of 'effectiveness' within that system. The report stated: 'Attempts at defining an effective planning service can easily open up a debate on the ideology and philosophy of planning itself' (Royal Town Planning Institute 1991).

It was acknowledged that statistics could be employed to measure procedural issues (for example the percentage of planning applications determined within a particular time period). However, such methods could not be used to measure the quality of decisions made, as this was a largely subjective matter. It is a paradox of the system that the more carefully a planning officer negotiates to improve an application, the less likely it is that a decision will be made within the eight-week statutory period that constitutes the only measure of quality control. The study therefore found that 'effectiveness' in the planning service does not necessarily equate with speed. With regard to development control, the study identified the following as the key attributes that contribute towards an effective planning service: clarity, speed, user involvement, openness and certainty. Recommendations were made, including several designed to improve service delivery, such as the need for concise reports to planning committee, encouragement to hold pre-application meetings, and greater delegation of decisions by planning committee to the chief planning officer.

In conclusion, the report emphasized that, for a planning service to operate effectively, a 'service culture' must be built upon the concept of customer care. In development control, such a concept of care requires the process to be both 'accessible' to developers and the public, in that decisions are clearly and easily explained, as well as procedurally efficient in that administrative targets are set for the speedy despatch of decisions or responses to enquiries.

The Audit Commission: Building in Quality 1992

Like the Dobry Report, the Audit Commission's report (1992) was concerned with the speed and efficiency of the development control function, but, unlike Dobry, its principal terms of reference were defined as improving the quality and effectiveness of the system. The report focused upon the attainment of quality outcomes. The Audit Commission had considered the views of developers and consultants, as well as existing statistical performance indicators, such as the net expenditure per application by the local authority, or the percentage of applications considered under delegated authority. These quality outcomes were similar to the RTPI (1991) study in that they identified a series of administrative areas of concern as follows:

- Service objectives need to be established – encompassing all the publications or policy documents of the LPA.
- Pre-application discussions and advice – should be encouraged and guidance published on applications, as well as the existence of an accessible planning department reception.
- Efficient administrative backup – to register applications upon receipt and pass promptly to a planner.
- Consultation and notification – encouraging the notification objectives to be clearly set out in correspondence, together with guidance on the relevance of particular responses to avoid replies with no planning relevance.
- Assessment and negotiation – following any negotiation it must be necessary to demonstrate the achievements gained from this process. LPAs should utilize the services of specialist in-house staff to ensure consistency and quality in specific areas (e.g. economic development, design, traffic or ecological matters).
- Documentation – written reports to committee upon a case, dealing with the merits or otherwise of the case; jargon is to be avoided.
- Decision-taking and committees – potential for greater delegation to chief planning officer and a frequent committee cycle.
- Decision notification – to ensure speedy delivery of decision reached.

Confederation of British Industry (CBI)/Royal Institution of Chartered Surveyors (RICS) 1992

This report was the result of a CBI-appointed task force of twenty-one business leaders and planning professionals, charged with examining the planning system and identifying areas where improvement would help the successful operation of businesses (CBI and RICS 1992).

The most far-reaching recommendation was for the creation of a 'National Framework of Strategic Guidance', with relevant central government departments producing a policy framework covering land use and infrastructure, over a projected five-year period and with the most immediate priorities identified for the next year, together with a funding commitment from the Treasury. This represented a call for greater direction by central government over strategic planning issues, together with associated financial commitment. The business community identified the need for a greater degree of direction regarding major land-use and transport proposals to ensure greater certainty for the property investment industry. Such a call was seemingly at odds with government philosophy, which in 1983 had proclaimed that strategic planning was an outdated concept of the

more engaging and that access to planning papers be both free (or at a low cost) and available by web access. Yet this more open process, based on greater public involvement, must not be achieved at the expense of jeopardizing increased speed in decision-making. In 2004 the government set a target that 90 per cent of applications be determined by the chief planning officer, i.e. delegated, and not reported to planning committee. Much debate as to the value of planning reform stemmed from the fundamental criticism that the system was mired in delay, which had a serious knock-on effect in diminishing economic performance and business productivity. While the system could be frustrating in its complexity, the value of this argument was built on weak foundations. In 2002 a report for the House of Commons Select Committee on 'Planning and Competitiveness' came to the informed view that 'there is no evidence that planning is a significant explanatory factor in the UK's low productivity compared to its main competitors'. The ability of the planning system to deliver timely and well-considered decisions would always be a significant factor in any public or user perception of its worth. Yet, national economic competitiveness was more a factor of issues like production costs than the ability of the planning system to respond to the commercial needs of business. All that said, unnecessary delay in decision-making would need to be avoided in both the future production of plans and the determination of applications.

The 2004 Planning and Compulsory Purchase Act heralded the new system, which set out to address some of these criticisms. Arguably it did not initially succeed because only some eighteen months later the Chancellor and Deputy Prime Minister appointed a senior civil servant at the Treasury, Kate Barker, to further review the planning system. The terms of reference included assessing ways of improving the efficiency and speed of the system as well as increasing the flexibility, transparency and predictability that enterprise requires. Such a review, hot on the heels of the new plan-making system, should have post-dated the 2001 Green Paper and not the introduction of the new system. While the Barker review gave great weight to the key role the planning system will play in tackling climate change it made recommendations on the plan-making system (such as speeding the early consultative phases of issues and options) that should have been more rigorously thought through in the period 2001–2004. Barker would be followed by a raft of new initiatives to free up new micro-generation renewable technologies (such as mini wind turbines and solar panels on domestic roofs) from the need for planning consent, a general speeding-up of planning appeals and fast-tracking of minor cases, a new system to deal with major infrastructure and some minor (but significant) tinkering with the 2004 reforms to speed the production of local planning policy and review of statements of community involvement. In May 2007 the essence of these future reforms was published in a White Paper entitled 'Planning for a Sustainable Future' (command 7120) which again repeated the language of Barker in seeking 'an effective and efficient planning system which is responsive to our needs as a society'. This time the White Paper set out key principles for future reforms involving a system that was responsive, streamlined, engaged with the community, was transparent and made a decision at the most appropriate national, regional and local level. The most stinging criticism was that the planning system was 'too bureaucratic, takes too long and is unpredictable'. In the eyes of the White Paper these fundamental flaws would ill equip the system for the major challenges ahead to increase housing supply and support sustainable economic development. In the same year, the housing Green Paper ('Homes for the Future: More affordable, more sustainable') raised the bar in respect of housing supply, when it set out to increase housing units to a target of 240,000 every year by 2016 and the ultimate goal of 3 million new homes by 2020.

Clearly, much more work is required to promote a proper and full engagement with the public. Work by Friends of the Earth in 2006 ('Listen Up: Community involvement in the planning system') demonstrated the value of meaningful public engagement, with local residents accepting change much more readily when they have been given a proper say in the development of a scheme. The 2007 White Paper resulted in legislative change in the form of the Planning and Reform Act 2008. Evidently the period to 2010 would be occupied by an increasingly modified and potentially streamlined system. The government will develop national policy statements for key infrastructure projects such as air transport and renewable energy. A push towards speed and efficiency will manifest itself with revisions to various statutory instruments so that micro-generation is freed up from the need for planning in a new general permitted development order, and the planning appeals system is revised to deal with householder appeals differently when compared to more significant proposals. Public participation would be improved by a range of measures, including developers being required to undertake their own public consultation exercises on major schemes, reform of planning inquiries to permit the public to speak without having to be cross-examined by lawyers and greater resources targeted to bodies like Planning Aid who offer free and impartial planning advice to residents affected by planning proposals. Arguably, the most controversial future reform is the creation of a national 'infrastructure planning commission' which would determine major schemes involving airport, seaport, road, rail and energy (power stations) planning applications. The Barker Review had been critical of the system in its inability to deal with major infrastructure proposals, identifying the time taken to determine Terminal 5 at Heathrow and a new container port at Dibden Bay (Southampton) as 'highly inefficient'. The corollary of taking such schemes out of the hands of local authorities would be that a clear set of national policies would need to be in place to guide the independent commission. Thus, the new system to 2010 will see a set of national infrastructure statements, considered by Parliament and with a strong element of public consultation. By creating effectively a national plan for infrastructure the future independent commission would be given a set of reference points for the future consideration of (most significantly) airport expansion and power station development. Both of these development sectors understandably produce considerable debate about a wider set of issues, notably climate change and sustainable development. It remains a concern that the government could lay down a set of national guidelines that effectively emasculates the ability of the independent commission to be truly objective in their assessment of the environmental impact of such far-reaching schemes as, for example, the construction of a new third runway at Heathrow or expansion of flying activity at Stansted airport.

'Modernizing' local government

During the late 1990s and into the new century the government issued a raft of new policy initiatives under the umbrella of modernizing local government or the planning function within local government. These initiatives have dealt with a broad range of topics from dispute resolution (such as mediation, see Chapter 5) to value for money (see 'best value' below). To accept the notion of modernization is to accept a preconception or premise, namely that the planning or local government system is itself dated and obsolete. This has clearly not been the case in past years and the system has undergone successive reforms since its post-war introduction. Nevertheless, the modernizing agenda has afforded a valuable opportunity to appraise many areas of the system, especially the impacts on businesses, to permit reforms to be based on a clear understanding of existing problems in service delivery. This process is almost entirely dynamic, with the 2007 White Paper continuing the current climate of reform to at least 2010 and most probably beyond. New constitutional arrangements in local government were put in place following the introduction of the Local Government Act 2000. This was accompanied by the introduction of a best value regime to monitor and appraise the performance of the Council when assessed against a whole range of targets addressing principally the speed of decision-making. Until 2000 the key constitutional framework of local government was a system of subject-led or responsibility-led committees (composed of around 10–15 elected councillors) and a full council (composed of all councillors). The planning function would normally be vested in one or more committees, with planning applications usually determined by a development control subcommittee. Fundamental reform to this structure was introduced in 2000 with the Local Government Act, allowing councils to adopt one of three broad categories of new constitution. They could restructure to include either an elected mayor, a cabinet with a leader, or an elected mayor with a council manager. The first two models give pre-eminence to elected politicians who would run council affairs, while in the third a considerable amount of responsibility would be delegated to the most senior council officer (Chief Executive).

In the pre-2000 arrangement, decision-making was diffuse, with many councillors taking an active part by sitting on one or several committees. With the post-2000 situation, by contrast, most key decisions would be taken by a cabinet and/or mayor. The remaining councillors outside this executive would be responsible for scrutinizing the actions of these key individuals as well as representing the interest of their local (ward) electorate. The impact on the planning system was mixed. However, a cabinet/mayor will decide certain strategic matters, such as housing allocations or local development framework policy. The determination of individual planning applications is unlikely to be affected. However, a cabinet or mayor would be soon be inundated by the sheer volume of work that this would entail, and it seems inevitable that, notwithstanding the new constitutional framework established in 2000, the role of a planning applications committee or subcommittee will endure for some considerable time to come.

The planning application process

Once it has been established that: the proposal constitutes development, in that it represents either a material change of use or operational development,[6] and that it would not otherwise be exempt from control by provisions within the General Permitted Development Order or Use Classes Order, then it is necessary to apply for planning permission by submission of a planning application to the local planning authority.

Two specific topics must be considered: the processing of the application, and how one arrives at the decision to grant or refuse planning permission.

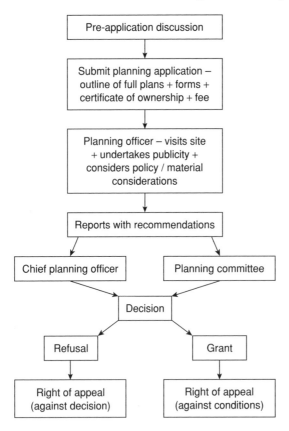

Figure 2.1 The planning application process

Processing the application

Pre-application discussions

Before the application is submitted, the developer may wish to approach the LPA to seek either the informal views of the planning officer on the likelihood of permission being granted, or to clarify whether permission is required for the proposal in the first place.[7] The developer would be well advised at this stage to check the planning history of the site or its surroundings (previous application approvals or refusals and appeal decisions, i.e. whether these were allowed or dismissed, and any Inspector's comments). Increasingly with the more complex schemes, developers are likely to undertake a more sophisticated public consultation, even detailed engagement with workshop and 'action planning' style approach (see Wates 1999).

Which application?

The application can be made in either full or outline. In both cases it is necessary to submit the following documents:

- **Plans** The exact detail or type of plan will depend largely on the proposal and whether the application is made in full or outline. Common to both will be an Ordnance Survey extract, showing the site outlined in red and any other adjoining land also owned by the applicant outlined in blue. Full applications will require detailed elevational drawings and floorplans together with a siting drawing (showing proposed access, parking, relationship of proposal to adjoining land and, possibly, landscaping). Outline applications may only require the Ordnance Survey extract, although a siting plan may also be submitted, depending upon which matters are to be reserved for subsequent approval.
- **Forms** The application must be made on standard forms issued by the LPA. From April 2008 one standard set of forms will apply nationally.
- **Certificate of ownership** A certificate – that only the applicant owns the land or has given notice of his application to all relevant landowners, and whether or not the land is on an agricultural holding – must be signed by the applicant or agent. It is therefore possible to make a planning application on land that is not within the ownership of the potential developer, although clearly you must have an interest in the land in question.
- **Fee** Charges for planning applications were first introduced in 1980, the government's view being that some part of the cost of development control should be recovered from the applicant and not solely borne by the LPA. The fee structure changes approximately every two or three years. Reference should be made to the current Town and Country Planning (Fees for Applications and Deemed Applications) Regulations to ascertain the current charges. The

planning portal at www.planning.portal.gov.uk has an online fee calculator facility.

Outline applications (Statement of Development Principles)

An outline planning application seeks to establish the principle of operational development on a particular site (applications for changes of use cannot be made in outline). The outline planning permission is one that is made subject to a condition requiring the subsequent approval by the LPA of reserved matters. These reserved matters cover five key areas of development control – siting, design, external appearance, means of access, and landscaping. The application form requests that the applicant nominates which matters are to be considered at the outline stage and which are to be 'reserved' for subsequent approval. It is possible for all of the five matters to be reserved, although it is common practice for the applicant to request (and supply necessary information) that siting and means of access are considered at the outline stage.

The LPA has powers to request that further details are required and that the application will not be considered until such details are received. However, it is rare for this request to go beyond the details required for access and siting.

Once outline planning permission has been granted, any application for the approval of reserved matters must be made within three years of the outline approval, and the development must be started within five years of that date, otherwise the permission will lapse.

The distinct advantage of outline planning permission is that it establishes certainty within the development process, namely that a particular scheme is acceptable, subject to reserved matters. This allows the developer the guarantee of a scheme without recourse to an appeal. Thus, outline approvals may enhance the value of land by establishing the principle of redevelopment without needing to draw up full plans. The government indicated in 2002 that outline permissions would be replaced by a certificate to be called a Statement of Development Principles. This idea was designed to give the developer greater flexibility but became unworkable and was subsequently dropped.

Full applications

An application for full planning permission is for detailed approval. Full planning applications will therefore require submission of elevational drawings and floorplans, together with site plans showing access, landscaping and other treatment, such as car parking or servicing areas. It is usually the case that, although a good deal of detail will be submitted, the full planning permission may be granted subject to some conditions. These conditions may, in a way similar to reserved matters on outline approvals, permit the proposal, while reserving for future consideration certain technical matters (e.g. details of internal matters such as soundproofing between converted flats). Conditions may also limit specific land-use matters – for example, hours of operation, or maintenance of an approved landscaping scheme.[8] The full planning permission must be begun within a period of three years from the date of the approval or it will lapse. To begin or implement a permission requires a 'specified operation' be performed, such as the digging of foundations. After that the permission is technically started and the consent cannot lapse.

Formal submission of a planning application

When the application is made to the LPA it will be checked to ensure that all the documentation is correct and the necessary fee has been submitted. The application will then be acknowledged by the LPA and the date of the application's receipt will constitute the starting date for the two-month statutory period, within which the LPA is required to issue a decision.

Following acknowledgement, it will be normal practice for most local authorities to undertake consultations with, and publicity to, various bodies or individuals.

Call-in powers

The Secretary of State under section 77 of the Town and Country Planning Act 1990 enjoys wide-ranging powers to make directions requiring applications to be referred to him/her without being dealt with by the planning authority. These powers are rarely employed. Around 786 planning applications were referred to government offices for decision in 2006–07 and thirty-six were called in for determination by the Secretary of State. This power is selectively used, and mostly in respect of applications deemed to be of more than local importance, such as departures from the development plan or significant proposals within the green belt. The principal criteria for assessment of call-in are the extent to which the application conflicts with national policies, the degree to which it has significant effects beyond its boundaries, the level of regional or national controversy it has created, whether it raises significant architectural and urban design issues, and if any issues of national security are raised. The Secretary of State had, over the years, passed a plethora of such regulations and after consultation (in early 2008) the regulations were revised, so that the key areas of call-in were confined to development of playing fields (to which Sport England had objected), development in excess of 5000 square metres of commercial/leisure or mixed, significant development in the green belt (over 1000 square metres), development within flood plains, and development affecting a World Heritage Site (to which English Heritage objected).

Publicity for planning applications

Publicity surrounding planning applications can be taken to mean advertisements in local newspapers, on site, or by neighbour notification.[9] Examples are shown in Table 2.2.

Table 2.2 Specified publicity for planning applications

Application	Publicity
1 Major development: 10+ dwellings, 1000+m² floorspace, waste processing or working of minerals	Advertisement by applicant in local newspaper and site notice
2 Developments affecting a conservation area and/or a listed building	Advertisement by LPA in local newspaper and site notice
3 Applications that depart from the development plan	Advertisement by LPA in local newspaper and site notice.
4 Applications involving submission of an environmental statement	Advertisement by applicant in local newspaper and on site
5 Minor development such as changes of use or extensions	Site notice or neighbour notification

Third parties

Until 1991, planning authorities were only encouraged to notify local residents who were neighbours considered to be affected by a proposal. However, it became increasingly apparent that different planning authorities adopted different internal practices towards such consultation. An RTPI report (RTPI 1991) discovered that over three-quarters of all authorities undertook discretionary publicity and notification of planning applications. Yet considerable differences existed between councils, with some only contacting immediately neighbouring occupiers, while others would contact widely within a set radius around the proposal site. Third parties did not enjoy any direct redress against the council for failure to consult them, as no statutory duty existed for notification to take place at all. Out of anger, or frustration, or both, many people lodged complaints with the Commissioner for Local Government Administration ('Ombudsman') on the grounds that the councils had been procedurally unfair in not consulting them.

In May 1991 the government accepted that all planning applications in England and Wales should receive some publicity, and regulations came into force in 1992.[10] Despite this, a problem still exists over the exact purpose of neighbour notification and publicity for planning applications. The Audit Commission (1992) identified a desire in many authorities to use neighbour notification as a public relations exercise, without informing the public about the exact purpose of such consultations. This devalues the process.

Third parties may draw the conclusion that the entire process is a waste of time if their comments are deemed irrelevant by the chief planning officer in the report to the planning committee. The Audit Commission recommended that authorities focus greater attention on providing the public with realistic expectations on both the process by which views will be taken into account, and the relevance of a particular type of response. Increasingly, LPAs do provide guidance to the public over the form and content of planning objections. A number of local branches of the Royal Town Planning Institute provide voluntary services of qualified planners for groups or individuals unable to afford professional fees. West Midlands Planning Aid Service and Planning Aid for London provide, arguably, the most well-known examples of such assistance for community groups and individual residents in their respective areas. This work was praised by the 2001 Green Paper, the government indicating that it may contribute resources in the future to achieve a better funding of the service. By 2008 national coverage was achieved for this planning aid function. The introduction of Statements of Community Involvement in the 2004 reforms greatly bolstered the emphasis given to seeking the views of local people and getting more people to engage in the system. These statements must address both applications and local policies. Many planning authorities embraced this new emphasis by grasping electronic communications such as web-based consultations and the online submission of planning comments. Planning Performance Agreements, rolled out on major applications, would also enhance more sophisticated methods of community engagement, provided by developers as a part of the application process.

Consideration by planning officer

The application passes to a case officer who will also deal with the results of the publicity and consultation exercise. The case officer will visit the site and consider planning policy and other relevant planning matters not covered by policy. The consideration of these issues is not the consequence of a haphazard interaction of factors but the discharge of a particular statutory duty imposed upon the decision-maker by planning legislation. This duty affects all decision-makers within the planning process, namely the local planning authority (i.e. planning committee or chief planning officer), the Secretary of State (as regards called-in applications or appeal decisions) and Inspectors appointed by the Secretary of State to decide planning appeals. This duty will be considered below. As a consequence of such considerations, the planning officer may seek amendments to the proposal. The desire for amendment usually results in some element of discussion and negotiation between the officer and applicant (or agent appointed to deal with the application).

What emerges from this consideration is a recommendation from the case officer to the chief planning officer either to grant planning permission, subject to conditions,[11] or to refuse permission, stating a reason or reasons in both instances. The consideration of the application may be deferred to allow for further information to be brought to a subsequent meeting (e.g. for amendments, details of proposed use or additional consultations). The planning committee may accept or reject (overturn) the recommendation of the chief planning officer. If it rejects a recommendation to grant permission, and refuses the application, this must be a decision based upon sound planning judgement. The introduction of the award of costs in planning appeals means that any unreasonable refusal of planning permission may result in the 'punishment' of the planning authority by an award of costs. However, overturning the recommendation of the chief planning officer does not automatically constitute unreasonable behaviour from which costs will follow. Circular 8/93 on costs states 'While planning authorities are not bound to follow advice from their officers . . . they will be expected to show that they had reasonable planning grounds for a decision taken against such advice'.[12]

Delegated applications (i.e. decision-making delegated by committee to officers) will usually be considered by the chief planning officer; the criteria that determine suitability for delegation will vary from authority to authority. Government targets require that 90 per cent of all applications be delegated.

The use of such delegated authority benefits the development control function in that, by avoiding the need to report the matter to committee, the decision time can be reduced. The officer simply reports, orally or by a short written summary, to the chief planning officer. If this is accepted, then a decision notice can be prepared and dispatched. When dealing with committees it must be remembered that such bodies function on a cycle of meetings throughout the year. To report, an application requires considerable administration, as draft reports must be prepared and circulated to senior officers and then placed upon the agenda for the forthcoming meeting. With most committees on a cycle of one meeting every three to four weeks, to miss one committee would take the decision period to between six and eight weeks, greatly increasing the chances of it falling outside the statutory period. The further complication of awaiting consultation and publicity responses before reporting to a committee provides additional procedural problems in determining applications within the eight-week statutory period. LPAs can improve their performance by increased use of delegated powers and shorter committee cycles.

The merits of the planning application

The power to determine planning applications is set out in the Planning and Compulsory Purchase Act 2004. Planning permission may be granted (either unconditionally or subject to conditions) or refused (giving reasons). This duty is best viewed as a discretionary one, in that the council or LPA must apply a variety of policy documents (the Local Development Document within the Local Development Framework) and site-specific circumstances in the decision to grant or refuse planning permission. The system allows for a measure of flexibility here, so that (for example) the plan need not always be followed, if material considerations suggest otherwise.

The duty to determine a planning application is a duty framed by law (hence sometimes referred to as quasi-legal) and was originally established by section 54A of the Town and Country Planning Act 1990 and now replaced by section 38(6) of the Planning and Compulsory Purchase Act 2004. This section established that:

> If regard is to be had to the Development Plan for the purpose of any
> determination to be made under the Planning Acts, the determination must

be made in accordance with the Plan *unless material considerations indicate otherwise*.

(Authors' emphasis)

The concept of a material consideration is one defined by the High Court in a lead case (Stringer v. Minister of Housing and Local Government (1971) All ER 65) in which Justice Cooke held that 'in principle it seems to me that any consideration which relates to the use and development of land is capable of being a planning consideration. Whether a particular consideration falling within that broad class is material in any given case will depend on the circumstances'. One key (perhaps philosophical) conclusion of both section 38 and the Stringer case is that a planning decision is based upon a wide range of issues and the person making that decision enjoys a very wide discretion within the strictures of the law. The deliberate consequence of this legislation is that the Development Plan is given greater emphasis (than previously existed pre-1990) in decisions on planning applications. The decision-maker (i.e. the council and in certain cases the chief planning officer or Inspector/Secretary of State on appeal of a decision) is steered towards an examination of policy, unless for some reason a 'material consideration' outweighs such policy. Material considerations are explored later on, although at this point it is worthy of note that the Act states they must 'indicate otherwise' and this has been interpreted by the Courts as meaning that the Development Plan does not have to be slavishly adhered to (see City of Edinburgh v. Secretary of State for Scotland (1997) in the House of Lords). So, section 38(6) of the Act is the essential starting point for all planning application decisions. Government planning policy in PPS1 (itself a material consideration) states, of this plan-led system:

> This plan-led system, and the certainty and predictability it aims to provide, is central to planning and plays the key role in integrating sustainable development. Applications for planning permission should be determined in line with the plan, unless material considerations indicate otherwise.

The new system

The 2004 Act introduced a considerable level of reform to the planning system. Structure Plans (produced by county councils) were scrapped, and a new level of regionally based guidance replaces them. Eight English Regional Assemblies (known as Regional Planning Bodies) will produce these 'Regional Spatial Strategies'. Local Development Frameworks (LDFs) will replace Local Plans or Unitary Development Plans (UDPs) as produced by local authorities. It should be noted that the longer-term future for Regional Assemblies hangs in the balance, with government now committed to the abolition of the Assemblies by 2010. It remains a matter of some speculation as to exactly where government will 'park' the Regional Planning Bodies (i.e. the body responsible for

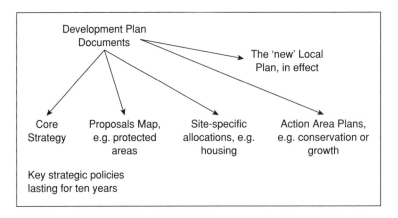

Figure 2.2 Contents of a development plan

producing the regional plan). The government's indication has been that, following what was coined the 'sub-national review', these powers will fall into the responsibility of the Regional Development Agencies.

The 'Local Development Framework' represents an umbrella term, covering a raft of local development documents, as shown in Figure 2.2. For detailed guidance on the production regime applicable to these documents, reference should be made to Planning Policy Statement 11 'Regional Planning' (2004), Planning Policy Statement 12 'Local Development Frameworks' (2008) and its companion guide as produced by the (then) Office of the Deputy Prime Minister in 2004.

This new system has been 'rolled out' over the period 2007–2010. When studying it in more detail, three key LDF documents are worthy of greater examination – the Statement of Community Involvement, the Development plan documents and the Supplementary planning documents.

The Statement of Community Involvement (SCI)

This is a formal document, which states how the authority intends to involve the community and other stakeholders in the production of the Local Development Framework. It sets out how the council will involve the local community in the preparation and revision of planning policy and planning applications. The Statement is subject to community consultation and, initially, the independent scrutiny by a Planning Inspector, although this requirement was lifted in 2008, following recommendations in the 2007 Lifting the Burden Task Force review and the Planning White Paper. The government have consistently said that they would like to create a 'culture change' in planning. Numerous policy documents have promoted greater community involvement – beyond mere 'box-ticking' exercises – by using local focus groups and stakeholder meetings

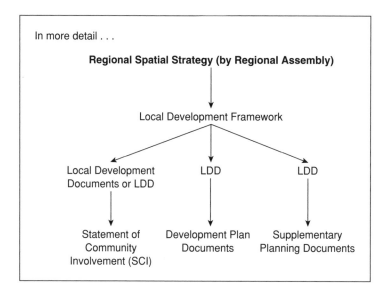

Figure 2.3 Hierarchy of regional and local plans

when producing policy and by promoting public speaking rights at planning committee meetings to create a meaningful engagement in the system.

Development plan documents

The development plan consists of (1) a Core Strategy, (2) Site-specific allocations of land, (3) Area action plans, and (4) a Proposals map. These four documents provide the key information governing the determination of a planning application and must be in 'general conformity' with the Regional Spatial Strategy (as currently produced by the Regional Assembly). The Core Strategy establishes key strategic policy (lasting for ten years) which consists of a vision and set of longer-term planning objectives. Site-specific allocations will identify land-use allocations, such as the exact locations for housing, employment, retail, and leisure development. Area action plans will deal with key areas of major change or conservation – for example, planned growth areas and regeneration projects. In areas of conservation, policies will deal with relevant development control matters and strategies to preserve or enhance historic areas or buildings. The proposals map reflects the up-to-date planning strategy for the area. It will show proposed allocations (e.g. areas identified for new housing or mixed-use development) and 'zoning' of various land uses. These documents will be the subject of a fairly complex production process in which the planning authority will prepare early-stage 'issues and options' documents, followed by a formal consultation and the right to make representations, then an examination in which the appointed independent inspector must convene a formal discussion of interested parties and determine if the proposed policies are sound. Indeed the sole purpose of the examination is to consider the soundness of the plan, which refers to a set of three broad principles of procedure – fits with sustainability appraisal and statement of community involvement, conformity (consistent with national planning policy and regional spatial strategy) and coherence (policies based on evidence and containing appropriate flexibility). The inspector's decision is final and binding. It will be that the plan is either sound or unsound; however, certain matters can be identified for further consideration. It may be that the need to revisit issues goes to the very integrity of the plan and a conclusion of 'unsoundness' must follow. This happened at the examination of the core strategy of the Royal Borough of Windsor and Maidenhead in 2007, in which the inspector deemed the plan unsound and recommended a review of green belt prior to its resubmission. Certainly the early indication of these examinations between 2006 and 2008 reveals a significant number of findings of unsoundness and a need for planning authorities to consider more carefully the evidence base and inherent flexibility of policy on which their plans have been created. The government, aware of these problems, moved to further revise the system, with a consultation paper in November 2007, entitled 'Streamlining Local Development Frameworks'. This introduced greater flexibility so that the planning authority could revise the plan, following public comments and ahead of the examination (presided over by an independent planning inspector). Prior to that, the planning authority were rather stuck with their chosen strategy and forced to defend this at the examination against any weight of objection by interested parties. Further revisions in 2008 (including a new version of PPS12) repackaged the tests of soundness that governed the examination, to focus on the key justification and effectiveness of the plan's policies, as opposed to the rather slavish adherence to prescribed tests of soundness and the government's aspirations for the system. The inspector would still look at the tests of soundness at the examination but would be more concerned with the strategic issue – that the plan would deliver on its own objectives while fostering key national objectives of sustainability. The core strategy would now last up to fifteen years and would, alongside its fundamentally strategic vision, be allowed to allocate strategic sites for development.

Supplementary planning documents

These documents cover a range of detailed and functional development control issues such as (most commonly) parking standards or design guides and urban design principles or codes. They permit the planning authority the opportunity to set out very detailed guidelines which, while not carrying the status of a development plan, do offer the necessary level of detail needed, especially in areas of design and layout. They will not fall within the umbrella of a development plan document but do constitute a material consideration.

Strategic Environmental Assessment and Sustainability Appraisal

In the 'new' (post-2004) system, European Community (EC) Directive 2001/42/EC requires that local planning authorities undertake a full appraisal of the environmental effects of their policies. This process is referred to as Strategic Environmental Assessment (SEA) and Sustainability Appraisal (SA). This applies to both the Regional Spatial Strategy and to the Local Development Framework. It is a process undertaken in the early public consultation stages of the plan and helps to evaluate its general 'soundness', bearing in mind the fact that the 2004 Act requires that a statutory duty exist when preparing plans to contribute to the achievement of sustainable development. Should a plan be unsustainable or propose environmentally inappropriate measures, then the SEA/SA would expose this. Such appraisals are commissioned of independent consultants and do contribute enormously to the robust evaluation of future planning policy. The independent inspector, who presides over the independent examination of the many development plan documents, will pay close attention to this document when deciding if policies are sound or not.

Preparation of a local development document

One of the government's principal objectives for the planning system is that the communities who will be affected by planning decisions become more engaged in the system than they have been previously. This means that there should be a 'front loading of involvement', so that local people can be involved at the earliest stage in the plan-production process. Therefore, when councils are identifying issues and debating options, local people are involved. This desire for greater (and earlier) public participation in planning was a key objective of the government when introducing the 2004 reforms. Each authority must produce a 'local development scheme', which is effectively a timetable for the production of these documents. The government's best value audit regime requires that all planning authorities have such a timetable in place by 2007, and reference to it will provide a useful route map in which the various component documents of the LDF are listed and their production process made plain. Four key stages are involved:

Stage 1: Pre-production

The council undertakes survey and evidence gathering. This means that they will prepare and maintain information on the social, economic and environmental characteristics of their area. Each will publish a 'local development scheme', which is a timetable for the production of local planning policy over the next three years.

Stage 2: Production

The council will now produce the development plan document. The 'frontloading' principle requires that the council consult with local bodies (as set out in the Statement of Community Involvement) at an early stage in the process and the Strategic Environmental Assessment/Sustainability Appraisal Directive establishes that options and alternatives are to be considered.

When the council have worked up their proposals they are required to publish a series of 'preferred options'. Initially this would require a formal consultation period but this was repealed following recommendations by Kate Barker and the Planning White Paper 'Planning for a Sustainable Future' (2007). Nevertheless, local planning authorities will be required to show that they have responded to public views during this consultation period and a more flexible system of engagement, workshops and community events is expected to deal with this initial stage of the consultation process.

After this, the local authority may proceed to publish the (formal) draft development plan document, receive public comments prior to the submission of the final version to the Secretary of State and move the process forward to the examination stage. From 2008 they are allowed the opportunity to revise the document ahead of the examination (the next stage) in response to public, developer and other representations received during the formal six-week consultation. At that point the document is submitted to the Secretary of State for examination.

Stage 3: Examination

An independent planning inspector will preside over the public examination. This will mean that he or she will scrutinize the contents of the plan, including reading the written comments of interested parties and hearing their oral evidence at the examination (if they exercise their right to appear). The inspector's final report will set out precise recommendations on how the development plan document and proposals map must be changed. These recommendations are binding. The inspector will be looking at a number of key tests of soundness which address its coherence, the evidence base on which it is founded, consistency with other relevant plans, proper regard to the SEA/SA process and its accommodation of the needs of the community. From 2008, he or she will also be looking, most strategically, at the ability of the plan to deliver on its policy aspirations.

Stage 4: Adoption

Providing that the Secretary of State does not intervene at this stage, the council will proceed to publish the plan (incorporating all the recommendations of the inspector) as an adopted plan. It now carries full weight in law as a material consideration in the determination of planning applications. The period to 2010 will witness a cascading of these new plans, and it is anticipated that the core strategy and allocated sites documents will proceed jointly through the process as local authorities both set out a vision and deal with the more day-to-day identification of new sites.

Subsequent review

The plan will be the subject of ongoing review in two ways. First, by reference to the council's own annual monitoring report which will check that its production is on schedule and, secondly, by establishing systems to regulate its effectiveness in delivering its objectives (e.g. in achieving sustainable patterns of development, or meeting local housing targets). The core strategy will be expected to have a shelf-life of fifteen to twenty years.

Material considerations

A material consideration is most definitively defined in case law as:

> Any consideration which, related to the use and development of land, is capable of being a planning consideration.
> (*Stringer* v. MHLG (1970) in the High Court)

The extent to which this consideration is material will depend upon the merits of the individual case. Thus a measure of interpretation is required.

More recent case law has established that while matters of, say, personal circumstance or hardship can, in exceptional cases, be relevant to planning, such cases are often seen as exceptions to the general rule. The economic viability of a proposal is not normally a matter for a planning authority but it may be material in certain circumstances where redundancy and re-use is part of the planning equation. To confuse the question, economics are very much a planning matter, albeit that they relate to the wider benefits arising from land use. Public opposition and/or support for an application is not, in itself, a material consideration, unless it is founded on valid planning reasons.

A number of key and/or significant material considerations may be considered. In many cases they have been defined by case law, in which Judges in the High Court, Court of Appeal and House of Lords have served to interpret and, therefore (hopefully) to refine planning law. Broad principles are established and they will not apply in all cases. For example, in a decision of the High Court dealing with the extension of an existing bail and probation hostel it was held that the residents fear of development was a material matter (West Midlands Probation Committee v. Secretary of State (1996)). Such fears would need to be justified and based on some objective assessment of the case. In many cases fear would be hard to prove and thus would not apply.

Precedent: the granting of permission and its influence on adjoining land

Case law	Issues
Collis Radio v. Secretary of State for the Environment (1975) 29 P&C R 390	When considering the grant of planning permission it is acceptable to consider the 'side effects' on other land, if it is granted.
Poundstretcher Ltd, Harris Queensway plc v. Secretary of State for the Environment and Liverpool City Council (1989) JPL 90	Where precedent is relied upon, some form of evidence must be required. Mere fear of precedent is not sufficient.

Comment: Every planning application and appeal site must be considered on its own individual merits. However, this does not exclude concern regarding the cumulative impact, whereby in granting permission on site A it will probably follow that permission will be granted on sites B, C and D.

Precedent can be material, yet caution is required here, as you should be more concerned with consistency of decision-making. It is not some kind of binding legal principle where the LPA must grant permissions on comparable sites. Remember, every site is considered on its own merits.

Balancing material considerations

Case law	Issues
Tesco Stores Limited v. Secretary of State for the Environment and others (1995) House of Lords	Made a careful distinction between a consideration being material (a matter of law) and the exact weight to be attached to it (a matter for the planning officer and planning committee). The decision-maker has wide discretion concerning how much weight to give a planning consideration.
R v. Richmond upon Thames LBC and Tom Dillon (2005) High Court 143	While the decision-maker was not bound by previous decisions to grant or refuse permission, it was important to be consistent, so reasons should be given when departing from previous decisions.

Comment: The history of previous decisions on the site in question is a matter of some importance. Unimplemented and expired (i.e. more than three years old) permissions will be relevant yet, as with precedent, the council are not automatically obliged to review such expired permissions. While case law and legislation will establish what is and is not a planning consideration, it will be a matter for the planning officer and committee to determine if it is material to the planning application in question and how much weight should be attached.

Planning obligations: Where an offer of 'planning gain' is made

Case law	Issues
Tesco Stores Limited v. *Secretary of State for the Environment and others* (1995) House of Lords	Dealt with the way a planning obligation should be considered. If the obligation was connected to a development proposal then it would be material. If material, the planning authority would have to take it into account *but* this is a matter for their discretion.
	Only if a planning obligation was unrelated to a proposed development could it be ignored by the planning authority.
JA Pye (Oxford) Limited v. *South Gloucestershire District Council* (2000) High Court	A similar decision to the Tesco decision (above) in which the Court took the view that the only test (in law) for a planning obligation was that it served a planning purpose and not unreasonable in what it sought to achieve.

Comment: Planning obligations are thus 'legal' if they serve a planning purpose and are related to the application site in some way. These are very broad principles. The Secretary of State has published policy guidance (Circular 05/05) which is more restrictive and must also be considered. This states that the planning obligation must be fairly and reasonably related to the development proposed. The offer of a planning obligation may help to control some of the external impacts of development (such as highway works) but cannot render unacceptable development as acceptable. While this system may be overtaken by the Community Infrastructure Levy (after 2009, at the earliest), it will no doubt remain where planning obligations are negotiated between developer and planning authority.

Government planning policy is a material consideration. Such policy is a combination of Planning Policy Statements (PPSs) and government circulars. PPSs are gradually replacing what were called Planning Policy Guidance Notes (PPGs).

Comment: Central government departments issue guidance to local government in the form of various policy statements and circulars. Such documents provide important, if broadly based, advice upon a range of development control issues and areas. Although local planning authorities are not duty-bound to follow this advice, they will need to show good reasons for any decisions that run counter to the government's view. It must also be remembered that if a matter proceeds to an appeal, the Secretary of State or an appointed inspector will take such guidance into consideration.

Some key PPSs/PPGs and circulars

Document	Year	Some key policy issues
PPS1	2005 Delivering Sustainable Development and Climate Change Supplement (2007)	• Statutory purpose for policy to achieve sustainable development • Guidance on the plan-led system
PPS3	2006 Housing	• Establishes national target that 60 per cent additional housing should be provided on previously developed land or by conversion, by 2008. • Minimum acceptable density is 30 dwellings per hectare and below that will require exceptional reasons. Each local authority will be required to have in place a five-year minimum housing supply from the date of plan adoption.
PPG8	2001 Telecommunications	• Health considerations and public concern can in principle be material considerations. A decision in the Courts in 2004 held that it would be sufficient for any phone mast application to contain a certificate that the international standards are complied with (the ICNIRP standards). See *T-Mobile* v. *First Secretary of State* (2005) 1 PLR 97.
PPS 12	2004 and revised 2008 Local Development Frameworks	• Processes to follow when preparing an LDF, especially for local development document.
PPG15	1994 Planning and the Historic Environment	• Conservation Area and Listed Building protection • The 2007 Heritage Protection Review and draft Bill are expected to result in a replacement PPS by 2010.
PPS 22	2004 Renewable Energy	• Promotion of renewable energy across UK
PPS 25	2004 Flood Risk	• Process covering development in flood plains
Circular 11/95	1995 Conditions	• Establishes the tests of a planning condition.
Circular 5/05	1997 Planning Obligations	• Establishes 'tests' of a planning obligation. Maintains past position that obligations must be 'fairly and reasonably related' to the application.
Circular 8/93	1993 Costs	• Establishes that a refusal of planning permission must be supported by some evidence of harm.

Consultations and objections

Most planning decisions involve the balancing or 'weighing up' of many issues. It is important to remember that the planning system involves an important democratic (or participatory) element. The planning committee must take into account any representations made by the public or various statutory consultees (e.g. the Environment Agency on water management and flooding, English Heritage on listed buildings and conservation areas, and Natural England on nature conservation and access issues). It follows that if such representations are to be given 'weight' then they must be relevant to planning.

When considering public representations, the officers/committee will, quite legitimately, be fulfilling an important function in representing local opinion. Elected councillors may be subjected to lobbying by local residents. This is perfectly acceptable; however a councillor on a planning committee should not have made up their mind on the issue before hearing the debate, so they should not make public pronouncements in advance of Committee, or this will be evidence of predetermination or bias. If a councillor has a personal interest in an application he/she must declare that interest, and if it is a prejudicial interest take no further part in the discussions surrounding that particular decision (usually by leaving the committee room). The test of a prejudicial interest is one where a member of the public, aware of all relevant facts, would consider the actions to be biased. After a fair and proper consideration of the merits of the application when measured against the development plan, a decision will be reached. This decision can be to either to grant permission unconditionally, or grant permission subject to conditions or to refuse permission. If permission is granted subject to conditions then they in themselves must satisfy six tests – relevance to planning; relevance to the development to be permitted; enforceability; precision; reasonableness; and being necessary.

If permission is refused, then reasons must be given which must be 'precise complete, specific and relevant to the application'. If permission is granted, (since December 2003) reasons are also required, so that the decision notice includes 'a summary of their reasons for the grant and a summary of the policies and proposals in the development plan which are relevant to the decision'.

Planning applications will come before the planning committee in the form of an agenda. This will contain a report (with recommendations) made by the chief planning officer and include a summary of representations/consultations received. Committee is entitled to disagree with the recommendations of their officers but, remember, the applicant has a right of appeal.

The best guidance here is from Circular 8/93 on Costs, which states that:

> while planning authorities are not bound to follow advice from their Officers . . . they will be expected to show that they had reasonable planning grounds for a decision taken against such advice.

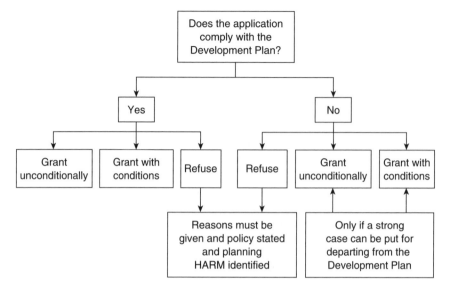

Figure 2.4 Flowchart indicating the most likely outcome of an application, when measured against the duty in the Act under section 38(6)

Decision-making near a listed building or in a conservation area or green belt

In a conservation area/green belt or when affecting the setting of a listed building, the duty imposed on the decision-maker is varied and by other legislation. This is not the same as listed building consent or conservation area consent but instead only the grant of a planning consent in these areas.

Application	Decision-maker's duty
When granting planning permission for development affecting a listed building or its setting. (This is *not* the same as listed building consent.)	To have 'special regard' to the desirability of preserving the building or its setting or any special features of historic or architectural interest (duty in Planning) Listed Buildings and Conservation Areas Act 1990.
When granting planning permission in a conservation area. (This is *not* the same as conservation area consent, which covers demolition.)	To pay 'special attention' to the desirability of preserving or enhancing its character or appearance (duty in legislation as above).
When granting planning permission in a green belt location.	To follow the guidance, in Planning Policy Guidance Note 2, that a general presumption exists against inappropriate development (which is by definition harmful to the green belt). Such development not to be approved except in very special circumstances. Policy in national planning guidance.

Procedures governing the determination of a planning application

The following points should be noted:

1.	Decision	The LPA decision must be given within eight weeks of receipt of a valid application. A decision issued beyond this period is still a valid one, but the applicant has a right of appeal against the failure of the LPA to determine the application.
2.	Delegation	The decision-making on a planning application may be made by a committee, sub-committee or officer of the council (the last being a delegated decision). Government targets seek that 90 per cent of all decisions are delegated to officers.
3.	Local Government Act 2000	This legislation changed the way that local government works by creating a cabinet style of decision-making (an executive). Decision-making on planning applications is not considered to be an executive function and is thus still exercised by the Planning (Applications) Committee.
4.	Natural justice in decision-making	Deciding a planning application is an administrative and not a legal act. There is no duty in law that an objector has a right to a hearing, e.g. to address the committee. However, if the LPA do allow the public speaking rights (and many do) then 'fairness' must be observed. No statutory duty exists to promote such public speaking rights, but it is increasingly being adopted by planning authorities as good practice.

The planning application process

The decision-maker's duty – how the decision to grant or refuse is made: Section 38(6)

The decision-maker in arriving at a decision on a planning application must discharge a legislative duty. Under the provisions of Section 29 of the Town and Country Planning Act 1971, which became incorporated into Section 70(2) of the Town and Country Planning Act 1990, this duty was that the decision-maker 'shall have regard to the provisions of the development plan so far as material to the application and to any other material considerations'.

In 1991 this was significantly changed by the introduction of Section 26 of the Planning and Compensation Act 1991, which introduced a new Section 54A into the 1990 Act as follows: 'Where in making any determination under the Planning Acts regard is to be had to the development plan, the determination shall be in accordance with the plan unless material considerations indicate

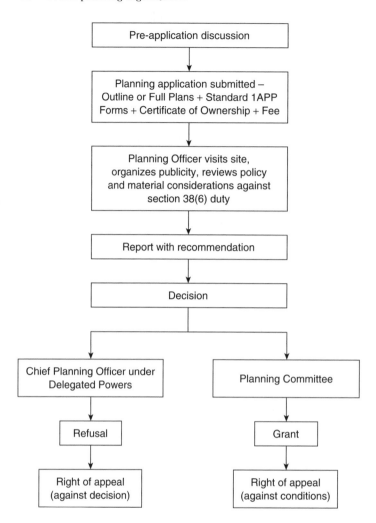

Figure 2.5 Flowchart of the planning application process

otherwise'. This provision has been carried over into the Planning and Compulsory Purchase Act 2004, section 38(6). A plan-led system has thus been created.

The general principles of the plan-led system are as follows:

- Great attention needs to be paid to development plan policy, especially to change a land-use allocation.
- Greater importance is given to adopted policy rather than emerging policy in the course of preparation. Section 38(6) only applies to adopted policy. Emerging policy passing through the adoption process does not benefit from these provisions, although policy is said to 'gather weight' as a material

consideration as it moves through the various stages towards formal Local Development Framework adoption.

- A greater degree of certainty in the development process is created as developers and planning authorities realize that, if a proposal is in conflict with policy, a presumption exists that permission will be refused and, if the proposal is in accord with policy, a presumption exists that permission will be granted.

- Greater attention will be focused towards the procedures by which policy is formulated, as developers and other interested parties realize that the weight attached to policy warrants greater attention to its content. Policy formulation will need to be monitored so that objections may be considered at the appropriate stage.

- Material considerations will still be of importance in the development process and capable of outweighing policy, yet where policy is adopted and up to date it will carry considerable weight in influencing the decision-making process.

Advertisement control

Control over outdoor advertisements is made under town planning statute and regulations.[13] Such control is self-contained – outside the rest of the planning system, with the creation of a separate category of advertisement control instead of planning permission. In addition to this, a series of exclusions and deemed consents are established, which reduce the need to seek consent for certain types of advertisements.

What is an advertisement?

An advertisement is defined by section 336(1) of the Town and Country Planning Act 1990 as:

> any word, letter, model, sign, placard, board, notice, or device or representation whether illuminated or not in the nature of, and employed wholly or partly for the purposes of advertisements, announcement or direction . . . and includes any hoarding or similar structure used, or designed or adapted for use, and anything else principally used, or designed or adapted principally for use, for the display of advertisements.[14]

In addition, certain modern forms of outdoor advertising fall within the definition and include rotating poster panels and advertisements displayed on permanent fixed blinds or canopies.

The need for advertisement consent

The Town and Country Planning (Control of Advertisements (England)) Regulations 2007 divide advertisements into three broad groupings:

Exclusions, i.e. applications excepted from deemed or express consent (see below), which fall within nine prescribed classes. These classes are defined as: (A) Displayed on enclosed land and not readily visible from outside; (B) Displayed on or in a moving vehicle (which excludes stationary vehicles in fields or lay-bys and specifically used for advertising purposes; (C) Incorporated into the fabric of the building, such as incised stonework lettering; (D) To advertise an article for sale; (E) To advertise a political election; (F) Any advertisement required by standing order of either House of Parliament; (G) A traffic sign; (H) Certain specified flags, including the National Flag and European Union Flag; (I) Displayed inside a building and not illuminated.

Deemed consent, i.e. would require consent, but this is automatically granted by the regulations, so no application is required. Sixteen such classes are defined as: (1) Functional advertisements for government departments, local authorities and public transport providers; (2) Relating to a premise, such as a means of identification, direction or warning; (3) Temporary advertisements, including a forthcoming event and 'for sale' boards (subject to size and location); (4) Adverts on business premises, with limitations on size and the nature of illumination; (5) Other advertisements on business premises, including notices, signs and means of drawing attention; (6) Adverts on the forecourt of a business premise, including a petrol station and terrace in front of a restaurant or café; (7) A flag advertisement displaying a company or trademark; (8) A hoarding advertisement to screen building or construction sites; (9) Adverts on highway structures, such as bus shelters or information kiosks; (10) Neighbourhood watch advertisements; (11) Directional signs (to residential developments); (12) Within a building; (13) Any advertisement displayed on the site for the preceding ten years without express consent; (14) After expiry of express consent (where permission is granted) the advert may be displayed for a further four years unless a previous condition forbids it; (15) Adverts on balloons no more than 60 metres above ground level; (16) Adverts on telephone kiosks.

Express consent is required when the advertisement is not covered by the deemed category. For example, this would cover most externally illuminated signs and multiple 'for sale' boards. If the LPA wishes to refuse permission for an application for express advertisement consent, it should only do so if it is considered that the advertisement will harm the amenity or public safety of the area. Amenity is defined as including aural and visual amenity, for example, because of its proximity to a listed building or its location within a conservation area. Public safety includes road safety as well as obstruction of highway surveillance cameras, speed cameras and security cameras. If, after considering the merits of the application, consent is given then this will (usually) last for five years. After the expiry of this period the advert may normally continue under the provisions of the deemed consent (see class 14 in the preceding paragraph) unless the planning authority seek discontinuance action, whereby they have subsequently decided that the advert now results in substantial injury to amenity or personal safety.

In the event that express consent is refused, a right of appeal exists to the Secretary of State. This right extends to include an appeal against a discontinuance notice.

Powers over contraventions

Display of an advertisement in contravention of the regulations is a criminal offence and if found guilty may be punished by a fine. The 2007 regulations identified a specific number of unauthorized advertisements, against which the planning authority could take action. These include fly-posting (the display of an advertisement without the owner's consent) and advertisements on vehicles or trailers parked in fields, verges or in lay-bys without consent. This has become an increasing problem, especially so in agricultural land traversed by motorways. Most such trailers and parked vehicles are used principally for the display of an advert and are illegal. The 2007 regulations make it clear that consent is required and unlikely to be given due to the associated safety and amenity issues associated with a proliferation of signage in rural areas and the distraction of drivers. The commonest form of enforcement will be the service of a discontinuance notice on the owner, occupier and any other interested person (such as the person who undertakes or maintains the display) in which reasons are explained for the removal of the notice with specific reference to matters of public safety and amenity.

Maladministration and town planning

Maladministration refers to faulty administration resulting in some form of injustice to a person or group of people. In 1974 the government created the Commissioner for Local Administration in England, commonly referred to as the 'Local Government Ombudsman',[15] with powers to investigate maladministration in all areas of local government. A Parliamentary Ombudsman had been created in 1967 to investigate complaints about central government departments.

Maladministration is not defined by statute. Examples include bias, delays, neglect, carelessness, or failure to observe procedure, which have all resulted in injustice. Separate Ombudsman offices have been established for England, Scotland and Wales. Once a complaint is received, it will be investigated to see if the matter falls within their jurisdiction and whether some maladministration is evident before a final investigation will be undertaken. The services of the Ombudsman are free and the staff are independent and impartial. If they find that maladministration has occurred, they may recommend a remedy to the matter, usually compensation paid to the complainants by the local authority. If the local authority decides to ignore the recommendation to pay compensation, no legal power exists whereby the Ombudsman may enforce payment.

Town planning matters often constitute the second most common area of complaints to the Ombudsman.[16] The lodging of a complaint does not mean that maladministration has occurred or been proven. It may be of little surprise that town planning does encourage complaints, because not all local people, some of whom may have been consulted on the application, will agree with a decision to grant permission. Although the system encourages public participation, such comment on applications is but one of the many material considerations. Frequently, public comment avoids planning matters and raises non-planning issues. Yet although some people feel aggrieved by planning decisions they consider 'unpalatable', this does not of itself constitute maladministration. Around 96 per cent of all complaints received do not proceed to a formal investigation. Matters found to constitute town planning maladministration have included a council's failure to enforce compliance with a landscaping scheme on a site; a delay of ten years to deal with unauthorized tipping of soil in an Area of Outstanding Natural Beauty; delay and conflicting advice by a council in deciding whether to save a tree protected by a Tree Preservation Order; and failure to take account of town planning history on a site and incorrectly informing the owner that a matter was permitted development when it was not.

A finding of maladministration in town planning is rare. Around 500,000 planning applications are dealt with every year in England, and around 4000 planning-related complaints are submitted to the Ombudsman. The Local Government Ombudsman Annual Report for the year 2006–07 revealed that planning was one of the more popular subjects for complaint, accounting for 24 per cent of the 18,320 complaints received across the entire local government service. Yet, some perspective is required here, with only 132 investigation reports (across the whole caseload) arriving at a finding of maladministration with injustice having occurred.[17] The Ombudsman plays a limited role in town planning, albeit an important one, in providing a mechanism for the investigation of bad practice and the ability to expose procedural problems. This may result in financial compensation to the complainant, but it also allows the local authority the opportunity to introduce reforms to its working practices to prevent a repeat in the future.

Probity

The planning system involves governmental regulation over the 'private' right to develop land, in the wider public interest of environmental and amenity protection. Since the late 1990s the system has increasingly been the subject of review and reflection with respect to matters of probity. Probity refers to qualities of uprightness and honesty. In public life, such as in land-use planning control, a high standard of probity is necessary to carry public confidence. This confidence is needed to give legitimacy to the precedence of public regulation over private interest in property development.

The UK planning system places the responsibility for decision-making on planning applications squarely on the shoulders of local elected politicians (councillors) who are not required to have any expertise in planning in order to take office, albeit that they are now required to undertake some training. This key principle gives a powerful democratic endorsement of decisions. However, many tensions arise, as councillors on planning committee must make decisions based exclusively on planning reasoning yet must also serve their constituents and reflect local opinion. Such local opinion may not be based on planning-related argument, and in the last decade or so development has increasingly been viewed negatively by local people as representing something undesirable and to be resisted. Since the economic boom period of the 1980s such tensions have become acute, as 'nimbyism'[18] has spread among local residents, who in turn will lobby their local councillors to help them in opposing development proposals.

This administrative duty on councillors is tempered by much planning law and locally produced policy. The chief planning officer and his professionally qualified colleagues advise the committee and make recommendations on individual applications. Clearly additional tension exists here as officers may make recommendations, based on policy and other material considerations, that councillors find unpalatable in the face of strong local opposition. It is acceptable for a planning committee to overturn officer recommendations to grant permission, although this must be on the basis of sound planning argument and not, for example, the volume or vociferousness of local opposition.

Since the 1970s the system has been monitored by the Ombudsman with respect to maladministration. During the mid-1990s, however, two major scandals received widespread media coverage and promoted tougher regulation in the policing of the system. While these two cases were numerically insignificant in terms of the total number of decisions made by the respective councils, the ramifications that followed had wider consequences in denting public confidence and influencing changes in respect of probity.

Regulation of the planning system has traditionally been threefold. First, the behaviour of officers and councillors has been shaped by codes of conduct dealing with the competence, honesty and integrity of officers[19] and their duty to serve the local community and to act within the law for councillors.[20] Second, statutory duties[21] are imposed to establish a series of moral and ethical standards. Third, officers and councillors must declare any interest that may affect their duty to determine a planning application. Such interests cover both financial (pecuniary) or other gains (such as the promotion of a private or personal interest). The division between pecuniary and non-pecuniary interest was established in the 1970s. The Local Government Act 2000 introduced a new system of ethical conduct in which any personal interest must be declared (including those of a relative, friend or employer). If that interest would be considered to be prejudicial to public confidence in the system, a councillor should play no part in consideration of the relevant planning application.

Reference to direct, indirect or remote pecuniary interest is therefore historic as a much wider test now applies:

Type of interest	Definition	Example
Direct pecuniary	Personal and financial position will be directly affected by a decision.	To grant permission on land you own, or refuse on land which adjoins yours.
Indirect pecuniary	Personal and financial interest of a person or body in close relation to the decision-maker (matrimonial or professional).	As above, with benefit to a company in which the decision-maker has some interest.
Remote pecuniary	Interest to include a wider remit of sons, daughters, siblings or parents of members.	Some benefits to these interests.

In North Cornwall District Council a number of decisions made by the planning committee in the late 1980s and early 1990s were questioned by journalists, culminating in a television documentary screened in 1991. It was alleged that a high number of planning permissions were granted to councillors sitting on planning committee (or their close family) and further that inappropriate development was granted in either the open countryside or Areas of Outstanding Natural Beauty, both against officers' guidance to refuse consent. Coincidentally, complaints to the Ombudsman from residents of North Cornwall rose to thirty-nine in 1990–91, compared to six complaints three years earlier. In 1992 the (then) Secretary of State, Michael Howard, appointed an independent expert to conduct an administrative enquiry into the control of planning in North Cornwall. In her report the following year (DoE 1993) Audrey Lees made eighteen recommendations, dealing mostly with the conduct of councillors. In particular, the enquiry dealt with how public confidence had been deeply damaged in circumstances where officer recommendations were ignored and councillors appeared to have acted unfairly by granting a large number of planning applications to fellow councillors. Audrey Lees clearly drew a line between such bad practices and any allegation of corruption. She explicitly stated that such matters fell outside her jurisdiction, although she did conclude that 'I cannot state categorically that there was no criminal corruption or conspiracy, only that I found no indication of it'. Nevertheless, in dealing with the conduct of the planning committee she set out guidance that 'it is not only the actual conduct of affairs which is important but also the *appearance* to the public' (her emphasis). The detailed recommendations made plain the fact that elected councillors had a wider responsibility to their local community, and extreme caution was required when voting on planning applications submitted by fellow councillors or when acting as a result of lobbying from applicants or constituents. While councillors may, quite legitimately, disagree with the recommendations of their officers, they would need good reason based upon sound planning judgement. One criticism levelled at officers in North Cornwall was that their reports on planning applications lacked sufficient detail on matters of planning policy. Councillors would need more guidance in these areas in the future.

In Bassetlaw (North Nottinghamshire) allegations of impropriety by the planning committee surfaced in 1995 and culminated in an independent inquiry at the instigation of the council.[22] The allegations centred on planning permissions, all granted against the professional advice of officers and all benefiting, in some way, the same developer. It was estimated that the total increase in land value on these sites was in the region of £6 million. Mr Phelps, the appointed investigator, drew the damning conclusion in his report that 'a reasonable outside observer must conclude that the Committee has been manipulated in some way'. As with North Cornwall, his conclusions avoided any direct charge of corruption, although he did state that 'whether or not there was any corrupt wrongdoing, some persons stand to gain several million pounds through increases in land values by the granting of outline planning permission on sites against a whole range of professional advice and considerations'. His central recommendation was that, in the interests of public confidence, 'the present Planning Committee should resign en bloc as soon as practicable'. Beyond such a dramatic reform, itself subsequently accepted and implemented by Bassetlaw, Mr Phelps called for the revocation of several previous planning permissions and reversals of local plan allocations. The council would need to introduce a new code of conduct as well as provide better training to councillors in the workings of the planning committee.

Both North Cornwall and Bassetlaw represented ad hoc or 'one-off' attempts to deal with, thankfully rare, cases of impropriety in the planning system. In both cases it appears that councillors failed to understand their responsibilities as imposed in codes of conduct or in statute. This situation was compounded by an ignorance of town planning law and a failure of council procedures to establish good practice, such as requiring councillors to provide detailed reasoning when departing from officer recommendation to refuse permission. Cases like North Cornwall and Bassetlaw were themselves perhaps indicative of other, more structural, problems in the planning system. The relationship between councillors and officers was sometimes poorly defined and some councillors on planning committee did not have much knowledge of planning policy or process.

In October 1994, the (then) Prime Minister, John Major, established a Committee on Standards in Public Life under the chair of Lord Nolan. The committee produced three reports between 1995 and 1997, 'Standards of Conduct in Parliament, the Executive and Non-departmental Public Bodies' (covering the activities of MPs, government ministers and their civil servants), 'Local Public Spending Bodies' (covering school and higher education and training/enterprise councils) and 'Standards of Conduct in Local Government in England, Scotland and Wales' (covering activities of councillors and officers and the planning function at a local government level). The first report did not establish that standards of behaviour in public life (for example in Parliament) had declined, but it did assert that codes of conduct were not always clear and enforcement of standards was sometimes inadequate (Committee on Standards in Public Life

1995). The Committee established seven principles to guide the behaviour of those in public life (see the table below) and laid down that maintenance of high standards should be achieved by the adoption of independent scrutiny of decision-making, the drawing up of codes of conduct, and education to promote and reinforce standards.

Seven principles	
Selflessness	Decisions made in the public interest
Integrity	Avoid any financial or other obligation to an outside body
Objectivity	Make a decision on merit only
Accountability	Open to scrutiny
Openness	Provide reasons
Honesty	Declare private interests
Leadership	Promote these principles by example

The third report (Committee on Standards in Public Life 1997) dealt extensively and, on occasion, contentiously with the planning system. The Committee had invited representations from the public and professionals. Planning produced the highest volume of letters drawn from any local government area and the Committee reported, somewhat anecdotally, that 'public satisfaction with the planning system does not seem to be particularly high'. The report itself was critical of the planning system. Training of councillors was patchy, the allocation of duties and responsibilities between officers and councillors was not always clear, planning gain amounted to the 'buying and selling' of planning permission, and there was insufficient scrutiny of planning decisions, especially when local authorities grant themselves planning permission. The Committee examined the responsibilities of councillors, concluding that it was acceptable for them to disagree with their officers, where appropriate, and that it is a duty of such elected people to listen to their constituents but to act properly when determining applications. Planning decision-making was viewed as an administrative and not a legal or judicial process.

Councillors were, therefore, free to balance community interests with other matters, while remaining within the constraints of planning law. Nolan's thirty-nine detailed recommendations divided themselves into three distinct areas, comprising the creation of a new ethical framework, clear reporting regarding declaration of interest, and achieving best practice in planning. Under the provisions of an ethical framework, councils would write their own codes of conduct (with a framework approved by Parliament), establish a standards committee and be accountable to a new tribunal with powers to arbitrate on disciplinary matters (for instance, to clarify interpretation of the code of conduct or deal with appeals when councillors sought to challenge any assertion that they had acted improperly). Councils would therefore benefit from a regime of much tighter internal self-regulation than had existed previously.

The third Nolan report focused on a desire for greater openness and account-ability in local government, with new statutory penalties and the creation of a culture of more effective 'whistle-blowing' in cases of misconduct. It would be wrong to conclude from Nolan that the system prior to this report (in 1997) lacked such accountability. Indeed, the Nolan Committee in drafting best prac-tice guidance did not claim originality for such ideas, as these recommendations were drawn from existing procedures already in place in many councils. Nolan, however, did crystallize these ideas and heightened awareness of them by seek-ing to raise the profile of local government generally and the town planning function in particular. Such reforms have been viewed as 'far-reaching'[23] and 'the vital tonic which the planning process requires in order to re-establish its authority and reputation' (Winter and Vergine 2000). The report's findings estab-lished an agenda for change. Nolan's call for a new ethical framework in local government was incorporated into Part III of the Local Government Act 2000. Each council would be required to adopt a code of conduct for councillors and a Standards or Scrutiny Committee and tribunal to uphold such standards, and to investigate allegations of failure to maintain the expected ethical behaviour.

Once adopted, all councillors must sign an undertaking to comply with the code and complete a register of their financial and non-financial interests (for example, employment or company interests). All codes must comply with a nation-ally set 'model code' issued by the Secretary of State under section 50 of the 2000 Act, ensuring a degree of consistency across authorities. Any interest in a planning application must be declared. The decision as to whether a councillor should withdraw from the Committee (i.e. has a prejudicial interest) is deter-mined by the hypothetical test that a member of the public with knowledge of the relevant facts would consider this personal interest to be prejudicial. The application of the principles of natural justice has ensured that a member of a planning committee must not engage in predetermination, that is to say making up his or her mind before the planning committee sits. Common law requires that the planning committee and its members exercise a proper discretion and that this is not 'fettered' in some way by a councillor making up his mind and declaring as much ahead of the meeting. Further, the code imposes a high moral standard on councillors such that in both their official and private capacity their actions must not bring local government into disrepute. Regulation of the potential misconduct is a matter for the independently established Standards Board in England and the Ombudsman in Wales. Sanctions available to the Standards Board include suspension or disqualification. Excellent detailed guidance on best practice within the workings of this new system was developed, in 2008, by the Government Office for London. This guidance states, for example, that a councillor on a planning committee can attend consultation events – even meet the applicant – but must avoid expressing a view on an application's merits (Government Office for London 2008).

The third Nolan report raised awareness of probity in planning. Its sometimes critical stance was tempered by the report's own acknowledgment that in its examination of local government it found:

an enormous number of dedicated and hardworking people. . . . We are of course well aware of the relatively few, but highly publicised, cases where things have gone wrong or people have behaved improperly. But it is important to set such cases in the context of more than 20,000 councillors and 2,000,000 employees in local government.

(Committee on Standards in Public Life 1997)

It is of fundamental importance that the planning system carries public confidence. Nolan and subsequent legislation maintained vigilance in this area, as clearly more can and should be done to promote openness and raise standards in planning decision-making. An important principle must be established by which even if people disagree with the granting or refusing of a planning application, they accept that the decision was made openly and fairly after due consideration of all relevant issues.

Case study 2.1   Planning and Property Development in the City of London

The ancient heart of London, 'The City of London', comprises one square mile in area (2.6 km^2) and incorporates the capital's financial sector. The Great Fire of London in 1666 destroyed approximately 75 per cent of the medieval City, and bombing during the Second World War destroyed approximately 30 per cent (Marriott 1989).

The City Corporation is the local planning authority for this area. In the immediate post-war years the City Corporation was subject to the newly introduced planning regulations of the Town and Country Planning Act 1947. A statutory development plan was approved in 1951 under the guidance of Charles Holden and William Holford, who were themselves previously responsible for development of the London transport system (Holden) and for the redevelopment of the Paternoster district within the City (Holford – Refer to study on Paternoster).

Since the early 1950s the City has been the subject of two property booms, those of the 1960s and the 1980s. The nature of each boom and its influence upon commercial development was shaped by the town planning system, and the buildings resulting from each boom may be distinguished by their contrasting architectural styles.

In the 1960s the demands for new office accommodation in the financial heart of London fuelled a building boom that was able to use newly acquired building methods involving concrete and steel construction to build high-rise office blocks. Architects, such as Mies Van der Rohe (1886–1969), considered that concrete used in construction should be 'seen and not screened' (Ross-Goobey 1992). Redevelopment around London Wall and Paternoster Square provides good examples of the style of the age, notably external concrete facings and curtain walling, whereby the external walls are hung like curtains from the concrete floors.

Town planning policies were an influence, mostly by the imposition of plot ratio controls. These controls restricted the amount of lettable floorspace as a portion of every square metre of land within the plot. This would restrict the resulting height and bulk of a building, so that a common ratio of say 5:1 or 3:1 would allow 5 or 3 m^2 of lettable floorspace for every 1 m^2 of site area. Conservation area controls were not introduced until the late 1960s and the City Corporation made few design-related decisions during this period. The architect and developer were allowed a free rein to design the fashionable brutalistic-looking tower blocks of the age, so long as they satisfied the plot ratio criterion.

During the 1980s the City of London was to experience a second boom, yet one whose impact upon development was to be far more dramatic than that experienced during the 1960s. The growth in information technology, increased levels of economic activity, financial deregulation, a reaction by many people against the architectural style of the previous boom, and a relaxation of town planning controls, were all to contribute towards a second boom in commercial development. The rate of property development is largely controlled by the town planning system, because the amount of floorspace permitted will influence the level of market activity. During the 1980s the City Corporation relaxed the application of its own planning policies and increased plot ratios to permit more floorspace on individual sites in an attempt to encourage developers to come forward with redevelopment schemes. It was hoped that a relaxed town planning regime would be perceived by many developers as a positive move. In 1986 the City Corporation made provision for an increase in office floorspace. At that time the City accommodated around 2,694,000 m^2 (29 million ft^2) of office floorspace. Taking the development cycle between 1986 and 1994, 2,276,050 m^2 (24.5 million ft^2) of office floorspace was completed. At June 1994 a further 1,263,440 m^2 (13.6 million ft^2) was the subject of unimplemented planning permission.

This almost relentless drive by the City Corporation planners and planning committee to permit new offices was not motivated by some desire to accommodate the needs of property developers but instead was a reaction to the threat posed by massive office development in the London Docklands, only a few kilometres to the east. Canary Wharf, the 244 m high tower on the Isle of Dogs created 929,000 m^2 (10 million ft^2) of new offices alone, and the London Docklands Development Corporation created a total of 1,208,000 m^2 (13 million ft^2) of new office floorspace between 1981 and 1994. The London Docklands Development Corporation (LDDC) and the Enterprise zone within it, were established by the Conservative government in 1981 to redevelop the designated 2226 ha (5500 acres) of derelict former docks to the east of the City of London. The LDDC saw office redevelopment as a key part of its strategy. The new office floorspace could offer cheaper rents than the City, and new floorspace incorporating all the necessary information technology and modern services. The City, fearing an exodus of office occupiers, fought back by granting as many office planning permissions as it could. The LDDC itself was a deregulated planning body whose planning powers overrode the existing London boroughs. The City Corporation, although not a deregulated planning body, merely served to throw away many of its own development plan policies to achieve the same effect. With the following economic slump in 1989, the permissions of the 1980s created a massive oversupply in the 1990s, resulting in both much empty floorspace and a considerable drop in rents. Some of this new office floorspace may never be let. In 1994, it was estimated that in Docklands some office floorspace had a vacancy rate of 50 per cent with rents as low as £0.92 /m^2 achieved in the late 1980s. LDDC's own statistics put this figure at 418,050 m^2 (4.5 million ft^2) or 35 per cent of all floorspace being vacant (LDDC Property Facts Sheet, updated periodically and available from LDDC Information Centre). No comparable figure is available for the City.

In the City itself some of the new office floorspace may also never be let. Before market demand can be found, new technology may render obsolete some of the schemes of the 1980s. Their glittering architectural styling incorporating postmodern hi-tech and classical revival styles may serve as a monument to the inability of the planners to predict an oversupply and to apply a braking mechanism to the ferocious activity of the property developers combined with the planning policies pursued by the London Docklands Development Corporation to permit large-scale office redevelopments such as Canary Wharf.

Notes on architectural styles

'Hi-tech' buildings are characterized by exposed steel structures, use of glass, and external siting of piping and ducting, a good example being the Lloyd's Building in London, by Richard Rogers.

'Classical revival' employs plentiful use of Greek and Roman decoration, sometimes called 'fake Georgian', a good example being Richmond Riverside, London, by Quinlan Terry.

'Postmodern' employs a mix of historic detailing with 'symbolism', where the building incorporates unusual shapes and forms, a good example being Alban Gate on London Wall by Terry Farrell.

3 Town planning law and regulation

A system of comprehensive control over all development was introduced by the TCPA 1947, which required that all building development and any material changes in the use of a building and of land would, henceforth, require planning permission, to be issued by the local planning authority. The legislation established just what would or would not require planning permission. Since 1947 all town planning legislation has provided a definition of 'development'. To understand the workings of the system it is necessary to understand just what falls within the provisions of the definition of development to establish what does and does not require planning permission.

This chapter will examine the principal legislation that defines what does and what does not require the submission of an application for planning permission. Detailed reference will be made to the TCPA 1990, Town and Country (Use Classes Order) 2005 and Town and Country Planning (General Permitted Development) Order 1995 and 2008, and consideration given to further changes to accommodate domestic renewable energy within certain freedoms from planning permission. The final section of the chapter will deal with the enforcement of town planning control, a specialist area of planning legislation that deals with remedial action against the development of land undertaken without the benefit of planning permission. The chapter will be subdivided as follows:

- The definition of development
- Use Classes Order and General Permitted Development Order (as amended)
- Enforcing town planning control.

The definition of development

Section 55(1) of the 1990 TCPA defined 'development' as:

> the carrying out of building, engineering, mining or other operations in, on, over or under land, or the making of any material change in the use of any buildings or other land.

This definition of development provides the very basis for the development control system and introduces a distinction between operations (building, engineering, mining or other) and material change of use (activity). The definition is itself broad in content and must be considered alongside the General Permitted Development Order (GPDO) and Use Classes Order (UCO). Read in isolation it would result in a vast number of operations and uses falling within the definition. The GPDO and UCO create a whole series of exceptions to the need for planning permission, effectively releasing many types of development from the need for planning permission (Grant 2003).

The TCPA 1990 does help clarify some issues that either do or do not fall within the definition. For the avoidance of doubt, the matters that do not amount to development are:

- Any internal works or external works that do not result in a material impact on the appearance of a building. Such external works would depend upon the circumstances of an individual case but include the addition of guttering and downpipes and repointing of mortar between bricks.
- Maintenance/improvement works within the boundary of a road undertaken by a highway authority or the laying out of an access to a highway.
- Inspection/repair/renewal of sewers.
- The use of any building or other land within the curtilage of a dwelling-house for an incidental use – for example, the use of a garden shed for hobby activities.
- The use of land for agriculture[1] or forestry (agricultural or forestry-related buildings may require permission).
- The change of use within the same use class in the Use Classes Order.
- The construction of various structures within the terms of the General Permitted Development Order (technically development but granted by the order, thus no need to make an application), including domestic micro-generation.

However, an operation that specifically does amount to development is the conversion of one dwelling into two (e.g. subdivision of a house into flats). The Act does not list all matters that may or may not require planning permission beyond these specific groupings. The decision whether or not any other proposal falls within or outside the definition of development will be the subject of interpretation. The following section will now set out some guidelines that will aid such judgements.

Operational development

The principal characteristic of operational development is that it results in some permanent physical change to the appearance of the land concerned. The works may be building, engineering, mining or other operations, and these will be considered in turn.

Edinburgh Napier University
Merchiston Library

**Customer name: OLUBUKOLA
OLUMUYIWA TOKEDE**

Title: Urban planning and real estate
development /
ID: 38042007758616
Due: 04/02/2016 23:59:00 GMT

Total items: 1
28/01/2016 10:31

Renewals:
http://librarysearch.napier.ac.uk
0131 455 6021

Give us your comments at
libraryfeedback@napier.ac.uk

Building operations

Building operations include the demolition of buildings, rebuilding, structural alterations and extensions, and are works usually undertaken by a builder. Case law dealing with what is and is not a building operation has established three tests of a building operation, namely:

- Does it have size?
- Does it have permanence?
- Is it physically attached?

In practice, if two of the three tests are satisfied, the matter in question will constitute a building operation. For example, we may conclude that the erection of a new warehouse, industrial unit, a block of flats or a dwelling house each constitutes a building operation as they incorporate size, permanence and physical attachment. They all fit the common everyday use of the word 'building' and we should experience little difficulty in establishing that they are operational development. However, it is important to recall that a structure need not look like a normal building to constitute a building operation, so that erection of a radio mast aerial, satellite antenna, and metal security shutters on a shop front all constitute building operations. In 1986 a fibreglass shark sculpture was erected on the roof of a terraced house in Headington, Oxford. In similar vein, a marlin was attached by a homeowner to his roof in Croydon. The works constituted a building operation and required planning permission. The argument that they constituted works of art and would thus be exempt from control, was clearly a false one.

Engineering operations

Engineering operations are taken to include operations normally undertaken by a person carrying on business as an engineer. This has been interpreted in case law as not meaning that an engineer need always be employed but instead that the works in themselves call for the skills of an engineer.

Table 3.1 Summary of building operations

Definition	Key points to remember	NB
§336(1) and §55(1A) of the TCPA 1990 to *include* demolition, rebuilding, alteration, extension, or addition, to *exclude* any plant or machinery comprised within a building, structure or erection	Three tests: • size • permanence • physical attachment. If any two are decisive then it will usually follow that the proposal constitutes a building operation.	Does not have to *look* like a building to be a building operation, e.g. Oxford shark

Table 3.2 Summary of engineering operations

Definition	Key points to remember	NB
§336(1) of the TCPA 1990 states it *includes* the formation or laying out of a means of access to a highway.	The limited definition in the Act has been *interpreted* as including any works requiring the skills of an engineer.	Many engineering operations may be any tied in with building operations. It is acceptable to consider them together.

It is sometimes difficult to distinguish between engineering and building operations. For example, in the construction of a new office development an engineer may be called in to survey the subsoil and deal with the foundation details (clearly an engineering operation) and then the office is constructed (clearly a building operation). In such cases it would be acceptable to regard this as both an engineering and building operation, thus amounting to development, although only one grant of planning permission (to cover both aspects) will be required. Other examples of engineering operations include the creation of a hard-standing, excavation of soil to form an artificial lake, or the deposit of soil to form a golf course or embankments.

Mining operations

Mining operations, although specifically mentioned within the definition of development, are not defined within the Act. 'Mining' can be taken to include the winning and working of minerals in, on or under land, whether by surface or underground working.[2] 'Minerals' are defined within the Act as including 'all minerals and substances in or under land of a kind ordinarily worked for removal by underground or surface working, except that it does not include peat cut for purposes other than sale'.

Other operations

The inclusion of 'other' within the definition of development is rather unhelpful to both student and practitioner, because of its vague 'catch all' quality. The concept of 'other' defies adequate definition. It may be useful to consider it where works involve some form of physical alteration to land, which appears to constitute an operation yet does not sit easily within the previous definitions of building, engineering or mining operations. For example, it was held in one appeal decision that the tipping of soil on to land for the purpose of raising the level of the land did not, in that case, constitute an engineering operation, but did constitute 'other' operations. The decision as to whether raising of ground level constitutes an 'engineering' or 'other' operation will depend upon the merits of the individual case. However, as a general rule, it would appear that the creation of embankments or larger-scale projects such as golf courses would

Table 3.3 Summary of mining operations

Definition	Key points to remember	NB
Not defined in the Act but taken to include surface or underground extraction of minerals	Coal, iron ore, china clay extraction	Any extraction of minerals

Table 3.4 Summary of other operations

Definition	Key points to remember	NB
Works that result in some permanent physical change to land yet do not easily fit within engineering, building or mining operations	Consider only in exceptional cases, or as a last resort.	Rare. Not a helpful concept for students or practitioners.

constitute engineering operations, whereas smaller-scale tipping and raising of ground level would fall within 'other' operations.

Demolition and operational development

Considerable legal debate has prevailed[3] over the question as to whether demolition of buildings falls within the definition of development. Certainly, if we go back to the definition of an operation as something resulting in a change to the physical characteristics of the land, then demolition works would be covered. Demolition may involve the work of a builder or engineer and may be considered to constitute either a building or engineering operation, yet, on examination of the tests of a building operation, demolition would not easily fit within the criteria of size, physical attachment and permanence. Case law has in the past resulted in conflicting findings on this issue. The definitive statement on the subject was made in 1991 by Mr David Widdicombe QC, sitting as a High Court Judge in *Cambridge City Council* v. *Secretary of State for the Environment and Another*. It was held that demolition would constitute development where it was an operation that a builder normally carried out. Thus, demolition was found to be a building operation. To avoid a vast additional burden of planning applications on local planning authorities, the government issued a specific direction to clarify the matter. Demolition of the following would not constitute development and therefore would not require submission of a planning application:

• Any listed building or unlisted building in a conservation area (remember that Listed Building Consent and Conservation Area Consent respectively would be required) so that some measure of control is exercised, but is not achieved by a planning application.[4]

- Any building except a dwellinghouse (includes a flat) or building adjoining a dwellinghouse.
- Any building smaller than 50 m^3 volume.
- Any gate, wall, fence or other means of enclosure.[5]

Material change of use

Taking the second limb of the definition of development, it is necessary to consider material changes of use. These have been defined as activities done in, alongside or on land, but do not interfere with the actual physical characteristics of the land. It is therefore important to understand the concept of a material change in the use of land and that this deals only with activity (uses) and does not deal with physical works on the land, such as building operations. In dealing with material change of use it is important to establish primary uses, ancillary uses and mixed uses, and to define the 'planning unit' – the exact area of land affected by the change of use.

What is material?

Determining whether or not a material change has occurred will depend upon the merits of the individual case. For a change or shift in use/activity to result in a material change it will be necessary to establish that the change has been substantial or significant, rather than some minor shift in activity.

To determine a material change in use it is necessary to examine the character of the use. For example, is the character retail (sale of goods to the public) or non-retail (services such as banking or 'food and drink' users such as pubs, restaurants). Following this, it is necessary to examine the consequences of the use in terms of planning issues (e.g. noise, smells, hours of operation, traffic or pedestrian generation). If either the character or consequences have changed to a significant degree, then it can be established that a material change of use has occurred.

In determining a material change, two problems are usually encountered. The first relates to the choice of the unit of land to be considered (the planning unit), which will influence the decision on materiality. For example, if we consider an industrial estate which comprises ten factory buildings and a small office building and the office is then converted to a warehouse/storage use, the decision as to whether this is material will very much depend on the planning unit considered.

The main principle derived from case law[6] is that the planning unit should be taken to mean the unit of occupation or ownership. However, a separate unit is created if within one unit of occupation two or more physically separate and distinct areas are occupied for unrelated purposes.

Taking the previous example, it would follow that, if each industrial unit and the office building are within separate ownership, then the office building

Table 3.5 The relationship between primary and ancillary uses

Primary	Ancillary
(i) Hotel with . . .	Bar, restaurant, laundry, swimming pool, sauna, open to hotel residents
(ii) Shop unit with . . .	Office at rear dealing with associated administration
(iii) Retail warehouse or departmental store . . .	Associated café/restaurant
(iv) Office building with . . .	Staff gym

forms its own planning unit and a material change of use has occurred, within that unit. If the whole industrial estate was within one ownership, it could be argued that the whole estate is one planning unit and no material change of use has occurred to that unit as a whole, by alteration in the use of such a small component. The second problem relates to the fact that, within any one site, several uses may take place. To help establish a material change of use it will be necessary to establish the primary (main or principal) use of the land. It will often be the case that ancillary (second or incidental) uses may function alongside such a primary use.

Consider the examples in Table 3.5. Provided that the ancillary activities remain functionally related to the primary activity, then no material change will have occurred. If the ancillary activities increase to such an extent that they could no longer be said to be ancillary, then a mixed use has occurred.

'Intensification' is a widely misunderstood concept within consideration of change of use. The intensification of a use may occur (e.g. increased levels of production output in a factory), which in itself does not result in a change of use. Intensification can be said to result in a change of use only where the intensification itself results in a change in the character and town planning consequences of the land. For example, if a clothes shop sells more clothes, it has intensified its activity, but no material change of use has occurred. It is a better practice to look for a material change in use rather than intensification.

Summary of material change of use

- To establish a material change of use, consider the character of use and consequences of that use.
- Define the area to be considered by establishing the planning unit (unit of occupation in which uses are functionally linked).
- Remember that in dealing with character/consequence of a use the primary use will need to be identified, together with ancillary uses that are secondary to it. If no primary/secondary relationship can be established, then a mixed use is created. If a secondary use grows to such an extent as to create a mixed use, then a material change of use has occurred from primary to mixed.

- Intensification of use is a misleading concept. Consider instead the characteristics of a material change of use.

The General Permitted Development (Amendment) Order 2005 (SI 2935) and 2008 (SI 675) and 2008 (SI 2362) and the Town and Country Planning (Use Classes) (Amendment) (England) Order 2005 (SI 84)

The GPDO and the UCO establish a series of freedoms from the need to apply for planning permission.

The General Permitted Development Order (GPDO)

The GPDO has two principal benefits for the planning system:

- It covers classes of development that are considered to be of relatively trivial planning importance and, in most cases, are environmentally acceptable.
- It relieves local planning authorities of a vast administrative workload for (generally) acceptable operations.

Article 3 of the current order (the current order being 2005 and revised in 2008) grants planning permission for a variety of the operations and some identified changes of use. In other words, any operations or uses that adhere to the criteria laid down in the thirty-three separate clauses of Schedule 2 constitute development, but permission for that development is automatically granted; that is, it is permitted by the Order without the need to submit a planning application and is therefore known as 'permitted development'.

The most important classes are:

- Part 1: Development within the curtilage of a dwellinghouse, e.g. extensions to a dwellinghouse of a certain size and siting are permitted development.
- Part 3: Changes of use, e.g. to change from A3 (Food and drink) to A2 (Financial and professional services), from A3 or A2 to A1 (Retail), from B2 (General industry) to B1 (Business) and from B1 or B2 to B8 (Storage and distribution). This was updated in 2005 so that the new classes of A5 (Hot food takeaway) and A4 (Drinking establishments) could revert to A3/A2/A1 without the need for planning permission. This was sometimes referred to as the 'ratchet' effect, and it only works in one direction within the A class of uses in which the numbers must fall for it to be exempt from planning. Thus, to go from A5 to A3 would not require planning (as the numbers fall) but not in reverse (A3 to A5) where the numbers rise and planning permission is required.
- Part 8: Industrial and warehouse development, e.g. small extensions to such buildings.

- Residential permitted development does not apply to flats, only to dwellinghouses.
- Residential permitted development rights are reduced on Article 1(5) land, i.e. in National Parks, Areas of Outstanding Natural Beauty, or conservation areas.
- Where the local planning authority has served an Article 4 Direction.[7] Such Directions require the direct approval of the Secretary of State. Normally Article 4 Directions withdraw permitted development rights for a particular class of development within a specified area. This is mostly employed in conservation areas; it protects the amenity and gives the planners greater control over development – for example, requiring planning permission for such activities as exterior painting or the installation of double glazing.

The local planning authority in granting planning permission for new development may seek to remove future permitted development rights by imposing a condition. However, they must have good reason to do this; for example, in high-density residential developments this will protect the amenities of the neighbouring occupiers. As we have seen, we must refer to the General Permitted Development Order with operational development, whereas with the vast majority of material changes of use, we refer to the Use Classes Order.

Review of the General Permitted Development Order 2007

A wide ranging review of permitted development was instigated in 2007, with consultation papers on 'permitted development rights for households' and 'micro-generation' covering respectively domestic extensions and small-scale domestic renewable energy. The government had previously commissioned consultants to address these issues, together with a wider review designed to reduce bureaucracy for householders and entitled the 'Householder Development Consents Review'. The combined result was a call to broaden the freedoms offered to householders in their ability to extend to the side or rear. The existing limit of 70 cubic metres volume was considered an artificial limit on the extension of larger properties. The appointed consultants had recommended that domestic permitted development be the subject of an assessment of impact as opposed to a 'one size fits all' approach based on volume tolerances. This would means that extensions would be permitted at single- or two-storey level, provided that certain key conditions were met regarding distances to boundary, materials to be matched, lack of balconies and pitched roofs if two-storey. By contrast, the review considered that the treatment of roof extensions under provision of the 1995 Order was too generous, leading to overlarge dormers and potential to harm the amenities of neighbours. Again, an impact-based approach would impose limits on size, location and materials within the roof pitch. While the General Permitted Development Order would remain a somewhat dry and dull set of legal principles, the underlying philosophy would change from a set of percentage tolerances to a series of detailed rules over impact, to protect residential amenity while freeing up unnecessary planning applications from the system.

Climate change and sustainability would also influence reforms. Entec Consultants were vested with the responsibility to review the freedoms that could be given to domestic renewable energy. This work fed into a government review and consultation in 2007 that recommended in favour of such micro-generation, which it was estimated could account for up to 40 per cent of UK electricity demands by 2050. Such technologies cover solar water-heating systems (usually on roofs but they can be stand-alone), ground–air–water heat pumps, wind turbines, biomass, and combined heat and power. In broad terms these would be accommodated into the permitted development regime so that solar panels/photovoltaic cells would be exempt from planning control, provided that they did not project more than 150 mm from the existing roof plane or stand more than 150 mm from a wall. If they were stand-alone panels they would need to be no greater than 4 metres high and set back by a distance of 5 metres from each boundary of the property. Wind turbines on a domestic roof would be exempt from the need for planning permission, provided that they were no greater than 3 metres above the highest part of the roof or 11 metres stand-alone, and in both cases the blade diameter did not exceed two metres. This would provide a reasonable balance between the need to harvest wind energy and the amenities of neighbours. The report dealt also with biomass (commonly wood-burning stoves), heat pumps and combined heat and power technologies but found that in most cases these would fall within the existing permitted development regime and be exempt from control. Most of these recommendations were incorporated into the 2008 amendments, in which a vast array of domestic renewables (wind, heat pumps and photovoltaic-solar) were granted exemption from formal planning controls in the wider interests of sustainability and the promotion of non-fossil-fuel energy sources.

These reviews would result in changes to permitted development in 2008. The planning system is not best placed to promote a take-up of domestic renewable energy, but these documents would provide much greater clarity as to what would be permitted without the need for a planning application. A new Part 40 of the GPDO was introduced in 2008, to exclude most domestic micro-generation equipment (such as solar panels, ground source heat pumps and biomass' heating) from the need for planning permission. The planning system would play its part by avoiding the need for an application and the consequential uncertainty that permission would follow.

The Use Classes Order

The UCO places certain planning uses into classes, with a total of thirteen classes and a variety of subdivisions within each class. To move from one use to another *within* a class is not development (Grant 1989, Home 1989). Conversely, to move between any of the thirteen classes is development and therefore requires planning permission. (The current order is the 2005 amended order and Statutory Instrument number 2005/84.)

The twofold purpose of the Order, as stated in the original Circular 13/87 (which is now out of date in so far as the 2005 revisions are concerned), is first to reduce the number of use classes while retaining effective control over change of use, which, because of environmental consequences or relationships with other uses, needs to be subject to specific planning applications; and, second, to ensure that the scope of each class is wide enough to take in changes of use that generally do not need to be subject to specific control.

The Use Classes Order is not comprehensive. Any use not covered by the Order (and therefore outside the provision of the Order) is considered to be *sui generis* (of its own kind). Any movement to or from a *sui generis* use is outside the provision of the UCO and would require planning permission. The 2005 revisions are helpful here and specifically identify a number of *sui generis* uses such as amusement arcades, car showrooms and launderettes.

The relationship between the GPDO and the UCO

Consider, for example, Class A1 (shops) of the UCO. The Order states that Class A1 use is for all or any of the purposes shown in Table 3.6.

Therefore, to change from a book shop to a travel agency is within the A1 class and would not require planning permission. To change from a book shop to a use outside A1 would require planning permission. It follows that, in the vast majority of cases, to move between individual classes is a material change of use for which planning permission will be required. In a few cases, such movements, although accepted as constituting a change of use and therefore development, are themselves automatically granted planning permission by Part 3 of the GPDO, so that to move from A5 (Hot food Takeway) to A1 (Retail) use is development, but it falls within the provision of Part 3 of the GPDO and therefore constitutes permitted development for which no planning application

Table 3.6 Summary of examples within the UCO

Use class	Principal examples (not exhaustive)
A1 Retail	Any shop selling retail goods to public → post office → travel agent → off licence → sale of cold food for consumption off the premises
A2 Financial and professional services	Bank → building society → estate agent
A3 Restaurants and cafés	Sale and consumption of food
A4 Drinking establishments	Public house, wine bar and drinking establishment
A5 Hot food takeaway	Sale of food to take away

Note
→ Denotes a movement 'within' the use class, which is not development and therefore would not require planning permission

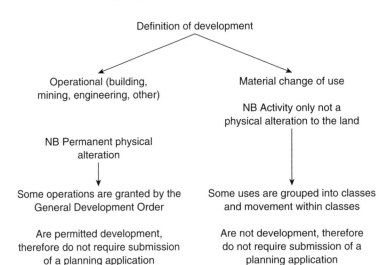

Definition of development

Operational (building,
mining, engineering, other)

NB Permanent physical
alteration

Some operations are granted by the
General Development Order

Are permitted development,
therefore do not require submission
of a planning application

Material change of use

NB Activity only not a
physical alteration to the land

Some uses are grouped into classes
and movement within classes

Are not development, therefore
do not require submission of a
planning application

Figure 3.1 A summary of the General Permitted Development Order and the Use
Classes Order

is required. Although it is somewhat confusing to include provisions relating
to use in the GPDO, the simplest way to remember these issues is that, after
establishing that a proposed use results in movement between use classes, cross-
reference to Part 3 of the GPDO to ascertain whether this is permitted development. Figure 3.1 illustrates a summary of this. The overall relationship can
be summarized in a flowchart (Figure 3.2).

Enforcing town planning control

> When the development of land is undertaken without the benefit of planning
> permission, the local planning authority has enforcement powers to seek a
> remedy to those breaches of control that they consider to be unacceptable.

A breach of town planning control is defined as the carrying out of development without the required planning permission, or failure to comply with the
terms of any condition attached to a grant of planning permission.[8] Such an unauthorized development does not automatically constitute unlawful development.
It will only become a criminal offence in the event of enforcement action being
taken by the LPA that is subsequently ignored or not complied with by the
landowner, or if works have been carried out to a listed building. It should also
be remembered that carrying out development without planning permission is
not automatically followed by enforcement action. The LPA has discretion in
deciding whether or not to enforce, i.e. they must deem the enforcement action
to be expedient and this decision is usually based on the breach being harmful
to amenity and/or contrary to planning policy. If the LPA considers the breach to

be acceptable, they may invite the owner to submit a retrospective planning application, so that the matter can be decided through the normal development control procedures. Once such a retrospective application is granted, then the matter becomes regularized. The established time limits for taking enforcement action effectively create immunity against action. This means that operational development (building, engineering and mining) or changes of use to a single dwelling substantially completed over four years ago or any other breaches completed over ten years ago are immune from action to remove them or cease the activities undertaken.

The Carnwath Report

In 1988 the Secretary of State for the Environment appointed an eminent planning lawyer, Robert Carnwath QC, to undertake a review of enforcement procedures (Carnwath Report 1989).

The findings were published in 1989 as 'Enforcing Planning Control' with a series of recommendations designed to make enforcement more effective when dealing with unacceptable breaches of control. These recommendations were introduced into the system by the Planning and Compensation Act 1991

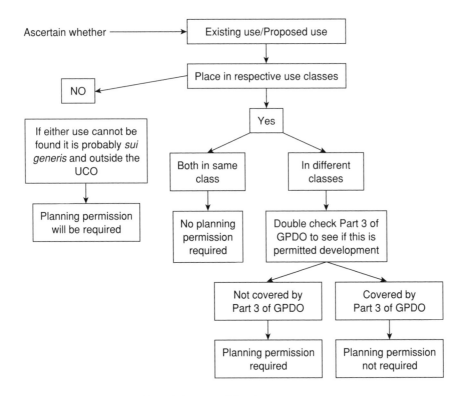

Figure 3.2 A summary of the definition of development

(Sections 1 to 11), which added new powers and amended those existing under the TCPA 1990.

The post-1991 system was based on eight key areas of change:

- The introduction of immunity, as previously explained, so that development falling outside the specific time period for enforcement action would automatically become lawful. This would remove an element of uncertainty over the lawful or other status of such land.
- The introduction of a new procedure to establish the lawfulness of an existing or lawful use in which a landowner could receive a clear and binding decision by the planning authority.
- The creation of new powers to allow a local authority to enter land in pursuit of an enforcement function.
- The newly acquired ability given to a local authority to obtain information about potential breaches.
- A simplification of the various rules and technical requirements for the drafting of an enforcement notice and clarification of grounds of appeal to the Secretary of State.
- An increase in the financial penalties for non-compliance with an enforcement notice.
- The introduction of express powers to apply to the Court when seeking an injunction to restrain an actual or threatened breach of planning control.
- The creation of a ceiling on the amount of compensation likely to be paid following a stop notice.

The various enforcement powers available to the LPA in the post-1991 system can be summarized as follows:

Planning contravention notice (PCN)

Prior to taking formal enforcement action, the LPA needs to determine whether a breach has in fact occurred. This may not always be an easy matter to ascertain. To assist, the LPA may serve a Planning Contravention Notice requiring information from the owner or other people with an interest regarding operations, uses or matters in respect of planning conditions relating to the land.[9] For example, a landowner or operator may start digging a trench on a site or may begin to service/maintain motor vehicles. A PCN can help to ascertain whether the trench is for the construction of a building or that the motor repairs undertaken in a domestic garage are for a commercial purpose and not merely a hobby. From this response, the LPA may initiate formal enforcement action, but the service of the notice will alert the owner to the council's concern, from which further dialogue between both sides may overcome the problem without recourse to any further action. The decision to serve a PCN is an option available to the LPA. They do not have to serve one as a precondition of future action. The notice may require information as to ownership of the land, operations or activities being carried out, any use of the land or any matters related to a breach of planning control. Once served, failure to comply with its requirements within twenty-one days constitutes a criminal offence, which can be charged on a daily basis to a maximum of £1000 on summary conviction. It is also an offence to knowingly or recklessly give false or misleading information.

Enforcement notice

The enforcement notice constitutes the principal and most commonly used enforcement mechanism at the disposal of the LPA when seeking to remedy a breach of planning control. Such action is entirely discretionary and is derived from the Town and Country Planning Act 1990 which establishes that any such notice may be issued if a breach of planning control is apparent and if it is considered expedient to pursue that course, having regard to the development plan and other material considerations.

Prior to the service of such a notice the LPA will need to be sure of its case and thus gather evidence. In the post-Carnwath era this was made much easier by virtue of the planning contravention notice. Additionally, the planning authority may serve a Section 330 notice, which requires the occupier of the land to provide information of interest in the land or the interest of other persons. The enforcement notice is issued by the LPA and served upon the landowner or any other person with an interest in the land who will be affected by the enforcement action. It will identify the breach of planning control, stipulate a course of action (steps to be taken) to remedy that breach and will indicate a time period within which such steps are required to have been taken or any activities ceased.

The Town and Country Planning (Enforcement Notices and Appeals) (England) Regulations 2002/2682 require that when the notice is served reasons are given as to why it was deemed expedient, plus a list of those served notice and their addresses, a plan showing the precise boundaries of land affected, details of all relevant policies and proposals, and details relating to the landowner's right of appeal.

The chosen remedy may seek the alteration or removal of a building or works, the carrying out of building works, activity to be ceased or performed within certain limits, or the construction of a replacement building. Enforcement notices do not take immediate effect. The notice is the subject of a twenty-eight day period following 'service' of the notice. The notice must therefore specify a date on which it is to take effect. Any appeal lodged must be made within this twenty-eight day period; otherwise failure to comply with the notice, once effective, constitutes a criminal offence. If an appeal is lodged, then the notice does not take effect but is held in abeyance and the matter determined by the Secretary of State or an appointed inspector – who may quash, uphold or vary the notice in some way. Any appeal must be submitted against one or more of seven grounds as stipulated on the form. These grounds deal with the merit of the action (i.e. the alleged breach is acceptable on its planning merits), the potential for immunity to exist (four-year or ten-year lawful status), that the alleged breach has not occurred as a matter of fact, that it is permitted development, that it is too late to take action, that the legal notice was not properly served, that the steps to take in remedy are excessive or that the time given is too short.

The enforcement notice appeal may be pursued by written representation, informal hearing or public inquiry method. The decision of the Secretary of State or inspector is the final decision on the matter, unless a further appeal is lodged to the High Court. Such an appeal, however, must be solely made on a point of law, with the Court's leave obtained. It is not an opportunity to reopen the matters raised at appeal unless they go to the heart of the legal case – for example, that the Secretary of State or inspector erred in law when determining the previously considered enforcement appeal.

Summary: characteristics of an enforcement notice

- Deals with remedying unacceptable breaches of planning control.
- Provides for a timescale within which the matter should be rectified.
- Allows for an appeal, in which case the effect of the notice is suspended and the matter is dealt with by the Secretary of State or inspector. An appeal must be lodged within twenty-eight days of service of the notice, otherwise the notice becomes effective.

Stop notice

The stop notice provides the LPA with an option to take immediate or almost immediate action to stop activities being carried out in breach of planning control. Unlike the enforcement notice, which allows for a reasonable period for compliance, the stop notice requires a halt to activities (uses) within three days of its service upon the landowner or other person with an interest in the land who will be affected by the stop notice. It is therefore served only in cases of serious breaches of planning control requiring immediate cessation. A stop notice can be served only if an enforcement notice of similar content has also been served and before the enforcement notice takes effect. The stop notice 'piggy backs' on the enforcement notice and while the former will almost immediately halt any specific activity, only the latter can be appealed. This distinction between stop (no appeal) and enforcement (right of appeal) derives from past experience of the appeals process being used to simply delay and frustrate enforcement action, while many people accept that the planning system must be allowed to halt some forms of development that are highly detrimental to environmental quality or residential amenity.

The two notices are usually served simultaneously, although this is not a legal requirement and the stop notice can follow the enforcement notice so long as the enforcement action has not taken effect. Certain limitations apply in that a stop notice may not be served if an enforcement notice has come into effect, it cannot be used to stop the use of a building as a dwelling house and it cannot be served to stop an activity that has been carried out for four years previously. If on appeal the Secretary of State or inspector either quashes the enforcement notice or varies it to the extent that the matter 'stopped' no longer constitutes a breach of control, then the LPA is liable to pay financial compensation to the owner for the loss incurred by the imposed cessation of activity. Compensation is an oft quoted reason for planning authorities declining to 'stop' certain activities (in preference to only serving an enforcement notice), although compensation is limited to certain circumstances in which either (a) the stop notice is withdrawn or (b) the accompanying enforcement notice is quashed or varied to exclude the activity prohibited in the stop notice. Such compensation is the loss in value (excluding the depreciation of land value) which must be directly attributed to the activities so stopped.

Section 52 of the Planning and Compulsory Purchase Act 2004 introduced the procedural innovation of a temporary stop notice, which gave planning authorities new powers to stop activities for a maximum period of twenty-eight days. No 'piggy back' enforcement notice is required and no right of appeal is available. The twenty-eight day or lesser period may resolve the matter but it also allows the planning authority the opportunity to consider enforcement action. Such temporary stop notices are very useful in cases where planning conditions have not been discharged prior to the implementation of the scheme. These 'conditions precedent' require, for example, agreement of site levels or materials prior to construction. Should the developer unwisely proceed without agreeing such matters, then the service of a temporary stop notice will allow for such details to be submitted and resolved ahead of implementation.

Summary: characteristics of a stop notice

- Deals with remedying unacceptable breaches of control that might require immediate cessation.
- No appeal, but because a stop notice can only be served alongside or after an enforcement notice (of similar content) then an appeal may be made against the enforcement notice.
- Compensation payable if enforcement notice appeal is successful in authorizing the breach stopped by the stop notice.
- From 2004, provision of a temporary stop notice permits an immediate halting of activities for a maximum period of twenty-eight days.

Breach of condition notice (BCN)

This procedure permits specific action against failure to comply with a planning condition imposed on a previous grant of permission by service of a breach of condition notice.[10] As with the enforcement notice, the LPA must specify steps to be taken to remedy the matter, together with a period of compliance, with a minimum period of twenty-eight days. The notice must be served no later than ten years from the date of the breach. Failure to comply with such a notice is a criminal offence and liable on summary conviction to a fine. No right of appeal is available against such a notice; therefore, if an onerous condition is imposed on a planning permission, the landowner is well advised to pursue an appeal against the condition rather than await any future breach of condition notice.

Certificates of lawful existing use or development and proposed use or development

Such certificates are considered by LPAs in the same way as applications for planning permission. They allow an owner to have a ruling as to whether an existing operation or use of land, without the previous benefit of planning permission, is lawful or to ascertain that a proposed operation or use would also be lawful and therefore not require the need for a grant of planning permission.[11] This would remove any uncertainty about whether a matter was outside the realm of planning control – for example, it was either permitted development (e.g. a small residential extension), or not development at all (e.g. movement within a use class), or was immune from enforcement action whereby an operational development was substantially completed for at least four years,[12] or, if a change of use, for a minimum period of at least ten years. These decisions are based on legal principles and the planning authority has no discretion as to whether or not to issue a certificate. They do, however, have to act on the civil test of the 'balance of probability' and the onus of proof rests with the applicant. Thus if an applicant for a certificate can prove that the time for enforcement action has expired (four-year or ten-year rules) then the planning authority must issue the certificate.

Both certificates help to remove any uncertainty that an owner may have about the planning status of a site. The LPA can refuse to grant either certificate, which carries a right of appeal to the Secretary of State.

Injunctions

The local planning authority also enjoys powers strengthened by the Planning and Compensation Act 1991[13] to seek an injunction in either the High Court or County Court to halt an actual or anticipated breach of planning control. Such injunctions are generally, but not necessarily, employed by LPAs as a second line of attack, although such a legal mechanism is a very effective way of controlling any contravention of the planning system, because, if an injunction is granted by the courts and if its terms are subsequently ignored by the owner, then the person involved risks possible imprisonment for contempt of court. The power is available whether or not the authority proposes to take enforcement action, and the planning authority must consider any action they take to be 'necessary or expedient' under powers vested in section 187B of the 1990 Act. Prior to the introduction of the Human Rights Act 1998, courts were readily willing to grant such injunctions to halt breaches of planning control, as they considered that the merit of such action rested with the planning authority or Secretary of State. Following the Human Rights legislation and in particular its introduction of Article 8 (the right to respect for private and family life, the home and correspondence) they have been more constrained to the extent that any such interference to private and family life must be in the interests of national security, public safety, the economic well-being of the country, preservation of order, protection of health or protection of the rights or freedoms of others.

Discovering breaches of planning control

The majority of breaches of planning control are discovered by the LPA following the receipt of a complaint from a member of the public, usually a neighbouring occupier. Local planning authorities usually establish a specialist in-house team of enforcement officers who investigate such complaints and advise both owner and complainant on the possibility of action being taken. Decisions to pursue enforcement matters involve legal judgement (establishing facts to determine that a breach has occurred) and planning judgement (to remedy the situation to overcome any loss of amenity that results from the unauthorized use or operation).

For this reason, enforcement activity involves both town planning and legal personnel, and government guidance encourages a strong level of cooperation between such staff to ensure effective implementation of this important planning function. In 2002 the Secretary of State published a consultation paper 'Review of the Planning Enforcement System in England'. It recommended that the profile of the enforcement function be raised and that a culture change be initiated to enhance the training and career structure of planning enforcement staff. On procedural matters the review recommended that certain key principles be maintained, for example that enforcement action remain discretionary, but that further review be undertaken to consider introduction of new powers to curtail unlawful activity in the form of an 'unlawful development certificate' and 'planning contravention notice'. More work and background research would be required before any such ideas were taken forward. The foundations of the Carnwath-inspired enforcement regime were deemed sound and will no doubt continue in their current guise for many more years to come.

Conclusions

Town planning legislation creates the procedures by which control may be exercised over the use of land and operations that take place on, over or under that land. Such legislation is applied consistently across England and Wales and it sets out to create a regulatory system, yet it must also establish freedoms or exemptions from the system where 'development' would not result in any harmful environmental impact. Thus, a balance must be struck between necessary environmental protection and unnecessary bureaucratic burden. Such decisions

are not easy and are particularly contentious in the realm of residential permitted development, where some homeowners will resent any form of planning
control that will restrict their desire to extend, or otherwise alter, a dwelling.
The introduction in 1988 of town planning control over external stone cladding
to dwelling houses illustrates the problem, with the government finally being
convinced, after many years of debate, that the residents' right to alter their property in this way was eroding the quality of the environment.

4 Planning appeals

A planning appeal is an administrative challenge to the merits of a planning decision made by a local authority and should be viewed as a decision of last resort.

Most decisions made by local planning authorities carry with them the right of appeal to the Secretary of State for the Environment. Such appeals provide a form of binding arbitration on the town planning merits of a decision and represent the final stage of the development control process. Any further appeal is a matter of legal submission in which the decision is challenged in the courts on grounds of procedural unreasonableness or perversity in decision-making, namely that matters were taken into account by the decision-maker that should not reasonably have been taken into account or were not taken into account when they should have been, or the decision was so manifestly unreasonable that no reasonable decision-maker could have come to it. This last test of unreasonableness is commonly referred to as 'Wednesbury' unreasonableness, in which a decision was so unreasonable that no reasonable authority could have imposed it. In other words the decision made was based upon a perverse and/or illogical approach. In planning appeals this would ordinarily mean that the decision-maker (planning inspector or Secretary of State) did not clearly or adequately explain the reasoning behind a decision to grant or refuse a planning appeal. Such legal appeals fall within either statutory review or judicial review, with the former commonly employed to legally challenge planning appeals and the latter to challenge planning applications. Judicial reviews are most commonly employed by aggrieved third party residents who wish to stop a grant of planning application (by a council) whereas statutory review is used by either side in a planning appeal to overturn the decision of a planning inspector/Secretary of State.

Such legal appeals are made to the High Court, Court of Appeal or House of Lords. In the event that such a legal appeal is successful, then the respective planning decision is quashed and sent back for a fresh determination. Thus to succeed in the courts and quash a decision is not the end of the story and can result in the application/appeal being granted anew after due process has been properly observed at a second opportunity.

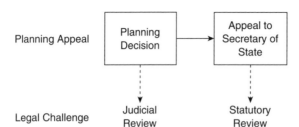

Figure 4.1 Distinction between a planning appeal and a legal challenge

A planning appeal, however, is *not* a legal appeal and deals solely with the technical town planning merits of the case. It does not involve legal argument unless that would exert some influence upon the technical planning merits of the appeal. It is important to draw this distinction from the start. Planning appeals involve disputes over the merit of a decision – in effect, should planning permission be granted for this development? That is an administrative judgement and thus the planning appeal forms a tribunal (in a number of guises) and not a legal appeal, heard in the courts.

This chapter deals with appeals based exclusively on matters of planning merit. Any further reference to case law is employed to assist in the clarification of planning issues only. This emphasis reflects town planning practice, where a grasp of law is employed to throw light on matters of process (how the system works) and matters of substance (the contents of the decision). So, in starting the chapter it is necessary to draw an important distinction between planning appeals and legal appeals.

Legal appeals are submitted by means of two mechanisms:

- First, there are matters for statutory review (section 288 of Town and Country Planning Act 1990), in which an appeal decision issued by the Secretary of State or an inspector is challenged. Such a challenge is most commonly made on the grounds that a decision was taken that was either procedurally unreasonable (for example the inspector failed to comply with relevant procedural requirements, such as maintaining impartiality) or included a matter which did not fall within the purview of planning law (for example an inspector gave weight to a non-planning matter when deciding the appeal). This latter concept is also legally referred to as *ultra vires* or acting beyond one's powers.
- Second, there are matters for judicial review (under part 54 of the Civil Procedure Rules 1999) in which the local planning authority or Secretary of State/inspector has acted unlawfully. Judicial review relates to issues of procedure but can extend to where a public body (such as a planning authority) has come to a decision considered perverse by the person or organization making the legal challenge. This mechanism is employed by

third parties (local residents) to challenge a grant of planning permission on the basis that the decision was not valid because procedural matters were not correctly followed by the planning authority. To proceed in judicial review the High Court must grant 'leave to appeal' – in other words, a judge accepts that an arguable case has been presented and may be submitted before a court for interpretation and determination.

These two matters of legal challenge may, therefore, be contrasted with the planning appeal. The main right of appeal is enshrined in the Town and Country Planning Act 1990 (section 78), which established that 'a right exists against the refusal of a planning permission or the failure to take such decision'. This right is available only to the applicant (the person or body who made the original planning application that is now the subject of an appeal). High-profile pressure groups like Friends of the Earth have called for this right to be extended to third parties so that, in other words, the public can appeal against a council's decision to grant planning permission. Government policy appears to be firmly and consistently against such a change. Evidently government fears that to extend the right of appeal in this way would clog the system with numerous appeals where residents were merely attempting to block acceptable development for non-planning related reasons such as loss of view or reduction in property value. Reference will be made to further consultations on improving the appeals process, issued in summer 2007.

The planning appeal system

Historical background

The TCPA 1932 introduced the right of planning appeal, whereby someone could challenge the decision of a local authority to refuse planning permission. The 'Public Inquiry' had been introduced twenty-three years before in the Housing, Town Planning, etc. Act 1909. However, at that time it did not represent a method of planning appeal as it does today, but instead was a means by which the public could voice objection to town planning schemes. The TCPA 1947 introduced a limited system of planning appeal that was tightly controlled by the Minister of Housing and Local Government. All appeals were considered by Public Inquiry. The rules governing the conduct of such inquiries were not publicly available because the relevant government department was unwilling to publish them. Although the ultimate decision – either to allow or to dismiss the appeal – was published, the reasoning upon which the decision had been based was kept secret. Such a system was not only secretive in its procedures but also largely excluded the public from the area of appeal decision-making.

This was all set to change in 1958 (Franks 1957) following the implementation of recommendations made by the Committee on Administrative Tribunals and Inquiries (the Franks Committee) (Layfield 1993) of the previous year. These reforms introduced statutory rules for procedure in Public Inquiries and publication of the inspector's report, and established the key attributes of openness, fairness and impartiality in all appeal proceedings. These three 'Franks' principles' still apply today and have governed all procedural reforms since 1958. Further changes in the early 1960s and 1980s introduced new appeal methods in the form of the 'Written Representation' and 'Informal Hearing'. In 2001 a government Green Paper countenanced the introduction of alternative means of settling planning appeals by recourse to mediation. No progress was subsequently made, although the idea was reignited again in 2006 with recommendations made in favour of its introduction by Kate Barker (HM Treasury 2006a).

The planning appeal is a critical stage within the development process. Unnecessary delay will frustrate both developer and local planning authority. However, it is important that every decision is made in full knowledge of the proposal to enable the appeal system to produce the correct decision and therefore enhance the development control process.

Key characteristics of the planning appeal system can be identified. There are many different rights of appeal against LPA decisions, and these rights are exercised by the applicant (person making the planning application) and, in enforcement matters, the person who occupies or has an interest in the land. The decision to appeal is free of charge (although future fees are proposed in a consultation paper issued in 2007) and the appeal is considered by the Secretary of State or an inspector. Administration of the appeal is coordinated by the planning inspectorate which covers both England and Wales (on behalf of the National Assembly for Wales). The Secretary of State will issue a decision either to allow (grant) or to dismiss (refuse) the appeal, with the system being paid for by the government, at a cost of around £30 million a year.[1]

Four principal purposes may be advanced. First, planning appeals provide a form of binding arbitration, whereby an aggrieved applicant or owner may seek an independent assessment on a wide variety of decisions made by the local planning authority. Second, they ensure that there is a degree of consistency in decision-making across the country. Inspectors will consider each case on its own merit but will take some account of national planning policy in the form of circulars and planning policy statements. Third, they provide an opportunity for public participation by which third parties can view the decision-making process and make their own representations. Third parties have been defined as 'those other than councils or appellants who, in relation to a particular appeal, think they will be affected by its outcome'. Third parties are therefore members of the public who consider that they may be affected by a development proposal (Keeble 1985: 80). Third parties enjoy no right of appeal. They are consulted about the appeal and may participate. At (Informal) Hearing and Public Inquiry they appear at the discretion of the inspector and are usually allowed to ask questions of the appellant. Fourth, planning appeals provide a safeguard against unreasonable decisions by the local planning authority. Appellants are expected to pay their own costs in all appeal proceedings. An award of costs can be made against either party if unreasonable behaviour is evident. This unreasonable behaviour would cover failure to follow relevant appeal procedures or to provide evidence to support the case.

Who considers the appeal?

All planning appeals are submitted to the Secretary of State. In practice, the jurisdiction for considering such appeals is split into either 'transferred' or 'recovered' decisions. Decisions are transferred to a planning inspector appointed on behalf of the Secretary of State. This applies to all Written Representations, most (Informal) Hearings and about 95 per cent of Public Inquiries. The planning inspector is an 'arbitrator', with a property-related professional specialism, who is employed by government but is entirely independent in determining appeals. Decisions 'recovered' (i.e. not transferred) are determined by the Secretary of State. Such appeals are usually heard by Inquiry and involve major proposals and/or ones that raise significant legal difficulties or public controversy. Although some of these may be personally referred to the Secretary of State for a final decision (as in the case of sensitive appeals like major development proposals in the green belt), it is usual practice for a senior civil servant within the office of the Secretary of State to make the decision upon receiving a recommendation from an inspector who has been appointed to hold an Inquiry and make a recommendation. In some very high-profile cases, such as the green belt proposal for an animal research complex (by the University of Cambridge) the Secretary of State made the determination personally – the appeal was granted, against the recommendation of the inspector who had presided over the Inquiry.

The necessary administration and processing of appeals is undertaken by the planning inspectorate, an executive agency of the Department of Communities and Local Government and vested with this duty by the National Assembly for Wales. The planning inspectorate was established in 1909 and became an agency in 1992. Today it employs around 300 planning inspectors, with gross running costs of approximately £30 million. Its work covers around 200 different types of appeal, with planning appeals comprising around 60 per cent of its workload.

The decision will be conveyed in a letter format, addressed to the appellant or agent and will set out in summary the case as presented by either side and any third parties, followed by the reasoning of the Secretary of State or inspector, dealing with policy matters and other material considerations, and concluding with the decision to allow the appeal (with conditions) or to dismiss the appeal. Any appeal beyond this point is based on a point of law and is made to the courts.

In the appeal decision letter the inspector will deal with findings of fact, such as whether the plan is up-to-date, and findings of opinion, such as whether the proposal is in character with the surrounding development. A distinction between the two may not always be easily apparent – for example, whether something was visible may appear as a matter of fact, although it is possible that it could be a matter of opinion. By contrast, a judgement whether some proposed development was visually intrusive would reasonably form a matter of opinion.

Nevertheless, in many cases, especially those concerning appeals against the refusal of planning permission, the decision is based on a balance between findings of fact and matters of professional judgement. Clearly the inspector's ruling on matters of fact must be based on a correct understanding of the issues.

Using past appeal decisions

A past planning appeal decision may constitute an important material consideration and may, therefore, be of sufficient value to allow the provisions of the development plan to be set aside (i.e. that material considerations should 'indicate otherwise' when considering the duty imposed by section 38(6) of the 2004 Act, see Chapter 2). Planning appeal decisions, while important, do not set a 'precedent' that binds the decision-maker – it is necessary to rely on the fact that decision-making should be consistent. However, a distinction has to be drawn between 'precedent' and 'consistency'.

Precedent is undoubtedly a material planning consideration, yet it refers to somewhat restrictive circumstances in which a planning authority refuse planning permission because to grant it 'would be likely to lead to a proliferation of applications for similar developments, which the authority would find difficult to refuse'.[2] In other words, to grant permission on a given site may create pressure to develop a wider area. Once this pressure is unleashed the council would be unable to resist it. In practice this claim is difficult to prove as most sites are dealt with on their own individual merits.

The courts have accepted that mere fear of establishing a precedent or some generalized concern is not sufficient and that some evidence must exist before reliance on such grounds may be justified. It follows that the courts have sought to define precedent in a relatively narrow way. The existence of a previous planning appeal decision on a given site would not of itself create a precedent. Rather, when using past appeal decisions it is preferable to examine consistency in decision-making.

Consistency refers to circumstances in which detailed examination of the planning history of a development site reveals the existence of past decisions (application or appeal decisions). When reading past planning appeal decisions, their relevance in establishing matters of consistency may not always be immediately obvious. What if you have an interest in a site and you want to examine other appeal decisions, either in the locality or which deal with similar issues? How much weight should you give to a planning appeal decision in such circumstances?

As stated earlier, many planning decisions involve matters of professional judgement where a planning inspector will weigh up a series of factors (some legal, some factual and others of development control merit) in arriving at his or her determination. Indeed the whole planning process is built upon such determinations and judgements. When using a past appeal decision you may wish to rely upon it in support of granting a fresh consent on the same or another site. Additionally you may want to use a past favourable appeal decision (i.e. granted) when pursuing a current application or appeal that is deemed contrary to provisions of the Local Development Framework (development plan). The existence of this past appeal, you argue, constitutes a material consideration that 'indicates otherwise', in effect that it outweighs any objection contained in the plan. (If unsure on this legal point, go back to Chapter 2, 'The decision-maker's duty' in section 38(6) of the Planning and Compulsory Purchase Act 2004.)

It is necessary to rely on the argument of consistency in decision-making and not precedent. Consistency in decision-making is a matter of importance. This was acknowledged in a decision of the High Court in 1990 and again in 2005 (*R v. Richmond upon Thames LBC and Tom Dillon*) in which the High Court held that the decision-maker (in this case a planning committee) was not bound by previous decisions to grant or refuse permission, but there was a need for consistency. This consistency required that reasons must be given when departing from a previous decision. The courts have previously held that 'the principle [of consistency in decision-making] is justified by a need to ensure that developers know where they stand'.[3]

Key guidance in this area is provided by the judgement of Lord Justice Mann in the decision of *North Wiltshire District Council* v. *Secretary of State for the Environment and Glover* (in the Court of Appeal, 12 April 1992).[4] This provides helpful clarification as to when a previous appeal decision may constitute a material consideration. Lionel Read QC, sitting as a Deputy High Court Judge, had previously quashed an appeal decision on the grounds that the inspector, in granting permission, failed to explain why he did not follow a previous appeal decision, some seven years earlier, in which his inspectorate colleague had dismissed an appeal dealing with an identical proposal on a similar, albeit larger, site. The Judge considered that this omission in the decision amounted to inadequate justification and he quashed the planning appeal (by Lionel Read QC). The Secretary of State and appellant sought to reverse this High Court decision by appeal to the Court of Appeal (before Lord Justice Mann). In dismissing this challenge and thus upholding the decision of the High Court, the Court of Appeal established some important features of general applicability to developers and their professional agents when relying on past decisions.

First, in relying on a past decision, the merits between past and present cases must be materially indistinguishable. The inspector in writing his decision benefits from a wide-ranging discretion. Yet, as Lord Justice Mann observed in the North Wiltshire case, 'like cases should be decided in a like manner so that there is consistency in the appellate process'. The fact that every case is determined on its own individual merits must take account of this. The Court of Appeal established in this judgement that for a previous appeal to be 'material' it must be 'indistinguishable' in (at least) critical areas. Such 'indistinguishable' decisions may be 'gold dust' in the pursuit of cases because, although they are no guarantee of victory, they will persuade the inspector or planning officer to look very carefully at the issues you set out to target. Second, the Court of Appeal in the North Wiltshire case stressed that such areas could not be defined, 'but they would include interpretation of policies, aesthetic judgements and assessment of need'.

The Court was not saying that consistency must always be applied but rather that a lack of consistency must be explained. Analysis of this case (reported in the Property, Planning and Compensation Reports No. 65) stated that Lord Justice Mann accepted that 'there is a presumption that there shall be consistency in decision-making but that it cannot always be achieved'. Consistency must therefore be an important objective of the system, but this must not lead to excessive rigidity in decision-making. The existence of a previous appeal decision was an important material consideration and may be advanced by developers to support consistency, where this would assist their case. Yet the inspector enjoys sufficient discretion to disagree with such earlier judgements, but must give reasons. Such reasons can be short, such as 'I disagree', but this will depend on the case merits.

Types of appeal

The most common type of planning appeal is against a refusal of planning permission. It is a common misconception that this is the only type of appeal. In fact, many different types of appeal are available under the provisions of town and country planning, listed building and advertisement legislation (Table 4.1).

Submission of appeal

All planning appeals are submitted on standard forms issued by the Secretary of State and coordinated by the planning inspectorate or government regional office. Any appeal against refusal of permission, planning conditions or reserved matters must be submitted within six months of the LPA decision. Appeals against enforcement notices must be submitted within the prescribed period (usually twenty-eight days) indicated on the notice. The appeal forms require submission of supporting documentation, including plans, notices of refusal, correspondence and certificate of ownership. The right of appeal is free of charge, although in some enforcement matters the appellant may be required to pay a fee and (in a 2007 consultation paper) this may be extended to all appeals. This may change as a result of the Planning and Reform Act 2008, with the introduction of a fee, when exercising the right of appeal.

The choice of appeal method is an important decision. It will affect the procedure for deciding the case, the overall time over which a decision will be reached and the costs involved – not in lodging the appeal, as this is free, but in the professional time required to pursue each method. The choice of method is unfettered by the type of case or nature of evidence to be produced, although the agreement of both parties will usually be required. It is conceivable, if rare, that the most minor appeal may go to Public Inquiry. The appellant may exercise a 'right to be heard' by an inspector, i.e. to convene an Inquiry or Hearing. It is not possible, when submitting an appeal, to insist that an Inquiry be held, while the planning inspectorate may impose a Hearing upon the parties if they deem this to be the most appropriate method. It is the common practice of the inspectorate to consult with the parties before such a decision is made, although this

Table 4.1 Types of planning appeal

Type of appeal	Example
Refusal of planning permission	Refusal to build on or change the use of land
Against a condition on a grant of permission	Hours of opening condition imposed on a grant of hot food takeaway
Against refusal of reserved matters application following grant of outline planning permission	Reserved matters – siting, means of access, external appearance, design and landscape, e.g. refuse submitted landscape details
Against refusal of any details required by a planning condition	A condition may require details of proposed materials to be submitted, which may subsequently be refused
Against failure to determine a planning application (non-determination)	LPA do not issue decision within eight weeks or an extended period, as agreed by each party
Against the issuing of an Enforcement Notice requiring some remedy against unauthorized development	Notice to remove a building or structure or cease a use – all undertaken without permission
Against failure to grant a certificate of lawfulness of existing or proposed use or development	LPA refuse applications to establish that a building without planning permission has existed for four years minimum or a use has existed for ten years minimum; any appeal would need to produce evidence to prove otherwise
Against refusal of Listed Building Consent	Refusal of application to extend or alter a listed building
Against conditions on a grant of Listed Building Consent	A listed building condition may require specific materials or methods of construction to be used to match existing
Against the issuing of a Listed Building Enforcement Notice	Specific grounds similar to a planning notice, e.g. requires removal of extension built without Listed Building Consent
Against failure to grant Conservation Area Consent	LPA refuse consent to demolish an unlisted building in a conservation area
Against refusal of permission to display an advertisement	Consent refused as advertisement may be too large or result in highway problems
Against an application to top, lop or fell a tree preserved under a Tree Preservation Order	Permission is refused to alter a preserved tree usually due to the loss of amenity involved and/or good health of existing tree

is likely to change in the future with the inspectorate imposing a fee on all types of application.

The appeal methods

Following the initial decision to pursue an appeal, the most important decision on the appeal forms is the choice of appeal method. The choices available are Public Inquiry, Written Representation or (Informal) Hearing. Only one method may be chosen. The planning inspectorate has always sought to encourage use of the written method, which is quicker and cheaper to implement.

All three methods are designed to embody the rules of natural justice. Such rules state that the decision-maker (inspector or Secretary of State) is impartial and that, before a decision is taken, individuals should be given a chance to put their points of view. All three methods are governed by statutory rules of procedure.[5]

These three appeal methods each represent a balance between the need for administrative expediency and for a proper examination of the planning issues of the case. It is widely accepted that the Public Inquiry results in a greater rigour of detailed examination than the written method (McCoubry 1990, Purdue 1991, Moore 2007).[6] However, it also takes longer to process and it costs more to both the Secretary of State for Communities and Local Government (in inspector time) and the appellant (in professional fees). Not all planning appeals involve complex policy or other issues. Therefore, it may be expedient to sacrifice the detailed examination of issues in preference to a quick and less expensive method of appeal. An appraisal of the three planning appeal methods is shown in Table 4.2.

Which method to choose?

Determining factors can be identified that will influence the choice of appeal method (Table 4.3). The decision to appeal is a decision of last resort. Around

Table 4.2 An appraisal of planning appeal methods

	Advantages	Disadvantages
Written Representation	• Cheapest method • Shortest period to get decision.	• Evidence is not rigorously tested • Written evidence only – little opportunity to clarify issues or allow Inspector to ask questions.
Informal Hearing	• Informal atmosphere • Some oral discussion – testing of evidence and clarification of issues • Avoids time-wasting – usually half-day duration • Opportunity for costs.	• Role of Inspector is central to proceedings. If an Inspector does not control the discussion then this method loses its advantage • Discussion based, is not adversarial and may help to readily identify issues • Costs may also go against.
Planning Inquiry	• Cross-examination allows for a rigorous testing of evidence and clarification of issues • Opportunity for costs.	• Formal and sometimes excessively adversarial • Most expensive • Longest period of time to get a decision • Costs may also go against.

Table 4.3 Factors to consider when choosing a method of appeal

Determining factor	Method
(a) Magnitude of case: the size and scale of development proposed	Public Inquiry suitable for major proposals,* Written Representation for minor ones
(b) Complexity of case: the number or depth of policy and material considerations involved	Public Inquiry for complex and Written Representation for straightforward cases
(c) Financial considerations (professional fees) imposed by (a) and (b) above	Public Inquiry will involve greater professional input to prepare evidence and appear at Inquiry
(d) Time available to appellant	Written – 18 weeks[†] average from submission of appeal to decision notice being received Informal – 26 weeks[†] Inquiry – 44 weeks[†]
(e) Possibility of seeking costs for unreasonable behaviour	Costs applications only available at Inquiry and Hearing, not at written method
(f) Level of third-party involvement (number of objections at application stage prior to appeal)	All appeal methods permit the appellant to deal with third-party comments. However, if many are expected the Hearing is an unsuitable method within which to deal with many objections – consider either Inquiry or written

Notes
* 'Major' is 10+ houses or 10,000 ft^2 floorspace for industrial, commercial or retail.
[†] Expressed as overall handling time in 80% of cases. See *Planning Inspectorate Annual Report* for year-to-year fluctuations.

30–35 per cent of all appeals are allowed, so, crudely speaking, the appellant has a one in three chance of success, although the Inquiry on its own gives slightly better odds, at around 40 per cent allowed.[7] If the LPA would give favourable consideration to some form of amended proposal, then this would be a more secure way of realizing development potential. Although some appeal proposals will stand a better chance than others, the appeal pathway will always remain a lottery to the developer, as the inspector is making an entirely fresh (*de novo*) development control decision.

Procedures involved in each appeal method

Written Representation

> These are rough justice, greater speed of determination being purchased at the cost of less thorough exploration.
>
> (Keeble 1985)

Case study 4.1

Proposal: The LPA refuses planning permission for a two-storey extension to a dwellinghouse for the reason:

> 'The proposal by reason of its excessive bulk would result in a loss of light and overshadowing of the neighbouring property, detrimental to the amenities enjoyed by the occupiers of that property.'

Appraisal: The planning issue is clearly defined. The case is of little magnitude or complexity. On this basis it would not warrant a great deal of professional input and the owner is keen to have a decision as soon and inexpensively as possible. In this case a Written Representation would be the best method.

Case study 4.2

Proposal: The LPA refuses planning permission for a change of use of a retail shop (A1 use class) into a restaurant/food and drink use (A3 class). The proposal satisfies local plan policy and was recommended for a grant of planning permission by the case officer. The committee overturned this recommendation and refused permission.

Appraisal: A straightforward case involving one policy issue. Although A3 uses involve the potential for several material considerations (especially odour emissions, late-night activity, traffic generation and non-retail frontages), they are not considered to represent complex cases of great magnitude. Such a proposal could be adequately dealt with by Written Representation. However, there is some evidence of unreasonable behaviour and the possibility of an award of costs being made against the LPA.* In such a case, only Hearings/Inquiry allow either party to pursue such an award. A Hearing provides the better forum for dealing with costs in relatively straightforward or minor cases, whereas the Inquiry is the most suitable method for dealing with costs in the more complex or major cases.

* The award of costs is considered at the end of this chapter. The overturning of the recommendation of the chief planning officer does not of itself constitute unreasonable behaviour, resulting in costs. However, if evidence is not forthcoming at the appeal to support the committee's action, there is a strong chance costs may be awarded.

Table 4.4 Timetable for the Written Representation appeal process

Time	Procedure
Decision to appeal is made	Appellant submits appeal forms and supporting documents to Inspectorate
Start date	Issued by Inspectorate after checking to ensure appeal is valid and documents correct
Two weeks	LPA returns questionnaire and key documents (extracts of policy and correspondence)
Six weeks	• LPA submits statement of their case (optional as they may rely on questionnaire only)* • Appellant submits statement of their case* • Third parties (objectors) to submit their case*
Nine weeks	Observations on case advanced by other party or any third party must be made*
Close of representations Site visit	• Date set for site inspection if site cannot be seen from public land. The site inspection permits both sides to show the Inspector various features and not to deal with arguments over the merits or otherwise of the appeal Decision letter issued either granting (allow) or refusing (dismiss) the appeal

Note
* These time limits are the subject of statutory provision. Failure to comply may result in them being ignored (if late) or the Inspector proceeding to a decision in their absence.

Such criticism, in past years, has been levelled at the written method on the basis that, in pursuing a relatively quick decision, the procedures inhibit a rigorous exploration of the planning merits of the case (McNamara *et al.* 1985). Such a view must be qualified by the fact that the written method is best employed in minor cases with straightforward planning issues (Case study 4.1). The planning inspectorate encourages use of this method. Since this method was first introduced in 1965 as an alternative to the Public Inquiry, it has increased its percentage share of all methods from 30–35 per cent to 80–85 per cent of all appeals. The written appeal has many benefits for the planning inspectorate in that the cost of each appeal is less, involving generally less administration or inspector's time to reach a decision and therefore the combined advantage of offering a cheaper unit cost per appeal. The inspectorate themselves estimated in 2007 that the total cost of a written appeal consumed £462 of inspector and administration costs, compared to an equivalent sum of £1477 for a Hearing and £2341 for an Inquiry.

Since 1987, Written Representation procedures have been governed by statutory rules,[8] which established a timetable to govern the operation of the appeal (Table 4.4). It is intended that this timetable should establish a set of deadlines

---

Summary: Written Representations – key characteristics

- Suitable for minor cases
- Written exchange of evidence
- Quickest appeal method
- Cheapest appeal (in professional fees)
- Preferred by planning inspectorate and least costs involved for them
- Procedure (timetable of events) governed by statutory rules
- Most used method: 80–85 per cent of appeals.

---

to be followed by parties to the appeal. Such time periods are strictly observed, with the inspectorate now empowered to disregard late evidence.

The written procedure allows for a single exchange of written statements and the opportunity to comment on that evidence. However, additional written exchanges beyond this point are discouraged. Nothing is gained from having the last word. One frequently expressed criticism of this procedure is the inability of local authorities to adhere to the procedural timetable and the unwillingness of the planning inspectorate to enforce it.[9] This criticism perhaps best explains the motivation behind the 2000 reforms and the draconian measure of allowing inspectors to proceed to a decision in the absence of (late) evidence by one party. It is doubtful that such a penalty will be used on every such occasion for fear of the criticism that it prejudices fairness in decision-making.

In August 2000 a revised timetable was introduced with the intention of improving the system. Nick Raynsford, the (then) Planning Minister, stated in a written reply to a Parliamentary question that 'The changes being introduced will improve the speed and efficiency of the system without impairing the quality, fairness or openness of the process or people's ability to participate'. Also refer to Circular 5/00 'Planning Appeals: Procedures', for a full explanation of the processes involved.

Hearings

(Informal) Hearings were first introduced in 1981 as an alternative to the Public Inquiry. They have been described as a 'half-way house' (Morgan and Nott 1988: 310) between the other methods, although the Hearing does have its own tangible advantage, in that discussion is allowed on the site visit, provided that no party would be disadvantaged by this. The procedure involves an exchange of written evidence between the parties prior to the Hearing, and at the Hearing the inspector leads a discussion between both parties and any third parties who attend. Legal representation and formal cross-examination is discouraged but not prohibited. The inspector plays a pivotal role in proceedings, leading the discussion, structuring the debate and intervening when the procedure departs

Table 4.5 Timetable for Informal Hearing process

Time	Procedure
	Appellant submits appeal forms.
Start date	Questionnaire issued by Inspectorate after checking to ensure appeal is valid and documents correct.
Two weeks	LPA returns questionnaire and key documents (extracts of policy and correspondence).
Six weeks	• Both LPA and Appellant submit statements of their case and (wherever possible) evidence on which they agree. • Third parties (objectors) submit statements of their case.
Nine weeks	Observations on case advanced by other party or any third party must be made.*
Twelve weeks (or earlier)	Hearing[†] (3–4 hours duration), followed by site visit and subsequently a decision letter issued, granting (allowing) or refusing (dismissing) the appeal.

Notes
* These time limits are the subject of statutory provision. The Inspector may disregard comments which fail to satisfy the nine-week target. First statements (i.e. six-week deadlines) are not the subject of this measure.
[†] If at any time before or during the Hearing one party deems the Hearing method inappropriate and the Secretary of State/Inspector agrees, then it will be suspended and an Inquiry held instead.

from the code of practice. The Hearing has been described as a 'round-table discussion led by the inspector' (Purdue 1991) or as a 'significant business meeting, free from archaic ritual but not by any means an unconstrained social gathering' (McCoubry 1990). The inspector does have considerable discretion to structure the discussion, which may result in differing approaches by different inspectors (Stubbs 1994). Most certainly, the Hearing gives the inspector greater control over the exact workings of the process compared to either the written method or the Inquiry. The procedure is shown in Table 4.5.

Since 2000, Hearings have been governed by statutory rules, having previously been enshrined in a non-statutory code. This change gives greater force to the rules that shape this method, while continuing to reinforce the central characteristic that an informal discussion takes place to examine evidence without the more formal employment of cross-examination. The Hearing method was itself the subject of legal scrutiny in a 'landmark' judgement of the Court of Appeal in 1998 in *Dyason* v. *Secretary of State for the Environment and Chiltern District Council*.[10]

In his judgement, Lord Justice Pill established that the absence of an accusatorial procedure, as in the seminar-style hearing, places an inquisitorial burden on an inspector to ensure that all issues are examined thoroughly. In discharging this burden and in its conclusion that a fair Hearing did not occur in this case, the Court sounded a warning that 'the "more relaxed" atmosphere could lead, not to a "full and fair" Hearing but to a less than thorough examination of the issues. A relaxed Hearing is not necessarily a fair Hearing'.

The Dyason case examined the way that evidence is tested in the Hearing, namely by virtue of discussion and not cross-examination. Lord Justice Pill established something of a 'benchmark' against which hearings in particular and planning appeals in general may be measured when he stated that:

> Planning permission having been refused, conflicting propositions and evidence will often be placed before an inspector on appeal. Whatever procedure is followed the strengths of a case can be determined only upon an understanding of that case and by testing it with reference to propositions in the opposing case. At a public local inquiry the inspector, in performing that task, usually has the benefit of cross-examination on behalf of the other party. If cross-examination disappears, the need to examine propositions in that way does not disappear with it. Further, the statutory right to be heard is nullified unless, in some way, the strength of what one party says is not only listened to by the tribunal but is assessed for its own worth and in relation to opposing contentions.

While this case of itself did not result in reform of the Hearing method, the judgement of Lord Justice Pill made inspectors acutely aware of their inquisitorial duty to examine evidence at the Hearing. After Dyason, it was more often the case that inspectors would rather play an active than a passive role in the discussion of planning merits. Research into perception of the Hearing by Stubbs (1999–2000) revealed favourable endorsement of this method by planning consultants and planning officers alike. Dyason, when set alongside these findings, was viewed as an isolated case of bad practice. Stubbs (1999) found that following a survey of planning practitioners they were 'more than content that Hearings can maintain high standards of openness, fairness and impartiality within an informal setting'. Two years after Dyason the government revised the guidance covering conduct of the parties at the Hearing.[11] It countenanced the limited introduction of cross-examination at Hearings, where deemed appropriate by the parties, to test evidence. Apart from such a somewhat odd innovation (which may potentially compromise the informality of the Hearing method) no material revisions were made to the guidance following Dyason. More recently (2006) the method has again been the subject of legal scrutiny, with the case of *Tapecrown Ltd* v. *First Secretary of State*, in the Court of Appeal (EWCA Civ 1744) in which it was noted that a written appeal reduces the ability of an inspector to act inquisitorially, as would be the case at a Hearing. Further, it was noted that a long site visit with lots of questions (as was the case in the enforcement appeal that led to this case) would still be no substitute for a Hearing.

Public Inquiry

The Public Inquiry is the most formal, as well as formidable, method of planning appeal. Procedure is governed by a set of statutory rules, which establish

Table 4.6 Timetable for the Planning Inquiry (transferred case)

Time	Procedure
	Appellant submits appeal forms Secretary of State (Inspectorate) issues an acknowledgement letter, establishing start date (referred to as relevant notice or RN)
Two weeks	LPA return questionnaire
Six weeks	• Both LPA and Appellant submit statements of their case (full particulars of the case including relevant statute and case law, but not detailed evidence) • Third parties to submit any comments/observations
Nine weeks	Observations on case advanced by other party or any third party must be made. Inspectorate may send the parties a list of the matters
(By) twelve weeks	Inspectorate may send the parties a list of the matters about which it wishes to be informed
4 weeks *before* Inquiry	LPA and Appellant submit proofs of evidence (detailed professional evidence) and statement of any common ground reached between the two sides (agreed factual information).
Inquiry – No later than twenty weeks (Inspector cases) or twenty-two weeks (Secretary of State cases) from start date/relevant notice	Each witness presents evidence by reading from proofs of evidence (or a summary) which is then open to cross-examination.
Site visit	Accompanied site visit, similar to that conducted for the Written Representation site visit
Decision letter issued	No target set (i.e. minimum number of weeks after decision).

that written statements of evidence shall be exchanged by both sides prior to the Inquiry. At the Inquiry, each side will appear with an expert witness or witnesses who will be open to cross-examination by, in most cases, trained advocates (see Case study 4.4 and Table 4.6).

The exact procedure varies between cases decided by inspectors (transferred cases) and those decided by the Secretary of State (recovered and 'called in' cases). What they both share is a system based on an exchange of evidence, including statements of common ground, prior to the testing of that evidence at the Inquiry.

Cross-examination

The Inquiry procedure rules are designed to ensure that the Inquiry time is used most effectively in helping the inspector in arriving at an informed decision. Successive reforms of the rules have been designed to avoid wasted time, while allowing each party to fully present its case and 'test' the planning evidence presented by the other side. In 1992 the rules were reformed to require a written summary to accompany any proof of evidence exceeding a threshold of 1500 words. Summaries themselves should not exceed 10 per cent of the length of the proof. Brevity in evidence was thus encouraged, and if this were not possible then only the summary and not the full proof would be read out at the Inquiry (although all evidence is open to cross-examination). The 2000 rules, in similar

---

Summary: Informal Hearings – key characteristics

- Written exchange of evidence followed by 'round the table' discussion
- Inspector plays important inquisitorial role in controlling the decision
- Increasing popularity from mid-1980s onwards; since mid-1990s more popular than Inquiry
- Procedure governed by statutory rules since 2000
- Half-way house between Written Representations and Public Inquiry in speed of decision, and professional fees involved
- An award of costs is available at a Hearing and dealt with at the end
- Increasingly popular and growing to around 20 per cent of all appeals.

Case study 4.3

Proposal: The LPA refuses planning permission to build two new houses within a backland site in a conservation area. At the application stage, considerable local opposition is voiced against the proposal. The application is refused permission for several reasons:

> The proposal is contrary to the nature and form of development within this Conservation Area.
> The proposal would result in an unacceptable loss of existing trees within the site, which make an important contribution to the appearance of the Conservation Area.
> The proposal is contrary to conservation policies within the local plan.

Appraisal: The magnitude and complexity of the case are greater than in Case study 4.1, yet the matters are still relatively straightforward – principally the impact on the character and appearance of the conservation area. However, the possibility of considerable third-party representation rules out the Informal Hearing, leaving either a Written Representation or Public Inquiry. If the developer is happy to bear the additional cost and time involved, an Inquiry allows the opportunity to deal effectively with any third parties who wish to appear by means of cross-examination.

Case study 4.4

Proposal: The LPA refuses planning permission for an office redevelopment within a town centre location for the following reasons:

> The proposal is considered to be contrary to local plan policy that identifies the site as being suitable for retail development.
>
> Insufficient parking is provided within the site, resulting in congestion on the neighbouring highway.
>
> Excessive height, and mass, of proposal, resulting in a form of development out of scale with surrounding development.
>
> In the absence of any contribution towards highway improvements on surrounding roads, the LPA considers that the additional traffic generated will result in an unacceptable increase in congestion, detrimental to the free flow of traffic and highway safety.

Appraisal: This appeal raises several complex technical issues (policy, material considerations and possible need for planning obligations) and a proposal of some magnitude. The financial cost of professional representation would be high, involving possibly several different professionals (planning, highway engineering and architectural) to deal with the different reasons. The Planning Inquiry presents the best method with which to deal with these issues, with the significant benefit of being able to cross-examine the other side.

vein, required submission of a 'statement of common ground' between LPA and appellant. This would cover matters of fact (site dimensions, planning history) and technical methodologies (such as how design standards or air-quality standards were arrived at). By therefore identifying matters not in dispute, valuable Inquiry time is saved. In 2007 further mooted reforms were geared to improving future efficiencies by speeding the submission of evidence. Such reforms do not diminish from the central and most tangible advantage of the Inquiry, notably the ability to cross-examine witnesses who appear on behalf of the LPA, appellant or third parties (see Case study 4.3). In this respect the Inquiry may take on the appearance of a court, with the adversarial stance taken by either side and the frequent use of barristers or solicitors. It is not, then, uncommon for the Inquiry to be viewed as a judicial hearing, but this is misleading. A court hearing involves strict rules of evidence that may rule some evidence inadmissible – hearsay evidence, for example. A planning Public Inquiry, although governed by statutory rules, deals with a good deal of opinion-based argument, for example the professional judgement of a witness in how to interpret a particular policy, or the relative balance between policy and other material considerations in arriving at a land-use decision.

Summary: Planning Inquiries – key characteristics

- Suitable for more complex cases
- Written exchange of statements and proofs of evidence followed by Inquiry with formal rules of procedure involving evidence in chief, cross-examination, re-examination and submission
- Appeal method of longest duration
- Most expensive (in professional fees) for appellant and inspectorate (in administration and inspector's time). Involves around nine times more hours per inquiry decision compared to a written equivalent
- Procedures (exchange of evidence and inquiry conduct) governed by statutory rules
- Least used method but tends to deal with the most important cases
- Smallest proportion of all appeals: 5–10 per cent.

In an Inquiry, cross-examination should not be used to discredit any witnesses but instead to test the validity of facts or assumptions, explore how policy relates to the merits of the case and to identify and narrow the issues in dispute. The inspector enjoys powers to refuse to hear evidence or to permit cross-examination which is irrelevant or repetitious. At the Inquiry only the applicant (or appellant), local planning authority and any statutory party (such as English Heritage or Natural England, who are consulted on specific heritage or nature conservation matters) are entitled to cross-examine. The inspector enjoys the discretion to allow other persons to do so, notably third parties (objectors). In 2002 it was agreed by the planning inspectorate and Planning Bar (representing advocates) that barristers would remain seated during cross-examination of witnesses. This change to protocol was introduced to reduce the adversarial nature of Inquiries.[12]

The format of an Inquiry – on the day – is outlined in Table 4.7.

The nature of evidence

In all methods of planning appeal, 'evidence' may be produced in several ways. In all appeals this evidence may comprise both fact and opinion/judgement. For example, note the distinctions between facts and opinion in Table 4.8.

Instructing an advocate

The professionals who appear at a Planning Inquiry divide into two distinct kinds: the advocate and the expert witness. The advocate principally presents and leads the case by making speeches and submissions to the inspector and by examining and cross-examining witnesses. The advocate is 'neutral' with respect to the case merits. He or she does not express a personal view and need not even believe

Table 4.7 Planning Inquiry format 'on the day'

Format	Details	Tactics
Inspector opens Inquiry	Statement that Inquiry is to be held and short explanation of procedure. Inspector notes names of advocates, witnesses and any third parties. The Inspector will identify the principal issues to be considered at the Inquiry.	
Local Planning Authority's case		
LPA Evidence in Chief	As below	As below
Appellant may cross-examine		
LPA may re-examine		
Inspector may ask questions of witness		
Appellant's case		
Appellant's Evidence in Chief	Each witness reads proof or summary plus any additional oral explanation.	Deal with reasons for refusal point by point
LPA may cross-examine each witness	Opportunity to test evidence by oral examination.	• Agree common ground • Focus on differences • Test validity of differences
Appellant may re-examine	Advocate may deal with issues raised in cross-examination.	Must avoid leading witness or introducing fresh evidence
Inspector may ask the witness questions		
*Third Party evidence**		
Closing submissions by LPA, third parties* and appellant	Summary of case as has emerged from evidence/ cross/re-examination.	An extremely important opportunity to target what has been conceded in cross-examination. The appellant enjoys the last word.
Inspector will close Inquiry, then . . . Site visit		No discussion of the merits of the case, while on site.

Note
* At discretion of Inspector. Third Party individuals or groups may be permitted to present their own case and question the appellant.

Table 4.8 Examples of evidence produced in planning appeals

Facts	Opinion
Planning policy issues, i.e. the site is or is not covered by policies A, B or C. This is a matter of fact. It is a matter of fact that the site is within a conservation area.	Some policies are vague in detail or broad in their application and require opinion to decide on how they should be interpreted. Conservation policy states that development must preserve or enhance the character/appearance. It may be a matter of opinion that a proposal satisfies such criteria.
Car parking or amenity space standards, i.e. does the proposal satisfy such standards? This is a matter of fact, e.g. proposal provides five spaces and standards require seven spaces – fails standards by two.	Whether rigid adherence to car parking standards is required is a matter of opinion, e.g. surrounding roads contain plenty of parking on the kerbside, so two additional cars would not result in any harm to the free flow of traffic.

in the merits of the case. While advocates must not knowingly mislead or deceive the inspector, their main goal is to present their case in its best possible light. The advocate can be a barrister, solicitor, planner or surveyor. Planning Inquiries are not the subject of strict rules of audience, so anyone may appear as an advocate, although a professional grasp of advocacy skills is desirable. With the increased formality or 'judicialization' of planning appeals over the last forty years, specialist planning barristers or solicitors have emerged as the most commonly used advocates. Most are members of the Planning and Environment Bar Association (PEBA) or the Planning Panel of the Law Society and their principal work involves environmental and planning law and advocacy.

Members of a number of property-related professional bodies, including the Royal Town Planning Institute, Royal Institution of Chartered Surveyors and Royal Institution of British Architects, may instruct a barrister without reference (as was required in the past) to a solicitor. This 'direct professional access' means that the instructing planner, surveyor or architect must brief the barrister concerned with all relevant papers and is responsible for the payment of fees.

The witness must provide an expert view consistent with a professional opinion. This will require the witness to present a distinct body of expertise in a proof of evidence and oral defence of it under cross-examination at the Inquiry. This evidence must be consistent with the witness's own professional opinion. The expert planning witness is not a 'hired gun' who will simply say whatever the client or planning committee wish them to say. Such matters of professional conduct or ethics are dealt with by the various professional bodies. The Royal Institution of Chartered Surveyors[13] guidance in such matters is that 'The Surveyor's evidence must be independent, objective and unbiased. In particular, it must not be biased towards the party who is responsible for paying him. The evidence should be the same whoever is paying for it.'

In similar vein, the Royal Town Planning Institute's professional code states that 'The town planner as a witness at an Inquiry is there to give evidence which must be true evidence . . . if the evidence is . . . given in the form of a professional opinion it must be the planner's own professional opinion if it is to carry weight as expert evidence'.[14]

It may be the case that the planning officer is giving evidence after the planning committee had overturned a recommendation to grant permission. This situation may appear rather odd, in that the planning officer who recommended a grant of permission is now given the onerous task of defending that refusal at appeal. Professional guidance is unambiguous:

> Care must be taken to avoid giving the impression that any statement made or views expressed at the Inquiry represent a planner's own view if these are contrary to his or her bona fide professional opinion . . . [the planning officer should be] . . . frank and open about his or her professional opinion.
>
> (RTPI 2007)

This situation is a product of the democratic process in which a planning committee may reject an officer recommendation, provided that they have sound planning grounds for so doing. It is preferable that a member of a planning committee gives evidence in these circumstances. However, officers are on occasion called upon to represent their council without compromising their own personal and professional views.

The award of costs

In all planning appeal proceedings, each party is expected to pay their own costs. The power to award costs in planning appeals was first introduced in 1933. Since 1972 the Local Government Act has enabled the Secretary of State or inspector to require that one party pays the costs of another in planning appeals.[15] Key features of this provision are that:

- It is available in all public Inquiry and (Informal) Hearing appeals[16]
- It is also available in all enforcement appeals or listed-building enforcement notice appeals submitted by Written Representation. This power may be extended to all written appeals in the future.
- Applications for an award must usually be made within the appeal procedure; at Public Inquiry or Hearing this is usually before the close.
- The award covers the costs of attending and preparing for the appeal. It does not deal with the financial costs relating to the purchase of a site, the development of which has been delayed by the fighting of a planning appeal, loss of profit, and so on.
- The award is made because of unreasonable conduct by a party, which has caused another party unnecessary expense.

- The award does not automatically follow the appeal decision, e.g. if the decision of the inspector is to allow the appeal, it does not imply that costs will follow. If an LPA fails to support a reason for refusal with evidence, this can constitute unreasonable behaviour, and costs may be awarded to the developer. However, the merits of the appeal and merits of costs are dealt with entirely separately.
- Costs are rare, amounting to an average of one award in every twenty-eight appeal decisions.

The award of costs represents a penalty against either party for unreasonable conduct in appeal proceedings. During the 1980s the majority of awards were made against local planning authorities. Research undertaken between 1987 and 1990 indicated that costs had been awarded against an LPA 6.5 times more frequently than against appellants (Blackhall 1990, Association of Metropolitan Authorities 1990). During this period the government was seeking to 'deregulate' the planning system by establishing, in policy guidance, a presumption in favour of granting planning permission. A development boom resulted in the submission of many more planning applications, and planning committees found themselves overturning officer recommendations and refusing planning permission in order to pacify local opposition to this 'tide' of new development. The research indicated that costs were more likely to be awarded in cases where the planning committee had rejected a recommendation by the chief planning officer, albeit not by a great margin.

The volume of costs awarded in favour of the appellant or the LPA has fluctuated over the years. Both government planning policy and the level of property development in the economy has influenced these statistics. For example, during the property boom of the 1980s, when policy established a 'presumption in favour of development', appellants were winning around 90 per cent of all cost applications. Local government planners at the time understandably viewed the costs regime as a penalty against them and the planning committee. By the 1990s, with boom turning to recession and policy changing to a presumption in favour of the development plan (as still applies), the 90 per cent statistic fell to 60 per cent. During the 1990s and into the 2000s the level of awards granted has stabilized at around two-thirds to appellants and the remainder to LPAs. Consequently the professional perception of costs has changed among LPAs and the current regime is increasingly viewed as a more even-handed sanction against unreasonable behaviour.

Costs were only marginally more likely to be granted in favour of the appellant after a planning committee had rejected a recommendation by the chief planning officer. Stubbs (2000 and 2001) concluded, after analysis of a sample of 500 costs decisions, that 'Costs were granted in 35 per cent of all councillor-led decisions, compared to 27 per cent of officer-led ones . . . a straightforward conclusion is that a refusal based upon a reversal of the Chief Planning Officer's recommendation is absolutely no guarantee of success on a costs application'.

Table 4.9 Examples of the award of costs

Facts		Evidential	
(A) Unreasonable behaviour	(B) Resulting in unnecessary expense	(A) Unreasonable behaviour.	(B) Resulting in unnecessary expense.
Failure to provide adequate pre-Inquiry statement, i.e. not setting out case or documents to be used. Both sides.*	Waste of Inquiry time to establish the case produced by one side, or results in need for adjournment.	Failure to provide evidence to support refusal. Award against LPA.	Planning application should not have been refused in the first case, or LPA have not justified their case so appeal unnecessary.
Failure to provide supporting information, or late submission of proof of evidence.	Waste of Inquiry time to establish the case produced by one side, or results in need for adjournment.	Planning policy† establishes that proposal was in accord with policy and therefore planning application should have been granted. Against LPA.*	Matter should not have proceeded to appeal in the first place.
Introduce at late stage a new ground of appeal or legal ground in an enforcement appeal (Appellant)* or reason for refusal (LPA).*	Waste of Inquiry time to establish the case produced by one side, or results in need for adjournment.	It was apparent from a previous appeal on the site that a resubmission with amendments would be acceptable. Against LPA.	Matter should not have proceeded to appeal in the first place.
Unreasonable/late withdrawal once Inquiry/Hearing has been arranged.	One side has wasted time in preparing for Inquiry unnecessarily.	It was apparent from a previous appeal on the site that a resubmission with amendments would be acceptable Against LPA.*	LPA should have granted resubmitted proposal, following the material consideration of the previous Inspector's decision.

Notes
* Party against whom costs would be awarded if an application for costs was made at the Inquiry/Hearing and the Inspector agreed.
* Some caution is required when considering this case. Most planning policy requires a good deal of interpretation and of course material considerations may 'indicate otherwise', making it difficult to establish unreasonable behaviour against either an appellant who proceeds to appeal on a matter that appears contrary to policy or an LPA that refuses an application that appears in accord with policy.
† Planning policy...

Evidently during the ten-year period after the work by Blackhall (1990) the incidence of cost awards between LPAs and appellants had narrowed – while the chances of regaining costs following planning committee's rejection of an officer's recommendation made a decision more vulnerable to an award.[17]

Examples of costs

To gain an award of costs, it is necessary to establish that one party has acted unreasonably, vexatiously or frivolously and that this behaviour has resulted in unnecessary expense for the other side (LPA, appellant or, in rare cases, third party).

In the majority of cases, applications for costs can be divided into those based on procedural issues and those based on evidential issues. Table 4.9 shows a series of examples to illustrate some common features of costs applications – but they are by no means exhaustive. It is important to remember that criteria as stated under headings (A) and (B) must be satisfied for an award of costs to be granted

---

Case study 4.5

Blackacre Holdings apply for planning permission to erect a block of flats with accommodation in the roofspace, at Sylvan Avenue, Melchester. The planning officer recommends approval to the Melsham District Council planning committee. The Sylvan Avenue Residents Association (SARA) mount a vigorous campaign against the application. At the committee meeting the Sylvan Ward councillor pleads with the committee to refuse permission. The committee decide to defer the application and visit the site to assess the impact of ten proposed dormers in the roofspace. At the next meeting, they decide to refuse permission on the grounds that 'The design of the roofscape is harmful to the character of the streetscene on Sylvan Avenue, which is predominantly of two-storey detached dwellings without dormer windows.'

Appraisal: The recommendation of the chief planning officer has been overturned by the planning committee but this of itself does not mean that costs will follow. If the LPA can bring to an Inquiry/Hearing some evidence of harm they should be able to defend any application for costs by the appellant. The matter for the inspector in deciding the planning merits is both a professional and subjective assessment of design-related issues. The committee visited the site and thus formed their own view on this matter. This case involves assessment of evidential and not procedural matters, and the extent to which the LPA can put forward a case (such as photographs and plans showing the character of the area and visual impact of the proposal). If they can present such a case then an inspector will in all probability refuse any application for costs made by the appellant.

in favour of one party. For an application for costs to succeed it may be helpful to consider the notion of a 'threshold'. In procedural matters this threshold is crossed when it can be demonstrated that by failing to follow various rules the other party was put to some tangible waste of time and, importantly, expense. In evidential matters the threshold is crossed where the evidence fails to have substance in its own right (see Case studies 4.5 and 4.6). It is not necessary for the inspector to be sufficiently persuaded by this evidence to rely upon it when determining the appeal. It is conceivable that an LPA may lose an appeal yet save costs by producing some evidence of demonstrable harm. What matters is that the LPA have produced some evidence, because to do so, even if the inspector is not swayed by it in his decision, will render the LPA to be immune from any costs application mounted by the other side.

Case study 4.6

The fast-food chain, Tasty Burger, apply to change the use of an existing retail shop to a restaurant (A3) in the historic town centre of Wykham-in-the-Vale. Wykhamstead District Council, the LPA, refuses permission because

> 'The proposed ventilation ducting is unacceptably close to neighbouring residential property, resulting in a loss of amenity to those occupiers.'

Tasty Burger appeal. At the Hearing the appellant produces a report commissioned from an acoustic engineer, which concludes that noise transmission would be minimal and insufficient to be audible by neighbouring occupiers. The planning officer representing Wykhamstead District Council produces no technical report but argues that he has observed ducting at other A3 takeaway uses while on his holidays at Compton-on-Sea and concludes that noise levels would be unacceptable.

Appraisal: The LPA have refused consent on a technical ground, dealing with noise levels arising from fume extraction ducting. To defend this at appeal, technical acoustic evidence must be produced. The appellants have produced this evidence but the Council have failed to do so and rely on mere observation made by the planning officer when on his holidays (thus unrelated to this site).

The LPA have failed to produce any technical evidence and have not crossed the necessary evidential threshold. The appellant was put to unnecessary expense in paying for an acoustic report. If the appellant can demonstrate this then an inspector will, in all probability, grant an application for reimbursement of the costs incurred in producing the acoustic report.

Conclusions

The planning appeal process plays a vital role in the town planning system, granting power to challenge the decisions of the LPA. The procedures upon which the system is based are themselves shaped by the needs of natural justice and administrative efficiency. Most appellants seek speedy decision on appeal, but they also seek a system that allows for a full explanation of their case, and requires the LPA to account for its decision. All three methods of appeal contain a balance between administrative efficiency and the rules of natural justice. The written method is quickest, with the least rigour in its examination of evidence, and the Inquiry is the longest, with the most rigour in its examination of evidence; the Hearing falls somewhere between the two. Changes to procedures have increasingly sought to improve efficiency by introducing timetables, rules and the award of costs.

It is important to recall the need for appeal decisions to be made in a cost-effective way (for the Exchequer, which funds the system at an annual cost of around £26 million) and a speedy manner (for the benefit of appellant or LPA) as delay in the appeal system will delay the development process and act as a disincentive to any applicant seeking a review of a development control decision. The inspectorate is required to meet a series of performance indicators agreed with the Secretary of State for Communities and Welsh Office, together with its own internal 'Quality Assurance' standards. In a typical year such targets deal with both speed of decision-making (50 per cent of Written Representations in sixteen weeks, Public Inquiries in thirty weeks and Hearings in thirty weeks). A 'quality' target is also imposed, in which 99 per cent of appeal casework is free from justified complaint (i.e. any factual error in a decision letter or inadequate or incorrect reasoning). In the year 2006–07, of 28,534 decisions by the inspectorate only 228 fell within the category of a justified complaint, out of a total of 2287 complaints made. A mere fifty-one cases were successfully challenged in the High Court (i.e. an error in law was deemed sufficient for a Judge to quash the decision and return it for re-determination). Such matters are independently vetted by an independent advisory panel on standards.[18]

In past years, this drive towards procedural efficiency has resulted in some reforming proposals that have subsequently been dropped by government, following criticism that they would compromise the ability of appeals to deliver natural justice. Such ideas have included dropping the automatic entitlement to a Public Inquiry, issuing policy guidance to the effect that pursuing an Inquiry instead of an alternative method could be grounds for the award of costs, curtailing the opportunity to cross-examine at Inquiry, and widening the power to award costs to Written Representation. None of these ideas have yet been acted upon,[19] and both the planning inspectorate and the Secretary of State have consistently supported the appellant's automatic right to insist on a Public Inquiry. However, critics of the system are concerned that the increasing support of alternatives, such as Hearings, is only the tip of the iceberg to reduce both the costs of appeal and the length of time to reach a decision, by ultimately either restricting access to the Public Inquiry method or the ability to cross-examine within that method.[20]

The key defining feature of the English and Welsh appeal system remains that it is essentially an adversarial system of dispute resolution, in which the parties seek to challenge the evidence presented by the other side in a variety of written and oral exchanges, considered by an independent decision-maker (i.e. the inspector). Further, with the inspector's decision binding all parties, the current planning appeal orthodoxy is best encapsulated as a form of 'independent professional decision-making' in which the inspector brings an independent, objective and impartial determination of disputed facts or issues to the evidence presented by all sides (Bevan 1992). The planning inspectorate performs their duties to a very high standard indeed, and inspectors apply the Franks principles of openness, fairness and impartiality in the conduct of their duties. This high standard was recognized by the House of Commons Environment, Transport and Regional Affairs Select Committee report of 2000, 'The planning inspectorate and Public Inquiries' (House of Commons 1999–2000). The Committee noted that 'The planning inspectorate performs an extremely important task and we conclude that, in most aspects of its work, it is doing an excellent job'. Any criticisms were not levelled at the conduct of inspectors but were a call for more transparency in their training, the handling of complaints, recruitment practices, and use of technology (such as the Internet). Such concerns dealt more with a desire to break down a perception by the Committee that the inspectorate was secretive than to challenge the very high standards it achieves in the discharge of its decision-making functions. In 2005 the inspectorate introduced an Internet portal allowing appeals to be submitted electronically and progress monitored.

The establishment of the Franks principles of openness, fairness and impartiality have created valuable quasi-judicial guidelines to establish due process in the conduct of planning appeals. The importance of these principles cannot be overstated. Yet, one notable consequence of them has been a trend towards increasing levels of judicial control over planning. It is perhaps arguable that the recovery of costs at Inquiries and Hearings and the introduction of strict timetables for the submission of evidence fit into this trend by imposing greater mechanisms of control over the conduct of a case. Planning appeals are, however, also responsible for the discharge of an administrative/development control function, notably to determine the merits of a case. Hearings may be seen as representing a refreshing diversion from or counter to this trend of progressive judicialization. Michael Howard, when Minister for Planning, said (in 1988) of the Hearing method: 'there are obvious limits to its use but it is a development I welcome which I believe in many ways gets nearer to the original intention of an inquiry than the much more formal way which has developed over the years' (Howard 1989).

It is arguable that Hearings allow for a more direct way of uncovering development control issues than by cross-examination at Inquiry. Part of the concern, as expressed in the Dyason and Tapecrown cases, was that planning issues may not be exposed to sufficient enquiry or testing, the corollary of which is that unfairness may result and the inspector be unaware of all relevant issues.

Consideration of the Dyason case may help us to focus future debate about planning appeals towards certain key areas. 'Informal dispute resolution' has a role to play in the planning system. Set against a post-Franks trend towards greater judicialization of planning appeals, the favourable endorsement of hearings uncovered by research by Stubbs (1999) demonstrates that it is possible to depart from an adversarial and formal testing of evidence and maintain a professional view that the process is fair and that an adequate discovery and testing of development control issues is undertaken. One of the most meaningful lessons to emerge from the work by Stubbs (1999) is that informality of method and delivery of fairness are not mutually exclusive. Striking an acceptable balance between them, as hearings do, facilitates an acceptable uncovering of appeal merits in a manner that obviates the need for judicial techniques such as cross-examinations to test a case or expose an argument.

Future directions

The planning appeal system is the subject of almost continuous review and reform. During the twelve-year period 1988–2000, three sets of procedural timetables were introduced. External pressures imposed by both government (in targets for decision-making) and by 'users' of the system (in their expectation of efficiency and fairness) result in an almost constant 'drip feed' of new initiatives. In past years such changes have maintained the central foundation of planning appeals, notably the traditional method of dispute resolution previously encapsulated as 'independent professional decision-making'. Since 2000, two new developments may serve to change this traditional landscape of dispute resolution. First, the introduction of the Human Rights Act 1998 (enacted in England and Wales in October 2000) may 'open a can of worms [and] nobody had any idea of the size of the can.'[21] Second, the result of a pilot study of Alternative Dispute Resolution in 2000 and subsequent recommendations by Kate Barker in 2006 may herald future reforms that set out to change the 'traditional' culture that influences the way in which planning appeals are resolved.

In 2007 the government published a wide-ranging review of the appeals process, under the banner title of making the system more 'proportionate, customer focused, efficient and well resourced'. Such a review was forced upon government by the sheer volume of appeals, rising dramatically from 14,000 per year in the late 1990s to more than 22,000 in 2006, and predicted to top 25,000 by 2010. The consultation paper (DCLG 2007h) made plain the fact that 'the existing system is not equipped to efficiently handle such large appeal numbers, leading to delays in decision making'. The published proposals represented a somewhat piecemeal attempt to reduce unnecessary appeal volumes and to increase revenue to the planning inspectorate by imposing a fixed fee for the right to appeal. Panels of councillors would form 'Local Member Review Bodies' which would determine only minor appeals (such as household extensions or small change of use proposals) but significantly remove such decisions from the planning inspectorate and give it to local councillors. This was deleted from the Planning and

Reform Act 2008. Such a change, while not that dramatic, would have required a greater grasp of the Franks principles, for instance, when councillors were presiding over appeals concerning householder applications. It must be remembered that these appeals would be against their own planning authority – in other words their planning officers had refused consent and the householder appealed to the Local Member Review Body. This proposal was deemed too controversial.

Appeal methods would therefore – and for the first time – be tailored to individual circumstances so that householder appeals (usually involving domestic extensions) would be 'fast tracked', resulting in a process that was less bureaucratic and much faster. This would, almost overnight, speed up one quarter of all appeals. On more complex appeals the planning inspectorate, on behalf of the Secretary of State, would be able to determine the appeal method. The costs regime, while not dramatically overhauled, would be bolstered by the introduction of fixed fees which would be imposed against late evidence as well as widened to include all written appeals. A fixed or proportionate fee would be levied against the appellant and would yield an estimated £7 million revenue for the planning inspectorate.

Most of these mooted reforms were floated in an attempt to free up some space by taking many small appeals out of the system and/or reducing time-consuming procedures for the simpler cases. By charging a fee, the inspectorate would 'claw back' some resources, crudely estimated at around 20 per cent of their operational costs. The 2007 review, at best, represented an attempt to fend off the severe resource gap that would emerge in the event of rising appeals numbers, combined with the increasing popularity of the Hearing method. The 2007 consultation paper would, if carried forward, require legislation – in the introduction of fees, for example. It lacked any wider ambitions geared towards a modernization of planning jurisprudence as would follow from the introduction of mediation or an environmental court. Nevertheless, the reforms it would probably herald were required to prevent the planning appeal system from requiring an enormous injection of extra funding from the Exchequer to maintain its high-quality standards when confronted with a dramatic rise in the volumes of appeals submitted.

5 The future for dispute resolution in planning

Two distinct areas will be considered, namely those of 'alternative dispute resolution' (mediation) in planning, and human rights legislation and its consequences. Both challenge current thinking and provide innovative solutions to some existing problems in the appeal system. Over the next few years both planning practitioners and casual spectators of the system are well advised to monitor developments in these two areas.

Introduction to alternative dispute resolution

Alternative dispute resolution (ADR) is a convenient, if imprecise, expression by which a whole raft of dispute-resolution procedures may be classified. Mediation is one of the best known methods of ADR. The methods covered are considered to fall outside traditional litigation and arbitration (including planning appeals). Brown and Marriot (1993) provided a good definition: 'ADR may be defined as a range of procedures which serve as alternatives to the adjudication procedures of litigation and arbitration for the resolution of disputes'.

Mediation, therefore, represents but one method of resolving disputes within the broader spectrum of ADR. ADR has been viewed as an umbrella term (Bevan 1992) to cover a variety of dispute-resolution systems that share a common aim of seeking to act as alternatives to traditional methods in which disputes are resolved by the imposition of a decision upon the parties. Such traditional methods (i.e. litigation or arbitration, mostly in courts) have been criticized, for the high cost imposed on parties, the delay in getting a case heard and the formality and adversarial nature of the proceedings (Rogers 1990). ADR mechanisms have been credited with many advantages, perhaps the most frequently cited ones being that they seek a consensual outcome that is acceptable to both parties, in which each party enjoys ownership of the decision (thus increasing the likelihood of improved user-satisfaction) and that they are administratively expedient because they may save time and expense to the disputing parties.

The Land and Environment Court of New South Wales introduced town planning mediations in 1991, representing one of the first such innovations to be used in environmental disputes worldwide. They were introduced for a number of reasons. First, there was a growing awareness and promotion within Australia of the benefits of ADR in general to solve disputes (Astor and Chinkin 1992). Second, there was an increasing awareness of the costs involved in litigation and the fact that a major source of costs in local government legal expenditure was accounted for by litigation to defend council planning decisions on appeal to the Land and Environment Court (Parliament of New South Wales 1991). Finally, there was a desire to make decision-making more open, accessible and less formal (Pearlman 1995), coupled with the fear that litigation, environmental or otherwise, was becoming increasingly lengthy, complex and prone to delay (Fowler 1992). This lead taken by the Land and Environment Court established an important prototype that has subsequently influenced the system in England and Wales. This section will consider the theory and practice of ADR, to be followed by discussion of how this process may affect planning decision-making.

Establishing a definition of ADR

Literature on ADR abounds with many definitions. This material provides a useful starting point by establishing common terms and allowing certain technicalities to be unravelled.

At the most elementary level, ADR represents a generic term (Mackie 1997) or convenient label, as claimed by diverse interests, under which a whole series of non-binding dispute-resolution techniques may be collected (Heilbron 1994). Such techniques have evolved as a reaction to the formal determination of disputes by means of litigation (Street 1992, Briner 1997). Litigation is viewed as a sovereign remedy of dispute resolution, in which a judicial determination in a court of law will produce a transparent and binding settlement built upon the traditional adversarial principle, where the parties dictate at all stages the form, content and pace of proceedings. Arbitration, by contrast, is based upon the parties to a dispute giving power to an independent third party to make an adjudicatory award which will, in similar terms to litigation, determine the dispute and be binding upon both sides (Miller *op. cit.*). The UK literature considers arbitration to fall outside ADR and within the traditional system.

It has been argued that it would be more accurate to refer to ADR as 'complementary' dispute resolution (Harrison 1997), 'appropriate' dispute resolution (Acland 1990, Mackie *et al.* 1995) or even 'additional' dispute resolution, in that they reflect more accurately the desire for ADR to provide for a series of subsidiary processes that are often pursued simultaneously with court proceedings, rather than seeking to compete with the established legal system (Astor and Chinkin 1992, Street 1991). Further employment of an approach based upon adjudication and adversarial encounter may be viewed as inappropriate where personal or working relationships need to be preserved between the parties to a dispute (Brown and Marriot 1993: Chapter 2). ADR has a defined role to play in providing appropriate methods of dispute resolution when a settlement is to be based upon consensus, in which relationships are to be maintained between the respective parties. This means that ADR will not replace litigation but would necessarily be employed to make traditional adjudicatory or adversarial systems work more efficiently and effectively.

ADR theory

A whole raft of literature deals with process and mechanism. A series of individual ADR systems has been described and evaluated against ADR theory or against other 'traditional' methods of dispute resolution. The whole machinery of ADR has commonly been viewed as referring to a series of processes such as conciliation, mediation, mini-trial, or neutral evaluation (Mackie 1991, Mackie *et al.* 1995). The outcome of the process is determined by mutual consent of the parties, with varying assistance from a neutral facilitator. In Britain, as many as thirteen possible derivatives of ADR have been identified (O'Connor 1992) drawing upon the variations of techniques adopted by specialist ADR organizations and hybrid methods that amalgamate a selection of procedures, such as 'med-arb' and 'concilo-arb', mediation/conciliation and arbitration methods (Newman 1996). The subject area can easily become confusing. It is therefore often easier to focus upon a number of shared characteristics, namely that processes are largely informal (Folger and Jones 1994) in content with no prescribed or set method (Beckwith 1987, Kendrick 1995) and that consent will be required from all parties. Such features are key to establishing the fundamentals of ADR. ADR techniques may be classified broadly into those directed towards reaching agreement over an issue or set of issues, and those that seek to develop greater understanding, while falling short of actual agreement (Dukes 1996). As a consequence, ADR techniques may produce a settlement outright, or serve to narrow the dispute, combined with greater understanding of the stance taken by the other party.

Mediation is a 'facilitative' process (Brown and Marriot 1993: 99) whereby a neutral third party (mediator) assists the parties to a dispute to reach a self-determined agreement (Dana 1990) based on consensual solutions (MacFarlane 1997). The mediator enjoys no authoritative decision-making power to assist the disputing parties, who must reach their own mutually acceptable settlement (Moore 1996: 14), but strives to create conditions that are conducive to concluding a successful negotiation (Moore 1996).

Definitions of mediation concentrate on how it incorporates techniques that assist parties to explore and/or achieve a voluntary negotiated settlement after consideration of the alternatives. Such settlement may be identified as an 'early stage procedure' to prevent disputes entering the courts or as a 'settlement conduit' after legal proceedings have been commenced (Roberts 1995). The most straightforward purpose of mediation has been viewed as the creation of an atmosphere favourable to negotiation (Curle 1990). No set procedure is prescribed, and it would be misleading to infer that the term 'mediation' implies one consistent and uniform procedure adopted by all practitioners (Brown and Marriot *op. cit.*). The mediator will, however, be responsible for helping to establish a number of key features governing the confidentiality of the technique, the way in which joint discussions and negotiations are held, and the holding of private caucus meetings between mediator and individual party (Williams 1990). The neutrality of the mediator ensures that he or she is impartial towards all sides, but it does not prohibit the mediator from expressing a view on the merits of the case (i.e. from being evaluative), although this is not a precondition of the mediator's role and he or she may seek to act in a purely facilitative capacity (Dana 1990) by seeking to foster negotiation and settlement between both sides without expressing an opinion. Some commentators view mediation as being exclusively within the realm of facilitative settlement, indeed referring to it as 'facilitated, collaborative problem solving' (Burton 1988).

The distinction between facilitative (interest-based) mediation and evaluative (rights-based) mediation does itself establish a division of methodologies in the mediation process, and this is reflected in the literature and the theory. A spectrum is established in which some commentators hold that a mediator should only facilitate, and others that evaluation is the principal means by which settlement can be created, with yet other commentators holding a midway position, in which both methods are employed, to varying degrees, in an attempt to move the process forward (Brown and Marriot 1993: 114). The role of the mediator is central to the process, assisting each party to examine and highlight the respective strengths and weaknesses of their case (O'Connor 1992) and to explore options that may lead to a settlement. To achieve this, the mediator must possess different qualities and skills from that of a judge (or planning inspector) – principally the ability to act in a facilitative capacity (Robertshaw and Segal 1993). Such facilitation by the mediators is used to build and secure a settlement and is best considered as a three-tier process. This comprises information gathering (to understand priorities), diagnostic tactics (to make predictions about the basis of settlement) and movement tactics (in which the mediator attempts to tackle power relationships between the parties) (Kolb 1983). Such movement tactics involve fostering communication by procedures such as chairing joint and private sessions and by reporting between each side.

Many advantages and disadvantages have been attributed to ADR (Heilbron 1994, Newman 1996, Mackie *et al.* 1995, Shilston 1996). One of the most commonly cited advantages is the saving of time and expense to participating parties (O'Connor 1992, Acland 1995a, 1995b, 1995c, Dukes 1996), usually a benefit claimed without any real evidence in support of it. Again, limited research into this area during the 1980s (Williams 1990), together with the reported findings of specialist mediation centres such as the Centre for Dispute Resolution (CEDR) (Mackie 1997), have reinforced the perception that ADR can produce settlements in more than 70 per cent and sometimes as high as 90 per cent of cases. Furthermore, the suitability of case is determined not by the issues or legal questions involved but by what the parties want to achieve (ADR Group 1993). Alongside such benefits to the participants are the tangible benefits to the courts, as a backlog of cases may be cleared and the general level of litigation reduced (Heilbron 1994). The other body of advantages tend to focus upon how ADR improves the quality of decision-making by seeking an outcome that is based on consensual settlement and not imposed arbitration (Kolb 1983) and in which harmonious relationships may be maintained between the parties.

ADR and justice

A distinctive body of literature identifies a fundamental concern over the procedural fairness of ADR systems. This material also examines the relationship between ADR and the courts, seeking to identify problems in, for example, court-annexed ADR. Such concerns are important, and attention needs to be drawn to them at an early stage before considering how this process may be accommodated in the planning system. Justice may itself be perceived as relating both to procedural matters and to the distribution of resources in society. Literature on jurisprudence (the philosophy of law) establishes that procedural justice is heavily dependent upon the individuals' perception of fairness in the rules or procedures that regulate a process or produce a decision. This may require that legislation result in a generally beneficial consequence for at least one party and that most people will obey such rules or guidelines. Justice is often held to involve adherence to a judicial process and its outcome (Harris 1980). Justice is not the same as fairness and, indeed, a number of influential works in the early 1980s dealt with the central criticism that justice was not routinely achieved by litigation (Twining 1993), also that ADR was unlikely to deliver greater access to justice within 'American' society (Abel 1982, Auerbach 1983: 146). Such work may reflect wider inequality in society than just that related to legal mechanisms. Nevertheless, in delivering judicial fairness or a wider access to justice, it is important that public perceptions of the process are taken into account.

Mediation, for example, involves the possibility of a series of private caucus meetings between one party and the mediator, designed to encourage greater candour in establishing the criteria for settlement of a dispute. In addition, the combined informality and confidentiality of mediation/conciliation may restrict the proper disclosure or discovery of expert evidence (O'Connor 1992). Third parties may appear only at the discretion of the principal parties and the wide discretion given to the mediator may result in considerable inconsistency across the number of cases considered.

It has been reported that the greatest cause of concern among lawyers is a mediator in private caucus with one side, because it is impossible to assess the impact on the mediator in the absence of the right to question or rebut what is said (Elliott 1996). Natural justice concerns are seen to be raised most often in mediations that rely heavily on private caucusing. The caucus may greatly assist the mediator to broker a settlement by allowing for the ventilation of grievances/justifications, consideration of respective strengths and weaknesses, and exploration of bargaining or settlement positions. Much of the literature focuses on such attributes, albeit that several commentators dealing with the ethical foundations of mediation acknowledge the sensitivity of the caucus and the problems it raises for delivery of natural justice (because the mediator hears one side in the absence of the other) and public perceptions (a potential misconception that deals are being struck in private).

Associated with these concerns about the inclusion and measurement of fairness of some ADR methods is the view that such criticisms render ADR obsolete as a dispute resolution procedure to be employed within court jurisdiction. Mediation is gradually being used as an adjunct to the court system in England and has spread into a variety of civil cases and commercial matters. Some lawyers have expressed concern that mediation practices like caucusing run counter to the openness and fairness required by the courts in the maintenance of procedural justice (Street 1992, Naughton 1992). One of the most important and sensitive questions, therefore, is 'who should be responsible for the mediation process?' The exact location of the process is a key factor in shaping people's perception of mediation. Should it be part of a court or appeal body like the planning inspectorate or should it be entirely separate and independent?

ADR in practice

The task of the mediator is to 'oil the wheels of communication' (CEDR 1997). The parties are responsible for solutions and discussion of merits, while the mediator is responsible for the process. What is fundamental to achieving a settlement is that the parties move from what is referred to as 'positional bargaining' to 'principled negotiation'. Fisher and Urry (1997) have written the most important single work in this area. They advanced the view that in most disputes parties adopt an initial position (often an extreme one) and in negotiation reach a mid-way compromise after entrenched positions have been adopted. Such an outcome is often unsatisfactory and arrived at only after much haggling and often anger. Fisher and Urry (1997) developed the concept of 'principled negotiation' based upon an understanding of the 'best alternative to a negotiated agreement' (BATNA). The key to unlocking the respective BATNAs of the disputing parties is to grasp their underlying interests so that the ultimate settlement satisfies those interests and is therefore fair in its outcome.

This method of negotiation may be broken down into four key components (set out in Table 5.1) which are designed to ensure that the ultimate settlement is fairer and more durable than one reached by positional bargaining.

The process itself involves a number of key stages (see Figure 5.1) although no rigid or set model is imposed, and a more flexible interpretation is a matter for the mediator and the disputing parties. One fundamental principle is that

Table 5.1 Basis of principled negotiation

People	Separate the people from the problem.
Interests	Focus on interests, not positions.
Options	Generate a variety of possibilities before deciding what to do.
Criteria	Insist that the result be based on some objective standard.

Source: Fisher and Urry (1997)

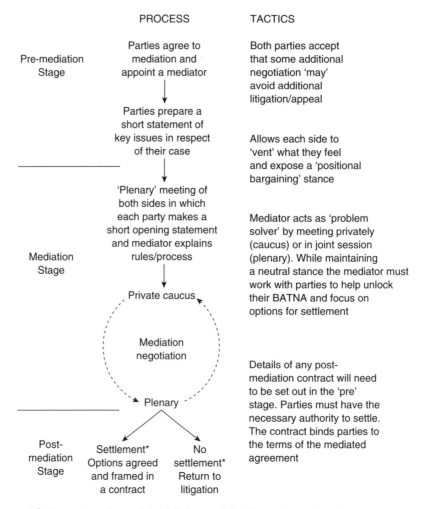

PROCESS

TACTICS

Pre-mediation
Stage

Parties agree to
mediation and
appoint a mediator

Both parties accept
that some additional
negotiation 'may'
avoid additional
litigation/appeal

Parties prepare a
short statement of
key issues in respect
of their case

Allows each side to
'vent' what they feel
and expose a 'positional
bargaining' stance

Mediation
Stage

'Plenary' meeting of
both sides in which
each party makes a
short opening statement
and mediator explains
rules/process

Mediator acts as 'problem
solver' by meeting privately
(caucus) or in joint session
(plenary). While maintaining
a neutral stance the mediator must
work with parties to help unlock
their BATNA and focus on
options for settlement

Private caucus

Mediation
negotiation

Plenary

Details of any post-
mediation contract will need
to be set out in the 'pre'
stage. Parties must have the
necessary authority to settle.
The contract binds parties to
the terms of the mediated
agreement

Post-
mediation
Stage

Settlement*
Options agreed
and framed in
a contract

No
settlement*
Return to
litigation

* Settlement may be partial or full. In a partial settlement a number of
issues may be agreed, thus reducing the areas in dispute that remain.

Figure 5.1 Mediation process (typical model)

commitment to a mediation is entirely voluntary and that either party may walk
away from the negotiations at any time and return to a more traditional model
of dispute resolution (i.e. back to court or planning inquiry).

Mediation in town planning

Two trends running in parallel may be identified over the period 1995–2008,
which have shaped a number of reforms culminating in the potential introduction of planning-based mediation. These trends may be distinguished as 'legal
push' and 'planning pull'. Each will now be considered.

'Legal push' in favour of ADR/mediation deals with the growing cultural awareness of ADR and in particular, with the emergence of court-annexed ADR over the period 1996–1998. The Woolf Report of 1996 'Access to Justice' and subsequent reforms to the civil justice system in England and Wales were influential in promoting greater awareness generally of mediation. ADR/ mediation is not without its sceptics in the legal profession, but the profile of civil law mediations is certainly rising. For example, 'Practice Directions' promoting the employment of ADR are in place in the Court of Appeal, High Court and Commercial Court. Such directions thereby oblige lawyers to review cases for their ADR suitability at the commencement of court proceedings. Two pilot mediation programmes ran in the Central London County Court (CLCC) and Patents County Court, in 1996. In July 1999 a family mediation pilot project was instigated whereby solicitors, in certain areas of London, had to advise clients to consider mediation when seeking legal aid for family disputes. The introduction of mediation into such legal jurisdictions has pushed the legal profession into a greater awareness and employment of such an alternative mechanism of dispute resolution.

Research work has also influenced awareness among lawyers. Findings drawn from the Central London County Court pilot were published by Professor Hazel Genn (1998). These research findings were significant. For example, it was reported that despite rigorous attempts to stimulate demand for the available mediation option, demand for it among disputing parties remained consistent at about 5 per cent of all cases. Take-up was highest among disputes between businesses and lowest in personal injury cases. Where mediation was employed, it resulted in settlement and withdrawal of court action in 62 per cent of all cases. Genn (1998) concluded that:

> mediation appears to offer a process that parties on the whole find satisfying and, handled carefully, can lead to a situation in which a sense of grievance is reduced [and that] there is also strong evidence in this report that mediation at an early stage can reduce the length of cases even when cases do not actually settle at the mediation appointment.

Yet the report was also aware that actual take-up was 'pitifully small', and that greater promotion and a 'cultural shift' by lawyers away from traditional litigation would be required for it to increase in its popularity.

Such a cultural shift was evident even in its early stages, between 1998 and 2000. The Lord Chancellor, Lord Irvine, endorsed the benefits of mediation in civil justice on several occasions, and new Civil Procedure Rules implemented in Spring of 1999, on the back of recommendations by Woolf (1996), required judges to promote the use of ADR in civil courts. The pre-eminence of such Law Lords as Woolf and Irvine, and endorsement by researchers like Professor Genn and practitioners like Professor Mackie, have raised a high profile for mediation that far exceeded its numerical impact on civil justice (measured by the number of cases mediated). This has kept a constant spotlight on mediation in legal journals, periodicals and books. While this means that mediation may be 'punching above its weight', the consequences are that this has influenced other disciplines in which disputes are to be settled. A number of government departments have introduced mediation pilots, including the Department of Trade and Industry, the Department of Health and (the then) Department of Environment, Transport and Regions. Town planning has been no exception to this trend.

In 1996, the Chief Planning Inspector promoted a discussion on the merits of planning mediation at the Royal Town Planning Institute National Conference. Later that year, speaking to the North West Branch of the Royal Town Planning Institute,[1] he said of ADR: 'It is a technique which is spreading rapidly. . . . It should be considered as part of the planning process.' Three years later, also at the National Conference, he hosted a workshop session on a simulated planning mediation. His enthusiasm for a debate in this area followed similar lines to the approach of many lawyers, as previously addressed, namely that it is an innovation laden with sufficient benefits to render it worthy of further employment.

'Planning pull' deals with the way mediation is drawn or pulled into the planning system by government for the less than utopian desire to reduce the burden of appeals to be determined by the planning inspectorate. By reducing this burden, the appeals remaining in the system would be dealt with more efficiently (i.e. quickly) as resources were freed. Government and the planning inspectorate have set out, over many years, to improve the service provided to appellants, third parties and local planning authorities at appeal. An appropriate balance must be struck between delivery of the Franks principles (dealt with in the previous chapter) and efficiency (unit cost of each appeal to government and time taken to reach a decision). Between 1990 and 2000 various measures have been considered in pursuit of the goal of efficiency. Some have been implemented (such as adherence to procedural timetables for the exchange of evidence), while others have not (such as dropping the automatic right to cross-examine at Inquiry). Mediation in planning may be part of this general trend, in which reform of the system is principally designed to promote speed and reduce the cost of decisions. Perhaps not surprisingly, governments have promoted consideration of mediation in planning more in terms of its wider benefits to disputing parties. In May 1998 Richard Caborn, the (then) Planning Minister, in heralding a pilot programme of planning mediation said 'This pilot study will consider whether greater use of mediation can help to modernize the planning system'. By placing mediation within the modernizing agenda of government policy, Caborn set out to establish a more utopian vision of mediation than one framed within the more grubby policy of cost-cutting and efficiency savings. The reality may fall somewhere between the two.

The potential for ADR in planning

Clearly, the planning system is capable of accommodating some kind of ADR, with mediation being the most probable method. Research in this area presents a case in favour of its introduction but also draws attention to significant problems that must be addressed. The planning system is distinctive in having a democratic base, especially when compared to, say, purely commercial decisions. A planning mediation will decide upon matters that have been the subject of public comment or scrutiny and are usually made by locally elected councillors in a planning committee. In a commercial mediation the two parties may settle the matter, sign a mediation contract and walk away from the negotiating table. In a planning mediation a similar outcome would affect the powers of the planning committee and public perception of the local democratic process. In the 'worst-case scenario', the planning committee would lose control in determining an application and the local electorate would perceive the mediation as a private deal struck between developer and LPA. Such potential criticisms must be addressed in any model of planning mediation. Indeed, the corollary of this is that planning mediation will need to be a tailor-made version of the commercial or court-annexed mediation to reflect this distinctive democratic constitution.

The potential enjoyed by planning mediation has been explored in two areas of research work by Stubbs (1997) and by Michael Welbank (DETR 2000e). These works examined respectively the potential to 'import' the New South Wales model of planning mediations and the findings of a pilot study of forty-eight planning-based mediations conducted in England and Wales.

The work by Stubbs (1997) was based on examination of 108 town planning appeals. A matter of some significance is that the planning system in New South Wales is comparable to that in the UK (especially England and Wales), with appeals being determined on their development control merits (see Case study 5.1).

These 108 planning mediations represented about 5 per cent of all planning appeals submitted over a four-year period, a figure comparable to the take-up experienced by the Central London County Court in its 1998 pilot study (Genn 1998). Similarly, once a mediation was held, settlement of the dispute was more than likely to follow, with 70 per cent of cases subject to settlement (compared to 62 per cent in the Central London County Court pilot). A questionnaire survey of practitioners within New South Wales did not reveal opposition to mediation, but the reverse: 'the opinions expressed by planning officers and consultants provided favourable endorsement of mediation of town planning appeals, with a significant amount of agreement on the suggested advantages of this option and some emphasis on the savings in time and money' (Stubbs 1997).

The findings of the study suggested that mediation, while demonstrating the benefit of saving time and money to the parties involved (assuming that settlement was reached), also improved the quality of dispute resolution by avoiding the adversarial and confrontational nature of the traditional appeal. The low take-up was not a function of unpopularity but rather of the number of cases in which negotiation was possible. In other words, 5 per cent reflected the volume of cases suitable for mediation, i.e. where additional assisted negotiation would yield agreement. This would work only in cases where the dispute was over

Case study 5.1   The planning appeal system in New South Wales

In New South Wales all planning appeals are dealt with by the Land and Environment Court. This specialist court was established in 1980 with jurisdiction over a range of planning, environmental and enforcement matters. The creation of a single court, by the Land and Environment Court Act 1979, was itself a rationalization of a number of appeal tribunals and powers previously exercised by the Supreme Court and District Courts of the State, so that the new court enjoys powers to determine both matters of administrative appeal and of judicial review. In recommending the relevant legislation to the New South Wales Parliament, the Minister for Planning and the Environment stated: 'The proposed new court is a somewhat innovative experiment in dispute resolution mechanisms. It attempts to combine judicial and administrative dispute resolving techniques and it will utilize non-legal experts as technical and conciliation assessors.'

Appeals to the court are heard by both Judges and Assessors. Assessors are professional experts, with relevant qualifications in town planning, engineering, surveying, land valuation, architecture, local government administration, or natural resource management. The principal method of appeal is by a Full Hearing in the court, in which evidence is presented in both written and oral form and is tested by adversarial cross-examination. The Assessor or Judge will decide the appeal, with Assessors determining the vast majority of appeals that deal with the planning merits of the case, and Judges ruling on matters of civil and criminal enforcement and cases raising points of law. The decision to allow or dismiss the appeal is binding upon both parties and constitutes a form of independent expert arbitration. The Full Hearing is a lengthy and expensive form of appeal determination, involving many professionals and usually taking several days to hear a case. One council located on the Sydney metropolitan fringes defended fifty-seven planning decisions in the Court in the financial year 1994–95, with a total professional cost (comprising legal fees and production of planning evidence) amounting to A$1,144,533.

Mediation was introduced in 1991, by means of an amendment to the Land and Environment Court Rules. The Rules state that at a 'call over' meeting the Court Registrar may refer proceedings to mediation in accordance with the court's practice direction. A practice direction, published in April 1991, stated that mediation would be offered in matters within the jurisdiction of town planning, building and rating appeals. This guidance was incorporated into the court's revised practice direction of 1993. Under its provisions, optional mediation was available, if both parties requested. The mediation is held before an officer of the court (the Registrar or Deputy Registrar) who conducts the mediation as a neutral and independent party to assist negotiations between the principal parties.

No record is kept of any content of the discussions, only a record of the outcome, relating to whether the matter was settled, and some data on the type and location of the development proposal.

In 1994, by an amendment to the original 1979 Act, statutory procedures dealing with mediation came into force and, importantly, this process was defined as follows: 'A structured negotiation process in which the mediator, as a neutral and independent party, assists the parties to a dispute to achieve their own resolution of the dispute'. The mediation lasts on average three to four hours and is held either in the court or on site. Seven days prior to this, each side will exchange a summary of the principal issues, which should be only two to three pages in length. As part of the process, the mediator may caucus with each party, meeting with them privately to discuss their side of the case. Such discussions are confidential and designed to assist the mediator by providing the opportunity for frank and open statements to be made on a 'without prejudice' basis, from which options can be explored and ideas for settlement proposed.

The caucus is an important procedural device to be employed in the conduct of a mediation. The fact that mediation within the court results in a court officer becoming involved in a private meeting with one side has been subject to the criticism that it devalues the court, in that 'views are expressed in the absence of the other party, [which] is a repudiation of basic principles of fairness and absence of hidden influences that the community rightly expects and demands that the courts observe' (Street 1991). Such criticism has been rebutted by the Chief Justice of the Court.

matters of detail and not principle, such as in design layout, siting, landscaping, and materials. If a policy objection was raised against the very principle of the development, then mediation would be inappropriate. By concentrating upon cases with potential for negotiated settlement it was perhaps a matter of little surprise that agreement was reached. Cases involving objections in principle were siphoned off from this pool of potential mediations. The most popular mediated cases, measured by land-use category, involved minor residential schemes (less than ten units) and domestic extensions. Matters in dispute frequently centred upon amenity-based arguments, such as the relationship of a building to neighbouring builds, the shape of a landscaped area, the position of windows, car parking layout, and proposed materials. Negotiated outcomes included the reconfiguration of housing layouts/siting, amendments to materials and reduction of bulk, and deletion of windows in extensions. The mediation itself provided a valuable opportunity to continue negotiations or simply to begin them for the first time, and to extend them (with the benefit of the mediator's influence) until a successive conclusion was reached.

The work by Michael Welbank (DETR 2000e) reported and analysed the findings of a pilot study of forty-eight planning mediations coordinated by the planning inspectorate and conducted between 1998 and 1999. The mediations were drawn from existing planning appeals and applications, either following a direct approach by the research team to LPAs asking them to take part or in response to a mail-shot distributed with planning appeal forms.[2] The format followed the 'facilitative' model in a similar style to that set out in Table 5.1. The outcome (settlement or otherwise) was recorded as a 'memorandum of understanding'. Of the forty-eight cases, half of the disputes dealt with design-related issues, and the majority (54 per cent) dealt with householder applications (mostly domestic extensions). In 65 per cent of cases an outcome was recorded (taken to be an agreed solution or action plan for future steps designed to achieve an outcome). Participants' views were sought. The overriding majority of participants reported satisfaction with mediation, whatever the outcome. Many endorsed the value of mediation in establishing an effective channel of communication between LPA and appellant. In similar fashion to the experience in New South Wales, detailed development control issues were the most common matters to be resolved, and householder applications the most popular case by land-use type. The principal issues for negotiation in these planning mediations dealt with domestic extensions (to side, rear or front), porches, conservatories, garages, sheds, and outbuildings. Beyond this, the mediations dealt with a variety of 'house improvements' such as insertion of new windows, addition of dormer windows and replacement of wooden windows by PVC alternatives. In a number of cases it became apparent that certain works as proposed fell within the provisions of the General Permitted Development Order (see Chapter 3) and therefore planning application was not required.

Where mediations dealt with the construction of a new dwelling, negotiations centred on a number of amenity considerations, such as the relationship to neighbouring properties with regard to the massing, scale and layout of the proposal. In four cases the matter in dispute dealt with replacement dwellings in green belt locations and negotiations dealt with the size of the replacement with regard to the existing building.[3] All such matters constitute 'classic' development control negotiations in which the details of a planning application are agreed once the planning officer has accepted the development in principle (by reference to the development plan). The research concluded on this matter that 'These are all matters on which a degree of subjective judgment can be exercised and do not normally produce conflicts with key land use policies. . . . sitting down with an applicant in the atmosphere of a mediation can allow a more creative mood to be established'.

This research produced six recommendations. The key recommendation (the first) was that 'the use of [planning] mediation on a voluntary basis . . . should be encouraged'. Analysis of the forty-eight mediations conducted during 1998–99 reported a benefit to householders submitting planning applications (i.e. people who were not represented by professional agents). The mediation process and particularly the conduct and presence of the mediator created a valuable and 'user-friendly' 'communication linkage' (DETR 2000e) between householders and planners. The householders were able to put their case to the planner and benefit

Case study 5.2   Planning mediation

Chris Wren, Architect, submits a planning application to the London Borough of Richville, an outer suburb authority of distinct low-density character. The application seeks consent to replace an existing dwelling and rebuild with some additional accommodation in the roof space. The clients, Geoffrey and Gloria Green-Sward, want the new dwelling to be in accord with 'sustainable and ecological' principles. Chris consults the Richville Local Development Framework prior to the submission of the application, and draws comfort from a policy which states that 'the Council will support applications that use "green" architecture'. He informs Geoffrey and Gloria that the plan supports their proposal.

The planning case officer, Penny Wise, telephones Chris to inform him that she likes his design and welcomes his use of solar panels and timber frame construction. Chris awaits his permission and informs Geoffrey and Gloria accordingly. They are delighted, as this means construction will be completed before their baby is born the following summer.

Two weeks later Geoffrey is dismayed to receive a notice of refusal of permission, stating that 'the height and bulk of the proposal is considered to be out of scale with its surroundings and detrimental to the amenities of neighbouring occupiers'.

Geoffrey and Gloria consult Chris. He advises them that an appeal will take anything between four-and-a-half and six months to determine and, statistically, has only a 30 per cent chance of success. He suggests mediation. At the beginning of the mediation Chris, Geoffrey and Gloria feel a mixture of anger, hurt and bewilderment at the way they have been treated.

Positional bargaining: Each of the parties (Chris, Penny and Geoffrey/Gloria) would begin the mediation from a positional stance. Geoffrey/Gloria are baffled and hurt by the process, Chris is angry with the planning officer for 'misleading' him over the telephone, and Penny feels she has acted within her professional and ethical standards, which allows her to alter her position in this way, albeit that she regrets being quite so enthusiastic to Chris on the telephone. Such positions are revealed in the opening 'venting' stages of the mediation proper. The mediator will need to manage this and set out to channel any anger expressed into more productive dialogue.

Unlocking their BATNAs: As a problem-solver, the mediator will meet with each party and get them to appraise their own stance. It transpires that Geoffrey/Gloria seek a speedy decision without recourse to appeal, Penny is willing to negotiate on detailed design matters and Chris wants to save face with his client, following his embarrassment over the refused consent. If the mediator can get the parties to confront these positions and reveal them to the other party, movement from initial positions to principled negotiation may follow. If all three parties confront their BATNAs, it will

> become evident that they could agree on a revised planning permission as
> the solution. In such a case the acceptable revisions can be agreed at the
> mediation, subject to ratification by the LPA planning committee. Where
> matters of detail (such as in design of materials) and not principle are at
> stake, mediation in town planning is an appropriate mechanism.

from the presentation and unravelling of any technical matters (such as those
involving permitted development rights – see Chapter 3). In other areas, mediation still had the potential to resolve or reduce planning disputes, but based
on the reported results, benefits were much more likely to be felt in small-scale
design and detailed development-control matters, like extensions and small-scale
residential schemes. This study thereby produced a seminal finding in England
and Wales, that mediation in some areas of planning dispute would produce
tangible benefits to the system.

A model of planning mediation

The work of Stubbs (1997) and Welbank (DETR 2000e) led to the construction
of a hybrid model of (facilitation-based) mediation, designed with particular regard
to the democratic nature of the planning process. In this model a number of key
features must be accommodated. Six may be distinguished:

(a) Mediation is voluntary

A key principle established by both the 1998–99 pilot programme in England
and Wales and the mediation option available in the Land and Environment
Court of New South Wales is that the process is entirely voluntary. Any party
may simply walk away from it at any time. Compulsory mediation would diminish its effectiveness and constrain the parties from engaging in the proper level
of discussion.

(b) Mediation is case-dependent

Mediation is unlikely to succeed in cases involving any objection to the very
principle of development (established by planning policy). As mediation itself
is no more than assisted negotiation, some common ground must exist between
appellant and LPA. This common ground is invariably based on matters of detail,
such as design and layout considerations.

(c) Mediation is confidential

No record is made of the discussion, only the outcome. In New South Wales
such an outcome would be expressed in an agreed contract (if successful). In

England and Wales the DETR (2000e) pilot programme recorded the result as a 'memorandum of understanding' in which a plan of future action was minuted, if some agreement had been reached.

(d) Mediation is binding

To ensure that planners or applicants use mediation in the first place, they must be confident that what is agreed during the mediation will subsequently be implemented. In New South Wales a frequent problem was that planners lacked sufficient authority to settle, once some agreement had been reached. This proved to be a major obstacle because in such cases, the appellant may consider the process to be a futile waste of time. Yet planning officers are not 'supreme' decision-makers. They are servants of the planning committee, who bear ultimate responsibility in decision-making. The public will also need to be involved, as the outcome may require a fresh round of public consultation. These issues will need to be addressed in any planning mediation. If the mediation were to fail then the excursion into ADR would have served to increase and not diminish time taken to reach a decision, for the appellant would have to revert to the traditional appeal method. Research indicates that this will occur in around one-third of all mediations. This constitutes a powerful disincentive, for in such cases the entire mediation will have been a waste of time or at best a 'fishing expedition' (perhaps to explore the merits of the case put forward by the other side, but with no real incentive to settle).

(e) Mediation is inclusive

Third parties (the public) will need to be accommodated in any mediation process, if they so desire. It would, however, be inappropriate for third parties to block the achievement of a successful outcome if the appellant and LPA agree. In such circumstances it would be acceptable to note that various individuals dissented from the mediation outcome.

(f) Mediation is a sovereign method of dispute resolution

Planning mediation as a constituent method of ADR is an alternative to the traditional appeal pathway. It follows that the organization of a mediation service should be at 'arm's length' from the traditional method to which it provides an alternative. Ideally, this means creating a separate body to coordinate the conduct of mediators. The alternative of creating a 'mediation arm' of, say, the planning inspectorate is not in itself unacceptable, but the complete independence of the mediator and mediation process must be preserved. Court-annexed mediation services exist (as in the Land and Environment Court of New South Wales and Central London County Court) in which traditional and ADR mechanisms are located within the same institution. They can only do this if disputing parties perceive and discover each distinct wing of the organization to be wholly independent. As discussed earlier, such court-annexed systems have been criticized for diminishing the authority of the court in the eyes of the public. If, for example, a planning mediation service were to sit within the inspectorate and LPAs, and appellants or the public perceived this to lack independence, then the system would collapse. The assertion that the inspectorate only employed mediation to reduce its workload of traditional appeals would be difficult to refute. So, if mediation is to grow in the planning system it must be placed within the control of an independent body. If this is not the case then, in the words of the DETR (2000) report, it must be shown to be 'demonstrably independent of other functions [of that organization] . . . with its own distinct image and status'.

The model of planning mediation presented below (Figure 5.2) adapts the facilitation model set out in Figure 5.1 and accommodates a number of the

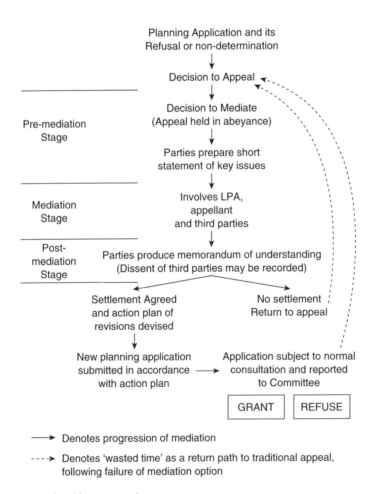

Figure 5.2 Planning mediations

previously discussed key principles. The establishment of mediation within the planning system in England and Wales provides an important and extremely significant 'first step' towards greater employment of ADR.

Supporters of mediation often portray its advantages in dramatic language: 'mediation can be magical' (Higgins 1997); 'mediation . . . has grown like a silent revolution across the globe' (Mackie 1997); and 'mediation is a process which offers commercial disputants meaningful, creative solutions at a fraction of the cost of the litigation system' (Choreneki 1997). Statistics to some extent support this enthusiasm, with 73 per cent of cases in the DETR pilot programme resulting in some kind of 'resource saving' to the LPA (i.e. settling or narrowing any future conflict) and Stubbs (1997) reporting that in New South Wales some 736 hours spent in mediation sessions resulted in approximately 405 days saved in court time. On receiving the DETR 2000 report, the (then) Planning Minister, Beverley Hughes, said 'I would like to see further investigation of the use of mediation at other stages in the planning system, for instance, at development plan stage or in resolving particular issues in cases going to inquiry'.[4] In 2001 the (then) Secretary of State, Stephen Byers, further reinforced the government's enthusiasm for this idea by incorporating it in the planning Green Paper. This endorsement in effect ensured that mediation would be in 'pole position' for planning reform, sometime in the future.

It has been anticipated that mediation will permeate into the development plan process, with initial experimentation in this area in 2000–01.[5] Beyond further deployment of mediation in planning it is conceivable that the next few years will see other innovations drawn from the ADR toolbox. Pearce (2000) speculates on the intriguing possibility of 'med-arb' (or 'mediappeal'), which combines arbitration with mediation:

> where the arbitrator (the inspector in our case) functions first as a pure mediator, helping the parties to arrive at a mutually acceptable outcome and then, but only if the mediation fails, reverts to her normal role, arbitrating between the parties' cases and argument and issuing a final and binding decision. In effect the parties would first seek to reach agreement through assisted negotiation (mediation) but agree to submit to binding arbitration (i.e. a conventional appeal procedure conducted by an inspector) should they reach impasse.

The post-2004 reforms to the production of Local Development Frameworks/ Local Development Documents, means that planning authorities are expected to establish a dialogue with those who have made representations on the preferred options (i.e. the council's desired choices for development). The document that progresses to the independent examination will also be the subject of round-table discussions, in effect a far less adversarial system than its predecessor and one that is readily conductive to the introduction of a mediation pathway at either the examination stage or the production stage. Kate Barker's 2006 review of the land-use planning system (HM Treasury 2006a) reignites this interest with a recommendation that further attention is, once again, focused on the benefits of mediation to resolve planning disputes. An eminent lawyer, Sir Henry Brook, gave further emphasis to this when delivering the annual Boydell Lecture of 2008, in which he concluded that great merit lay in the introduction of mediation within the planning system.

Problems exist in such an amalgamation of traditional and alternative processes, notably that parties will be less likely to reveal their underlying needs and concerns (i.e. unlock their BATNAs) in the initial mediation phase for fear that this may 'backfire' and adversely influence the subsequent arbitration phase (should the attempt at a mediated settlement fail).

Pearce (2000) demonstrates the value of continued reflection in this area. Alternative Dispute Resolution has arrived in town planning. Its future will be assured when applicants and LPAs experience its benefits, whether they be time and cost savings or improved quality of decision-making achieved by a process based on building consensus and not adversarial exchange.

Town planning and human rights

Introduction

In December 1948 the United Nations agreed a 'Universal Declaration of Human Rights'. Such action came as an essential component of post-war reconstruction, motivated by the powerful desire to protect against a repetition of the many atrocities committed during the Second World War. Two years later (1950), the Council of Europe applied these principles to the Member States of the European Community in the European Convention of Human Rights (ECHR), designed to guarantee some sixteen specified civil rights and freedoms as enshrined in the UN Declaration (see Table 5.2). The following year (1951), the Convention was ratified by the UK government, although for a further forty-seven years (until 1998) the UK government resisted proposals to incorporate the Convention into domestic law (Grant 2000). Instead, these various rights were adapted by virtue of 'ministerial discretion', so that, for example, the principles were referred to in planning and environmental policy without specific reference being made to their existence in planning statute. Prior to 2000, if a UK citizen sought redress against the government, or any other public body, for their failure to comply with the rights and freedoms contained in the ECHR, then this would ultimately require legal challenge in the European Court of Justice.[6]

Over the years, the Strasbourg court adapted a number of principles in relation to the ECHR, notably that the detailed language of 1950 be subject to broad interpretation. Indeed, the court has described the Convention as a 'living instrument' that must be interpreted in the light of present-day conditions.[7]

The UK government changed the constitutional position of the ECHR in passing the Human Rights Act 1998 (Royal Assent, September 1998), which came into force on 2 October 2000. The Human Rights Act 1998 (HRA)

Table 5.2 European Convention on Human Rights

Article or Protocol	Rights guaranteed
Article 2	To life
Article 3	To freedom from torture
Article 4	To freedom from slavery or servitude
Article 5	To liberty
Article 6*	To a fair and public trial
Article 7	To no punishment without law
Article 8*	To respect for private and family life and home
Article 9	To freedom of thought
Article 10	To freedom of expression
Article 11	To freedom of assembly
Article 12	To marry
Article 14	To prohibit discrimination
Protocol 1 – Article 1*	To peaceful enjoyment of possessions/property
Protocol 1 – Article 3	To free elections
Protocol 2 – Article 2	To access to education
Protocol 6 – Articles 1 and 2	To abolish the death penalty

Note
*Of key relevance to the planning system

therefore served to perform a relatively simple structural reform by adopting into domestic law all the rights identified in the Convention – in other words formally 'importing' provision of the ECHR so that it was incorporated into UK law. This reform was subsequently described as 'not exactly a major constitutional resettlement' (Grant 2000), although the longer-term ramifications for planning have been considerable and far-reaching. The Human Rights Act 1998 will influence both the process and substance of planning control and, for the first time since the enactment of the Town and Country Planning Act 1947, its implementation heralded a fundamental rethink in the relationship between the powers held by the Executive (government), Judiciary (courts) and individual citizen. The key consequences would be that some planning functions (especially appeals) would become more autonomous of government, while third parties (objectors) would benefit from increased power and representation in the system. Legal opinion differed on the consequences of these reforms, and when the HRA was debated in the House of Lords its impact was viewed both as an opportunity 'to freshen up the principles of common law' and 'a field day for crackpots' (speech by Lord McCluskey).

Running alongside this increased focus on environmental civil rights, the United Nations introduced guidance on freedom of information. The UN Economic Commission for Europe adopted the Aarhus Convention in June 1998, which stipulated that:

In order to contribute to the protection of the right of every person of present and future generation to live in an environment adequate to his or her health and well-being, each Party shall guarantee the rights of access to information, public participation in decision-making and access to justice in environmental matters.[8]

Such a document reflected an awareness of growing public participation in environmental decision-making and reflected principles previously agreed by the UN (in its Rio Declaration). Indeed, Article 9 of the Aarhus Convention, in parallel with developments like the ECHR, considered the increased momentum gathering in favour of access to justice in environmental decision-making, by stating that all members of the public should have access to a review procedure (i.e. court of law or independent tribunal) that allows a review of both the substance of, and process followed in, environmental decision-making.

The ECHR thus 'imports' (or repatriates from European to UK courts) (Grant 2000) a number of individual rights that protect the citizen from unacceptable actions by the state (usually the national government). To protect individuals in this way, the HRA places an obligation on the state (including public bodies) to uphold convention rights. After its introduction into UK legislation in 1998 (and operative after 2000) the citizen can assert such individual rights by challenging actions, decisions or indeed omissions by public bodies in the UK and not European courts, thus avoiding the time-consuming, complicated and costly excursion to Strasbourg that had previously been required.

The HRA incorporated a number of central provisions that exacted fundamental change in the actions of national government and the judiciary. All new legislation passing through Parliament would require scrutiny to ensure compatibility with Convention rights. Ministers will be required to address this directly by making a statement with regard to the compatibility of any proposed legislation to the Convention. All UK public bodies must act in a manner that is compatible with Convention rights and freedoms. Failure to do so can be challenged in UK courts by any person, individual or company. The courts cannot 'strike down' any legislation they consider incompatible but may make a 'declaration of incompatibility to encourage swift revision of it by Government and Parliament' (Hart 2000).

Three articles in particular addressed the regulation of land use, dealing with procedural guarantees, such as Article 6 (fair trial), protection of substance as contained in Article 8 (respect for home life) and Protocol 1: Article 1 (peaceful enjoyment of property). Their impact was spread over a wide area, because the HRA made it unlawful for any so-defined public authority[9] to act in a way considered incompatible with the Convention. Many planning organizations were thus affected. Provisions were both far-reaching and deep-rooted, by affecting the actions of numerous public and semi-public bodies in a fundamental way. The Convention and subsequent HRA set out to protect individual citizens' rights by allowing complaint to the courts. It was, therefore, possible for a person, individual or company (not a group, such as an interest or amenity group) to bring an action against a public body, only if that body had violated a Convention right (Purchas and Clayton 2001). That person must constitute a 'victim' in the strict definition within Article 34 of the Convention, which restricts such qualification to someone 'directly affected' by the action or omission at issue (Hart 2000).

If the actions or omissions of a public body are the subject of challenge, the courts[10] are duty-bound to consider the 'proportionality' of that action when addressing the remedy to the situation. In other words, any interference with a Convention right must be both fair and specifically designed to pursue a legitimate aim: 'The underlying idea is that a sledgehammer of interference with rights should not be used to crack a nut of social need' (Hart 2000). It follows that a balance will need to be struck between the rights of the individual and the interests of the community. This means that some infringement of individual civil rights may be permissible in justifiable cases, but that this interference must not be excessive (in other words, it must be proportionate). For example, certain rights (freedom of assembly in the case of a public demonstration) might be acceptably limited to prevent criminal damage or riot. Such restrictions must be proportionate – a total ban on all public meetings would be a disproportionate response to the potential threat of, say, a single gathering leading to civil unrest. Such a disproportionate response would, in all probability, be an unacceptable erosion of civil/human rights, whereas by contrast the banning of one meeting (on the basis of evidence of unrest) would be proportionate. In town planning, enforcement proceedings against unauthorized development are a common example of this principle in action (Purchas and Clayton 2001). The question is posed, are the remedies against such breaches of regulation 'proportionate' to the offence? It is possible to appeal against an enforcement notice on grounds that the steps required (to make the matter acceptable) exceed what is necessary to remedy the breach.[11] If, for example, the notice requires total removal of a building without planning permission in a case where the key area of harm relates to an inappropriate roof design (bulky with overlooking windows) then such a requirement could arguably be disproportionate. A more proportionate response would require revisions to the roof.[12] The HRA establishes that a landowner may seek remedy against such matters by virtue of the proportionality principle contained in the ECHR. Judges in matters of judicial review will make decisions that go beyond interpretation of such legislation as existed previously and become embroiled in judgements on the 'value' attached to legislation in its defence of human rights. In dealing with legal challenges on the basis of disproportionate interference with Convention rights, judges will need to decide upon the balance of competing factors and not just mere interpretations of the law.

Human rights: applications to planning

The Human Rights Act and the ECHR have several implications for the operation of the UK planning system. Specific reference is made here to the impact on the system in England and Wales. Grant (2000) reflects upon how the relatively simple 'importation' of the ECHR to domestic law has changed the whole foundation of the planning system. A seemingly straightforward legislative reform has undergone a seismic change. This change has altered the very basis of policy formulation.

The post-war planning system withdrew a landowner's right to develop land and replaced it with the right to submit a planning application, with subsequent appeal should the LPA refuse to grant consent (Grant 2000). Applications were then, and still are today, assessed against planning policy and other material considerations. The key powers of regulation over land-use control were given to the executive (government, both national and local). The whole system was constructed on the basis that government ministers assumed key supervisory responsibility. A government department produced statements of national planning policy (in PPGs and circulars), enjoyed a right of 'call-in' to determine certain major or controversial applications and had the power to 'recover' jurisdiction over certain appeals, similarly for determination by the Secretary of State. The planning inspectorate formed a part of the executive as an agency of a government department (the DETR). It was, therefore, not wholly independent of government. A 'settlement' was thus achieved in which the executive assumed an administrative responsibility for control of the system and the courts, through the exercise of judicial review and statutory challenge, protected against abuse of power and sought to respect citizens' rights.

The ECHR fundamentally changed that post-war compromise between executive and judiciary. Article 6(i) of the Convention provided for the most significant reforms, followed by Article 8 and Article 1 of the First Protocol. Each will be considered in turn.

Article 6 deals with process, i.e. the manner in which the system allows for a fair and equitable representation of people's interests. Five key components are identified, such as that individuals enjoy civil rights, the opportunity of a fair and public hearing (by way of an independent impartial tribunal) and a decision within a reasonable time. A third party's civil rights are affected by a planning decision. Under the current planning appeal system they are not a principal party and have no formal rights of challenge. The right to challenge a decision by way of judicial review falls within Article 6 and complies with it.

Article 8 and the **First Protocol** deal with matters of substance (the right to enjoy property). Fairness, openness and impartiality have been fundamental principles in post-war planning appeals, indeed are described as both the 'mission and hallmark of the planning inspectorate' (Grant 2000). Article 6 will further promote this mission and hallmark across the entire system and requires that everyone has the right to respect for his private and family life, home and correspondence. It also extends to prevent interference by a public authority with the exercise of this right, except as is in accordance with the law and is necessary in a democratic society in the interests of national security, public safety, economic well-being, prevention of crime and disorder, protection of health or morals and freedoms of others.

Article 6(i): Right to a fair trial

In the determination of his civil rights and obligations or of any criminal charge against him, everyone is entitled to a fair and public hearing within a reasonable time by an independent and impartial tribunal established by law. Judgement shall be pronounced publicly but the press and public may be excluded from all or part of the trial in the interest of morals, public order or national security in a democratic society where the interests of juveniles or the protection of the private life of the parties so require, or to the extent strictly necessary in the opinion of the court in special circumstances where publicity would prejudice the interests of justice.

Article 8: Right to respect for private and family life

(1) Everyone has the right to respect for his private and family life, his home and his correspondence.

The First Protocol: Article 1: Protection of property

Every natural or legal person is entitled to the peaceful enjoyment of his possessions. No one shall be deprived of his possessions except in the public interest and subject to the conditions provided for by law and by the general principles of international law.

The preceding provisions shall not, however, in any way impair the right of a State to enforce such laws it deems necessary to control the use of property in accordance with the general interest or to secure the payment of taxes or other contributions or penalties.

In town planning, a fair and public hearing by an independent and impartial tribunal (Article 6) affects planning applications, plan making, enforcement action, and the appeal process. Article 8 (and the First Protocol) restricts government in how far it may influence private property. This will similarly affect planning decisions, especially on applications. A number of key areas will be considered in respect of planning applications, plan making, planning enforcement, and planning appeals.

As regards planning applications, the immediate ramifications of the HRA relate to citizen rights in the application process. Private or individual interests have not traditionally been placed 'first' in the priorities of the system (as the ECHR tends to dictate in Article 8). Indeed, government guidance in PPS1 of 2005 states:

The planning system does not exist to protect the private interests of one person against the activities of another. . . . the basic question is not whether owners and occupiers of neighbouring properties would experience financial or other loss from a particular development but whether the proposal would unacceptably affect amenities.

By contrast, the Convention puts private interests first, and places emphasis on individual rights (including property rights) in respect of planning decisions. Lowes (2000) speculates that, as a consequence, LPAs will need to show they had taken such convention provisions into account. One manifestation of this is that planning committee reports will be not only longer, but much more precise, in detailing how matters in respect of Article 8 and the First Protocol have been complied with.

As regards plan making functions, the LPAs and other relevant bodies (such as county councils and regional planning bodies) will need to pay closer regard to personal circumstances and private interests when producing regional planning guidance and development plan policy. It follows from the Convention that those individuals who deem that their health, property or commercial activities could be affected by the outcome of such plans may seek to rely on Article 6(i) as a means of gaining audience to participate fully in the decision-making process. Article 6 requires reasons to be given (i.e. 'judgement shall be pronounced publicly').

In a local plan inquiry, the inspector responsible for the inquiry will make recommendations on land-use allocations (such as a greenfield site being allocated for housing), after consideration of representations by the LPA and other interested parties. The LPA is now obliged to follow the inspector's recommendations (i.e. they are binding). Initial speculation on this process concluded (in 2001) that the development plan process was 'potentially' incompatible with principles established in Article 6(i). A planning authority may have a strong political or financial interest in the outcome of the process and is the judge and jury of the process. No independent review process exists by which an individual may challenge the planning merits of the planning authority's action, in this regard. Compliance with Article 6(i) may require that this is a necessary post-HRA reform.

In planning enforcement, the test of 'proportionality' (previously discussed) will affect the nature of enforcement action. Planning authorities must have regard to this part of the Convention and be prepared to demonstrate that the action taken to remedy a breach of planning control is in proportion to the legitimate aims pursued. Such 'proportionality' must balance the interests of the community against the individual's right to respect for their home (Article 8). This principle equates to 'reasonableness', i.e. whatever a public body may do, it must be proportionate (Samuels 2000).

In planning appeals, Article 6(i) has had the most significant and far-reaching impact. The right to an independent and impartial tribunal is one of the most important features of the Article and has considerable significance in the planning and environmental context (Hart 2000). Grant (2001) considers the key ramifications of this Article on the appeal process. First, prior to HRA the public (third parties) enjoyed only restricted rights of access in appeals. They appeared only at the discretion of the inspector and enjoyed no right of appeal themselves (against, for example, a grant of planning permission). Such a lack of civil rights 'does not reflect the ideals of a participative democracy of the twenty-first century' (Grant 2000). Second, the ideal of an independent tribunal is not undermined by virtue of the reserved intervention powers of the Secretary of State, who may himself determine planning applications (call-in) or appeals (recovered jurisdiction). While this may amount to only a small volume of appeals (1 per cent recovered or around 100–150 appeals per year), it deprives the planning inspectorate of the necessary appearance of independence. The ideal of independence (as interpreted by the European Court and set out in the Article) is arguably not met by the planning inspectorate, which sits as an agency under the ultimate control of the Secretary of State. The strict legal position is that the Secretary of State appoints planning inspectors to assist him in conducting and discharging the appellate decision-making process. The planning inspectorate is thus not a sovereign independent body, as Article 6 would require. While the inspectorate has an established and widely acknowledged reputation of impartiality in decision-making, this lack of independence provides something of a stumbling block to the complete implementation of the Convention in planning appeals.

The HRA vests in the courts strong powers to 'police' the implementation of the Convention. At its most extreme, a UK higher court (such as the House of Lords) may declare domestic legislation incompatible with Convention articles. In other cases it is possible for a court to strike down a piece of subordinate legislation. In town planning such subordinate legislation covers statutory instruments, which set out detailed procedural guidance (in, say, appeals) or detailed policy matters (in, say, requirements of permitted development thresholds in a domestic dwelling). A number of court rulings have already brought valuable judicial guidance to bear on the future functioning of the Convention in town planning. Some legal decisions (as in *Bryan v. UK* – see Case study 5.3) pre-date the HRA 1998, being made in the Strasbourg Court. Others (as in *R v. Secretary of State for Environment, Transport and the Regions, ex parte Holding and Barnes plc*)[13] post-date HRA 1998 and were issued by a UK court (in that case the House of Lords). In both cases they perform the same task in giving valuable interpretation of the Convention with HRA 1998. Such legal determination will be pivotal in shaping the future direction of human rights legislation in planning. In the key decisions made to date, it appears that the compatibility of Article 6(i) to planning appeal systems is a matter heavily dependent upon the right of legal challenge (Judicial or Statutory Review) after the planning appeal has been determined. This particular interpretation may not endure – indeed, eminent commentators (Grant 2000) viewed the decision in *Bryan* (and by implication in *Alconbury*) as 'unsatisfactory' due to the courts being restricted in what they can do, i.e. they cannot rehearse the planning merits of the case, only consider the grounds of legal challenge. An aggrieved third party cannot use a legal challenge in the courts as a means of reopening the case merits (i.e. whether planning permission should or should not be granted) but only to achieve a review of the legality of a decision or the process by which it was made. The outcome of the *Bryan* case appears unlikely to last in the longer term. Indeed, Grant (2000) looks towards more structural change, with a number of far-reaching (even tantalizing) reforms. Such ideas countenance broadening the jurisdiction of the courts to hear merit appeals and making the inspectorate wholly independent of government. The findings of a (then) DETR-sponsored research project of 2000 (DETR 2000e) rather opportunely considered the potential to introduce an Environment Court to the UK. Such a court would combine both merit appeals and legal challenges, in similar fashion to other jurisdictions (notably New South Wales). The report itself acknowledged that the HRA 1998 may promote a review of the relationship between planning inspectorate and government and also 'creates an opportunity for the development of a new

---

Case study 5.3   Human rights case law: *Bryan* v. *United Kingdom*

An enforcement notice was served on Mr Bryan requiring the demolition of two buildings on his land. Mr Bryan appealed to the Secretary of State against the merits of this decision. The appointed inspector subsequently dismissed the appeal and upheld provisions of the notice. Following this, Mr Bryan mounted a legal challenge in the High Court, also subsequently dismissed. He then took his case to the European Court of Human Rights in Strasbourg. The European Court of Human Rights held that the decision made by a planning inspector was not consistent with Article 6(i) and did *not* constitute an independent and impartial tribunal, since the Secretary of State could at any time revoke the powers of the inspector and deprive that inspector of the appearance of independence required by the Convention. Yet the European Court of Human Rights went on to determine that this deficiency was *cured* by the opportunity given to a planning appellant to challenge the decision of a planning inspector in the courts and was content that the grounds on which the court could review the decision of a planning inspector 'were wide enough to provide the necessary safeguards' (Grant 2000).

Key issues: That Article 6(i) 'fair tribunal' is satisfied in spite of the planning inspectorate *not* being wholly independent of the Secretary of State *because* of a 'cumulative effect' (Hart 2000) in which the proceedings held before an inspector may be challenged in the High Court (by judicial review or statutory challenge), which *is* wholly independent but cannot rule on issues of planning merit, only legal irregularity.

jurisprudence in relation to environmental rights'. In any event, such structural reform (a new Environment Court or the total splitting off of the inspectorate, to give it complete autonomy) will create a more 'Convention-friendly' system than the one that existed when the Human Rights Act 1998 came into force in October 2000.

Case study 5.4   Human rights organization: An bord Pleanála

An bord Pleanála, the body responsible for determining planning appeals in the Republic of Ireland, has been much praised by UK commentators in respect of Human Rights legislation. Much of this praise has been directed at its independence from government. Established in 1977, An bord Pleanála is currently vested with appellate powers by the (Irish) Planning and Development Act 2000. Individual planning inspectors, when determining appeals, offer a recommendation to a Chairman and Board. While responsible to the Minister for the Environment and Local Government, in terms of organization, efficiency and finances, the Chairman and Board or inspectors are wholly independent in their decision-making responsibilities. Indeed, the Chairman's annual report for 2005/06 celebrated this fact when stating 'the Board remains at all times acutely conscious of its stated objectives to carry out its work in an independent manner [and] I wish to stress the fact that there is no political or other interference in decisions by the Board in individual cases' (An bord Pleanála (2006) *Annual Report*, p. 11). Under the terms of the Act, while the Minister appoints the Chairman and all seven Board members (usually nominated by various prescribed organizations), they enjoy complete autonomy in the decision to allow or dismiss any individual planning appeal that comes before them. The Minister can submit representations on appeals, as indeed can any individual, but the Board enjoys ultimate decision-making authority. This contrasts markedly with the strong, if infrequently used, intervention powers enjoyed by the Secretary of State in the equivalent system in England.

Case study 5.5   Human rights case law: The Alconbury case

The independence of the planning inspectorate was reviewed further in three High Court appeals heard together in the House of Lords in 2001. These three appeals are referred to as the 'Alconbury judgement'* and owing to their importance in respect of human rights they were passed direct to the House of Lords, leapfrogging the Court of Appeal along the way.

As with *Bryan*, the ability of the planning appeal system to deliver the rights enshrined in Article 6(i) was again brought into question. As the judgement of the House of Lords established, no complaint was raised over the independence and impartiality of planning inspectors, or indeed the very fairness of the Inquiry method as measured in, say, the ability to make representations, or call or challenge evidence. Instead the central issue related to the potential interventions in decision-making made by the Secretary of State, whose independence and impartiality was compromised by the fact that he lays down national planning policy in circulars and PPGs: 'all of these are bound to affect the mind of the Secretary of State when he takes decisions on called-in applications or on appeals which he recovers'. Lord Slynn of Hadley quoted from paragraph 24 of judgement in (2001) UKHL 23, or (2002) 1 PLR 58.

This lack of independence in these appeals was further compromised, it was argued, by the fact that the government itself was a landowner in one case (the Alconbury site being owned by the Ministry of Defence) and had promoted a road improvement scheme in another (the Department of Transport having previously promoted a road at the Newbury site). All four Law Lords hearing the appeal were unconvinced by such argument, relying on the provision (as established by *Bryan*) for legal review (by virtue of judicial or statutory review of a planning appeal decision) rendering any decision taken by the Secretary of State as compatible with Article 6. Further, this scope of review power was deemed sufficient to comply with standards set by the European Court of Human Rights. Their Lordships accepted the point put by the Secretary of State's barrister, that the key issue was not the existence of complete independence or impartiality of the Secretary of State but the decision-making process within which such powers were exercised. In other words, the fact that the Secretary of State lacked independence by virtue of being both policy-maker and decision-taker (Holgate and Gilbey 2001) was not the deciding issue. What was material here was not the existence of an independent and impartial tribunal but the existence of sufficient opportunity to scrutinize any decision made by the Secretary of State by way of statutory challenge or judicial review to guarantee an acceptable discharge of rights contained in the Convention. Their Lordships concluded that this level of review was adequate and, as a result, 'the Secretary of State's powers to intervene in the planning process . . . remain undiminished' (Holgate and Gilbey 2001).

This endorsement of the status quo received a 'mixed press' among planning and legal commentators. Some felt this decision represented an opportunity missed (Grant 2001) to embrace the Environmental Court approach, that it was pragmatic in tone in order to achieve a political solution to the dilemma facing the Secretary of State (Holgate and Gilbey 2001) while others argued that its reasoning was consistent with decisions previously made by the European Court of Human Rights (Elvin and Maurici 2001). Grant (2000) perhaps comes to the most robust judgement in arguing that *Alconbury* was not just a simple endorsement of the status quo. Instead it helped to clarify the future role of the Secretary of State, permitting ministerial involvement in planning appeal decision-making. The Minister is thus able to come to a different view to that of a planning inspector.

* R. (*Alconbury Developments Limited and Others*) v. SSETR, R. (*Holding and Barnes*) v. SSETR, and SSETR v. *Legal and General Assurance Society Limited*. Legal references to the House of Lords Decision are [2001] 2 WLR 1389 and [2001] 2 All ER.

Summary of Possible Revisions

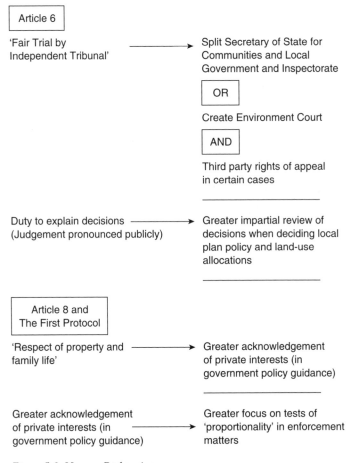

Article 6

'Fair Trial by Independent Tribunal' ⟶ Split Secretary of State for Communities and Local Government and Inspectorate

OR

Create Environment Court

AND

Third party rights of appeal in certain cases

Duty to explain decisions (Judgement pronounced publicly) ⟶ Greater impartial review of decisions when deciding local plan policy and land-use allocations

Article 8 and The First Protocol

'Respect of property and family life' ⟶ Greater acknowledgement of private interests (in government policy guidance)

Greater acknowledgement of private interests (in government policy guidance) ⟶ Greater focus on tests of 'proportionality' in enforcement matters

Figure 5.3 Human Rights Act

Pre Human Rights Act 1998

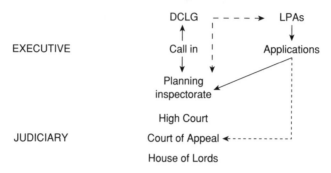

Post Human Rights Act 1998

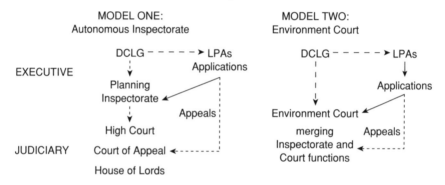

⟶ Determination of planning application and appeal

----➤ Legal challenge of application and appeal

– –➤ Policy guidance issued by Department for Communities & Local Government

Figure 5.4 Planning decision-making

6 Planning obligations, the planning gain supplement and the community infrastructure levy

> Government should consider the granting of planning permission as a suitable point in the development chain in which to levy a charge based on local land prices that aims to capture part of the windfall development gain.
>
> (HM Treasury 2004)

This recommendation by a senior civil servant, appointed by the Chancellor of the Exchequer to review and to achieve a 'step change' in housing supply, heralded a policy shift in favour of land taxation. Such taxation would be based upon the uplift in land value following from the granting of planning permission. The pendulum of 'planning gain' was swinging away from a system of informal negotiation in which developers and planning authorities would work out a settlement based within certain policy limits and towards one of standardized and uniform charging for the funding of infrastructure.

'Planning gain' is a term familiar to many professionals working in property development and provides a convenient, if colloquial, umbrella to cover a multitude of issues whereby developers make contributions (in cash or kind) as a part of the planning process. While this should not amount to the buying and selling of a planning permission, the external perception of this process has been poor (Committee on Standards in Public Life 1997) and today the practice of planning obligations, to import the correct technical language, is the subject of wholesale reform. This chapter will outline the system for the period 1968–2008 and detail the (anticipated) reforms for the post-2008 introduction of what will be called the 'planning gain supplement'. These reforms are only partially motivated by a desire within government to modernize planning obligations. More significantly they are the consequence of a more sophisticated objective, seeking to fund the vast amount of infrastructure required to pay for housing growth over the next twenty years. The need for affordable housing, transport improvements and open/natural spaces is viewed as key in the need to create new communities on the back of housing growth. The sums involved are huge, estimated at some £37 billion in the South East and East of England regions (Roger Tym & Partners 2005). The need to pay for this new infrastructure was the principal driving force behind the need to introduce what amounts to land taxation, which fundamentally reshaped the landscape of planning gain.

This chapter will, therefore, involve the following: discussion of the negotiated system and its replacement after 2008, an examination of betterment in which the granting of a planning consent raises land values, a review of the many alternatives to a negotiated system, and a description of the reforms in the Community Infrastructure Levy. The practice of planning gain, planning obligation and the introduction of a levy or tax (the planning gain supplement) exposes the many tensions that exist between the town planning system and the property development industry. At its most fundamental it involves examination of who should pay for the wider environmental impact of a development proposal, the developer or the local authority? In recent years the government has countenanced two broad areas of reform, based around an 'optional planning charge' (also known as a tariff or planning contribution) (DETR 2001a) or the introduction of a levy on development uplift (or betterment) (HM Treasury *et al.* 2005). The new system, designed for a comprehensive roll-out after 2009, will be detailed and set within the historic context of the system.

Background

Historically, this subject has been surrounded by a confusing array of terms, in part explained by the lack of a single and widely used definition and the use of a variety of titles relating to the practice of planning gain. Research (Healey *et al.* 1993) discovered the use of twelve terms to describe the same function.[1] The term 'planning gain' provides a convenient umbrella under which benefits in either cash or kind are offered to a local planning authority by a developer, following the grant of planning permission and controlled by a legal agreement between the local planning authority and landowner or (rarely) by planning condition. This implies a situation in which the local planning authority benefits from something for nothing, that is, by simply granting planning permission the developer will provide benefits or indeed money to secure a consent. Such a view would be an unsatisfactory start to the topic. At this stage, it is vital to acknowledge the important procedural role played by this system in its ability to mitigate the external impact of development on the wider environment (i.e. the environment outside the planning application site).

This mitigation of environmental impact enables planning permission to be granted in cases where, without these controls, it might have been refused. Planning obligations thus bring to the system the very powerful benefits of allowing the developer the opportunity to remedy a planning problem (such as inadequate site access or provision of bus facilities in the neighbourhood) or to enhance the quality of a development (such as provision of communal facilities for sports use or schools). The most popular types of planning obligation dealt with provision of open space, transport works, community and leisure facilities, affordable housing and education (DCLG 2005). Development schemes impact on their surrounding environment and the planning obligations allows a legal mechanism within which essential off-site mitigation can be delivered. The problems experienced by this pre-2009 system were its apparent lack of national consistency.

Regional variations mean that in southern England the average value of an obligation was almost double that of one secured in the north of England. This disparity is a consequence of land and development values but is also a product of the level of (in most cases) financial contribution expected by local authorities, based upon local policy frameworks and the expectation of individuals (DCLG 2005). Such variations fuel the perception that such a system is unfair and inconsistent.

Provision for agreements relating to the development of land have existed in planning legislation since 1909.[2] The current system can effectively be traced back to 1968 when the need for ministerial consent was removed and such agreements were left for straightforward negotiation between the local planning authority and landowner/developer, as exists today.

In 1980 the government commissioned the Property Advisory Group (PAG)[3] to examine the practice of planning gain. Their report (Property Advisory Group 1980) concluded: 'We are unable to accept that, as a matter of general practice, planning gain has any place in our system of planning control.'

However, the government did not accept such a finding, and in 1983 they issued a circular, 'Guidance on Planning Gain', which offered for the first time a definition:

> 'Planning gain' is a term which has come to be applied whenever, in connection with a grant of planning permission, a local planning authority seeks to impose on a developer an obligation to carry out works not included in the development for which permission has been sought or to make payment or confer some extraneous right or benefit in return for permitting development to take place.

The circular introduced a series of broad rules or 'tests' of reasonableness, to establish what could be considered to be acceptable practice. These tests established that any gains should be reasonable in content, and both geographically and functionally related to the development to be permitted. This approach would depend upon negotiation and interpretation of just exactly what would be deemed reasonable and unreasonable within the government's prescribed policy. Despite many subsequent pronouncements that this system would be reformed, successive governments adhered to the principles set out in the 1983 circular and only served to tinker with reforms by revising the circular in 1991, 1997 and 2005.

Towards the end of the property boom in the 1980s, a growing suspicion emerged that both local planning authorities and developers had violated the 'tests' in the pursuit of planning consent or wider benefits by the local authority. In 1989 the Royal Town Planning Institute raised doubts over some activities that were purporting to manifest as planning gain. The problem was neatly encapsulated in the conclusions which stated that:

> Planning gain is a somewhat misleading term. A key element of our statutory land-use planning system in this country is action by local planning

authorities to influence developers to come forward with proposals which are in accord with the authorities' development plans and other policies. This may include essential infrastructure provision of various kinds. This should quite properly be termed planning gain. However, the term has more recently been applied to agreements, entered into by local planning authorities and applicants, to ensure that a development when permitted includes wider benefits.

(Byrne 1989)

The Planning and Compensation Act 1991 replaced 'planning gain' with 'planning obligation' (Redman 1991) perhaps in a vain attempt to alter perceptions. New circular guidance (in 1991) again grappled with definitions:

The term planning gain has no statutory significance and is not found in the Planning Acts. . . . In granting planning permission, or in negotiations with developers and other interests that lead to the grant of planning permission, the local planning authority may seek to secure modifications or improvements to the proposals submitted for their approval. They may grant permission subject to conditions, and where appropriate they may seek to enter into planning obligations with a developer regarding the use or development of the land concerned or other land or buildings. Rightly used, planning obligations may enhance development proposals.

(DoE 1991)

Further revisions introduced six years later (1997) acknowledged, for the first time, that a negative perception was becoming apparent, when stating that 'To retain public confidence, such arrangements [for negotiating planning obligations] must be operated in accordance with the fundamental principle that planning permission may not be bought or sold'. In the same year Lord Justice Nolan was to conclude, in a wide-ranging review of probity in the planning system, that obligations amounted to the buying and selling of planning permission (Committee on Standards in Public Life 1997). In July 2005 the Office of the Deputy Prime Minister (now Secretary of State for Communities) issued the fourth (and most probably the last) circular on planning obligations (5/05), which sought to update the concept by stating that planning obligations are an established mechanism used to bring development in line with the objectives of sustainable development. Considerable emphasis was attributed to the need to avoid delay when devising and agreeing such obligations.

The legal issues

Planning obligations

Planning obligations are created under Section 106 of the TCPA 1990. A new Section 106 was introduced into the 1990 Act by the Planning and Compensation

Act 1991,[4] together with a new Section 106A (powers to modify or discharge an obligation) and Section 106B (appeal against refusal to modify or discharge an obligation). The Section 106 obligation forms the legal contract by which the objectives of the planning obligation are legally honoured and enforced.[5]

In addition, local planning authorities may enter into legal agreements with developers under Section 111 of the Local Government Act 1972.[6] It is common practice for such legal agreements to recite that they are made in compliance with both statutes. It is possible for a planning condition to be used to control various land-use matters instead of a planning obligation. However, a condition may be of limited use because in the majority of cases it may deal only with land-use-planning-related issues within the application site[7] and, this notwithstanding, many local authorities simply prefer the legal enforceability associated with Section 106 and Section 111. If a proposal involves a financial payment or an off-site matter such as a highway improvement, then a legal agreement will normally be required. With the very limited use of conditions, it follows that Section 106 planning obligations provide the most popular and effective method of control. Section 106 establishes that any obligation used specifically to restrict the development or use of land may require specific operations or activities to be carried out or that a sum of money is paid to the LPA.

The solely system in operation to 2009 was based on the following:

- Planning obligations were introduced on 25 October 1991.[8] The new concept of the planning obligation comprised either a Planning Agreement, whereby the developer/landowner enters into a (bilateral) agreement with the local planning authority, or a unilateral undertaking, whereby the developer/ landowner gives an undertaking to the LPA.
- Such obligations may restrict the development or use of land, require specific operations (works) or activities (uses) to be carried out on land owned by the applicant, which may be within the application site or may be on neighbouring land, require land to be used in a particular way, and require payments to the local authority periodically or at one time. (This was the first statutory recognition that an obligation may include an undertaking to make a financial payment, although the practice had existed since the 1970s.)
- While, initially, unilateral undertakings were anticipated to be used only rarely, they have become increasingly popular over the years because they are quicker to expedite and often preferred because developers commit a specific sum of money to fund local amenities (Jansen and Pattinson 2007).
- The avoidance of delay due to the deletion of negotiation gives the unilateral undertaking a significant advantage over the planning agreement. Both planning agreements and unilateral undertakings are binding on successive owners and will be recorded in a public register for inspection at the relevant planning office.
- There are powers to modify or discharge a planning obligation. Following a period of five years from the date the obligation is agreed, an application can be made to the local planning authority on the grounds that the

planning obligation no longer serves a useful planning purpose or should be modified in some way. The right of appeal to the Secretary of State is available in the event of the local authority either failing to determine the application or deciding that the planning obligation should not be modified or discharged.[9]

- No right of appeal exists in the event that a planning authority seeks an obligation and the developer disagrees. The only way to challenge the planning merits of this is to submit a planning appeal in the event that the planning authority imposes a reason for refusal which attributes the lack of an obligation as a principal reason for objection.

Examples of planning obligations

Government planning policy establishes that, if properly used, planning obliga-tions may both enhance the quality of development schemes and permit the granting of planning applications that would otherwise have to be refused. The government was, however, keen to state that acceptable applications should never be refused because an applicant is unwilling to offer benefits, or conversely that simply because benefits are proposed does not render an unacceptable scheme to be automatically acceptable. Instead the relevant circular establishes a number of relevant 'tests' or pre-conditions that must be satisfied. Yet, and somewhat confusingly for the student of planning, failure to satisfy these pre-condition tests does not render any subsequent obligation 'unlawful' rather, it effectively invalidates the merits of what is agreed as a material town planning considera-tion. In practice, this means that such an obligation (which will be 'tied' to a planning permission) will carry little weight if LPAs or developers wish to rely upon it in future years to justify a repeat of the principles as established. Circu-lar guidance is broad in its content, but does establish that any obligation must be both 'necessary' and 'fairly and reasonably related' directly in proportion with the requirements of the site in question. Circular 5/05 made it clear that planning permissions must not be bought and sold.

Prerequisites of a planning obligation

Circular 5/05 paragraph B5 'Test for planning obligations' requires that they are:

- Relevant to planning
- Necessary to make the proposed development acceptable in planning terms
- Directly related to the proposed development
- Fairly and reasonably related in scale and kind to the proposed development
- Reasonable in all other respects.

Circular 5/05 paragraph B31 states that 'it is important that the negotiation of planning obligations does not unnecessarily delay the planning process, thereby holding up development'.

Very little is specifically ruled inside or outside the guidance. Instead much is left to the individual interpretation of planning officers, planning inspectors and developers or their professional representatives. Considerations as to the circular's prerequisites of 'need' or 'reasonable relationship' allow a wide discretion over what obligations are within or outside government policy. Ultimately negotiation will play a part, which may result in the unsatisfactory situation in which the public consider that private deals are being struck. The planning officer (and planning committee) will need to arrive at a professional judgement as to whether an obligation is appropriate and, if so, the nature of its content. The system is thus based on local discretion within a framework of policy, established by government. The 2005 circular encourages local planning authorities to use set formulas and standard charges (set out in policy documents) to add a measure of transparency and consistency in the calculation of a developer's contribution. Such quantitative estimates of a planning obligation must be flexibly applied, to reflect local site circumstances. A 'one size fits all' approach is not the desired objective of this system.

Planning obligations have been neatly encapsulated in the past as land-use/amenity-related gains and social/economic-related gains (Debenham, Tewson and Chinnocks 1988). Certainly, in the latter category it is harder to satisfy all the tests of reasonableness, and such provision of social and economic infrastructure within planning obligations tends to produce greater controversy and provides critics of the system with an easy target. The starting point should be that an obligation is required only to overcome some legitimate planning objection to a proposal. Yet, the British system in general and the planning obligations system in particular, are based upon negotiation and bargaining. If a developer wishes to offer land or financial payment towards social and economic infrastructure beyond the strict requirement of the consent, then that is the prerogative of the developer. This may be viewed as 'buying planning permission' on the one hand or as an acceptance of the need towards betterment in society. Either way, it does not make the obligation illegal within the rules of the system.

The lack of detailed guidance by government will result in difficulty in interpreting the tests. The system has been described as 'fuzzy' (Lichfield 1989). It will continue to be fuzzy as long as the government maintains such policy guidance, which is based upon the application of 'tests' to the vast array of suggested planning obligations that arise from consideration of planning applications.

Stronger criticism has been expressed by two eminent former Chief and Senior planning inspectors, respectively Stephen Crow and John Acton. Crow (1997) argues that while developer payments towards infrastructure provision is a legitimate activity, the 'gain' system brings the planning profession into disrepute by promoting a culture in which planning permissions may be bought and sold. Acton (1998) goes further, arguing that the system fuels public suspicion and cynicism about the planning process. Some developers and LPAs manipulate the system to either buy (or enhance chances of gaining) their consent or by extracting benefits without good reason. Lord Justice Nolan (Committee on Standards in Public Life 1997) added further authority to such opinion when, set against the background of standards in public life, he found with respect to planning obligations (and gain) that 'The potential problems have little to do with corruption, but have a tremendous impact on public confidence', and that, should the post-1991 regime continue, 'planning permissions will continue to be "bought and sold"'.

As with many critics of the system, Nolan was not opposed to the principle of the wider community (via the planning system) imposing a charge against developers for infrastructure. The key issue was the means by which such a charge was levied and public scrutiny or confidence in that system. Nolan recommended that government should reconsider the wording used in Section 106 of the Town and Country Planning Act 1990 to make more explicit the fact that permissions should not be bought or sold. Arguably this has been taken on board in the 2005 circular. It was not until 2000, in the Urban White Paper, that a fresh review of planning gain was heralded. A consultation paper reviewing the 1991–2000 system of planning obligations was issued in 2001 (DETR 2001a). In large part this was in response to calls for reform made by the Urban Task Force (1999 and 2005). The Task Force was generally supportive of the notion of planning gain: 'our main conclusion is that the use of planning obligations to secure planning gain is necessary and justified', although they then added 'but that the process is not currently being applied consistently'.

The Task Force reported three principal problems[10] in the system: that Section 106 Agreements were taking too long to process, were not produced to standard formats (in drafting) across the country and often revealed little grasp of commercial reality by planners. The Task Force made three specific recommendations: that national guidance be revised, arbitration be introduced when Section 106 negotiations were not proceeding to a conclusion, and standardized impact fees be introduced to extract 'gain' in smaller urban development schemes. Such influential lobbying for reform galvanized government to set in progress a review and subsequently reform. While the government subsequently agonized over a variety of alternatives, the use of planning obligations became increasingly popular to the extent that research revealed that the proportion of planning permissions with a planning obligation attached had risen from 1.5 per cent (1998) to 6.9 per cent (2004) and that in South East England they are attached to 40 per cent of all applications, mostly the more significant development proposals (Department for Communities and Local Government 2006e).

Case law

An examination of relevant case law dealing with legal challenges involving planning obligations provides an interesting commentary as to what may be deemed 'lawful'. Such an examination, based upon a legal interpretation of Section 106 statute, is much more precise than the guidance as set out in the circular. It is worth remembering, at this juncture, that government circular guidance is policy-based and does not represent a set of legal principles. While the previously detailed 'tests' are an important material consideration and the Secretary of State will apply them when determining an appeal, the local planning authority is not bound to follow this advice. In essence, we find that the circular tests are much more demanding that the legal interpretation of Section 106, established by case law.

In *Newbury District Council v. Secretary of State for the Environment* (1988),[11] the Court of Appeal said that any planning obligation should serve a planning purpose, related to the development and not be unreasonable (to the extent that no reasonable planning authority could have imposed it). In *R v. Plymouth City Council and others ex parte Plymouth and South Devon Co-operative Society Limited* (1993),[12] the Court of Appeal, in supporting a previous decision by the High Court, cast doubt on the role of the 'tests' as a legal guideline (which are now replaced by the prerequisite of an obligation). The legal test was the one stated in *Newbury* – the tests themselves only represented government policy and not statute, and as such the local planning authority was under no obligation to apply the circular. In essence the local planning authority would need to consider the circular guidance but could give it 'zero' weight when balancing planning policy and other site-specific matters.

The contention that planning obligations amount to the 'sale of a planning permission' was considered in *R v. South Northamptonshire District Council ex parte Crest Homes Limited* (1994). The LPA was seeking to finance infrastructure provision in the absence of sufficient public funding. The Court of Appeal held that, in this case, such a policy was lawful. Particular emphasis was laid on the fact that the LPA had identified specific infrastructure projects and sought to distribute the infrastructure cost equitably among a consortium of developers and landowners in the area.

In *Tesco Stores Limited v. Secretary of State for the Environment*[13] (1995), the House of Lords upheld the Secretary of State's decision to grant planning permission to Sainsbury's for a site in Witney, Oxfordshire (where Tesco were also promoting a superstore site). In so doing, the Secretary of State had overturned the decision of the inspector hearing the original appeals, who had recommended in favour of the Tesco proposal, which included the offer of a £6.6 million contribution to highway works for their store. It was held by the House of Lords that the starting point was whether or not the obligation was a material consideration. Such a legal decision would be based on the degree to which the obligation was connected with the development. If it was more than *de minimis* (insignificant) the local planning authority must take it into account. The amount of weight they gave to that obligation, however, would then be a matter for their own discretion. Thus the Secretary of State was perfectly entitled to take the view that the proposed road only had a tenuous connection to the proposed superstore. To reject it was to properly exercise discretion in decision-making. This position was confirmed again in 2001 in *JA Pye (Oxford) Limited v. South Gloucestershire District Council* (Court of Appeal, 29 March 2001) when the Court of Appeal held that the only test of legal validity of a planning obligation was that it (a) served a planning purpose and (b) was not unreasonable.

The *Tesco* case is perhaps the most definite judgement and casts some doubt on the value of circular guidance in interpreting what is, and what is not, a reasonable offer of planning gain. The courts thus have relied upon a simpler test: that providing a planning obligation serves a planning purpose and is not unreasonable, then a planning authority is free to decide what weight should be given and this decision involves an application of the policy tests in Circular 05/05. This throws a very wide net indeed. It is clear that, with such large sums of money involved, litigation in this area of planning law will continue. The outcome of all this litigation, especially the consequences arising from the *Tesco* case, is that while the LPA and developer should follow the guidance laid down by the circular, failure to so do does not render the obligation somehow 'unlawful', but merely bad practice. What is strictly required is adherence to the terms laid down in Section 106 of the Town and Country Planning Act 1990, i.e. that it involves financial payment to the LPA or details specific restrictions on or requirements to construct buildings or regulate use(s).

We may go on to consider the wider philosophical issues surrounding this system in the knowledge that interpretation of the circular's rules is a matter left to local planning authorities and developers, and the rules themselves are by no means clear cut.

Summary: planning obligations – characteristics

- Section 106 of the TCPA 1990 provides legal powers to enter into planning obligations.
- The 1991 reforms to the system introduced the new term 'planning obligation' to cover both agreements between the LPA and the developer/applicant, and unilateral undertakings offered only by the developer/applicant, as well as the power to discharge or modify an obligation.
- Cash payments are detailed as permissible in the 1991 Statute.
- Planning obligations may restrict the development or use of land, require specified operations to be carried out, require land to be used in a particular way or require a sum to be paid to the LPA on a specified date(s) or periodically. They are tied to a planning permission.
- Circular guidance has sought to promote best practice. Adherence to the guidance is a matter for the decision-maker. The strict legal test of a Section 106 planning obligation is that it is relevant to planning and not unreasonable.
- In 2009 the system will be replaced (in the most part) by the 'community infrastructure levy' (see the section below on reforming planning obligations).

The philosophical issues

> For some, 'planning gain' was a legitimate contribution from developers to community development, but it has been viewed by others as both an unconstitutional tax and a form of negotiated bribery corrupting the planning system.
>
> (Healey *et al.* 1993)

> The government believes it is fair in principle to capture a portion of the value uplift arising on development land and use it for the benefit of the wider community.
>
> (HM Treasury 2006a)

The practice of developers offering a variety of benefits to local authorities has resulted in many emotive, if easy to remember, phrases, such as 'planning blackmail' or 'cheque-book planning'. Such a response to the system tends to ignore the more significant issue of whether or not a developer should pay something back to the community after taking profits from a development that will inevitably have some impact on the locality. It also ignores the procedural reality of planning obligations whereby they actually benefit the developer by allowing the grant of consent to develop land where it may be otherwise unacceptable in planning terms. The question for debate should be whether a developer should pay anything towards alleviating the impact of a development and then in what form should this charge be levied? Although these points are being considered, it should also be remembered that the planning obligation gives the developer a legal mechanism within which planning objections may be overcome, therefore improving the chances of gaining permission.

Historical background

In considering such issues, it is important to recall the historical development of the British planning system. The TCPA of 1947 nationalized the right to develop land. The ability to build or change the use of a building became a decision for society to exercise by means of the decisions of local planning authorities. However, land with planning permission would, in a country with limited land resources, carry a premium. The planning system introduced a new control mechanism, which means that obtaining planning permission would both enhance the value of land and increase the value of adjoining land that benefits from the 'amenity' created by development. These benefits introduced by the planning system or indeed any other activities of government are referred to as 'betterment'.

The 1947 Act was based upon the key philosophical position that, alongside the nationalization of the right to develop land, any future increases in the value of land following the granting of planning permission should be the property of the state (Ward 1994: 108). The new legislation introduced by the Labour administration resulted in a 100 per cent tax on betterment (i.e. all of the increased value of land resulting from gaining planning permission would be taxed). This has been described as a contradiction at the heart of the Act (Ward 1994), because private ownership of land would be maintained, yet any increases resulting from the speculative grant of planning permission would be taxed, thereby killing off a good deal of private sector activity by attacking the profit motive. Not surprisingly, this proposal was unpopular and the incoming Conservative administration of 1951 soon announced their intention to end it. The Planning Act of 1953 abolished the development charge without introducing any alternative tax measure to collect betterment.

A betterment tax was not to return until the late 1960s with the Land Commission Act 1967. This time a levy of betterment at 40 per cent was introduced. A new agency, the Land Commission, would oversee the system. The new 1970 Conservative government abolished the Land Commission after one year in office. The final betterment tax came with the Development Land Tax Act 1976, which introduced a new tax on land value increases, initially set at 80 per cent of betterment, with the intention that it would eventually rise to 100 per cent. However, this Development Land Tax suffered from a poor level of implementation, hampered by a serious property recession in the mid-1970s. This, then, represented the third post-war attempt at taxing betterment and it was itself abolished in 1986.

To assess the role of the planning gain/obligations system we must examine the extent to which a developer should pay towards the environmental impact of their proposal and, if the answer is yes, then whether this should be deemed a matter of taxation (by virtue of a betterment levy) or instead as a legitimate development cost, to be factored into the calculation of residual land value. The 2005 consultation announcement by HM Treasury and following the Barker review into housing supply of the previous year (HM Treasury 2004), recommended that the planning process be amended so that a proportion of uplift in value be captured when planning permission was granted and payable when work commenced. This consultation reopened an evolving debate (commenced in 1947) which examined the virtues of introducing a tax on development value.

Betterment tax?

Arguably, planning obligations represent a form of indirect betterment tax in that a charge is imposed on development which is linked to an assessment of its impact. The actual cost of developer contributions will vary dramatically across the country and across development proposals, with the values secured in London and the South East at about double that of the North of England (Department for Communities and Local Government 2006e). The measure of tax will crudely depend upon the size of a development proposal – the exact nature of the proposal will greatly influence the value of the gain required, with affordable housing provision at the most, and open space provision the least expensive (Department for Communities 2006e). It is unlikely that planning authorities undertake detailed economic appraisals of development proposals and then 'top slice' a percentage towards community 'goodies' in the form of obligations.

Instead, practice is much more varied and the subject of nationally inconsistent performance as development plans differ and their respective planning officers must exercise a measure of judgement in the interpretation of these policies. Yet successive governments have persisted with this somewhat 'hit and miss' system which is characterized by considerable uncertainty for the developer as to the likely stipulations of the planning authority and the consequential cost. Yet it has creaked along and, subject to minor revisions (encapsulated in the new circulars of 1983, 1991, 1997 and 2005), has remained largely unchanged. Of course the government would be at pains to say that a planning obligation is not a tax on betterment and Circular 05/05 does explicitly make this point. Further, in the previously quoted *R* v. *South Northamptonshire District Council ex parte Crest Homes* case the High Court deemed the council's attempt to enshrine a 20 per cent capture of enhanced development value in a housing scheme as 'equivalent to a development tax being imposed without lawful authority'.

A betterment tax imposes a set of uniform criteria to be applied nationally and consistently. An obligation does not work in this way and the ultimate outcome reflected in cash terms will depend upon the merits of the case and the negotiation and bargaining between the two parties, influenced by government circular advice. Planning gain/obligation may be viewed as at best a crude form of land taxation. It is not a continuation of a tax on betterment as introduced in 1947, 1967 and 1976, but in the absence of any other form of levy or development land tax it becomes associated with this subject. The question remains, would such a formalized system be better than the negotiated obligations?

The idea of developer contribution is based on the view that the planning obligation system represents a legitimate cost to a developer, who must accept that all development has some impact on the environment and that some level of contribution should be made towards either controlling or alleviating this impact. Such an impact may be physical (roads, landscaping, drainage, sewerage measures) or social (provision of social housing, community uses, access to open space or recreation facility). Government circular advice is more aligned with this view than the notion of a tax on betterment, in that it establishes guidelines for a negotiated solution based upon compliance with a series of policy tests. These tests are based on the creation of a functional or geographic link between the development site and the offered planning obligation or gain.

It seems reasonable that the developer should make some form of contribution to the impact of a development proposal. In some ways the current system, when correctly applied, permits a developer to overcome matters that would otherwise result in refusal of permission.

To determine fully the extent to which legitimate obligations have been pursued by local authorities or indeed developers, reference should be made to research on this topic. Before the 1968 reforms, little real use was made of such legal agreements. It has been estimated that between 1932 and 1967 only some 500 such agreements were made. A dramatic increase followed over the next few years. A survey of 106 English planning authorities revealed that more than 50 per cent admitted seeking some form of planning gain (Jowell 1977).

Research into the use of planning agreements by district councils (MacDonald 1991) revealed that around 70 per cent of all respondents were intending to include planning obligation policies in emerging local plans to strengthen their stance in negotiation with developers. The most comprehensive survey in recent years was published in 2006 (Department for Communities 2006e). This extensive study of 3940 planning obligations estimated that the proportion of planning permissions accompanied by a planning obligation quadrupled in the five years to 2004 and in that year alone the total value of all planning obligations amounted to about £1.15 billion, the most popular obligation, by type, being the creation and/or funding of open space, with payment towards affordable housing resulting in the highest cost at some £250,000 average developer contribution per agreement. A study the previous year (ODPM 2005) had specifically examined the delivery of affordable housing by means of planning obligations. This work appraised the planning obligation as an appropriate mechanism for the delivery of affordable housing (mostly in the social rented sector) and concluded that 12,700 affordable units (44 per cent of the total provision) were delivered nationally through the planning system; 2000 of these units were completed without any public subsidy, i.e. the developer funded the complete construction and land cost of (mostly) social rented housing (managed by a housing association). The negotiation of these obligations, it was estimated, could amount to 5 per cent of the total gross development value of a scheme. Clearly, planning obligations were making a significant contribution towards social provision and promotion of mixed tenure in development schemes. Work commissioned by the Joseph Rowntree Foundation (Watson 2006) examined a selection of affordable housing schemes and reported some concerns about the quality of such housing in terms of design and workmanship. That conclusion notwithstanding, the overall research base in recent years demonstrates that planning obligations are significantly increasing in terms of both numbers and the value of 'gain' extracted. Their application to planning applications delivered a vast array of benefits involving open-space provision, transport and travel services, community and leisure provision, educational provision and affordable housing. Would a direct land tax be a better means of funding such a range of social and physical infrastructure?

Reforming planning obligations

Three models of future reform may be advanced, notably those of impact fees, tariffs and betterment taxation/community infrastructure levy.

Impact fees

The introduction of (US-style) impact fees is not a new idea. Such a system may indeed be something of a panacea for the many problems of planning gain, most often encapsulated as its arbitrary case-by-case approach (Estates Gazette 1999). Professor Malcolm Grant, one of the leading advocates of impact fees, argued as long ago as 1993 that 'planning gain can be rationalized, and made

Figure 6.1 How impact fees would work

more predictable, and impact fees are a step in the right direction'. Indeed Grant (1993) concluded that while impact fees were by no means perfect, they performed far better than planning obligations when measured against criteria of transparency, equity, predictability, and efficiency.

A conference organized by the Royal Institution of Chartered Surveyors in 1999 considered both criticism of planning gain and the potential to introduce impact fees in its place. A paper presented by Professor Chris Nelson from the University of Georgia considered the functioning of US-style impact fees.[14] The starting point is that the local government must consider that a need exists for infrastructure. Such need is most commonly associated with growth, in which an urban area is projected to grow over the next twenty to twenty-five years. Local government planners are thus vested with the responsibility to devise growth plans and related infrastructure requirements. Such infrastructure must be costed and account taken of existing federal (i.e. national), state and local taxation that may (partially) fund such necessary services. The impact fees provide the 'gap' or 'bridge' between identified infrastructure (and its cost) and existing revenue allocated to local government, via taxation. As Professor Nelson pointed out, 'The shortfall in revenue becomes the basis for assessing . . . impact fees'. The shortfall is then broken down into an 'impact fee schedule' of necessary works. Each development project, therefore, is responsible for paying a proportionate share towards the identified infrastructure.

It was noted by Professor Nelson, that 'Impact fees are the last step in a planning process', in that they deliver on strategic infrastructure requirements as set out in the local land-use plan. An example he cited is set out in the box below.

The local land-use plan establishes standards for recreational and open space at 5 acres per 1000 residents. It is projected over the plan period that a town will grow by 10,000 people, creating the need for 50 acres of parkland. As housebuilders come forward they will need to pay a proportion of this cost. The local council will need to identify and implement these parks, acknowledging the source of their funding.

Professor Nelson divided US-style impact fees into four categories of infrastructure: that directly required (such as water supplies); that providing public services (such as schools, roads, parks); or a social function (such as subsidized public housing); and that providing for the maintenance of the whole process (mostly in payment of professional time to devise such schemes).

In summary, this system of collecting infrastructure charges against develop-ment proposals is vested with several benefits over planning gain. First, impact fees are collected for a specific purpose and may be used only for that prescribed project. Planning gain is less tightly defined and may be used for a vast array of matters, provided that council and developer agree. Second, impact fees are based on equality, being applied in a proportionate and fair way. Planning gain is less clear-cut, with the exact proportion falling on the developer dependent upon individual negotiations between developer and council, and varying on a case-by-case basis. Third, impact fees are simple to calculate and transparent in application. This assists all parties to understand the process and presents a favourable image to the public. By contrast, the planning gain process is opaque, sometimes shrouded in private negotiations and the subject of public mistrust (as noted by Lord Justice Nolan). Finally, impact fees are deemed flexible. The calculation of fee is based on the relative proportion of infrastructure required. Planning gain can also be flexible, based as it is on negotiation. Such a benefit of impact fees may also be attributed to gain. Taken overall, however, planning gain appears at a disadvantage compared to the tangible benefits attributed to impact fees. Such benefit may account for the growing popularity associated with impact fees over recent years. The government-appointed Urban Task Force (1999) did not call for planning gain to be abolished but that standardized impact fees be introduced 'for smaller urban development schemes (for example, an end value of less than £1 million)'. The impact fee is, therefore, a standardized fee that applies in certain locations, mostly in areas of identified growth. A tariff is a similar concept but one applied more universally across all developments and locations.

Tariffs

Tariffs at one time represented the planning mechanism most likely to replace planning obligations. Importantly, their employment was significantly endorsed in the 2001 consultation paper 'Reforming planning obligations' and two years later, this time incarnated as the optional planning charge in another consul-tation 'Contributing to sustainable communities: a new approach to planning obligations'. This was couched as an alternative to (but not a replacement of) a planning obligation. The consultation paper proposed that a developer could either pay such a charge or tariff in preference to negotiating a Section 106 agreement. The optional charge would be known as the 'planning contribution'. The response to this paper was mixed with some criticism that it would result in a confusing two-tier system. Subsequently, however, the review of housing supply undertaken by Kate Barker in 2004 eclipsed such a favoured alternative due to her endorsement of the planning gain supplement (PGS). Barker did, however, discuss the notion of an optional planning charge, a derivative of the tariff and a potential (if unlikely) replacement of the planning obligation. What subsequently emerged in legislation was a derivative of the PGS.

Tariffs or optional planning charges themselves involve a schedule of planning obligations, seeking various works and/or financial contributions. They are given foundation, even authority, by virtue of their integration into the Local Development Framework. Each council would be able to tailor its own tariffs to the prevailing development circumstances that it confronts. If an element of negotiation were to be required in small sites, say, then this could be written into the policy to allow a measure of local discretion. National planning policy guidance would be issued (say, in a PPS) in which the government would establish some broad rules regarding the setting of a tariff (i.e. when it would/would not apply) and the monitoring and accounting involved (i.e. by a standard form of legal contract between the parties). Otherwise, government would effectively devolve powers to the local planning authority. The community infrastructure levy would allow councils to raise funds to spend on infrastructure to (mostly) support new housing, by virtue of an agreed levy or tax.

This system would arguably involve more clarity, certainty and even transparency than the planning obligation system introduced in 1991. The levy would be set in local planning policy within a series of broad rules as established nationally. A somewhat prickly issue would be the exact calculation of the levy. Government themselves implicitly acknowledge this in the 2001 consultation paper regarding the optional planning charge, by providing four options for calculation as: (i) cost measured by floorspace; (ii) cost measured by unit (e.g. dwellings); (iii) cost as a proportion of development value; or (iv) a combination of these. The ultimate calculation of the (then) and (now) levy will be difficult, even controversial. It will obviously influence the nature and pattern of development. Such an approach can be used to encourage sustainable development, itself a necessary attribute of any new system. For example, the levy could be higher for greenfield housing schemes compared to brownfield land and equivalents. Nevertheless, potential exists for conflict in a number of areas. First, there are cross-boundary issues, when two councils either side of a local government boundary set wildly differing tariffs. This may greatly encourage commercial, industrial and residential development in one council to the exclusion of the other. Second, disputes could arise over valuation matters. If the development value of a planning application forms the basis of a tariff calculation then disagreements may arise as to the assumptions employed in arriving at those figures. Finally, there could be controversy surrounding how the levy is spent. They would need to be carefully formulated to ensure that any financial contributions collected were used directly towards the necessary infrastructure works, as dictated by the published schedule. The government's earlier idea of an optional planning charge (also known as the planning contribution) was based on a standard tariff which would be paid in lieu of a negotiated planning obligation. The government consulted on this in 2003, in 'Contributing to Sustainable Communities: A new approach to planning obligations', in which a schedule of charges would be calculated and based on environmental/social/

community costs resulting from the scheme, such as the need for schools and community buildings as a consequence of new housing. The charge would not, therefore, be based on the capture of land value. Implementation (for the government at least) would be relatively painless as the Planning and Compulsory Purchase Act 2004, Sections 46–48 made provision for the implementation of such a charge or contribution, should the government seek to take this forward. Such a reform would not have replaced planning obligations but would have sat alongside the existing system, offering an alternative which would appear more persuasive, should planning obligations continue to be dogged by delay in their negotiation and production.

The 'community infrastructure levy', with anticipated introduction in 2009, appears a second choice to the introduction of more local taxation, yet shares a similar pedigree to the (dropped) planning gain supplement. Both will now be considered, and the new system will be the subject of some conjecture as to its future direction.

Betterment tax and the community infrastructure levy

The Kate Barker review of housing supply, which manifested itself in an interim report (2003) and a final list of recommendations (HM Treasury 2004), promoted the planning gain supplement (after consideration of a wide range of alternatives) centred around the central notion of capturing a portion of land-value increase following the grant of planning permission for development. Barker examined four options in the quest for an increased supply of land for housing. First, that of a 'land value tax' whereby land would be taxed according to its market value, so that land in the greatest demand for use would attract a higher tax liability to encourage its development. The tax could be honed to apply exclusively to undeveloped or vacant land, land allocated for development or land with the benefit of outline or full permission. The current use of capital gains tax (CGT) works in a similar fashion because it applies when land is sold. The Barker review considered that CGT was not the best way to capture the 'windfall' in land value with its associated tax relief rendering it a 'low tax liability'. Taken overall, Barker considered a land value tax (geared to planning) as unlikely to stimulate housing supply. Secondly, Barker considered the option of a 'development gains tax', in which taxation is applied to a proportion of the increase in land value attributable to changing to residential use. This option was dismissed because it increased the damaging possibility that landowners might hold back land in anticipation that a future government might reverse such a tax. Previous complexities associated with the failed Development Land Tax of 1976 appeared to have coloured Barker's judgement of such an option. Thirdly, Barker considered the introduction of Valued Added Tax (VAT) on new housing (currently zero-rated) but this was also dismissed because, notwithstanding the well established credibility of this existing tax, it would result in significant regional imbalances and considerably reduce land coming forward for residential development in the North of England. Finally, the Barker review considered the idea of moving the point at which a tax is applied to the planning permission. A levy calculated on the proportion of residential land would fall on the landowner and/or developer. If such a levy were 'applied at a sensible rate' then it would not significantly affect development profit nor dent the amount of land coming forward for development, especially compared to the other options. One significant advantage compared to the uniform application of, say, VAT was the ability to tailor such a levy to either provide economic incentives or even disincentives to development such as favouring brownfield over greenfield development.

Government in its initial response to the Barker review accepted the central foundation of its recommendation, namely that it was considered fair to fund future infrastructure by applying a levy to the uplift in land value experienced during the planning process. Further, that a tax levied on the basis of a grant of planning permission was the most effective way of capturing land-value uplift. These broad principles were developed in a consultation paper issued at the end of 2005 which heralded the introduction of a new system to replace planning obligations. The basis of the tax would be the difference between the land value with full planning permission (PV – planning value) and its current use (CUV – current use value). Thus a 'modest' levy would apply to all planning applications (except for home improvements) and be imposed on the difference or uplift, and the total amount payable would be derived from multiplying the uplift by a prescribed amount (the PGS rate). Thus, this new form of betterment levy could be simply expressed as:

Uplift = Planning value *less* current use value
Planning gain supplement = PGS rate *multiplied* by uplift

Two key features are worthy of examination. First, the exact nature of this tax and secondly the means by which it is paid and distributed. The exact rate at which the PGS rate would be set remained a critical feature – and ultimately one that would sink the idea. The development industry were highly critical, and argued that the intended duel objectives of bringing forward land for housing development while also adequately funding necessary social and physical infrastructure, would not be achieved. A study undertaken to test the PGS, and published some nine moths after the consultation report (Knight Frank 2006), suggested that such a tax would not deliver the level of funding sought for new local infrastructure. Further, it found that such a mechanism could render small developments unviable, which would threaten housing supply and undermine the objective of increasing the delivery of new housing by the market. The research base for this work was a persuasive study of eighteen developments in which a hypothetical PGS rate was set at 10 per cent, 20 per cent and 30 per cent of the uplift in value following the grant of planning permission. One worrying conclusion of the research was that:

There is great concern that the community infrastructure required for these large-scale developments, which under PGS would be supplied by local authorities or other government agencies, would not be adequately funded or provided in time to serve new developments.

(Knight Frank 2006)

While the government did not set an indicative levy in the consultation paper, the fact that this conclusion applies from a PGS rate as low as 10 per cent of uplift, remains a deep concern when speculating on the future impact of the new system.

The second matter to consider here is the means by which payment is captured. The government clearly signalled, in the consultation paper, that it would be inappropriate for payment to apply immediately following the grant of planning permission as not all permissions are implemented. Instead payment would be required following the commencement of development and paid by an identified chargeable person (developer and/or landowner) who would make a PGS return to HM Revenue & Customs within a specified time (HM Revenue & Customs 2006). This revenue would be recycled back to the local level in the form of either direct grants or by application of a set formula. Some significant sums of money would be held back for delivering strategic or regional infrastructure by transferring this to the Community Infrastructure Fund (CIF), a body created in 2004 to support transport infrastructure costs in the four growth areas identified by government in the Sustainable Communities Plan. The South East England Regional Assembly estimated that the PGS would raise £1 billion annually but themselves expressed concern, in response to the consultation paper, that income raised from such an economically active region would be siphoned away to pay for national infrastructure or work in other regions (SEERA 2006).

The consultation paper, as may be expected, produced a mixed response. While some commentators felt that the idea was correct in principle and geared to the delivery of sustainable communities (Butt 2006), others were critical of the potentially iniquitous situation whereby small and/or marginal projects would shoulder a disproportionate share of the tax burden and therefore would be rendered unviable (Gilman 2006). While one poll of social housebuilders revealed general contentment with the concept, property market commentators focused on the problems associated with valuation in a calculation of the PV figure, leading to further uncertainty in light of the many variables that affect a site's value (Jansen 2006, Knight Frank 2006). While this debate raged, the government also consulted opinion on the future of planning obligations and in particular whether or not to keep a scaled-back and greatly reduced system, geared exclusively to site-specific issues and payment towards affordable housing (Department for Communities and Local Government 2007c). It was important that a developer avoid double helpings of gain in which payments are against both the planning gain supplement and a planning obligation. Thus government proposed creation of a series of set criteria dealing with key functional issues to resolve, such as site access, protection of biodiversity and provision of landscaping. The government were content that affordable provision stay within the realm of a planning obligation as this would permit implementation of a system already well understood by social housing providers, developers and planning authorities.

After much consultation and debate as to the merits and mechanics of a tax on development uplift, the proposed new tax was suddenly and dramatically dropped in the summer of 2007. Instead the government returned, in their thinking, to the original concept of a schedule of charges linked to development proposals. This would pay for wider infrastructure, services and amenities. Planning obligations would continue in a very limited set of circumstances whereby they would mitigate the impact of development – for example, creation of an access road to a site, dealing with on-site archaeology or the protection of endangered species which may exist within the application site but migrate from a much wider area.

The Planning and Reform Act 2008 makes provision for the passing of detailed regulations that will govern the detailed mechanics of the system. Release of the detailed regulations is anticipated by mid-2009. Government issued an initial scoping paper in early 2008, which set out the philosophy behind the reforms. After much consultation and debate surrounding the previous proposals for both the optional planning charge (2001–02 and 2003–04) and planning gain supplement (during 2007) progress on the Community Infrastructure Levy was both rapid and arguably in haste. Almost as a 'bolt from the blue', the development industry discovered in the wording of the Planning and Reform Act (then Bill) that from 2009 planning authorities would be able to set a standardized charge on development that would (in the words of the 2008 scoping paper) 'raise hundreds of millions of pounds of extra funding for infrastructure'. Government rather sidestepped the issue of consultation on this new scheme by implying that it had emerged following reaction to the previous optional planning charge/planning gain supplement consultations. In essence, a twin-tracked system of negotiated planning obligations (mitigating detailed impacts of development) and standard charges set by individual councils (to pay for major and identified infrastructure) would be established. The government were clear that affordable housing would still be provided by means of negotiated planning obligations as currently exist. Yet beyond this, issues like transport infrastructure, green space and community uses (including educational uses) would be funded by virtue of set charges, levied at a local level after each council had costed its future infrastructure needs based on the amount of anticipated growth and even regeneration in the planning pipeline. In support of this tilt away from a taxation-based system (i.e. planning gain supplement) and in favour of a set charge or contribution, the government deemed this system as both fair and predictable, in that developers would know just what they had to pay and exactly when they would have to pay it.

The pendulum had swung back, somewhat, in favour of a set amount of money, to be determined locally. Thus, and without the fanfare of previous consultations, the government moved quickly to introduce the Community

Infrastructure Levy (CIL) into legislation in the Planning and Reform Bill 2008. After 2009 each council would be empowered, rather than required, to introduce a community infrastructure levy. To implement a set of standard charges (which would vary from council to council), they would need to produce evidence to back up the exact levy (i.e. the costs of required infrastructure and anticipated level of development) and to set out a formula for calculation (i.e. per dwelling or per square metre of development). Government would set the broad rules in the regulations, including powers of enforcement should the developer fail to pay, and the 'reserve power' held by the Secretary of State to direct a council to amend its scheme, if for example it was setting an unrealistic levy or one calculated against criteria that fell outside the regulations. The charge would be paid upon implementation of development and the developer would not benefit from any rights of appeal in the event that they did not like the very principle of a charge being imposed.

From 2009, a much more broadly based planning charge (or levy) would thus be used to capture income that would be applied to most forms of development (excluding domestic extension) and ring-fenced to pay for essential infrastructure. In growth areas these sums would be significant. In the pre-2009 system of negotiated planning obligations only an estimated 14 per cent of housing planning permissions made a contribution to 'planning gain', via a linked planning obligation. In the post-2009 system, all new residential developments would be captured by this new levy and the proportion of development contributing to infrastructure would be dramatically increased in both developments affected and in the amount of revenue thus raised. It would remain to be seen if such a levy would be imposed fairly and realistically and the extent to which the development industry would be consulted on the proposed amount. The anticipated regulations would need to allow for necessary consultations, to permit an appropriate level of robust scrutiny of the evidence base upon which the levy is set. This would allow the development industry to feed back valuable information and meaningful appraisal of the nature of the proposed levy and its associated formulas, so that it would not inhibit development by being too high and create a situation in which it prevented development, instead of promoting it.

Conclusions

The system in which developers contribute towards social and physical infrastructures in return for obtaining planning permission remained largely unaltered for a forty-year period between 1968 and 2008. In spite of some important procedural changes introduced in 1991, this system was largely based on negotiation between developers and planning authorities with, since 1983, 1997 and 2005, some broad policy guidance issued by the government. Nothing was specifically prescribed as either acceptable or unacceptable, and the application of government guidelines or tests resulted in considerable uncertainty as to just what exactly was acceptable and what was not. Developers may have felt that they had little choice but to comply with the planning authorities' demands for benefits, with pursuit of an appeal offering no guarantee of success. Yet, within this somewhat imperfect system and in the absence of any formal betterment taxation, both sides in the development process made the system work. Research in the early 1990s had indicated that the tests were generally followed by the planning authority, and in the majority of cases the obligations were required to facilitate the grant of planning permission. As long as the system operated at this level, then it clearly constituted a legal mechanism by which a developer was able to rectify the physical and sometimes social impact of the proposal. In this respect planning obligations clearly fall within the category of a development cost. Problems principally occurred when the system was used as a means by which planning authorities could extract wider social benefits. Although research in the early 1990s has demonstrated that this was evidently not the case in the overwhelming majority of proposals, when it does occur it creates frustration and fuels the misconceptions of 'planning blackmail'.

Several alternatives have been proposed – for instance, the American model of impact fees (Grant 1993, 1995b) and the tariff or optional planning charge, and most recently the community levy. These involve, in effect, a reshaping of the aspirations set for the planning obligation, to take a prescribed and allocated amount to fund infrastructure. The government exhibited an appetite for major reform with the reincarnation of a betterment tax in 2007. Following the recommendation of Kate Barker, in pursuit of the combined objectives of financing vital infrastructure, supporting growing communities and increasing housing supply, the planning gain supplement was viewed as the most preferred future reform for the system. The system would move from a somewhat informal site-specific system of negotiated obligations, to a uniform taxation of uplift in land value to be applied nationally and consistently across all planning authorities. Yet, this idea was suddenly and swiftly dropped in the late summer of 2007. A void opened, in which government was still proposing to raise annual housebuilding targets but lacked any mechanism to pay for infrastructure beyond its owns coffers. The 'community infrastructure levy' appeared to be quickly cobbled together as a solution and one that drew heavily upon the optional planning charge that had been discussed some five years previously. The exact detail of the levy remains to be determined in the published regulations (expected mid-2009) and the amount of charge will vary from council to council in response to their particular circumstances. Planning obligations will remain and will, in particular, be used to mitigate the direct impact of a development site – for example, the need for a new road access. Yet, the scope of planning obligations when compared to the pre-2009 system will be dramatically scaled back to more of a legal mechanism, while the remit of the community infrastructure levy will be a much broader one in gathering income to fund significant new community and transport infrastructure. This change is significant, as government moves toward a system in which the development industry is expected to pay for infrastructure needs across a much wider spectrum of applications and in which a clear expectation is made that a charge or levy is collected upon implementation of a planning permission. After forty years of negotiated planning obligations the 2009 revisions would herald in a totally different system for the collection of funding, while the expression 'planning obligation' would remain as a more strictly applied legal mechanism for the control of a direct off-site impact from a development site.

Part Three

Urban planning issues

7 Specialist planning controls

'Specialist planning controls' provides an umbrella term under which we can examine topics dealing with the preservation of the built and natural environment. In urban areas in particular, listed building and conservation area controls seek to protect historic and architecturally significant buildings and spaces, whereas urban design seeks to improve the quality of urban fabric when those areas are developed. In rural locations those considerations also apply, but many additional controls seek to ensure the protection of the natural environment for its beauty (i.e. National Parks, Areas of Outstanding Natural Beauty or National Scenic Areas) for its flora and fauna (i.e. Sites of Special Scientific Interest, Special Areas of Conservation, Special Protection Areas and Nature Reserves) and for its recreational value to Britain's mostly urban-based population (i.e. the development of what is now called 'accessible natural green space'). Other environmental controls applicable to both urban and rural locations include Ancient Monuments, Areas of Archaeological Importance and Tree Preservation Orders. Green belt designation applies a multi-faceted approach – and one familiar to many members of the public, who are reassured by its inherently anti-development stance (see Table 7.11 for a summary of these policies). This chapter will deal with these topics and will be organized as follows:

- Listed buildings
- Conservation areas
- Design control
- Green belts
- Nature conservation and countryside planning
- Accessible natural green space and green infrastructure.

Listed buildings

Buildings or groups of buildings considered to be of special architectural and historical interest are included in a list compiled by English Heritage and are protected from demolition, alteration or extension without obtaining Listed Building Consent from the local planning authority. After 2010 (it is anticipated at the time of writing), the Listed Building Consent procedure will be replaced by the Heritage Asset Consent. The system has grown, incrementally, since the very first legislative recognition of special buildings and monuments, with the passing of the Ancient Monuments Act of 1882. Today, the system is the subject of wholesale review, albeit that certain key principles remain. These principles establish that whatever is protected must be deemed of 'special' quality. The determination of what is special is decided nationally and by one body (formerly the Secretary of State and now English Heritage) and the decision to allow alterations or even demolition is made locally, by the Local Authority, following consideration of national guidance and expert opinion.

> A building, eligible for listing, can thus be as large as a palace or as small as a bollard, provided it is at least a 'structure'. And indeed a surprising variety of structures have been listed over the years, including, for example, statues, grave stones, lamp posts, train sheds, water troughs, mews arches and tunnels.
>
> (Mynors 2006)

Procedure for listing

The list is administered by English Heritage on behalf of the Secretary of State for Culture, Media and Sport (DCMS). The introduction of the Heritage Protection Review between 2004 and 2008 resulted in passing the decision to list a building entirely to English Heritage (after 2010) and for the nature of that listing description to be far more comprehensive in its identification of what is special than had been the case previously. A summary of the review and its implications is set out later in this chapter.

Historically, the decision to list a building was shrouded in mystery for fear that the structure being considered might be demolished or significantly altered if knowledge of this became public, albeit that in recent years and as matter of good practice English Heritage would engage in some publicity before a survey was conducted. The consideration of a potential entry to the list was, until 2008, undertaken without notice to the occupier or owner. Such an approach was greatly influenced by the demolition of the Firestone Building, an Art Deco 1930s factory near Heathrow, during the weekend prior to its listing coming into effect. To avoid further recurrence of this, powers were introduced to allow the service of a Building Preservation Notice to prevent demolition, alteration or an extension of a building without consent for a period of six months, while the building is considered for listing. The owner or developer may seek a certificate that a building is not intended to be listed (a Certificate of Immunity) to avoid any uncertainty regarding its future potential for development. This immunity certificate, if granted, lasts for five years, after which the building may be considered afresh. Such a certificate was issued against the former Bankside Power Station on the South Bank of the River Thames in London in 1994. This allowed the owners of the site, Nuclear Electric, to market the building for sale and redevelopment without the possibility of listing (until 1999 at the earliest). In

2000 the building re-opened as Tate Modern, housing the Tate's collection of twentieth-century international art and contemporary exhibitions. The building's vast internal spaces and boiler house were well suited to providing gallery space, at a cost of some £80 million, but without the need to obtain Listed Building consent. In the post-2010 regime a new process, called the 'interim protection order', will provide temporary protection against demolition or alteration while a structure is being considered for listing.

The principles of selection for listing were amended in 2007 under Circular 1/07 which selectively updated Planning Policy Guidance Note 15 and established that the building must have 'special' interest, taken to be directly related to architectural or historic value. This might involve, for example, the design of the building and/or innovation in its construction method, its decoration or craftsmanship used (architectural) and social, economic or cultural links to history or individuals, together with some quality of interest in the physical fabric of the building (historic). When listing a building, English Heritage will also take into account the extent to which the exterior links with its neighbours, to create a group value. English Heritage themselves publish a comprehensive series of papers on criteria for selection, ranging from commercial to residential sectors and including much detail on the age and architectural or historic features necessary for a building to make the list. This information is easily accessed on their website at www.english-heritage.org.uk.

General principles for listing

Specific groups may be identified in terms of listing:

- All buildings prior to 1700 that survive in anything like their original condition.
- Most buildings erected between 1700 and 1840.
- Buildings erected after 1840 are listed only if they are of definite quality and character – for example, the principal works of important architects, or those exhibiting particular design quality of workmanship employed in the building's construction and ultimate external or internal appearance.
- Buildings of high quality, erected between 1914 and 1939 – for example, Hoover Building, Perivale, London, which has an Art Deco façade on a 1930s factory, and Battersea Power Station (a unique power station in the middle of London). These buildings represent examples of high-quality design during the inter-war period. However, listing is no guarantee of preservation – Battersea Power Station has lain empty and increasingly derelict since it ceased operating.
- Post-war to present day: only outstanding buildings. This criterion applies to buildings more than thirty years old. Buildings less than ten years old are listed exceptionally and if under threat of alteration/demolition and of exceptional quality. The consideration of such exceptional buildings less than ten years old was only introduced in 2007. The first building to be listed under

the thirty-year rule was Bracken House in the City of London (former home of the Financial Times newspaper and designed by Sir Albert Richardson), built 1956–59 and listed in 1991. Other examples include Centre Point in New Oxford Street, London (by Seifert and Partners) built 1961–65 and listed (at the third attempt) in 1995. The listing criteria acknowledged this building's architectural innovation and pre-cast sculptural concrete curtain walling to decorate the external elevation. This tower block of offices, flats and shops was admired as a symbol of 'swinging London' (Harwood 2000). Post-war listing has resulted in many unique and unusual structures being protected, such as a vast concrete sugar silo in Liverpool (Grade II*), a road viaduct near Wakefield (Grade II), a university engineering building in Leicester (Grade II*), and a new Civic Centre in Newcastle (Grade II). The architectural or historic rationale behind these listings may not always be apparent. Arguably it is the case that 'listing has to be one step ahead of fashion' (Harwood 2000). The consequence is that such buildings are protected ahead of any threat of demolition and that the next generation will appreciate them more than the existing one for their preservation of the past. Table 7.1 gives further examples.

What is listed?

Once a building is listed, then listed building consent (LBC) is required for any works that would result in its demolition, alteration or extension in any manner likely to affect its character as a building of special architectural or historic interest. The need for planning permission is entirely separate from listed building consent and, in practice, LBC extends far beyond what would require planning permission, because it deals with 'any matter' affecting the character of the listed building. Demolition was defined in *Shimizu UK Limited* v. *Westminster City Council* (1997) as meaning clearing a site for redevelopment, in effect removing all or nearly all of the structure. All proposed demolitions required listed building consent and no room for interpretation or judgement exists. Partial demolition, by contrast, is interpreted in listed building legislation as an alteration, itself taken to be a change in position, size, and shape or form of a building. This only requires listed building consent if it would affect the character of the building as a building of special architectural or historic importance. In other words, a measure of interpretation is required, with the local authority and sometimes English Heritage vested with the responsibility of making that decision.

The entire building is protected and this includes both internal and external fabric. For example, a period plaster ceiling or a particular type of historic (usually lime) mortar used between brickwork or external paintwork may be considered to be of historic or architectural importance, and works to them will affect the character of the building and therefore require listed building consent. General cleaning and repair works would not require listed building consent, whereas

Table 7.1 Examples of listed buildings

	Building	Reasons
Prior to 1700	Hampton Court	Begun by Cardinal Wolsey in 1515 and later enlarged by Henry VIII in 1531, using Renaissance architects.
1700–1840	Radcliffe Camera, Oxford. Part of the Bodleian Library, University of Oxford	1739–49 by James Gibbs. A unique building in England with a circular form and strong Italian influence in its design.
1849–1914	Midland Hotel, St Pancras railway station and Eurostar terminal since 2007, London	Gothic revival architecture (1868–72, Sir George Gilbert Scott)
1914–1939	Penguin Pool at London Zoo	Novel use of moulded reinforced concrete to create curved form (1934–38, Berthold Lubetkin)
	Red telephone box (Kiosk No. 2 or K2)	Design by Sir Giles Gilbert Scott, 1925. The wooden prototype is outside Burlington House, Piccadilly, London.
	Stockport Plaza	1932 Art Deco cinema with dramatic white terracotta façade and 100m of neon lighting. Grade II*
1945 + 30-year rule	Bracken House, City of London	Highly decorative façade, 1956–59
10-year rule	Wills Faber office building, Ipswich, Suffolk	Excellent example of a modern office building with external appearance strongly influenced by lighting technology. Built 1975 and listed in April 1991, following proposals to alter the interior to construct a swimming pool within the interior.

painting (in a different colour) probably would require consent. Any object or structure fixed to the building that is either external (e.g. guttering downpipes) or internal (e.g. wall panelling) is also protected, as is any object or structure within the curtilage and forming a part of the land since before 1 July 1948; that is, any outbuilding (garden house, statues, gazebos) will be listed only if it was constructed before 1948. A celebrated case involved the removal of a statue (*The Three Graces*) at Woburn Abbey in which the Secretary of State came to a considered view that the degree to which an object or structure is deemed to be fixed depends upon the degree of annexation, in effect the extent to which it was permanently fixed or (relatively) easily removed. Certain problems do arise over the nature of ancillary buildings and especially so where the object or structure within the curtilage is itself a building. This has, perhaps understandably become an area ripe for legal challenges (see Mynors 2006: Chapter 4).

Table 7.2 Listed building grades

Grade I	Of exceptional interest (around 6000 buildings or 1.4 per cent in England)
Grade II* (referred to as 'two star')	Of particular importance more than special interest (around 18000 buildings or 4.1 per cent in England)
Grade II	Of special interest (around 417,000 buildings or 94.5 per cent in England). In Scotland 37,000 buildings are listed within a different classification of A, B and C. In Wales around 14,500 buildings are listed and classified in the same manner as in England.

Grading of buildings

A grading system applies which does not affect the level of statutory protection but does reflect the importance of the building. Three grades exist, as shown in Table 7.2.[1] Once it has been determined that a building is listed and that the proposed works affect the character of that building, then it is necessary to apply to the planning authority (LPA) for listed building consent. Grades I, II* and II thus fall within a national list. It should be remembered that some 5% of planning authorities will compile a local list of locally significant buildings. The status of such buildings falls outside the national system and is a matter for consideration within the remit of local plan/local development framework planning policy. After 2010 the government have proposed that planning permission would be required for the demolition of a locally listed building. (Prior to that date no such consent was required and local listing rendered a very weak method of protection.)

Although many churches are themselves included as listed, listed building controls do not apply to works for the demolition, alteration or extension of an ecclesiastical building that is currently used for ecclesiastical purposes. This would cover the place of worship and not any building used by a minister of religion for residence. The government have proposed that this exemption continues following the 2010 reforms.

The planning authority may grant listed building consent, subject to conditions, or refuse it. The planning authority must notify English Heritage (or CADW, Historic Scotland) of all applications dealing with Grade I and Grade II* buildings or involving the total or partial demolition of a Grade II building. In London, English Heritage must be notified of all applications. English Heritage has powers of direction in respect of Grade I and Grade II* buildings. In extreme cases, English Heritage will request that the application be called in by the Secretary of State for his or her decision. While rarely used, this power tends to affect significant high-rise development proposals in London and has resulted in some criticism of the organization, mostly by the former Mayor of London. Two major commercial (with lesser retail and some public access) high-rise developments succumbed to this fate in recent years at London Bridge

Tower in 2003 (310 metres) and 20 Fenchurch Street (160 metres) in 2007 as well as the demolition of unlisted buildings within Smithfield Market in 2008. All three cases involved English Heritage as the principal protagonist arguing against these schemes on the basis that they adversely affected both the setting of the Tower of London and the London skyline or represented unacceptable demolition of buildings in a conservation area. Both high-rise schemes were granted by the Secretary of State following planning inquiries and had previously received the support of the Mayor and CABE as well as their respective local authorities (London Borough of Southwark and the Corporation of London). The Smithfield Market demolition was refused on grounds that the buildings were still capable of conversion and had architectural and historic value within the context of a conservation area.

Every year English Heritage processes around 6500 such consultations. If an application involves the complete demolition or works of alteration that include demolition, then the planning authority must notify six national amenity societies who each have a specific concern regarding various periods of architecture or historic interest.[2] Refusal or failure to reach a decision within eight weeks carries with it the right of appeal to the Secretary of State.[3] All these listed building matters are considered separately from applications for planning permission. It is a common occurrence that many development proposals involve both listed building and planning proposals, and this will require separate applications and decisions. It should also be noted that some planning applications beyond the boundaries of a listed building may affect its setting. Such applications must be publicized and English Heritage consulted, should the proposal affect the setting of a Grade I or II* building.

Other listed building powers

Unauthorized works

It is a criminal offence to carry out unauthorized works to a listed building. Therefore, the planning authority may prosecute under criminal law, or it can issue an enforcement notice[4] seeking restoration of the building to its former state. Such unauthorized works constitute either demolition or alteration/extension that would affect its special character. A local planning authority will need to decide whether to pursue enforcement or prosecution. It is often more appropriate, even sensible, to pursue enforcement action and not prosecution, due to the differing burdens of proof between these alternatives (Mynors 2006). To achieve a criminal conviction requires evidence of proof 'beyond reasonable doubt' that an offence has occurred and that the accused person is, in fact, responsible. In an enforcement case that burden of proof is reduced to 'on the balance of probabilities' which takes away the need to identify who was exactly responsible for the damage. Thus, unless the works carried out are irreversible (for example, total or partial demolition or removal of a significant feature such as a fireplace) then prosecution has few benefits over and above enforcement, which enjoys the

Case study 7.1   Repairs notice and compulsory purchase: St Ann's Hotel, Buxton, Derbyshire

The hotel was built at the end of the eighteenth century as a principal attraction in the Duke of Devonshire's attempt to make Buxton a spa town to rival Bath. The hotel's fabric was neglected during the 1970s and 1980s, ending with its forced closure on environmental grounds in 1989.

In 1992 the Secretary of State, in consultation with High Peak District Council and English Heritage, served a repairs notice, followed by the compulsory acquisition of the property and works of repair and restoration. At the time there was some speculation among property professionals that this case heralded a new interventionist stance by the Department of National Heritage, and willingness to serve notices/acquire listed properties that had fallen into neglect and involved repairs that the LPA on its own could not afford to pay. Such speculation was unfounded and, since 1992, the Secretary of State has used these powers in only a handful of other extreme cases. If they were to be more widely used, then the Department for Culture, Media and Sport or English Heritage budget would need to be greatly increased.

additional benefit of specifying a remedy. Such a listed building enforcement notice can require removal of unauthorized works and indeed the restoration of the building to its former state, should that constitute a practical option. Criminal prosecution can, of course, result in a penalty or even imprisonment. Most unauthorized works to a listed building are limited to £20,000 or six months imprisonment, upon summary conviction. Research undertaken by the Institute of Historic Building Conservation (cited in Mynors 2006) examined criminal convictions against unauthorized works since 1991 and discovered that prison sentences are extremely rare and imposition of fines increasingly common, albeit that the level of fines is pegged by the courts and rarely appeared to extend beyond about £10,000.

Buildings falling into disrepair

If a building has been neglected, the LPA or English Heritage may serve an urgent works notice, stipulating that the owner performs these repairs or undertake the necessary repair works themselves and recover their costs from the owner. This applies to both occupied and unoccupied buildings and is usually restricted to emergency repairs to keep a building wind and weatherproof and safe from collapse. Further action involves the authority acquiring the building itself, against the wishes of the owner. Service of a repairs notice commences this process, in which works are specified for the necessary preservation of the building. If this request is ignored, then, after two months, the planning authority may acquire the building by compulsory purchase, subject to the consent of the Secretary of State. Should objections be raised against this action (usually by the owner) then a public inquiry will be convened to hear them. Compensation is payable in favour of the owner and this is calculated on the 'open market' value of the building and any associated land.

These powers are used only rarely, and on average each planning authority will serve a repairs notice every five years, resulting in about 300 such notices nationally served over such a period. Such powers of repairs notice and compulsory purchase are also available, exceptionally, to the Secretary of State and were first used in 1992 to acquire the Grade I St Ann's Hotel in Buxton and again in 1998 to acquire the Grade I Apethorpe Hall in Northamptonshire. These cases involve the most prestigious listed buildings and, by inference, the most celebrated cases. Apethorpe Hall is a fifteenth-century building which was acquired by compulsory purchase (following a planning inquiry) in 2004 and the freehold transferred to English Heritage. It represented a rare but notable case of the government interfering in private property interests in light of the greater public good of heritage protection. Incidentally, after English Heritage had acquired and repaired the building, it would be sold on to a private buyer and not opened as a visitor attraction. The repairs notice and acquisition system is not geared to the purchase of publicly accessible heritage but instead the sole protection of crumbling heritage icons and their return to health and then disposal. The objective of securing public heritage for the benefit of the nation is vested in the National Trust for Places of Historic Interest or Natural Beauty under provision of The National Trust Act of 1907. Many special charitable trusts have been established to preserve and permit public access to a variety of previously vulnerable structures. Yet, public funding is constrained, notwithstanding the valiant efforts by the Heritage Lottery Fund (HLF) in recent years. One key criterion for HLF funding is public access, as this funding stream is derived from National Lottery income. Much active campaigning and income generation to protect a number of key buildings has come from Save Britain's Heritage (SAVE), a small but highly effective charity who compile a register of vulnerable and neglected buildings and have fought actively to prevent demolition of listed buildings via the planning application process. Charitable work to save historic buildings is not divorced from commercial realities. HLF funding usually has to be matched by an equal sum raised by the recipient, which focuses the mind on active and economically viable reuse of the buildings. Dean Clough Mills in Halifax is such an example, in which an innovative project team worked on the reuse and renovation of an empty and vast Grade 1 structure to create offices, arts and hotel accommodation, together with the establishment of a charitable trust to maintain the structure and continue the work.

Listed buildings and the development process

When a building is listed, it has consequences for the owner or developer. Listed building consent is required for the alteration, extension or demolition, covering both internal and external fabric. This control is in addition to planning permission and may be perceived as either an additional bureaucratic burden or important control over the nation's built heritage. Decisions on listed building control involve detailed architectural and historic appraisals, and decision-making on applications takes longer than for most planning applications. Government policy establishes a presumption that listed buildings should be preserved. It is highly unlikely that listed building consent will be granted for demolition but it does rarely occur (see Case study 7.2 on the Mappin & Webb site). Development potential is invariably restricted, with greater attention required to architectural design, interior detail and materials used, resulting in higher costs. Grants are available from the Heritage Lottery Fund (administered by the National Heritage Memorial Fund) for projects that involve the 'public good' and from English Heritage for matters of restoration and repair. Around £30 million is available in grant aid every financial year from English Heritage and about £318 million from the Heritage Lottery Fund (HLF). However, no legal duty exists whereby the owner must keep the building in good repair and all such grants are the subject of the discretion of the awarding body. In the case of the Heritage Lottery Fund the criteria for awards extends beyond an assessment of the buildings fabric (which English Heritage would be primarily concerned with) and include widening access to heritage, which includes the history, natural history and landscape of the nation, as well as furthering the objectives of sustainable development. HLF awards are usually contingent upon levering in funding from other sources. The overwhelming source of funding for repairs rests with the owners and, inevitably, developers who find listed properties central to or by coincidence within their redevelopment schemes. Yet, it is often the case that listed buildings are sometimes seen as a barrier to development or regeneration due to their inherent complexity, with developers 'nervous about protracted discussions on restoration and high maintenance costs' (RICS *et al.* 2006). While much research data exists to suggest that many commercial listed buildings yield the same returns as their unlisted counterparts (Investment Property Databank 2006), the fact remains that the system largely relies on owners to conserve these structures and buildings. In 2000, the government-commissioned review of heritage (undertaken by English Heritage) speculated that a 'duty of care' be imposed on owners (English Heritage 2000) and while such an idea undoubtedly has merits (Sharland 2005) the de facto situation currently is that the legislation imposes this in a negative way, by default, should a building fall into disrepair or unauthorized works be undertaken.

The fact remains that listed status may enhance value because of the cachet of period features or, conversely, reduce value as many institutional investors perceive such buildings as resulting in higher costs and poorer returns compared to unlisted ones. In recent years, mostly dating from the new millennium, listed buildings and the heritage sector generally have undergone a review of policy priorities. Increasingly, heritage has been viewed as not just historic bricks and mortar (accepting that these are inherently of importance in any event) but as fundamental to the quality of life, to achieving sustainability, promoting

Case study 7.2   Demolition of listed buildings: The Mappin & Webb site, No. 1 Poultry in the City of London

The site comprised a group of eight Grade II listed buildings located within the Bank of England conservation area in the ancient heart of the City. The buildings were listed between 1970 and 1975, but towards the end of that decade the upper storeys, previously used for small offices, became vacant. Such small office suites were no longer required in the City of London, and the site's owner, Lord Palumbo, sought to redevelop it for modern office floor-space. Lord Palumbo's first proposal, in 1985, involved demolition of all the buildings and their replacement by a 90-metre tower designed by the modern architect Mies Van der Rohe. The planning authority, the Corporation of London, refused listed building consent, and planning permission and subsequent appeals were dismissed.

In 1986 a second proposal was submitted, by the architect Sir James Stirling. This also incorporated demolition of the existing buildings, but replacement with a modern building of similar bulk. Again, listed building consent and planning permission were refused, but the Secretary of State granted a subsequent appeal. Save Britain's Heritage (SAVE), a heritage pressure group and third party at the appeal, challenged the decision in the courts. The matter was finally considered by the House of Lords* in 1991, five years after the submission of the original planning application. The key legal issue was whether the Secretary of State was entitled to permit demolition, contrary to his own policy in circular guidance, in which a presumption was established in favour of the preservation of a listed building. The inspector's decision letter, accepted and supported by the Secretary of State, concluded that the Stirling scheme was an 'architectural masterpiece' and that this was considered sufficient to override that presumption. Their Lordships accepted that the Secretary of State was entitled to take this view on the merits of the case, although this did not establish that in future the demolition of all listed buildings would be permitted in the event of the replacement being considered to be of greater architectural merit.

The presumption remained intact if perhaps a little 'dented' by this outcome. The appeal decision, supported by legal judgement, illustrates the wide discretion in decision-making within the British system to permit the demolition of a listed building in certain cases.

* *Save Britain's Heritage* v. *No. 1 Poultry Ltd and the Secretary of State* (1991) 1 WLR 153, *The Times* (1 March), *Estates Gazette* (Case summary 24), *Chartered Surveyor Weekly* (28 March).

Case study 7.3   The Hoover Building, Perivale, West London

The Hoover Building was built in 1932 and formed part of a complex of several buildings comprising factory, offices, staff club and canteen, commissioned by Hoover for its British headquarters and designed by the architectural practice of Wallace Gilbert & Partners. The frontage building incorporated into the Art Deco style of the 1930s Gilbert's love for Egyptian decoration, to create a spectacular façade. The factory buildings were hidden behind this elaborate façade.

Hoover vacated the building in 1980, and in 1985 the frontage buildings were listed as Grade II* which resulted in the automatic listing of all the factory buildings (either attached to the frontage or within the curtilage and built before 1948). The buildings remained vacant until 1990, when the entire site was acquired by Tesco Stores Limited, with a view to some form of superstore development.

The London Borough of Ealing, in consultation with English Heritage, granted a series of listed building consents and planning permissions, following a change in their own policies that had previously resisted a loss of industrial employment uses on this site. The Tesco scheme involved demolition of rearward factory buildings and construction of a 41,500 ft² superstore, together with extensive refurbishment and restoration to the frontage buildings. Work was completed during late 1992.

By permitting the new superstore, this outstanding landmark listed building could be returned to the glory of its original 1930s architectural splendour.

regeneration/urban and rural renaissance, as well as making a key contribution to economic and social well-being. This reappraisal began with a series of reviews comprising 'The Power of Place' (undertaken by English Heritage) and 'A Force for our Future' (Department for Culture, Media and Sport 2001). Both reviews acknowledged the contribution made by heritage to regeneration, sustainable tourism and educational/community work. A collective vision was presented in which heritage was very much a key component of a broader sustainable agenda. Yet, it was also noted that a substantial number of people saw heritage as having no relevance to them, and greater attention needed to be paid to its role in achieving social inclusion (Stubbs 2004). Professor Stuart Hall, former professor of sociology at the Open University, encapsulated this brilliantly when he said 'National heritage is a powerful source of meaning: those who can't see themselves reflected in the mirror are therefore excluded' (Benjamin 2007). One consequence of this shift in policy was the production of annual 'State of the Historic Environment Reports' (SHERs) which, amongst other things, assess the contribution made by historic assets towards cultural, economic and social dimensions of contemporary life. A recurring theme in these reports has been the key benefit provided by the economic value. English Heritage themselves have moved to the vanguard of this new policy direction. A host of new policy initiatives have sought a fundamental reappraisal of heritage. This has manifested itself in a number of ways, notably in positioning heritage as a key part of the government's growth strategy (with initiatives like characterization, to record historic assets ahead of growth planning) as well as producing an overhaul of the entire listing process (see below). 'Heritage Counts', produced by English Heritage in the second year of the SHERs initiative (2003) stated, in the foreword, that 'our heritage is all around us. It permeates daily life, enriching its quality and helping to define who we area'. In the same year, English Heritage produced guidance on tall buildings, which gave a new emphasis to the notion of conservation (as opposed to preservation), by arguing that this involves acceptable change providing that the historic context is respected. Work on regeneration followed (2005) in which the benefits of heritage as a catalyst of change were combined with the reuse and sustainability benefits provided by the sector (English Heritage 2005). The benefits of reuse were supported by a host of statistics and, very memorably, the fact that repairing a typical Victorian terraced house uses 40–60 per cent less energy than replacing it with a new home. Even the historic value of suburban development was celebrated (focusing on the period 1840–1939) and concern expressed that a push to raise the density of new development may introduce a significant change to some celebrated residential suburbs (English Heritage 2007b). The value of regeneration was comprehensively examined in a 2006 report (RICS *et al.*) which helpfully divided the benefits between direct and indirect value, that is to say the creation of economic rent or capital value (direct) and less tangible values of identity and inclusion derived from physical, community and employment benefits (indirect). A key conclusion was that 'there is a strong economic case for regenerating historic buildings. The benefits relate not only to the individual building but also to the wider area and community' (RICS *et al.* 2006). In seeking to take this entire historic sector forward, English Heritage developed (in 2007–08) a set of conservation principles. These set out to harness the entire spectrum of benefits derived from the historic environment and geared to delivering a sustainable management of assets. Conservation is enshrined as 'the process of managing change in ways that will best sustain the significance of a place in its setting while recognising opportunities to reveal or reinforce its value for present and future generations' (English Heritage 2007b). It was argued that the historic environment is highly relevant to the creation of local significance and the development of a 'power of place' (National Trust *et al.* 2004). A new emphasis was given to the management of acceptable change and in assessing the key significance of heritage buildings, spaces and landscapes. This collective reappraisal of value would need to be accompanied by a new legislative framework. The necessary legal revisions to achieve this were contained within the 'Heritage Protection Review' which commenced in 2004, reported (in a government White Paper) in 2007 and created legislative reform in 2009.

Listed building control and the Heritage Protection Review

By 1970, some 120,000 buildings were listed. By the mid-2000s the figure had increased to 372,039 listed building entries on the register, of which only around 8 per cent were Grade I or II*. Thus, protected heritage buildings in England amounted to about 1 in every 40 of the country's total stock of buildings. It was estimated by English Heritage in January 1992 that 8.3 per cent (36,700) of all the listed buildings in England were 'at risk' (i.e. in very bad or poor condition and unoccupied) and that a further 16.5 per cent (72,850) were 'vulnerable to neglect' (i.e. in a poor condition but occupied); 2400 Grade I or II* buildings were considered to be at risk (including at the time the Grade I Midland Hotel at St Pancras Station in London, which was subsequently extensively renovated and now forms the Eurostar terminal with shops and luxury apartments). This lamentable situation meant that around 25 per cent of all listed buildings were in an unsatisfactory state of repair at the beginning of the 1990s (English Heritage 1992a).

This sorry state of affairs led English Heritage to monitor the progress of Grade I and II* buildings and Scheduled Ancient Monuments considered to be at risk or vulnerable to becoming so. The 2007 survey recorded a fall in the numbers, with 1273 Grade I and II* buildings at risk. This represented a significant reduction on the equivalent figure for 1992 (2400 Grade I/II* found to be at risk). Nevertheless, this is still a high figure, especially so when it relates to the top two categories of heritage building. A number of factors may be identified as influential on the future preservation of listed stock, although ultimately the solution lies with funding, because English Heritage themselves have estimated that around 87 per cent of those buildings 'at risk' require some form of subsidy to return them to a viable economic use. Grade II buildings in a parlous state are recorded on local lists compiled by local authorities. Their prospects of receiving grant-aid are remote, with local authorities having limited budgets, albeit that some may fit within Heritage Lottery Fund criteria, especially those within areas of anticipated growth in which heritage 'building blocks' will assist greatly in forming communities. A notable example is within the Thames Gateway growth corridor where Grade II 'at-risk' buildings may provide a vital link to both public access (a key criterion for HLF) and the creation of a sense of place and a feeling of belonging for new and existing residents. The vast majority of Grade II listed buildings, therefore, fall upon the owner's income to sustain their physical survival.

In July 2003 the government published a consultation paper 'Protecting our historic environment: Making the system work better' and so embarked on a discussion of future reform. Such reform would be geared to deal with the very 'nuts and bolts' of heritage protection by addressing the system of recording the special interest of buildings and monuments. Control over the protection of heritage assets had grown incrementally and was increasingly viewed as lacking transparency and a measure of openness. The following year a series of formal proposals were put forward in the 'Review of heritage protection: The way forward'. Future reforms were divided into the short-term and long-term. In the short term, the government would introduce a series of minor and/or policy reforms to enhance the powers of English Heritage (who became responsible for all listing decisions in 2005) and to review the selection criteria involved in those decisions (undertaken in 2007). In the longer term, legislation would be introduced to comprehensively overhaul the statutory (i.e. listing) regime that constitutes the very bedrock of the system. A further three years would pass until the publication of the, by then, much awaited 2007 White Paper which signalled the structure of future legislation. The period between 2004 and 2009 formed something of an interregnum, with informed commentators speculating on the ultimate final completion of these reforms by 2010 at the earliest (Mynors 2006) or indeed the missed opportunity of a more radical vision based on stronger enforcement powers and a rethink of selection criteria (Sharland 2005).

The government's White Paper 'Heritage protection for the 21st century' was published on 8 March 2007, with a consultation period of nearly four months. On reflection, it did not present a radical vision but one that sought to rationalize the many different protection regimes, and one that sought to introduce some transparency and judicial fairness in the determination of special interest and therefore, the decision to protect a building or site. Three core principles were advanced:

First, the principle of a unified approach to heritage protection. The original 2003 consultation paper posed the question 'how can the system be made to work better?' and the government's firm view in response was that too many systems existed, leading to confusion and complication. Instead the White Paper proposed 'a new holistic approach towards the historic environment by creating a single designation regime' (DCMS 2007). One single designation regime would replace several former systems of listing buildings, scheduling ancient monuments/ archaeological areas or registering parks and gardens or historic battlefields and historic marine sites. English Heritage would be responsible for all the decisions for inclusion on the newly established register. World heritage sites would continue to be designated by UNESCO but would be included within the unified register. All designations of Grade I, II* and II will be maintained and extended to all entries within the register. This represented a shift away from initial ideas floated by government which had proposed to delete a national designation of Grade II and remove these from national protection to 'local lists', administered solely by local councils. Listed building consent and schedule monument consent would be replaced by a single permission, known as the historic asset consent.

The second principle advanced was that of improving public involvement in the system. The White Paper noted that 'the system can be perceived as opaque and complex' and required greater levels of consultation and scrutiny. Reforms here were based around a combination of more information to explain how English Heritage would select future assets and a procedure to reflect the need to make 'designation' (as it would now be known) more open and fair. Should a building or site be considered by English Heritage for its special value, then the owners, local authority and national amenity societies would be formally consulted. While this was underway, the site would be given a special interim legal protection (replacing building preservation notices), to protect against any hasty demolition or inappropriate alteration. Should that building or site be formally recommended for designation, then the owner will be able to exercise a right of challenge in the form of an appeal, thus referring the decision to an independent panel of experts.

The third principle was that of engaging with the planning system. The White Paper acknowledged that the historic environment constituted 'an essential element of building sustainable communities'. The policy emphasis previously given to the benefits of heritage in fostering a sense of place would now be a part of the new legislative system. A new statutory management agreement (to be known as the heritage partnership agreement) would be created to allow strategic management of large sites without the need to seek multiple consents over a period of many years. Such agreements could be tailor-made for regeneration and growth projects and/or include complex sites. Greater certainty could be built into such projects with the prior consent of owners, managers, developers, local authorities and English Heritage. Such work was piloted by English Heritage (in 2005) to assess what was a favourable outcome on a number of large and complicated sites. Research commissioned by English Heritage indicated that this idea would work best for large sites and/or those with more than one type of asset.

The overarching aims of the White Paper were designed to improve the speed at which decisions were made and (perhaps more significantly) introduce a system that both made logical sense in its unified regime and would cut unnecessary red tape and allow the historic environment to deliver significant gains to regeneration and growth. Fresh legislation would be required, and a significant resource would need to be devoted to the introduction of much new information, including publication of selection guides for buildings, updating the national register and new training. English Heritage would rise to this challenge with the launch of a new heritage portal website in addition to further development of its excellent Historic Environment Local Management (HELM) website. The desire of the organization to update the existing entries to the register (i.e. all list descriptions for buildings, monuments and landscapes) would take many years and, arguably, be a highly unrealistic target in view of current resources. What appears the case is that when the new designations are incrementally introduced they will be models of the new system, which will be partially grafted on to the former listing, monuments and landscape designations.

New legislation is expected to come into effect in 2010, with a draft Heritage Protection Bill published in late spring 2008. The Bill and then Act is anticipated to cover a number of key areas, including guidance on new principles for the selection of listed buildings, introduction of the unified Heritage Asset Consent (HAC), introduction of Heritage Partnership Agreements (HPAs), new approaches to local designations and conservation areas, publication of new principles in marine designation and a refinement of ecclesiastical exemption. English Heritage will receive additional financial resources to deliver training and to implement the new designation programme. A draft Bill was published on 2 April 2008. The draft nature (prior to its formal parliamentary progress) indicated that the Department of Culture, Media and Sport was open to further suggestions as to improvement or revision. The gist was as expected from the White Paper, notably a single system for designations to replace listing, scheduling and registering, the power to designate formally passing to English Heritage, creation of a Heritage Asset Consent, introduction of interim protection while the building was considered for listing, and merger of conservation area consent with planning permissions. In announcing the draft bill, the Secretary of State for Culture encapsulated the changes as 'Unifying the protection regime, encouraging wider participation and making the system more transparent'.

Post-war buildings and management agreements

Since the late 1980s, English Heritage's survey of post-war buildings has sought suitable examples of architecturally or historically important buildings drawn from all major building types. In 1993, ninety-five school, college and university buildings were recommended to and accepted for listing by the Secretary of State.[5] In March 1995, further recommendations were submitted by English Heritage, dealing with many other uses, including out-of-town offices, and commercial, industrial and railway buildings. In addition, some post-war buildings have been listed under the thirty-year or ten-year rule. The merits of post-war listing generated fierce debate between developers, heritage groups and members of the public. Most post-war buildings were built for a particular purpose and a limited lifespan. Such buildings do not always easily lend themselves to conversion into alternative uses, which results in dereliction when the original use becomes redundant, and conversion to another use may destroy the fabric of the original building and with it the very reason for listing.

Critics argue that such listings create an obsolete building, unsuitable for reuse, which remains empty for many years until the LPA, English Heritage or the Secretary of State accept that demolition is inevitable to release land for redevelopment. Thus, the listing only serves to delay the agony; but this argument should not be used to resist all post-war listing, otherwise an important period of history would not be recorded in its built form. Instead, it should be used to justify a careful selection in which the viability of economic and acceptable reuse is taken into account in the decision to list. An example of failure to adhere to such principles was evident at Brynmawr in Gwent, South Wales. The 1951 former Dunlop tyre factory, with its dramatic vaulted concrete roof, was listed Grade II* in 1986. For fourteen years the building lay empty and became increasingly derelict, with new occupiers discouraged by its vast size and high costs of remedial repair. In 2001, after some bitter rows regarding preservation of the building, the decision was taken to permit its demolition to make way for a purpose-built business park. Ironically, the business park was not built. Failure to take into account economic reuse means that post-war additions to the list will serve to increase the number of buildings 'at risk' or 'vulnerable to neglect'.

In 1995 the Secretary of State for National Heritage (now DCMS) announced that, for the first time, further additions to the list would be the subject of a wide-ranging public consultation of proposals to include professionals, amenity societies, private citizens and owners of the buildings. The post 2009 Heritage Protection Review would ensure that in future, all decisions to list were the subject of a right of appeal and therefore an independent review of the special interest of that building.

Notwithstanding the introduction of this additional right to challenge the recommendations of English Heritage, the decision to list a post-war building remains a controversial one. Officers at English Heritage have themselves acknowledged that after an initial concentration on the period 1940–1957, they have (since the 1990s) turned their attention to an eclectic range of 1960s and 1970s architecture. It seems inevitable that some of these 'little known but exciting buildings' (Harwood 2001), which do not share any single overall style, movement or period, should invite outrage and support in equal measure. Scruton (1996) and Harding-Roots (1998) have previously argued that a requirement of listing is the need for a measure of flexibility. In other words, the structure, both internally and externally, must be capable of change to accommodate new uses:

> To list a building is not merely to endorse its aesthetic or historic merit. It is to express confidence in its versatility. A listed building must be able to change its use, for human uses last on average no more than three decades.
>
> (Scruton 1996)

It follows that most post-war buildings have been constructed for a specific purpose, such as offices, railway stations, schools, and industrial buildings. Consequentially they are not flexible and do not lend themselves to other uses without higher costs and considerable structural alteration, which itself compromises the rationale behind listing. It is more often the case, therefore, that such buildings will fall into disrepair. Commercial buildings are seen as being more vulnerable to such a problem, being 'frequently constructed of materials with a limited life expectancy. They fulfil a role of providing modern commercial floorspace – nothing more – and they have little in the way of any wider purpose in attracting, for example, recreation- or tourist-related activities' (Harding-Roots 1998).

A number of solutions have been proposed during the last ten years or so, including limiting the jurisdiction of post-war listing to the exterior only, initiating periodic reviews of post-war buildings so that derelict and/or empty ones could be removed from the list and, finally, the notion of a specific category of 'M' listing to denote a modern building and indicate a differing status to the other grades. A Channel 4 television series, in 2006, even countenanced the notion of an 'X' listing, signifying a building's identification for demolition because of its brutal ugliness. None of these potential suggestions were ever adopted as reforms or new legislation. English Heritage themselves have, since 1995, placed emphasis on the deployment of 'management agreements' to facilitate preservation and economic reuse of such buildings (English Heritage 1995b). Such agreements between English Heritage, the relevant LPA and owner of the building provide detailed guidance on matters of particular merit in the building, stipulate various minor works that may be undertaken without listed building consent and detail works where listed building consent will be required and is likely to be forthcoming. Greater certainty is established as the owner is made aware of just what will or will not require consent and the likelihood of listed building consent being granted. One of the best examples is the agreement made in respect of the Willis Faber (now Willis Corroon) building in Ipswich, a Grade I office block (built 1972–75). It was listed in 1992 after a threat of inappropriate internal works and is the subject of a comprehensive management agreement which specifically details matters of little importance (such as the basement) compared to key architectural features (the internal partitioning and roof terrace). Yet, in spite of a considerable fanfare of interest following the adoption of this agreement, few other leading heritage buildings followed the lead set by Willis Corroon. The idea resurfaced, albeit in a slightly modified form, in the 'Heritage Partnership Agreement' within the 2007 Heritage Protection Review. This time the idea had been the subject of a more rigorous review of options, which began with a research report in 2003 and then a pilot study of large complex sites the following year. The research report (Paul Drury Partnership/English Heritage 2003) plotted the existing eighteen such management agreements, together with a detailed examination of four case studies involving the Alexandra Road Estate, Camden (1978 local authority housing, listed II* in 1993), the Willis Corroon building (see earlier), University of Sussex (1959–69 campus in a park setting, with ten II* and II listings in 1993) and Newcastle Civic Centre (1956–68 Scandinavian offices, listed II* in 1995). The research noted a shift in government thinking in favour of more cooperative and active management of the historic environment (as set out in 'A force for our future'). Management agreements offered a means of implementing such a vision but had been thwarted by a combination of limited local authority resources, a lack of national planning policy in support of their deployment and (most importantly) a lack of appropriate legal powers. The last issue related to the fact that it was not possible for a local authority or even the Secretary of State to make a binding legal determination that listed building consent was not required. Should this be possible, then a management agreement would offer real and tangible benefits to an owner and/or developer because it would be able to offer a series of 'express' consents in advance, to avoid the need to apply for listed building consent at a later date. The subsequent pilot of Heritage Partnership Agreements sought to address this significant barrier to change by promoting the idea of prior consents being agreed in advance and covering a large number of agreed works within a complex site. In light of the findings reported in the Paul Drury study (2003) it still remains uncertain as to whether these new Heritage Partnership Agreements will overcome the problems that have beset management agreements, namely a lack of legal teeth in which local authorities can give a binding assurance (incorporated into the agreement) that specified future works will not require listed building consent. Removing this problem may still be the principal barrier to effective reform in this area.

The future direction of post-war listing requires greater deployment of such management agreements and Heritage Partnership Agreements in pursuit of greater certainty and predictability, so that owners become more engaged in the process (English Heritage 1995b). Further, the decision to list a post-war building must be made with greater regard to issues of future reuse and the avoidance of its potential redundancy. While the decision to list is made on decisions of architectural or historic merit only, it may be necessary in the future to bring to bear an economic criterion to prevent situations as found at Brynmawr from being more commonplace. A government consultation document on listed building control (Department of National Heritage 1996) argued that 'major difficulties' would follow if economic, financial or even personal considerations were allowed to be taken into account in the decision to list. The government expressed a strong endorsement of the existing system of listing, based only upon architectural or historic merit: 'the current regime is clear and defensible'. This position was reiterated in 2007 with the issuing of a revised circular dealing with the principles of selection for listed buildings (Circular 01/07). Once a

---

Summary of issues concerning listed buildings and future directions

- The 2007 Heritage White Paper 'Heritage Protection for the 21st Century' sets out a new vision for a unified system of consents in which a single 'historic asset consent' will replace listed building consent and scheduled ancient monument consent. This will require new legislation, published in the draft Heritage Bill of 2008 and subsequent Act. The new protection regime, it is anticipated, will come into effect from 2010.
- New style Heritage Partnership Agreements will replace the (1992 introduced) management agreements and will set out to reduce bureaucracy and delay for the owners/developers of large sites with complex and/or multiple heritage assets.
- A new and emerging policy area increasingly promotes the relevance of historic building and heritage in pursuit of quality of life and a sense of community. Bodies like English Heritage and the National Trust are increasingly promoting the value of heritage in pursuit of sustainable development and in engendering regeneration, renewal and a sense of place. Indeed when commenting on the publication of the draft Heritage Bill on 2 April 2008, the Chair of English Heritage stated that 'Our heritage is a glorious national asset that gives us a sense of belonging and of local and national identity'.

Table 7.3 Examples of post-war buildings

Category	Building date	Built	Listed	Reasons
Educational	Templewood School, Welwyn Garden City; Herts County Architect; still in educational classroom use.	1949–55	1993	Use of prefabricated building systems – an architectural innovation in post-war construction methods
Commercial, industrial	Centre Point, Charing Cross Road, London WC2	1961–65	1995	1960s office block illustrative of London speculative office development of the period
30-year rule (Grade II)	Brynmawr Rubber Factory, Gwent; Architects Co-Partnership; Grade II*; Derelict since 1980, and demolished 2001.	1952	1986	Roof involved nine spectacular roof domes, the largest of their kind in the world. Example of architectural form.
	Keeling House, New Lane, East London; Sir Denys Lasdun; Grade II; vacant and derelict, subject to a dangerous structure notice in 1994, renovated by a developer.	1955	1993	Post-war council housing tower block. Example of social housing policies in post-war years and early example of high-rise tower block architecture.
10-year rule (usually Grade I – exceptional and under threat of alteration)	Alexandra Road Estate, Camden; Camden Borough Architects; Grade II*; listed during council renovation works, still in residential use.	1978	1993	Medium-rise council housing block of 1972. Unique low-medium rise design
	Wills Faber Domas Building, Ipswich; Norman Foster; listed Grade I, following threat to interior; still in office use.	1975	1992	Novel use of a curving glass skin on the exterior to create an entirely glazed façade. The glass is not divided by mullions, but by translucent silicone to enhance the effect.

building was listed, however, such matters as economic performance could be entertained in any decision to alter or extend or even subsequently demolish it. Introduction of such criteria at an earlier stage (i.e. in the decision to list) would result in protracted and often inconclusive debate over matter of repair costs, maintenance requirements, and a building's potential for restoration and economic reuse. In light of this definitive view (as restated in 2007) the government appears resolute in its opinion that decisions to protect certain post-war buildings will not, in the future, benefit from the added consideration of economic factors.

Conservation areas

A conservation area is an area of special architectural or historic interest, the character or appearance of which it is desirable to preserve or enhance. 'Special' implies being set apart from or excelling others of its kind.[6]

Conservation areas were introduced by the Civic Amenities Act 1967. Local planning authorities were provided with statutory powers to designate such areas, resulting in a stricter regime of planning control over development proposals. The first conservation area was in Stamford in Lincolnshire, designated by Kesteven District Council in 1967. Since that date, planning authorities have been enthusiastic about the additional powers that flow from conservation area designation, and every year has seen an additional number of designations. 1975 witnessed the highest number of individual designations, with 602, resulting in a total of 3000 conservation areas. By the mid-1990s this figure had risen to 8315 in England (English Heritage 1995b), covering an estimated total of 1.3 million buildings – 4 per cent of the nation's buildings (Rydin 1993: 108) and in 2007 the total figure had reached 9374, with an average of around 28 conservation areas per planning authority in England (Shelbourne 2006).

Types of conservation area

No standard specification exists beyond the statutory definition of special architectural or historic interest. It is not always easy to separate the two limbs, and many conservation areas contain a mixture of both components. For example, Shipley Saltaire in Yorkshire is a conservation area designated by Bradford City Council in 1971. The area represents an important piece of both social and town planning history, created by Titus Salt as a 'model' community in the mid-nineteenth century. The architectural layout combined good quality Victorian workers' houses and a park, church, shops and library. The design and location of its buildings reflect (and are a result of) the social ideas of Titus Salt in seeking to create a better environment for his workers. Therefore, both architectural and historic issues are closely linked.

Conservation areas are designated for a whole range of reasons. The one factor common to all designations is that they are based on areas, not individual buildings, whether listed or not. The historic spaces within these areas are just as important as the built heritage. These spaces may include parks or open land, streetscapes, public squares and village greens, or simply relate to the separation between buildings and historic layout and the pattern of development or 'grain'.

The following examples illustrate the diversity of such areas:

- Oxford City and the University of Oxford, including many ancient and historic buildings of the university and historic streetscapes; designated 1971 and extended 1985.
- Durham: ancient cathedral and university; designated 1968, extended 1980.
- Undercliffe Cemetery, Bradford; Highgate Cemetery, London; Necropolis, Glasgow: examples of Victorian cemeteries; designated 1984.
- Leeds–Liverpool Canal; designated 1988: example of Victorian engineering, not based around buildings.
- Hampstead Garden Suburb, London; designated 1968 and extended 1988: uniformity of architectural design and use of open space. Important post-Howard example of the Garden City planned layout.
- Bloomsbury (Fitzrovia), London: groups of Georgian town houses with square and open spaces; designated 1969 and extended 1985.
- Thame, Oxfordshire: medieval street pattern; designated 1969 and extended 1978.
- Royal Crescent, Bath; designated 1969 and extended 1985: Regency terraced houses with open spaces as an integral part of the layout.
- Finchingfield, Essex; Church Green, Witney, Oxfordshire; designated respectively 1969 and 1968: traditional English village greens with buildings around.
- Leicester Square, London; designated 1984 (within Soho conservation area): highly varied architectural, economic and social character.
- Swaledale, North Yorkshire, designated 1989: rural area in Dales National Park with characteristic pattern of Dales barns and walls.

Implications of conservation area designation on development control

Conservation area designation enables many additional development control powers to be exercised and will therefore influence the decision to grant or refuse planning applications.

Schemes of enhancement

The planning authority is required to formulate and publish proposals, from time to time, for the preservation and enhancement of conservation areas. Such schemes must be submitted to a public meeting for consideration, and regard shall be paid to any views expressed. Proposals may include traffic calming measures to reduce and restrict car access, tree planting schemes, provision of street furniture (litter bins, streetlights, seating, bus stops, etc.) or works to improve pavements and road surfacing (e.g. cobbles) to enhance the appearance of the area. Although many planning powers are viewed as 'negative', in that the planning authority may refuse permission to develop, these enhancement schemes allow for a 'positive' role in improving environmental quality in the conservation area. Unfortunately, financial squeezes on local government funding have restricted such works in recent years, and many planning authorities have ignored their duty under the Act to bring forward such schemes of enhancement. English Heritage has pushed, in recent years, for the wholesale application of character assessments and appraisals. Increasingly, planning authorities are producing such guidance (in the form of supplementary planning documents) for the majority of conservation areas. In more complex (often urban) locations more detailed management plans may be produced to deal with future strategy. Reforms introduced to local planning policy (in 2004) mean that planning authorities can introduce area action plans for some conservation areas, most typically those affected by regeneration and renewal proposals. It remains to be seen exactly how this will be taken up in planning practice, but this new-found ability of the planning authority to consider the development of longer-term strategies for new development within historic areas, bodes well for the acceptable fusion of new development with more historic designs or layouts.

Duty when considering planning applications

Conservation area legislation imposes a duty on the decision-maker (planning authority or Secretary of State/inspector on appeal) when considering development control in conservation areas as follows: 'Special attention shall be paid to the desirability of preserving or enhancing the character or appearance of that area.'[7] This section of the legislation enables the planning authority to exercise far greater control than would otherwise be possible over matters such as design or materials. 'Appearance' refers to the visual impact of a proposal and 'character' refers to the use or activity within a proposal. The terms 'preserve' or 'enhance' have proved more problematic in their definition, and the period 1988–1992 witnessed considerable legal argument regarding the exact meaning of these terms in the exercise of development control. The matter was finally clarified in a decision of the House of Lords in *South Lakeland District Council v. Secretary of State for the Environment and the Carlisle Diocesan Parsonages Board* (1992).[8] Their Lordships relied upon the meaning of 'preserve' in the Oxford English Dictionary – i.e. 'to keep safe from harm or injury' – and therefore, where character and appearance were not harmed, they were preserved. Thus 'preservation' would imply a neutral impact, and positive improvement goes beyond what is necessary to meet that requirement.

The meaning of the term 'enhance' was not considered in the *South Lakeland* judgement. However, following from part of an earlier decision in *Steinberg v. Secretary of State for the Environment* (1988),[9] 'enhancement' is taken to produce a positive outcome, so to 'enhance' would imply a positive effect. See Table 7.4

Table 7.4 Examples of how to apply conservation area legislation

Planning proposal	Harm (negative)	Preserve (neutral)	Enhance (positive)	Character (use)	Appearance (visual)
Externally refurbish existing hotel in conservation area by rebuilding part of structure and repaint, repair elevations	–	–	Benefit, because previously in a poor state of repair	No impact	Benefit to visual and external impact of building
Conclusion: Enhancement of appearances of the conservation area (positive)					
Remove ugly metal shop front and replace with wooden painted version in conservation area	–	–	Benefit, because it was previously an eyesore	No impact	Benefit to external impact
Conclusion: Enhancement of appearances of the conservation area (positive)					
Change of use: shop to bank in conservation area	–	No difference in impact, with similar hours and activity	–	No impact	No impact, because shopfront the same
Conclusion: Preserves existing character of the conservation area (neutral)					
Change of use: shop to pub in conservation area	Late night noise and activity	–	–	Change in character with more activity	No impact
Conclusion: Harms existing character of the conservation area (negative or harmful result)					

Overall conclusions: A finding of either no impact or a positive impact to either character or appearance would satisfy the statutory duty imposed by Section 72 of the Planning (Listed Building and Conservation Areas) Act 1990. Any finding of harm (negative impact) fails the duty and planning permission would be refused on grounds of unacceptable harm to the conservation area in question.

for examples of how such legislative wording is applied to practical examples. For more guidance on development control powers in conservation areas see Suddards and Hargreaves (1996) Chapter 3, and Mynors (2006). Notwithstanding the many legal arguments advanced in these cases, it is clearly apparent that this duty is a fundamentally important statutory provision from which much necessary control and rigour follow, a duty to. The litigation involving the Steinberg and South Lakeland cases demonstrates how important the preserve and/or enhance duty is which planning authorities must devote careful attention (Mynors 2006).

Summary of conservation area powers

Statutory duty

If a proposal results in either neutral or positive impact on the character or appearance of the conservation area, it will pass the duty and should be granted planning permission. If a proposal results in neither a neutral nor positive impact, it will invariably result in *harm* and planning permission should be refused. These decisions are not always easy ones. They require both a thorough examination of the merits of the case and the application of professional judgement.

Complete demolition of any unlisted buildings within a conservation area always requires conservation area consent. Partial demolition has been held to constitute an alteration and conservation area consent is, therefore, not required for this (see *Shimizu* case below). Certain minor demolition works are specifically exempted from the need for conservation area consent. These include any building smaller than 115 cubic metres, any agricultural building erected since 1914 or any gates/walls erected before July 1948. Listed buildings are already protected by listed building consent, so this provision applies only to unlisted buildings. This conservation area consent was introduced in 1974[10] and it allows planning authorities to protect buildings that, although not worthy of listed status, do contribute to the character of an area. Government policy advice states that 'consent for demolition should not be given unless there are acceptable and detailed plans for any redevelopment'.[11] The decision to grant conservation area consent is like any other development control decision in a conservation area and is subject to the statutory preserve/enhance duty. The decision-maker will need to consider whether the loss of existing building and the proposed replacement would preserve or enhance the character or appearance of the conservation area. In the 2007 Heritage White Paper it was proposed that conservation area consent be scrapped and merged with planning permissions, so that the decision to demolish an unlisted building in a conservation area would require planning permission. The White Paper suggested that this would not weaken this power in any way. The draft Heritage Bill (published 2008) takes this proposal forward. This will diminish the perceived importance of unlisted buildings in conservation areas although it remains to be seen if legislative change would actually weaken controls and allow for more demolitions in such historic environments.

Shimizu *and Demolition*

In the case of *Shimizu (UK) Ltd* v. *Westminster City Council* (1997), the House of Lords greatly altered previous interpretations of demolition and alteration as they affect both listed buildings and conservation areas (Blackie 2004). Their Lordships held, in a case involving the removal of chimney breasts in a listed building in central London, that demolition meant the removal of a whole building or nearly all of it. Anything less than that would be an alteration. The distinction is more than a semantic one because demolition of a listed building always requires consent whereas an alteration would only require consent if it were deemed to affect the character as a building of special architectural and historic interest. In conservation areas the legal fallout from *Shimizu* meant that conservation area consent will only be required for the total or almost total demolition of a building. Anything less will not require conservation area consent. Mynors (2006) comprehensively encapsulated this subtle but significant change, stating that consent would be required for the removal of an entire building or all of it except the façade whereas the removal of a single window, a whole shop front, one wall of a building, a porch, removal of architectural details or even knocking a hole into a wall would all be deemed alterations and outside conservation area consent. It should be emphasized that these matters only apply to unlisted structures in conservation areas and not listed buildings.

Restrictions on permitted development rights

Freedom from the requirement for planning permission in respect of certain development in a conservation area under the General Permitted Development Order (GPDO) is much more restrictive, especially in terms of the volume tolerances for the enlargement of a dwelling house (reduced to 50 cubic metres or 10 per cent of the original volume for a side or rear extension to all types of property) and the exclusion of any external cladding (stone, timber, plastic or tiles) or any alteration to the roof which would materially alter its shape (i.e. a dormer window) from permitted development.

Many planning authorities seek to restrict permitted development still further by means of an Article 4 Direction. These Directions under the GPDO take away selected permitted development rights and must be approved by the Secretary of State. Without an Article 4 Direction, permitted development rights, albeit restricted, can dramatically alter the appearance of residential property. Works of maintenance are still permitted in a conservation area and can include extensions, re-roofing, double glazing, painting of brickwork and some satellite dishes.[12] By bringing such work within control and introducing a formal Direction, many house-owners are angered by the need to obtain planning permission to alter their own property and by the fact that the planners may insist on expensive materials being used in construction, such as handmade bricks or slate roof tiles to match existing period details. Yet, a balance has to be struck between individual freedoms and acceptable environmental impact.

Control over trees

All trees within a conservation area, whether or not they are already protected
by a Tree Preservation Order, are given limited protection. Six weeks' notice
must be given to the planning authority prior to cutting down, lopping or topping, uprooting, wilful damage or destruction of such a tree.[13] If the planning
authority considers that the tree is of amenity value and should remain, they
can then serve a Tree Preservation Order to protect it.

Any applications that in the opinion of the planning authority would affect
the character or appearance of a conservation area must be advertised in the
local press. This will be in addition to any neighbour notification that may also
be required.

Conservation area advisory committees

Planning authorities are encouraged to set up committees of local residents to
advise on conservation policy and individual applications. These committees are
usually composed of people drawn from local historic amenity or civic societies,
as well as resident professional architects, planners or surveyors.

Exploding some myths about conservation areas

Do conservation areas prevent development?
No: conservation area designation only prevents unacceptable development.
Although the planning regime is made tougher in a conservation area, government advice clearly states that 'Although conservation of their character or
appearance must be a major consideration, this cannot realistically take the form
of preventing all new development: the emphasis will generally need to be
on controlled and positive management of change' (PPG15, *Planning and the
historic environment*, paragraph 4.16).

Conservation areas are based around listed buildings
No: they may often be centred around listed buildings, but not always. The
reasons for designation do not stipulate that the inclusion of a listed building is
a necessary requirement for a conservation area to be set up.

Conservation areas help preserve buildings
Yes: but they also preserve areas; therefore, open spaces and the separation
of development, street patterns and historic urban or rural layouts are just as
important as the buildings within.

Conservation areas remove all permitted development rights
No: some permitted development rights remain. The only way to remove such rights
is for the local planning authority to put in place an Article 4 Direction (see
section above). The approval of the Secretary of State is required in certain cases.

Character and appearance represent the same thing

No: character tends to relate to use, and appearance tends to be visual (e.g. the buildings' elevations). Conservation areas introduce a restrictive planning regime. A planning authority may designate as many conservation areas as it deems necessary. There is no statutory duty to consult anyone prior to designation, although the government considers consultations with local groups to be 'highly desirable'. The agreement of the Secretary of State, following notification by the planning authority, is only required for certain (not all) Article 4 Directions, and not for the designation of conservation areas. In London, English Heritage enjoys such powers of designation in addition to the local authority. However, the restrictive planning regime that follows designation may make planning permission harder to obtain and, subject to many factors, that will influence development cost by imposing the need for a high quality of design and materials. Conversely, this designation gives effect to valuable protection of the built environment. It must also be remembered that many of the early conservation area designations contained boundaries that were narrowly drawn (Suddards and Hargreaves 1996), leading to a desire to extend or add fresh conservation areas around them. Since 1967 local planning authorities have become more adept at appraising areas, enabling them to define more accurately the special architectural or historic qualities on which a designation depends.

Summary: key characteristics of conservation areas

- More rigorous planning regime over new development compared to land outside a conservation area
- Development proposals must preserve or enhance the character or appearance
- Conservation area consent required for demolition of entire buildings, which may be replaced by simply the need for planning permission following recommendation in the 2007 Heritage White Paper and draft Heritage Bill 2008.

Design control

Design control within the planning system operates at two levels, covering, first, aesthetic control and, second, urban design or townscape. These will be considered in turn.

Aesthetic control

The dictionary definition of 'aesthetic' concerns an appreciation of beauty. In town planning, the term 'aesthetic' refers to the external design of a building. Many architects and other design professionals would argue that planning authorities should not be permitted to exercise any aesthetic control over development proposals and that such matters should be left to the architect and his client, owing to the subjective nature of design. During the last thirty years or so successive governments have issued a variety of policy statements that reflected the many tensions here between 'necessary control' and 'excessive intervention', in details that remain largely a matter of personal opinion. The most recent position is set out in 'Planning Policy Statement 1: Delivering Sustainable Development' (2005) which makes clear that 'Good design is indivisible from good planning.'

Yet, design is a more broadly based notion than mere aesthetics. The former refers to the way that a development can link places and include all sectors of society into a scheme, while the latter deals more exclusively with the visual appearance of an individual building.

A refusal of planning permission based solely on an aesthetic judgement, such as the design of a window or door, could constitute unreasonable behaviour, sufficient to warrant an award of costs on appeal in favour of the appellant. This should be distinguished from matters of good design which address the scale, integration and even sustainability of developments. PPS1 is clear that new environments should seek high-quality and inclusive design, which refers to the creation of sustainable, locally distinctive, safe and accessible places. Paragraph 35 of PPS1 states that 'although visual appearance and the architecture of individual buildings are clearly factors in achieving these objectives, securing high quality and inclusive design goes far beyond aesthetic considerations'. Thus a broader net is cast, and one that covers issues of connections to services and employment, integration with urban form, the creation of safe and inclusive places, inclusion of access for all society and careful regard for the impact on the natural environment.

Design control is increasingly contained in a variety of local policy documents and especially in supplementary guidance (more commonly referred to as design guides, area action plans and supplementary planning documents). Essential components for content include matters of local distinctiveness or vernacular design, covering materials, style, and scale of buildings as well as local plot patterns, landscaping, enclosure, fencing and tree and hedgerow protection. Many give guidance on such matters as the use of traditional materials and methods of construction, the historic 'grain' of development – the pattern or arrangement of the buildings – or the creation of public realm links between new developments and existing areas. Design and access statements have been required for all planning applications submitted after 2006. Guidance issued by government in Circular 1/06 and by the Commission for Architecture and Built Environment (CABE) 'Design and access statements: How to write, read and use them', establishes that these documents must clearly explain the design principles and concepts that have been applied to the proposed development, while also addressing matters of layout, scale, landscaping and visual appearance. The design and access statement must identify the steps employed to appraise the context of the site. A common theme found in both PPS1 and the circular

Table 7.5 A glossary of modern architecture

High-tech	Plentiful employment of glass and steel with exposure of building techniques, e.g. external siting of piping and ducting.
Classical revival (or neo-vernacular)	Plentiful use of Greek and Roman architectural decoration in treatment of the façade.
Post-modern	A mixture of historical details/styles to create unusual shapes and forms.

on design and access statements is the extent to which a development responds to local context and creates or reinforces local distinctiveness. This is not merely a challenge for the author of any such document, but more meaningfully for the designer (or team) who must identify matters of context and distinctiveness when devising and evolving the design. This task will be undertaken prior to any submission of the planning application. The design and access statement will thus explain the thought processes from which the application was created and honed.

Some definitions of modern architectural terms are set out in Table 7.5.

The 1980s and 1990s witnessed a period of intense and at times acrimonious debate about the quality of architecture. Some of the most stinging and well received (by the public, at any rate!) criticisms of modern urban redevelopment and aesthetic control were expressed by HRH Prince of Wales (Prince Charles).

While some of the subject matter was particularly British in content, much comparison was made with good practice in other countries. This debate was very much international in perspective, although its foundation was primarily based upon a critique of British architecture and urban planning, at that time.

Study of this topic began in earnest on 30 May 1984 when Prince Charles delivered a speech at the 150th anniversary of the Royal Institute of British Architects (RIBA). The guiding principles of the Prince of Wales's architectural and aesthetic pronouncements, throughout the 1980s and beyond, were established in this speech. The key points, which are still of application today, may be identified as community involvement, symbolism and decoration. On community and public involvement in town planning, Prince Charles said:

> For far too long, it seems to me, some planners and architects have consistently ignored the feelings and wishes of the mass of ordinary people in this country. . . . a large number of us have developed a feeling that architects tend to design houses for the approval of fellow architects and critics, not for the tenants.

By contrast, he advocated community architecture, wherein architects act more as servants than as masters, helping local communities to redesign their local environments. On symbolism and ornamentation in design he made his (now famous) jibe at the high-tech extension to the National Gallery (in Trafalgar Square):

Case study 7.4   Aesthetic control and urban design: Paternoster Square redevelopment, the City of London

The Paternoster area is located to the north of St Paul's Cathedral. The area developed around the original St Paul's, which was founded in AD 604 and rebuilt by the Saxons in the late seventh century. The Paternoster area has been destroyed and rebuilt on two occasions. First, following the Great Fire of London in 1666, which also destroyed the Cathedral, which was replaced by Wren's masterpiece design, completed in 1710; and, second, by incendiary bomb attack in 1940. In spite of the extensive rebuilding following the Great Fire, Paternoster retained its original medieval street patterns, including principal thoroughfares and a series of tightly packed lanes and squares/courtyards incorporating three- and four-storey buildings used for residential and commercial purposes. The post-war reconstruction ignored this form and layout, with a series of 1960s high-rise buildings constructed on a grid layout. The brutal architectural style, use of concrete and separation of vehicles from pedestrians reflected the prevailing architectural and town planning thinking of the time, but it soon became unpopular among the people who worked in or visited Paternoster.

In 1992, outline planning permission was granted for the redevelopment of 1.7 ha (4.2 acres) of the total 2.8 ha (7 acre) site, which, with its location alongside St Paul's, is one of the most sensitive planning sites in Britain. The scheme submitted by Paternoster Associates proposed to re-establish the traditional street pattern, employing many urban design techniques to create a diverse and interesting street layout and provide 70,000 m^2 (750,000 ft^2) of offices and eighty shops. The architectural form employed neoclassical aesthetic treatment of keystones, round windows, brickwork, limestone detailing and metal railings, drawing inspiration from the work of many classical architects. This ultimate choice of design has not been without a degree of controversy, illustrating how aesthetic judgement is a matter of personal opinion. The approved scheme has been described as 'the most outrageously theatrical classical-style architectural development London has ever seen since the construction of the titanic Ministry of Defence headquarters in Whitehall' (*The Independent*, 3 February 1993) and the Royal Fine Art Commission has compared a part of the scheme to Disneyland. A previous proposal by Arup Associates, incorporating a modern architectural solution, was dropped following strong criticism by HRH Prince Charles in 1987 (Mansion House speech, 1 December 1987). Detailed planning permission was granted in early 1995.

The debate surrounding the redevelopment of Paternoster illustrates that the exact choice of a building's external treatment can, especially in sensitive locations, raise heated debate about what are matters of personal taste. Most property professionals and members of the public would agree on what may constitute good urban design, but it would be impossible to gain a consensus of opinion on what constitutes good architecture. Aesthetic decisions are important in conservation areas and when dealing with listed buildings. However, the many views expressed over Paternoster show that aesthetic control is a subjective matter and that local planning authorities should avoid becoming arbiters of taste concerning the external appearance of a building.

The design battle for this prestigious site was finally settled in 1998 when a second planning consent was granted. The scheme by architect Sir William Whitfield was chosen, largely due to his close links with the views of Prince Charles. Aesthetic treatment is modern. Six office buildings of 88,275 m^2 and associated retail space have created a new public square and restored views of St Paul's.

What is proposed is like a monstrous carbuncle on the face of a much loved and elegant friend.

He advocated greater attention to the scale and decoration of new architecture, identifying deficiencies, and bemoaning the post-war destruction of the London skyline:

It would be a tragedy if the character and skyline of our capital city were to be further ruined and St Paul's dwarfed by yet another giant glass stump, better suited to down-town Chicago than the City of London.

During the period 1984–1988 Prince Charles was to make several more speeches on architecture, including the notable Mansion House speech. His views were the subject of further elaboration. A summary of some key points is set out in Table 7.6.

The Mansion House speech was arguably the most reported of his many architectural pronouncements during this period and produced the most vociferous backlash from professional groups (notably from architects). It contained some of the most widely quoted passages:

In the space of a mere fifteen years in the 1960s and 70s, and in spite of all sorts of elaborate rules supposedly designed to protect that great view, your predecessors, as the planners, architects and developers of the City, wrecked the London skyline and desecrated the dome of St Paul's.

[The] Department of the Environment [now the Secretary of State for Communities and Local Government] does not encourage planning authorities to set firm aesthetic guidelines in development. As things stand, they are only justified in rejecting a proposal if it is absolutely hideous; anything merely ugly must be allowed to get through.

Table 7.6 Key speeches on architecture by Prince Charles

Speech	Key points	NB
26 February 1985	Promoted community architecture and gave examples. Called for architecture to 'lift the spirit'.	'Developers are coming to realise that good design produces a sound investment.'
13 June 1986	That 'good architecture both makes money as an investment' and creates a better environment.	Endorsed classical revival architecture in inner city renewal.
27 November 1986	Brown-land to be used for new housing in preference to green fields. Promoted architecture with a 'human scale'.	Emphasized beauty and harmony of classical Greek architecture.
3 July 1987	Desire for greater partnerships in urban regeneration between public, private and voluntary sectors.	Professionals to act as enablers/facilitators to promote quality design.
1 December 1987 (Mansion House speech)	Dire post-war redevelopment in the City of London, especially Paternoster Square, especially in the 1960s and 1970s	Need for a 'sense of vision' in our system of architecture and planning.

Source: Jenks (1988)

> I am sometimes accused by architects of always being negative, so here is my personal vision. . . . [build] at a human scale . . . at ground level . . . materials . . . ornament and detail of classical architecture . . . [add] character and charm [and] . . . ennoble commercial buildings . . . reassert a sense of vision and civilized values amidst all the excitement of the city.

These concepts were put into practice at Poundbury in Dorset for the twenty-five year project which began in 1996. This site involved some 180 hectares of agricultural land owned by the Duchy of Cornwall and located on the western edge of Dorchester. A master-plan produced by the architect-planner Leon Krier was designed to create an urban and traditional townscape. Traditional street layouts would incorporate terraced housing, courtyards, alleys, and squares to foster a traditional urban feel or 'grain'. Krier was keen to avoid the suburban layouts of the post-war years in which housing was spread out and of a low density. The community theories of Prince Charles were to be realized by a mixture of tenure (housing association/owner occupier) and house type. The urban design master plan gave rise to an 'urban style' using local materials and with vernacular detail, combined with a series of public spaces and community uses.

Table 7.7 Ten principles of good design

1 The place	Respect for landscape. All new buildings must respect their setting and avoid visual intrusion into the surrounding landscape.
2 Hierarchy	Size of building to signify its importance
3 Scale	Relate to human proportions and respect buildings which surround them.
4 Harmony	Respect for the size/setting of a neighbouring building
5 Enclosure	Enclosed spaces to create a community spirit
6 Materials	Use of local materials and avoidance of concrete, plastic cladding, aluminium, machine-made bricks and reconstituted stone
7 Decoration	Detailed ornamentation to soften the appearance of buildings and enhance their visual appearance
8 Art	Public art including sculpture and painting
9 Signs and lights	Avoid corporate imagery and promote individualistic design, notably in shopfronts and signage.
10 Community	Closer consultations by property professionals with the users/occupiers of those buildings

Source: HRH The Prince of Wales (1988)

Poundbury presents a model of housing development that accentuates the aesthetic but is also based upon a robust design, with the creation of an inclusive and connected community. Its construction has resulted in much comment and debate among planning and other property professionals. It also displays Prince Charles's personal vision and has influenced much debate on the design and layout of residential environments. In this respect the development of only a small parcel of land in West Dorset has been highly instrumental in shaping an appraisal of how planners and developers may improve the aesthetics and design of urban development.

Prince Charles gave zest to a debate about the quality of British urbanism. His architectural and design legacy in this area is immense and has had some far-reaching implications. Three, in particular, spring to mind. First in raising awareness of bad planning and design he greatly influenced a debate on the subject, leading to the creation of bodies like the Commission for Architecture and the Built Environment (CABE) and the Academy for Urbanism. Secondly, his design commandments were an early stage attempt at 'design coding' which subsequently became much more commonplace in the creation of development strategies and policies. CABE itself was created in 1999 as the government's principal champions of well designed buildings and public spaces (CABE 2008). Since its creation, CABE has produced numerous publications dealing with the design of public space, design of industrial commercial development, design of public buildings (including hospitals and schools) and the significant process of public engagement in the whole design process. Their work is a combination of research and promotion of good practice. The CABE design review panel, comprising a variety of experts, was initially non-statutory (i.e. it had no formal powers based on planning legislation) but has subsequently (since 2004) been given limited powers in that they may insist on offering opinion on the merit of certain planning applications. In the vast majority of cases they are informally approached by planning authorities to offer such views. CABE themselves will, in most cases, only consider offering feedback on applications that affect either large buildings, sensitive sites or ones that may be deemed 'out of the ordinary' in which their view may set out important future principles and precedents.

Thirdly, Prince Charles's views have influenced the introduction of design appraisal and reflection techniques, such as, for example, 'designs coding'. Design(s) coding refers to 'a set of three-dimensional, site-specific design rules or requirements for development' (CABE 2005a). Prince Charles was an early advocate of such an approach, when offering his ten principles we can build upon. A methodology is offered which can provide an effective appraisal tool within which a place may be appraised and priorities set to provide new development at an appropriate scale – one that promotes local distinctiveness in the creation of a new community or regeneration of an established one. Work by CABE (2004a) promoted this method as a way of both promoting the integration of architecture and public space (as well as key public engagement) and subsequently (2004b) as a key issue for success and speed in the planning process, albeit one that is poorly understood by designers and architects even if they do implement key principles in a variety of ways (CABE 2004b). Prescribing the most appropriate layout of a city is not new and (in the UK at least) can be traced to the rebuilding of London after the Great Fire of 1666 when regulations were introduced to govern the height of buildings and their pattern or arrangement. Codes have established some of the most striking urban layouts in Britain, including Edinburgh's New Town and Georgian as well as Regency proportions in London, Bath and Brighton. The design code is an attempt to set the rules for new development and thereby establish the principles of the block, vista and urban structure (i.e. urban design and layout) as well as the proposed building elevation or materials (architectural form). A series of specific rules or requirements are crafted to indicate the acceptable layout and form of future development. It is easy to confuse this process with that of the 'master-plan' but it must be remembered that the master-plan is the essential vision for future development and the design code deals with the operational principles of how to implement that vision (Murrain 2002). Therefore, the design code builds upon the master-plan and is the result of a wide range of consultations including local stakeholders. CABE in their 2004 research advocated that this approach be formally recognized in the planning process by upgrading the value of such documents to supplementary planning status or even by the creation of local development orders. They even countenanced the idea that section 106 agreements could be employed to enforce the content of design codes. All very laudable in their objectives, it will probably remain the case that design codes are best delivered as material planning considerations, and for them to succeed and indeed flourish they will require the enthusiastic adoption by the developer and/or applicant. It is unlikely, except in the most significant or large-scale applications, that the planning authority

Table 7.8 Good and bad urban design

Urban design principles	A reaction to 1960s and 1970s architecture and town planning
Build on a human **scale**, low- or medium-rise development with regard to the nature of the surroundings. Use of traditional and local **materials**, e.g. stone, local brick.	High-rise commercial and residential buildings, with a brutal and intimidating appearance. Use of concrete in facing and roofing materials, with a harsh external appearance.
Ensure pedestrian **access** and **priority** within urban areas, e.g. traffic restrictions, and pedestrian-only areas.	Dominance of the car, with only secondary consideration to pedestrians (Ministry of Transport 1963).
Create a **community** with a mix of land uses (shops, residential and employment) and housing ownership (rent or buy), together with community participation in planning decisions.	Subdivision between council rental estates and private housing estates and different uses in different zones in planning policy. Local people feel isolated from planning decision-making.
Reflect the importance of the **function** of a building, so a civic building is identifiable by its grand design and decoration.	Similarity of buildings, making it difficult to distinguish the function of each.
Make the urban form **diverse** and **stimulating**, with the use of squares/ piazzas, narrow and winding streets, landscaping and traffic calming.	Urban form dictated by rigid and detailed road layout, creating uniformity of width and building plots, resulting in a boring and monotonous urban form.

will be able to insist upon them in the planning documentation, albeit that they do benefit the application.

Urban design or townscape

Urban design represents the subject area where town planning and architecture meet, that is, the design and layout of urban spaces. In the 1960s a distinct urban design subject area emerged as a reaction to the many failures of comprehensive redevelopment during this period and the realization that both the architectural and the planning professionals were ignoring the design of public space (Tugnett and Robertson 1987) – 'the void between buildings, the streets and spaces which constitute our everyday experience of urban places' (Hayward and McGlynn 1993).

Works by Nairn (1955), Cullen (1961) and Jacobs (1961) warned against mediocre town planning and architecture, and sought to establish a series of urban design principles. During the past thirty years, various people have added to and refined such principles, including HRH The Prince of Wales (1989). A summary of urban design principles is shown in Table 7.8. Perhaps the most seminal work in this area was undertaken in the mid-1980s, culminating in an influential text that set out to create responsive environments or environments

Table 7.9 Responsive environments

Permeability	'the number of alternative ways through an environment.'
Variety	'variety of uses is . . . a second key quality.'
Legibility	'how easily can people understand its layout.'
Robustness	'places which can be used for many different purposes.'
Visual appropriateness	'places as having meaning.'
Richness	'details' such as materials and construction techniques.
Personalization	'people can put their own stamp on their environment.'

After Bentley *et al.* 1985

that offered both visual and pedestrian choices to their inhabitants (Bentley *et al.* 1985).

The principles previously promoted by people like Cullen and Jacobs were to be incorporated into an action plan of ideas, in an attempt to make environments more 'responsive'. But what did this term imply? The starting point, in the eyes of the authors, is that the urban environment should 'maximize choice to urban occupiers'. One of the authors has subsequently argued that choice in the urban environment is very heavily influenced by economic power (McGlynn 1993). The fact that public space has been seen to decline in the last thirty years reflects decisions made by property developers (and the ultimate consumers of that property, the occupiers) who determine that, for example, a building should maximize use of the site to the detriment of other wider environmental issues, like design of public space or external appearance of the building. So, while the concept of 'responsiveness' may provide for choice in the built environment, the importance of other economic and social factors must not be ignored. Seven criteria of what it means to be responsive are advanced in Table 7.9. A combination of these will make an environment suitable with respect to choice and mobility of urban dwellers.

The period 1985–2000 witnessed gathering momentum in favour of quality design in urban environments. Assessing the success or failure of design schemes (measured against criteria laid down by, say, Ian Bentley or Prince Charles) is not easy. Such decisions are based upon an individual's sensory response to a combination of factors involving an historic attachment to a place (or our 'sense of place'). Ultimately these factors (as identified earlier) combine to give 'meaning' to urban quality. Such judgements may not be easy yet nevertheless we know what urban environments we like and dislike: 'the element of meaning in our surroundings is essential to our psychological well-being. A meaningless environment is the very antithesis of what we need and expect our urban surroundings to be' (Parfect and Power 1997).

Arguably the most significant issue for urban design in the twenty-first century will be the incorporation of urban design principles into the renewal of certain 'cultural quarters' in major cities (such as the Smithfield-Farringdon area of inner north London or the Jewellery Quarter in Birmingham, Ancoats urban village in central Manchester or Chimney Pot Park in Salford), and into the redevelopment of both brown-land inner-city sites and greenfield urban extensions, as well as in identified major growth poles (such as in the Thames Corridor between London and north-east Kent/southern Essex) (Smith-Morris 1997), which will accommodate some 160,000 new dwellings by 2016.

By the late 1990s and into 2000 government policy caught up with this new mood in favour of quality in urban design. Two documents have been influential: *Places, Streets and Movement: A Companion Guide to Design Bulletin 32* (DoE 1998d) and *By Design – Urban Design in the Planning System* (DETR and CABE 2000). *Places, Streets and Movement* acknowledged the poor-quality residential urban design created by previous adherence to a 'roads first and houses later philosophy' (Prince's Foundation 2000), in which 'The geometry of road design and the highway authority's adoption standards have frequently created places which relate badly to their locality and are indistinguishable one from another'. The document drew upon good practice (with many examples drawn from Prince Charles's development at Poundbury) to demonstrate how the technical requirements of radii and visibility could be achieved in a way that protects local context, sense of place and creates a 'high-quality public realm'. In effect and consistent with other policy directions (such as in the Urban Task Force Report) in which an urban renaissance would be created, *Places, Streets and Movement* promoted higher density 'urban'-style housing around public space and discouraged the low-density suburban pattern built around a hierarchy of estate roads, as had predominated in the past. *By Design*, in similar vein, promoted regard for local context and character in the redevelopment of urban areas, with an urban design emphasis that promotes character in townscape, defined public and private space, quality public-realm accessibility, and pedestrian permeability, a diversity of uses and development that can adapt to social, technological and economic change. English Partnerships similarly promoted the value of well-conceived urban design in their 2000 compendium of urban design (English Partnerships 2000). A sequence of decisions and appropriate appraisals of urban design required an appreciation of context (building on historic character), creating the urban structure (between blocks, streets, landscape and open space), making the connections (physical and transport-related) and the detail (especially between buildings and public realm). The compendium set a number of key principles, with the opportunity to strengthen local communities, create places of distinction, harnessing site assets and resources, integration with surroundings and providing a vision. All new development must, in essence, respect the context of an existing place, which refers to the 'character and setting of the area within which a projected scheme will sit' (English Partnerships 2000).

In 2007, policy guidance was further reinforced by the publication of *Manual for Streets* (Department for Transport 2007).

Such reports are statements of 'best practice' and do not carry the same statutory weight in a planning consideration as, say, a Local Development Framework policy or a PPG/PPS, although the need for high-quality urban design is itself acknowledged in PPS1, paragraphs 33 to 36. Nevertheless, these reports illustrate the growing importance attributed to urban design by government, on the back of previous work by eminent practitioners like Ian Bentley. As a new urban renaissance takes grip in the period 2000–2010, increasing emphasis will be placed on the design of public space or realm and the relationship between buildings as created by quality urban design. Research undertaken for the Commission for Architecture and the Built Environment (CABE 2001) found that 'good urban design brings better value'. Property developers, funding bodies, occupiers and planners have become increasingly aware of the interrelationship between urban environments and economic and social value. This relationship is symbiotic and provides an important foundation upon which an urban renaissance may be built.

Green belts

A green belt forms a highly protective land buffer around the urban area which restricts the vast majority of development in an attempt to both thwart urban sprawl and protect the very character of the urban area it envelopes.

Green belts were first mooted by Ebenezer Howard in his theory of the Garden City, published in 1898, and they were subsequently introduced around Letchworth and Welwyn Garden City. The somewhat simple theory was that by limiting the outward expansion of his developments into the surrounding agricultural land, which was also owned by the Garden City Corporation, the green belt would preserve the very character of the towns he wished to plan. It was, therefore, a self-imposed restriction on future expansion. Such early examples represented isolated cases, in which undeveloped land provided a 'buffer' around the Garden Cities – there was no national or statutory system of green belts in existence. Movement towards a national statutory system began with Raymond Unwin, who took this green belt concept and applied it to the problems of London's rapid growth during the inter-war years (Oliver *et al.* 1981). Unwin advised the Greater London Regional Plan Committee in 1933 and recommended that an estimated 250 km² of open space was required to restrict urban expansion within the belt of land surrounding London's urban fringe. Patrick Abercrombie echoed these ideas in his Greater London Plan of 1944. In 1947 the modern town planning system was created and, for the first time, a system existed whereby, through the exercise of planning policy, green belt restrictions could be imposed by local authorities.

In 1955 the government introduced planning guidance that established the purposes of green belt policy. In heralding this guidance, the then Minister for Housing and Local Government made a statement in the House of Commons:

I am convinced that for the well-being of our people and for the preservation of our countryside, we have a clear duty to do all we can to prevent the further unrestricted sprawl of the great cities.

Table 7.10 Green belt policy since 1955

Purpose of green belts (1955, 1988 and 1995 policy)	Policy objectives for land use (1955 and onwards)
Check unrestricted urban growth	Provide access to open countryside
Prevent neighbouring towns from merging	Promote use of land near urban areas for sport and leisure use
Safeguard countryside from encroachment	Retain attractive landscapes near urban populations
Preserve the special character of a town	Improve derelict land around towns
Assist in urban regeneration	Secure nature conservation and retain agricultural, forestry and related land use

This heralded the beginning of the current system. That vision is still valid today, and since 1955 fourteen separate green belts have been introduced, covering a total of 1.8 million hectares (4.5 million acres) of land in England, and five have been introduced in Scotland, covering a total area of 15,000 hectares (37,000 acres) of land. No green belts have been designated in Wales, though the coalescence of Cardiff and Newport is prevented by a strategic gap policy – the 'green wedge' between these two distinct urban areas. The majority of this land is in agricultural use, although this is not an essential prerequisite of green belt designation. The important issue is that the land enjoys an essentially open character, so that land may be woodland or farmland, or may incorporate some buildings as long as it maintains its open character (Thorne 1994). Indeed, derelict or waste land without a use, and even unattractive in appearance, may still serve a green belt purpose, although the existence of such land in the green belt serves to weaken the effectiveness of the policy.

Following an extensive review of green belt policy commissioned by the (then) Department of the Environment and reported in 1993 (Elson *et al.* 1993, Elson and Ford 1994), the government published a new policy guidance in 1995,[14] superseding the earlier guidance issued between 1955 and 1988. The 1995 guidance repeated the principal purpose of green belt policy, but for the first time set out objectives for the use of land within green belt designation (Table 7.10).

Green belts: post-1995

The period since 1995 has witnessed implementation of a new green belt policy agenda. The 1995 guidance heralded this new approach with a greater emphasis towards enhancing the quality of green belt land and making greater use of its recreational potential for use by neighbouring urban dwellers. Since the mid-1950s green belt policy has been very successful in restricting urban sprawl. It has been less successful in protecting the quality of land on the urban fringe, and the proportion of derelict land has increased. Little evidence has been produced to show that if developers cannot build on green belt land, then they consider inner-city sites. It has been estimated that about 61,000 ha

(157,000 acres)[15] of derelict land still exists in the urban areas of Britain, and in England the estimated annual loss of rural land to urban uses stands at about 11,000 ha (27,170 acres) (Sinclair 1992). More recent estimates still calculate a considerable area of derelict and/or vacant land, with the Urban Task Force (1999) suggesting some 58,000 ha of brown-land was available for redevelopment, albeit that they themselves acknowledged a reduction in this figure after a subsequent review of their own policy recommendations (Urban Task Force 2005).

It therefore appears the case that developers refused permission on green belt land were, in the past, more likely to leapfrog the belt and look for sites beyond, instead of redirecting their attention towards the inner city. A report by the Regional Studies Association (1990) argued in favour of 'green areas', that is, green belts covering a far wider area to prevent this leapfrogging and to create a more sustainable regional or even sub-regional planning policy. Such ideas have not found favour with the government, which in past years has expressed a desire to maintain green belt policy but not to widen its geographical scope beyond current limits around the major cities, mostly due to its highly restrictive schedule of what may be developed. The 1995 guidance links green belt policy with the promotion of sustainable patterns of development so that planning authorities should 'consider the consequences for sustainable development (for example in terms of the effects on car travel) of channelling development towards urban areas inside the inner green belt boundary, towards towns and villages inset within the green belt, or towards locations beyond the outer green belt boundary'.[16] Green belt policy may contribute to such sustainable objectives, although in isolation from other strategies it will have little real impact on development patterns beyond its own boundaries. Most certainly the government's own push towards 'recycling' urban and/or previously developed land for development (in PPS3 of 2006) has arguably been more successful in redirecting development patterns to urban areas than the essentially negative anti-sprawl restriction on development as promoted by the green belt.

Green belts or concrete collars?

Green belt policy will continue to operate for many years to come due more to the political popularity of such a policy and its easy understanding by the public, instead of its effectiveness in redirecting development to the urban area. This policy is not without its critics, however, who are positioned at either end of the planning and environmental spectrum. At one end, it is suggested that such a policy should be scrapped in favour of free market economics in which the market would itself recognize the importance of undeveloped and open countryside on the edge of cities (Pennington 2002). At the other end, lobby groups like the Campaign for the Protection of Rural England (CPRE) have consistently argued that green belts are one of the cornerstones of the planning system and should be more rigorously applied (CPRE 1994 and 2007).

Green belts impose a necessary restriction on the outward development of settlements. In rural areas 'washed over' by green belt designation, this designation may prevent various local needs (such as provision of low-cost affordable housing) from being properly accommodated, and a shortage results. Planning Policy Guidance Note 2, Annex E (of 1995) permits, in exceptional circumstances, the release of small-scale low-cost housing schemes on sites within existing settlements and covered (washed over) by the green belt. Yet research in this area (Elson *et al.* 1996) covering implementation of such rural exceptions concluded that very few houses had been built in such locations. In the period 1989–1996 only 300 new low-cost homes had been built in villages in English green belt locations. The research concluded that among other things, both national and local planning policy needed to be more sympathetic to this problem. For example, development plan policy could be clearer in establishing necessary pre-conditions for such affordable housing locations with reference to need, location, scale, design, and maintenance of an affordable component. Further, this could be achieved without compromising green belt objectives or indeed eroding or encroaching upon such protected land (Elson *et al.* 1996). Generally speaking, the production of housing policy in Local Plans/Local Development Frameworks produced after this research has included certain policy criteria that may permit more rural exceptions linked to local needs within such green belt locations. Such occupation of these dwellings will need to be tightly controlled by planning obligation, to prevent the assertion that this is a loophole in the otherwise highly restrictive control of inappropriate development within the green belt.

Such a restrictive land-use designation is a popular planning tool, especially in south and south-east England beyond the existing metropolitan green belt outer boundaries (Elson *et al.* 2000 and DETR 2001b). It is argued that the alternative of strategic gap/green wedge policies provides a more flexible, even sustainable, way of achieving urban restraint than a green belt (with its more rigid adherence to checking unrestricted sprawl). Kate Barker, in her review of housing supply (HM Treasury 2004), did call for a wide-ranging review of green belt policy, albeit that the Secretary of State moved quickly to quash any suggestion of any such examination.

The alternative notion of a strategic gap (protecting the setting of a settlement) and green wedge (preserving important open land on the edge of a settlement) allowed for tight controls with a measure of flexibility to permit small-scale and insignificant changes when an appropriate case for development can be advanced. Yet, few politicians would move to amend the status quo of such a well understood and long serving policy. The long-term rigidity of green belt policy may, in the future, lead to a decline in any real reflection on the benefits of alternatives such as the use of alternative regimes involving strategic gaps, green wedges or any other options. Finally, this leads conveniently to the review of green belt policy. Nationally, green belt policy serves an important purpose, but it must be the subject of continued review and reflection. By 2008, if government policy has failed to deliver 60 per cent of new housing on brown-land or through conversion, then green belts may be viewed as something of a villain, unable to effectively contain urban sprawl and foster an urban renaissance. An interesting study of the Edinburgh green belt (Llewelyn-Davies 1998) made

the point that green belts were 'conceived in an era before sustainable development became the over-riding objective of planning policy'. Indeed, citing
comments made in the Lothian Structure Plan (1997), the Edinburgh green belt,
it was argued, promoted unsustainable development patterns by encouraging new
development to 'leapfrog' the green belt in favour of less sustainable car-reliant
outer suburbs. The report itself concludes that green belts are a fundamental
component of sustainability but accepts that the existing Edinburgh green belt,
largely unchanged since drawn up by Sir Patrick Abercrombie in 1949, is in
need of substantial revision. Such revision would be based upon a dramatic
increase in width from the existing 4–5 km (and at its narrowest only 1–2 km)
to 6–8 km, comparable with cities like York (7 km) and Cambridge (6 km).[17]
The conclusion of this study is to call for more and not less green belt, but also
to acknowledge the need for an association between such policy and sustainability. One of the commonest criticisms of green belt boundaries is their inherent
inflexibility or, to be more precise, their infrequent updating and review.
Government planning policy has been largely consistent that any review of
such boundaries must be the subject of careful appraisal in circumstances where
the land in question no longer serves a green belt function. Yet the growing
pressure to find development land and allocate sufficient housing to address growth
projections puts undue stress on councils to release some green belt land. The
South East Plan, for example, sets a target housing supply at 32,000 homes
per year for every year to 2026 (raised to 33,500 by the Secretary of State for
Communities and Local Government in 2008). Kate Barker in her review of
the planning system (HM Treasury 2006a) while not arguing for a review of green
belt policy, did suggest a comprehensive review of boundaries because undue inflexibility was stifling necessary development in some urban fringe locations. CPRE,
by contrast, argued that some 80,000 hectares were 'nibbled away' at every year.
In any event Barker's ideas regarding green belt review were swiftly rejected by
the Secretary of State only days after its publication. Such an immediate and
damming response to any hint of change perhaps reflects the political pressure
(itself reflecting public opinion) which will always prevent any comprehensive
rethinking of green belt policy in the UK.

Countryside planning powers

> The statutory purposes of National Parks are to conserve and enhance their
> natural beauty, wildlife and cultural heritage, and to promote opportunities
> for public understanding and enjoyment of their special qualities.[18]

National parks in England are designated by Natural England, in Wales by the
Countryside Council for Wales and in Scotland by the Scottish Parliament.
Natural England was created in October 2006 and inherited powers from the
(former) English Nature, Rural Development Service and parts of the Countryside

Agency. Principal legislative powers stem from the National Parks and Access to the Countryside Act 1949 and more recently the National Park (Scotland Act) 2000. With two Scottish parks designated in 2002 and 2003, the Scottish Parliament turned their attention to the designation of the UK's first marine national park (anticipated in 2009). The first park to be designated in England was the Peak District in April 1951, followed in the same year by the Lake District, Snowdonia and Dartmoor. The most recent designation was the New Forest in 2005 and the future designation of the South Downs is anticipated with a planning inquiry into the boundary of the proposed park expected to report in late 2008. This new national park would result in the deletion of two areas of outstanding natural beauty (East Hampshire and Sussex Downs). This results in a total of eight national parks in England (together with the Norfolk and Suffolk Broads which carry similar status), three in Wales and two in Scotland (approximately 10 per cent of the land mass of these countries). Protection of the natural beauty of these landscapes is a major reason for this designation but not the only one. Cultural significance and public access are also of fundamental importance and the purpose of such designation is usually couched in terms of the conservation, enjoyment and well-being of these areas, which itself includes matters of socio-economic importance as well as the protection of landscapes and built heritage from inappropriate development (Pearlman 2005). Provision of affordable housing illustrates the problems associated with the need to provide for economic and social welfare (for example, housing for local people) and the protection of very special places.

National Park Authorities

Each park is administered by a National Park Authority (NPA). Reforms in 1972, 1991 and the Environment Act 1995 have resulted in enhanced powers for these bodies, so that they are now responsible for development control, preparation of a national park management plan and countryside management activities. Each NPA must produce its own local plan and will determine all planning applications submitted within the park. Such local plan policies will need to consider the conservation of the high standard of the natural environment and the economic and social needs of the local population. Government planning advice states that major development should not take place in national parks except in exceptional circumstances. The higher duty imposed on development within a national park (to conserve or enhance natural beauty) means that the decision to designate a new park can be a controversial one. The position of the New Forest boundary led to a legal challenge and the area covered by the proposed South Downs park produced numerous objections, which were considered at a formal planning inquiry in 2006 and a reopening of sessions dealing with boundary revisions in 2008.

In 1997 the Council for National Parks, a charity vested with responsibility to promote public enjoyment of parks, set out its own vision for the next forty years or so (Council for National Parks 1997). National parks were viewed as being critical to achieve national and international sustainable development objectives, notably in respect of biodiversity, countryside management and cultural heritage. Yet, future delivery of such objectives was threatened by a number of sustainability trends. Seven such trends were identified: demand for energy (with climate change resulting in soil-vegetation and biodiversity loss in national parks); acidification (acid pollution in soils caused by burning fossil fuels); intensive agriculture (and consequential loss of semi-natural habitat); increased demand for aggregates (mostly from the extension of existing quarries, with 116 active surface mineral workings in existing parks); road traffic growth (with consequential pressure to make roads more urban to accommodate such growth); development pressure (mostly to increase housing provision); and finally threats to water quality and supply caused by pollution in groundwater (such as wildlife loss caused by the introduction of phosphates as a by-product of sewage treatment). The report concludes that to maintain and enhance the longer-term protection of national park areas requires strong support at governmental level, with adequate funding and new designations (such as the New Forest and South Downs). More recently, the Council for National Parks has promoted the economic benefits which derive from designation and promoted more sustainable travel modes to such places. The Environment Act 1995 gave National Park Authorities greater and more unified powers in respect of matters like sustainability. From 1995 (in force from 1997) each Park Authority became a free-standing local government body, responsible for drawing up a management plan and a development plan and for determining planning applications. By integrating such powers with an increasingly sustainable agenda, the report sets out the key objective that national parks become 'models for the whole countryside and pinnacles of environmental achievement' (Council for National Parks 1997). Considerable evidence already exists to suggest that the protection of these high-quality landscapes results in economic benefit through recreational tourism and rural diversification activities based around a growing leisure-based economy (Powell *et al.* 2002, Hyde and Midmore 2006).

Areas of Outstanding Natural Beauty (AONBs) and National Scenic Areas (Scotland)

An AONB is a countryside conservation area of high landscape beauty which must be conserved and enhanced and equivalent in quality to that of a national park.

Areas of Outstanding Natural Beauty are designated by Natural England, the Countryside Council for Wales and the Heritage Service for Northern Ireland, subject to the confirmation of the Secretary of State, and in Wales by the National Assembly. Grounds for designation are the same as those of the national parks in seeking to protect areas of high landscape importance. The principal difference from a national park is that no duty exists to promote recreational use and public access. Further, AONBs tend to cover smaller areas and are principally in lowland areas. The AONB is not automatically governed by a special AONB authority, although following legislative changes in 2000 a conservation board may be established to promote certain objectives. All planning controls remain with the local authority. Policies to protect the landscape quality are usually incorporated into development plan policies. A strong presumption exists against any major development in these areas, and with the promotion of the conservation and enhancement of natural beauty. Increasingly, the production of AONBs management plans are being used to influence planning decisions (Owen and Alexander 2006).

Forty-nine AONBs have been designated in England, Wales and Northern Ireland, covering a total of 2.7 million ha of land (18 per cent of the total land area). Examples include the Chilterns AONB – which follows a natural escarpment from Oxfordshire to Bedfordshire, and Bodmin Moor (Cornwall AONB) – based around a granite landscape in south west England. A total of thirty-five have been established in England, four in Wales, plus one shared together, and nine in Northern Ireland. Designation of AONB is based on an appraisal of landscape character and not size, thus the smallest is a mere 16 km^2 of the Scilly Isles and the largest is the Cotswolds, at a much more extensive 2038 km^2.

In recent years, increasing importance has been attached to the coordinated management of such areas, and government (prior to 2000) encouraged the creation of 'joint advisory committees' to bring together local authorities, amenity groups, farming and other interested parties to agree a common strategy for protection of the landscape, while facilitating activity such as agriculture, forestry and public access. This somewhat informal alliance of interests was to change with the introduction of the Countryside and Rights of Way Act (CROW) 2000. The CROW Act, apart from extending public access to the countryside and improving greater protection of Sites of Special Scientific Interest (SSSIs) set out to improve the management of AONBs. Two key consequences were, first, that each planning authority which hosted an AONB would be responsible for producing a management plan. This responsibility would be passed to a specified AONB Conservation Board, should support exist for its creation and the Secretary of State agree. To date, two have been established – to manage the Chilterns and the Cotswolds AONBs. These Boards come with the added purposes of increasing the understanding and enjoyment of the natural beauty of their areas and fostering the economic and social well-being of the communities within their boundaries. Secondly, a duty was imposed (in Part IV of the CROW Act) upon *all* public bodies, ministers, statutory undertakers and those holding public office when doing anything so as to affect land in an AONB, in which they were required to have regard to the purpose of conserving and enhancing the natural beauty of that area. This was not only a specific legal test (i.e. to conserve/enhance natural beauty) but was far-reaching and covered any public office, thereby ranging from planning applications to the routing of over-flying aircraft.

During the last fifty or so years since the inception of this policy, AONBs have been the subject of much change. Holdaway and Smart (2001) have categorized such changes as those affecting landscape, tranquillity (unspoilt by urban influences such as traffic noise) and rural communities (provision of shops and services). It must be remembered that the visual quality of many of these areas is affected greatly by agricultural and forestry management, matters themselves 'largely beyond the ambit of planning control' (Garner and Jones 1997). Such activity can dramatically change the quality of landscape. For example, it has been estimated that between 1947 and 1983, 95 per cent of lowland grassland and hay meadow in England has disappeared or been affected by agricultural intensification (Evans 1997). Other changes in similar vein have resulted in a loss of hedgerows, lowland heathland, heather moorland, chalk downland and wildlife habitats. As a consequence, the visual (as well as social and economic) characteristics of AONBs have changed, 'all too frequently for the worse' (Holdaway and Smart 2001). Long-term monitoring and a possible reappraisal of legislative control over land-use changes in such areas may be required as the solution to this creeping erosion of the environmental quality of these areas. The Campaign for the Protection of Rural England (CPRE) issued a press release in 2006 which argued that protected landscapes (including AONBs, national parks and world heritage sites) were 'threatened as never before' by development either within or in close vicinity of their borders. These tensions are played out most acutely in the south east region of England where the most development pressure is concentrated and yet in which around 36 per cent of the land area is protected by either AONB or national park status. As towns and cities such as Portsmouth–Southampton, Brighton or High Wycombe expand they collide with protected landscapes, causing many planning arguments as to the adverse impact on these special areas.

In Scotland, similar powers are vested in forty National Scenic Areas, covering much of Scotland's beautiful landscapes, such as extensive parts of the Highlands. Planning controls, as with AONBs, are held by planning authorities, although extensive consultation is required with Scottish Natural Heritage before any planning applications may be granted. Some 13 per cent of Scotland's land mass, amounting to just over 1 million ha, is protected by such designation. Scottish National Heritage may also designate National Heritage Areas to manage recreational and conservation needs in other parts of the country.

Special Areas of Conservation, Special Protection Areas and Ramsar Sites

In 1998 the European Commission adopted a formal policy stance on biodiversity which set out a future strategy for long-term protection (set to 2010) to arrest and reverse the loss of biodiversity. A 'Natura 2000' network of European-wide nature conservation sites was established by virtue of the EU Habitats Directive (Directive 92/43) and EU Birds Directive (Directive 79/409), with which member states must comply. A collection of three designations fall within this Natura 2000 umbrella as Special Areas of Conservation (SACs), Special Protection Areas (SPAs) and Ramsar wetlands. In the UK, some 237 SPAs have been classified, covering just over one million hectares of habitat, and 567 SACs, covering just over two million hectares.

An SPA designation establishes a strict regime of protection for rare and vulnerable birds identified under the Birds Directive. Examples include both terrestrial and marine sites such as the Norfolk/Suffolk Brecklands and the Mersey Estuary. An SAC designation identifies non-bird habitats of special nature conservation value identified under the Habitats Directive. Again this applies to both terrestrial and marine habitats, such as heath and scrubland in Sussex (Ashdown Forest), bogs and marshes in Scotland (Ben Nevis) and salt marshes and estuaries in Wales (Anglesey).

Provisions of the Habitats Directive were transposed into UK law by the Conservation (Natural Habitats) Regulations 1994. Regulation 48 restricts the granting of planning permission for development which is likely to significantly affect a European site by requiring that an 'appropriate assessment' be carried out to assess the impact. Natural England provides specialist guidance in this highly technical area (see ODPM Circular 06/2005). In essence, this deals with the nature conservation issues in light of the specific conservation objectives and values of the site affected. This process requires consultation with the general public and other specialist nature conservation bodies. It must also be remembered that a similar approach is applied to the production of planning policy, and the European Habitats Directive casts a long shadow over the production of Regional Spatial Strategies. The South East Plan has been scrutinized by an appropriate assessment (Hughes *et al.* 2007) regarding the impact of new housing on the Thames Basin Heath within Surrey, Berkshire and Hampshire. This location is protected by virtue of the Birds Directive. The special quality of these heath habitats supports rare ground-nesting birds (such as the Dartford Warbler) whose survival is threatened by additional recreational pressures associated mostly with dog walking. A complex series of land-use mitigation measures have been devised by Natural England and given regional emphasis in the South East Plan to limit the impact of new housing around the SPA. A series of zones is devised, subject to their proximity to the SPA, to both resist new development and mitigate its impact. This mitigation mostly extends to providing new, or enhancing the existing, natural green space to provide alternative recreational space, thus preventing people visiting the SPA especially for the purpose of dog walking. The planning system thus became embroiled in a debate about the future behaviour of new residents and the degree to which they would use alternative space in preference to the Thames Basin Heath. The nature conservation importance of this location was given considerable weight and attention and most certainly resulted in new housing being set away from the habitat to limit the incidence of dog walking and its dire consequences for the rare groundnesting habitats. The debate surrounding the Thames Basin Heath represented one of the first real instances where nature conservation issues (elevated by the relevant EU directives) effectively thwarted the location of new housing and other forms of development within its hinterland.

Sites of Special Scientific Interest (SSSIs)

> SSSIs are areas of special nature conservation interest that are designated to protect habitats and wildlife/plantlife. They are nationally designated sites of nature conservation value.

SSSIs are designated[19] by Natural England (the nature conservancy body for England), the Countryside Council for Wales or Scottish Natural Heritage, on the basis of detailed scientific criteria. Once a site is so designated, Natural England is obliged to notify the relevant local authority of the flora or fauna or geological or physiographical features of the site, and any operations likely to damage such matters of special interest. Anyone performing such operations in contravention of this is liable to criminal conviction 'carrying a curiously low maximum fine of £2500' (Garner and Jones 1997). Today some 4000 sites exist in England, 900 in Wales and 1400 in Scotland, covering a total of 9750 km^2 (6.5 per cent of the land area). Examples include Oxleas Wood in Greenwich, London, and Loch Sheil in Scotland. This land is not excluded from development pressures. Most of the reported damage to SSSIs is short-term, from which sites recover. Natural England produces an annual audit of condition, and the most recent data (2007) reveals that while very few are in serious decline, nearly one-third are 'unfavourable recovering' which means that while their condition is not satisfactory, a longer-term management plan is in place to ensure their recovery. The Wildlife and Countryside Act 1981 imposes a duty that 'reasonable steps' are taken to conserve and enhance a SSSI in the discharge of planning functions. This includes dealing with planning applications and producing planning policy. If the planning authority is considering the grant of planning consent for development that is likely to damage the special interest of the SSSI, they must notify Natural England in advance. In exceptional cases Natural England can secure legal action to challenge the validity of such a permission. Assessing the impact of development proposals is not always easy, and specialist nature conservation evidence is required. For example, sand and gravel extraction can alter surrounding hydrology over a considerable distance. Therefore, a wetland site may not immediately abut such a site but can be adversely affected as the water table around it is altered by an extraction site some distance away. The effective management of an SSSI requires a positive partnership between both the owner (and there are some 26,000 of them) and Natural England. Guidance on effective management is crucial and very much encouraged by government (DEFRA 2003 and 2006).

Nature reserves

Nature reserves are habitats considered to be of national and local ecological and habitat importance.

Nature reserves are designated by Natural England, Scottish Natural Heritage and the Countryside Council for Wales[20] and may deal with protection of habitats of rare and migratory birds or waterfowl, by the introduction of specialist habitat management policies. Such nature reserves may be terrestrial (national or local nature reserves) or marine (marine nature reserves). To date, 273 terrestrial and two marine reserves have been designated. Where the nature conservation issues are not deemed to be of national importance, a local authority may so designate its own local nature reserve, which it will usually control or manage. To date, 519 such local reserves have been designated and they provide many essential living green spaces in towns, cities and villages which support a rich and vibrant wildlife. Additionally it must be remembered that numerous non-statutory and privately owned reserves exist – for example, the seventy-six reserves managed by the Royal Society for the Protection of Birds (RSPB). For a history of nature conservation in Britain see Sheail (1998). Examples include Lundy Island (marine) and the Island of Uist, Shetland (terrestrial).

Tree Preservation Orders, Protected Hedgerows and High Hedges

A Tree Preservation Order (TPO) constitutes an order imposed under town planning legislation to protect trees or woodland considered to be of amenity value and including consideration of their nature conservation interest.

Neither 'amenity' nor 'tree' is defined within town planning legislation. Planning practitioners therefore, most readily, apply a dictionary definition to the interpretation of amenity, where it is often viewed as the creation or protection of pleasant circumstances or features. In most cases a TPO will seek to protect a fine or rare specimen, usually mature in growth and exceeding 20 cm in diameter. The decision as to what constitutes 'amenity value' is left entirely to the local planning authority although they are expected to show that a reasonable degree of public benefit would result because the tree is visible from a public place, road or footpath. Under provision of Town and Country Planning (Trees) Regulations 1999 the LPA must serve a notice on owners/occupiers of the relevant site, stating that they intend to make a TPO. A period of twenty-eight days is then given for any representations or objections to be submitted, after which the LPA may confirm the Order. No right of appeal is available against the service of a TPO. Once a TPO is in force, consent is required from the planning authority before the tree can be cut down, topped, lopped, uprooted, wilfully damaged or destroyed. A right of appeal exists against a refusal of such consent or failure to issue a decision. Unauthorized removal, topping, lopping or uprooting is a criminal offence, usually punishable by a fine. The planning authority may also require the planting of replacement trees of the same maturity. In a conservation area, six weeks' notice is required to cut, lop, top or uproot *any* tree above a diameter greater than 75 mm, measured 1500 mm above ground level.

Under provision of the Environment Act 1995 (section 97) the government introduced legislative reform to provide limited protection of hedgerows. The Hedgerow Regulations 1997 set out a somewhat complicated set of legal hurdles to satisfy before a hedgerow can be protected. In the first instance the hedgerow must be a minimum of 20 metres length and thirty years of age, and not within the grounds of a dwelling house. The local authority must consider specific criteria relating to landscape, archaeology, history and wildlife before deciding if it contains sufficient value to be worthy of preservation. Detailed guidance can be found in Statutory Instrument 1997/1160 (The Hedgerows Regulations 1997). Removal of a hedgerow requires forty-two days prior notice to the local planning authority. The authority, within this time period, may duly serve a hedgerow removal notice or hedgerow retention notice, subject to their appraisal of the previously mentioned criteria.

Part 8 of the Anti-Social Behaviour Act 2003 (in force from summer 2005) gives the planning authority powers to seek removal or reduction (to less than 2 metres) of a high hedge. Such a high hedge is defined in the legislation as being an evergreen tree or shrub exceeding 2 metres. A remedy must be required because the offending hedge, due to its height, is causing an unreasonable obstruction of light to a neighbour. To get to the service of a remedy notice is a means of last resort and it must be demonstrated that reasonable steps have been taken to resolve the matter (involving negotiation, even mediation) and that the planning authority are satisfied that a serious harm to amenity and reasonable enjoyment of property is taking place. A right of appeal exists against the notice of remedy and a handful of such notices are served every year.

Ancient monuments, scheduled monuments and archaeological areas

> An ancient monument may constitute any building structure or work, including a cave, excavation, or remains, considered to be of public importance. If 'scheduled' this usually denotes national importance.

The Secretary of State for Culture, Media and Sport is responsible for compiling a list[21] of ancient monuments, usually following the recommendation of English Heritage in England or specialist boards established for Scotland and Wales. The vast majority of the 13,000 scheduled ancient monuments in Britain comprise archaeological sites incorporating ancient structures and buried deposits. However, other examples include various bridges, barns, castles and other fortifications. Scheduled monument consent is required to undertake any works, including repairs to such monuments, and this is permitted only by application to the Secretary of State. No right of appeal exists if consent is refused, although compensation is payable. Unauthorized works are liable to criminal prosecution. Government policy establishes a presumption that such monuments shall be preserved. In a number of cases, structures are both listed and recorded as scheduled monuments and in most cases these are unoccupied buildings or structures such as barns and ancient city walls. Scheduled monument consent is required for all works affecting these structures.

In areas of known archaeological remains, developers may be required by the planning authority to permit an investigation of the ground before redevelopment and this can be acceptably controlled by planning conditions. The designation of an area of archaeological importance by a local authority or Secretary of State delays any construction work, to allow a full site investigation to extract sufficient archaeological information from the site. This status has been conferred upon the historic centres of the five English towns of Canterbury, Chester, Exeter, Hereford, and York. The legislation requires that appropriate notice must be served on the local authority prior to commencing certain building or other operations.

Natural green infrastructure

Since about 2006 a number of UK-based environmental bodies have become increasingly involved in the promotion of what has almost universally been referred to as 'green infrastructure'. This work has dealt with both the physical provision of such infrastructure and the benefits derived from the associated recreational opportunities. A significant body of knowledge has emerged that has promoted an array of environmental, social, economic and health-related benefits of natural green space, itself an area with the established presence of natural habitats. The new structure for the production of planning policy in England and Wales, introduced by the Planning and Compulsory Purchase Act 2004, is based upon a hierarchy of regional (Regional Spatial Strategies) and local (Local Development Framework) planning policies. The government has introduced a requirement that all new local planning policy be 'evidence-based', whereby plan content is 'underpinned by comprehensive and credible evidence' (ODPM 2004). Thus, much emerging spatial planning policy is based increasingly on survey evidence, or land-use statistics (such as open space deficiency, or access to recreational space). The government's substitution of 'land-use' for 'spatial' planning, in the post-2004 plan-making system in England and Wales, reinforces a desire to integrate environmental, economic and development criteria when producing policy. Regional planning policy must both promote a 'vision' and 'add value' when delivering spatial strategies for the next twenty years (ODPM 2004).

Work by Box and Harrison (1994) and Burgess et al. (1998) has been seminal in the current development of policy geared to the provision of what is referred to as 'natural greenspace', defined by Harrison et al. (1995) as 'an area naturally colonised by plants and animals which is accessible on foot to a large number of residents'. Such a definition is clearly distinct from the more widely interpreted term of 'green space or infrastructure' held to be 'publicly accessible land which is environmentally pleasant from a human point of view, including parks, footpaths, urban squares and pedestrian streets' (Turner 1991: 2). The term 'green space' or 'green infrastructure' is thus a generic expression, which is also identified as covering 'countryside, formal parks, green chains, green corridors and wildlife parks' (Countryside Commission 1991: 2).

The notion of *natural* green space is based around the presence of flora and fauna. Such natural space can be either 'planned', in that natural open areas are preserved within residential development projects, or 'unplanned', which is otherwise referred to as 'encapsulated countryside', whereby an informal landscape around an urban area offers wilder (and accessible) landscapes, for the enjoyment of nearby populations. Furthermore, it can also be 'unofficial countryside', in which brownfield (previously developed) land has become sufficiently colonized to create 'urban brownfields, rich in wildlife, providing a refuge for many plants and wild animals' (London Wildlife Trust 2002).

It has been argued that too much development of previously developed land may 'divorce city dwellers from the nature that they crave', thus denying residents necessary 'emotional and psychological sustenance' (New Economics Foundation and Nicholson 2003: 10). Indeed, national planning policy is sensitive to the potential dilemma that a push to build on brownfield land runs the risk that some biodiversity will be lost. It states that 'Local Planning Authorities, together with developers, should aim to retain this [biodiversity] interest or incorporate it into any development of the site' (New Economics Foundation and Nicholson 2003). Thus, 'natural green space' is a term that covers land colonized by plants and animals, whether by accident or design, and from which public benefit is derived.

English Nature concluded (in 1995) that local nature reserves should be provided at a minimum threshold of 1 hectare per 1000 head of population and that a provision of 2 hectares 'would provide children with an opportunity to experience and enjoy more than one habitat type in a site'. In October 2006 English Nature was merged with the Rural Development Service, together with the landscape, access and recreational functions of the Countryside Agency, to create Natural England. Other work by the Forestry Commission, Urban Green Spaces Task Force (2002) and others (such as the National Trust, the Wildlife Trusts and East of England Assembly) reinforce this growing 'evidence base' in support of natural space within a more broadly based provision of green infrastructure.

Traditionally, land-use planning policy has concentrated upon the delivery of the National Playing Fields Association Standards (the NPFA or 'six-acre' standards) which dealt with the provision of playing fields – in effect, open space for sports use. These standards are based upon a functional provision, itself dealing with distance and population criteria – in other words, the walking distance to open space and its provision per head of population. The six-acre standard has become widely accepted by planning authorities when preparing local planning policy. This may be explained by the fact that such recreational open space standards have a long-established pedigree, dating to 1925 (Turner 1991) and, in part, influenced by the Abercrombie London Plan of 1944 (Turner 1991) when a blueprint for the planning of post-war London and its hinterland was published.

The period since the mid-1990s has witnessed a reappraisal of the importance of, for example, urban public parks and countryside access issues, in public policy and the promotion of accessible natural green space standards (often referred to with the acronym 'ANGSt'). Work on functional provision has dealt with the creation of targets for the provision of natural green space in urban areas, with Box and Harrison (1994) suggesting two minimum targets. First, that an urban resident should be able to enter a natural green space, of at least 2 hectares, within 500 metres of their home, and secondly, that provision should be made for local nature reserves at the minimum level of 1 hectare per 1000 population. Woodland parcels are the subject of similar size criteria, with a threshold size of around 2 hectares before adults look on them as a wood worth visiting (Harrison *et al.* 1995).

The notion of accessibility to woodland and natural green space is more complicated than just a consideration of distance, involving the concept of both barriers to movement, such as severance caused by physical constraints, and social/cultural issues – fear of crime, for example. Yet, the principal justification for these threshold (minimum) size standards is largely based upon biodiversity criteria and not recreational rationale. In effect, the need for a 2 hectare minimum size is a function of what is necessary to permit biodiversity to flourish and cope with pollution. Since the launch of this area of work, in the early to mid-1990s, this underlying principle has become widely accepted. Few studies have gone beyond an examination of biodiversity and set out to appraise how people interpret and value such space, or how natural green space (as opposed to open space) should, or could, be accommodated into planning policy. English Nature (Harrison *et al.* 1995) set out to distinguish such natural green space standards from their NPFA counterparts and stated that, 'neither approach to open space planning recognises provision of natural greenspace as a requirement and both approaches ignore the question of site quality and its relationship with the sense of well being people experience when seeing or visiting a natural site'. The House of Commons Environment sub-committee (1999) in supporting networks of green space (including natural space), concluded that 'human beings need to make contact with nature in the course of their daily lives and no special effort (or journey) ought to be required for obtaining it', and continued, when dealing with standards for open space provision, that 'they only emphasize the quantitative provision of greenspace and fail to address the issues of greenspace quality' (in itself an endorsement of work by Kit Campbell Associates (2001) which was submitted in evidence to the sub-committee).

In 2007, Natural England did some exploratory follow-up work, examining comparative levels of natural green space provision and potential visitor pressures in a number of wards, districts and sub-regions within the English south east region. They discovered an unequal distribution of natural green space within the region, with only 20 per cent of households enjoying accessible natural green space (2 hectares or more) within walking distance of home. A detailed report published in 2007 established a far-reaching evidence base for south east England, in which areas of accessibility and deficiency were geographically plotted across the region. Such an approach provided the first real audit of provision and a robust evidence base for future advocacy work (McKernan and Grose 2007) and a method to be rolled out across other regions confronted with both growth and regeneration challenges.

For an essential guide to the necessary context of natural green infrastructure, reference should be made to a wide-ranging review of literature by Land Use Consultants (2004) on behalf of Scottish Natural Heritage, and to a report by the Royal Society for the Protection of Birds (RSPB 2004). The Land Use Consultants study advanced the consideration of four relevant sub-groups, which provide an essential starting point for the examination of other material. The four sub-groups were (a) environmental, (b) social, (c) health and (d) eco-nomic factors. Such umbrella terms cover, respectively; the contribution of natural green space to air quality/bio-diversity and water run off (environmental); the creation of civic pride/community involvement and empowerment (social); exercise, mental health and physical well-being, interaction and involvement (health), and links to land values, economic development and business oppor-tunity (economic). The RSPB (2004) study provided a wide-ranging review of literature dealing with the health implications of insufficient physical exercise and the relationship between emotional well-being and physical activity. It concluded that physical inactivity was adding a 'catastrophic burden to society' (RSPB 2004: 3) leading to a host of health problems and placing additional (and unnecessary) burdens on the health and social care sectors. Proximity to natural green space was viewed as a fundamental resource, especially so for large urban populations. One central conclusion was that local access to safe natural green space can help individuals sustain levels of physical activity and that, to increase physical activity levels in a green space, the space should be accessible (within 2 km of home), have a good surface, with no obstructions such as stiles, but, above all, it should feel safe (RSPB 2004). There is a need for imaginative ways to promote wildlife-rich green space – 'the green space must appear attractive; being natural, but access routes and facilities must be well kept. It is possible to have sensitive wildlife-rich areas visible from smaller well kept areas, without promoting physical access to them, as the view of nature is a main motivator' (RSPB 2004).

Work by Edinburgh College of Art, on behalf of the Department for Com-munities and Local Government (DCLG), set out to map existing and future research into public space and green space, so that gaps could be identified and future priorities set (DCLG 2006f). Six subject themes to encapsulate previous work were identified: 'economic', 'health and well-being', 'social and community', 'environmental quality and biodiversity', 'physical aspects' and 'maintenance and management'. The majority of work dealt with the physical dimensions of public/open space (planning, landscape, access and nature conservation topics) with a significant, but lesser, volume of work devoted to economic values (property prices, economic regeneration). The weakest area identified was health-related studies (taken as physical and psychological health and well-being).

A study some five years earlier by the Greater London Assembly had, following evidence submitted by the King's Fund, reported that a need for research into the health implications of green space should 'involve both epidemiological research and also practical recommendations as to how the design, facilities and activities available in parks can be made conducive to good health' (Greater London Authority 2001: 56). The DCLG study itself also identified a number of areas for future work. These included work on valuation implications (for residential house prices as well as commercial property) of a host of health issues, dealing with benefits in relation to key target groups and the relationships between linkages and movement, to promote green space use without reliance on any transport (DCLG 2006f). These previous studies only dealt with natural green space as a constituent element of green infrastructure, a much wider concept, covering all natural, restored and man-made green space with a measure of public access. They provide a contextual framework of issues from which a more focused study of natural green space emerges.

Other work by the Countryside Recreation Network (CRN 2005) provided a synthesis of much international work, and undertook a UK study based upon a quantitative analysis of ten countryside activities and the effect upon social capital – for example, criteria based upon self-esteem, depression and tension/ anxiety. Based on a study of 263 people, and spread over ten different activities, the researchers concluded that green exercise has important implications for both public and environmental health. A fitter and emotionally more content population would clearly cost the economy less, as well as reducing individual suffering. This work identified barriers to promoting exercise, but also, in its recommendations, argued that planners and developers should take account of the vital role that local green space (or nearby nature) plays for all people. Green exercise was identified as having important implications for public and environmental health. It has been estimated that some 5 billion day-visits are made to natural green space (in English countryside locations) annually and that there are about 2.5 billion visits to urban parks.

Future delivery of natural green space can most readily follow the model advocated to the Milton Keynes and South Midlands (MKSM) Growth Area Study, by a broadly based alliance of ten planning and environmental bodies.[22] The MKSM study proposed that this British post-war new town and its hinterland would grow by an additional 210,000 dwellings between 2001 and 2021.[23] In this evidence was advocated the delivery of the 1995 English Nature model, and it was argued that:

> it would be simple to calculate the amount of natural green space required to match the growth, based on average household sizes, and compare it with

Table 7.11 Summary of specialist planning control topics

Title	Year control was introduced	Statute today	Town and country planning objectives	Numbers in force and percentage of land or building stock
Green Belt	1955 (limited introduction in 1940s)	No green belt statute – control exercised under Town and Country Planning Act 1990	Maintain open character around urban areas and prevent sprawl	15 1.6m hectares (13%) England
Listed Buildings	1947	Planning (Listed Building and Conservation Areas) Act 1990	Preserve buildings of historic and architectural importance	372,039 in England 37,000 in Scotland 14,500 in Wales
Conservation Areas	1967	As above	Preserve/enhance areas of historic and architectural importance	8000 in England 550 in Scotland 350 in Wales
National Parks	1949	Environment Act 1995	Conserve natural beauty and allow public access enjoyment	14 + South Downs 9% England 20% Wales 7% Scotland
Areas of Outstanding Natural Beauty or National Scenic Areas (Scotland)	1949	As above	Conserve natural beauty	36 in England (15%) 4 in Wales (18%) 11 in Northern Ireland 40 in Scotland (13%)

Designation	Year	Act	Purpose	Figures
Sites of Special Scientific Interest	1981	Wildlife and Countryside Act 1981	Nature conservation of plants, habitats, wildlife	4000 in England 1450 in Scotland 1000 in Wales
Environmentally Sensitive Areas	1986	Agriculture Act 1986	Protect landscape wildlife and agricultural features	22 in England 10 in Scotland 6 in Wales
Nature Reserves, National (Land) and Marine	1971 and 1981	Wildlife and Countryside Act 1981	Nature conservation of habitats	*National* 150 in England 71 in Scotland 52 in Wales *Marine* 1 in England, 1 in Wales *
Country Parks	1986	Town and Country Planning Act 1990	Public recreation	*
Special Landscape Value	1971	Town and Country Planning Act 1990	Development plan policy to keep landscape quality.	*
Tree Preservation Orders	1947	Town and Country Planning Act 1990	Protect trees of amenity value.	*
Ancient Monuments and Archaeological Areas	1913	Ancient Monuments and Archaeological Areas Act 1979	Preserve ancient monuments in the public interest.	20,000 monuments Covering 35,000 sites

Note
* Figures/data not available. All figures for Britain unless otherwise stated.

the current supply, to measure the amount of shortfall that needs to be made up. These shortfalls could be included as delivery targets within the sub-regional strategy.

It must be remembered, however, that provision of natural green space is not a matter exclusively limited to growth areas – it also applies to existing locations. For example, it is a key starting point for the Mayor of London in developing a 'Green Grid' of natural and other green space in areas of open space deficiency within East London. This is an exciting area for future development in spatial plans and policy. It links to quality of life and associated benefits like health and even property valuation. Debate continues as to how certain standards or thresholds should be applied – for example, in respect of Natural England's advocacy of local nature reserves at a minimum provision of two hectares within 500 m of home. It remains to be seen if regional spatial strategies or local development frameworks will pursue such ambitious targets. Nevertheless, the evolution of the accessible natural green space standards (ANGSt) has placed provision of green infrastructure in general – and natural green space, in particular – in the spotlight of new policy issues which planners must confront when devising strategies for both regional growth and regeneration.

8 Sustainable development and climate change

'Sustainable development', 'sustainability' and 'environmental stewardship' are all terms that refer to the relationship between environmental protection and the economic development associated with industrial society. Just as the early public health legislation of the nineteenth century was a reaction against disease associated with slum housing, so in the 1990s the introduction of sustainable development was a reaction to the environmental degradation of the latter half of the twentieth century, which is associated with pollution, depletion of non-renewable resources (fossil fuels, minerals, aggregates), erosion of the ozone layer, and the warming of the Earth's atmosphere because of the production of carbon dioxide and other greenhouse gases (global warming). Consequently the world's climate will change, with profound implications for agricultural production (as some areas become more arid and others more wet) and the ability of cities to support their populations (with limited water or energy supplies). In the UK it has been forecast[1] that by 2020 average temperatures will increase by 1 °C, increasing to 1.5 °C by 2050. Average global surface temperature has increased by between 0.4 °C and 0.8 °C since the end of the nineteenth century. The evidence for such climate change is compelling. Such rises may appear inconsequential in themselves but the resulting climatic change could produce more erratic weather systems, so that winter storms and flooding in the UK would be more commonplace.

Sustainable development is difficult to define and can mean different things to different people. As a subject area it deals with the relationship between economic growth and environmental protection. In some ways it represents a marriage between these two issues, seeking to ensure that future economic growth and development is achieved without longer-term environmental degradation. As Blowers (1993: 5) suggests:

> Sustainable development requires that we have regard to the Earth's regenerative capacity, the ability of its systems to recuperate and maintain productivity. Thus, the conservation of resources is a strong component of sustainable development.

The following definition, provided by the United Nations World Commission, (commonly referred to as the Brundtland Commission after its chairperson,

Mrs Gro Harlem Brundtland) is the most quoted, and has been adopted by many national governments in their own policies on the matter:

> Sustainable development is development that meets the needs of the present without compromising the ability of future generations to meet their own needs.
>
> (World Commission 1987)

A strategy of sustainable development will, therefore, deliver economic growth and development without resulting in long-term damage to environmental resources. How does urban planning and property development fit into this equation?

In Britain the town planning system has, since its post-war origins, been concerned with decisions relating to land use. Sustainable development has the following implications for British town planning. It will influence the existing nature of land-use decisions so that new developments will be assessed against environmental planning criteria, such as the need to halt processes that lead to global warming or ozone depletion. It will broaden the realm of material town planning considerations so that environmental issues become important in decision-making. It will influence the very nature of that decision-making process, with greater public involvement in the production of local policy and other initiatives. The planning system is ideally placed to engage the public, given its long-established practice of public participation in planning applications and policy production. Planning policy will be widened to take such matters into account. This chapter is organized as follows:

- Background
- Current environmental problems
- Future directions.

Background

In 1972 a report entitled *The Limits to Growth* (Meadows 1972) was published by the Club of Rome, a group of industrialists who had commissioned research into the relationship between industrial growth and environmental protection. It argued that economic development associated with a modern industrialized society was resulting in environmental damage. The choice had to be made to continue with economic growth and create further environmental degradation or halt further economic activity and preserve the environment. It was argued that it would not be possible to 'balance' economic needs with environmental protection. This was the real beginning of modern environmentalism.

In 1980, a report on World Conservation Strategy (United Nations 1980) identified an increasingly alarming trend towards damage to ecological systems by economic development. However, unlike *The Limits to Growth*, the report concluded that, instead of a 'no growth' strategy, a balance was required so that economic development could be continued as long as ecological interests were unharmed. A strategy of sustainable development would deliver this 'equilibrium' between the economy and the environment, so that future industrial growth with its associated urban growth could be achieved without a continued erosion of natural resources and environmental quality. In 1987, the United Nations World Commission on Environment and Development published a report of proceedings entitled *Our Common Future* (the Brundtland Report: World Commission 1987). Sustainable development was defined in a way that implied that future generations would still be able to use and benefit from environmental resources. Action would be required to arrest environmental problems of global warming, acid rain, pollution, consumption of non-renewable resources and reduction of the ozone layer. As with the 1980s report, further economic growth and development were not viewed as incompatible with such objectives.

In 1992 the UN held a Conference on Environment and Development in Rio de Janeiro.[2] The tangible outcome of the conference was published as 'Agenda 21', in which national governments committed themselves to an 'action plan' of strategies for sustainable development. The document[3] set out policy areas dealing with social and economic issues (combating poverty, protecting and promoting human health and promoting sustainable human settlements) and conservation of resources to allow for future development (meeting agricultural needs without destroying the land, protecting ecosystems, safeguarding the oceans and halting the spread of deserts). A United Nations 'Commission on Sustainable Development' was established to monitor the progress made by countries in implementing Agenda 21 within their own political systems.

In Britain and in the European Community, Agenda 21 has found its way into several policy initiatives. The European Community published the fifth Environmental Action Programme (1993–2000) 'Towards Sustainability' and the fifth Environmental Action Plan. Both documents set out a broad range of policy areas in which sustainability must be considered by member nations, including control of industrial pollution, spatial land-use planning policy, education and training. The British government published discussion documents, notably the White Paper, *This Common Inheritance* (DoE 1990a), that set out the broad policy agenda for sustainability in Britain, including tackling global warming and the role of land-use planning decisions. In addition, the government commissioned a series of environmental studies, notably the 1993 joint DoE and Department of Transport study 'Reducing emissions through planning' (DoE 1993c) and the introduction of new legislation, notably the Environmental Protection Act 1990, which imposed a duty on Her Majesty's Inspectorate of Pollution and on local authorities to establish registers of data on potentially polluting processes, which are open to public inspection. A requirement, under Section 143 of the Act, that all local authorities maintain a register of contaminated land (e.g. sewage sites, former industrial sites and completed landfill sites) was never introduced by the government, following opposition from the development industry, especially housebuilders. The Environment Act 1995 imposes a duty whereby a local authority must designate sites of serious contamination. The issue of government policy guidance to influence the planning system has been recognized, with several planning policy statements being revised to accommodate sustainable policy objectives and PPS1 the subject of a new annex dealing specifically with climate change (released in 2007). Finally, the government has published a series of strategy documents to set out its aims for the implementation of sustainable development, following on from its commitment to Agenda 21 at the Rio Earth Summit (formerly referred to as the Rio Declaration on Environment and Development). Four documents were published in January 1994, dealing with sustainable development,[4] climate change,[5] biodiversity,[6] and sustainable forestry.[7] Each document takes a long-term view of the various environmental problems to the year 2012 (twenty years from the Earth Summit). As with Brundtland, the UK policies have always taken the view that economic development and environmental protection can be achieved together. In many ways the British government went further than Brundtland, when they stated in the *UK Sustainable Development Strategy: A Better Quality of Life (2005)* (UK Government 2005):

> Sustainable development does not mean having less economic development: on the contrary, a healthy economy is better able to generate the resources to meet people's needs and new investment and environmental improvement often go hand in hand. . . . what it requires is that decisions throughout society are taken with proper regard to their environmental impact.

This is not a universally accepted view. Although the views of the Club of Rome are not given wide support today, many commentators on the subject still argue that sustainability brings with it a *conflict* between economic activity and environmental quality. To improve and protect the environment requires a curb on some economic activities.

A growing awareness of sustainability in the post-Rio Summit world has been translated into local Agenda 21 strategies, whereby local government has sought to adopt policies on sustainability in many topic areas. In town planning, local government is well placed to develop and codify these local ideas into planning policy. During the 1990s, with momentum increasing in this subject area, growing numbers of local councils published such strategies, either incorporating Agenda 21[8] concepts or introducing fresh planning policies geared to a sustainable agenda. By the mid-1990s some county councils took a lead on this by reviewing the environmental content of policies in their structure plans. Beyond this more strategic application of sustainable principles, district/city and unitary councils increasingly formulated local sustainability policies in their local or unitary development plans and subsequently Local Development Frameworks. The Climate Change Act applies a new test to statements of national planning policy. From 2009 all such policy must have regard to the needs of sustainable development and the mitigation of climate change, in arriving at recommendations for action.

During the late 1990s and into the new century, government policy became increasingly influenced by the sustainability agenda. The genesis of this policy was influenced in two ways. First, government was reacting to international policy and, second, it was embracing the findings of many eminent reports and influential think-tanks, some themselves government-sponsored.

In 1998 the Kyoto Agreement (Framework Protocol on Climate Change) established a series of international targets to limit the increase in production of carbon dioxide, already running at around 3 billion tonnes of carbon released into the atmosphere annually. The UK government committed itself to reduce national production of such gases by a figure of 12.5 per cent, so that by the period 2008–2012 the volume of such emissions would be reduced to 1990 levels. To deliver on this binding commitment, the government would be required to introduce a raft of new policies.

Among the influential reports and findings of respected bodies that raised awareness of sustainability issues, a common theme was evident: that the planning system had a central role to play. The Commission on Sustainable Development (previously, prior to 2000, the British Government Panel on Sustainable Development and the UK Round Table on Sustainable Development) constitutes the single most influential body in this area. Being appointed by the Prime Minister and able to discuss a wide array of issues, the Commission's findings enjoy authority and respect. The land-use planning system was described by the Commission as 'crucial' in securing sustainable development objectives and importantly, as 'one of the few current mechanisms which clearly links national goals with local ones' (UK Round Table 1999). Indeed, the Commission recommended that planning guidance should increasingly reflect the growing sustainability agenda and become much more integrated with other public policy areas, notably economic policy. Such a 'holistic' or cross-disciplinary approach to sustainability was highlighted in 1999. The UK Round Table had argued in favour of stronger powers of implementation for the planning system and greater reliance on 'economic instruments', such as fiscal measures to tax greenfield development and fund infrastructure benefits to brown-land alternatives (UK Round Table 1999).

Government policy has become increasingly sympathetic to such an approach. In 2001 the Chancellor of the Exchequer embraced this 'holistic' concept, introducing new taxation measures to encourage restoration of historic buildings,[9] greater conversion of empty space over shops[10] and increased levels of conversion/ refurbishment of existing residential stock.[11] This was a start, but much more remains to be done. Indeed, the UK Round Table, prior to their absorption into the Sustainable Development Commission, argued in favour of a more dramatic set of reforms, in which the planning system incorporated a set of stronger 'tools' to achieve more effective implementation of the sustainability agenda. Such powers would cover matters of land assembly (for instance, to create suitable redevelopment sites from previous vacant and/or brown-land sites) and decontamination of previously polluted land after previous industrial and/or commercial activity. Historically, local planning authorities have enjoyed few significant powers in such areas. In the medium to longer term, therefore, it is important that the planning system moves beyond its traditional land-use 'base' if it is to tackle the demands of sustainable development. Many emerging core strategies (established in the 2004 reforms) have policies that reflect this new policy emphasis dealing with the mitigation of and adaptation to the effects of climate change. Indeed a key reform introduced by the Planning and Compulsory Purchase Act 2004 was the requirement that all Regional Spatial Strategies and development plan documents (except for the Statement of Community Involvement) are the subject of a sustainability appraisal. This process allows for positive improvement of policies to ensure they reflect sustainable development principles and itself requires a comprehensive gathering of baseline information and consideration of options. The profile and delivery of sustainability in planning was thus raised considerably. Further, the 2004 reforms truly embedded sustainability into the system by imposing a duty that all policies seek to promote the objectives of sustainable development.

Since the mid-1990s new thinking has indeed emerged. After 1998, with the publication of a major piece of work in this area (DoE 1998c) and subsequent reporting of the findings of the Urban Task Force (1999 and 2005) and Urban White Paper (DETR 2000b), the notion of sustainability in planning policy became commonplace. The impact of such work will be considered later in this chapter and in the following chapter on urban regeneration. Suffice it to say at this stage that these reports have been instrumental in affecting this new thinking towards sustainable development, but that the implementation of this agenda (by virtue of changes in planning policy) will to some extent be constrained by the system in which planners react to the development proposals of developers (planning applications) without recourse to the more 'proactive' ability to assemble land, engage in its remediation (from contamination) or control taxation benefits in its sustainable promotion. Globally, much remains to be done, yet most western and/or industrialized nations are now signatories to Kyoto, although America is still outside. The UN Climate Conference in Bali in late 2007 was ostensibly about 'processes' and not 'outcomes'. The conference agreed what would, in the future, be known as the 'Bali Roadmap'. This was an agreed protocol for future discussions on climate change. Bali was not about the adoption of more rigorous international targets for cutting greenhouse gas emissions but instead the methods and means by which all nations could come together to achieve this. One significant stumbling block to achieving international consensus is the considerable disparity between the needs and aims of richer compared to poorer nations. Bali agreed to establish an adaptation fund in which developing countries could seek funding for projects to implement mitigation strategies

Sustainability and town planning

In 1998 it was reported that 'The planning system has a vital part to play in promoting some sustainable land-use patterns and use of resources' (DoE 1998c). The notion of sustainability is indeed a broad one and is often perceived as a 'process' as much as a 'set of solutions' (UK Round Table 5th Report). The planning system is well placed to address matters of process by involving many interested groups in the formulation and implementation of planning policy. As for substance (policy and decisions) the verdict is less certain. Indeed, it may be too early to judge the system on this. Nevertheless, it is appropriate that consideration is given to current environmental problems and the role of town planning in providing a solution. A number of key areas will be considered.

Current environmental problems

Use of urban land

In Britain, post-war development patterns have increasingly been influenced by the rapid growth in private car ownership. This has resulted in increasing levels of out-of-town development, such as retail warehousing or business parks, not easily served by public transport. As a consequence, people and businesses have relocated away from existing urban locations. It has been estimated that by the late 1980s between 60,000 and 110,000 ha of wasteland existed in urban areas of Britain.[12] During the 1990s the calculation of such statistics became more accurate. In 1993 a Derelict Land Survey estimated that there were about 39,600 ha of derelict land in England. Five years later (1998) the government-commissioned Compilation of National Land Use Database (NLUD) statistics reported 28,800 ha of previously derelict land and 16,200 ha of previously developed vacant land, a total of 45,000 ha. While not all of this land would be suitable for redevelopment (in around 10 per cent of these sites it would remain economically unviable to reclaim or remedy) the Urban Task Force (1999) cal-culated that around one quarter was suitable for housing, yielding just over two million new housing units. This would make a substantial inroad into the oft-quoted headline figure of 3.8 million new units required between 1996 and 2016 as a result of population change. Groups such as the Friends of the Earth and the Campaign for the Protection of Rural England have argued for many years that 'Cities have great capacity to be more resourceful' (Houghton and Hunter 1994: 45). Clearly, sustainable planning policies can contain urban growth (e.g. by green belt policies) and ensure that derelict urban land is developed while existing land is recycled through redevelopment. However, this strategy alone will not accommodate all future land-use needs. It was estimated by the DoE that between 1981 and 2001 the urban area of England would increase by 105,000 ha.[13] When one considers that 40 per cent of all urban expansion in Britain during the 1980s was on previously agricultural land, it becomes apparent that the planning system must balance competing demands for finite land resources and make difficult decisions regarding urban containment or expansion.

In 2000 the government announced a 'step change' in policy, designed to deliver new housing on previously developed land or through conversion. By 2008, 60 per cent of all new housing would be required to be built on previously de-veloped land or through conversion. To achieve this would require a new focus on urban redevelopment, in effect an 'urban renaissance'. Densities would need to be higher than previously and a new emphasis would be placed upon making more 'efficient' use of land, whether on urban brown land or on greenfield land. To reach a 60 per cent target posed a considerable challenge when it is recalled that between 1995 and 2001 this figure remained static at 57 per cent with little improvement, notwithstanding much effort to do so. Reliance upon a target alone with the absence of other measures like taxation (tax on greenfield schemes and tax relief for brown-land equivalents) would render delivery of the 60 per cent figure less likely. The 60 per cent brown-land target was exceeded by the target delivery date of 2008, with around 65 per cent of all new homes on previously developed land. Local Development Framework policies would continue to adopt strategies for maximizing urban and/or previously developed land, including expressing this as a priority for future locations and increasing housing densities beyond 30 dwellings per hectare.

Global warming

The production of carbon dioxide, methane, nitrous oxide and chlorofluorocarbons creates a heat blanket around the Earth, trapping some of the sun's energy and producing a rise in global temperature. Such increases in temperature have been predicted to be around 0.3 °C every decade, resulting in changes in weather patterns (affecting agricultural production) and rising sea levels, in the range of around 6 cm every ten years (Houghton *et al.* 1992). During the 1970s, UK emissions of greenhouse gases declined as a result of restrictions on industrial production and domestic heating. However, the dramatic rise in the number of motor vehicles meant that by 1984 any further decline was arrested and soon greenhouse emissions were rising again. By 2006 it was evident that transport emissions were growing faster than any other sector (such as energy production or industry). Reports like the Stern Review on Climate Change (HM Treasury 2006b) and the Eddington review of transport policy (Department for Transport 2006) were pushing for dramatic reductions (as high as 80% by 2050). By 2010 it is anticipated that government policy would target commuter and business car travellers, who at 2008 levels accounted for nearly 40% of all miles driven by car. Such policy would promote more efficient vehicles and/or modes, by charging against use, for example by the introduction of road pricing or a road tax regime based on emissions.

To achieve its agreed target at Kyoto[14] the government has agreed to cut UK emissions of greenhouse gases by 12.5 per cent relative to the 1990 level over the period 2008–2012. This target was achieved by 2002 (DEFRA 2003a) leading the government at the time to estimate and project that by 2010 UK greenhouse gas emissions could be reduced to 23 per cent below their levels in 1990. This would exceed the government's own domestic target (which is not legally binding, as Kyoto is) to cut carbon emissions by 20 per cent below 1990 levels (DoE 1999a (*A Better Quality of Life*)) and the longer-term target of 60 per cent reductions by 2050 and real progress by 2020 (DEFRA 2005 (*Securing the Future*)). Climate change is recognized as 'one of the greatest environmental threats facing the world today' (DoE 1999a). Such a conclusion has not been reached without debate – even disagreement among some scientists as to the reality of global warming. An overwhelming evidence base now exists to suggest that mankind is changing the climate and to the detriment of the environment. Politicians and policy-makers are now acutely aware of the importance of this issue, Indeed, Sir Crispin Tickell, panel convenor for the Sustainable Development Commission, summarized the situation thus: 'When the panel was first established in January 1994 the somewhat slippery concept of sustainable development was peripheral to mainstream thinking and policy on the environment. That is no longer so' (British Government Panel 2000). Research in 2002 concluded that while the policy objectives of sustainability were unavoidable it was unlikely that there would ever be one agreed definitive or standard set of indicators by which it could universally be measured (RICS Foundation 2002). Policy-makers have neatly side-stepped such a debate and gone for targets as an indicator of success. The aim is the creation of a low carbon economy, as the government sought in the energy White Paper of 2003.

The ozone layer protects the Earth from excessive levels of ultraviolet radiation. This layer is being reduced by chlorofluorocarbons (CFCs), which are found in chemicals such as halon, used in the manufacture and operation of air-conditioning solvents, refrigeration and aerosols.[15] An international commitment was made in 1987 to reduce such substances.[16] Depletion of the ozone layer is measured by the effective chlorine loading in the atmosphere. UK measurements during the 1990s showed a gradual reduction, and predictions based on 1996 data (DEFRA 2003b) appear accurate in their forecast that chlorine loading will decline substantially after 2050. Al Gore's film and subsequent book, *An Inconvenient Truth*, released in 2006, both reported the devastating impact of climate change but drew hope from past triumphs over political and environmental threats, including the international consensus to tackle the production of CFCs. The UK government was at the forefront of delivering national sustainable development strategies that would filter down to the planning system. The originally created 1999 strategy (*A Better Quality of Life*) set out the four aims for sustainable development as those of social progress, effective protection of the environment, prudent use of natural resources and maintenance of high and stable levels of economic growth and employment. By 2005 a review and publication of a refreshed strategy (*Securing the Future*), amended these aims to key principles, encompassing living within environmental limits, ensuring a strong, healthy and just society, achieving a sustainable economy, promoting good governance and using sound science responsibly. While the UK government is committed to targets that far exceed Kyoto and realistically reflect what needs to be done (Flannery 2005), it has also promoted policy that seeks best practice. This includes a mixed bag of initiatives that include, by way of example, raising urban density and promoting mixed use schemes, reuse of buildings and a modal shift away from the private car and in favour of public transport or cycling and walking. Government thinking is ranged at both a macro-level, dealing with major infrastructure projects (like off-shore wind farms) and at a micro-level, dealing with promotion of small-scale renewable energy in domestic dwellings (by changing the General Permitted Development Order, to exclude such works from requiring planning consent). A truly effective strategy will need to extend beyond land-use planning, and indeed the UK Strategy of 2005 accepts this by promoting a host of measures ranging from environmental education to giving greater powers and responsibilities to the Sustainable Development Commission. Yet, decisions made on land use and the application of renewable/low carbon solutions to new development will go a long way to delivering real change in this area.

Deforestation

Trees, woods and forests absorb carbon dioxide, which helps to reduce the effects of global warming. Tropical forests have been destroyed annually for a variety of reasons, including the harvesting of timber. In Britain around 10 per cent of land (2.4 million ha) has tree cover, compared to an average of 25 per cent in the European Community. Nevertheless, this figure represents a dramatic increase on the situation prevailing at the beginning of the twentieth century and is largely the result of planting undertaken by the Forestry Commission, which was established by the government in 1919.

Biological diversity

Activities such as the burning of forests, draining of wetlands and growth of urban areas and road networks have led to the loss or near extinction of many species of plant or animal life, resulting in the loss of sources of food, medicine and industrial materials. It has been estimated that about 2 per cent of agricultural land is eroded by city growth around western European cities every ten years (Houghton and Hunter 1994: 7). In Britain the amount of land occupied by urban areas continues to grow. Urban growth is usually accompanied by an increased demand for infrastructure, especially roads, and development pressure on urban fringes becomes intense. Between 1985 and 1990 around 14,000 ha of land were used to build new roads in Britain (DoE 1994c). The growing value attributed to nature conservation or biological diversity (biodiversity) is reflected in a newfound emphasis placed on such matters. For example, when appraising the relationship between the growth proposed in the South East Plan and the protection of relict heathland in Hampshire, Surrey and Berkshire which supported a ground-nesting bird habitat of international importance (the Thames Basin Heath), planning authorities devised a visionary solution. This involves the creation of alternative natural green space within a radius of between 400 m and 5 kilometres of the nesting habitat. Thus, the logic goes, residents of new and existing housing in this zone will be less likely to walk their dogs within the Thames Basin Heath and more likely to use the alternative sites in their neighbourhood. Such special and (at the time of their development) contentious policies demonstrated an increasing awareness of the value of nature conservation when threatened by new development, either within or close to sites of importance.

Industrial pollution

Industrial pollution is discharged into the air, sea and ground, and includes the dumping of industrial waste at sea. Many industries in the former Soviet Union are responsible for a heavy discharge of pollutants. 'Acid rain' refers to rain, snow, fog or mist that has become contaminated by contact with sulphur and nitrogen dioxide, which are produced by industrial processes. Motor vehicles account for about half of all nitrogen oxide emissions. While such emissions have fallen since 1970 levels (by around one quarter), traffic volumes accounted for an increasing proportion of this figure. Indeed this situation is unlikely to change as statistical projections point to an increase in car ownership, to 30 million by 2025. Levels of sulphur dioxide, produced mostly by power stations (burning fossil fuels) have fallen far more dramatically since 1970 levels (by around three-quarters) as a result of alternative energy supplies, most notably a switch to gas as an energy source. UK sulphur dioxide emissions surpassed UNECE targets for 2006 (85 per cent reduction from 1980 baseline or 676,000 tonnes per annum), with future reductions anticipated by 2010, so that total emissions would fall to around 625,000 tonnes every year.

The role of town planning

Following an examination of these various environmental problems, it is necessary to pose the question 'How can the UK land-use planning system affect these environmental issues?' Several key areas may be examined (Table 8.1). Each environmental issue will be considered, and reference will be made to the influence of town planning.

Greenhouse effect

The UK government's adherence to the principles agreed to at Rio (1992), Kyoto (1998) and most recently Bali (2007) have resulted in ambitious targets being set for reductions in carbon emissions and the 'roadmap' agreed in which new discussions and targets will be identified in future years. To deliver on such commitments required both a reversal of the upward trend in emissions of recent years but also real cuts in carbon production. Such a policy agenda was given further emphasis at the World Summit on Sustainable Development in Johannesburg (2002). The 2002 Summit permitted appraisal of global, national and local sustainability initiatives in the ten years since the Rio summit. Johannesburg re-emphasized the pivotal link between the developed and the developing world in the implementation of sustainable development. It is important to remember that implementing sustainability is not solely confined to effective protection of the environment (albeit that this is important) but also extends

Table 8.1 Town planning and sustainable development

Environmental use	Land-use planning influence
Greenhouse effect/global warming Use of urban land	• Planning policies to restrict use of the car • Green belt policy to contain urban areas • Urban density policies to ensure urban land is used efficiently • Strategies such as urban villages and an urban renaissance to reduce car use by ensuring a mixture of employment and housing or shopping land use within close proximity
Pollution/ozone depletion/ deforestation	• Control over industrial emissions when deciding new planning applications • Use of procedures such as Environmental Impact Assessment to assess the exact potential for pollution and other environmental harm

to matters of social progress, prudent use of natural resources and maintaining high and stable levels of economic growth. A reduction in global inequalities (say in health provision, education and maintenance of a stable economy) will themselves influence how the environment is managed in future years. Sustainability is a holistic subject and it would be folly to consider environmental issues alone, although this chapter is primarily concerned with land-use planning issues. Bali (2007) raised, perhaps for the first time, the need to address issues of development inequalities, when devising sustainable solutions. To create a sustainable city requires appraisal of urban planning but also of health, transport, production, agriculture, urban design, and resource management issues. Such interdependencies must not be forgotten when considering land-use matters, and the 2004 Act does require a more joined-up approach, especially in the creation and implementation of Regional Spatial Strategies and Local Development Frameworks.

In pursuit of the Agenda 21 strategy agreed at the Rio conference, the UK government pinned great hopes on the implementation of sustainable patterns of future land-use planning, to control and restrict motor vehicle usage and therefore carbon emissions. By 2006 this perspective had been broadened, when the government consulted on relaxing planning controls to allow domestic renewable energy (such as small wind turbines and solar panels) without the need for planning consent.

Reducing global warming has been identified as the environmental imperative to sustainability.

> The land-use planning system can be employed to influence the siting of new shops and offices, where we work, where we go to enjoy ourselves and where we go to shop – these choices are all significant for the use of the car. . . . We need to deliver development patterns over the next twenty years

that will enable people to continue to choose to walk or cycle or use public transport. We should stand firm against the urban sprawl that would deny those choices.[17]

In 1999 the government published its strategy for the implementation of sustainable development, *A Better Quality of Life* (DoE 1999a) and this was revised six years later in *Securing the Future* (DEFRA 2005). Both documents advanced policy goals first established in the *UK Strategy of Sustainable Development*, published in 1994. Contrary to the conclusions published by the Club of Rome in 1972, the UK government did not accept the argument that continuing economic growth would be incompatible with environmental protection. Indeed this mix of objectives led to the coining of the phrase 'sustainable economy' in the 2005 publication. These apparently conflicting objectives could be reconciled and economic growth would not be contrary to the implementation of environmental protection. A key priority was established in respect of the built environment, 'improving the larger towns and cities to make them better places to live and work'. The effective implementation of sustainable cities and their resident communities would require action at national, regional (via Regional Development Agencies and Regional Spatial Strategies) and local (via Local Development Frameworks) level to achieve a 'basket' of sustainable objectives.

Such objectives included the need to reduce car travel (in part by siting major developments alongside good public transport) and to improve various land-use and design standards in pursuit of higher-density greenfield development. A key factor would be the need to direct 60 per cent of new housing on to brown-land (converted land) by 2008, but in so doing to create a balanced community. Indeed the 2005 UK strategy is built upon the five principles or aims of living within environmental limits, ensuring a strong, healthy and just society, achieving a sustainable economy and promoting good governance. In addition, the government have set out four policy priorities of promoting sustainable consumption and production, applying climate change adaptation strategies to energy policy, promotion of natural resource protection and the creation of sustainable communities. Yet, delivery of truly sustainable development patterns would challenge many previous planning practices. Future development patterns would require more concentrated urban areas, with extensive reuse of previously developed land, considerable attention to the maintenance of urban amenity (by, say, provision of green space and through urban design) and giving preference to sustainable urban extensions instead of building isolated new settlements in circumstances where greenfield development must be countenanced. Planning policy would need to promote regeneration as well as more sustainable patterns of land use, for example by locating high-density development in or near transport corridors and through promotion of mixed-use schemes (such as in urban villages). Further, it would need to promote energy-efficient buildings with good architectural and urban design. Design is indeed more than just an aesthetically pleasing development.

The 1999 and 2005 UK strategy documents committed the government to report annually on progress made in delivering sustainable development. Such appraisal itself requires the establishment of indicators or benchmarks against which sustainability can be measured. The Department for Food and Rural Affairs (DEFRA) is the government department vested with this responsibility. It must be remembered that a whole industry of sustainable targets has evolved in recent years, with the introduction of Sustainability Appraisal of all regional and local policy in compliance with EU Directive 2001/42/EC, requiring a Strategic Environmental Assessment of development plans.

Some policy areas would lend themselves to easy measurement, such as a 60 per cent brown-land target. Others would be less easily appraised, such as the improvement of quality in architecture and urban design, themselves matters of personal opinion. Nevertheless, the government have sought to identify a series of key statistics, notably fifteen headline indicators out of a total of sixty-eight indicators, whereby implementation of sustainable development and quality could be measured in local communities (DETR 2000g). With regard to land use, such indicators were restricted to the solitary quantifiable factor of how many new homes were built on previously developed land. Others were drawn from a variety of topics, including economic issues (such as employment or output levels), social issues (education, health, social exclusion) and environmental issues (climate change, air quality, road traffic levels, biodiversity, and land use). Such headline indicators are not the only means by which sustainability can be measured. Research published by the Royal Institution of Chartered Surveyors (RICS Foundation 2002) uncovered a 'bewildering array of approaches which are sometimes in contradiction' to the measurement of sustainability, itself a reflection of the different political, social and economic forces affected by the sustainability agenda. The report additionally concludes with respect to the property and construction industries that for a limited investment such sectors 'can embrace sustainable development, and thereby gain a considerable advantage'. Such an approach emanated from work commissioned by the Secretary of State six years earlier, in which a government interdepartmental working group produced a number of key indicators to monitor sustainability (DoE 1996a). Key land-use indicators included household growth, reuse of brown land and loss of rural land to development. Appraisals based upon more subjective (or opinion-based) assessment, such as the quality of new architecture or urban design, could not be so readily measured and were not included as key indicators of sustainability.[18] Nevertheless, the importance of such policy areas should not be overlooked, even if it is acknowledged that easy measurement is not possible.

Implementation of strategies in such new policy areas would necessitate a cross-cutting or 'cross-cultural' approach. This would require integration across what are known as Community Strategies (CS), which seek to develop a wide range of initiatives that all contribute to the objectives of sustainable development. Planning is a component of this but not the only one, and such work falls within the remit of the Local Strategic Partnership (LSP) which will bring together a broad range of stakeholders and community interests. The outcomes of the

Community Strategy should be used to inform the development of local planning policy and, significantly, marry the key aims of sustainable development with the needs of the local community. Furthermore, land-use decisions, such as raising urban density or promoting mixed use, would need to be linked to other policy areas like transport (such as mixed-use development around transport nodes) and social policy (so that new development brings with it economic opportunity and helps redress social imbalance). The government set the planning system the ambitious target of promoting urban regeneration, social inclusion and the creation of more sustainable patterns of development. Additionally, the system would be vested with the responsibility of engaging the public in the process by virtue of public consultation and participation, albeit that the Community Strategy and Statement of Community Involvement now promote such mechanisms to more powerfully engage with local opinions, needs and aspirations.

Urban growth

The Earth Summit considered how sustainable development could be applied to patterns of human settlement to create the 'sustainable city'. This urban sustainability deals with the achievement of urban development, subject to the condition that natural resources are not depleted so as to threaten their long-term future.

The sustainable city must enjoy a harmonious relationship with its region or sub-region, so that its existence and potential for growth are balanced against the long-term maintenance of water supply, air quality, land in agricultural production, and drainage/sanitation. Thus, urban sustainability is directly influenced by land-use controls, which ensure efficient use is made of urban land and which protect non-urban land from urban encroachment (Jenks *et al.* 1996).

In Britain, some land-use policies have emerged that address such issues. Although they largely predate the first introduction of sustainable development policies (in 1994) they can be adapted to reinforce the implementation of a sustainable strategy. For example, until 1994, green belt policy had been principally concerned with checking urban sprawl, so that only a restricted schedule of development activity had been permitted around the major conurbations of Britain. In 1995 the government issued amended policy guidance with a new emphasis on how such policy, by operating at a regional and sub-regional level, can deliver sustainable patterns of development. Green belt policy, while continuing to resist outward urban expansion, thus can play a positive role in retaining attractive landscapes, promoting outdoor recreation, improving the quality of spoilt land (subject to tipping or extraction) and encouraging development within the existing urban envelope, whether by development of derelict land or redevelopment of existing sites within towns and cities. One problem is that such areas of restraint are 'leapfrogged' by developers. Additionally, the planning policy emphasis in favour of carefully planned town extensions or even self-contained satellite development away from existing urban areas, has moved up the policy agenda.

The (now replaced) Planning Policy Guidance 3 (of 2000) allowed the consideration of such schemes after all previous options had been exhausted, and an (informal) sequential test was established with a clear preference for development within urban areas before other options could be considered. The replacement PPS3 (of 2006) deleted this policy test in favour of a broader minded approach in which sustainable extensions could be considered, if they were both appropriate and well planned. A final example is the ways that transport policy has evolved with Planning Policy Guidance Note 13 (2001) on transport moving away from the past notion of minimum parking standards (i.e. a baseline standard that has to be met) to maximum standards, in which provision is ultimately limited to a set ceiling. Further, the guidance now states that it should not automatically be assumed that meeting parking standards renders a scheme necessarily acceptable. Government policy is now pushing hard for reliance on alternative modes to the private car, and reducing parking – as well as offering other choices – is all part of the equation. A push to increase sustainability has been at the genesis of these changes.

Efficient land use

Various planning policy initiatives, including urban villages and new settlements have championed the cause of sustainability and set new goals and aspirations for the system. New settlements, and sustainable urban extensions provide for a mixture of residential, commercial, industrial and leisure-related activities. Urban villages promote the idea of medium- to high-density (not high-rise) mixed-use redevelopment. Such proposals offer redevelopment within the existing urban fabric and appear to minimize commuting by providing for both employment and housing within an area limited to approximately 40 ha (100 acres), with most parts of the urban village within a walking time of around ten minutes. The consequence is that urban land can be 'recycled', providing for industrial and residential needs without eroding land outside the city. The new settlement can create a more self-sustained community, less reliant on the car, as homes and workplaces can be provided side by side (Neal 2003). Clearly our urban areas have the potential to be more sustainable. The urban village presents this vision in a cogent way, namely provision of a high-density, mixed-use 'quality' environment in which residents enjoy both employment opportunity and local amenity. Consistent with the findings of research commissioned by DETR (1998c) and Lord Rogers (Urban Task Force 1999 and 2005), such development could be used to 'retrofit' or repair existing urban fabric damaged or blighted by either dereliction and vacancy or by past planning of either low-density, single-use suburbia or by high-rise housing without access to local amenities. Work commissioned by DoE (1998c), entitled *Planning for Sustainable Development: Towards Better Practice*, addressed this policy area and argued that 'the approach to increasing sustainability in urban areas essentially involves improving accessibility, raising densities and achieving a mix of uses in selected locations'. A key threshold was established in which an area or district was determined by a radius of 800 metres from a 'node' such as a bus stop, shop or local park, or other focal point. This rather simple concept was somewhat revolutionary in determining the shape of cities and residential areas. It is often stated in support new density-led planning policies that a minimum housing density of 25–30 dwellings per hectare is needed to sustain a bus route. The evidence-base for such an assertion is unknown, but it does illustrate the point that the economic viability of facilities and services is contingent on the number of residents within any given area of a town.

The drive for sustainable land-use is based on a number of assumptions. First, that a flexible application of many planning standards in respect of parking, density (i.e. habitable dwellings per hectare) and overlooking/separation of development, is applied. In past years a criticism of the system has been that planners adhered too rigidly to standards which prevent innovation in density or design. Secondly, it requires that density standards are themselves raised due to the simple economic truth that 'as densities rise, it becomes increasingly viable to provide facilities, such as shops, health services and public transport, within walking distance of the population necessary to support them' (DoE 1998c). Yet density itself is no guarantee of achieving sustainability and requires that increased provision of public transport is linked with such developments.

Research work commissioned by government (in 1997) examined the relationship between housing density and area of land consumed. This work made fascinating reading in a subject that is somewhat dry and technical. It concluded that as density increases the amount of land saved is not commensurate – in other words, the proportionate savings in land diminish once a certain point is reached. The research found that the best savings were achieved by increasing density from 10 to a minimum of 20 dwellings per hectare, for provision of 400 dwellings (a land saving of 50 per cent). Yet, as the density standards were increased the amount of land saved diminished. So it followed that to achieve the optimum savings on density would require only a modest increase from low to medium, that is to say by reaching a minimum threshold of 40 dwellings per hectare. Subsequently (in 2006) a new PPS3 (Department for Communities and Local Government 2006c) would advocate raising housing density to between 30 and 50 dwellings per hectare. Therefore, to achieve a noticeably more efficient use of land would not require a dramatic shift in density policy. Finally, it requires that if development is to be acceptably accommodated outside existing urban areas then this must replicate key principles of sustainability in land use. Such principles encompass development around nodes such as transport corridors well served by rail and bus, to ensure that residents benefit from the choice of a non-car-based transport mode.

This concept of 'sustainable urban extension' is not new. It has previously been promoted in UK planning as both Garden Cities on the model designed by Ebenezer Howard in 1898 (Ward 1994) and by private companies like Eagle Star in their sponsoring of a new settlement at Micheldever in Hampshire. It is very much back on the map with the government's 2008 announcement that ten 'eco-towns' would be considered (from a list of some fifty options) with the

Secretary of State for Communities and Local Government due to announce the five most favoured sites in 2009, after which they would have to be progressed via the normal planning process of policy allocations and planning applications. The noticeable departure of sustainable urban extensions from these previous models, apart from their linkage or proximity to existing urban areas, is their emphasis on efficient land use, with a much higher density profile at 30–50 houses per hectare than, say, that advocated by Howard himself at 37 houses per hectare (Hall 1992). More efficient land use is thus achieved by raising density around key nodal points, greater integration between land use and public transport networks, and ensuring that, if greenfield development is to take place, it strictly adheres to such principles while also linking to existing urban centres. The promotion of numerous new settlements undertaken during the 1990s, in which free-standing and self-contained towns were promoted on greenfield and some previously used land (mostly disused airfields) is likely to be a launch pad for more satellite developments or urban extensions based upon sustainable principles. While considerable energy will be devoted to 'retrofitting' higher-density schemes into existing urban areas, sufficient demand exists for new housing on otherwise undeveloped countryside. Developers, especially housebuilders, have embraced such thinking, and centrally located and brown-land sites are increasingly being developed for medium-density and mixed-use schemes. Considerable opportunity exists here, especially in the so-called 'Golden Belt' area of predicted higher rates of change to urban areas, stretching from south-western England to East Anglia via Wiltshire, Oxfordshire and Northamptonshire (Hall 1988 and DoE 1995) but also with the launch of the 2009 'eco-towns' programme in which five schemes, with the benefit of the Secretary of State's expressed preference (but no detailed planning approvals as yet) will promote new sustainable living within new development on greenfield sites, including a number of redundant airfields.

Government planning policy

The culmination of influential reports like *Planning for Sustainable Development: Towards Better Practice* (DoE 1998c) and *Towards Urban Renaissance* (Urban Task Force 1999 and 2005) helped to shape the future direction of a sustainable planning policy agenda, as established in statements of national planning policy. Such works were also supplemented by a series of research findings and best-practice reports that contributed empirical findings and promoted good practice. Several cascaded on to the desks of practitioners during the period from the late 1990s and into the new century. Work on the relationship between density and efficient land use has been previously cited (DoE 1997). Additionally, work by Llewelyn-Davies examined practical ways in which density could be raised (DoE 1998b). Parking policies were scrutinized in a comprehensive study of standards completed in 1998, also by Llewelyn-Davies, consultants for the DETR and the Government Office for the South East (DoE 1998b). The report, while accepting that it is 'unreasonable to rely solely on parking standards to bring

about . . . sustainability', promoted a more structured approach to the application of standards. While parking requirements would in future be based on
maximum (i.e. ceilings) as opposed to minimum standards, the key recommendation was that parking policy should be more closely integrated to location
in preference to the mere blanket application of standards, as had previously
been the case. A locational matrix was proposed in which development plans
geographically divide areas into zones, with differing maximum standards. Such
an approach was subsequently implemented in Edinburgh in 1999, whereby
the zone covering the urban centre or other high-density areas well served by
public transport (such as a district centre) could entertain car-free or dramatically reduced provision. In fringe or rural areas a maximum standard of one space
per dwelling is then set. Parking policy is, as a result, more flexible and able to
respond to a sustainable agenda in which car-free/reduced development can be
acceptably accommodated in central nodes or other areas well served by public
transport.

Alongside such research findings additional best-practice documentation set
out to improve standards in urban design (DETR 2000d) and the relationship
between development layout and car parking/highway considerations (DoE
1998d). Sustainability was promoted by the concern to improve urban spaces
and to ensure that, in future, parking provision and layout did not encroach upon
the importance of creating a high-quality public realm.[19]

By 2000 such a body of work had gathered considerable momentum amongst
policy-makers in the (then) DETR. The PPSs issued from this point on would
step up the national implementation and the new focus. It should be remembered, however, that sustainable inputs to PPGs go back to the mid-1990s.
In 1996, PPG6 was issued, establishing a sequential test in assessment of retail
development, clearly favouring town-centre retail and discouraging out-of-town
developments (as much favoured during the 1980s). Town centres, with their
traditional focus of bus and rail interchanges, are less likely to rely on car-based
shoppers than an out-of-town equivalent. Similarly the (now cancelled) PPG13
of 1994 sought to discourage out-of-town business parks or leisure/retail complexes,
with their almost total reliance upon car-based transport modes, in preference to existing centres where people are more likely to arrive by a variety of
modes. So a sustainable agenda is not of itself an entirely new concept. What
significantly changed after the introduction of the Planning and Compulsory
Purchase Act 2004 was the depth and breadth of this agenda.

Protection of the ozone layer, conserving resources and forests, and reducing pollution

Conservation of resources such as minerals and aggregates, and reduction of
industrial emissions, with consequences for the ozone layer, fall within the realms
of planning consideration.[20] Since the introduction of the modern system of
planning controls in 1947, planning authorities have enjoyed considerable planning powers to control industrial pollution. However, until recent years, with the

introduction of a new 'sustainable' agenda, these powers were largely unused, because of inadequate training for planners in this subject, lack of effective government guidance, attempts by council environmental health departments to deal with such issues, and the fear that such planning restrictions would result in job losses. Sustainability has provided the much-needed incentive to 'kick start' many planners into a reconsideration of their role in this area. Such a new awareness of pollution issues within town planning has been accompanied by a wider range of controls over the regulation of industrial pollution. The Environment Act 1995 introduced new procedural systems for the regulation of industrial and water pollution, establishing a new Environment Agency to coordinate implementation of such powers. New Planning Policy Guidance as well as case law[21] accepts that potential pollution from a proposed development is a material consideration to be taken into account when deciding to grant or refuse planning permission. In particular, the planning system should consider matters such as location, impact upon amenity, impact upon other land, nuisance, impact on road or other transport networks, and feasibility of land restoration in the longer term, when considering potential pollution issues.

The increased employment of environmental impact assessment in large-scale development proposals allows for an examination of potential pollution emissions from industrial development. However, a planning authority enjoys power to refuse planning permission for any type of development proposal, with or without an environmental impact assessment, which may result in unacceptable pollution (DoE 1994d). The Earth Summit identified the contribution of industrial activity to causing airborne pollution, which is harmful to human health as well as damaging to forests and trees, creating acid rain and resulting in depletion of the ozone layer. PPS12 (2008) heralded a much more proactive approach in this area by including matters such as energy conservation, global climate change and reduction in greenhouse gases squarely within the purview of planning policy. Coupled with this, PPS22 (2004) promoted renewable energy at both regional and local level and reinforced the government's strategic objective of generating 10 per cent of all UK energy from renewable sources by 2010, rising to 20 per cent by 2020. This would require a step-change in mostly the provision of solar, wind and combined heat and power energy sources.

Between 1995 and 2004 this initial trickle of 'sustainable' policy became a flow of new ideas and initiatives. Since 2004, all development plans and frameworks contain an amalgam of sustainable policies designed to address global warming by means of land-use planning decisions. It is also inevitable that planning permissions will be refused for such environmental reasons and, when these decisions are the subject of a challenge at appeal, then the Secretary of State or an inspector will be required to arbitrate on the outcome. The government's resolve will be tested in the degree towards which it supports local councils who seek to use planning policy to protect the ozone layer or the finite supply of fossil fuels and the means by which they deal with attempts to calculate the environmental impact of schemes, for example, due to carbon emissions (Pearce 1994). Such an issue was dealt with in a decision of the High Court in 1994 regarding the construction of a new regional shopping centre at Trafford Park (also called Dumplington), in Manchester. Mr Justice Schiemann stated:

> The evidential problem of establishing the amount of CO_2 to be generated by the Trafford Centre and establishing how much of this would have been generated by shopping trips that would no longer take place if shoppers went to the Trafford Centre instead of their habitual shops is manifestly enormous. The results would inevitably have to include a vast range of error. Such a result if it turned out to show that there would be a net increase in such gases, would then need to be balanced against the undeniable benefits of the proposal.[22]

More recently the Secretary of State had to consider an appeal against the refusal of Uttlesford District Council to vary a planning condition at Stansted airport to increase the number of flights. One of the reasons given was the climate change implications of increased air traffic movements – a bold step by the planning authority and one that was subsequently challenged at an appeal heard in 2008. The Secretary of State disagreed and allowed the appeal in late 2008.

Climate change and a new direction for land-use policy

Climate change refers to the changes to annual weather patterns across the world, influenced by human behaviour. This influence is, for the most part, caused by emissions of greenhouse gases, resulting in the greenhouse effect. Some sixteen such greenhouse gases have been identified, with the most significant six being: carbon dioxide, methane, nitrous oxide (produced by burning fossil fuels), hydroflurocarbons, perflurocarbons and sulphur hexafluoride (produced by industrial processes). The worldwide production of carbon dioxide equates to about 6.5 billion tonnes annually, resulting from the burning of fossil fuels to derive energy (coal, oil and gas). Europeans produce about one-third to one-half of all their carbon in heating their homes and heating domestic water. In the UK the one significant area where carbon dioxide emissions have been increasing (over the last ten years) is in the transport sector.

These greenhouse gases absorb energy from the sun and prevent its escape back into the atmosphere, thus trapping this energy and causing heat to radiate back to the Earth's surface. This greenhouse effect causes global warming. An overwhelming majority of scientific opinion supports the conclusion that human activities are changing the climate. The ten warmest years globally have all occurred since 1994 (records began in 1861) with the two warmest years on record in 1998 and 2005. In 2008 the government published a framework for change, which dealt with necessary adaptation to climate change impacts (under the title 'Adapting to Climate Change in England: A Framework for Action'). As global temperatures rise, weather patterns alter, and sea levels rise. The UK Climate Impacts Programme (UKCIP) have undertaken modelling of future impact and predicted that, for the UK, climate change means warmer temperatures, wetter winters with severe flooding, drier summers with more drought conditions, less snow, and flooding of some coastal areas as sea temperatures rise. Some of these impacts are inevitable because carbon dioxide, methane and nitrous oxide have long lifetimes (around a hundred years). Therefore, we will have to implement adaptation strategies to cope with these impacts, such as avoiding building on flood plains or within coastal landscapes. We will also have to adopt mitigation strategies to contain the impact of climate change and to stabilize the amount of carbon and other gases being produced in the future. This is to prevent the impact of 'runaway (irreversible) climate change' in which the impacts cannot be stopped and, as a consequence, vast areas of the Earth become uninhabitable due to severe climate events, like drought and flooding. In Europe during 2003 several major floods were followed by extreme heat which killed more than 35,000 people. Predictions of climatic impact without any mitigation suggest that summers of such exceptional warmth will occur every two or three years by 2050.

Internationally and nationally, targets have been set to reduce greenhouse gas emissions. These reductions are usually set at the baseline of 1990 levels. Work really began in 1992, with the United Nations Framework Convention on Climate Change, in which 188 countries agreed to a commitment to stabilize greenhouse gas emissions in the atmosphere to a level that would avoid dangerous levels of climate change gases. Subsequently the Kyoto Protocol of 1997 (ratified by over 150 countries) set legally binding emissions reduction targets for six greenhouse gases (as listed above). The targets required a reduction of 5 per cent below 1990 levels, to be delivered by 2012. The European Union committed to a deeper cut of 8 per cent below 1990 levels. This would be divided up across member countries, with some taking a larger share and others a smaller one. For the UK it was agreed that the cut would be 12.5 per cent below 1990 levels, although the government have set their own ambitious target of a 20 per cent reduction. The EU has committed to a 60–80 per cent reduction by 2050.

The UK government has estimated that by 2010 their emissions cutbacks will be double that agreed at Kyoto. A good proportion of this will be achieved by switching electricity supply from coal-fired power stations to gas-fired ones. Currently the vast majority of UK greenhouses gas emissions are carbon dioxide (77 per cent, of which nearly half is energy used in buildings) and these are mostly produced by energy supply but also industry, vehicles and domestic heating/water. In 2006 the government published *Climate Change The UK Programme 2006*, which sets out the strategy to achieve domestic targets. The foreword stated that 'The Government believes that climate change is the greatest long term challenge facing the world today. There is strong and indisputable evidence that climate change is happening and that man-made emissions are its main cause.' Key areas for action involve carbon reduction in the energy supply, transport,

The UK Programme commitments

Energy supply sector

Issues to address: Responsible for about 36 per cent of all UK carbon in production of electricity. Significant reductions achieved by switching from coal to gas. Push to alternative sources and a reduction in demand for energy.

UK Programme strategy
- The Renewables Obligation, in which energy supply companies must increase percentage of supply from renewable resources
- Research into wave/tidal technology
- Bioenergy/biomass (crops) grants to promote energy crops, agricultural residues and forestry.
- Combined heat and power (CHP) to be promoted
- Micro-generation promoted in domestic property
- Energy from waste promoted (e.g. anaerobic digestion of food waste).

Business sector

Issues to address: Responsible for about 35 per cent of UK carbon in the activities of commerce and industry.

UK Programme strategy
- Climate Change Levy: a tax on energy used in industry, commerce and the public sector and designed to provide incentives to improve energy-efficiency levels
- Climate Change Agreements represent significant discounts from the levy for meeting strict reductions in emissions
- UK Emissions Trading Scheme, whereby reductions achieved can be 'traded' with other sectors
- Activities of the Carbon Trust who provide independent information on energy saving and low carbon technologies
- Building Regulations 2002 and 2005 which with a new part 'L' have promoted more energy efficient construction methods.

Transport sector

Issues to address: Responsible for around 27 per cent of UK carbon and *rising*. Car fuel economy is getting more efficient yet transport-related carbon levels are growing (at 8 per cent every ten years) as people travel by car in greater amounts.

UK Programme strategy
- Renewable Transport Fuels Obligation, in which the production of fuels from renewable sources will be promoted. These are called biofuels.
- Low Carbon Vehicle Partnership, in which the government promote new technologies. The EU has set voluntary targets to reduce new car carbon emissions by 25 per cent over the next few years.
- Policies designed to promote non-car based transport use
- Aviation emissions are currently *not* included in Kyoto targets, and remember that the climate change impact of aircraft emissions is two to four times greater than ground level emissions.

Domestic sector

Issues to address: Responsible for about 27 per cent of UK carbon and *falling*. (Note that this figure overlaps with energy supply.) The domestic sector is viewed as an effective way of reducing emissions and achieving social and economic objectives (such as reducing fuel poverty).

UK Programme strategy
- Seeking energy-efficiency, such as installing low-energy light bulbs, high efficiency appliances or boilers
- Use of Building Regulations for new and refurbished buildings, for example use of condensing boilers and windows/doors designed to reduce air leakage
- Code for Sustainable Homes, a voluntary standard that goes beyond Building Regulations, such as the use of micro-generation technology
- Encouraging 'Consumer Choice and Raising Standards', whereby producers of electrical goods are encouraged to produce more energy-efficient alternatives.

business and domestic sectors. The UK Programme commitments can be summarized as above.

Climate change adaptation and mitigation strategies have implications for sustainable development. In other words, when we decide to build on land, one of the most significant planning issues should be that it makes for the best use of resources and will result in minimal pollution. Since 2007 climate change issues have been a relevant planning issue in the decision to grant or refuse a planning application. A number of planning authorities are now promoting 'climate neutral development' (see www.bedzed.co.uk) defined as:

> Development that is neutral risk to the climate, by not contributing to greenhouse gas emissions [i.e. mitigation of global warming] and is at neutral risk from the climate, by ensuring it is resilient to the changes in climate

that are expected over the lifetime of a development [i.e. adaptation to global warming].

Remember that the planning system deals with the location, design, and siting of built development. Activity associated with development, including how energy is supplied, can affect the level of greenhouse gas emissions. In 2007 a new annex to PPS1 was issued that dealt specifically with climate change and the planning system. Yet, remember that climate change issues are but one consideration. Promoting new housing on the flood plain is clearly related to adaptation strategies and the incidence of greater floods as impacts are felt. However, promoting climate neutral housing in the green belt is unlikely to succeed because the very principle of development is not established, and climate neutral development does not constitute a 'very special circumstance for setting aside green belt policy'. Table 8.2 indicates how climate neutral development can be applied to the planning system.

The planning system may have (at first sight) only a limited role to play in the reduction of greenhouse gas emissions. The planning system is not responsible for taxation (climate change levy), construction methods (building regulations) or behavioural change (Carbon Trust). It is principally concerned with the external design and location of a building. One key area will be the extent to which the location of new development reduces reliance on the private car. Landuse decisions can give people 'choice', such as to cycle, walk or take convenient and accessible public transport. Further, the government made micro-generation exempt from planning control in 2008 – that is to say, small-scale domestic wind turbines, solar panels, biomass (wood fuel) boilers

Table 8.2 Climate neutral development

Climate neutral development	Climate change impact
Location and transport	• Lowering/reducing carbon emissions by reducing dependence on private car-borne transport. • Promoting alternatives to fossil fuelled transport. • Locating development away from areas liable to flooding.
Site layout and building design	• Lowering carbon emissions by reducing energy demands for heating and cooling. • Building in adaptation to high summer temperatures.
Reducing energy consumption	• Use of generation within a site (e.g. micro-generation and ground source heat pumps).
Sustainable drainage systems	• A drainage system that holds and releases a controlled amount of water to natural systems.
Water conservation and recycling	• Use of rainwater harvesting and recycling of grey water.

Table 8.3 Planning and climate change

Land use policy or objective	Climate change implication (A) – adaptation or (M) – mitigation
Density of development	Supports services/bus route, so residents can walk to a local shop or have the option of public transport (M)
Priority to develop 'previously developed land'	Again, supports local services and avoids 'sprawl' which tends to be more reliant on the private car (M)
Design and layout of development	Promotes energy-efficient design, e.g. passive solar gain whereby south-facing elevations receive increased levels of sun (M)
Location of development	Avoids development in areas of flood risk (A)
Parking standards	Suppress demand for car use (M)
Micro-generation	Promotes mini wind turbines by making them (generally) exempt from planning control (M)
Sustainable urban drainage systems	Required by planning condition in new development (A)

and various heat pumps that source natural energy supplies will fall outside planning controls.

So climate change and planning have the key policy areas shown in Table 8.3. This table is for guidance and can be universally applied across a variety of applications and projects.

Conclusions

In 1991, legislative reforms[23] introduced a presumption in favour of the development plan, which superseded the 'presumption in favour of development' that had reigned throughout the 1980s property boom. Planning authorities have, since the mid-1990s, been encouraged to adopt sustainable strategies within all emerging planning policy, and the DoE, DETR, Office of the Deputy Prime Minister and now Department for Communities and Local Government have produced increasing volumes of guidance, with a strong emphasis on sustainability, especially in respect of using planning policy to discourage use of the private car. The 1994 *UK Strategy* (DoE 1994c), as a response to the Earth Summit's Agenda 21, represented a further move in the direction of this 'greening' of the planning system, whereby environmental considerations are given considerably more weight in the decision-making process than would have been the case in the 1980s. Yet the *UK Strategy* contained few detailed targets or timetables to establish guidelines by which government policy can be assessed. The climate change document (HMSO 1994a) set out a programme for curbing carbon emissions up to the year 2000 and the *UK Strategy* identified the important role that town planning can play in helping to change land-use patterns and reduce car dependency. The publication in 1999 of *A Better Quality of Life: A Strategy for Sustainable Development* (DoE 1999a) and its 2005 replacement *Securing the Future* as well as the revised Local Development Framework system (in PPS11 and PPS12) have consolidated this policy foundation. This direction has increasingly pointed towards mixed-use, higher-density, well-connected urban environments. More efficient use of land is now focused, by means of the sequential test, towards urban land use that helps sustain local communities by ensuring proximity to shops, services and transport networks.

The objectives of such policies, as laid down in *Planning for Sustainable Development* (DoE 1998c) and *Towards an Urban Renaissance* (Urban Task Force 1999 and 2005) are twofold. First, they seek to reduce the need to travel, or at least the need to travel by car, and thus contribute to agreed reductions in greenhouse gas emissions (as required by the Kyoto Protocol). Second, they contribute to a new 'urban orthodoxy', in which the planning system redirects development not simply back to urban areas but into an urban renaissance of our towns and cities.

Critics have argued that government pronouncements merely serve to 'shoe-horn' previous planning policies into a sustainable setting, that the strategy delivers nothing new and instead just 'repackages' existing commitments to the environment so that they *appear* to be pro-sustainability. Such a view may have held sway in the 1990s, when sustainable policy was in a somewhat embryonic state. Since 2004 that view has significantly diminished as sustainable land-use planning has become the 'norm' and not the 'exception' for the new Local Development Frameworks. A host of background studies have reinforced the key principle of 'sound science' and how the activities of mankind are changing the climate. This anthropogenic (man-made) climate change is now the subject of an international scientific consensus. The Third Assessment Report (TAR) of the Intergovernmental Panel on Climate Change reviewed a basket of scientific, technical and socio-economic data, to conclude that strong evidence already existed to confirm that human activity was resulting in a raising of global temperature and that future emissions of such gases were likely to raise global temperature by between 1.4 °C and 5.8 °C during the current century. In 2005, DEFRA sponsored an international conference on 'avoiding dangerous climate change'. This examined the science which would direct action towards dealing with the impacts and how to stabilize concentrations of carbon dioxide and other gases within the environment. For example, a global increase of 3 °C above current levels will result in possible destabilization of the Antarctic ice sheets. Put another way, if concentrations of carbon dioxide (measured by the quantum of parts per million – ppm) were to rise to 550 ppm then the global mean temperature increase would be unlikely to stay below 2 °C. Currently the figure is around 350 ppm. The 2005 conference on avoiding dangerous climate change set a stabilization concentration at around 450 ppm, a range within which scientists were confident that a global increase in temperature would be less than

2 °C. A similar approach was adopted in the Stern Review of 2006, which examined the implications for economic growth of runaway climate change and the central conclusion that action now would be considerably cheaper than action in twenty years or so. The 2005 conference also examined some of the techno-logical options for reducing emissions. They concluded that there are no 'magic bullets' and a portfolio of actions is required together with major investment in both mitigation and adaptation.

The government's own aspiration for a low carbon economy resulted in another energy White Paper, setting out a host of energy-efficiency initiatives (in 2007) and the Climate Change Bill (and subsequently Act), published in March 2007. This legislation was the subject of a pre-parliamentary public con-sultation between March and June 2007, resulting in some 17,000 responses. The subsequent legislation put in place a mechanism by which successive governments may set and report on the implementation of climate change tar-gets. Governments would, following enactment of this legislation, set national legally binding targets for cuts in carbon emissions. The already published and longer-term commitment to 60 per cent cutbacks by 2050 would thus be set in law. An interim target of between 26 per cent and 32 per cent was indicated by government at the time the Bill was published, causing some concerns within the environment sector that government was watering down its commitment here. The Climate Change Act would establish an independent climate change committee to advise on the setting of a five-year carbon budget, which will limit total emissions over that period. The first is set to run from 2008 to 2012. Once set, the budgets can only be changed with the agreement of Parliament, and following the recommendation of the committee. The committee is to be wholly independent of government and if the government of the day disagree with their five-year carbon budget or fail to meet the previously set targets they will have to justify this to Parliament. Further, under provision of the Act they will have to report annually on emissions from international aviation and shipping as well as regular assessments of the risks of climate change to the UK and how adaptation strategies are being rolled out. In anticipation of what may lie ahead, the government initiated a series of mitigation measures on the back of the 2007 energy White Paper, with a combination of reduction targets and energy commitments. These would involve the setting of carbon emission reduction targets for 2008–2012, to promote domestic energy reduction and a carbon reduction commitment to require large commercial organizations to reduce their emissions. Further, more information would be made available on energy use and a biomass strategy implemented to increase the supply from this sector. The landscape of sustainable development was recast by the new legally imposed targets in the Climate Change Act of 2008.

Any planning strategy must be linked to broader areas of public policy, if such objectives are to be realized. The Climate Change Act 2008 makes this a reality. For example, reducing the use of the private car will require a combination of planning policy with financial matters (subsidy to public transport) and a coherent transport strategy (reduce new road building) before the real growth in car ownership can be arrested, as people will opt for other modes of transport that provide greater accessibility at lower cost. The planning system operating in isolation of these other areas will not make any significant impact on such environmental issues as global warming. The Royal Commission on Environmental Pollution (1994: 159) concluded that 'In isolation, land-use planning is a relatively blunt instrument for changing travel behaviour, critical though it may be in the long term. . . . The problems of traffic growth and congestion must, in the first instance, be tackled by more direct means.' In considering the role of the land-use planning system, the report acknowledged the interaction between land use and transport issues, but emphasized the role of a coherent transport policy framework alongside purely planning-based strategies.

Planning authorities are being encouraged to adopt sustainable policies in their regional spatial strategies or development plan frameworks. After 2004 it is evident that such policies will be widely applied throughout the system. Councils like the London Borough of Merton are, in many respects, leading the way here with adoption of a benchmark of 10 per cent renewable energy in new commercial development in excess of certain floorspace thresholds. The 'Merton rule' as it is colloquially known, perfectly encapsulates the new policy emphasis in land-use planning, which takes broader climate change/sustainability issues and applies them to local policy and the determination of planning applications 'on the ground'.

Sustainable development has been, and will continue to be, a buzzword in town planning. Land-use decision-making is an important arena, within which a balance may be struck between economic development and environmental protection; town planning, therefore, plays a vital role. Although it alone cannot deliver sustainable development, it enjoys considerable potential to direct key areas towards these goals. The key test for the future will be the political will of national and regional governments to support such a role for the town planning system. The potential loss of future planning powers from Regional Assemblies, as mooted by government in late 2007 (but subsequently shelved for future review), could be potentially damaging to this aspiration.

The term 'sustainable development' is not subject to one universally agreed definition. This may be of little surprise when one considers the broad subject area encompassed by the term 'sustainability', namely that of the relationship between economic development and global environmental conservation. This chapter has focused upon the role of land-use planning in delivering sustainable development. That in itself is a broad subject area. Nevertheless, the UK government has sought to initiate some debate, as well as action, on the role of the planning system. It is too early to judge whether such policy has been a success or failure, and a meaningful reassessment should really begin after 2010. Nevertheless, the threat of severe environmental degradation posed by global warming necessitates that the implementation of such policy cannot come too soon.

Table 8.4 Summary of key statistics

Issue	Statistics	Source
Global warming		
Previously developed land Urban growth	64,000 ha brown-field land Projected change of urban area of England from 10% land use (1981) to 12% by 2016. Between 1991 and 2016, 169,000 ha will change from rural to urban use.	DCLG (2006) Indicators of Sustainable Development (1996) and Office for National Statistics
Agricultural land	77% land area (Britain) appears the easiest way forward of all urban increase, around 40%, was previously in agricultural use.	DEFRA land-use change statistics
Forestry	2.4 million ha (Britain)	UK strategy
Road building	12,000 ha used for road building in the period 1985–90 (66% on rural land)	Indicators of Sustainable Development (1996)
Re-use of urban land	Around 66,000 ha per year available and 29,000 ha suitable for housing, 60% of this being vacant or derelict	Statistical Bulletin: Land Use Change in England (1995 & 2002)
Household projections	Household formation in England and Wales expected to grow to 2.5 million by 2006 and over the period 1991–2016 the total increase in households is projected to be 23%, and 232,000 new households every year	DoE Projections of Households in England to 2016 (1995) and DCLG statistics (2008)

Issue	Statistics	Source
Global warming		
All greenhouse gases (methane, nitrous oxide and carbon dioxide)	Government target: all emissions to be at 1990 levels by 2000 + 60% cutbacks by 2050	Climate Change Act 2008 and Climate Change – UK Programme 2006
Carbon dioxide emissions	1990 calculated at 160 million tonnes carbon. By 2000, between 157 and 179 million tonnes carbon	UK Strategy
Road traffic	84% increase in road traffic from 1980 to 2006.	Transport Trend Statistics and Friends of the Earth
Pollution	Sulphur dioxide/black smoke fallen by 70% 1970–93. Nitrogen dioxide fallen by 37% 1990–2000 and projected to fall by a further quarter by 2020.	Climate change statistics from DEFRA
Climate change	Estimate: 3 °C increase in temperature and a 6 cm rise in sea level every 10 years at 1990 rates.	Climate change statistics from DEFRA and Houghton et al. (1992)
Changes in land-use patterns 1982–92	Out-of-town retail: 4.1 million m^2 and 3.4 million in town (Compare 1960–81: 1 million out-of-town and 6 million in town)	UK strategy

9 Urban renaissance and urban renewal

Background

On 16 November 2000 the Deputy Prime Minister launched a new Urban White Paper, entitled *Our Towns and Cities: The Future* (DETR 2000b). This document laid down a vast array of policy initiatives dealing with the social, economic and environmental dimensions of urban life. It was billed as presenting a new 'joined-up' and long-term approach to the coordination of financial/fiscal measures, policy agendas (including planning), and the functioning of various government and non-governmental agencies, all seeking to promote urban 'renewal' and arrest long-term decline and under-investment. Such a document, the first White Paper to exclusively address urban policy issues for some twenty-three years, was constructed upon other works, notably the findings of the Urban Task Force, chaired by Lord Rogers (Urban Task Force 1999), and research reports into the *State of English Cities* and *Living in Urban England: Attitudes and Aspirations* (DETR 2000c). The White Paper set itself a number of ambitious targets, with detailed monitoring by a newly formed cabinet committee and Urban Summit in 2002. The following year the government launched its amalgamation of policy initiatives in the form of the Sustainable Communities Plan. This would have a wide-ranging impact on urban policy, combining £38 billion worth of investment with significant housing growth (in the South East). The oft-repeated mantra of this strategy was 'to create communities and not housing estates'. A government appraisal of this strategy, after three years, reported success measured against a whole basket of indicators, albeit an independent review in 2007 by the Sustainable Development Commission raised concern that too much emphasis was placed on the delivery of housing to the exclusion of other issues, notably sustainability and a community aspect. In 2006, a second *State of English Cities* report was published, together with the creation of a database that captured much information on various indicators, policies and spatial patterns relevant to cities and urban areas. Since the millennium the urban areas of England, in particular, had been the subject of White Papers, Green Papers and a plethora of legislation on housing, planning, regional government and local government.

The creation of 'environmental sustainability', 'local participation' and 'mixed communities in urban area renewal' represented key themes that reverberated throughout the White Paper and Sustainable Communities Plan. In twenty years time, it seems reasonable to conclude, commentators will look back to 16 November 2000 either as a day when new thinking emerged to shape the fundamental approach to urban renewal, or when yet another raft of regeneration initiatives was launched that failed to understand the complex interrelationship between economics, planning and society. This chapter will focus primarily on the implications of these new initiatives for physical planning, although other (social and economic) policy areas will be dealt with where appropriate.

The context of urban change

Demographic change over the last hundred or so years has resulted in a population movement from rural to urban areas. At the start of the twentieth century around 10 per cent of the world's population lived in towns and cities. A century later this figure exceeds 50 per cent. This urban population accounts for almost all pollution (Urban Task Force 1999), while England's urban areas (in which 90 per cent of people – 47 million – live) accounts for 91 per cent of total economic output and 89 per cent of all employment (Urban Task Force 1999).

Urban areas predominate in the economic and social life of the nation. While Britain is highly urbanized, land-use patterns are increasingly viewed as 'inefficient'. For example, while London and its hinterland constitute the second most densely populated region in Europe, prevailing post-war density standards in Britain have (up to the 1990s) produced housing layouts as low as 5–20 dwellings per hectare. A clear link is drawn between density and car usage, in which 'land-grabbing' low-density housing encourages car use (as shops and services are beyond an acceptable threshold of five minutes/500 metres distance) and discourages public transport (it is uneconomic for a bus route to serve sprawling low-density areas). In post-war Britain the planning system has encouraged this low-density suburbanization around many small- to medium-density towns, while at the same time restricting the outward expansion of the major conurbations (where 40 per cent of the population live) by the imposition of green belts and open countryside designations. England thus has vast areas of protected and otherwise 'development-restricted' landscapes and an urban population that renders it the third most densely populated country in the world.

It may come as little surprise, therefore, that these development patterns (coupled with peripherally located business and leisure uses) have promoted car dependency. Between 1980 and 1996, Britain's roads experienced a 63 per cent increase in motor vehicle traffic (almost entirely composed of car use), and between 1992 and 2021 car ownership is projected to increase from 24.5 million to 30 million. The planning system and housebuilding industry has hitherto operated on a model of regulation dominated by conformity to prescribed road layout, density and parking standards, and separation of development (typically 21 metres rear-to-rear elevation). This has produced some uninspiring layouts in which a low-density, low-rise suburbia predominates. Further it has, in the past, catered predominantly to achieve the delivery of private sector market 'volume' housing.

Demographic change and its implications for land use have brought into sharp focus the problems created by continuing to replicate this model. The government's prediction in 1996, that over the following twenty-five years 3.8 million new households will be required (a product of increasing numbers of single-person households, coupled with a population drift away from urban areas of around 90,000 net outward migrants every year) has resulted in a reassessment of priorities. The spectre emerges of satisfying the call for 3.8 million new dwellings on a density model of less than 20 dwellings per acre and creating over the next fifteen to twenty years an additional urban area the size of the West Midlands conurbation (Urban Task Force 1999). Alongside this powerful statistic it should be remembered that around 700,000 homes were empty by 2006 (with 250,000 of them having been so for in excess of one year) and that by 2003 some 66,000 hectares of brown-field land was available for redevelopment. This reassessment of past town planning values led to calls for an 'urban renaissance'. It is this renaissance that must be given detailed attention today and how it affects both existing cities (whose centres continue to suffer population decline, albeit at a slower pace) and the creation of growth areas in the green fields of southern England.

The task is by no means an easy one to achieve. Past and current drift away from urban areas (especially among more affluent social groups) must be reversed, standards of urban development and design must be improved, greater low cost market and socially rented affordable housing must be constructed, and the private sector must be encouraged (and actively supported) to recycle urban land that may be derelict, vacant and even contaminated. Consideration must be given to a number of important policy documents that have established an agenda for change as well as to several case studies of best practice. Specific attention is given to matters of urban density, urban design, local democracy, sustainability and mixed use/mixed-tenure projects, principally presented as case studies.

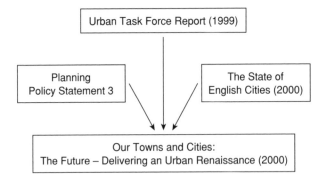

Agenda for change

The Urban White Paper, *Our Towns and Cities: The Future*, constitutes the key background document, itself being influenced by the findings of the Urban

Task Force chaired by Lord Richard Rogers, a think-tank created by the Deputy Prime Minister in April 1998. Further, it has been shaped by (the then) DETR-sponsored reports into the state of urban life (DETR 2000b) and a review of the way housing has been allocated by the planning system (now in PPS3). The Urban Task Force (UTF) made some far-reaching criticisms and called for a radical rethink of many urban planning policies. The UTF report, *The State of English Cities* and its 2006 update – as well as the Sustainable Communities Plan of 2003 and subsequent five-year plan for delivering homes (entitled *Sustainable Communities: Homes for All*) – will all now be considered. (PPS3 (2006) and the more gritty site-specific topics addressing housing layout and design are considered in greater depth later, in Chapter 19 on residential development.)

The Urban Task Force reports (1999 and 2005)

The UTF findings were critical of several failings in the planning system, although not all blame was laid at the door of planning authorities because the overall direction of the system (created by government) was also responsible. The first report championed the status and importance of the city in supporting key cultural, educational and welfare institutions 'to perform a unifying civic function' (UTF 1999). The future of the city will be influenced by technical innovation (such as in information technology), ecological threat (i.e. sustainability) and social transformation (as life patterns change and the level of one-person households increases). The UTF identified a number of threats to the future of cities, notably the economic decline of many (northern English) cities, their weakening manufacturing base, and disproportionate percentage of poorer social groups and less productive manufacturing capacity. Such structural weaknesses combine to create a vicious spiral, which generates a poor public image and unfavourable perceptions of city life, whether justified or not by the facts. These influences on future success are set out in Table 9.1.

The report confronted the problem of accommodating an additional 3.8 million households in England by 2021. Cities (and urban areas) contain vast swathes of derelict and vacant land, with estimates ranging between 17,000 and 39,000 ha derelict land and 16000 ha of vacant land being available for redevelopment. Public opposition to greenfield development is increasing and a significant

Table 9.1 Future success of urban area (from Urban Task Force Report 1999)

1 Quality	→ In design and the promotion of compact urban form
2 Economy	→ To achieve sustained investment to target economic decline and social exclusion
3 Environmental responsibility	→ Use resources more efficiently; energy-efficient buildings: awareness of biodiversity and housing on recycled land
4 Governance	→ Promote participatory democracy through urban government
5 Society	→ Give priority to social well-being to ensure neighbourhoods have a balance of tenure and income groups

proportion of housing demand is from one-person households. The UTF, in a highly creative strategy, identify the potential to satisfy this demand on urban land in such a way as to repair 'current tears in our urban fabric' and create a renaissance in both the physical fabric of and attitudes to our urban areas.

Such repair is to be achieved by the creation of mixed, diverse and well-connected urban areas in ways that regenerate or 'retrofit' existing environments. A strong commitment is attributed to design in this report: 'successful urban regeneration is design-led'.

The UTF gave a great deal of attention to the physical ways in which the planning system may 'repair' the city. The way forward is set out in a number of key recommendations. First, they judge that past reliance on rigid planning standards has stifled creativity. For example, adherence to highway standards (such as road widths, radii and visibility at junctions)[1] has dominated urban layouts by establishing a 'roads first, houses later' priority. The ease of car movement predominates over pedestrian or cycle priority. By contrast, they recommend that streets should be seen as places and not transport corridors. The 2007 publication of the 'Manual for Streets' was a consequence of such a shift in policy, with its fundamental starting point that streets need to be designed for people and not the unimpeded movement of vehicles.

Second, to foster both sustainability and urban quality, the UTF promoted the notion of a compact city. Sustainability would be achieved by linking urban density to a hierarchy of urban centres/local hubs providing shops and services within well-connected public transport and walking routes. The report declared that 'there is a proven link between urban densities and energy consumption'. An appropriate integration of density and the 'connected compact city' would reduce the reliance on the car. Urban quality would be achieved by improved urban design – that is to say, the design of public space and proper acknowledgement that quality public space provides vital 'glue' between buildings, creating integrated city spaces. The report laments a recent demise in the quality of city space (i.e. the public realm between buildings) that demonstrates the loss of a rich urban tradition evident in medieval and Georgian civic planning in cities such as York and Bath.

Third, and related to the compact city, they recommend that the previous adherence to density standards must be dropped: 'density is not an indicator of urban quality'. The report sets out to destroy the previous orthodoxy that density dictates an acceptable urban form. Indeed, it argues that higher densities (and not necessarily high-rise developments) contribute to urban sustainability and support a greater number of public amenities and transport facilities. Previously, half of all land used in England for new housing has been at prevailing densities of 20 or fewer dwellings per hectare, equating to 54 per cent of all land used providing just one quarter of all housing units completed. Not only is this form of housing highly inefficient but it is no longer a viable means of providing housing when confronted with the dual priorities of providing 3.8 million units while people continue to leave urban areas. In raising density levels, quality need not be diminished. Indeed, the UTF makes reference to

Table 9.2 Density comparables (from Urban Task Force Report 1999)

Barcelona	400 dwellings per hectare
London (Islington/Bloomsbury)	100–200 dwellings per hectare
Most of UK	5–10 dwellings per hectare
Post-war 'norm'	20–30 dwellings per hectare

the density of a city like Barcelona, compared to Britain's post-war norm, as summarized in Table 9.2.

New government policy on housing (PPG3 of 2000 and then PPS3 of 2006) attempted to lift density standards, albeit modestly, to at or above 30 dwellings per hectare. The UTF report recommended imposition of a planning presumption against excessively low-density urban development, and its 2006 update (see later) would recommend that density and brown-land targets were raised further still, a position also taken by the Sustainable Development Commission when reviewing the Sustainable Communities Plan in 2007.

Finally, regard is given to the utilization of urban design to facilitate mixed-use/mixed-tenure development to foster sustainability (by living and working in close proximity) and allowing people to change tenure type to meet changing circumstances while remaining in the same locality. The report raised the status of design in urban regeneration as a pre-eminent consideration. Good urban design should encourage people to live near to the services they require on a regular basis. Key principles to be employed include consideration of the context/density/sustainability of the site and the promotion of mixed-tenure/mixed-activity development built in an environmentally responsible way (see Case studies 9.1 and 9.3).

The UTF set out to deliver this new vision by a combination of measures dealing with taxation, planning policy and urban design. Such integration across physical and economic policy, and the establishment of government agencies, may not be new. The report, reflecting its overall emphasis on design, promoted the spatial master-plan as an 'engine' of change, set within a national urban design framework. This master-plan would promote a three-dimensional model for urban regeneration, prepared by a local authority, combined with newly developed techniques like design coding, in which a checklist of design issues would be set out and robustly appraised.

Design coding is now frequently employed in many regeneration master-plans or significant regeneration projects and is used to focus on the integration of buildings and spaces. This methodology is viewed as more dynamic and design-led than the traditional two-dimensional approach, in which plans were produced that dealt with 'zoning' of use, density and access, and largely ignored the shape of the consequent urban form/public space, building design and integration between pedestrian, vehicular and public transport routes. The subsequent creation of bodies like CABE, then CABE Space and the use of design coding and creation of the Greenwich Millennium Village were all a consequence of the UTF review.

Case study 9.1   Urban renaissance: Good practice In urban design

To promote excellence in urban design, between 1999 and 2003 the government sponsored a series of Millennium Communities or Villages (development projects following design competitions) and Urban Regeneration Companies (government-sponsored agencies to target investment in deprived cities and link public with private action).

The Greenwich Millennium Village was one such project, located on London's Greenwich peninsula and involving a 'high-profile international competition' (Urban Task Force 1999) to create a mixed-tenure community comprising high-density, energy-efficient development, integrated with a variety of public spaces (streets, square, open spaces, and communal gardens). The nature of the resulting development was commended by the Urban Task Force as a model of design-led regeneration that harnessed a competitive process to produce innovation in design and sustainability (energy efficiency).

Between 2000 and 2003, fifteen Urban Regeneration Companies (URCs) were established, following the successful pilot of 'Liverpool Vision'. This URC was funded by three public agencies and the private sector, and established a 'Strategic Regeneration Framework' to stimulate sustained long-term investment in the city. A coordinated strategy recommended action in a wide variety of areas, including urban design projects, cultural projects (seeking nomination as European City of Culture) and public participation to engage local people in the new strategies. Such an approach established a new agenda in which physical and economic regeneration was no longer viewed as the exclusive preserve of the public sector. Instead a partnership was formed between public and private sectors, in close liaison with the views of local people.

Urban Task Force – the way forward

The Urban Task Force report was highly design-oriented and viewed quality urban design and urban form as an essential engine of change in bringing about urban regeneration. While not ignoring other considerations (economic policy, fiscal incentives and matters of local governance), the report placed design at the centre of all issues. The report's promotion of the compact city is not new (Jenks *et al.* 1996, DoE 1998c, Coupland 1997) but is part of a dynamic attempt to change the low-density suburban and 'non-place' orthodoxy of much post-war British residential town planning (see Case study 9.2). Perhaps the most exciting recommendation to emerge from this work centres on the deployment of the 3.8 million new homes to be built by 2021 to repair the existing residential fabric, utilizing this to connect and thus integrate existing environments to

Case study 9.2 Urban renaissance: Urban extensions

In 2000, the Prince's Foundation published a report, *Sustainable Urban Extensions: Planned through Design*, which advocated an alternative model of community involvement deemed preferable to past public participation, in which local people merely commented on a completed scheme instead of getting involved with its formulation. The Foundation's own mission was to promote 'a return of human values to architecture, urban design and regeneration' and their report took a critical view of much in the design of past residential environments, railing against the piecemeal low-density outward expansion of towns and cities. Private-sector housing estates offered little choice of house type and were predominant in creating 'placeless' low-density suburbs. The rigid enforcement of highway rules (seeking vehicular visibility) prevented innovative urban design because of creating cul-de-sacs, visibility splays and radii in a low-density suburban style. This 'roads first, houses later' approach and the consequent inefficient low-density suburban form, is unable to justify bus services and so increases car dependency.

The report argued that a consensus was emerging among planners and the public that greater priority needs to be given to urban design, environmental sustainability and public involvement. New greenfield development will continue (40 per cent is accepted by government in its housing projections) so a new approach is needed. The Foundation holds 'Enquiry by Design' community workshops, in which landowners, council officials and public and other interested groups assemble to devise new-build residential layouts on an anti-sprawl and sustainable agenda. Workshop facilitators help the 'stakeholders' to debate, discuss, enquire, and design collaboratively, usually focused on the key criterion that housing is organized into walkable neighbourhoods of a five minute/500 metre radius from public transport or community facilities.

The approach was employed in two English case studies, Basildon and Northampton. Two urban extensions into greenfield sites designed on the model of a traditional low-density volume householder were redesigned to create significantly greater housing yields and more sustainable layouts. In Basildon, a 35 ha site would yield 1120 houses (preserving 7 ha open space) at 40 dwellings per ha, compared to 875 units of traditional low-density detached houses. In Northampton, 6400 houses were located on a site of some 250 ha, compared to 3700 on the traditional model. This 70 per cent increase in the yield of dwelling units was achieved not by compromising the amenities enjoyed by future occupiers but the very reverse, in which quality urban design (based on urban and not suburban principles) allows for higher density with integration of public spaces and transport networks. Such an 'Enquiry by Design' approach creates better, more sustainable and more democratic environments. It is unsurprising, therefore, that this approach should be strongly endorsed by the Urban Task Force when the direction of government policy (as expressed in PPG3 and then PPS3) accepts that urban extensions will occur in the future. Taking this on board, such an approach will need to be brought to bear on the future development of the many green fields that will need to be ploughed up for housing by 2021, in order to render that development more sustainable and more efficient in its use of land. This focus on the importance of urban design has been reinforced by research published by the Commission for Architecture and the Built Environment (CABE 2001). Following detailed examination of the literature in this area and appraisal of six recently completed developments, the CABE research concluded that good urban design not only added economic value but also social and environmental value. (Economic value in this context means higher profits for owners and investors, by virtue of higher capital values and rents. Social value refers to job creation, while environmental value refers to the urban realm and its infrastructure.) Further, the cost of such urban design need not be high. One of the case studies dealt with Standard Court in Nottingham, a 2.6 ha mixed-use office, retail, leisure, and residential redevelopment of a former hospital site in the city centre. A public space is created (the public arena), defined by both new and refurbished buildings (mostly listed). The researchers considered the scheme to be 'a disconnected place', poorly integrated into the neighbouring historic environment of Nottingham Castle and with the main entrances of the office buildings not facing on to the arena. The result is an unused, desolate space that does not benefit from passing trade, with detrimental effects on the retail/catering premises in the scheme. Office rents have been below the best Nottingham levels, indicative of a satisfactory but not excellent economic performance for Standard Court. Compare this with Barbirolli Square in central Manchester, another case study in the research. This involved a 1 ha redevelopment of former railway land to create a concert hall, two office blocks and a café/bar. Again a public space is created, linking and opening up a former canal basin. The site was considered to be reasonably well-connected and creates 'a new landmark gateway to Manchester'. The offices have commanded high rents and an economic/social ripple effect is evident, in which five new restaurants have subsequently opened up in the surrounding area.

Such case studies demonstrate that the design, configuration and use of urban space can either hinder or enhance the economic, social and environmental prosperity of the surrounding area. Good architecture, while important, is not the sole factor in creating success. Design of buildings must be linked to design of space, so that redevelopment schemes connect with their surroundings and link to the neighbouring morphology (the shape and features of the urban space), such as that found in historic areas. The importance of urban design is thus critical in fostering successful and sustainable urban renaissance.

create higher-density well-planned places. This would challenge the system to produce many things, including the timely release of land for development and/or housing as well as better design and an increase in building by housebuilders. After the work of Kate Barker, geared to increase housing supply, the government was (by 2008) seeking to increase the annual rate of housebuilding to about 220,000 new homes per year. Historically, from the mid-1990s to the mid-2000s this rate of annual completions had bottomed out at between 130,000–150,000 units annually. Thus much remained to be done to increase housing supply.

Considering the fact, as the UTF report establishes, that more than 90 per cent of our urban fabric will still exist in thirty years time, then such a 'retrofitting' approach, while a significant policy change, will only bring about a limited spatial change, measured in hectares affected. The report issued a series of qualified warnings that the government's target for 60 per cent new housing by 2021 on previously developed sites is unlikely to be met, concluding instead that 'from our models we have estimated that based on current policies and trends just under 2.1 million dwellings will be developed' on such land. But given that, in 1996 for example, only 40 per cent of urban housing was provided on such sites, a step-change is required in planning policy and other areas (taxation and subsidy) to prevent the then (at 2000) achievement of around 50–55 per cent built on recycled land falling back to the 40–45 per cent equivalent of less than a decade before. (For details of how new housing land is allocated, see Chapter 19.) As it would transpire, this prophecy appeared incorrect with the 60 per cent target (all housing) exceeded by 2005 and the creation of an all-time record of 72 per cent of new development being built on previously used land by 2006 (up to 89 per cent in the Thames Gateway growth area). Architects likes Sir Terry Farrell published a vision of the Thames Gateway in which a new national park would be created and the vast majority or 90 per cent of the 160,000 proposed dwellings by 2021 would be located within the existing urban footprint of outer London and a series of Medway Towns, with the vast majority of the allocated land area devoted to landscape regeneration and public access. This vision, published in 2008, while not a formal planning document, made a strong impression on the public and politicians alike, and demonstrated that the need to create a 'place' required a new way of thinking about planning, landscape and the creation of identity.

Urban Task Force – conclusions

The Urban Task Force report gave fresh momentum to an urban renaissance in our towns and cities. It accepted that a cultural change would be required, in which people perceived urban living more positively than previously, but argued that a new focus on the urban fabric (by means of better urban design) will assist greatly in bringing about this change in attitudes. The planning system needs to be less concerned with rigid adherence to set standards on density, parking or layout of development. Instead planning authorities should adopt a more three-dimensional and flexible approach to policy standards, should promote mixed uses and refuse permission for low-density schemes. The overall strategy for accommodating new housing projections in the system needs to be more flexible and the report endorsed the government's decision (of 1998) to adopt a more flexible stance on housing allocations and their delivery over the plan period. The Barker Review of Housing (in 2005) reinforced this objective, with its call for a more flexible planning system and one that responds more readily to market forces.

The Urban Task Force report made 105 detailed recommendations for change. A summary of the key ones is set out at the end of this chapter. While it contended that the 60 per cent brown-land target was unlikely to be met (although it may be possible upon implementation of the report's recommendations) it was ultimately optimistic that an urban renaissance could be delivered and could effect lasting change in the planning of urban space in England.

The State of English Cities (1999 and 2006)

This report addressed the change in intellectual orthodoxy over the last twenty years in the nature of urban policy. For the period from the mid-1970s to the 1990s, the predominant thinking at government level involved targeting of resources specifically at the poorest areas, in pursuit of redistribution of wealth. A new agenda, evident towards the end of the 1990s, attempted a more connected (or 'joined-up', to quote from the Urban White Paper) approach. The work of many agencies would need to be integrated and connected.

The report established an 'urban asset base' of factors that have influenced the success or failure of cities, including location, age, economic structure, company characteristics (growth potential), skills and innovation, communications, environmental quality, and nature of local governance. It reports that cities have endured – 'whilst there is some evidence of the continuing relative economic weakness of British cities, there are also signs of a renaissance in their roles as centres of economic strength'. The report appraises the economic and social dimensions of cities. Economically they exert a powerful 'propulsive' or wealth-generating impact upon their regional hinterlands. This impact goes beyond just employment opportunities to include provision of learning, education and a better regional image. Economics and demography (population change) are interlinked. The annually accelerating population losses from urban centres of the 1980s slowed in the 1990s and became population growth by the late 1990s. It is worthy of note, however, that 'in most conurbations, rates of net out-migration are highest for the better-off. While central Manchester has enjoyed an urban renaissance (a consequence of the policy initiatives of the council and innovation in development by developers like Urban Splash), the trend measured across the entire city is still one of population decline.

Socially, it is apparent that cities perform badly when measured against indices of socio-economic deprivation: 'unemployment, educational levels, health, crime, and poverty tend to be worst in the big cities'. Evidence cited on poverty and social exclusion shows beyond doubt that there is a widening gap between 'comfortable' Britain and the poorest, as factors like child poverty and above-average mortality (in poor areas) increased at the end of the 1990s. The 1999 State of English Cities report called for some hard thinking if child poverty is to be ended in the next generation. Tackling social exclusion (from employment opportunities) is a priority. A cyclical problem emerges, in which low levels of educational achievement and related social/life skills are a major source of social exclusion. This cycle is reinforced by the inability of poorer families to relocate to the catchment of schools with good social infrastructure. Conversely, those who can move away from the catchment of schools with poor educational records, entrench the problem. In the report, emphasis is placed on the importance of neighbourhood-led or community-led action to engage residents in the implementation of projects to tackle local problems. One important area of city regeneration is the way the various agencies operate. In reflecting on many past policies, the report established that a number of key features may be identified. For example, appraisal of City Challenge[2] (1992–1998) and the Single Regeneration Budget[3] (SRB) Challenge Fund (from 1994) identified key benefits in their partnership of public, private and community groups. Further, these groups adopted a cross-disciplinary approach, linking across several agencies and/or professions to target resources at key problems. Greater partnership across the work of all regeneration agencies, combined with a regional focus, were identified as key features, leading the report to state that: 'At the end of the 1990s the key principles of regeneration policy were partnership, spatial targeting, integration, competition and a commitment to combined economic, social and environmental regeneration'.

The report called for greater clarity in the role of the Regional Development Agencies (RDAs) and financial resources available to them. The eight RDAs were established in 1999 to provide a regional dimension to regeneration strategies, although little fresh money was made available because their resources were largely transferred from SRB and English Partnership funding. The principal focus of RDA strategy was to be delivered by local partnerships (reflecting many lessons learnt from City Challenge and SRB projects), but in their early years they lacked the 'joined-up' dimension so sought-after by government, and suffered from an ill-defined relationship with the other big regional agencies for regeneration, the government regional offices. The government announced in 2008 that Regional Planning Authorities would be scrapped in 2010 and their powers transferred to the Regional Development Agencies.

A comparative study of regeneration strategies in other European countries endorsed the model of targeted and local spatial initiatives, based upon partnership. Further, it confirmed that policy solutions to the problems of regeneration are not easy – 'achieving the goal of regeneration is proving as great a challenge to [other European countries] as it is for the British'.

The 1999 report concluded by explicitly stating the key principles of regeneration, given the experience of the previous twenty years. Four key principles were identified: integration of policy approach across agencies and areas; the establishment of public–private–community partnerships; a pivotal role to be taken by local government; and policy initiatives to be carefully linked to both regional and local implementation strategies. Qualified endorsement was given to the twelve urban regeneration companies, with their cross-disciplinary and city-wide focus. A key feature of successful integration policy is that all agencies integrate their work. Failure to adopt this holistic view can have far-reaching (if not always readily apparent) consequences. For example, government decisions on the brown-land/greenfield targets 'can have profound effects on the likelihood of urban regeneration', because in northern cities demand is less buoyant for new housing, resulting in less incentive to develop recycled urban land.

Key principles of urban policy based around the need to maintain partnerships, local governance, and for a wider grasp of socio-economic factors (especially social exclusion), were established. All regenerative agencies were vested with the responsibility to work together, at neighbourhood, city and regional levels to create the conditions for local partnership considered necessary for effective implementation of renewal policies. Figure 9.1 provides a summary. In 2006, the next *State of English Cities* report made for mostly upbeat reading of the progress made, with five key areas of appraisal identified and the central conclusion that 'England's cities are now better placed than at any time since the end of the nineteenth century to become motors of national advance'. The five identified areas were social cohesion (with a reported narrowing in the gap between poor and the rest), liveability (with better urban spaces and streets), governance (with more joined-up agencies), economic performance (with increased levels of activity expressed in gross value added) and demographics (with a reverse in population decline). Yet, much remains to be done, and the 2006 report was clear that while urban regeneration is well developed, it needs to be both sustained and widened. Levels of deprivation, unemployment, worklessness and crime are all higher and more widespread in cities. The European Union's vision for the creation of a prestigious knowledge-based economy spread across all member states, would act as a key point of regeneration and renewal in some city-regions. In England, national government became increasingly aware of a gap in regional growth, with most economic growth measured as gross value added (GVA), being largely confined to the south and east of England, with the notable exception of Manchester. London's GVA, at over 40 per cent above the national average, would not be repeated elsewhere, due to its unique status as a capital city and one influenced by international economic relations. Yet, the gap with cities in traditional manufacturing locations (estimated at £29 billion difference in prosperity) was a worry, and attempts to improve prosperity, jobs and investment in the eight major city-regions in the north of England led to the publication of *The Northern Way* in 2004. This strategy, developed by the three northern RDAs, would benefit from an additional £100 million provided to fund projects. The 2006 *State of English Cities* report made a significant comparison with the renaissance of many competitor cities within Europe (such as Barcelona). Decision-making was generally decentralized in many European cities and combined with greater regional government and autonomy from national governments. The report identified a number of key principles, including the need for increasing regionalization. Other principles dealt with the need to discourage

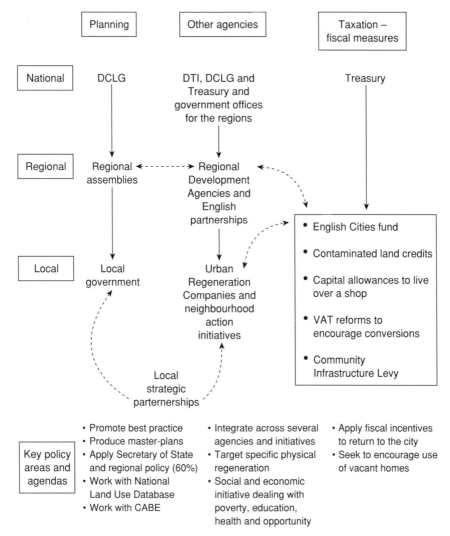

Figure 9.1 Key agencies in the urban renaissance

suburbanization by promoting brown-field development, promoting better supply in housing and improving the links between government departments who were vested with responsibility to tackle urban problems dealing with urban quality, skills training and social exclusion. The report viewed cities as 'dynamos' of national and regional economies but also as assets with great capacity to promote community development, social cohesion and civic or cultural identity. The task for the next period of review (set to 2010) would be to ensure continued economic growth and population growth within urban areas as well as a narrowing between the regions, notably between the north of England and the south and east of England.

The Urban White Paper: Our Towns and Cities (2000)

This White Paper married a number of existing policies with a variety of current or forthcoming policy reviews. The document, therefore, presented itself as a vast amalgamation of policy areas and action plans. Key themes emerged, most notably its attempt to promote an integrated approach to urban policy by linking planning, sustainability, transport, economics, and social exclusion policies into one holistic framework. This ambitious remit may account for its sometimes confusing stream of initiatives and policies.

A key feature is that local leaderships and partnerships are seen as fundamental to achieving an enduring change in urban renewal projects. In response to the House of Commons Environment Committee's observations on the (then proposed) Urban White Paper,[4] the government accepted the need for an urban renaissance to create sustainable mixed neighbourhoods and economically powerful cities, by emphasizing that alongside physical regeneration, 'strong and effective local leadership and close partnership working both locally and between tiers' are required. When considering the future direction of urban policy, regard must be paid to the government's emphasis on local political structures and the coordination of initiatives. The need for local democratic processes reverberates across the many policy areas in the White Paper. An element of 'self-help' is often an underlying theme behind an array of policies, and the White Paper declares that 'a clear message from the regeneration initiatives of the last 30 years is that real sustainable change will not be achieved unless local people are in the driving seat'. Emphasis is placed on reforms of local government democracy within the provisions of the Local Government Act 2000 (such as the appointment of directly elected mayors or cabinets) and for greater deployment of Local Strategic Partnerships (linking community and voluntary groups to tackle social, economic and environmental issues).

The White Paper incorporates many of the conclusions of the Urban Task Force, although it is less hard-hitting in certain areas. As with the Urban Task Force, a clear relationship is established between density in urban areas and consumption of energy (petrol), and in similar fashion a strong conclusion is drawn that past development patterns must be changed to secure sustainable cities and halt the trend towards a decline in the urban population.

A key theme was to create a vision for the repopulation of the urban core (based on greater physical attractiveness and enhanced economic opportunity) and provide greater flexibility in housing allocations (by scrapping the 1990s 'predict and provide' approach in favour of 'plan, monitor and manage').[5] This 'vision' is encapsulated, for example, in the championing of the recovery of Manchester's urban core in recent years and resulting population increase from 300 to 6000 in the two years between 1998 and 2000, and to 25,000 by 2007, in part a consequence of conversions of existing stock and mixed-use schemes. No real strategy is presented to address the anxieties of the Urban Task Force in respect of recycled urban land, notably the historically poor take-up of such land for housing and associated problems of long-term dereliction. Instead the White Paper adopted a fourfold strategy to meet the projected 3.8 million new homes target.

Case study 9.3   Urban renaissance: Best practice in urban design

The Urban Task Force placed considerable emphasis on improving urban design standards, calling for greater promotion of good practice and innovation by bodies such as the Commission for Architecture and the Built Environment (CABE). Contemporaneous with such recommendations, the DoE promoted 'best practice' in two reports, *Places, Streets and Movement* (DETR 1998d) and *By Design* (DETR 2000d). Both demonstrated a fresh awareness of the urban realm and the importance of creating a sense of place in urban development that reflected the local historic context and traditions.

Manual for Streets (Department for Transport 2007) replaced *Places, Streets and Movement* with a central aim that streets are about the creation of place and not merely for movement. The 'roads first, houses later' approach of past planning (see the critique by the Prince's Foundation in Case study 9.2) has not only contributed to car dependency but also to the design of layouts that give priority to the car. Matters of vehicular visibility and passing capacity (road widths and radii) have promoted low-density and predominantly suburban housing models. The local (urban) historic context and sense of place have been destroyed by the proliferation of these suburban layouts. A series of technical solutions are put forward (see Table 9.4 below) to create 'a network of spaces rather than a hierarchy of roads'. Many examples in the Report are drawn from Poundbury (Prince Charles's urban village in West Dorset) and Coldharbour Farm (a mixed-use satellite urban village in Aylesbury, providing 1500 houses – also referred to as Fairford Leys).

By Design: Urban Design in the Planning System: Towards Better Practice (DETR 2000d) drew much inspiration from work such as *Responsive Environments* (Bentley *et al.* 1985) which argued for greater attention to 'form' (the physical fabric of the city). To be 'responsive' an environment would need to offer appropriate choice to its citizens. *By Design*, in similar fashion to the Urban Task Force, views urban design as providing 'a key to creating sustainable developments [and] lively places with distinctive character . . . that inspire because of the imagination and sensitivity of their designers'. Successful urban design and its employment in master-plans (see also the Urban Task Force findings) must be employed at an early stage in the planning process and not as an afterthought. The report proposed seven principal objectives of urban design (see Table 9.4 below) and describes them as 'prompts to thinking', in which they influence good practice without necessarily constituting 'rigid formulae to be followed slavishly'. The report drew attention to how the planning process can be shaped by the inclusion of urban design policies in development plans, development briefs and master-plans, and in urban design frameworks (detailed urban guidance for areas undergoing change). *By Design* is an important material consideration in the determination of any planning application.

First, government planning policy would implement a step-change in the way we plan for housing. PPS3 (2006) would raise density standards and adopt a sequential test[6] in Paragraph 30, in accord with the Urban Task Force. The Secretary of State would reserve the power to 'call-in' and himself decide on any greenfield housing applications in excess of five ha or 150 dwellings that the LPA seeks to grant. Alongside such new policy directions the establishment of a National Land Use Database would permit more accurate monitoring of the amount of brown-land available for development. Work by Dixon (2007) employed this new resource to examine the role of the development industry in the regeneration potential of such land.

Second, the dissemination of best-practice guidance (on urban design) would promote better design and management of urban space without recourse to policy. Third, there would be a greater role for master-planning (as sought by the Urban Task Force) coupled with more resources allocated to the Commission for Architecture and the Built Environment to promote design training and establish twelve regional centres of excellence. The Academy for Sustainable Communities was established in 2005 to promote 'place-making' when development occurs. This was in response to the Egan Review of 2004 which reviewed the existing skills training to deliver sustainable communities and concluded that a new national centre of skills development was needed. Finally, there is a combination of financial and fiscal measures, including an exemption from stamp duty for disadvantaged communities (covering property transactions), tax credits for cleaning up contaminated land, capital allowance for creating flats over shops, and a reduced VAT tax burden on residential conversions. Alongside this the government encourages public–private partnerships (English Cities Fund) to fund mixed-use development projects in certain priority areas. The government's intention was that this should provide a framework, so it is simply impossible to assess whether this would meet the 60 per cent target (which includes conversions). The document lacks the radical and reforming edge of the Urban Task Force. The national taxation measures were reported as amounting to a £1 billion package in the 2001 budget, but the government avoided more contentious measures, such as a property tax on greenfield development or vacant land. The Sustainable Communities Plan (commenced in 2003) resulted in the creation of a Growth Area Fund (GAF), which was linked to provision of community infrastructure in areas identified for significant amounts of housing growth.

In 2003 the government published its vision for urban development in the form of the Sustainable Communities Plan. It combined planning growth (four and later five key growth areas in the South East Region), a £38 billion commitment to infrastructure delivery including £5 billion for affordable housing and a commitment to protect existing green belt and other special landscapes. The planning system would need to accommodate around one million homes in the South East region by 2026, but additionally would need to address 'market failure' in the Midlands, North West, Yorkshire and North East regions where a lack of demand had created decay and dereliction. These 'Pathfinder' projects

Table 9.3 Best practice in urban design

Places, Streets, Movement and Manual for Streets		By Design	
Technical innovations	• Variation in road width between 4.1 and 5.5 metres • Use of tracking, i.e. changing carriageway width • Junction design with an urban form, e.g. tight angles with 'raised tables' (bumps) to calm traffic • Use of traffic calming by employment of street parking, chicanes, raised junctions and tables	Objectives of urban design	• Character: promote townscape • Enclosure: continuity of street frontage • Quality urban realm: accessible public space • Ease of movement: promote pedestrian movement • Legibility: recognizable landmarks and easy to understand environment • Adaptability: can respond to changing social, technological and economic conditions
Overall emphasis	• Parking in rear courtyards and squares • Look for the place and not the car • Look for local context, e.g. density, layout of buildings and spaces, scale, mass and local materials • Give priority in movement to foot, bicycle and car	Applied to planning system	• Diversity: mixed uses and diversity of environment • Development briefs • Urban design frameworks • Development plan policy

would spend money to refurbish, demolish and rebuild housing stock to eradicate the blight imposed on these districts. Thus the housing market in England was split between the old industrial heartlands with a declining manufacturing base and loss of demand and that of the South East region (including London) where increasing economic buoyancy created a demand for housing that was 'boiling over' and causing severe problems of affordability and acute environmental pressures (Power and Houghton 2007). The overall strategy would be floated on a combination of government funding to address market failures (in the North) and government funding to provide some (but not all) infrastructure to facilitate growth (in the South) and to lever in much needed private sector investment. Locations like the Thames Gateway, stretching from East London to the North Sea, presented the only location that crossed this spatial divide, with many areas of poor housing, contaminated land and creaking infrastructure, yet located within the South East economic powerhouse and incorporating the

Table 9.4 Key recommendations of the Urban Task Force

Number	Policy areas	Subsequent action
3	Density – avoiding low-density schemes	PPG3 (2000) then PPS3 (2006) established new thresholds of 30–50 dwellings per hectare (paragraph 47 of PPS3)
5	Spatial master-plans – basis of all area-regeneration schemes and linked to public funding	Approach endorsed in the Urban White Paper, Chapter 4
6	Significant area-regeneration projects to be the subject of a design competition	Approach endorsed in the Urban White Paper, Recommendation 8
7	Develop a national Urban Design Framework to promote good practice	PPS1 (2005) to place greater emphasis on urban design, and creation of CABE
8	Promote design-led regeneration	Approach endorsed in the Urban White Paper, Chapter 4
11	Establish legal status for Homezone environmental areas	The Urban White Paper supports pilot studies of the operation of Homezones (car-free or reduced) and clear zones (low-emission zones) in town centres
19	Establish maximum parking (i.e. ceiling) standard of one space per dwelling	PPS3 (2006) encourages no greater than 1.5 spaces per dwelling
31	Creation of urban priority areas to facilitate neighbourhood renewal	Little government reform to support this, with reliance upon local participation and action at neighbourhood level
41	Production of detailed planning policy guidance to support urban renaissance	Carried across into a variety of national planning policy statements
42	Increase regional planning guidance (RPGs) to foster brownfield (recycled) development	Regional Spatial Strategies emerging from 2005 and regional targets set within those frameworks
44	Achieve comprehensive development-plan coverage in England by end 2002	2004 Planning Act and PPS11 and PPS12 to speed adoption of new planning policy
45	Encourage speed and efficiency in decision-making on planning applications	Best value regime introduced 2000 (see Chapter 4 of this book)
49–51	Revise planning obligations/gain system to seek a more streamlined system with a standardized system of impact fees	Considered in policy reviews 2001–03 with new guidance emerging, and by 2006 a 'Planning Gain Supplement emerges as favoured option
54	Support a new 'plan, monitor and manage' approach to housing demand	Push for urban land over rural land and 60% brown-land target set nationally

Table 9.4 (cont'd)

Number	Policy areas	Subsequent action
56	Support a sequential approach to used housing land release (i.e. green field, only after inner and edge urban capacity is exhausted)	PPG3 (2000) and new emphasis on LPAs conducting studies of that urban capacity (as above)
64	Prepare a scheme for taxing vacant land to deter vexatious delay of its development	None (with respect to tax) because the government questioned effectiveness of this method
75	Establish a national framework to deal with remediation of contaminated land	The Urban White Paper supports the existing assessment regime. A new database on condition of such land was established (2001) and tax relief granted (2001)
81	Measures to encourage restoration/reuse of historic buildings	Reduced VAT for listed places of worship (2001) and a review by English Heritage (2001–02)
84	Encourage property conversions by tax and VAT inducements	Reduced VAT (on conversions) and zero rating (on renovations after ten years and empty) (2001)
100	Give Regional Development Agencies (RDAs) more freedom to establish funding programmes	Greater budgetary flexibility introduced from 2001

2012 Olympic site. The coordination of the Thames Gateway would fall within a mosaic of control involving existing local authorities and two development corporations with selective planning powers (over mostly larger-scale development). Leading architects like Sir Terry Farrell proposed a development vision involving the creation of a new Royal Park as a focal point for this disparate corridor of existing communities, derelict land and considerable tracts of land with nature conservation value. Well-respected planning academic Professor Sir Peter Hall had consistently promoted the need for a sophisticated rail and public transport network, from which new development would be integrated. Yet, following some notable concerns raised by the Sustainable Development Commission (in 2007) and based on the experience of Ashford in Kent where dormitory housing developments lacked community services, justifiable fears arise that the Thames Gateway could become a poorly planned housing-dominated project without wider regeneration outcomes. Government appeared aware of this potentially devastating pitfall, which would turn the vision from flagship of the Sustainable Communities Plan to one of a model of unsustainable planning. In 2006 the Secretary of State published interim development prospectuses which, while not a formal regional strategy (remembering that the Gateway crosses three regions) constitute an attempt to recognize the need for some serious joined-up thinking about regional planning and the key integration between employment, land-use and transport strategies.

The 2003 Sustainable Communities Plan would present an immense challenge to government in its attempt to regenerate on the one hand, and to plan for major growth with limited environmental impact, on the other. These new growth strategies would need to be approved within the new Regional Spatial Strategies for the East of England and the South East. New planning language was to emerge, such as the concept of 'water-neutral' development (in the Sustainability Appraisal for the East of England Plan) and 'sustainable urban extensions' for the growth in South Hampshire around Southampton and Portsmouth. Problems were to emerge along the way, including the shelving of a major urban extension to the post-war new town of Harlow in north Essex (due to the unsustainable nature of the development) and the lack of funding to put in place the rail infrastructure to link the many 'pockets' of development that would form the Thames Gateway. Yet, the Sustainable Communities Plan would greatly shape the nature of future development over the next twenty years and probably beyond as the government increasingly became wedded to the need for more housing to tackle the acute problem of affordability. The national target for the period to 2020 would be three million new homes, with an annual target raised from 200,000 new dwellings (Barker in 2006) to 240,000 (2007). The difficulty would be delivering both community and sustainability so that people felt uplifted by the design and services as well as the reduced or zero carbon in their use, pointing the way to the future. Continually tougher building regulations (in Part L) and best practice codes (like the code for sustainable homes) have been identified as essential components here. Yet, the development sector has been wary of some of the more innovative design solutions (for example as employed in BedZED) as the perceived risk of a negative consumer reaction puts off major housebuilders. Maybe this is inevitable as the more innovative schemes should be pioneers for the future. The Sustainable Communities Plan will require a real step-change in government policy to link growth with zero carbon development.

In 2005 the Urban Task Force decided to review progress on their report and take stock of their 109 recommendations. Their original vision still remained valid, with the urban renaissance of English cities constituting 'well designed, compact and connected cities supporting a diverse range of uses where people live, work and enjoy leisure time at close quarters in a sustainable urban environment, well integrated with public transport' (Urban Task Force 2005). Much progress had been achieved, and for the first time in fifty years a measurable change in culture was evident in respect of English cities. By 2005 the population of central Manchester had risen to nearly 25,000 from a base of only ninety residents fifteen years before. Development of brown-field land and a demonstrable increase in density had both been achieved, together with greater levels of private investment in urban regeneration. The findings were upbeat, noting that 'English cities have established themselves as powerhouses in the UK economy and centres for cultural innovation. They stand more confidently on the international stage'. New problems had emerged and certain vigilance was also required to maintain this key policy direction. The supply of social housing (i.e. affordable rented accommodation) was too low, with around an additional 17,000 new units required every year to address the backlog in supply. Design standards were not always high and more expert professionals were required in this area. Regeneration was a function spread across too many bodies with overlapping but differently funded backgrounds. As a policy, the need to push for creation of sustainable communities was overshadowing the need for regeneration. Key transport infrastructure decisions were made solely on the basis of financial investment criteria and not wider regeneration objectives, resulting in the loss of key catalysts of change. A more joined-up approach was needed in which transport underpins regeneration. The loss of more affluent groups from cities was creating a problem of racial segregation while, in spite of progress on standards of sustainable construction, more remains to be done by raising density levels and brown-field targets further.

The summary of the 2005 review, below, reveals a template of key issues to address in English cities to 2010.

2005 Urban Task Force review

Key areas	Problems identified	Recommendations
Design standards to be raised	• Poor design still prevalent for majority of new development. • Quality of 'new' public realm also poor.	• More design professionals to be employed in government, regeneration sectors and local authorities. • Transport investment must be used to act as a catalyst for regeneration.
Social well-being to be improved	• Middle-class exodus from cities and social polarity/racial segregation as a result.	• Need to promote balanced communities. • Government to set a target for all social housing estates to be transformed to mixed-tenure communities by 2012.
Environmental responsibility	• Need to increase environmental performance in this area and build on past work.	• Raise brown-field target to 75 per cent of all new homes by 2010 and increase density to 40 dwellings per hectare. • Apply sustainable standards to existing homes with an estimated 22 million of them being structurally sound and potentially re-usable.
Delivery, fiscal and legal framework	• To speed the system and make the regeneration process quicker to implement.	• Simplify compulsory purchase of land for regeneration purposes. • Provide more incentives to develop brown-land. • Reduce VAT on repairs and renovation. • Provide strong financial incentives for developing 'infill' within urban areas under 2 ha.

One highly damaging trend in existing cities is the apparent exodus of the more affluent social groups from the inner cities, resulting in a concentration of poorer groups 'who have least choice, [creating] high dissatisfaction among the very groups we are helping, leading eventually to low demand and abandonment' (Power and Houghton 2007). The creation of a mixed ownership or tenure community creates a more stable social and economic environment. Work by government in 2005 looked to develop the previously established 'millennium community projects' (such as at Greenwich) to address redevelopment and regeneration issues in some of the UK's most deprived neighbourhoods. This work took place under the umbrella of the 'Mixed communities initiative' and would tackle a series of severely deprived communities in which works of physical improvements would be combined with the introduction of mixed tenure (homes to rent and buy) for a variety of income groups with or without children and linked to shops, services and schools/public transport. The incorporation of green spaces and introduction of longer-term management would maintain quality and maintenance as well as security issues.

The immediate to longer-term solution for a viable regeneration of inner city housing stock rests with the development of communities, built upon existing ones and not resulting in their displacement. Anne Power and John Houghton advance six essential steps and outcomes to achieve this:

Essential steps to develop communities (from Power and Houghton 2007)

Essential steps	Beneficial outcomes
Engage in close consultations with existing residents.	Produce a flow of new and renovated affordable homes within the existing community.
Design with care and to high environmental standards.	Create more green space to provide physical improvements and facilities.
Look for ways of creating mixed uses.	Upgrade housing to cut energy use.
Cost physical works, looking at (i) improving public spaces, (ii) recycling empty buildings and land, (iii) refurbishing existing homes to high standard (iv) modernizing remaining homes.	Make area look cared for by the 're-modelling' of eyesores, derelict buildings and land.
Identify public and private investment streams to transform the neighbourhood.	Increase population or stem decline and support local shops and local transport.
Devise a longer-term management structure.	Slow climate change by cutting materials, transport and land use to a minimum.

The government's 2003 initiative of the Sustainable Communities Plan proposed new growth. While much of this applies to greenfield development, it must not be forgotten that existing urban centres need immediate action to arrest a decline in their resident populations and to provide much-needed housing and the regeneration of mixed ownership and flexible housing to create meaningful and long-term regeneration. Many hurdles and pitfalls stand in the way of this policy, and the consequences are far-reaching when you consider that the Sustainable Communities Plan will affect some 10 per cent of the total housing stock in England. Yet, again one returns to the central problem that the construction of just housing to the exclusion of transport and community infrastructure and employment raises an ugly spectre for the future of the South East, while physical works of regeneration in the Pathfinder areas without economic growth will fail to address the steady and continuous population drift away from all major conurbations, with the one exception of London where incoming migration tends to cancel out the domestic population drift from the capital to the regions – and mostly the South East region. On top of this, the piercing need for climate change mitigation requires zero carbon housing (in use and not necessarily production) to reduce carbon emissions. The overall challenge is thus both technical (construction methods) and policy-led (integration of land-use and transport). Further, its implementation will require the integration of many agencies, both governmental and private sector, to deliver on a hugely ambitious but very necessary vision for the future.

Part Four

The real estate
development process

10 Sustainability and property development

As has been discussed above, attempts to achieve sustainable development are shot through the planning system and therefore affect developers at every turn when they are seeking to bring schemes forward. More than just a regulatory issue, however, it is a theme which cuts across every aspect of the work of property developers these days, because those who fund, purchase and occupy them, as well as those who build them and provide the necessary professional advice, increasingly require sustainability issues to be fundamental.

Much has been written about how sustainability affects the property development process, including specialist books and journal articles. The purpose of this chapter is briefly to summarize the key sustainability issues as they affect the property developer, rather than to provide a fully comprehensive analysis of the history and philosophical foundation to them. The chapter is divided into the following topics:

- Sustainability in the property lifecycle
- Principal sustainability issues affecting property developers
- The regulatory environment for sustainability
- Commercial sustainability considerations
- Practical sustainability issues for developers
- Key issues for property sectors.

Sustainability in the property lifecycle

The property lifecycle can be described in various ways, but a simple schematic description is provided below in Figure 10.1. Every aspect of the property lifecycle is affected by sustainability, and those who are involved in decision-making at every stage of the lifecycle need to consider its implications. They must also appreciate that, to greater or lesser degrees, because of the very cyclical nature of the lifecycle, their decisions and actions will have consequences in all other stages of it. This is perhaps more true for developers than all or most other actors within the property lifecycle.

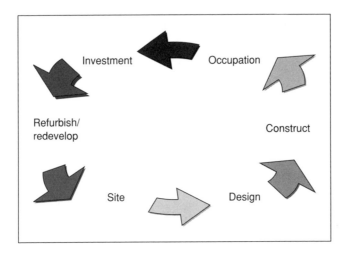

Figure 10.1 Schematic representation of the property lifecycle

Sustainability and the property lifecycle stages

We can see how sustainability affects each aspect of the lifecycle by asking simple questions, the answers to which have consequences for sustainable development at least, as follows:

Site
- Where is it in relation to other developments?
- How will people get to it?
- Will development lead to loss of greenfield land?
- Could other amenities be lost or gained by the development?
- Will development lead to brownfield use and possible decontamination?

Design
- Will the scheme incorporate 'green buildings'?
- Does layout and orientation maximize the beneficial use of natural resources?
- Will materials used minimize the negative use of natural resources?
- Can ecological resources be enhanced?
- What effect will the scheme have on water use and purity?
- How much energy will the scheme require to build and operate?

Construction
- How much waste will be created by contractors?
- Will water courses be affected by construction activity?
- Are the contractors likely to be considerate to the scheme's neighbours?

Occupation
- Have tenants' aspirations been considered?
- Could 'green lease' clauses be relied on to reduce environmental damage?
- Are effective environmental and building management systems in place?

Investment
- What is the obsolescence risk of the building?
- Are environmental issues considered as components of a prime property?
- What are the value implications of 'green' specifications?

Redevelopment/refurbishment
- Is saving resources via refurbishment rather than redevelopment an option?
- Are materials going to be reused or recycled?
- Does the site need decontamination?

Vicious circle of blame

For some time, there has been an ignorance surrounding sustainability issues in the property world, but this is diminishing. As with many 'new' concepts, this ignorance was a contributor to a general unwillingness to adopt change. For some time, people sought to apportion blame for this on different actors within the property development process, and the 'vicious circle of blame' was drawn up, as shown in Figure 10.2 below.

As the concept of sustainable development has progressed, the property world has become more amenable to the production of appropriate buildings. The first wave of demand for the procurement of sustainable buildings came from the public sector, at both national and local governmental levels, as edicts from central government for the public sector to reduce its environmental impact took effect. Subsequently, as the private sector began to see the benefits of sustainable buildings, the next wave of procurement of them came chiefly from owner-occupiers. These organizations were able to derive maximum benefits from the buildings because of their long-term involvement in them. Herein we see one of the problems commonly perceived with sustainable buildings – investment in them often requires the ability to wait for relatively long-term payback periods. Developers, particularly those involved in speculative schemes, do not have the time to wait for long-term returns on capital employed which are anticipated and therefore have to front load the returns into higher prices for completed schemes or to leave out those elements which have higher upfront costs. This is very often a matter of perception and anticipation based upon a poor understanding of how to procure sustainable buildings which is still not uncommon, but is thankfully less so than was the case.

The next wave of procurement of sustainable buildings has come from speculative developers of commercial buildings who now appreciate that they do not necessarily require significant additional costs to build, so long as sustainability is considered as an integral part of their procurement from the very outset of

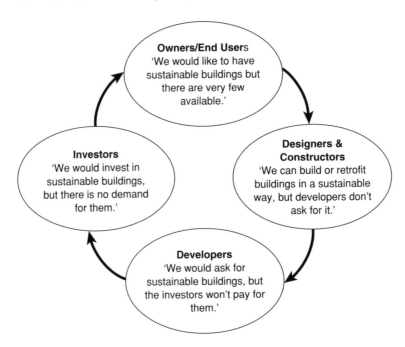

Figure 10.2 The vicious circle of blame (adapted from Cadman 2000 (quoted in Keeping 2000))

the scheme. Sustainable buildings do cost more than their conventional coun-terparts *if* sustainable features are retrospectively included in their design or, worse still, their construction.

Speculative developers are now seeing that good returns flow from sus-tainable buildings and the vicious circle of blame is moving more towards a virtuous circle, as promoted by the RICS and shown in Figure 10.3 below.

Principal sustainability issues affecting property development

As has already been discussed, definitions of sustainable development generally refer to the three 'pillars' of economy, environment and society. As far as the property industry is concerned rather than, say, the town planning community, there is an almost total focus on environmental concerns rather than the others. Indeed, the terms 'sustainable' and 'environmental' (and also 'green') are used synonymously.

There are many reasons for this but probably the most relevant is that regu-latory drivers have pushed developers, investors and their professional advisers in this direction. Another reason is because of media fascination with 'green' issues – some call it 'climate porn' – often with a view that the planet is going to hell in a handcart unless radical steps are taken to remove us from the mire of environmental degradation. It is, therefore, climate change which most

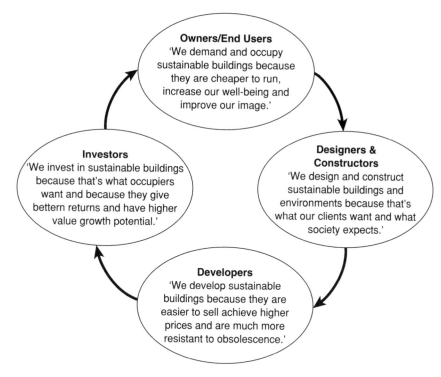

Figure 10.3 The virtuous circle (RICS 2008)

property people consider when they are asked about sustainability and, in particular, the imperative to reduce the amount of carbon which is emitted as a consequence of buildings being built and used.

New stock and the existing stock

There has also been a fascination within the property industry with consideration of sustainability in the context of 'green buildings' and in particular, new green buildings. Much of the discussion within the industry has been about how the procurement of new buildings can do much to reduce the carbon impact of buildings once they are being used because they can be built to very thermally efficient standards, for example. There is a growing awareness, however, that it is in the existing stock that much more needs to be done if carbon emissions are to be reduced because new stock only ever accounts, in the commercial property world for example, for up to a maximum of about 2 per cent of the stock when it is counted on an annual basis (the figure used in this sort of discussion varies).

If the UK more strongly wishes to pursue sustainable development and to make significant reductions in terms of its contribution to climate change, then it will have to invest far more heavily in making its existing stock of buildings more energy-efficient. Because investment finance is limited, this would have to mean that a shift in the balance between new-build and refurbishment of buildings in favour of the latter would have to be made. In turn, this would probably require a much more stringent regulatory environment than we have at present.

The regulatory environment for sustainability

The preceding chapters about the town planning system have shown that it is now and has been for some time fundamentally concerned with delivering sustainable development. We can see that strategic policy, from legislation and PPS1 downwards, considers that planners have a duty to enforce sustainable decision-making on those who wish to develop land and buildings.

Sustainability and development control

Inevitably, therefore, it is at the development control end of the planning system, where developers and planners most often interact, that sustainable property development is keenly considered. Developers are increasingly recognizing that sustainability is an issue which they must have included in their initial thinking about proposed development schemes because their early pre-application discussions with planners and consideration of development plans will confront them with sustainability requirements at the very first step.

In this regard, developers are looking for advice from specialist consultants who can help them to ensure that they have a suitable proposal to discuss with planners that has addressed the necessary range of sustainability issues well before negotiations commence.

Sustainability checklists

Assessing the sustainability of designs for individual new homes and buildings is one thing (and is discussed further below) but discussing sustainability in the round, as development control teams will want to, let alone ensuring that meaningful consideration of relevant matters has been undertaken, is another matter. Some developers and their advisers therefore find it helpful to use sustainability checklists for schemes, certain in the knowledge that development control teams will have their own checklists ready and waiting. One such checklist has been developed by the Building Research Establishment (BRE) (Brownhill and Rao 2002) which provides tools and indicators that measure the sustainability of developments at site or estate level. This publication also enables developers to frame their discussions with local authorities and other stakeholders. Versions of this checklist have been adopted by regional authorities. The South East England Development Agency (SEEDA), for example, has an online version intended to 'guide the design of new developments by making sense of current policy' (http://southeast.sustainability-checklist.co.uk/). The checklist enables developers and local authorities to consider whether the following sustainability issues have been considered in development proposals:

Climate change and energy
- Flooding
- Heat island
- Water efficiency
- Sustainable energy
- Site infrastructure

Community
- Promoting community networks and interaction
- Involvement in decision-making
- Supporting public services, social economy and community structure
- Community management of the development

Place making
- Efficient use of land
- Design process
- Form of development
- Open space
- Adaptability
- Inclusive communities
- Crime
- Street lighting/light pollution
- Security lighting

Buildings
- EcoHomes/BREEAM or Code for Sustainable Homes

- **Transport and movement**
- General policy
- Public transport
- Parking
- Pedestrians and cyclists
- Proximity of local amenities
- Traffic management
- Car club

Ecology
- Conservation
- Enhancement of ecology
- Planting

Resources
- Appropriate use of land resources
- Environmental impact
- Locally reclaimed materials
- Water resource planning
- Refuse composting
- Noise pollution
- Construction waste

Business
- Competitive business
- Business opportunities
- Employment
- Business types.

Sustainability and building control

As well as considering sustainability issues in a planning context, developers also need to include such considerations in the context of the Building Regulations.

Building Regulations

Part L of the Building Regulations was introduced in 2002 and details how buildings must perform in terms of their thermal efficiency. Minimum values are required to be achieved in terms of the insulation of buildings, measured by way of potential energy loss during their occupation. Part L was revised in April 2006 and legislation, currently in the Climate Change Act 2008, provides for it to be revised at least every five years, with significant energy-efficiency improvements (by a factor of one quarter) being required in each subsequent revision.

Developers need not only to comply with the current Building Regulations but also need to consider the effects of future changes indicated above. If, for example, a building is being designed to meet the requirements of a current set of Building Regulations but will not be completed until after the next revision of Part L, it is possible that it will be released on to the market place at or just before newer buildings which are compliant with the subsequent Regulations and are therefore more energy-efficient. This is likely to have the effect of focusing the minds of developers on 'future-proofing' their schemes by ensuring that their designs clearly exceed extant Regulations.

It is also now the case that during certain refurbishments, depending upon the size and cost of the work, part of the expenditure on the works will have to be earmarked to be spent on improving the energy performance of the rest of the building up to current Part L standards. Known as 'consequential improvements', this is an attempt by regulators to enforce improvement of the existing stock of buildings in energy-efficiency terms.

Energy Performance of Buildings Regulations

Developers also have to contend with the Energy Performance of Buildings (Certificates and Inspections) (England and Wales) Regulations 2007 and associated Regulations elsewhere in the UK. These were implemented because of the EU Energy Performance of Buildings Directive 2002, which sought both to try to level the European playing field in terms of energy regulations in buildings and also to require each member state to implement rules which would force buildings to become more energy-efficient. As far as developers are concerned, the principal element of the 2007 Regulations is the requirement for newly completed residential and non-residential buildings to have an Energy Performance Certificate (EPC), akin to those which appear on new white goods and cars. The certificates will rate the intrinsic energy performance capability of the building on a scale of A (best) to G (worst), as shown in Figure 10.4 below.

These Regulations will be another factor that developers must consider at the design stage. They would be well advised to consider how investors will respond to EPCs – for example, whether they will have minimum requirements in terms of the energy rating of buildings that they will be prepared to fund and/or purchase.

Commercial sustainability considerations

Much of the discussion above has focused on the regulatory drivers for developers to consider sustainability options in their decision-making. If these were the only drivers, the norm would probably be for many developers to resort to 'clearing the hurdle', i.e. just achieving the regulatory minimum. We can see in the marketplace, however, that this is not what is happening in many cases. The reasons for this are that investors and occupiers have demonstrated that they have an interest in procuring sustainable schemes because of the business case which makes them attractive.

Business case factors

In general terms, we can observe the following factors as indicating that sustainable buildings are 'a good thing':

- Saving energy: Energy is in short supply, it is expensive and use of non-renewable resources leads to climate change. Sustainable buildings use less of it.
- Attracting people: Companies which occupy green buildings indicate that this is a key factor in recruiting people who share their values.
- Increasing property values: Evidence is building in the USA, UK and elsewhere that certified sustainable buildings are attracting a premium in terms of investment yield. This is partly because demand from occupiers is also increasing, often as a response to companies' Corporate Social Responsibility policies.

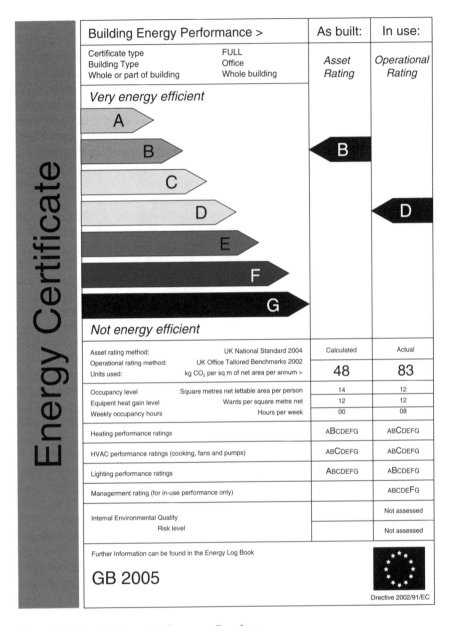

Building Energy Performance >		As built:	In use:
Certificate type	FULL	*Asset Rating*	*Operational Rating*
Building Type	Office		
Whole or part of building	Whole building		

Very energy efficient

A

B

C

D

E

F

G

B (As built)

D (In use)

Not energy efficient

		Calculated	Actual
Asset rating method:	UK National Standard 2004		
Operational rating method:	UK Office Tailored Benchmarks 2002		
Units used:	kg CO₂ per sq m of net area per annum >	**48**	**83**
Occupancy level	Square metres net lettable area per person	14	12
Equipent heat gain level	Wants per square metre net	12	12
Weekly occupancy hours	Hours per week	00	08
Heating performance ratings		ABCDEFG	ABCDEFG
HVAC performance ratings (cooking, fans and pumps)		ABCDEFG	ABCDEFG
Lighting performance ratings		ABCDEFG	ABCDEFG
Managerment rating (for in-use performance only)			ABCDEFG
Internal Environmental Quality			Not assessed
Risk level			Not assessed

Further Information can be found in the Energy Log Book

GB 2005

Drective 2002/91/EC

Figure 10.4 Sample Energy Performance Certificate

- Mitigating risk: Sustainable buildings mitigate various types of risk, including regulatory and obsolescence risk.
- Green buildings no longer carry cost premium: As discussed above, it was the case that sustainable buildings were considered to be more expensive to procure than others. As awareness and expertise have increased, however,

and as developers consider sustainability at an earlier stage, costs differentials need not appear.

- Professional expertise: For some years, universities have been graduating trainee design and construction professionals who are far more aware of sustainability concepts and ideas than previous generations were. These people are now often in decision-making positions and are better able to advise developers and shape their approaches to sustainability than was the case previously.

Pressure from stakeholders

It is worth mentioning that as well as pure financial considerations, of course, developers have to contend with different sorts of pressures coming from a variety of quarters. Figure 10.5 demonstrates who the more common stakeholder groups are, any or all of which could, with different motivations, apply pressure to developers to reconsider their approach to sustainability. Developers increasingly have to be alert to the benefits of stakeholder engagement in all of their operations.

Cost and value issues

The foregoing discussion has referred to attitudes which were, and to an extent still are, predicated on the view that sustainable or green buildings cost significantly more to build than their conventional counterparts. It has also been discussed that if sustainability is retrofitted or 'bolted on' to existing designs or buildings then this does add greatly to the overall cost of the amended scheme – but why wouldn't it? Almost any variations to a building design contract will

Figure 10.5 Examples of stakeholder groups that can exert pressure on developers

mean extra cost to the developer, whether the variations mean extra sustainability or not.

The costs of sustainable buildings

In order to determine whether, and if so how much, sustainable buildings do cost more to build, research has been undertaken by the BRE and the Cyril Sweett building consultancy (Building Research Establishment and Cyril Sweett 2005). This research found that there are, understandably, many variables at play in determining costs associated with one scheme or another, but sought to strip out as many variables as possible in order to determine the key issues. The findings were essentially that:

> One of the principal barriers to the wider adoption of more sustainable design and construction solutions is the perception that these incur substantial additional costs. A costing analysis, using real cost data for a broad range of sustainability technologies and design solutions, contradicts this assumption. ... significant improvements in building sustainability performance can be achieved at very little additional cost. In addition, more sustainable buildings can offer major in-use cost savings.
>
> (BRE and Cyril Sweett 2005)

The research methodology involved assessing the capital costs of each design, management or specification option and comparing them with a 'Building Regulations compliant' standard building. In order to make the comparison as realistic as possible, the capital costs analysed include all construction works, as well as preliminary works, overheads, profits and contingencies. Furthermore, the costs were based on design stage implementation rather than retrofitting, and the most cost-effective options were favoured.

The costs of achieving different levels of environmental performance (using BREEAM or EcoHomes standards) were investigated for four different types of building in three different location types (because BREEAM and EcoHomes standards award credits depending on location):

- a house
- a naturally ventilated office
- an air-conditioned office
- a healthcare centre.

In brief, the results of the research are outlined below in Table 10.1 and Figure 10.6.

The value of sustainable buildings

Of course, the cost implications of procuring sustainable designed buildings need to be seen within the context of their value if developers are to be convinced of merely

Table 10.1 Indicative costs of sustainable buildings compared to non-sustainable alternatives (Building Research Establishment and Cyril Sweett 2005)

Property type and location	Percentage increase in capital cost to achieve an EcoHomes/BREEAM rating			
	Pass	*Good*	*Very Good*	*Excellent*
House				
Poor	0.1	0.9	3.1	–
Typical	0	0.4	1.7	6.9
Good	0	0.3	1.3	4.2
Naturally ventilated office				
Poor	−0.4	−0.3	2.0	–
Typical	–	−0.4	−0.3	3.4
Good	–	−0.4	−0.4	2.5
Air-conditioned office				
Poor	0	0.2	5.7	–
Typical	–	0	0.2	7.0
Good	–	0	0.1	3.3
PFI Healthcare centre				
Typical	–	–	0	1.9
Good	–	–	0	0.6

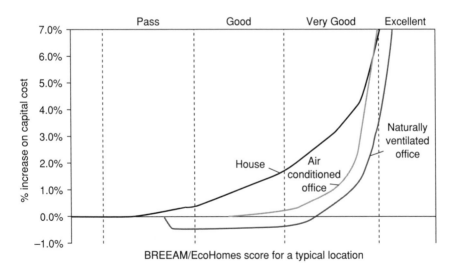

Figure 10.6 Indicative costs implications of attaining different levels of BREEAM ratings (Building Research Establishment and Cyril Sweett 2005)

clearing the regulatory minimum by complying with extant Building regulations and the requirements of local planning authorities. Assessing the value of sustainable buildings is not easy – certainly not as 'easy' as defining what they cost to build – because valuation, whilst not exactly a black art, often involves a certain amount of subjectivity and manipulation of data to suit individual circumstances.

Another problem associated with assessing the value of sustainable buildings is the paucity of transaction data. This will improve with time, but at present and in the short-term this situation will confound those trying to prove a link between sustainability and value in buildings. In 2008, a pan-European network of RICS members began to consider how the issue of data collection could be addressed, and their findings are awaited with interest.

In the meantime, it is useful to consider the general drivers of value in buildings and how sustainability features might either add to a building's value or detract from it. Research undertaken on behalf of the RICS (RICS 2005) attempted to establish the link between sustainability features of buildings and their value. This research, which looked at buildings in North America and the UK, showed that in their case studies there was a relationship between the market value of a building and its sustainability features (as shown in Table 10.2 below), i.e. that they can:

- command higher rents and prices
- attract tenants more quickly
- reduce tenant turnover
- cost less to operate and maintain.

Although relatively few case studies were investigated, it is important to note that the research also concluded that the main benefits of sustainable buildings are achieved by occupiers and that chief amongst these, i.e. where there is the biggest return on investment, is probably in increased employee productivity (given that labour costs are by far and away the major cost to a business).

A common theme which is revisited at intervals in later chapters of this book is that developers need increasingly to understand and respond better to the needs of occupiers if they are to offer products which really suit occupational needs. This situation applies in relation to the sustainable features of buildings as much as any other.

It is not just occupiers' requirements that developers need to satisfy, however. Investors' and regulators' demands and wishes also need to be heeded and, as the above discussion suggests, it is increasingly clear that all three of these most important stakeholders are increasingly requiring attention be paid to the procurement of sustainable buildings.

Practical issues for developers

As has been discussed above, it is beyond the scope of this book, or indeed any book, to provide a highly detailed discussion and explanation of every aspect of

Table 10.2 Possible linkages between sustainable building features and building value (RICS 2005)

Green objectives	Green strategies/features	Green impact	Theoretical linkage to value
Sustainable site development	• Reduce site disturbance and soil erosion during construction • Use of natural drainage systems (e.g. swales) • Preserve or restore natural site features • Landscape and orient building to capitalize on passive heating and cooling	• Improved site aesthetics • Greater public support for the development and accelerated local approval process, hence lower carrying costs • Lower energy costs	• Reduced development costs, improved marketability, reduced ongoing maintenance costs, improved natural appearance, higher sales/rents, absorption and re-tenanting, NOI*/ROI** benefits. • For gross leases, higher NOI. • May have impact for net leases *** if benefit can be demonstrated to tenants
Water efficiency	• Use captured rainwater for landscaping, toilet flushing, etc. • Treat and reuse greywater, excess groundwater and steam condensate • Use low-flow fixtures and fittings (pressure-assisted or composting toilets, waterless urinals, etc.) and ozonation for laundry • Use closed-loop systems and other water-reduction technologies for processes	• Lower water consumption/costs	• Lower tenant CAM**** charges, Direct NOI benefit for gross leases, potential for net leases requires communicating benefit to tenants
Energy-efficiency	• Use passive solar heating/cooling and natural ventilation • Enhance penetration of daylight to interior spaces to reduce need for artificial lighting • Use thermally efficient envelope to reduce perimeter heating and size of HVAC	• Lower capital costs • Occupant benefits • Lower energy costs	• Reduced operating costs, longer lifecycle, lower development costs • Improved occupant productivity, lower churn, turnover, tenant inducements, etc. • Higher net income for gross leased buildings, improved yield.

Table 10.2 (cont'd)

Green objectives	Green strategies/features	Green impact	Theoretical linkage to value
	• Use energy-management systems, monitoring, and controls to continuously calibrate, adjust, and maintain energy-related systems	• Operational savings (can offset higher capital costs) • Reduced capital cost of mechanical systems because control systems reduce the need for over-sizing	• Lower operating costs. On gross leases, higher ROI/NOI • On net leases, potential for improved ROI/NOI
	• Use third-party commissioning agent to ensure that the installed systems work as designed • Develop O&M manuals and train staff	• Lower operating costs • Lower maintenance costs.	• Marginally higher initial soft costs should be offset by long-term operating cost benefits, higher ROI
Indoor environmental quality	• Control pollutant sources • Use low-emission materials • Ventilate before occupancy • Enhance penetration of daylight and reduce glare	• Superior indoor air quality, quality lighting and thermal quality • Fewer occupant complaints • Higher occupant productivity.	• Risk reduction • Greater marketability • Faster sales and lets • Improved churn/turnover • Higher ROI/NOI
Reduced consumption of building materials	• Select products for durability • Eliminate unnecessary finishes and other products • Reuse building shell from existing buildings and fixtures from demolished buildings • Use salvaged/refurbished materials • Design for adaptability	• Longer building lifecycle • Lower maintenance costs.	• Lower depreciation typically after higher investment costs • Lower construction costs, probable lower operating/maintenance costs, higher ROI/NOI

Notes
* NOI: net operating income
** ROI: return on investment
*** Net lease: a lease that requires a lessee to pay all their operating costs resulting from their occupation of the premises
**** CAM: common area maintenance

Table 10.3 Sustainability considerations at key stages in the development process
(adapted from Building Research Establishment and Cyril Sweett 2005)

Feasibility	Planning and design	Construction	Occupation	Demolition
Ecologist	Sustainability adviser	Commissioning	Environmental policies	Reclamation of materials
Environmental consultant	Building form	Considerate Constructors Scheme	Monitor energy	Recycling
Renewables	Cycle storage	Minimize waste	Monitor water	Reduce impact of redundant materials
Location	Material specifications	Off-site construction	Maintenance	
BREEAM target	Orientation	Use of local suppliers	Occupant satisfaction	
Site conditions	Services Waste		Recycling Transport policies	

sustainability in every aspect of the property development process. The purpose
of this next section is to give an overview of some of the practicalities with which
developers have to contend when they are assuming a sustainable approach to
their work.

Earlier in this chapter, sustainability checklists were considered in terms of
enabling developers and others to ensure that they had considered sustainability 'in the round' and were able to frame discussion with stakeholders on the
basis of compliance or otherwise with checklist criteria. Table 10.3 above provides another set of criteria which is much more general than those discussed
above but does provide a quick view of the key practical issues that developers
will need to consider.

Key issues: Location, design, construction

If developers are to deliver a more sustainable development than would otherwise be the case, they would be well advised to think about the three key issues
of location, design and construction. In this regard, several factors need to be
considered.

Location

Given that about one-third of carbon emissions in the UK are generated by
vehicles, i.e. more than homes or the non-domestic property sector, designing
and locating buildings which reduce the need to travel would make a significant

contribution to the country's attempts to reduce its impact on climate change – probably far more than tinkering with buildings' thermal efficiency, for example.

There are many factors to consider here, including the in-town and out-of-town debate (which is discussed in previous and subsequent chapters), investment in public transport networks and even investment in technological changes to the engines and use of fuels in vehicles, which are within developers' control. It is certainly the case that developers can decide whether or not they will build homes a long way from places of work and amenities (and vice versa). It is also true that developers can decide whether or not they will invest in public transport networks (and sometimes they do not have any option to do otherwise). It is even true that developers can invest in technologies within vehicles which have a lower environmental impact, such as through green travel plans.

Design

The necessity to improve the condition of the existing property stock through sustainable refurbishment has been discussed above, but whether or not it is refurbishments or new-builds that are being considered, the next most important thing, after sorting out transport-related environmental impact, is to consider the sustainable design of the buildings themselves.

In this respect, designers should these days be deeply familiar with the concept of sustainability and how best to achieve it. If they are not, they are probably not worth engaging. Advice is certainly necessary from designers on this aspect of developers' requirements and reference to suitable design tools will be essential.

An essential item in every designer's toolkit these days should be *The Green Guide to Specification* (Anderson and Shiers 2008), which provides guidance for specifiers, designers and developers on the relative environmental impacts of over 250 elemental specifications for building components, such as roofs, walls and floors. Use of this tool will enable designers to compare the environmental and cost profiles of these components and thus demonstrate more precisely to what degree they are engaging with sustainability.

Having designed a scheme which is constituted by sustainable components and is in a sustainable location, developers would be advised to ensure that their building is assessed and 'badged' as being sustainable in order that potential occupiers and investors will be aware of this (i.e. to achieve marketing advantage) and that other stakeholders, such as the press, local authority and shareholders are also aware of this (i.e. to achieve public relations advantages).

In the UK, the best means of assessing and badging buildings comes in the form of Building Research Establishment Environmental Assessment Method (BREEAM), of which there are versions for different buildings types, including the Code for Sustainable Homes and BREEAM Retail, Offices and Industrial specifications. All versions examine the same environmental impacts:

- Management
- Health and well-being
- Energy

- Transport
- Water
- Material and waste
- Land use and ecology
- Pollution.

Credits are awarded in each of these areas according to performance, and an overall score is awarded in a certificate, which rates the building on a scale of:

Pass; Good; Very Good; Excellent; Outstanding.

The benefits of achieving a BREEAM rating to developers are listed to include:

- Enhanced marketability
  - Recognized brand associated with quality buildings and organizations with active corporate social responsibility agendas
  - Represents a low-risk investment choice
- Increased flexibility
  - Reduced letting voids
  - Increased investment security
- Good return on investment
  - Desirable buildings give a high rate of return and a low void rate.

(Source: www.breeam.org)

Construction

The UK construction industry is a wasteful one. It is responsible for about half of UK landfill waste and 13 per cent of all raw materials use (BERR 2007). This situation has not gone unnoticed by regulators, and the government intends that the following targets will be achieved to rectify it:

- By 2012, a 50 per cent reduction of construction, demolition and excavation waste to landfill, compared to 2005
- By 2015, zero net waste, at construction site level
- By 2020, zero waste to landfill (BERR 2007).

Various pieces of guidance are available for developers and their contractors to use in managing construction waste. WRAP (www.wrap.org) is a company which has been established to encourage and enable businesses to be more efficient in using materials and recycling. Its work in the construction sector has enabled it to provide practice guides and technical manuals for waste minimization and management.

The key benefits of having effective Site Waste Management Plans are that they not only enable developers and contractors to comply with legislation but can also realize benefits, which include:

- Cost savings through reduced requirement for materials, disposal costs and sale of materials
- Demonstration of good environmental performance and corporate social responsibility
- Reduced impact on the local community and better public relationships
- Improved company performance, allowing differentiation from competitors (www.wrap.org).

Developers, as clients of the construction industry, have a real opportunity to ensure that construction waste is reduced. They would be well advised to insist upon effective Site Waste Management Plans being used and that conditions are included with construction contracts to enable this.

Key issues for property sectors

Much of the foregoing discussion relates to every property type. All sectors of the property industry are affected by sustainability, and developers in all of these sectors need to be alert both to the regulatory situation pertinent to sustainability in their sector and to the different opportunities flowing from sustainability that exist within them. This section focuses on some of the key issues and emerging trends that are relevant to the sectors of the property industry which are considered later on in this book.

Retail

It is in the retail sector of the economy that most regard has been had to sustainability. This is partly because shareholders of large companies are demanding change and expect retailers (and others) to have strong Corporate Social Responsibility (CSR) credentials which translate into their business decision-making. It is also the case that regulatory change has had a part to play in this but the overwhelming reason is a more direct business driver – changing consumer attitudes. Evidence of this comes from the government's Survey of Public Attitudes and Behaviours toward the Environment (DEFRA 2007), which found that it is a 'socially acceptable norm' to be 'green'. Importantly, the survey also identified the extent to which customers are assessing businesses based on their environmental performance. Half of interviewees try not to buy products from companies performing badly in environmental terms and nearly half would be prepared to pay a premium for 'green' products. The retail world is extremely competitive, and margins are often tight. Retailers can use sustainability strategies as marketing tools to help them to win customer share.

Perhaps it is for these reasons alone that the country's largest retailers have bought into the sustainability agenda (and particularly the climate change agenda) and realize that their properties need to reflect their green aspirations. Others might argue that retailers are making genuine attempts to address climate change because it needs to be addressed. In a speech in January 2007, the Chief Executive of the UK's largest retailer spoke about climate change:

> I am determined that Tesco should be a leader in helping to create a low-carbon economy. In saying this, I do not underestimate the task. It is to take an economy where human comfort, activity and growth are inextricably linked with emitting carbon and to transform it into one which can only thrive without depending on carbon. This is a monumental challenge. It requires a revolution in technology and a revolution in thinking.
>
> (Leahy 2007)

Given that retailers have adopted certain themes as the environmental issues that they must address, energy use being chief amongst them, developers need to understand the role that they can play in providing retailers with a means of reducing their carbon footprints. In this respect, it is again location and the fact that many stores require (and encourage) visits by car which is probably the chief issue that retailers need to address. Furthermore, they need to address the logistical infrastructure which keeps them supplied with goods and where stores are located in relation to warehouses and depots. Independent developers, whilst they can assist in site finding and procuring facilities in locations which have lower carbon impacts, have relatively little to do in retailers' locational decision-making. Where they can make a difference is in the design and construction of the buildings themselves.

If developers need convincing of major retailers' positive intentions in this regard, then it is worth considering how the major food retailers are behaving in terms of managing their carbon impact. The following three examples provide just some of the evidence (Keeping 2008):

- Tesco has committed itself to reducing its carbon impact by 50 per cent by 2020 in its stores and distribution centres.
- Sainsbury has (since 2001) a commitment to reduce carbon levels by 10 per cent. By managing this aspect of the business, Sainsbury has realized over £8 million worth of savings.
- ASDA has focused upon designing a viable prototype store that is considered to be between 25 and 30 per cent more energy-efficient than 'usual' stores and subsequently has 30 per cent fewer greenhouse gas emissions.

Offices

According to market opinion, of the costs associated with procuring and operating a commercial building over a twenty-five year lifespan, about 2 per cent is spent on construction, about 6 per cent on operation (rent, maintenance, taxes, etc.) and 92 per cent on staff wages. In terms of how occupiers of these buildings think, therefore, uppermost in their minds is not the rent or the energy bills but the effect of the building upon the productivity of employees. As an area of research, employee productivity has been studied for some time, and work was particularly active from the 1950s onwards. However, measuring the effect of building design and specification on employee productivity is relatively new. For proponents of sustainability, this is somewhat of a 'holy grail' because it is felt that if the anecdotal evidence that sustainable buildings boost the performance of employees can be proved much more broadly to be true, procurement of sustainable buildings is likely to become another standard requirement for companies.

Often the anecdotal evidence is, while limited, compelling. Much of it originates from the USA. For example, at communications company Verifone's offices in Costa Mesa, California, an energy-efficient design which derived 50 per cent energy savings through use of daylighting and natural cooling also meant that absenteeism dropped by 40 per cent and productivity increased by 5 per cent due to improved comfort. The return on investment of the additional costs associated with this scheme meant that it was paid back within one year (Romm 1999). As stated previously, there is a growing body of this sort of anecdotal evidence, but more empirical work needs to be done to identify which elements of sustainable design result in what sort of employer benefits.

Advice as to how to approach sustainable office design is varied, both in terms of scope and quality. Other than the excellent *Green Guide to Specification* (Anderson and Shiers 2008), a useful guide for those beginning to think about refurbishing and fitting out office space, which works well for those specifying new build schemes as well, has been produced by the Ministry for the Environment in New Zealand (Ministry for the Environment 2005), which comments that:

> The definition of sustainability as applied to buildings is not fixed, but 'green' or sustainable buildings are sensitive to:
> * the environment – local and global
> * resource, water and energy consumption
> * the quality of the work environment – impact on occupants
> * financial impact – cost-effective from a long-term, full financial cost-return point of view
> * long-term energy-efficiency over the life of the building.
>
> When looking at what's involved with refurbishing or fitting-out a building, this could mean:
> * using resources efficiently – getting more from less
> * minimizing waste
> * focusing on energy and water use
> * choosing products carefully to ensure they are not harmful to the environment or to occupants' health.

The main other issue which the developers of office premises need to consider is, yet again, that of location and transport. Out-of-town business parks are carbon intensive, given that they have high car parking ratios and often have limited public transport provision. Given the direction in which transport policy is going, it seems that the days of large new out-of-town business park developments are numbered. Furthermore, it is likely that achieving BREEAM ratings of 'Excellent' will become difficult, and 'Outstanding' nigh on impossible for buildings in such locations in the near future. This will have consequences in terms of occupier preference.

It has been interesting to see a number of speculative office development schemes being undertaken in recent years which have achieved 'Excellent' BREEAM ratings. Notable schemes which stand out include those at:

- Merchant Square and Kingdom Street in Paddington, London
- Calthorpe House and 11 Brindleyplace in Birmingham
- Temple Back and The Paragon, Bristol
- Lattitude in Leeds
- 3 Hardman Street and Piccadilly Place, Manchester
- Interpoint at Haymarket in Edinburgh.

The reasons behind this sudden rash of speculative BREEAM 'Excellent' buildings have undoubtedly included a shift in the attitudes of large corporate occupiers. PricewaterhouseCoopers (PwC), for example, which is one of the largest office occupiers in the all-important financial and business services sector in the UK, states in its environmental policy that it will:

> Give due consideration to environmental issues in the acquisition, design and location of buildings, and apply BREEAM standards for building specifications, features and construction wherever possible
>
> (PwC 2005)

Furthermore, in their Corporate Responsibility report, PwC says that:

> For the buildings we occupy, we always aim to site them in locations easily accessible by public transport. We also insist on buildings with a good environmental performance – for our new London building architects BDP produced a sustainability specification which means that this building will meet the highest BREEAM standard of 'excellent', as must any new building we specify. Refurbished buildings will be brought up to the next best rating of 'very good'.
>
> (PwC 2007) (http://www.pwc.co.uk/eng/aboutus/
> corporate_responsibility_environment.html)

Developers need to think about changing occupiers' attitudes and monitor them carefully. The BREEAM 'Excellent' schemes noted above all came to the market quickly, helped by the investment boom of the mid-2000s, which shows how quickly the property juggernaut can actually respond to trends and demand.

Industrial

Logistics operators, whether third party providers or in-house operations for retailers or other businesses, undertake to provide their clients with a service which is nearly wholly reliant upon road transport. By their very nature, therefore, they have a large carbon footprint. In order to reduce this significantly, they could switch to alternative forms of transport, such as rail or even canal. However, the capacity of these systems is considered insufficient to meet the needs of modern businesses which generally require more rapid and flexible movement of goods, although some goods do travel by such routes (rail freight interchanges are discussed in Chapter 18 on industrial property development).

Otherwise, developer can assist logistics operators to reduce the carbon intensity of their operations by providing facilities which are designed to reduce energy use (and make other environmental savings).

In terms of the means by which the design of logistics facilities can contribute to reducing environmental impact, both Prologis and Gazeley have produced buildings which are market leaders. Gazeley's 'EcoTemplate', for example, includes:

- Local provenance vegetation
- Wall vegetation
- Pervious paving
- Pre-cast concrete dock faces
- 15 per cent rooflights
- Recycled and rapidly renewable finishes to office
- Photovoltaic panels
- Wind turbine
- Solar thermal hot water system
- Roof water collection
- Low flush volume products in WC area.

Further discussion and examples of sustainable industrial development are provided in Chapter 18 on industrial property

Residential

In as far as making significant contributions to reducing carbon emissions and thus to the causes of climate change, it is undoubtedly the case that it is the residential sector to which most attention ought to be paid. Figure 10.7 shows why this is the case.

In considering the data evident in Figure 10.7, one might not unreasonably wonder why governments pay so much attention to the commercial property world's contribution to climate change relative to that of the domestic sector. It might be that it is politically expedient to make businesses address climate change reduction measures rather than the voting public. Nonetheless, governmental attention has been focused on the domestic sectors and to residential

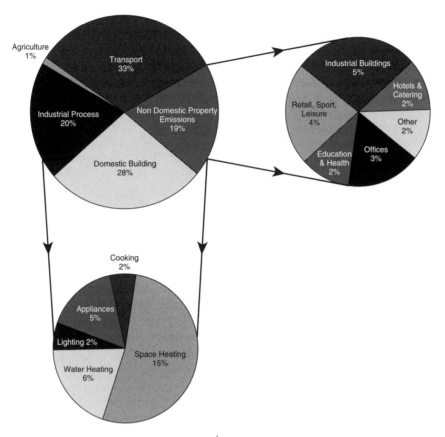

Figure 10.7 Indicative energy use by sector (Source: Keeping and West 2008 (Note: includes rounding error))

property development in particular (again, one might wonder why more attention is not paid to the existing stock rather than new-build).

It is undoubtedly regulatory drivers that are pushing progress in terms of sustainable residential property development rather than purchase or occupier demand. In the private sector, dominated by owner-occupiers, demand for sustainable properties is limited. In the social housing sector, there is more demand for sustainable housing from Registered Social Landlords (RSLs), but this is largely driven by demands from public funding bodies (i.e. Communities England, Communities Scotland, etc.).

Recent changes in the regulatory landscape for and the mainstreaming of sustainable residential property were largely prompted by the 'One Million Sustainable Homes' campaign led by WWF. The campaign was supported by regulators, government agencies and private sector developers and its most significant result was the driving through of the Code for Sustainable Homes as the standard against which the sustainability of residential schemes should be measured. This has replaced EcoHomes and is likely to develop further.

The Code for Sustainable Homes measures the sustainability of new homes against categories of sustainable design, rating the whole home as a complete package. The Code uses a 1-star to 6-star rating system to communicate the overall sustainability performance of new homes, setting minimum standards for energy and water use at each level (Department for Communities and Local Government 2007b). Level 6 of the Code requires homes to be 'carbon zero', a decision which was contentious after it was announced, partly because definitions of 'carbon zero' are many and various, but chiefly because it required buildings to rely upon on-site renewable energy technologies. It is suggested by policy that all new homes will be 'carbon zero' by 2016. All new homes require measurement against the Code, as of May 2008.

The theory behind compulsion to have on-site renewable technologies for residential schemes is not without some merit – it is efficient if generated power is not lost during transmission – but fails to account for the expensiveness of it and the limited scope of developers to afford it. The mathematics are quite straightforward. If costs increase in a scheme, developers have either to increase revenue (by putting up house prices) or to decrease other costs. The former option is not really possible, developers say (with justification) because purchasers will not bear the extra cost – house prices have been way too high for many to afford for many years. The latter option, to reduce costs, is only really possible in two ways – by reducing profit margins or by paying less for the land (other costs, like building construction, fees and finance are largely fixed by others, and the first two tend to inflate over time, rather than reduce).

The economic circumstances of residential property developers and the property market of the 2000s was certainly a 'game of two halves' and one which demonstrates that neither increasing sales prices nor reducing profit margins really works in this respect. The boom experienced by developers up until 2007 occurred because house prices were increasing steeply – adding to these prices with expensive on-site technologies would not have been in purchasers' interests (and thus not in developers' interests). The market turned quickly and, by 2008, many developers were struggling to survive (some did not even manage this), with profit margins non-existent because house prices were falling. At the same time, land prices were falling as well (as some developers put it at the time 'through the floor . . . and the basement'). Thus even suggesting a reduction on land prices encouraged land owners to sit back and wait for the market to change.

The result of the requirement to have on-site renewable energy technologies is, developers say, that though they are willing to provide them, they cannot do so without making losses on schemes, which of course they are not prepared to do. It is likely, therefore that one or both of two situations will occur. First, it will be up to public sector agencies to provide land at no or little cost for zero carbon schemes. Whilst this might suit Communities England and sister bodies elsewhere in the UK for this to occur, it is doubtful if the likes of the Ministry of Defence or NHS Trusts disposing of surplus land to meet Treasury revenue guidelines will be so keen. The other situation, of course, is that the policy changes and off-site renewable energy technologies are allowable within the definition of 'zero carbon'. This would seem a sensible situation – but that does not necessarily mean that regulators will adopt it. Developers would be well advised to keep engaging with regulators to ensure that the regulatory environment allows for sustainable homes to be developed.

Conclusions

Sustainable development is an issue which has rapidly come to affect property development and will continue to do so over the foreseeable future. No developers worth their salt have ignored this and those who have invested in it and engaged successfully with various stakeholders, such as Hammerson, Gazeley and Crest Nicholson, have quickly consolidated their reputations as recognized market leaders. These and other developers have recognized that early engagement with the raft of issues which are encompassed within sustainable property development leads to profitable returns. In the commercial and industrial property worlds, developers must recognize and respond to the fast-moving and constantly changing requirements of occupiers, for it is these stakeholders who are driving change most significantly there. In the residential property sector, drivers are most significant in the regulatory context, and understanding the Code for Sustainable Homes and influencing how it might develop will be important to all developers.

For all property developers, whichever sector they are operating in, deciding early on in schemes how sustainability issues will be addressed is absolutely vital. Bringing in such considerations too late in the day will delay schemes because development control officers will insist on schemes being rethought and will also mean that schemes become more expensive as designs are revised and money is borrowed for a longer scheme. Table 10.4 sets out how different sustainability issues can be considered at the conceptual stage of a development scheme and for every potential phase of the scheme.

Looking to the future, developers will need to get better at anticipating regulatory change, in order to 'future-proof' their schemes and thus make them attractive to occupiers and investors. The pace of change in terms of stakeholders' expectations is significant, as it is as far as regulations are concerned. The Code for Sustainable Homes was first introduced in 2006 and was made a mandatory requirement in 2008 for the assessment of energy and water performance in domestic buildings. Commercial property developers would do well to ensure that a stand-off similar to the one that occurred between government and residential property developers does not happen in their sector regarding on-site renewable technologies.

All developers should also realize that if sustainable development policy moves in a direction which seeks to increase sustainability significantly, then the development of new schemes is likely to get more expensive compared to the refurbishment of existing buildings. Furthermore, the development of

Table 10.4 Property lifecycle sustainability issues (John Lewis Partnership 2007)

Phase	Definition of phase	Key issues to be considered
Strategic business need	*Do we need the building?* • Identify demand for changes in service provision • Review local community needs • Develop a business case	• Integrate sustainability issues into decision making • Explore service delivery models • Assess options rigorously • Assess wider local community needs and possibility of buildings fulfilling some of these • Influence prospective business partners
Feasibility of project	*Can we build it?* • Prepare strategic brief and project objectives (including plans for stakeholder engagement and procurement) • Confirm main contractor/developer	• Integrate sustainability criteria into procurement strategy and selection criteria • Provide clear statement of intent • Develop sustainability objectives and targets for project (Sustainability Action Plan) • Consider fiscal incentives for developer/contractor to achieve high sustainability performance
Planning and design	*What will it look like?* • Develop outline design • Carry out sustainability appraisal and consultation • Win planning approval • Specify performance	• Consider whole-life value and social and environmental issues within design • Consult with key stakeholders, including local community, chambers of commerce, local training organizations, etc. • Include clear sustainability selection criteria for selecting materials and products
Construction	*How should we build it?* • Select subcontractors • Plan and manage construction • Monitor performance • Hand over to building users	• Include sustainability performance and whole-life considerations in selection criteria for subcontractors and suppliers respectively • Implement site management procedures on key issues such as waste and health and safety
Operation and maintenance	*How should we use it?* • Incorporate in facilities management • Carry out post-occupancy evaluation • Consider end-of-life options	• Monitor and report against sustainability targets • Be a good neighbour • Monitor and audit performance • Feed back results and transfer knowledge across estate • Conduct a detailed post-occupancy evaluation within the first year of use and at regular intervals thereafter

certain types of buildings, like 'glass box' office buildings, will become very difficult because of their environmental inefficiency.

Developers will need increasingly to ensure that they are not promoting the 'vicious circle of blame' but are a component of its 'virtuous' counterpart. If they do not, regulators will come down hard, heavy and hastily upon them.

11 The real estate development process

In the previous chapter, we have seen how property development sits within the property lifecycle and how, increasingly, sustainable development has significant influence over developers, the development process and development schemes themselves. This chapter considers two key questions – how does property development take place? – and who does it?

The property development industry is both complex and diverse: complex, in that there are many agencies, public and private, large and small, undertaking development in a variety of organizational forms and legal entities; diverse, in that it involves a vast number of businesses across a wide range of sectors, having different aims, objectives and modes of operation.

The property development industry is also risky, cyclical, highly regulated and lengthy in production. In addition, it comprises three major groups: consumers, producers, and providers of public infrastructure. This seeming imbroglio thus requires close consideration and understanding, so that the process of property development can be managed in a way that optimizes the benefit to all concerned. The point has been made more eruditely by one of the leading thinkers in the field of real estate development, as follows:

> Unlike many mass production industries, each real estate project is unique and the development process is so much a creature of the political process that society has a new opportunity with each major project to negotiate, debate and reconsider the basic issues of an enterprise economy, i.e. who pays, who benefits, who risks, and who has standing to participate in the decision process. Thus, the development process remains a high silhouette topic for an articulate and sophisticated society. The best risk management device for the producer group, which is usually the lead group in the initiation of a project, is thorough research so that the development product fits as closely as possible the needs of the tenant or purchaser, the values of the politically active collective consumers, and the land-use ethic of the society.
>
> (Graaskamp 1981)

The growing intricacy and sophistication of the property development industry has led to the need for a deeper understanding of public policy, physical planning, municipal regulation, market research, the legal framework, site appraisal, economic evaluation, financial arrangements, contractual procedures, building design, construction techniques and marketing strategy dimensions of a development scheme, together with a much more professional approach towards the management of projects in terms of time, quality, cost and asset value.

To facilitate the study and understanding of property development, several models of the development process have been devised since the mid-1950s. These have been grouped as follows (Healey 1991):

(i) **Equilibrium models,** which assume that development activity is structured by economic signals about effective demand, as reflected in rents, yields, etc. These derive directly from the neo-classic tradition in economics.

(ii) **Event sequence models,** which focus on the management of stages in the development process. These derive primarily from an estate management preoccupation with managing the development process.

(iii) **Agency models,** which focus on actors in the development process and their relationships. These have been developed primarily by academics seeking to describe the development process from a behavioural or institutional point of view.

(iv) **Structure models,** which focus on the forces which organize the relationships of the development process and which drive its dynamics. These are grounded in urban political economy.

For the sake of clarity, and in order to respect the principal aims of the text, this chapter essentially adopts an 'event sequence' approach. Nevertheless, mention is made of the various agencies involved in the property development process, the respective members of the professional team responsible for development projects and those other parties concerned with or affected by development decisions. Furthermore, the point is made that the development of real estate may be seen as a set of interrelated processes and not merely a single sequential process. Indeed, it is important to recognize that, although it is helpful to distinguish a series of steps or stages in the property development process, such as in an apparently consecutive flowchart approach, it by no means reflects the concurrent nature of most, if not all of those stages. A successful developer must maintain a perspective overview of the whole process all the time and be prepared to undertake almost constant repositioning of the constituent elements of the development scheme, as well as continually negotiating agreements with the other participants in the process.

It should also be appreciated that there are any number of ways in which the development process can be described as a sequence of events or series of stages from the start to the finish of the project. There might be slight variations, but by and large the stages identified are similar and they embrace the same range of activities. By way of example, one relatively simple approach divides the development process into four phases (Cadman and Topping 1995):

1. Evaluation
2. Preparation
3. Implementation
4. Disposal.

Another, more detailed, model of real estate development distinguishes eight stages (Miles *et al.* 1991):

1. Inception of an idea
2. Refinement of the idea
3. Feasibility
4. Contract negotiation
5. Formal commitment
6. Construction
7. Completion and formal opening
8. Asset and property management.

To explore the process of development and those professional disciplines participating in it, this chapter is divided into two main parts:

• Property development – steps to success
• Participants in the development process.

Property development – steps to success

The process of property development is beset with practices that cause it to suffer from inefficiencies. Some of these inefficiencies were and always will be unavoidable because development does not occur within a perfect market. Many of these inefficiencies arose because of the traditional approach of adversarial positions being adopted by different parties, which were enforced by the evolving of legal contracts.

The relationships between developer, professional team, contractors and sub-contractors were once nearly always framed by adversarial contracts which were predicated on the fact that disputes between the parties were likely to occur. Whilst it is still true that construction-related disputes are fairly commonplace, much has been done to establish relationships where the ethos is to encourage teamworking and a partnership approach to problem solving rather than accusation and counterclaim. This change in attitudes and approaches has occurred because of actions taken across the construction industry after the Latham Review (*Constructing the Team*, 1994) and Egan Report (*Rethinking Construction*, 1998) examined the factors which were hindering the competitiveness of the UK construction industry and proposed changes to working relationships.

Following the publication of these reports and subsequent consultation with parties involved in the development industry, Egan produced more advice to speed up the process of changing the industry: *Accelerating Change* was published

(Egan 2002), following which a number of cross-industry bodies were formed to drive change which were subsequently amalgamated into 'Constructing Excellence'. This body provides support to different stakeholders of the construction industry (e.g. public and private sector, IT and other technology providers, contractors and developer-clients), including information and case studies which demonstrate how approaches to 'partnering' can and do assist in ensuring an efficient development process.

Construction clients are provided with advice about 'procuring successful projects', which maps out six necessary 'steps' (from Egan 2002):

Step 1 Verification of need
Step 2 Assessment of options
Step 3 Develop procurement strategy
Step 4 Implement procurement strategy
Step 5 Project delivery
Step 6 Post-project review.
(http://www.constructingexcellence.org.uk/sectorforums/
constructionclientsgroup/procurement.jsp gives more information regarding
these steps, including appropriate objectives, actions and outcomes for each one.)

Understanding these steps will give a good basis for the understanding of how property development processes should work. The remainder of the first part of this chapter will consider how common pitfalls within the activities listed below, which occur during the steps, can be avoided or mitigated:

1. Concept and initial consideration
2. Site appraisal and feasibility study
3. Detailed design and evaluation
4. Contract and construction
5. Marketing, management and disposal.

Concept and initial consideration

*Establishing objectives for the development organization and generating
ideas to meet them*

In the private sector of the property industry the overriding objective is unashamedly one of profit maximization. In the public sector, other objectives apply, depending on the raison d'être of the development organization – it might, for example, be seeking to remove people from a housing waiting list or provide some infrastructure as its 'return'. However, and in all cases, potential return must be weighed against potential risk and the degree of uncertainty. Operational objectives are paramount in the public sector, although strict budgetary constraints might be imposed. Image may also be an important factor in decision-making. In terms of the generation of ideas to meet established objectives, however, property development is at root about imagination, opportunity and venture. Successful developers are invariably those who arrive at different conclusions from others, against similar sets of information. So too, it should be said, are unsuccessful developers.

Determine a basic strategy for the development organization

Strategy determination will normally entail a consideration of several related factors:

- The very purpose of development activity, whether it is for owner-occupation or for speculation
- The size of a potential project in respect of financial commitment
- Acceptable locations in terms of function and project management
- Specialist knowledge related to selective sectors of the property market
- Portfolio 'fit', taking into account existing investments, holdings and other development proposals so as to maintain an appropriate balance
- A surfeit of capital resources leading to pressures to invest
- The need to sustain an active and credible development programme
- The capacity of the development organization to undertake the scheme *and, perhaps above all,*
- How auspicious is the timing?

Time, for example, might outweigh all other considerations, and the planning approval position may be of paramount importance, or acquisition itself could be a problem. Conversely, quality of design, construction and finish might be the overriding consideration, or cost the critical factor. Where the client is an industrial or business concern intending to occupy the completed property, great attention must obviously be paid to operational needs and balanced against the continued marketability of the building. In satisfying the requirement of the development organization, once established, different forms of management structure will be most suited to particular projects according to such variable factors as size, complexity, time, sophistication, economy, degree of innovation and extent of external forces. It will also be necessary to identify the key decision points in the process of development, such as when planning permission is granted, acquisition completed, building contract completed, or sale or letting agreements entered into, and to determine the consequences that flow from such events, dependencies that arise, involvements that occur and costs that are incurred. A critical path through the development will also usually be constructed at this stage to assist planning control in the decision-making process.

Undertake market research and find a suitable site

The significance of sound market research cannot be stressed too strongly. Indeed, market research and marketing underpin every stage of the property development process. Market research is fundamentally concerned with demand and supply – demand, be it proven, perceived or latent, being the most difficult element to investigate with confidence. Although market research is commonly considered to be formal, focused and systematic, it has been pointed out that market research for generating ideas for development has a very large informal component made up of experience, observation, reading, conversation, networking and analysis. Both formal and informal approaches are necessary, as recognized elsewhere:

> The generation of ideas, marketing and market research have both intuit-
> ive and rational elements. Successful developers are able to maximize both
> the intuitive and the rational. Formal knowledge of marketing principles
> and market research enhances the use of both facilities.
>
> (Miles *et al.* 1991)

Finding a suitable site involves establishing a set of criteria by which alter-native locations can be identified and assessed. These would broadly relate to market, physical, legal and administrative conditions and constraints. Once a shortlist of, say, three or four options has been drawn up, a preliminary appraisal will be conducted in order to determine the most suitable choice. This is the proverbial 'back of the envelope' analysis, which combines an objective assess-ment of likely cost against value with a more subjective judgement based upon experience and feel for the market. Ideally, of course, the right site looking for the right use meets the right use looking for the right site. But there is no magic formula.

Site appraisal and feasibility study

Undertake a more refined appraisal of the viability of
the proposed project, taking into account market trends and
physical constraints

Decide to what extent further enquiries, searches, surveys and tests will have to be conducted, by whom and at what cost, so that there is sufficient information available in order to analyse the financial feasibility of a development proposal. This will normally entail a more detailed assessment of market demand and sup-ply; a close examination of the changing character of the sector; projections of rents, values and yields; and estimations of costs and time. An initial consider-ation of the structural engineering design, foundations and subsoil will also be undertaken. At this stage, developers need to be aware of the potential for land contamination, the consequences of which, if it is present, can turn a poten-tially profitable scheme into one which will only ever mean financial losses. Having assembled all the data, a check should be conducted to ensure that the basic concept achieves the optimum use of the site or buildings and maximizes the amount of letting or operational space.

Consult with the planning authority and other statutory agencies with regard to the proposed development

Apart from making sure that all the initial inquiries are made in respect of preparing and submitting applications for planning approval and building regulation consent, it is also essential for the developer to create a positive climate within which the development can progress. This means that the right people in all the various authorities and agencies concerned with accrediting the proposal must be carefully identified, and approaches to them properly planned and presented. It is vital for the developer to galvanize the professional team in such a way that everyone involved generates an enthusiasm for the scheme and conveys that interest to those responsible for assessing it. This is particularly the case for schemes of such a size that they represent significant changes to the make-up of the built environment and economy within a locality. In such cases, a confident public relations exercise may be required which will need significant planning and marshalling of all those involved in the scheme.

First impressions are always important, and simple precautions can be taken, such as consulting with all the contributors to the project to compile all the preliminary inquiries together to avoid duplications, and despatching them to the authorities and agencies in sufficient time to allow proper consideration and formulation of response. Among the principal factors the developer will seek to establish are the prospects of being expected to provide elements of a planning obligation or community infrastructure levy contribute by way of legal agreements and the likelihood of obtaining a consent, the possibility of having to go to appeal, the chances of success, and the consequent probable timescales and costs resulting. At every stage of the development process, including pre-application, developers will need carefully to consider the required balance between costs and income and subsequent profitability or other benefit to be derived from the scheme.

Identify the likely response from other interested parties to the proposed development

The developer needs to have a heightened understanding of how a particular scheme of development will be received by those likely to be affected by it, or have a voice in how, and if, it proceeds. This implies a knowledge of the wider consequences of development and a comprehension of, say, urban renewal policy. They must, therefore, be able to predict who will oppose, why, how they might organize their opposition, what influence they exert, and how best to negotiate with them and reduce potential conflict.

Establish the availability of finance and the terms on which it might be provided

Because the parameters set by a fund can influence and even determine the design and construction of a building, great care must be taken in selecting a suitable source of finance and in tailoring the terms to meet the aims of both parties to the agreement. This will involve an evaluation of alternative arrangements for financing the project in question, including an assessment of the financial, legal and managerial consequences of different ways of structuring the deal. In doing so, it will be necessary to determine very closely the absolute limits of financial manoeuvrability within the framework of the development plan and programme, for, during the heat of negotiation, points may be conceded or matters overlooked, which could ultimately prejudice the success of the scheme. Different sources of finance will dictate different forms of control by the fund. The major financial institutions, for example, increasingly insist that some kind of development monitoring be undertaken by project management professionals on their behalf, whereas a construction firm might provide finance for development but demand more influence in the management of the building operation. The developer must be wary. Presentation of a case for funding is also a task deserving special attention, and any message should be designed to provoke a positive response. Subsequent to a loan being agreed in principle, it will be necessary for the developer, in conjunction with their lawyer and other relevant members of the professional team, to agree the various drawings and specification documents to be included in the finance agreement. These will normally comprise drawings showing floor layouts and cross sections of the entire project, together with drainage, site and floor-related levels, and outline heating and air conditioning proposals, as well as a performance specification clearly setting out the design, construction and services standards to be met. The financial dimension to project management is critical, for a comparatively small change in the agreed take-out yield can completely outweigh a relatively large change in the building cost.

Detailed design and evaluation

Decide the appointment of the professional team and determine the basis of appointment

It is essential that the developer, or an appointed overall project manager, has a good grasp of building technology and construction methods, together with an appreciation of their effect upon the development process. To this must be added a perception of the decisions that have to be taken and an ability to devise appropriate management structures necessary to carry them out. In deciding such questions as whether to appoint a small or large firm, appoint on the basis of an individual or a firm, select professionals for the various disciplines from the same or from different firms, choose professionals who have worked together previously or who are new to each other, or opt for existing project teams or assemble one especially for the job in hand – the respective advantages and disadvantages must be explored and weighed most carefully. The chemistry is all important, but the opportunity to take such a deliberate approach towards the assembly and integration of the professional team is one of the great advantages of property project management. In this context, however, it is essential that the contractor is seen to be a central member of the team, playing a full part in the design process and not somehow placed in a competitive position. Increasingly, moreover, a choice has to be made between different methods of producing building services, such as package deal, design and build, selective competitive tender, two-stage tender, serial tender, negotiated tender, management fee contract or separate trades contract.

However, a true project management approach might be said to be superior to all other methods. The members of the team, once appointed, will usually be required to enter into collateral warranties as to their professional obligations and be prepared to produce reasonable evidence of the adequacy of their professional indemnity insurance. It may also be that the fund as well as the developer will expect similar undertakings and will insist that the conditions of engagement reflect this part of the financial agreement.

Prepare a brief that outlines the basic proposals for design, budgeting, taxation, planning, marketing and disposal, and sets out all the management and technical functions, together with the various boundaries of responsibility

The preparation and agreement of an initial client's brief is an indispensable stage in the project management process. Misunderstandings are common without a clearly identified set of client's objectives being established. In this, the traditional responsibility of the architect as client's representative or leader of the professional team has been found seriously wanting. Therefore, it is very important to define the separate functions and management activities of individual members of the professional team, as well as those of any project manager, and how they all relate to one another. Equally, it is necessary to ensure that everyone understands the brief. Sometimes a very formal agreement at the outset allows for greater flexibility thereafter. Furthermore, time expended at this stage can often save much wasted energy and ire later. Likewise, fee negotiations must be conducted and terms agreed at this stage, including a clear understanding and record of any departures from standard professional terms of appointment. Frequently, it is beneficial to seek outside advice on certain matters such as town planning, taxation and space planning, so that the organization of the project and functional use of the building can be optimized, even if it is expensive and provided by specialists who will not be involved in the development itself.

At this stage, when crucial decisions are being made about the purpose and design of the scheme, developers need to decide how they are going to approach issues relating to the sustainability of the scheme. Is the scheme, for example, going to be designed in an attempt to achieve a high BREEAM or Energy Performance Certificate rating? If it is, then this decision needs to be made now if this has not already been done because such decisions made at any later stage will result in delays and costs due to subsequent redesigning of elements of the scheme.

*Arrange for the design team to prepare and submit preliminary detailed
drawings for the planning approvals and budget forecasting*

The most important aspect at this stage is to make sure that strong and effective liaison takes place between the architect, the quantity surveyor, the agent
and the fund.

*Submit the planning application and negotiate with the local authority,
statutory undertakers and other interested parties*

An enormous amount of time and effort can be spent on fruitless discussions
unless the right relationships are established with the right people. The presentation
of the submission can have a considerable effect, especially for significant
schemes of a sensitive nature. In such negotiations, steps should be taken to
preserve as much flexibility for future action as possible.

*Make any necessary changes to the scheme, adjusting the various
programmes and obtaining final approvals from all concerned*

It should be appreciated that changes may have to be made and incorporated
within the plans for the project at almost any time, which emphasizes the need
to maintain flexibility. For example, changes may have to be made in respect
of occupancy, division of space, time of completion, technology used, design,
layout, materials, finishes, contractor, costs, services, and even use.

Contract and construction

*Establish the preferred procedure for selecting a contractor, arrange the
appointment and approve the various contract documents*

As discussed above, a more open approach to 'partnering'-type arrangements
evolved in the early 2000s, after Latham and Egan. There is now much wider
acceptance of the benefits to be derived from selecting and involving the contractor at the earliest possible point in the design process. Alternative methods
of building procurement will demand different procedures for appointing a contractor, and it is ultimately for the developer to recommend or decide how best
to proceed, reconciling the two often countervailing factors of competitive cost
and quality of work. Using a team which is tried and trusted and which has
previously worked well as a cohesive unit should pay dividends:

> Integrated team working is key. Integrated teams deliver greater process
> efficiency and by working together over time can help drive out the old style
> adversarial culture, and provide safer projects using a qualified, trained
> workforce. It is self evident that teams that only construct one project learn
> on the job at the client's expense and hence will never be as efficient, safe,
> productive or profitable as those that work repeatedly on similar projects. I

want to see expert teams coming together to deliver world class products, based on understanding client needs.

(Egan 2002)

Where this approach is not adopted, or sometimes even where it is, a combination of tender and negotiation is the preferred approach for deciding upon which team to appoint for a particular project. Performance bonds (at a percentage of contract value) will also be negotiated with the selected contractor and any nominated subcontractors, and any specialists or suppliers offering a design service will normally be required to provide a design warranty.

Establish a management structure to take account of the communication between the parties and the responsibilities borne by all those involved, paying particular attention to administration, accounting, purchasing, approvals reports and meetings

Traditional relationships established during the construction process are not always the most suitable means of communication and collaboration between the various parties engaged in a particular project. However, although it has been suggested that the quality of work is best, and the efficiency in production greatest, where discretion over detailed design is highest, it is often the case that the setting up of a formal structure with a strict routine of meetings and reports to begin with, but allowing for subsequent and deliberate relaxation or amendment as matters progress, works best.

Set up an appraisal system to monitor the viability of the project throughout the building period

It is the fundamental responsibility of the project manager on behalf of the developer to ensure that the project brief is being satisfied. Because of the task of constantly relating the requirements of the brief to the programme of development and the constraints of the budget, it is necessary for the project manager to prepare some kind of master programme. The monitoring of this programme will mean that they must make certain that the members of the professional team are producing all the required information at the right time and in the proper form. It will also be necessary to liaise with other parties, such as the fund and the various statutory bodies, to reassure them that the building and its construction is in accordance with the requirements of the various consents and agreements. Careful control will also have to be exercised over interim and stage payments to those claiming them.

Ensure that on completion of the development, arrangements are made to check all plant, equipment and buildings before they are commissioned

It will normally be the duty of the project manager to accept the building on behalf of the client, sometimes their duty to prepare it for acceptance by the client or their advisers or the funding agency, and sometimes a mixture of both. In certain circumstances, it may be appropriate to make provision for a phased completion and handover. Generally, a minimum maintenance period of twelve months will be required of those responsible for supplying and installing building services and equipment.

Generally supervise all contractual affairs in order to anticipate and solve problems as quickly as possible

At the beginning of the construction process the development project manager should consider the desirability of appointing a nominated expert to settle any building disputes that may arise between the parties. Occasionally the project manager will assume a greater responsibility than normal for arbitrating between contributors to the building operation. In any event, part of the project management function will always be the sensitive oversight and control of the building and associated contracts on behalf of the developer. Very simply, the risks of the development vary in proportion to the degree of detail and commitment to the project produced by the members of the professional team, and to the level of successful orchestration achieved by the project manager.

Marketing, management and disposal

Determine the point at which a marketing campaign is best started, how it should be conducted and by whom

All too often, concern for marketing is too little and too late. However, the prime aim of any private sector development scheme is to produce a marketable building, even if that market is a client who is already identified. Right from the start, therefore, it is the job of the developer to focus the attention of all the contributors to the professional team upon the marketing dimension of the project. Many of those concerned with design and construction have, in the past, tended to neglect the demands of the market. However, now that clients are better informed they are, arguably, more demanding than hitherto. Couple this with the common requirement to achieve a pre-let to secure funding and it becomes apparent that market issues are at the top of everyone's agenda. It is imperative for the developer or his project manager to forge a close link between the selected architect and the instructed agents – it is the agents' role to influence the design and timing of a scheme such that the delivered project is what the market wants, when it wants it. Where the project is speculative, the keynote must be flexibility – in both physical and terms of tenure. In selecting an agent, the developer will be faced with almost the same set of questions as when choosing any other member of the team, such as, national or local, small or large, firm or individual, regularly retained or new, generalist or specialist, and sole or joint instruction. Decisions must also be made between the developer and those engaged in the actual marketing of the development about the size of the marketing and promotions budget and the pattern of expenditure during the selling or letting period. As part of the process of planning the marketing campaign, it will be necessary to determine what specialist services such as market research, public relations and advertising might usefully be retained and on what basis they will work.

Decide on the form of lease or sale contract, so as to preserve an optimum return on the investment

Given the changing conditions of the market, this decision will involve the developer considering very carefully such matters as how many tenancies can be accommodated, what lengths of leases might be accepted, on what terms in respect of rent review and repairing and insuring obligations might leases be agreed, what incentives might effectively be offered, and whether there are any tax advantages to be gained from conducting sale or letting arrangements in a particular way. In respect of a forward sale agreement transacted with a financial institution, it is important to ensure that the conditions are reasonable so far as the client is concerned. Too sanguine a view of the programme for development, and the prospects for letting can often lead to the acceptance of a contractual straitjacket. It should also be appreciated by those acting in a project management capacity on behalf of clients undertaking speculative commercial development that, with most funds, the issuing of an architect's certificate no longer automatically triggers the machinery to release development profit and the start of a lease. Normally it takes a separate document issued collectively by the architect and project manager, together with the fund's professional representative, to release payment.

Establish a management and maintenance programme and, where the development is to be retained or a prospective occupier agrees, recruit and train the necessary personnel to provide a smooth handover

Besides making sure that the necessary operating manuals have been prepared, and the drawings, plans and approvals are collected together for transmission to the client's or purchaser's management organization, the project manager might often now have to initiate and supervise recruitment and training programmes for continuing management staff. This has been the case for some while in the development of planned shopping centres and certain forms of leisure development. It is now spreading to other commercial sectors, such as multi-occupied office schemes, and industrial and business estate developments. Even in the residential sector, large-scale housing projects will require the establishment of selling, management and maintenance operations. Certain apparently minor, but in practice very important, tasks must be commissioned and checked. These include such matters as the provision of a fire insurance valuation, the effectuation of a defects rectification programme with appropriate liabilities and the verification of other insurance and maintenance policies.

Maintain the security and safety of the building at all times

It is essential to ensure that the site is both secure and safe during the construction period for any potential visitor to the site, whether they be contracted personnel, invited visitors (e.g. prospective purchasers) or illegal entrants (such as vandals or thieves). The Occupiers' Liability Acts of 1957 and 1984 place a duty of care on the person or business in control of a site to ensure that all visitors are adequately safe. Evidence of the importance of the need to improve site safety comes from the Health and Safety Executive which reported in 2006/07 that there were seventy-seven fatal injuries to workers in the construction industry, 32 per cent of all worker deaths in the UK. The Construction (Design and Management) Regulations 1994 (CDM) were designed to encourage greater site safety in the industry by coordinating health and safety across disparate contracting organizations, employees and agency workers. Under the CDM Regulations, the developer must:

- Appoint a 'planning supervisor' and a 'principal contractor' to carry out health and safety responsibilities
- Ensure that construction work does not start until a suitable health and safety plan has been prepared
- Ensure that the health and safety file is available for inspection by the end user after construction.

It is also increasingly important to produce a building that throughout its economic life complies easily and inexpensively with ever more stringent regulations regarding health and safety at work – for example the provisions of the Disabilities Discrimination Act require all buildings to be accessible to people with disabilities. Moreover, with the advent of more advanced IT systems and multiple occupancy of commercial premises, there is a growing need to create accommodation with adequate business security systems. The project manager must take this into account at all stages of development.

Monitor the performance of the retained agents

Given that marketing is a critical ingredient in the project management process, close contact must be maintained with the agent. Regular meetings must be held, detailed reports prepared, and explanations provided for disappointing or unexpected results. The developer or project manager should also be consulted about advertising material and its placement. The image of the project and the way it is presented can be significant. Commitment and care on the part of the agent must be watched, and the developer or project manager must not be reluctant to take alternative or novel advice regarding the sales potential and marketing of a building. It is also important that, once identified, the prospective tenant or purchaser is fully involved in decisions taken during the completion of the development.

Reorganize the financial arrangements where necessary

Depending upon the progress of the development programme, the state of the market and the success of the marketing campaign, there may or may not be a need to renegotiate the terms of the funding agreement, seek additional financial support or restructure the cashflow projections and budget allocations. Aspiring tenants or purchasers might have occupational requirements that dictate a reordering of the financial arrangements. Alternatively, the original funding agreement might have certain stipulations in the way of rental guarantees or priority yield, for instance, which are either incompatible with, or detract from, potential disposal terms. Furthermore, for a variety of reasons it may be beneficial to rejig the financial agreement because of the taxation position of the parties.

Summary: Procuring successful projects

The *Accelerating Change* process map for clients (Figure 11.1) sets out the essential steps of the generic processes which, if followed, will help developers to achieve excellence. As Egan (1998 and 2002) and other commentators have identified, it is good teamworking which leads to good projects. For property development

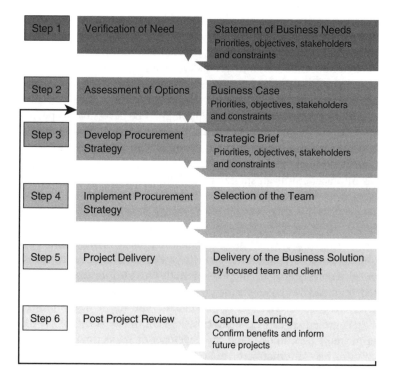

Figure 11.1 The client process map, from *Accelerating Change* (Egan 2002)
Source: http://www.constructingexcellence.org.uk/sectorforums/constructionclientsgroup/procurement.jsp

schemes, good teamwork requires the input of a diverse number of individuals from different disciplines, as the second part of this chapter explains.

Participants in the development process

The property development process involves the constant interaction of various agencies, groups and individuals. Given the all-pervasive nature of property in the lives of everyone, few, if any, are exempt from participating in the development process in one way or another.

A celebrated model of the real estate process collects the participants into three major groups:

- **The space consumer group** – which includes 'individual space users' attempting to rent or buy real estate space to house their specific needs; collective users generally pursuing their interests in real estate activity through the political systems that purchase open space, provide for public infrastructures, or regulate space production with pooled funds from taxation; and 'future users' who are typically represented by proxy, either by developers who anticipate the need to change the use of a building in the future, or by the judiciary or special interest groups, who perceive some trusteeship of the land for future generations. (Provision for future users is a hidden charge to present consumers.)
- **The space production group** – which includes all forms of expertise necessary to convert from space-time requirements to money-time. The system includes those who assemble the capital and those who prepare materials as well as those who contribute to their assembly on-site.
- **The public infrastructure group** – which comprises all those enterprises that provide a network of tangible and intangible off-site systems for the individual space user, including physical networks of roads, sewers and other utilities, services such as education, police and fire and operational systems for land registration, government regulation, adjudication and all forms of economic activity with efficiencies of scale that suggest off-site action (Source: Graaskamp 1981).

In a more prosaic manner, this book divides the participants in the property development process into 'development agencies' and the 'members of the development team'.

Development agencies

The generic term 'developer' embraces a wide heterogeneous breed of agencies, from central government at the one extreme to the small local housebuilder at the other. The aims and objectives of different property- developing organizations also varies enormously, as does their relative efficiency. Many indulge in property development as an ancillary function of a larger prime operation, such as the major retail chains and the principal banking houses, whereas others concentrate their efforts solely on the activity of land dealing and property development. Even within the mainstream of the property development industry, considerable specialization in respect of region, sector and size is experienced and a general description is difficult to manufacture. Nevertheless, the classification that follows serves to identify the principal agencies involved in property development.

Property development companies

As already stated, a great range in the type and size of property development companies can be discerned. There are large companies with extensive development programmes capable of undertaking complex major projects and there are small companies content to operate on a more modest and selective basis. Many large companies are publicly quoted on the Stock Exchange and portray a higher profile, as well as arguably bearing greater accountability for their actions than the bulk of others not so placed or exposed. Some specialize in particular sectors of the market such as office, shop, industrial or residential, where others spread their attentions and apply their skills across the market. There are also those who have established a niche market in such areas as church conversions, waterside developments, sheltered housing and historic buildings refurbishment. Some development companies concentrate upon projects in or around a particular town or city; others operate regionally, nationally or even internationally. There are also companies that trade predominantly in completed developments, whereas others are more concerned with building up a sound and balanced investment portfolio. In terms of organization and structure, it is hard to characterize the typical company, for some, even the very largest, run extremely lean operations, preferring to employ outside professional expertise for virtually the whole range of development activities, whereas others maintain substantial in-house teams. It is true to say, however, that most property development companies were originally founded as the result of one man's initiative, and the importance of the individual remains paramount in the private sector property development industry. They all, moreover, share a common goal: that of profit maximization.

Financial institutions

Since the mid-1950s many insurance companies and pension funds have involved themselves to varying degrees in direct development on their own behalf. The role of developer has often willingly been sought by the more venturesome funds, seeking to secure the full measure of equity return from development projects, but has also frequently been the result of having to take over the affairs of defaulting property companies to whom they advanced loans or purchased a significant interest. The extent to which such financial institutions become active developers in their own right is largely a function of the prevailing general investment climate and the particular performance of the property market. By the mid-1990s, it was a far more attractive proposition to acquire ready-made developments at a discount than indulge in the lengthy and speculative process of building from scratch. Conversely in a buoyant or rising market, or in antici-pation of one, there is much to be gained by financial institutions participating directly in development schemes.

The predominant characteristics of the financial institutions as developers are that they take a longer view of, and adopt a more cautious attitude towards, development proposals than would most private property companies, being con-cerned with future income and capital growth over a prolonged period of time. An inherent advantage enjoyed by institutions acting in a development capa-city is, of course, the financial confidence with which they can proceed, given the underlying capital strength they command. They also seem to attract a higher degree of respectability than their property company counterparts, because, no doubt, of their policy-holder, rather than personalized, ownership. Partnership schemes with local authorities and prospective owner-occupiers, as well as with property companies and construction firms, have also proved popular develop-ment vehicles for financial institutions where risks can be shared, attractive covenants gained and expertise acquired. Perhaps the major drawback that can be levelled at the insurance company or pension fund as a direct developer is that, although they possess all the attributes of a large corporate organization, they also suffer from some of the associated disadvantages in lacking a certain amount of flexibility, flair and enterprise. They tend to be very conventional in their approach towards location, design, covenant, tenure and management.

Construction firms

Traditionally, building contractors have always been closely connected with the positive promotion of speculative development. Of recent years, most major con-struction firms have all been active in the development field. Construction is a high-risk undercapitalized operation with very sensitive margins, and many con-tracting firms have built up property portfolios of respectable size in order to ensure greater continuity of income and a more substantial and secure asset base. The most obvious advantages derived from the horizontal integration of building and development is that it can internalize the risk of obtaining contracts, facilitate the borrowing of funds, and sustain the employment of a skilled workforce. Joint ventures have often been established between contracting firms and other prop-erty development companies on an equity-sharing basis. Likewise, with finan-cial institutions, one of the benefits gained by the builder as developer is that profitability can be viewed across both development and construction activities, providing a competitive edge in the bidding process for land.

Public sector agencies

The direct development activity undertaken by public sector agencies varies enormously according to their nature and function. Local and regional authorities provide by far the most diverse range of development experience, with some councils pursuing an extremely adventurous approach towards commercial schemes, particularly in the light industrial sector, in locations where small nursery factories have not been provided by the private sector. Others have attempted to engage in central area shop and office schemes, but with very mixed results. Residential development has, quite naturally, played a traditional role in municipal development, but has substantially diminished in significance after the introduction of the right-to-buy scheme for public sector tenants and the transfer of a significant proportion of public sector housing to Registered Social Landlords and the private sector. In general terms, the degree of involvement in different forms of development naturally varies between authorities, according to their geographical location, persisting problems, potential opportunities, landownership, financial resources and political complexion. Probably the main differences between public and private sector development are the degree of accountability that attaches to the former and the extent to which community consultation and participation takes place. Local authorities must demonstrate the highest levels of probity and disclosure in all that they do. They also have differing objectives in that such aims as the provision of shelter, the generation of employment, environmental protection and the supply of services outweigh the overriding profit-maximizing goal of the private sector. Sustainable development aspirations are central to much of what public authorities do and any scheme with which they are involved will have to demonstrate significant attention to this issue, as discussed in Chapter 10.

The positive part performed by central government in direct development is strictly limited, as opposed to the determination of a strategic framework and the promotion and control of the property industry by way of fiscal incentives and statutory regulation. Most state development, in fact, is confined to the provision of accommodation for their own purposes and, to this end, the Office of Government Commerce acts in the capacity of agent on the government's behalf.

Across the UK, different organizations are responsible for acting as strategic drivers of regional economic development in each region. Eight RDAs in England were established under the Regional Development Agencies Act 1998. The ninth, in London, was established in July 2000 following the establishment of the Greater London Authority (GLA). The nine English RDAs are:

- Advantage West Midlands
- East Midlands Development Agency
- East of England Development Agency
- London Development Agency
- North West Development Agency
- One NorthEast
- South East England Development Agency
- South West of England Regional Development Agency
- Yorkshire Forward.

RDAs aim to co-ordinate regional economic development and regeneration, thereby enabling regions to improve their competitiveness, with the main task of attracting business investment and stimulating employment rather than the direct construction of commercial premises. The RDAs are responsible for producing Regional Economic Strategies (RESs) and Regional Spatial Strategies after 2010, (RSSs) which have considerable influence not only on the types of occupiers who are attracted to the region and for whom developers will be required to provide accommodation, but also on local planning policies. Similar responsibilities exist in the rest of the UK under the auspices of:

- The Northern Ireland Assembly
- The Scottish Government
- The Welsh Assembly Government.

Public services such as health, prisons and education look to the private sector to meet their property development needs through the Private Finance Initiative (PFI) or Public Private Partnerships (PPP) as the preferred means of financing major public capital projects. Slightly different in kind are those public or quasi-public bodies who have a surplus of land for their own operational requirements, or who are able to combine their functions with other commercial endeavours on the same site and become energetic development agencies in their own right. Deserving of special mention in the context of public sector development agencies, albeit in a somewhat historic perspective, are the New and Expanded Towns, for, since their inception as part of post-war construction and interregional planning policy, they have played an ambitious and successful entrepreneurial role in providing civic, residential and commercial accommodation. In a similar vein, there have been the Urban Development Corporations and a host of other public and quasi-public agencies set up to tackle the task of regeneration in declining inner-city areas.

Another example of a public sector body is that which is created to deliver a one-off project, such as the Olympic Games. The Games will be hosted by London in 2012 and the focus of the London 2012 Games will be the Olympic Park in the Lower Lea Valley in east London, which will house the new sport venues and associated infrastructure. The Olympic Delivery Authority (ODA) is the public body responsible for developing and building the new venues and infrastructure for the Games and their use after 2012. It was established by the London Olympic Games and Paralympic Games Act 2006, which allows the ODA to:

- Buy, sell and hold land
- Make arrangements for building works and develop transport and other infrastructure
- Develop a Transport Plan for the Games, with which other agencies must co-operate, and make orders regulating traffic on the Olympic Road Network
- Be the local planning authority for the Olympic Park area.

The effect of the Games upon developers will be varied. It is certainly the case that some developers will benefit from being able to provide facilities for the Games, but some of the effects will be less positive. For example, the massive scale of the Games means that a huge amount of resources will be sucked into their infrastructure development programme. Consequently, many developers will find that materials and labour across the capital and wider region will become increasingly scarce and expensive up until completion of the associated schemes.

Large landowners

By dint of circumstance, many large landowners almost inevitably become property developers. Some of the most notable, such as the Grosvenor, Portland and Duchy of Cornwall estates, are long established and have set high standards in terms of building design and management. The Crown itself is, of course, a leading landlord and a major participant in the property market, as is the Church of England, another major landowner, property manager and developer.

Business concerns

Where there is a need for a highly specialized building or a non-traditional location is proposed, and there is likely to be little or no general market value attached to the completed development, then it falls to the prospective occupiers to provide their own premises. This can prove a hazardous affair, and professional expertise of the highest order is required. However, it should be stated that many businesses have opted to develop their own property, often in conjunction with a property development company and using some form of sale and leaseback arrangement. In fact, there has been an appreciable growth in the involvement of various business concerns in direct property development since the mid-1970s. Many major retail shopping chains have initiated, funded and managed the development of their own schemes. Other business organizations, such as breweries, have undertaken commercial projects on their own otherwise redundant property, an activity normally seen as outside their province. One developing area is that of total property outsourcing (sometimes known as corporate PFI) whereby companies outsource both their property and facilities management to an external organization (or consortium) in order to concentrate on the 'core' business.

Many of the activities that were traditionally part of the public sector, such as the privatized utilities – gas, water, electricity and telecoms – and the rail-operating companies are now part of the private sector. British Rail, in particular, implemented an ambitious development programme from the mid-1970s until privatization. Following privatization, Railtrack (now Network Rail) continued this programme, although to a lesser degree.

Members of the development team

It almost goes without saying that the quality of a development, and the level of efficiency by which it is produced, is dependent upon the ability and application of those involved in the process from inception to completion. Even where the individual contributions from the various disciplines are capable of producing work of the highest standard, it is imperative that their separate skills be coordinated in a manner that eliminates delay and harmonizes effort. Although the scale and complexity of particular projects will vary, and thus the professional demands will differ, the following catalogue of disciplines describes both the principal participants who would normally be involved in a major scheme of development and their respective terms of reference.

The developer

Developers vary enormously in the degree of expertise they bring to the development team. Their backgrounds may be in building, estate agency, engineering, finance, law, architecture or business management. They also differ in the extent to which they are involved in the actual process of development. Some assume total responsibility for the management of every stage of a project from start to finish, whereas others are content to delegate a substantial amount of responsibility to a project manager, retaining a more strategic policy role.

Above all, however, a developer is an entrepreneur – someone who can identify the need for a particular property product and is willing to take the risk to produce it for a profit. In stating this, a sharp distinction should be drawn between the private developer to whom this entrepreneurial tag truly belongs and the salary-earning corporate professional in either the public or private sector who really acts as more of a project manager. Thus, the developer is seen to play many roles, including:

- Promoter and negotiator with regulatory and approved authorities as well as other parties with an interest in the proposed development
- Market analyst and marketing agent regarding potential tenants or purchasers
- Securer of financial resources from the capital markets
- Employer and overall manager of the professional team engaged on the project.

The job description of the developer has been said to include:

> shifting roles as creator, promoter, negotiator, manager, leader, risk manager and investor, adding up to a much more complex vision of an entrepreneur than a person who merely buys low to sell high. They are more innovators – people who realize an idea in the marketplace – than traders skilled at arbitrage.
>
> (Miles *et al.* 1991)

With regard to general matters of concern in relation to the development function, one leading developer some time ago identified the following requirements, which still hold true today (Jennings 1984):

- **Motivation and leadership**. Probably the most important attribute of all, without which roles and objectives become confused and confidence eroded.
- **Selection of development team**. Another most important function because a considerable amount of collaborative work is required at all stages and mutual confidence is essential if misunderstandings and wasted effort are to be avoided.
- **Funding policy**. This will inevitably be a mix of market conditions and the developer's aspirations, but it must be kept constantly in mind and the relevant members of the professional team involved as appropriate.
- **Pre-letting objectives**. Since these can often have a material effect on various aspects of design and funding, they are bound to be at the front of items for close consideration.
- **Quality requirements**. These are not always easy to lay down in detail at an early stage and can tend to be rather subjective. Nevertheless, they are important to the team and can often best be defined by comparison with other existing buildings.
- **Who does what**. Although this should not be difficult, it is important to recognize that at the creative stage of a project the crossing of traditional disciplinary lines may often be beneficial.
- **Programme**. Although form and content will change frequently, it is imperative that at all times any activity should know where it stands both as to time and as to sequence.

From all this, it can be seen that, on a project, developers spend a large part of their time on managing the input of others. However, an alternative is the appointment of a project manager, to whom the developer, as client, devolves significant managerial responsibility.

Project manager

Project management has been defined as:

> The overall planning, control and coordination of the project from inception to completion, aimed at meeting a client's requirements in order that the project will be completed on time within authorized cost and to the required quality standards.

> (CIoB 1992)

Likewise, the duty of the project manager acting on behalf of the client has been stated to be:

Providing a cost-effective and independent service correlating, integrating and managing different disciplines and expertise to satisfy the objectives and provisions of the project brief from inception to completion. The service provided must be to the Client's satisfaction, safeguard his interests at all times and, where possible, give consideration to the needs of the eventual user of the facility.

(CIoB 1992)

Within the development industry, a project manager is the developer's representative who has to determine and implement the exact needs of the client, based on knowledge of the developer they are representing. The project manager will have to employ a variety of skills, including organizational, administrative and excellent human relations management in order to adapt to the various procedures of the various contractors. The project manager's key role will be to ensure that the key issues of cost, time and quality are achieved to the developer's satisfaction.

The function of project management and the role of the project manager have become increasingly important in the property development process since the mid-1980s. In practice, the project manager could be an in-house executive of the client development company or an external consultant specifically appointed to the project. It is also the case that each project is unique and the means by which the task of project management is fulfilled are subject to variation.

Construction manager

A distinction is drawn in this text between project management – where the span of control normally stretches from involvement in the initial development decision, right through to the eventual disposition of the completed building, covering every aspect of development in between – and construction management, where responsibility is restricted to the building-related stages of the development process. The appointment of a construction manager is most common where the developer acts in the capacity of total project manager and, for reasons of either managerial efficiency or lack of technical expertise, or both, prefers to delegate responsibility for overseeing all the construction activity to another.

The construction manager might be an architect, a builder, an engineer, a building surveyor or a quantity surveyor, and extensive practical experience in the type of project being built is essential. The prime task is similar to that of the project manager, seeing that the building comes in to time, to cost and to specification. In doing so, the construction manager is often called upon to reconcile conflicts between other professional members of the team involved in the building process.

The architect

The role played by the architect is critical to the development process. Invariably the design team leader, except where a project is essentially an engineering problem, the architect translates the developer's concept into a workable and attractive solution. Probably the best way of describing the various functions performed by the architect during the development process is to list the 'architect's services', as laid down by the Royal Institute of British Architects (RIBA) Outline Plan of Work. These services are summarized in Table 11.1, which divides the process of managing and designing building projects and administering building contracts into a number of key 'work stages'. The sequence or content of work stages may vary or they may overlap to suit the procurement method.

It can, therefore, be seen that the architect is fully concerned with several major elements in the development process – the acquisition of planning approval, the design of the building and the control of the building contract.

Table 11.1 RIBA Outline Plan of Work

	RIBA Work Stages		Description of key tasks
Preparation	A	Appraisal	Identification of client's needs and objectives, business case and possible constraints on development.
			Preparation of feasibility studies and assessment of options to enable the client to decide whether to proceed.
	B	Design brief	Development of initial statement requirements into the design brief by or on behalf of the client, confirming key requirements and constraints. Identification of procurement method, procedures, organizational structure and range of consultants and others to be engaged for the project.
Design	C	Concept	Implementation of Design brief and preparation of additional data.
			Preparation of Concept design, including outline proposals for structural and building services systems, outline specifications and preliminary cost plan.
			Review of procurement route.
	D	Design development	Development of concept design to include structural and building services systems, updated outline specifications and cost plan.
			Completion of Project brief.
			Application for detailed planning permission.
	E	Technical design	Preparation of technical design(s) and specifications, sufficient to coordinate components and elements of the project and information for statutory standards and construction safety.

Table 11.1 (cont'd)

RIBA Work Stages				Description of key tasks
Pre-construction	F	Product information	F1	Preparation of detailed information for construction. Application for statutory approvals.
			F2	Preparation of further information for construction required under the building contract. Review of information provided by specialists.
	G	Tender documentation		Preparation and/or collation of tender documentation in sufficient detail to enable a tender or tenders to be obtained for the project.
	H	Tender action		Identification and evaluation of potential contractors and/or specialists for the project. Obtaining and appraising tenders; submissions or recommendations to the client.
Construction	J	Mobilization		Letting the building contract, appointing the contractor. Issuing of information to the contractor. Arranging site handover to the contractor.
	K	Construction to practical completion		Administration of the building contract to practical completion. Provision to the contractor of further information as and when reasonably required. Review of information provided by contracts and specialists.
Use	L	Post-practical completion	L1	Administration of the building contract after practical completion and making final inspections.
			L2	Assisting building user during initial occupation period.
			L3	Review of project performance in use.

Source: http://www.ribabookshops.com/site/title_pdfs/08112007124207.pdf

Engineers

Several engineering disciplines are involved in the construction process of a development project. Working closely with the architect, they combine to ensure that the plans are structurally sound and that the mechanical systems will service the building adequately.

Structural engineer The role of the structural engineer is to provide the skills necessary to create structures that will resist all imposed forces over the lifespan of the structure, with an adequate margin of safety. The relationship between the structural engineer and the architect is inevitably a close one. A decision as to the choice of structural frame – reinforced concrete, pre-cast concrete or steel – has to be made early in the design process, as does the form of foundation adopted and the measure of resulting loads and stresses. Such decisions have consequential effects upon the basic design, construction, cost and use of the building. It is also important to provide sufficient flexibility in the initial design to permit changes during construction and even after completion. With the growing sophistication of modern commercial buildings, flexibility in routing services through floors, ceilings and vertical ducts is another prime consideration at the structural design stage. Attention must be paid to building cost throughout the process, and the structural engineer, together with the architect and other engineering consultants, needs to liaise with the quantity surveyor.

Geotechnical engineer Usually responsible to the structural engineer, the geotechnical engineer is retained to perform initial tests of the bearing capacity of the soil, evaluate drainage conditions and generally assist in planning to fit the proposed project on to the site in an optimum manner, balancing physical effectiveness with building costs.

Mechanical & Electrical engineer or Building services engineer Together, these engineering disciplines supply the life-blood of a building. It has been estimated that up to around 60 per cent of total building cost can be attributed to the provision of building services in some commercial development projects. Such facilities as heating, water supply, lighting, air conditioning, communications, fire precautions and lift services must be carefully planned and coordinated. Alternative systems must be assessed in respect of capital and running costs, energy conservation, main plant location and size, duct sizes and routes, partitioning flexibility, special computing requirements, control mechanisms and the facility to add on services or increase capacity. It should be noted that, given the singular service they provide and the potential problems, the specialist lift engineer is an important member of the professional team.

Part L of the Building Regulations was introduced to reduce energy consumption and therefore reduce the country's carbon emissions. We know already that each five yearly update of Part L will seek to reduce carbon emissions from buildings by around 25 per cent, which suggests that the significance of the role of the M&E engineer will increase in the coming years, particularly as the imperative to reduce carbon emissions intensifies. The low-carbon features that will become more common in the design of buildings are:

- Effective, adjustable external shading (motorized or manual), possibly integrated into a double-wall facade solution.
- More extensive use of narrow-plan spaces – for example, with a maximum centre to glass distance of 7.5 m. This will allow for optimal use of daylight with effective lighting and shading control, enabling lights off, blinds up operation when required.

- Use of exposed thermal mass and night-time ventilation for passive cooling, to allow design solutions featuring natural ventilation or mechanical ventilation with heat recovery only.
- Combined heat and power systems for mixed-use developments or small communities, including with bio-fuel, such as wood burning.
- Use of heat pumps for heating and cooling, particularly in areas with no gas supply.
- Greater use of solar thermal collectors and other building-integrated renewable technology.

(Source: Davis Langdon 2005)

Environmental consultant The environmental consultant is playing an increasingly important role on the design team. At one time, environmental issues were relatively straightforward, usually dealing with water and soil runoff on to surrounding property. Following the discovery that asbestos in existing buildings posed a serious health hazard, and with the advent of 'sick building syndrome', there are now a new set of environmental problems related to land contamination and a much wider range of concerns requiring environmental impact analysis and control.

The quantity surveyor

The quantity surveyor is charged with the task of cost analysis and cost control. It is advisable for the quantity surveyor (or building economist) to be included in the initial design deliberations and financial appraisal, particularly as the question of construction cost has become so critical over recent years.

The original function of the quantity surveyor was mainly restricted to the preparation of bills of quantities and the variations of accounts. However, they have progressively become more involved in providing cost advice throughout the development process, but they remain principally concerned with supplying cost information through the feasibility, outline and detailed design stages, culminating in an agreed cost plan linked to an acceptable preparatory design. This is followed by a process of cost checking; assistance on tendering procedures and contractual arrangements; the production of specifications for the main contract and nominated subcontractors; examination and report on submitted tenders and negotiations; and approval of variation orders, interim certificates and final accounts. However, it is worth emphasizing that the concept of cost-effectiveness is of greater consequence than ever before, and the application of associated techniques such as cost-in-use, life-cycle costing and value engineering have been in the ascendant.

The builder/contractor

The builder is not normally included as a full member of the professional team at the outset of the development process, but rather is viewed as a contracted

agent at the procurement stage. However, some more enlightened property developers, particularly those of large schemes which attract finance from major banks
and other lenders, have found that early, prompt and sympathetic advice on the
building aspects of construction and design, particularly such aspects as labour,
site management and materials, can be extremely useful in respect of savings in
both time and cost. The builder's function in the development process has been
described as follows (Somers 1984):

- **Feasibility.** Understanding the developer's overall timescale; preparing an
  outline network so that discussions relating to key dates can be meaningful at all principals' meetings; and providing general assistance to the whole
  team on matters relating to site conditions and construction.
- **Outline proposal.** Participate in site investigations and any surveys and
  schedules of dilapidations; produce initial method statements; liaise with the
  quantity surveyor on a range of cost information; supply examples of contracts
  and subcontracts; provide material samples; draw up alternative construction programmes; and develop the project network and report progress.
- **Scheme design.** Advise on design matters relating to trade sequencing and
  degree of difficulty; help in advising on the design details relating to weather-
  proofing, which must be guaranteed; consider long-term delivery aspects; continue with cost information advice; interview specialist subcontractors; and
  update the project network to include the detailed design stage and report progress.
- **Detailed design.** Prepare temporary support work designs; establish all special conditions to be included in subcontract documentation; prepare and
  agree the total budget for construction; detail all quality control and
  instruction procedures; update the project network to include construction
  activity and report progress; order long-term delivery items; advise local authorities, neighbours, local residents and unions of intentions; define the extent
  of all remaining details to be provided by the consultant teams and complete project network accordingly; and agree all work packages.
- **Construction period.** Follow the basic tenets of building safety, within
  budget, on time and to specification; update the project network to include
  show areas, letting procedures and key dates together with handover arrangements and maintenance period work; and be in a position to report time
  and financial progress accurately at all times.
- **Post-contract.** Monitor the users' acceptance and allocate a senior member
  of staff to be responsible for final certification and to act as a long-term
  contact for the client, consultants and users.

The real estate agent

It should be appreciated that the agent might be but one contributor to the
overall process of marketing, albeit an important one. Nevertheless, the agent
is an integral member of the development team, whose principal functions are
fully described and discussed in Chapter 15.

The valuer

Many development agencies supply valuation expertise from within their own organization. Where this is not the case, it is common for the estate agency firm retained also to provide valuation advice. Sometimes a separate consultant is employed. In essence, the valuer might be asked to estimate the likely value of land identified for a development project, the possible level of profit that might be derived from undertaking the scheme, or the capital value of the completed project. Again, the various components of the residual valuation, and the methods of conducting development valuation, are fully explored in Chapter 13.

There may be separate valuations that have to be conducted for such purposes as land assembly, compensation, taxation, funding, letting, sale and asset valuation. The initial valuation will almost certainly have to be revised and updated during the development process, as the picture of probable income and actual expenditure becomes clearer.

The solicitor

The services of a solicitor are unavoidable in the property development process, right from acquisition through the various stages of planning approval, contracts for construction, to eventual sale or leasing. How much legal work is involved in any particular project will naturally depend upon the complexity of the scheme and the number of parties concerned. It is also possible that specialist advice might have to be sought on certain matters. In simple terms, it has been said that the solicitor is well suited to undertake several roles: of adviser, especially in the complex area of planning law and construction contract law; negotiator, to explain, to persuade, to reach agreement and to discover for and between the various parties; advocate at meetings, representations of all kinds and inquiries; coordinator, between all parties to the project and all those who can regulate or otherwise have an influence upon it; and draftsman, of all the relevant formal documentation.

Other specialist team members

According to the nature of the proposed development project and the problems encountered, a need to bring in specialist consultants will often arise. The most common of these are:

- **Accountant**. An accountant might be called in to advise on certain tax issues, funding agreements, and disposal arrangements, as well as how the development relates to the overall position of the company.
- **Environmental planning consultant**. Employed in circumstances where the planning position is more complicated than a matter of pure design and layout, especially if the approval is likely to be difficult to obtain and there is a possibility of the proposal going to appeal. Sometimes an actual environmental impact statement or its equivalent is required.

- **Planning supervisor**. Ensures health and safety on site through compliance with the CDM regulations.
- **Landscape architect**. High-quality landscaping is increasing in popularity and importance, and a good landscape architect can promote the marketability of a project and enhance the value. When necessary, landscaping can also cover up defects in design!
- **Interior design**. The internal appearance of offices, houses and especially shopping centres is of utmost importance, and an interior designer might be called in to assist the architect in beautifying the building, especially the common parts, display units, reception areas and shopping malls.
- **Facilities manager**. The management of an organization's facilities, its built environment and its infrastructure must take into account the nature of the activities that take place within the building and which the facilities are serving. For an office building where the eventual occupant is known, the introduction of a facilities manager into the team is becoming increasingly common. Even where the occupant is not known, such advice is beneficial. The equivalent in the retail sector is the early inclusion of shopping centre management expertise into the development plan.

Other specialists might include PR consultant, accessibility coordinator, insurance, archaeology, party walls, traffic engineering and public relations consultants.

Conclusion

Although a description of the property development process and those professions participating within it can be relatively simple, the activity itself grows more and more complex. Increasingly, development requires more knowledge than ever before about prospective markets and marketing, patterns of urban growth, property legislation, local planning regulation, building procurement and disposal, elements of building design, site development and construction techniques, financing, controlling risk and managing time, the project and the people concerned. Greater complexity in property development has also resulted in more specialization, and as more affiliated professionals have become involved, the size of the development team has grown and the role of some of the professional disciplines changed. Fortunately, the most recent generation of professional advisers have grown up with knowledge and training about sustainable development, and developers will increasingly find this essential in procuring successful projects.

Methods and models of the development of real estate are constantly changing. Although developers may not continually address societal trends and changes in the short term, over the longer term such trends and changes have a tremendous effect on what developers build, where they build it, for whom and on what basis.

12 Development site appraisal

The previous chapter considered how we can view the development process – and who tends to be involved in it. This chapter examines how developers should consider analysing a site's potential, and this must be understood within the context of the foregoing chapters, particularly Chapter 10 Sustainability and property development.

Once a potential site has been identified, or a number of sites put up for selection, it is necessary to analyse the respective merits or otherwise of each before a formal appraisal can be conducted. In many ways, this stage of appraisal is one of the most important in the development process and, given the ever tighter margins within which development takes place, deserves more attention than it has sometimes received. Several well-reported cases of professional negligence highlight the need to undertake critical surveys and investigations with care and consideration. The project size, capital resource commitment and degree of community concern evoked determine the level of analytical detail required. This chapter does not cover in depth the extensive detailed analysis that would normally underlie summary calculations and recommendations undertaken for major development projects. Rather, the intent is to indicate the basic nature of the comprehensive methodology that should be employed in the appraisal of development sites.

The first step is to consider the developer's goals and objectives regarding the project. These must be clearly established and agreed before specific uses for the site are studied. This will require consideration of the developer's motivations, business capacities and financial situation. Increasingly complex objectives underlie the goals of development agencies. It is a fair assumption, however, that the private developer is motivated by financial considerations as opposed to the social or community characteristics of the project – although the latter should be of supreme concern to government agencies because of the public responsibility they bear. Even though developers are motivated primarily by financial considerations, their objectives may still vary substantially. Developers may have nothing more than an idea that a certain type of project may profitably be developed. They may or may not have a particular site in mind. Alternatively, they may have a site and be searching for the most profitable use. Some development agencies, such as Registered Social Landlords, may be socially motivated and concerned primarily with weighing social costs against social benefits within a given budget. In any event, once the developer's goals and objectives have been established, site appraisal may commence. For convenience, the principal factors that have to be studied at appraisal have been grouped as follows:

- Planning policy and practice
- Economic climate for development
- Site survey and analysis.

Planning policy and practice

It may seem an all too obvious starting point to state that a clear understanding of prevailing planning policies as they relate to the site or sites in question should be gained, but in one of the leading cases of professional negligence, involving a very substantial greenfield development site, it was not possible to prove that the surveyor responsible had spoken to the local planning authority, even over the telephone. It is vital to recognize, therefore, that planning policy provides the frame within which development takes place.

The formal procedures and practice of planning and development are examined elsewhere in this text (see Part Two). Developers will appreciate that a thorough understanding of a local planning authority's policies is essential to enable a planning application to be submitted that is likely to gain planning permission. Understanding all of the relevant provisions of the Local Development Framework is therefore vital to a successful application. What the following section seeks to do is to explore some of the less formal aspects of planning policy as they affect the appraisal of sites for development.

Planning documentation

The organization of planning systems and their policies has been discussed in Part Two of this book and it is not intended that this ground should be gone over again in detail. However, it is important just to reiterate, purely from a developer's perspective, how crucial a good understanding of the statutory process within which national, regional and local planning policies are formed is for development successfully to be undertaken. Furthermore, their involvement in strategic planning decision-making can be very much to their subsequent advantage.

Following the Planning and Compulsory Purchase Act 2004, at the local level, land planning policy is expressed within Regional Spatial Strategies (RSSs) and Local Development Frameworks (LDFs). The latter are 'folders' of local development documents prepared by the lower tier authority (district council, unitary authority or national park authority) which outline the spatial strategies for the area. It includes a core strategy, site-specific allocations of land, an adopted proposals map and, possibly, other documents such as Area Action Plans and documents which relate to specific aspects of the local economy (e.g. leisure, retail or offices). These are all classed as Development Plan Documents (DPDs) and outline the key development goals of the LDF. (For more on this process please refer back to Chapter 3.)

Much of the focus of the planning regime under the 2004 Act is upon public involvement in the generation of plans, both at regional and local levels. RSSs and DPDs are subject to pretty rigorous procedures of public involvement and consultation and also independent examination. The 2004 Act re-emphasizes the principle of the 1990 Town and Country Planning Act that planning decisions should only be made in accordance with material considerations, the development plan being *primus inter pares* in this regard. Once adopted, therefore, DPDs tend to dictate how a planning application will be treated (and because of this, DPDs are subject to a Sustainability Appraisal to ensure economic, environmental and social effects of the plan are in line with sustainable development targets, including those set by the RDA). Developers and their professional advisers are therefore well advised to get involved in public consultation exercises for RSSs and LDFs in order that their interests are considered by inspectors and, hopefully, respected in subsequent planning policy. (For more information and guidance, see http://www.planningportal.gov.uk/uploads/ldf/ldfguide.html.)

As well as the Core Strategy set out in the DPD, which expresses how community strategies relate to development priorities, developers will be particularly interested in the Site Specific Allocations, Area Action Plans, other planning documents covering sector-specific development policies and Supplementary Planning Documents (SPDs) such as design guides, development briefs and master-plans for larger sites.

Development briefs and master-plans can relate to sites owned by the council or other bodies which possess development or redevelopment potential. The brief is intended to bring together the requirements for a particular development, hoping to form a basis of agreement between interested parties before planning permission is granted. They usually contain information regarding the site and relevant planning guidance. It should be appreciated that development briefs can be prepared by landowners other than local authorities. Nevertheless, where they are produced by a local authority, several enquiries regarding their production are worth pursuing. Those briefs that have been the subject of consultation with all the relevant departments within the authority, with other statutory authorities and undertakers outside and with the public and their representatives, tend to be a great deal more dependable than those where they have not.

Despite the degree of detail and level of commitment given by the authority producing a planning or development brief, it is important to stress that they only represent the author's standpoint. According to the relative needs and bargaining strengths of the parties concerned, they should be seen as negotiable instruments, but at least they simplify appraisal by bringing together many different policy objectives in a single document.

A design guide and design code is prepared by some planning authorities for more detailed development control purposes and is most commonly in the format of a supplementary planning document backed, where applicable, by standards and statutory requirements. It describes preferred forms of development, giving advice on design techniques and materials to be used across an entire planning area. Less important at appraisal stage than other documents, it might influence market research and the choice of architect. Good examples of such design guides seek to conserve the local vernacular, promote local distinctiveness and context and to inspire good new architecture using sensitive materials, appropriate design density, form, style and landscape requirements.

Another common approach aimed at providing 'development briefing' relates to residential development. Often, the intention is to supply supplementary guidance to ensure that developers of residential areas know what is expected of them by using a system which covers social housing provision, requirements for open space, extra facilities and quality of design. They are often applied to specific sites prior to proposed schemes being submitted, using agreed checklists in an 'open process' – a trifle too interventionist and deterministic for some developers, especially as the idea is to fund such elements out of the development land value. Nevertheless, a more structured approach towards design issues is welcomed by many developers, particularly if the length of the process of negotiating planning permissions can be shortened with the use of such guidance.

The planning application

An examination of the past performance of a given planning authority can usually give a pretty reliable indication of the likely reception a particular development proposal will receive and the approximate length of time it might take to obtain a decision. The starting point for this examination is the online Planning Register (or hard copies for very historic applications), which records applications and decisions for all current and past applications, refusals and permissions. From this can be gained an overall impression of the authority's attitude towards development: the type of conditions they are inclined to attach to planning permissions, especially where they are unusual or generous; the refusals to approve applications and the general tenor of the reasons given; and the number of applications that have been called in by the Secretary of State and appeals made to him, together with the decision letters and inspectors' reports resulting from them.

Relevant ministerial circulars and Planning Policy Statements should be consulted and the manner in which these are interpreted by the local authority considered. It may transpire that the local planning authority pursues a particular policy towards certain forms of development that is apparently not in accord with central or strategic planning policy and are not perturbed by their failure rate at appeal, though this is less commonplace than prior to the 2004 Planning and Compulsory Purchase Act. In these cases it may be apparent that an appeal is inevitable and protracted negotiation futile except to judge the strength of the authority's argument, so that the procedural wheels are best set in motion early.

The planning history for the site in question should be studied carefully, with note taken of past applications, previous decisions, outstanding consents and current proposals. The same exercise should be conducted for neighbouring properties in order to identify any intended development schemes that could affect the site concerned. A more comprehensive approach might benefit all parties, on the one hand, whereas possible overdevelopment might detract from the viability of the proposed project, on the other. Either way, it could make a difference to the timing and presentation of an application.

One of the most difficult aspects of appraisal to describe in comparatively objective terms is the effect that personalities and politics have upon planning decisions. They can, however, be crucial. Many an application has foundered, or progressed less easily than it should, on the lack of awareness on the part of the developers or his advisers of certain individual or political sensitivities existing within the authority, its officers and its representatives. Where a developer is faced with an unfamiliar locality, it is often worthwhile compiling a scrapbook of cuttings from the local newspaper stretching back a year or so that deal with planning and development matters. The front page and the letters column are most productive. These extracts can help paint a most revealing picture, spotlighting issues and individuals in the forefront of local planning affairs. Slightly harder is the task of identifying those within the council who are most influential with regard to planning decisions. Time taken with finding informal contacts is rarely wasted. If the developer does not have those informal contacts, there are professional organizations that will investigate the political scene in a particular locality and provide a report on local politics and the movers and shakers in the planning and other committees. In politically sensitive situations it pays to check the date of local elections and the likelihood of political change – either way.

These days the authority and influence of various interest groups can play an important part in the planning process, and some consideration of their presence and power at appraisal stage is expedient. Apart from those local amenity groups formed to promote and protest about particular causes, there are established national bodies concerned with specific facets of our urban heritage. These include the Georgian Society, the Victorian Society, the Society for the Protection of Ancient Buildings, the Commission for Architecture and the Built Environment and the Town and Country Planning Association. A sympathetic attitude towards the views of such interests at an early point in the development process can often prevent unnecessary conflict and smooth the path to approval.

An absolute must in all appraisals of any significance is the holding of informal discussions with officers, and occasionally members, of the local planning authority. The main purpose of these enquiries is to elicit information and details that may not have been forthcoming from published documents, and to clarify the background to previous decisions and published statements so as to avoid confusion. Apart from those matters already mentioned, these discussions might usefully cover any relevant policy work in progress, the timetable for the production of any new plan or policies, suitable land-use survey information that could be made available, the relationships and need to consult the regional authority and other bodies, the dates of the appropriate committee meetings and agenda deadlines, the immediate reaction of the authority to the particular development proposal, and any special information that should be provided by the applicant. It is suggested that, at the conclusion of the meeting, the local authority be asked if there are any other matters to which the authority would like to make reference, and it is recommended that following the meeting the subjects discussed are confirmed in writing. It is a well-known axiom in planning and development circles that the quality or usefulness of an answer obtained from planning officers is only as good as that of the question posed – it is also only as good as the person answering, and their standing. Commonly, it has been found that developers are often concerned about the quality of advice they have received at pre-application inquiry. They frequently find that junior staff are used to deal with enquiries and that their views are overridden by more senior staff at later meetings, or when a planning application is submitted. As a result, they feel misled when committees do not support officers' recommendations. In particular, frustration is felt when proposals are amended before planning applications are submitted, in response to advice received from planning officers, and officers later recommend refusal of something that they appeared to support earlier (Taussik 1992). It has further been stated that officers are often unprepared, overly cautious and preoccupied with detail. Conversely, developers have been accused of being too vague in their proposals, over-expectant of the off-the-cuff on-the-spot responses, and tending to hear what they want to hear. Nevertheless, proper preparation prior to a meeting, an appointment with the appropriate officer, a careful agenda drawn up, sufficient information provided (preferably in advance), objectives identified, notes taken and written confirmation of the discussion made after the meeting – should help make pre-application inquiries fruitful.

These days, communication is of the essence – information or development proposals should be concise and frank, with a clear style of presentation that makes them easy to understand (Boys 1983). Developers and their consultants sometimes produce a single package of information for the authority and other involved parties. Typically, this would provide an introduction to the company's affairs, then give a history and summation of the development proposal, discuss the commercial background to the company's plans, explain the development proposals in relation to various topics, and provide annexes in support of earlier parts of the statement, together with any supplementary information. Later in the process this might be followed with a public exhibition, using additional aids such as enlarged plans, models and audiovisual programmes.

Consultations with other bodies

Most development projects of any size will involve consultations with at least two or three bodies in addition to any consultations with the LPA. If the proposal is thought to have strategic implications, it may be necessary to discuss it with the relevant regional authority or, in the case of London, the Mayor must give his approval for large-scale development and development that may affect strategic policies. Similarly, where development has traffic consequences, then having discussed the matter at first instance with the district or borough council, it may be advisable to check certain points with the highway authority. This may relate to possible changes in public transport routing, any required improvements or alterations to the road system, adoption and maintenance of new roads and appropriate parking and servicing standards.

In respect of large development schemes, generating a substantial amount of public transport travel, it will be necessary to consult the local passenger transport services if any rescheduling, rerouting or stopping provisions are required. Further, it is always worth checking with those services, or where appropriate with the relevant rail network operator, that local services are likely to be maintained at their present level of provision, especially where those travelling to the development for business, shopping, work, leisure or housing are dependent upon public transport.

In addition to detailed investigations regarding the supply of services to the site, it is incumbent upon the developer to approach statutory undertakers, such as the water authority and the gas and electricity companies, to ascertain if there are any capital programmes or proposals that they may have formulated and which could have a bearing on the project. Sometimes certain other bodies such as the Environmental Health Officer, the Health and Safety Executive, or the Environment Agency might have to be consulted if the circumstances of the scheme dictate.

With regard to infrastructure requirements, most statutory undertakers are governed by statutes that enable them to assist developers, either by rerouting existing services or linking-in with existing services up to the site boundary. However, the provision of major off-site infrastructure can bring major problems, financial and legal, so it needs to be assessed very carefully. For example, it is not unknown for an authority opposed to a development proposal on planning, or even political, grounds to find the most surprising highways, drainage or other service reasons for refusal. Conversely, a cooperative authority can be very helpful, even to the extent of being prepared to use their powers to assist a developer in acquiring any necessary land. The likely reaction of a local authority must, therefore, be carefully assessed.

Planning obligations and planning gain

Probably the most controversial issue surrounding planning and development since the mid-1970s has been that of 'planning gain'. Sometimes known as planning agreements (or S106 agreements) or planning obligations, the extraction of community benefits from a development project through the exercise of the planning approval mechanism has been the subject of continuing legislation, litigation and debate. This topic has been covered in Chapter 6, which should be referred to for a fuller treatment of this topic, but the key points are worth reiterating.

The most recent debacle concerning planning obligations reached a head in December 2005, following a review of the system for the UK Treasury by Kate

Barker (HM Treasury 2004), with the publication of government proposals on a Planning Gain Supplement (PGS). The PGS, it was proposed, would be a formalized levy on non-residential and residential developments, payable under a self-assessment regime upon commencement of development. After vociferous lobbying on behalf of property development interest groups, the 2007 Pre-Budget report indicated that the PGS, as proposed by Barker, would not be implemented and the system of negotiated contributions would continue alongside a reformed system of locally based development charges. In December of the same year a hasty consultation was undertaken (together with some minor legal tinkering of the Planning and Reform Bill) to introduce the Community Infrastructure Levy. This would allow individual planning authorities the right to set a charge on certain categories of development, to fund general infrastructure needs. Affordable housing would fall outside this system and together with the mitigation of mostly traffic impacts (such as new access improvements), the Section 106 mechanism would remain in a somewhat scaled-down format.

Over a decade prior to Barker's PGS proposals, several competing rationales justifying the imposition of planning agreements upon developers in return for the grant of planning permission were cogently set out in a 1993 report (Healey *et al.* 1993) and are now contained in Circular 5/05 ('Planning Obligations'). The first rationale is concerned with the implementation of planned development. Within such a framework, agreements may be used to address management problems with respect to development, or developers may be encouraged to contribute to the provision of planned infrastructure to enable their development schemes to proceed. The second rationale focuses on the adverse impacts of the development and the subsequent need to alleviate or compensate for the social costs of that impact. Unlike the first rationale, it is not so much concerned with making the development work on its own terms as with accommodating the development over a wider area. It is suggested that this rationale can be used to justify a wide range of community benefits.

Under a third rationale, the developer is seen as having a duty to return some of the profit from the development to the community – a form of local development charge. In both the first and second rationales, reasons can be established for refusing the proposal on the grounds that, without the planning gain or obligation agreement, the development would be unacceptable in planning terms, in the former by making the proposed development project fit with an already envisaged scheme, and in the latter by amelioration of the impact of the project. The third rationale, however, is founded solely on the perceived need to impose some form of local tax on the developer (Edwards and Martin 1993). It is often suggested that developers being required to provide affordable or social housing in a scheme, for example, is because of the third rationale, i.e. that in some way the 'planning system' is trying to penalize developers for making profits whilst others are homeless. More considered thought might lead to an appreciation that the second rationale is actually much more likely to be relevant and that which is applied, and as Circular 5/05 makes clear, planning obligations should never be used purely as a means of securing for the local community a share in the profits of development, i.e. as a means of securing a 'betterment levy'.

(Circular 5/05)

The position covering planning obligations is governed by the provisions of the Town and Country Planning Act 1990, as amended by the Planning and Compensation Act 1991, together with DCLG Circular 5/05 and the Town and Country Planning (Modification and Discharge of Planning Obligations) Regulations 1992. The general principle is that,

it will in general be reasonable to seek, or take account of, a planning obligation if what is sought or offered is *necessary* from a *planning* point of view, i.e. in order to bring a development in line with the objectives of sustainable development as articulated through the relevant local, regional or national planning policies.

The five 'tests' which a planning obligation must satisfy in order to be entered into are also set out in Circular 5/05, which states that a planning obligation must be:

(i)   relevant to planning
(ii) necessary to make the proposed development acceptable in planning terms
(iii) directly related to the proposed development
(iv) fairly and reasonably related in scale and kind to the proposed development
(v)   reasonable in all other respects.

(Circular 5/05)

One of the main changes introduced by the 1991 Act, amending the TCPA 1990, was a section allowing for the possibility of unilateral undertakings. It also provides a statutory regime for modifying and discharging such unilateral undertakings and other planning obligations. A system of appeal to the Secretary of State was introduced and Crown land was brought into the ambit of unilateral undertakings and planning obligations. Furthermore, certain new formal requirements were introduced. As Circular 5/05 dictates, for a planning obligation to have statutory force, it must be made by deed; it must state that it is a planning obligation for the purposes of the 1990 Act; it must identify the land to which it relates; it must identify the person entering into the obligation and their interest in the land; and it must identify the local planning authority by whom it is to be enforceable.

Planning obligations may be conditional or unconditional, and be either indefinite or limited in time. A planning obligation requires registration as a local land charge. As long as the formal requirements are met, then a planning obligation is enforceable against the person entering into it and those subsequently deriving title, unless otherwise specified.

Planning obligations can be positive or negative: positive, in that they might relate to the provision of services or facilities such as highways, sewerage, low-cost housing, open space, landscaping or other physical community benefits; negative, in respect of controls over the use and occupancy of the land or building. They can also require sums of money to be paid to the local planning authority, both one-off and periodic payments. Circular 5/05 provides guidance to local planning authorities on the use to be made of planning obligations. Properly used, planning obligations may enhance the quality of development and enable proposals to go ahead that might otherwise be refused. When used appropriately, they can be key elements in the implementation of planning policies in an area. For example, planning obligations may involve transport-related matters (such as pedestrianization, street furniture and lighting, pavement and road surface design and materials, and cycle ways).

Time and money spent negotiating, drafting and agreeing planning obligations can often come between a good development proposal and achieving planning permission. Given that planning obligations, after 2009, will remain as key tools used by local authorities and developers alike, the likelihood is that there will be a continued growth in their use and further refinement of their application by government. It is imperative, therefore, from the viewpoint of the developer at appraisal, that they identify the general policy and practice of a particular local authority towards planning obligations, and their success in implementing them.

Economic climate for development

A study of the market to estimate the range of specific land uses, and the rate of physical development that can be supported within the constraints imposed by demand and supply conditions, is perhaps the most important stage in the development process. However, it is one of the most difficult to undertake.

Market appraisal is used not only to inform prospective developers and to assist them in reaching a decision, but also to gain support from local planning authorities, leading financial institutions and potential tenants and purchasers. It must be conducted in a manner that is systematic, rigorous, logical, defensible and reasonably detailed. However, the degree of objectivity required is not always a trait most immediately associated with the natural optimism or bullish behaviour of the developer. Thus, the services of a more dispassionate consultant analyst are often felt advisable. Nevertheless, problems persist, most notably the basic lack of relevant data; the dated and non-comparable nature of such data as does exist; a frequent reluctance on the part of public authorities and their officials readily to cooperate; a similar, though natural, recalcitrance by competing developers, estate agents, property managers and occupiers or owners to share market knowledge; and the fact that there is often no direct precedence to act as a guidepost. In similar vein, the developer invariably wishes to act at this stage with a high degree of confidentiality, if not down-right secrecy. An independent consultant acting as analyst also often faces the problems of an inadequate budget for undertaking a thoroughgoing market appraisal, and sometimes a developer with a preconceived notion as to the preferred outcome of any analysis. Moreover, there is the somewhat invidious pressure placed upon the consultants themselves to produce positive results that may lead to further work on the project.

It should be appreciated that a market appraisal may be undertaken for one of two basic reasons – where the use is known, but the site has to be determined, or where the site is known but the use has to be determined. Many of the fac-tors to be studied remain the same, but the processes of analysis are somewhat different.

General market conditions

Overall economic climate

All development decisions are inevitably affected by the overall economic climate prevailing in the city, region and country concerned. Increasingly, moreover, international markets are exercising a considerable influence over national and local ones. A market appraisal should, therefore, start with an examination of global as well as national conditions and projected long-term trends, then narrow the focus upon the characteristics of the region, locality, neighbourhood and ultimately the site.

Business cycles

Within national economies, and even within regional and local economies, there are distinct business cycles that affect investment and development decisions in the property market. The reverse is also the case, because it should be borne in mind that there is also a situation of 'simultaneous causation', whereby events in the property market can impact upon other sectors of the economy as well as vice versa. In this context, four types of economic fluctuation bearing upon property investment and development decision-making have been identified (Barrett and Blair 1982). These are: random fluctuations, which are short-term irregular changes in business activity; seasonal fluctuations, which are regular and reasonably predictable; business cycles, which are fluctuations affecting the total economy having expansion, recession, contraction and revival phases; and secular trends, which represent the underlying economic conditions that might influence generations. Construction and property cycles do not normally match the average cycle for the economy as a whole, tending to peak before the total economy peaks, and bottoming out before the rest of the economy. This is mainly attributable to investor and consumer confidence, the fact that property is usually one of the first sectors to be adversely affected by rising interest rates and that a slowdown in construction and development activity itself depresses other parts of the economy. The important issue so far as analysing the economic climate for development is to make sure that the timing of the development is related to the turns of the business cycles.

Urban structure theories

In searching for a site, or deciding the highest and best form of economic assessment, developers are advised to reflect upon certain basic economic theories of urban structure and change. Some regard should be paid to the traditional concepts of concentric zone theory, axial theory, sector theory and multiple nuclei theory. Concentric zone theory states that, assuming no variations in topography, transport or land supply, land uses are sorted out according to their ability to benefit from, and therefore pay for, the position of greatest accessibility. Axial theory accounts for development along transport corridors, with accessibility considered in time-cost terms so that changes in transportation lead to changes in land use and land value. Sector theory also recognizes the importance of limited transportation in urban areas, but suggests that specialization of land use takes place according to direction rather than just distance from the position of greatest accessibility. Multiple nuclei theory observes that urban areas may have more than one focal point, each of which influences the location of certain land uses. One cautionary note – Schiller (2001) suggests that:

> Since the early days of the twentieth century, the movement from heavy to light industry has reached the point where this model [location based on the idea of cost minimisation, in particular proximity to markets and raw materials] is of little relevance. Improvements in transport and the globalisation of the markets for raw materials means that these costs vary little between different locations in Britain.

With changes to the use of transport networks (not least caused by increased congestion on road networks) typified by the attention paid to the logistical operations of the major retailers, it will be interesting to see how the relevance of proximity to markets changes in future.

Economic needs

There are also a set of urban economic models or concepts that provide a less descriptive and more analytical approach towards the examination of growth and change. These include economic base analysis, shift and share analysis, input–output analysis, econometric models, simulation, time-series and other hybrid models. Between them, these macroeconomic tools allow a perspective of general economic forces to be gained and translated into the demand and supply of urban land and property resources. The range of forecasting techniques is large, and the choice lies with the user, and with a sound understanding of the strengths and weaknesses of each approach, as well as an equally sound understanding of the particular forecasting or analytical problem facing the developer's consultant. Only through the exercise of informed judgement based on knowledge of local conditions, the problem to be studied, and the techniques available for studying the problem and the area concerned, is it possible to construct and present usable studies of urban economic systems.

Local markets

Most property development markets, however, are essentially local markets. Local developers will have a good understanding of their own area – the policy of the local planning authority towards property development; prevailing rents, values and costs; other projects in process or contemplated; and the potential for future expansion from contact with tenants, purchasers, financiers and the construction industry. Newcomers will obviously have to find out. Nevertheless, a broad understanding of the property market and an intuitive grasp of the particular situations should enable a prospective developer in unfamiliar surroundings to feel at the outset if they like the town, like the location and like the site. This personal judgement is not to be despised, for as in most lines of business, confidence in the final product is essential. Even without sophisticated analyses of the local market it should be possible to tell if, for example, a town is under-shopped, lacks sufficient housing, has a buoyant industrial base, is well placed for distribution services, or lends itself to office relocation.

Market delineation

It is important to define exactly what is the relevant local and non-local market area for the proposed project as a specific site. The local market might be contiguous, such as that for retailing, or diffuse, such as that for housing. Office and industrial development can be both. Apart from recognizing a geographical identity, it is also necessary to study market-area dynamics, taking account of the compatibility of the proposed use with surrounding land uses and in the light of neighbourhood growth trends, the location of competitive sites and the degree of spatial monopoly (Miles *et al.* 1991).

Any market study must focus on the determinants of demand and supply. It should be appreciated, however, that in doing so there is an inherent difficulty in differentiating the many economic factors influencing the property development industry between demand and supply. There are large areas of overlapping influence where certain factors can be said to affect both demand and supply. Nevertheless, there are certain basic forces that clearly affect one side of the demand and supply equation more than the other. These have been stated as follows (Barrett and Blair 1982):

- Demand = (population, income, employment, relative prices, taxes, interest rate, down-payment requirements and future expectations).

- Supply = (expectations of demand, planned supply, competitive environment, availability, and cost of land, labour and capital).

Demand for development

The demand for property is both derived from and driven by the market. It is
market-derived in that many occupiers locate in a given market area in order
to provide goods or services for that area, or be accessible to resources and
customers, and others, to secure employment within a reasonable commuting
distance. It is market-driven in that the local economy must remain competitive
to support sustained demand for accommodation, so that spatial arrangements
within an area become important in influencing firms' profitability and local
residents' well-being. A typical market study of demand for property development would analyse a number of basic factors, of which those below may be
considered to be of notable importance.

Catchment area

For most forms of commercial property development the demand for space
is a function of the catchment area or hinterland commanded by the site or
the activity proposed on it. The exact nature of the centripetal forces at
play will vary according to the size, use, location and accessibility of the planning developments. The prime concern at appraisal is to establish whether
or not those forces external to the scheme that affect the extent of the hinterland are likely to change. Rail and road closures, diversions and by-passes, motorway extensions and ringways, parking provision or restriction and traffic
management schemes of all kinds can have a major impact upon development
viability.

Population

The population factor would include an examination of past trends and current
estimates regarding population size, birth and death rates, age structure, migration, family size, and spatial distribution. In terms of forecasting, natural births
and deaths are relatively easy to gauge, but migration is more difficult. It is also
hard but necessary to categorize the population properly into consuming units,
especially for retail and housing studies.

Again, income data is mainly required for retail and housing studies, and include
a study of past trends and current estimates of personal income, socio-economic
distribution, household formation and change over time. In the housing market
it is important to distinguish between 'need' (the desire for a property) with 'effective demand' (the intention to occupy backed by the ability to pay) in respect
of affordability. In the retail market it is necessary to estimate actual consumer
expenditure between sectors, and forecast likely future disposable income on
consumer durable and convenience goods.

Employment

This would include an examination of past trends and current estimates of employment among different sectors and occupations, so as to give an overall picture
for a given community. This study is especially important in smaller communities, where dependence upon certain major employers can be high, and also in
larger urban areas where there is an agglomeration of businesses in the same field
of service or production activity. Comparatively small or selective changes can
have a significant and multiplier effect upon total employment. Predictions of
location and relocation of actual or potential employers, inwards and outwards,
can have a dramatic impact upon forecasts of effective demand.

Labour supply

In the context of employment, several different surveys have shown the importance of labour supply to those intending to occupy completed developments,
mainly in the industrial sector. In one survey, the calibre of staff required was
placed second, just after transport considerations, as the reason for selecting a
particular location, while in another it was put top, so some recognition of the
effect of labour supply upon property demand at appraisal is required.

Rents and values

The most reliable indicators of demand for space are rental values for commercial schemes and capital values for development land and housing. In analysing
values for property it is the general direction of rents and prices for the area
over a period of time that is important, and the broad pattern of their incidence
across the market, not individually quoted deals struck in isolation from the rest,
which might result from pressures to purchase unconnected with the prevailing
conditions of the property market. Moreover, care must be taken to ensure that
only achieved rentals are used in appraisal, and not asking-rents, which may
differ considerably. Any incentives to either party, such as rent-free periods or
premiums, should be taken into account. In the same way, where seemingly
comparable transactions are being analysed, adjustments must be made to take
account of variations in location, size, use and date. As with most preliminary
appraisal it is sometimes sufficient to employ a break-even rental figure as a rule
of thumb to find out if it is worth pursuing investigation further.

Vacancy rate

Another useful guide to effective demand is the vacancy rate persisting in a
chosen locality. Some degree of care must be exercised, however, in reacting
too immediately to a forest of estate agents' signs on high street frontages. It
may just be that old leases have fallen in at the same time. Nevertheless, where
a surplus of existing property development has been overhanging the market for
some time, it is obviously a warning sign not to be ignored.

Informal enquiries

Discussions with those actively involved in local property markets can give a good picture of the current scene. Existing tenants in competing projects, estate agents acting on behalf of buyers and sellers, property managers concerned with occupiers' requirements, investors involved with financial performance, and contractors providing building services can all provide informed and informative views of present conditions and prospects. However, it should be remembered that the picture they paint can be highly coloured.

Other factors

There are many other factors affecting the demand for development, including taxation, special incentives, interest rates, local amenities, leisure facilities and environment. All must carefully be considered.

Supply of development

An appraisal of actual and likely future supply of property is generally agreed to be easier than an appraisal of demand. It is conducted so as to compare resultant supply figures with those of demand so as to gauge the amount, if any, of excess demand and the prospects for development. Many factors need to be considered in any assessment of the demand for development.

Anticipated supply

> Put simply, anticipated supply = existing stock + (space under construction + expected starts + planned new projects + conversions of space) − (demolitions + removals of stock + abandoned projects).

Existing and planned supply

This involves an examination of past trends, current estimates and future forecasts of stock for the particular types of property under scrutiny. Data on existing stock are relatively easy to gather, but predictions of future supply beyond a three- to five-year time horizon are difficult to make reliably. Some important assumptions regarding market behaviour, and central and local government responses to any significant market changes, need to be made. It is also important to recognize that longer-term supply is sensitive to fluctuations in the business and construction cycles.

Competition

It is essential in appraising supply to study most assiduously actual and possible competition. In general terms, this necessitates an assessment of projects under construction, their size, number of units, quality, location, special features, management and stage of development. Competitors themselves must be studied in terms of their number, activities, aspirations, capacity, confidence, contacts, image and performance.

Land availability

It is imperative to ascertain the amount of land allocated in the development plans for the area under study, and the total amount of development that might result if taken up. Possible changes to land release, zoning policy and density control must be considered. Furthermore, the potential for conversion of existing buildings to a new use, and the refurbishment of older premises to provide competition to fresh development schemes, must be assessed.

A survey of cleared sites and other evident development opportunities should be undertaken, for latent supply can be just as telling on market conditions over time as that possessing formal recognition. Floorspace targets, land allocation and infrastructure programmes established by the local authority must be studied, so that a full picture of the potential supply of development land can be presented. In linking land release with permitted levels of commercial floorspace, a certain amount of circumspection is often advised about land owned by local authorities and the final resolution regarding the preferred location of commercial development.

The Planning Register

As already mentioned, one of the main sources of information is the Planning Register, which will show the number of outstanding planning permissions for various forms of development within the planning area. From this, a rough calculation of the probable proportionate increase in the existing stock of buildings and supply of floorspace can be performed. If possible, an attempt should be made to ascertain who the likely developer is and, even more pertinently, whether or not the scheme is designed with a prospective occupier in mind. Where the development is intended for a known owner-occupier, or has already been pre-let, it can be argued that there will be less impact upon the overall supply base. Conversely, the search of the Register might reveal one or more directly competing schemes, which, upon further inquiry, might prompt a complete reconsideration of the planned development. In any case, the prospect of the take-up of these competing schemes and their likely timing should be considered, for it might be possible to pre-empt them by swift action in progressing the planning approval and making an early start on site. However, care should be taken in scrutinizing the Register because several applications and approvals might relate to the same piece of land. Some official surveys have been distorted by adopting crude aggregates of potential floorspace with planning permission and neglecting to sift-out duplicate consents. A check should be run on permissions previously granted to ensure that they are still valid. Outline consents and full approvals last for three years, unless extensions are sought and approved.

Neighbouring markets

It is not always sufficient to restrict the appraisal of the supply of development to a particular authority area or presumed hinterland. Extensive land release and a profusion of planning consents in adjoining towns and areas can exert a very considerable influence upon property markets. This can apply across the board, but is especially significant in the retail development sector, where shopping patterns are notoriously vulnerable to changes in supply.

One aspect of market conditions that is sometimes overlooked when it comes to appraising the supply of development properties is the capacity of the local building industry, and its ability to cater for the level of construction required by the proposed development programme. This check should extend to the availability of materials as well as labour. The effect of swings in the business cycle can be profound on the construction industry, but major problems emerge for the developer, of course, during boom periods where skilled labour and experienced supervisory staff are short and delays in delivery materials long.

Absorption and capture rates

The rates at which supply soaks up demand (absorption rate) and the proposed project penetrates the market (capture rate) are of great consequence to the developer. There are three levels to such absorption or capture rates: the overall market for the type of property concerned, the relevant market segments, and the subject property – the intention being to ascertain what surplus or unfulfilled demand exists and the extent to which the project in question can attract that demand. Thorough market research should provide a good basis for appraisal, but it has been stressed that the capture rate of the project and its eventual profitability will actually depend on how well the developers understand demand and what the competition is doing, beyond cursory market studies (Miles *et al.* 1991).

Informal enquiries

As with the appraisal of demand, it pays an aspiring developer to talk to a range of parties who might be able to give insights into the supply side of the market. In the public domain, elected representatives, community associations and interest groups will give an indication of what might be favoured and what opposed. In the private sector, property owners, occupiers and managers can give an idea of what is preferred, where, when, why and how.

Other factors

Other factors also tend to affect the supply side of the development equation, including infrastructure costs, land assembly problems, land-holding issues and capital investment programmes, and the availability of grants and subsidies for development, urban regeneration and economic development projects.

With the appraisal of both demand and supply for property development, it is important to recognize the inherent risks that exist. Sources of information can be suspect, long-term forecasts are notoriously unreliable, policies towards land release and planning consent can change quickly, market studies do not necessarily determine the highest and best use for a site or the best site for a given use, and the attitudes and behaviour of owners and occupiers can be volatile. Some form of risk analysis or simulation to test the sensitivity of project proposals to change is well advised.

Site survey and analysis

Having considered the planning position, and explored the likely level of potential demand and the overall prospects for supply persisting within a particular town or given locality, a developer must assure himself about the capabilities of a selected site to meet his development objectives. For convenience, the various surveys and analyses that are necessary to achieve this can be grouped into those of a legal, physical and functional character.

Legal considerations

Ownership

To begin with, it is clearly essential to establish the ownership of all the various interests that may subsist in the land and property. If the site is offered as a freehold, it is necessary to ensure that full vacant possession can be obtained. It is possible that, in disposing of the freehold interest, the vendor might seek to impose legal requirements placing the developer under some form of obligation to fulfil certain conditions relating to the nature and performance of the development scheme. If the vendor is a public authority, for example, it might seek to retain certain rights to approve the layout or design of the development or to compel the developer to complete the project within a stipulated period of time. The developer will wish to be satisfied that such conditions are acceptable, that they are expressed in reasonable terms and that they allow enough flexibility for the proper execution of the scheme. If there are leasehold interests to be taken into account, then the developer will need to ascertain the period of any lease, the amount of rent payable, the review pattern, the main provisions of the lease, the position with regard to security of tenure, and the respective responsibilities on reversion. A check should also be made about any licences that might have been issued, and the terms on which they were granted. Unauthorized entry and occupation by squatters might have been effected, and both time and money could be expended in obtaining possession. Appearances of vacancy or dereliction can sometimes be deceptive. Land Registry Direct, an Internet-based service that allows instant and inexpensive access to tens of millions of registers of title, including title plans, has greatly increased the accessibility of this useful information and led to a reduction in bureaucracy and associated delays.

Land assembly

The process of land assembly in the private sector can be a somewhat secretive affair. The skill and guile of the developer, or more usually his agent, is employed to piece together a site in such a way as to acquire the various interests at the lowest possible price. Sometimes a developer who has identified a site containing many different interests will instruct more than one agent to act independently on separate plots in order to maintain anonymity and suppress expectations. One of the major problems faced by the private sector in the piecing together of a mosaic of plots is the creation of what have been called 'ransom' sites. These occur where a developer has been unable to secure all the land necessary for a scheme, and one or two key sites remain, such as those required for access or essential services, with the owner holding out for an extravagant price, only too aware of the 'blackmail' or 'marriage' value of his interest. Colourful stories can be related about commercial schemes developed above and around recalcitrant owners, but the lesson in terms of expeditious and economic assembly is that such key sites should be pinpointed and purchased at the earliest possible opportunity.

Many private purchases can be highly speculative in nature and be undertaken well in advance of likely planning permission. A common device in such transactions is the taking of an 'option to purchase', normally enforceable upon the grant of planning consent. The purchase of an option postpones the need to incur heavy capital investment in successful circumstances and it safeguards the developer where the scheme proves abortive. Care must be taken, however, to ensure that the figures determined in the option agreement are realistic, and do not unduly reflect the uncertainties of inflationary growth.

Boundaries and obligations

One of the earliest tasks to be performed in the survey of a site is the precise identification of the boundaries and the way in which they are defined. Although this may seem a somewhat obvious precaution, it is surprising how often in practice discrepancies are found with boundary alignments, and how relatively small, but frequently critical, parcels of land have been either omitted or wrongly included in the disposition.

Some very costly renegotiations have been witnessed. At the same time as identifying the boundaries of the site, the responsibilities for repair and maintenance should be determined. Furthermore, in some development situations, particularly those in congested highly developed parts of major towns and cities, it is necessary to consider rights of support that might have to be afforded to adjoining properties both during and after development. Highway agreements might also exist. In more rural locations, way leaves, such as those to accommodate overhead cables or underground public trunk mains can cause problems. Party walls should be considered with awareness that an award might have to be negotiated. It is essential, therefore, to obtain from the existing owners a copy of a plan showing their legal title, and to compare this with an updated Ordnance Survey sheet by walking the boundaries with the plans in hand. This may well show up anomalies between the title plan and the physical boundaries of the site. These anomalies must be checked out very carefully, for even Land Registry plans can be in error.

The Party Wall Act 1996 and the Access to Neighbouring Land Act 1992 lay down specific procedures for dealing with party wall, boundary and access issues. If a developer fails to recognize his obligations there could be significant financial and legal consequences. One developer in Manchester redeveloping two sites that shared supporting walls with a public house purchased the public house specifically to avoid party wall problems (and used it as the site office).

Covenants

Covenants running with the land that restrict its free use must be investigated and, where necessary, early steps should be taken to refer such matters to the Lands Tribunal to have them removed or modified. Rights of light, rights of way and rights of entry are the most common forms of easements encountered in a legal search for development land, and it may sometimes be possible to reach a satisfactory accommodation with those entitled to the enjoyment of the rights without recourse to the uncertainties and expense of the legal system. Again, it is important to carry out a careful inspection of the site for evidence of ease-ments that might have been acquired by prescription and will not necessarily be disclosed on title, such as gates, doors in boundaries, or drains crossing the site. With restrictive covenants, however, they are always expressed and never implied (save only those rights of indemnity implied by the Law of Property Acts). Nevertheless, there are some very complex rules governing whether or not restrictive covenants are still binding on the land. As a rule of thumb, the best approach at initial appraisal is to assume they are still effective and to try to gauge either the likelihood of getting them amended or discharged, or the cost of taking out an indemnity policy with an insurance company. The Land Registration Act 2002 aims to make easements more obvious on the register. Many types of easement that first arose after October 2002 must be entered on the register in order to bind the buyer.

Planning permission

It may be that the site being appraised has the benefit of an existing planning permission. Even if an alternative planning permission is to be sought, it is necessary to scrutinize the current consent and any conditions that are attached. Obviously, if the site is to be bought on the strength of a particular planning approval, a thorough perusal is essential – of the permission, the planning appli-cation and accompanying drawings, and all the subsequent correspondence leading up to the decision. Special considerations might have to be given to any planning conditions, and an assessment made of the need to have certain conditions struck out or modified, together with the chances of being able to do this. There may also be the question of an outstanding planning agreement or obligation that could constrain development and that might outlast the expiry of any existing planning permission.

Planning and preservation

Since the introduction of conservation areas in the Civic Amenities Act 1967, more than 8000 'areas of special architectural or historic interest, the character or appearance of which it is desirable to preserve or enhance' have been designated. Individual buildings can also be listed for protection, the current legislation being the Planning (Listed Buildings and Conservation Areas) Act 1990. Although it is clear that conservation areas can embrace acceptable change, and should not be regarded as 'preservation' areas, close attention must be paid by a prospective developer when considering a site within a conservation area, or where a conservation area impinges upon a site. Even more care must be taken where any buildings on the site are listed as being of special architectural interest, for they may well constrain development. A developer must obtain listed building consent before carrying out any demolition or renovation work that could affect the character of a building. The development of land within a conservation area entailing any demolition work will also usually require the express consent of the local planning authority. Further, any tree on the site that is protected by a tree preservation order, or any trees within a conservation area, must not be cut or damaged without special permission from the authority. Even if consents are eventually forthcoming for protected trees or buildings, there is often an effect on the development programme or a compromise with the proposed scheme.

Nevertheless, planning new development in a conservation area, or on a site containing protected buildings or trees, can be a particularly challenging and rewarding experience. Outstanding and profitable results can often be achieved, but this requires a sensitive and constructive attitude from both the planning authority and the private developer. Reference to PPG15 'Planning and the Historic Environment' and Circular 1/07 'Revisions to Principles of Selection for Listed Buildings' will provide appropriate guidance.

Environmental protection of the site

As is discussed in Chapter 10 (Sustainability and property development), developers must prepare prospective schemes with an approach which accounts for and fosters sustainability. That chapter provided guidance on how to consider this from a strategic point of view. When it comes to considering a site-specific appraisal, the environmental sustainability issues discussed below need to be considered.

Awareness of environmental issues has increased dramatically since the mid-1970s and particularly since the planning system embraced the principles and requirements of sustainable development in the early 1990s. PPS1 'Delivering Sustainable Development' provides guidance on matters from the preparation of development plans to the determination of development applications. Because the planning system is now required to deliver sustainable development, including that which embraces environmental sustainability, so developers must adhere to sustainable development principles in their schemes. It is important also to remember that significant drivers for incorporating sustainability in development schemes come from those who will finance, purchase and occupy them, so much so that increasing numbers of designs for speculative development schemes in the first decade of the 2000s have achieved top level environmental credentials. The previous chapter touched on basic issues relating to environmental issues in design, and subsequent chapters consider some sector-specific issues in more detail.

The sustainability of a proposed development scheme is a material consideration in its determination because of the provisions of PPS1 and because all RSSs and LDFs are subjected to sustainability appraisals before adoption. In terms of site appraisal, developers are required to be sensitive to the need to conserve and sometimes enhance sites' natural resources. This is particularly the case for certain types of major development proposals which are subject to mandatory environmental impact assessment (EIA) because of the provisions of the following legislation:

- In England and Wales: The Town and Country Planning (Environmental Impact Assessment) (England and Wales) Regulations 1999 (SI 1999/293) as amended by the Town and Country Planning (Environmental Impact Assessment) (England) (Amendment) Regulations 2007.
- In Scotland: The Environmental Impact Assessment (Scotland) Regulations 1999 (SSI 1999/1) as amended by the Environmental Impact Assessment (Scotland) Amendment Regulations 2002.
- In Northern Ireland: The Planning (Environmental Impact Assessment) Regulations (Northern Ireland) 1999 as amended by the Planning (Environmental Impact Assessment) (Amendment) Regulations (Northern Ireland) 2008.

The requirement for EIA originally comes from a European Directive (85/33/ EEC as amended by 97/11/EC). Under the above Regulations, the developer is required to compile an Environmental Statement (ES) describing the likely significant effects of the development on the environment and proposed mitigation measures. The ES must be circulated to statutory consultation bodies and made available to the public for comment. Its contents, together with any comments, must be taken into account by the competent authority (e.g. the local planning authority) before consent may be granted.

This mandatory requirement relates to very special types of development having obvious environmental consequences, such as crude oil refineries, thermal power stations, chemical installations, radioactive waste stores, major roads and the like. There is, however, a discretionary power under the Regulations where an EIA may be required that includes such proposed uses as energy production, processing of metals, manufacture of glass, chemicals, rubber, textiles, the food industry, infrastructure schemes and miscellaneous 'other projects'. This is more significant for the conventional developer since it can include industrial estate development projects, certain urban developments, yacht marinas, holiday villages and hotel complexes – although all of these would either have to be of a very large scale or be proposed on a sensitive site to warrant an EIA. The majority of EIAs have been concerned with waste-disposal sites and the extractive industries. Nevertheless, many development proposals already have to submit a form of EIA or environmental impact statement in support of a planning application. There is also more and more attention being paid to such ecological issues as water quality and resource management, air quality management, wildlife management, solid waste disposal control and noise control. Developers must increasingly be able to anticipate these issues and proffer acceptable mitigation measures, should their proposed scheme conflict with the requirements of nature conservation.

Recent amending Regulations have been implemented following decisions in the European Court of Justice in May 2006. These Regulations require that where development consent comprises a multi-stage process (e.g. outline planning applications), an EIA can be required before approval of reserved matters. The Regulations also apply to conditions attached to full planning permissions which do not permit development until the submission of certain detailed matters and their approval by the planning authority.

Physical considerations

Site measurement

The first physical survey to be carried out should be an actual measurement of the site and its boundaries in order to determine the exact area. Too much reliance should not be placed on third-hand reports, estate agents' details, or figures arrived at from measurements taken off Ordnance Survey maps. An accurate assessment of the area of the site is essential in arriving at the permissible density of the development in accordance with development control standards and any agreements made with the local planning authority. It is also vital where a financial offer based upon a design scheme is to be prepared, as will usually be the case.

Ground conditions

It is necessary to discover the character and stability of the land and subsoil. There are three basic deposits beneath a site: artificial ground created by man; drift deposits such as sand, clay, gravel, silt and peat; and rock such as mudstone, sandstone, siltstone and granite. If there is a shallow water table, this should be identified, especially when the site in question is located on the floodplain of a river. Particular attention should also be paid to the presence of any under-ground rivers, ponds or springs. The existence of any of these features will have implications for the kind of foundations that would need to be laid to support the development. For the same reason, the type of soil or soils covering the site should be classified and the degree of permeability investigated to check how easily water will drain from the site. The load-bearing nature of the subsoil should be ascertained, particularly where the site is composed of made-up ground, or has recently had trees removed.

It is sometimes also necessary to find out if any part of the site could be liable to subsidence because of the underlying geological formation or as a result of previous mining operations. Air shafts and walls of underground activities must also be located. The appraisal of one major development site revealed the exis-tence of a forgotten railway tunnel, another was found to mark the scene of a notorious mining disaster, and yet a further site, unbeknown to the prospective developer, concealed a vast lake not that far beneath the surface. In most circumstances, therefore, it pays to sink a few trial boreholes, or at the very least to do a little hand-auguring or probing at first instance to see what subsoil con-ditions are like, although more sophisticated techniques might have to be employed by geotechnical engineers at a later stage in exceptionally difficult or uncertain conditions. Ground investigations are often given too low a priority, especially in highly competitive situations where time is of the essence. Even a simple desk study, plus site visit by a specialist firm, is rarely undertaken, although the costs of a full site investigation should not exceed 2 per cent of building costs.

Any contamination of the soil by a previous use (e.g. gasworks or chemical works) should be recorded and investigated, especially if the proposed development is to be residential. Keeping and Shiers (2004) explain that land contamination:

- Can and does irreversibly harm living organisms, people, animals and plant life.
- Can cause building materials and components to fail, such that buildings may become unfit for their intended purpose.
- Often reduces the value of sites through a poor public image and reduced marketability.
- Usually means that redevelopment costs of certain sites are higher than otherwise, partly because it is less safe for contractors to handle the soil, and that alternative uses have to be considered for some sites.
- Can result in some highly and widely polluted urban areas becoming stigm-atized with a 'dirty' image, leading to no-go development areas (often where urban regeneration is most needed).
- May result in legal liability of polluters and owners or occupiers of land for the costs of cleaning-up pollution.

In terms of a site investigation, Table 12.1 provides an outline of the infor-mation required from site investigations that developers should be trying to uncover.

Table 12.1 Information required from site investigations (Keeping and Shiers, 2004 (adapted from the Welsh Development Agency's approach to site investigations in former mining and heavy industry areas in the 1990s))

An historical study
Many sources of information, such as Ordnance Survey and geological maps, newspaper records, town planning records, historical photographs and utilities' records. Checking for previously undertaken environmental surveys can save considerable time at this stage, although its current relevance must obviously be checked.

Site characterization
Pulling together initial evidence as to the hazards posed to the natural and built environments and human health. The source–pathway–receptor model should be employed.

Site reconnaissance
A visual survey of the site is necessary to check the veracity of documentary sources and to supplement them with apparent but unrecorded data.

Inspection and testing
This should only be necessary if the previous stages have been thorough and suggest so. More detailed inspection of the site than previously undertaken and some initial soil testing will assist in determining the objectives of future investigation and designing an appropriate and cost-effective ground investigation. Consideration of any ongoing activities on the site will be necessary.

Ground investigation
The purpose of this is to determine the presence, nature, distribution and amount of any contaminants. It will involve determination of systematic sampling patterns (before actual sampling is undertaken) and of the requirement for machinery and personnel to undertake the sampling.

Sampling and analysis
Various techniques might be employed, such as the digging of pits and trenches to expose and remove soil or the use of gas surveying equipment. On-site and off-site analysis of soil is recommended, the former to protect site workers and the latter for more thorough laboratory testing.

Supplementary investigation
This becomes necessary when, for example, unexpected contaminants are discovered, when a more detailed investigation of a certain area is required or when other on-site activities inhibit previous investigation.

The potential commercial consequences of not pursuing a rigorous risk assessment in investigating sites for contamination can mean financial ruin for schemes and individual developers alike.

Topography

The topography of a site can occasionally be a significant factor in appraisal. Certainly, extreme gradients can cause problems and, although some interesting design solutions might be produced by the architects, cost penalties can be high. Where widely varying and irregular levels exist on a site, it is essential to commission a proper land survey from which the constraints on building layout and design can be gauged and implications for both development cost and value assessed. In this context, physical site appraisal might also include a consideration of the aspect and climate relating to the land in question. Views to and from the site can again affect building design and development value, especially in housing schemes, and south-facing developments benefit very generally in terms of sunlight and rainfall evaporation. There may even be odd instances when local climatic conditions are worthy of appraisal, since, in the event of severe weather the development programme might be affected, and in singularly exposed positions marketing might be difficult and viability subject to modification. On the other hand, certain existing landscape features might enhance the site, and their careful retention and exploitation be reflected in the value of the development, either directly by an uplift in rents or prices or indirectly by easier letting or sale.

Of particular note in recent years is the issue of flood risk. For years, experts engaged in understanding UK rivers have been warning that progressive changes in river morphology and land management, together with increasing flood-plain development, will lead to problems. This prediction came true in many of the early years of the first decade of this century, with widespread demonstrations that rivers in flood are usually an unstoppable force. The need for preventive action has resulted in PPS25 ('Flood Risk') imposing a duty on LPAs to identify areas that are liable to flooding and to assess the likely extent and effect of that flooding. It also identifies developers' contributions for the provision of flood defence and mitigation work.

Archaeological remains

Since the mid-1970s it has become increasingly important to make sure if a selected development site contains archaeological or historic remains. Almost by definition, the interests of the developer and the archaeologist are diametrically opposed, but responsible developers have normally allowed reasonable access for excavation and provided funding for it. Ever since the introduction of the Ancient Monuments and Archaeological Areas Act 1979 there have been statutory powers enabling access and postponing the start of development to allow excavation. There are also designated Areas of Archaeological Importance such as the old town cores of Canterbury, Chester, Exeter, Hereford and York. In addition, the British Property Federation and the Standing Committee of Archaeological Unit Managers have drawn up a code of practice that is effective, and there is a British Archaeologists and Developers Liaison Group (BADLG) to further co-operation between the respective parties.

But even the best codes of conduct and collaborative agreements can go awry and give cause for conflict. Because of this, a few basic rules have been suggested for developers who might face the problem of archaeological remains (Thame 1992). First, make sure that a full site evaluation is undertaken. This includes trial excavations, remote radar sensing, boreholes and documentary research, so that, even if there are remains, any final archaeological agreement regarding access, an agreed timetable and financing is based on adequate knowledge of what is likely to exist below the surface. Second, organize an exploratory dig (Gregory 1989). There is not always a need to demolish a building for this, and the excavation of exploratory trenches in basements is standard practice in cities such as York. In any event, new government planning rules in the form of PPG16 mean that local authorities are very likely to insist on some modest evaluation work in propitious situations, and archaeological remains are now a material consideration in the planning process, Advice taken early usually pays off. Third, retain experienced consultant architects and engineers who can produce sensitive and economic design solutions. And fourth, be prepared to contribute, sometimes significantly, to the costs of excavation. The Rose ('Shakespeare') Theatre 'debacle' is a salutary tale that led to the introduction of PPG16, which makes archaeology a 'material consideration' in the determination of planning applications.

Building surveys

Most of the above searches and investigations are equally relevant where some form of refurbishment or rehabilitation of existing buildings is contemplated. In addition, of course, it will be necessary to conduct a physical survey ('referencing', as it is known) of the existing buildings. In brief, this will cover the following matters. An appraisal report on the buildings themselves will describe their design and construction, probable age, existing use, current occupation, present access, available services, provision of amenities and any special installations. Measurements of gross external, gross internal and net internal areas, as well as cubic capacity, will be calculated for different purposes, and particular attention paid to existing eaves heights, clear heights and column spacing. Performance standards will be assessed in respect of the general repair and condition of the building, together with specialist requirements relating to health and safety, fire, heating and ventilation, insulation and floor loading. A special eye will be kept open for defects such as the presence of high alumina cement, blue asbestos, woodwool roof slabs and other deleterious materials, as well as evidence of subsidence or flooding. The extent to which these investigations are pursued will depend upon the degree of redevelopment envisaged. The mere retention of a facade or external walls will call for a more restricted but highly specific survey, and the simple renovation of the existing structure will demand a comprehensive and thorough survey of the entire building. A record of existing and established uses for planning purposes might also be required. Even where existing buildings are to be demolished, there is a need to carry out a careful survey of the structure of the premises, along with any plant and machinery contained therein, to find out how much demolition will cost, how long it will take, what safety and security problems arise and whether or not much can be salvaged.

Functional conditions

Transportation

Transportation linkages to a project must be reviewed carefully at the preliminary stages of site appraisal. Proximity and access to motorways, connecting streets and the availability of public transport are all important to the competitive posture of the project. Time and distance to major sources of employment, commercial activities, schools, and health and recreational facilities should be plotted and compared to existing and planned competitive projects. In some cases, consideration will have to be given to the alteration of existing road configurations to accommodate the additional burdens imposed on the road network by the new development. As part of this appraisal process, a traffic survey may be needed, studying the traffic records of the local authority, traffic counts and patterns, delay analysis and noise levels. The provision of means of transport other than the private car is becoming increasingly important to the success of development proposals; many schemes are required to have travel plans in place at the application stage which promote public transport and demonstrate that the scheme will not add undue pressure to the road network nor pollution levels. PPS6 (relating to town centre development) and PPG13 (transport) demonstrate the government's commitment to reducing the public's reliance on car travel.

Mains services

Availability of mains services is crucial to development, and from the developer's point of view is likely to become more so, as utility companies are ever more alert to the possibility of extracting the costs of off-site infrastructure directly associated with the scheme from the developer. With gas supplies it should be established whether the local mains are high or low pressure and if governors will be required, With electricity, the probable loading capacity must be estimated and, when the scale or nature of the scheme dictate, the construction of a substation may be needed and a decision reached as to where and how it can be located. The only normal problem experienced with water supply, unless the scheme is particularly large or there are special industrial requirements, is with existing pressure. However, sewerage capacity can often be difficult, but at appraisal it should be ascertained whether the existing system is a joint drainage system, or a split foul and surface water system; if the size of sewer is sufficient to cope with the additional flow; and if the present configuration of the sewers is suitable for the proposed development. Alterations and improvements can be extremely expensive. It is, therefore, important to determine the need to stop up, divert or replace any such services and whether the utility companies will insist upon undertaking the work themselves. Where large distribution mains are involved, it is also common for the utility companies to insist on the work being carried out at a certain time of year; hence the need to coordinate this into the development programme. Where new mains services are being installed, utility companies sometimes demand that new mains are sized in excess of those required solely by the development in question, and financial contributions can be negotiated accordingly.

Other facilities

The proper and prompt provision of some facilities and services is often overlooked in development appraisal. Among these are telephone and data communication, refuse disposal and treatment, and postal deliveries and development nomenclature, and the availability of certain social amenities such as schools, shops, restaurants and banks. Leisure and medical services should also be taken into account. It may also be necessary to identify and measure the major sources of noise within the vicinity of the development.

Problems and pitfalls

Although the preparation of site appraisals and analyses has become more professional and reliable since the mid-1980s, there are still problems, shortcomings and pitfalls that have been identified (Eldred and Zerbst 1985). These can be summarized as follows:

- An over-optimistic developer unduly influencing the consultant's analysis
- An unclear set of objectives established by the developer, leading to resultant studies being incomplete, inconsistent and misleading
- Consultants too concerned with producing a positive recommendation, which might lead to further fees from the project
- Fragmented development planning where the full survey and analysis process has not properly been followed
- Inadequate analysis of indirect forces affecting the feasibility of the project, such as changing planning policies, consumer behaviour or community reaction
- Misrepresentation of data, either deliberately to enhance the prospects of the project, or inadvertently where key data may not be sufficiently substantiated by market fact
- Mis-specification of supply and demand by the indiscriminate use of aggregate data, such as population, employment, income, values and vacancy rates, coupled with a failure to correlate supply and demand factors
- Inattention to economic indicators regarding likely future conditions through the business cycle
- Underestimation of infrastructure costs
- Inadequate techniques of analysis
- Too much statistical data and not enough analysis or judgement
- Lack of primary data and over-reliance on secondary sources
- Lack of consumer surveys exploring preferences and attitudes

- Lack of sensitivity analysis testing the effect of potential changes to the constituent factors determining the feasibility of a project
- Overvaluation of land caused by too sanguine an approach towards income flows
- Faulty financial analysis and inadequate methods of computation
- Avoidance of responsibility on the part of consultants.

As a cautionary note to conclude the subject of development appraisal, it is recommended that anyone concerned with the valuation of development land should read, or re-read, the decision in *Singer & Friedlander*, which is reported in full elsewhere (*Singer & Friedlander Ltd.* v. *John D. Wood* (1977) 2 EGLR 84). The procedures and pitfalls are well described. Finally, it should be recognized that, although there is no unvarying approach towards appraisal, there is a necessary attitude of mind, which has been succinctly summarized by the American Institute of Real Estate Appraisers as follows:

> Making an appraisal is solving a problem. The solution requires interpretation, in terms of money, of the influences of economic, sociological and political forces on a specific real property. Characteristics of real property differ widely. This does not mean, however, that there is wide variation in the orderly procedure for solving appraisal problems. The best experience in the appraisal field has crystallized into the appraisal process.
>
> This process is an orderly programme by which the problem is defined, the work necessary to solve the problem is planned, and the data involved are acquired, classified, analysed, and interpreted into an estimate of value. It is a dependable method of making a thorough, accurate appraisal in an efficient manner. It can also serve as an outline of the appraisal report.
>
> (AIREA 1979)

These days, as is clear from an understanding of planning policy and market attitudes to sustainability, development site appraisal also needs to be set within a context which considers sustainability from the outset. Failure to do so will result in negative (not to say very surprised) responses from Local Planning Authorities, as well as other stakeholders such as investors and occupiers.

13 Development valuation

It has been said that property possesses development potential whenever an element of latent value can be released by the expenditure of capital upon it (Baum and Mackmin 1989). Generally, this may arise through the development of a bare site where planning permission has been, or is likely to be, obtained; by redevelopment through the demolition and replacement of existing buildings following the grant of planning consent; by renovation through the upgrading of an existing building, with or without planning approval for a change of use; or by a combination of new development, redevelopment or renovation.

There is nothing especially complex about the basic theory of development valuation, or indeed the traditional techniques employed. In fact, its very simplicity often attracts the disfavour of those seeking the mystical qualities of more advanced techniques of financial appraisal. In essence, development valuation merely involves the calculation of what can be achieved for a development once completed and let, less what it costs to create. It is, therefore, the most explicit and straightforward of valuation tasks, but can, at the same time, be the most prone to error and most responsive to individual supposition. Consequently, it depends above all upon sound professional judgement and a thorough investigation of all the circumstances prevailing in individual cases.

Fundamentally, the reliability of any development valuation depends entirely upon two things – the quality of the appraisal information and the manner in which it is used. Both of these are discussed in this chapter.[1]

The purposes

A development valuation or viability study can be undertaken for various different purposes, which include:

- Calculating the likely value of land for development or redevelopment where acceptable profit margins and development costs can be estimated
- Assessing the probable level of profit that may result from development where the costs of land and construction are known
- Estimating the required level of rental income needed to justify the development decision

- Establishing a cost ceiling for construction where minimum acceptable profit and land value are known.

A combination of the calculations can be conducted to explore alternative levels of acceptable costs and returns, but all valuations for development purposes require an agreed or anticipated level of income or capital value with which to work.

Several methods of assessing viability can be employed, with the appropriate choice of technique largely resting upon the individual circumstances and objectives of the developer concerned. The principal method used is that of capital profit, by which total development costs are deducted from gross development value and a residual profit is established. An alternative approach is the estimation of the yield or return produced by a development scheme. This can be a simple comparison of the anticipated initial income expressed as a percentage of the likely development costs; or it can be a more refined relationship between estimated income allowing for rental growth and the attainment of a specified yield by a selected target date. A further method, more commonly employed abroad, is that of loan requirement whereby the period it takes to repay a fixed interest loan is used as a comparative test of viability between alternative projects.

The process

It is worth mentioning that, these days, few developers or professional advisers will undertake full development valuations without either the assistance of a computer programme designed specifically to perform this task – there are several proprietary brands available – or a spreadsheet of their own making. Having a programme or spreadsheet available allows the data variables discussed below to be entered and the 'result' of the valuation (e.g. developer's profit or land value) immediately calculated. This has obvious benefits, chief amongst them the ability to obtain a swift valuation. Another benefit is an ability to obtain a degree of consistency in appraisals which is useful if processes are audited for quality assurance purposes or if reporting requirements are consistent with the outputs of the software.

Detractors of such systems, particularly proprietary ones, argue that their alleged chief benefit, i.e. the accuracy of the result, is questionable. As we know, the worth of any appraisal system or method is dependent upon the data inputs and how they are used. Consequently, errors in data inputting will lead to errors in results. It could be, and is, argued that such errors are more commonplace than might be assumed, partly because users of such systems have become so reliant on their use that they do not always realize when such errors have been made, why that may be problematic or what the consequences might be. Valuation is not a science – some call it a 'black art'. A proper appreciation of market nuances is a matter best gained through professional experience and with the application of professional judgement.

These points notwithstanding, students of development valuations would be well advised to be familiar with appropriate software. However, they would be even better advised to develop their own understanding of the fundamentals of the valuation process by undertaking valuations 'long hand' before reliance on technology to provide a solution to their appraisals.

Component variables

To conduct a development valuation, there are variable components about which quantitative data is normally required. These are explored in more detail later in the chapter, but typically can be listed as follows:

- rental income or sale price
- investment yield for capitalization
- gross building size
- net lettable area
- construction costs
- fees
- cost of finance
- land cost (if known)
- required profit (if not the purpose)
- development period
- construction period
- acquisition and disposal costs
- contingency sum
- void period.

In examining the valuation of development properties, the rest of this chapter is organized into three sections:

- The residual method
- Discounted cashflow analysis
- Risk and uncertainty.

The residual method

The technique most frequently employed in the financial analysis of development projects is generally known as the residual valuation method. In essence, the residual method of valuation simply calculates what you can get for a development scheme once completed and let, less what it costs to create. Put another way, the conventional approach to a residual valuation is based upon the simple equation:

Gross Development Value − (costs + profit) = residual value

Over the following pages, a number of examples of residual valuations have been provided to exemplify and explain their use. Attempts have been made to make the general scenarios within which the valuations are set to be realistic, but readers must expect that some of the variables used will not necessarily be appropriate for any one market at any one time. This is because the economic background to property markets is always changing, which means that things like rents, yields, interest rates, building costs and developers' expectation for profit margins also change. (N.B. A very good appreciation of this fact is what sets aside the very good developers and professional advisers from the 'also-rans'.)

What the valuations intend to show is how variables are used, whilst the text explains:

- What the variables are
- Why the variables are important
- Where the data for the variables might be found
- How the variables can be used
- What the limitations of the valuation method are.

Example 1: to find land value

A prospective developer finds it necessary to ascertain how much he can afford to offer for a small prime provincial site, which has planning permission for 2000 m^2 of offices, producing 1600 m^2 of lettable floorspace. The projected development period is expected to be twenty-four months and the building contract period twelve months. Six months have been allowed before building works start to take account of detailed design, estimation and tendering. Six months following practical completion have been allowed for any possible letting voids that may occur. Finance can be arranged at 1.2 per cent per month, comparable schemes have recently yielded 6 per cent, rents of around £185 per m^2 net of all outgoings have currently been achieved on similar properties and a developer's profit of 15 per cent on capital value is required. Construction costs have been estimated at £800 per m^2. A development valuation to assess the residual value of land can be conducted as in Table 13.1.

Example 2: to find development profit

A vacant and partially derelict deconsecrated church building in the centre of a large provincial town is being offered for sale at £2.5 million. A local property development company is interested in converting the building into a small speciality shopping centre on two floors. The reconstructed building will be approximately 3000 m^2 gross in size providing about 2000 m^2 of net lettable floorspace divided into eighteen units of between 50 m^2 and 250 m^2. Rental income is predicted to average out at around £300 per m^2. An investment return of 7.5 per cent is sought. Building costs are estimated at £550 per m^2. Bridging finance is available at 1.4 per cent per month and the development will probably take 21 months to complete and let. The development company is anxious to know what will be the likely level of profit (Table 13.2).

Table 13.1 Valuation to assess land value

	£	£
A. Capital value after development		
Anticipated net rental income	296,000	
YP in perpetuity at 6%	16.67	
Estimated gross development value		4,934,320
B. Development costs		
(i) Building costs:		
2000 m² gross floor area at £800 per m²	1,600,000	
(ii) Building finance:		
Interest on building costs 1.2% for 18 months × ½	191,606	
(iii) Professional fees:		
12.5% on building costs	200,000	
(iv) Interest on fees:		
1.2% for 18 months × ⅔	31,934	
(v) Promotion and marketing:		
Estimated budget (including interest)	50,000	
(vi) Contingency:		
5% on costs (including interest)	103,677	
(vii) Agents' fees:		
Letting at 10% on initial rent	29,600	
Sale at 3% on capital value	148,030	
(viii) Developer's profit:		
15% on capital value	740,148	
(ix) Total development costs		3,094,995
C. Residual land value		
(i) Sum available for land, acquisition and interest		1,839,325
(ii) Let land value = 1.00 x		
(iii) Finance on land:		
1.2% for 24 months = 0.33 x		
(iv) Acquisition costs:		
0.04 at 1.2% for 24 months = 0.053 x		
(v) 1.384 x = £1,839,325		
(vi) ∴ x = residual land value now		1,328,992
	Say	1,330,000

Component variables

Probably the most important part of the development valuation process is the analysis of all the determining factors that underlie and condition the various component variables.

Density of development

Having investigated the general climate for development and the broad planning policies in an area, it is a necessary first step in any residual valuation to establish the optimum amount of achievable gross floorspace or units of development.

Table 13.2 Valuation to assess likely level of profit

	£	£
A. Gross development value		
Anticipated net rental income	600,000	
YP in perpetuity at 6% — 7·5%	13.33	
Gross development value		7,998,000
B. Development costs		
(i) Building costs:		
3000 m² gross floor area at £550 per m²	1,650,000	
(ii) Professional fees:		
15% on building costs	247,500	
(iii) Contingency:		
5% on (i) and (ii)	94,875	
(iv) Promotion and marketing:		
Estimated budget (including interest)	50,000	
(v) Finance on (i) to (iv):		
1.4% pm for 18 months × 0.65	377,486	
(vi) Agents' fees:		
Letting at 10% on initial rent	60,000	
Sale at 3% of GDV	239,940	
(vii) Land cost	2,500,000	
(viii) Acquisition cost:		
4% of land cost	100,000	
(ix) Finance on land and acquisition		
1.4% pm for 21 months	881,532	
(x) Total development costs		6,201,333
C. Development profit		
(i) Residual value in 21 months		1,796,667
(ii) PV of £1 in 21 months at 1.4% pm		0.747
Value now		1,342,110

$$\text{Profit on cost in 21 months } \frac{1,796,667}{6,201,333} \times 100 = 28.97\%$$

$$\text{Profit on cost now } \frac{1,342,110}{6,201,333} \times 100 = 21.64\%$$

$$\text{Profit on value in 21 months } \frac{7,796,667}{7,998,000} \times 100 = 22.46\%$$

$$\text{Profit on value now } \frac{1,342,110}{7,998,000} \times 100 = 16.78\%$$

$$\text{Investment return on cost } \frac{600,000}{6,201,333} \times 100 = 22.46\%$$

Assuming that no improvements can be made by further land assembly, a consideration of the relevant density controls must take place. For residential development this will usually be expressed in habitable rooms per hectare. Habitable rooms or bedrooms are more popularly applied as a measure in concentrated urban areas; dwellings as the most familiar form of density control in private residential estate development; and bed spaces as a governing factor in public housing schemes. With regard to the commercial development of offices, and to some extent shops, the two major instruments of density control are floorspace index and plot ratio. The former is based upon the total area of gross floorspace measured externally and expressed as a proportion of the site, plus half the width of surrounding roads up to a usual maximum of 6.1 m (20 ft), whichever is the less. The latter is similar but excludes the half-width of surrounding roads.

Variations occur between authorities in respect of whether or not certain elements such as basements, vaults, car parking, plant rooms, fuel stores and other kinds of special storage are included or excluded from the calculation. It is also fair to say that many local authorities now place greater emphasis upon design and other environmental considerations than they do on arithmetical formulas. With industrial development, the conventional way of assessing density is by site cover. Most modern industrial estates are developed to meet an eventual coverage of 45–55 per cent. Some inner urban projects, particularly those creating small nursery units, can produce as high as 65 per cent site cover, and at the other end of the spectrum the new business and science park concept with high-technology operations is often designed to provide around 15–25 per cent cover.

Again, it should be stressed that there are many other planning, and design considerations that determine the permissible volume, bulk and massing of new buildings. Among these are such matters as car parking, access, height, landscaping and light. There might also be the question of conservation, and the existence of listed buildings or protected trees and views, either on or around the site, can exercise a stringent control over the density of development. On the other hand, it is sometimes the case that local planning authorities will be prepared to approve schemes of development that are in excess of normal density levels as a result of a planning obligation, and exceptional design or the peculiar nature of the site.

Where the development project involves the refurbishing of existing premises, either in whole or in part, a detailed survey should be undertaken to establish gross and net areas so that existing use rights can be appraised. By rearranging the internal layout of the building, making more efficient use of common space, redesigning stair and light wells and exploiting basement and roof-space, considerable gains in lettable floorspace can be made from these existing use rights.

Economic design

In the context of property development it has been written that 'The economic design is not necessarily the cheapest; it is the one that gives the best value for money'. Costs in the development equation used to be taken at too crude an average and with little recognition of real design and construction implications. All parties involved in the process of property development are becoming increasingly aware of the need to create an economic design. The developer is concerned with the costs that must be borne to obtain the best return on capital, seeking to maximize lettable floor area from a given gross area. The investor is more interested in the relationship between annual expenditure and the capital tied up in the project, looking for a building that is lettable and saleable and an asset that promises good rental growth with a sound economic and physical life. The occupier is concerned with the total costs of operating the building and the value it affords in terms of comfort, convenience and appearance, and the consequent effects upon business. Agents often speak of first impressions being very important when showing potential occupiers around buildings and that the quality of finishes in the 'lobbies, lifts and loos' are key in this respect.

There has been a 'flight to quality' in recent years. A paper, *Quality of Urban Design,* funded jointly by the RICS and the Department of the Environment in 1996 as part of the 'Quality in Town and Country' initiative, was an early attempt to define what was meant by quality in design. Work in this area has, since 1999, been pursued by the Commission for Architecture and the Built Environment (CABE), the government's adviser on architecture, urban design and public space which advises those who make and implement policy as well as those who design and develop buildings. CABE has produced many publications on the quality of design of urban areas and buildings themselves (www.cabe.org.uk).

In attempting to minimize non-lettable floorspace it is possible to make a few generalizations about the 'efficiency ratio' of different kinds of commercial development, that is, the relationship between gross external and net internal floorspace. With new offices, the target is to achieve around 80 per cent, but in refurbishment schemes this figure can drop to between 60 per cent and 70 per cent. Shopping development varies considerably, but somewhere between 65 per cent and 75 per cent is normally sought. In industrial and warehouse development it is possible to achieve 90 per cent and more. Naturally, there are various factors that influence the efficiency ratio and design economics of a building, and without going into too many details it is worth recording some of them.

To begin with, the plan shape of a building has a significant effect on cost. It is, therefore, necessary to have regard to the 'enclosing ratio' in order to compare the economics of various plan shapes, because the lower the ratio between the perimeter of the building and the floor area, the lower the unit cost. Heat losses can also vary according to layout, and change in shape may have an effect on the provision and cost of external works such as paved areas and drainage systems. Although the shape of a building is determined by a combination of factors, it has been ascertained that overall costs increase as the perimeter wall length increases in relation to floor area, and, further, that this becomes more marked when the building is increased in height by adding extra floors without altering the total floor area.

Because certain fixed costs connected with demolition, transportation and erection do not appreciate proportionately with increases in the size of a building, unit costs are usually reduced as a building becomes larger. Moreover, wall-to-floor ratios are again reduced with larger projects, and in some high-rise buildings there may be a cost advantage where certain services, such as a lift installation, serve a larger floor area and reduce overall costs. In certain forms of construction the grouping of buildings can affect cost. If, for example, buildings are arranged together rather than erected separately, there can be some cost saving by the combined use of separating walls between the two structures. This is particularly important when the facing walls are expensively clad.

Although a sensible balance has to be struck between space efficiency, aesthetics and marketability, a good economic design for a building will seek to reduce circulation and core space to a minimum. Entrance halls, corridors, stairs, plant rooms, lift wells and passages are all examples of dead space that cannot be used for any profitable purpose, yet all these areas have to be enclosed, heated, decorated or maintained in some way. Of course, cost is not the only criterion, because the value of the completed development will depend upon the appeal of the property to prospective tenants. Nevertheless, it is desirable to avoid unnecessary core provision and limit circulation space to an effective minimum.

Another factor is the height of buildings and, in very general terms, as storey height increases over about three or four storeys, upper floors become more expensive to provide. This is largely because of increased costs of scaffolding, the hoisting of materials and equipment, the extended provision of services and the need for formwork and additional reinforcements. Moreover, the demand for circulation space tends to increase slightly with height, and structural components are inclined to occupy a larger area. Wind is an important factor in high-rise buildings, which is not always considered as fully as it might be. Prevailing winds against the structure can cause eddies and whirlwinds affecting pedestrian flow at ground level, require the installation of plate glass windows at extra cost and dictate the incorporation of an air conditioning system. In addition, maintenance costs will usually be greater on high-rise buildings, but, on the other hand, heating costs can fall with the reduction in roof area, and economies can be experienced by repetition in the construction of successive floors through standardization and familiarity of work.

Therefore, it can be seen that the most economic design solution for a building is that which gives the best value for money, having regard to the need to contain initial, periodic and user costs, but taking into account the rental and capital values created. Depending upon the stage in the development process at which the residual valuation is being made, all the above design factors must be considered to varying degrees of detail in order to explore the cost-value implications.

Estimation of rental value

Possibly the most critical factor in the development equation is that of rental income, and yet all too frequently the chosen figure must rest upon hunch and intuition. Estimates of rent are usually based upon comparison with transactions conducted on similar properties in the locality, but, as already stated in the previous chapter, true comparables are sometimes difficult to discover. Adjustments will often have to be made to allow for differences in size, location, age, condition, occupancy and lease terms. It may seem obvious, but care should be taken to ensure that quoted figures used for comparison are achieved rents and not asking-rents, and that any premiums, discounts, rent-free periods or special lease terms are allowed for in analysis. Another problem is that, although some valuers are tempted to employ subtle zoning or apportionment techniques when comparing rental values for development proposals, this is not how the majority of commercial occupiers look at rent. In fact, it is increasingly common to find that prospective tenants tend to have greater regard to the full annual cost of occupying space, which on top of rent will include rates, maintenance and repair, insurance, cleaning, security, lighting and heating. For the purpose of valuation it is assumed that the tenant is normally responsible for all outgoings such as repairs, maintenance and insurance, or that a separate service charge would be levied to cover management costs.

Conventionally, rents are assessed on current rental values, but in practice the majority of developers also conduct valuations to take account of any likely rental growth, up to completion. The argument for this is that, if rental values, which are a significant and sensitive component in valuation, were not projected in some way, then a developer would invariably be outbid at auction or when a sealed tender offer was made. The percentage to be taken for growth would depend on the local market where the scheme was situated, and a demand assessment study would be required (Marshall and Kennedy 1993).

In the absence of comparables, or in certain other special circumstances, rent may be calculated as a proportion of profit. The most notable situation where this occurs is in the use of turnover rents in planned shopping developments. These fix the rent at a percentage of current rental value plus a proportion of takings according to use. Nevertheless, in the valuation of a development scheme where such rents are proposed, many valuers will ignore the turnover element but adjust the year's purchase to reflect additional security and potential growth, while others will adopt two different rates in capitalizing the rental income, one rate for the relatively secure base income and a higher rate for the riskier turnover income.

A further method of assessing rental value is by taking a percentage on cost, following the logic that rent is a return for investment risk. Very much a method of last resort, it is used occasionally in checking the viability of development projects.

The most certain conditions for establishing rental value are, of course, where a pre-letting of the development has been agreed. In this instance, it is likely that the tenant would have negotiated a preferential rent up to first review at a level something below full rental value at the date of occupation. Equally, however, it would be reasonable in any valuation to adjust the yield downwards so as to reflect the increased security conferred by a pre-let. Thus, there is a compensating effect.

Selection of capitalization rate

Most residual valuations rely upon the conventional 'all-risks' yield to determine the rate at which estimated rental income should be capitalized. Also known as the initial or investment yield, it is market-derived and, one can argue, price-dominated. As already intimated, the main complication arising from the use of yields produced by analysing allegedly similar market transactions is that prices often reflect special circumstances. Initial yields deduced from the analysis of existing investments in a current market should not be employed indiscriminately in the selection of capitalization rates for assessing the viability of development schemes. However, they do have to reflect factors including probable future rental growth, security of income, flexibility of use, ease of letting, likely economic life of the building, acceptability of design and layout and responsibility for management.

Although most projects are highly sensitive to small changes in yield, especially at time when prime commercial yields are running at very low levels, it is the component of the residual valuation over which the developer has least control. With all other factors such as costs, rents, fees, time, and even finance, much more scope exists for improving project performance by skilful negotiation or management. Invariably the yield, and thus the capitalization rate, are determined within very narrow margins by the funding institutions. Even so, it is always worth presenting a scheme to a variety of funds in the hope that the special nature of it, in terms of situation, size, tenure, covenant and use will exactly meet certain outstanding requirements of their portfolio, in which case they may be prepared to accept a slightly lower yield. As it is usually the asset value upon completion, and through time, that is the overriding objective to an investing institution, they will often take a longer-term view than the developing agency. It is not uncommon for funds to put together a package deal with a chosen developer that includes a forward sale commitment and demands a slightly higher return. In such circumstances it is vital to agree a specified yield rate at the take-out date.

For whichever party to a development proposal the valuation is being prepared, it is important to explore the possible range of yields that might be adopted by all other interested parties and to study the effects on value and profit levels. A vendor will wish to examine the likely spread of bids and a potential purchaser will want to identify the manoeuvrability of any competition.

In order to achieve a desired yield, a purchaser of the development as an investment would need to meet the costs of legal fees, agents' fees, stamp duty and other disbursements. These could amount to anything from 2.5 to 7 per cent of gross development value (GDV) and would need to be deducted from the GDV to arrive at the required net yield. However, it is sometimes assumed, as in the examples described in this chapter, that the yield is analysed net of purchasers' costs and so it would be double counting to deduct the costs again. In practice, especially where a developer has entered into a commitment to sell the project on completion to a fund, these costs would almost always be deducted.

Building costs

The precision with which building costs are gauged will differ according to circumstances, becoming more refined and exact as the valuation is worked up. At the outset it is likely that very indicative figures will be employed, drawn from roughly similar schemes on an overall basis. If the result is encouraging, then an outline scheme will normally be prepared by the architect, and slightly more detailed figures, calculated against a general specification, will be used. Several more stages of sophistication will follow if the auguries are propitious.

Again, a few very general factors merit attention. To begin with, demolition can be a very expensive item, particularly where heavy fixed plant has been installed, special foundations or superstructure provided, or the site is tightly positioned in a busy urban area. Likewise, in older central locations where existing and redundant underground services are present, or in fresh situations where the ground lacks stability or access to infrastructure, site preparation costs can be high.

Probably the largest single element in terms of the costs of development and the potential economic life of a building is the provision of mechanical and electrical services, and in the past too little consideration has been given to the environmental engineering aspects of a development too late in the design process. It has been suggested that over 60 per cent of building costs can be attributed to these services, and it has been argued that more problems arise around matters of power, lighting, lifts, air conditioning, heating, water supply, drainage and communications, than with any other aspect of development. The heating and ventilation system of a building, for example, should be designed in sympathy with the structure for which it is intended, and considered in respect of both initial capital costs of installation and future annual running costs. The advent of Energy Performance Certificates (EPCs) has focused the minds of developers and their designers on future-proofing buildings and ensuring that their systems' running costs are as efficient as possible.

One of the greatest irritants to occupancy is the lift system and, as a broad guideline, buildings exceeding three storeys usually have a passenger lift and those taller than six storeys require a second. In addition, where a substantial flow of goods takes place within a building, a separate goods lift will have to be provided, even at two storeys. The two most commonly used types of lift installation are electrical traction drive and oildraulic drive. From a development valuation point of view, the cost of installing an oildraulic lift can be approximately twice that of a conventional electrically driven lift. Running costs are about the same for both, but, because the oildraulic system has no large driving motor, maintenance costs during its working life are negligible, and it is a very much more flexible system to install in refurbishment schemes, tending to optimize lettable floorspace. Lifts can be of varying speeds, but faster lifts require the use of either two-speed or voltage motors to provide smoother acceleration and deceleration, thereby increasing capital, maintenance and running costs. On the other hand, the extra cost of high-speed lifts is usually justified by the saving of valuable floor area.

With regard to other services, the amount of artificial lighting will depend upon the use of the property and vary according to the depth of the building, its orientation and the type of windows incorporated. The accommodation of power and communications cabling to desk, check-out counter or operating position is a basic design consideration with both cost and value implications. Another fundamental factor is the supply of plumbing and waste disposal facilities, and any hot and cold water system, together with their related utilities, will be more economic the more compactly they are planned and the shorter the pipe runs that result.

To aid the accurate spread of building costs throughout the construction period, most experienced developers have drawn up cost profiles for the various sectors of the property development industry, but these are only used in an indicative way in the residual method of valuation, as opposed to DCF analyses where they can be employed more positively. Techniques for appraising total building costs, which have gained in popularity within the quantity surveying profession, are costs-in-use analysis, life-cycle costing and value engineering, whereby the initial construction costs and annual user costs of a building can be reduced to a common measure. Initial and future expenditures for selected alternative designs are discounted to their present worth and compared in the knowledge that small changes in design can often have significant effects upon running costs as well as capital costs.

Developers need to keep a weather eye on building cost inflation, which has at different times caused prices to increase dramatically. In the first decade of the 2000s, for example, shortages of labour and materials caused building price inflation to increase in the UK at a much faster rate than retail or consumer prices. Reasons for this included the increasing consumption of raw materials in rapidly expanding economies elsewhere in Europe (such as Ireland) and further afield (such as China), as well as the fact that during the 1990s, contractors competing for a limited number of projects absorbed a substantial proportion of increasing costs in order to win contracts. In practice, a majority of developers allow for an inflation in building costs in the same way as rental projections are made until practical completion.

Professional fees

Many developers prefer all fees to be expressed as a percentage of the total costs of construction. It is possible to provide indicative costs for professional fees although this is not straightforward, as the days of standard scales of fees have long since passed and everything is these days negotiable. The traditional allowance has for some time been around 12.5–15 per cent of total construction costs (excluding VAT and exclusive of furniture, fittings and equipment). This proportion will be higher for refurbishment works and for premises which are unique or particularly complex, such as theatres, laboratories and TV studios but will fall as the price of the works rises. For straightforward and repetitive work such as that in certain industrial and residential estate development, fee levels will be lower. Another factor to add to the mix is that cost-conscious developers and professionals eager to win contracts can cause professional fee levels to be below 'typical' rates but setting fees at too low a level can be counter-productive for those concerned.

In very broad terms and at the generous end of the scale, fees may be broken down among the various contributing professionals as follows. The architect usually receives about 6 per cent on construction cost, excluding disbursements, but this figure can easily rise to 10 per cent on refurbishment schemes, and there is an entitlement to stage payments. Quantity surveyors' fees vary but are normally in the range of 2 per cent to 3 per cent inclusive on cost, depending upon the value of the work, being a lower percentage the higher the value. It is traditional for consulting engineers to relate their fees to the cost of the relevant engineering works with which they are concerned, not to total construction costs, at a rate of around 6.5 per cent exclusive of disbursements, but pressure is applied by some developers to have engineering fees expressed as a proportion of the whole. Where this is done, structural engineering fees work out at approximately 2 per cent of total construction cost and other engineering fees at a further 2 per cent to 2.5 per cent. Project management fees are around 2 per cent.

Other 'design and construction' consultants who may or may not be involved in projects include those with specialisms in:

- CDM planning supervision
- Highways
- Landscaping
- Acoustics
- Fire engineering
- Fire risk assessment
- Security.

The majority of commercial agents act in a joint agency capacity (see Chapter 15 on marketing for more on this type of arrangement) and would seek to split a letting fee of around 15 per cent of the initial headline rent. Fees on sale are likely to be about 1.5 per cent of the sale price. All fees are negotiable, and where developers use regularly retained agents they will sometimes look to secure a discount but may on the other hand pay a bonus fee if agents secure a good or quick deal. It should be noted in most circumstances that, on sale, the tenant will pay the legal costs of the landlord. In some development projects it will be necessary to call upon specialist advice relating to such matters as planning, tax and party walls, in which case the fees are normally charged at an appropriate hourly or daily rate by the consultant concerned.

Apart from the agent's letting fee, the finance on fees tends to be somewhat front-heavy. Architects, for example, are entitled, in theory at least, to stage payments including during the pre-construction stages of their work. One reason for this is that architects' fees need to be protected when design work is done and the subsequent scope of the project is reduced. Also in these circumstances, abortive work clauses or contracts based on QS estimates or tender costs may come to the designers' rescue.

Finance for development

Chapter 14 is devoted to this topic in some detail. For the purposes of conducting a basic residual valuation it is pertinent to make a few comments regarding how the cost of finance is accounted for in an initial feasibility study. More complex calculations would follow.

In allowing for finance charges on construction costs in the residual valuation, adjustments are made to reflect that funds are borrowed only as they are required, cashflow being critical. Three basic alternative methods are variously employed, all being nothing more than rough estimates. Either half the rate of interest is applied for the full building period, or the full rate is applied for half the building period, or the full rate is applied for the whole period and half the result is taken as the finance charge. All three give different figures, the last quoted producing the highest. In calculating the finance on other components, similar proportions are adopted. For example, the accumulated debt charge on fees is often taken at two-thirds to three-quarters of the interest rate. In fact, a variable percentage, such as 60 per cent or 65 per cent, can be applied to building cost finance to take a rough account of higher charges resulting from such items as costly demolition or site preparation at the beginning of development, or void periods at the end. In practice, the most popular calculation is 50 per cent of total costs for the building period. Although this may appear to be a crude rule of thumb, which in all truth it is, experience suggests that this is a fairly good means of predicting the expense of borrowing money during a development scheme. Justifications of this method often include reference to S-curve analysis of typical construction cost patterns but it is important to remember that every scheme is different from all others and this method is only a rule of thumb.

Unless special arrangements have been agreed with the vendor, the finance charges on the cost of land and land acquisition are invariably compounded at the full rate of interest over the entire development period and, as stated above, it should be remembered that, if there are any void periods following completion, the total outstanding amount should be rolled-up at the full rate to account for interest on interest, not simply deferred.

The actual rate of interest by which the costs will be rolled-up depends upon the source of finance available to the developer. Conventionally, however, where these are not known or have yet to be agreed, a rate of interest some few percentage points above the base rate (such as London Inter-Bank Offered Rate, LIBOR) will be employed. Even where a substantially lower rate of borrowing has been negotiated or internal funds are to be employed, it is correct at earlier stages of valuation to adopt a full opportunity cost of finance approach so as to identify other possible bids and a minimum open market value for the land. Again, refinements will follow.

Promotion and marketing

The amount of the budget allowed for promotion and marketing in the development valuation varies considerably and depends largely upon the nature and location of the project concerned. Many schemes are either wholly or substantially pre-let and will require little or no additional funding during the development period. However, it should not be forgotten that an extensive marketing campaign may have been involved prior to construction, and the financing of those costs will have to be carried throughout the gestation period of the scheme.

Because marketing needs will vary so widely between projects, it is unwise to adopt an easy proportion or percentage of some other figure. Rather, a figure related to the probable costs of promoting the individual development must be estimated, and the early advice of agents is desirable.

Likewise, although it is often true that the larger the development, the larger the budget, there is no direct relationship with the size of the project, and some of the largest may be relatively easy to let. Nevertheless, it is possible to identify certain fixed costs, and even the very smallest development will rarely require less than £50,000 as a promotions budget.

Contingency

There is a certain amount of disagreement within the ranks of development surveyors whether or not a contingency sum should be included within a residual valuation, and if so, how much it should be. It is argued that a contingency should be set aside in the calculation to allow for any unforeseen and financially onerous occurrences that would take place during the development period and affect viability. This might cover such circumstances as the need to provide for unforeseen service requirements, overcome undiscovered physical problems on the land or supply special facilities for a particularly attractive tenant. On the other hand, some would argue that all the other components in the residual should be properly estimated, and that effective project management should ensure that a project or development comes in within total budget. On the whole, however, it is sensible to make provision for a contingency sum. The exact amount will vary, but a commonly accepted margin is around 5 per cent on construction cost or alternatively 3 per cent on gross development value. With schemes of refurbishment it is usual to allow much more. The amount of the contingency item can vary according to the date of the valuation. Prior to the preparation of plans or cost estimates it can be as much as 8 per cent of building cost; after the preparation of sketch plans and cost estimates it is more appropriately put at 5 per cent; and after the award of the building contract it can be reduced to as low as 3 per cent of building cost (Jolly 1979). As an alternative to allowing for a separate item in respect of contingencies, it is common practice to add a further margin to the developer's profit. In Example 1, for instance, a developer's profit of around 17 per cent instead of 15 per cent on gross development value would suffice. In any event, the actual figure should be determined by the degree of detailed research and survey work undertaken, both before and during appraisal.

Land acquisition

The very purpose of many residual valuations is to identify the likely price that may be paid or received in respect of an opportunity to develop land. On the other hand, sometimes the cost of land is ignored, sometimes it is known, and sometimes it is assumed. This is either because no change of ownership is contemplated, or because disposition has already occurred at an agreed sum, or because the calculation is being performed against an asking or offer price. In all circumstances, however, it should be remembered that the value of land is a residual, even if it resides from another or previous computation.

As stated above, in the majority of cases the cost of acquiring land is charged at the full rate of discount throughout the entire period of development. However, there may be instances when an arrangement is made between the vendor and the purchaser to phase acquisition or postpone payment. Conversely, an option to buy the land may have been taken out some time prior to purchase and must itself be charged in the calculation. In similar vein, special arrangements regarding the timing or phasing of payment might be agreed between the parties, and adjustments may have to be made to land acquisition costs as a result, depending upon the precise nature of the agreement. Refinements in the purchase agreement leading to delayed, reduced or staged payments should not be ignored, as their effect upon viability can often be quite dramatic.

Theoretically, a formula-based approach incorporating the notional costs and the consequential finance charges should be employed, although in practice some valuers simply apply a discount factor to the sum available for land acquisition at the end of the development period.

Developers' profit

A figure to take account of the reward expected by a developer for taking the risks associated with a scheme of development and applying his management expertise to the project is either included within the residual valuation or is the result of it. Sometimes, indeed, it may be a combination of both, where the calculation is being conducted to ascertain a surplus.

There are two conventional methods by which a developer's profit is included in a residual valuation, the choice depending upon whether or not the cost of land is known. Where land acquisition costs cannot be ascertained and are likely to be the result of the valuation, then a proportion of gross development value is taken, usually 10–20 per cent. Where land costs are known, and can be included as part of total costs, then a proportion of that total cost is adopted, normally 15–20 per cent. Research has previously suggested that a figure of 15–17 per cent is the minimum return on cost accepted by most developers (Marshall and Kennedy 1993) but these days it is clear that in terms of profit, 20 per cent is a benchmark that many developers aspire to. In reality, 15 per cent is acceptable for many developers and, where a pre-let has been secured, even 10 per cent will do. The key factors are a combination of the size of scheme, the developer's financial strength and the resilience of the scheme itself (i.e. the risk of it not letting or selling) that underlies the profit element. Any funder or tenant should want and expect developers of their schemes to make decent profits in order to avoid them going broke and leaving them with an unfinished scheme, or sometimes even worse, a hurriedly or poorly completed scheme.

If the purpose of the valuation is to identify probable levels of developers' profit, then the same proportions of gross development value and total construction cost can be used as measures. In addition, profit may be expressed as a proportion of the yield relationship between anticipated rental income and gross development value. Put another way, a developer will look for a percentage margin above the initial investment yield, normally between 1.5 per cent and 3 per cent, so that if the funding institution requires a 6 per cent return on the project at disposition, the developer will be seeking something between 7.5 and 9 per cent yield in total. Some smaller, more speculative developers might merely look for achieving a simple capital gain and not assess minimum acceptable profit as a percentage of cost or value. In other circumstances, certain development agencies may adopt different attitudes towards development profit. Financial institutions, building firms and major retailers are known at times to operate lower margins of profit, being respectively interested in creating new investment, ensuring continuity of construction work, and obtaining fresh outlets for retailing. In practice, it is also becoming increasingly common to see developers adopting a basic project management fee approach towards their first slice of profit and sharing additional equity in a predetermined manner with a funding institution.

Example 2 shows that the developer's profit on both cost and value can be calculated as being receivable either upon completion or as a discounted sum now. In practice, the former future figure is often used to judge acceptable levels of profit, whereas in theory, the latter discounted figure is more suitable for comparing alternative development schemes having varying periods until completion. In fact, most developers examine profitability from all angles before making a land bid.

The impact of time

The impact of time upon development valuation can be quite startling, particularly (but not exclusively) in periods of high interest rates, inflation and erratic changes in both costs and rents. In this respect, the residual method is arguably less sensitive to changes through time than the discounted cashflow analysis approach. The most important starting point is to ensure that the appropriate discount rate is employed to defer future income and expenditure. Whereas the initial investment yield is the proper rate to capitalize rental income once the scheme is completed and let, the correct rate at which to discount the residual sum during the development period, whether it represents land value or development profit, is the opportunity cost of capital for internal funding or the cost of borrowed finance for external funding. Any other rate should be based upon explicit policy assumptions made or approved by the client.

In conducting an appraisal it should be appreciated that, whereas rental growth during the development period will have the effect of inflating the value of the completed scheme by the whole amount of the increase, the total costs of construction will only increase by about half the rate of growth. This is because only a proportion of the debt charge is outstanding. This inherent gearing builds in a margin of enhanced profitability and explains why some developers undertake projects that on the face of it appear highly suspect.

Risk and uncertainty can be analysed easily in residual valuations by courtesy of suitable software and it must be stressed that all appraisals should be subjected to sensitivity analysis by varying the component factors of rent, cost, yield, finance charges and time in order to explore the effects of change and the different attitudes that might be taken by the market. At its very simplest a basic optimistic/realistic/pessimistic set of appraisals should also be conducted to establish the effects of changing multiple variables.

Taxation and allowances

Allowance for taxation is rarely made in residual valuations. The discounted cashflow technique described below, however, can be used to incorporate the effects of individual tax liabilities, as well as tax relief against interest charges and tax allowances for the installation of plant and machinery and for construction in assisted areas. In most other circumstances it has been held that the effects of tax on the residual valuation are ignored so that rents, costs and values are calculated on a before-tax basis. So far as the capitalization of rent is concerned, this is a well-established principle in any open market valuation where it is likely that potential purchasers will pay tax at the standard rate of corporation or income tax. Tax relief against interest charges and tax allowances for the provision of plant and machinery are again not usually taken into account in an open market valuation, because they are dependent upon the circumstances of the particular developer which can vary almost as much as the taxation arrangements for them (Jolly 1979). Likewise, value added tax is usually ignored in residual valuations, but there is evidence that, where appropriate, a majority of developers are allowing for VAT in any cashflow analysis (Marshall and Kennedy 1993).

Criticisms of the residual method

Most notable, and often quoted, among the critics of the residual method of valuation has been the Lands Tribunal, which has demonstrated a reluctance to accept the technique as a primary method of valuation within the aegis of their jurisdiction. Although it has employed the approach on a few very exceptional occasions, either in whole or in part, the Tribunal has stated that residual valuations are far from being a certain guide to values, because minor adjustments to constituent figures can have a major effect on the resultant valuation. Further, they have argued that 'once valuers are let loose upon residual valuations, however honest the valuers and however reasonable their arguments, they can prove almost anything (*First Garden City Ltd* v. *Letchworth Garden City* (1966)). A close examination of some of the cases placed before the Tribunal would seem to support a measure of criticism and, in the notable case quoted above, the continuous revision of figures between disputing parties caused the Tribunal to comment that their process of residual valuation 'continued like a seemingly endless game of battledore and shuttlecock, until even such a veteran player as the District Valuer was showing signs of exhaustion'. The criticisms made by the Lands Tribunal become even more understandable when one appreciates that the parties before them are not actually intending to use their quoted figures for purposes of disposition for actual development. As the Tribunal itself has stated in another case, the valuations they see are immune from 'the purifying fires of open market dealings' and 'with captive parties there can be no acid test'.

Setting aside the strictures of the Land Tribunal, the residual method was brought into greatest practical disrepute during the worst excesses of the property boom in the early 1970s. A phenomenon aptly described as '130 per cent valuation' was witnessed, whereby negligent, unnerved, and occasionally nefarious valuers sought to establish hyperbolic levels of value in order to secure for clients full funding from banks who would normally advance around two-thirds of the valuation figure. Bullish views of anticipated rents were combined with a bearish attitude towards costs, and compounded by a dismissive approach regarding potential planning problems. Unprofessional practices experienced at that time in the area of development valuation, only some of which have been exposed in the courts, have tended to cast a shadow over the residual method, and while it is true that in many respects it lacks degrees of precision, is often insensitive to changes of cost and value through time and many of the component factors are either crude averages or very approximate guesses, there is another side to the argument. When performed properly with carefully considered assumptions, well-researched figures regarding costs and rents, an informed view of the development programme and a justified set of decisions in respect of marketing, management and disposal, it becomes a comparatively overt and reliable means of appraising the viability of, and constructing, a valuation for a prospective development scheme relating to a specific site, a known developer and established conditions for finance, design and building. In any event, it is an appropriate valuation technique where no readily comparable transactions are available or where the scale of the scheme could itself distort the local market. The Lands Tribunal did concede that:

> it is a striking and unusual feature of a residual valuation that the validity of a site value arrived at by this method is dependent not so much on the accurate estimation of completed value and development costs, as on

the achievement of a right balancing difference between these two. The achievement of this balance calls for delicate judgement, but in open market conditions the fact that the residual method is (on the evidence) the one commonly, or even usually, used for the valuation of development sites, shows that it is potentially a precision valuation instrument.

(*Clinker & Ash Ltd* v. *Southern Gas Board* (1967) 203 EG 735)

There are really only two alternative ways to the residual method for valuing development properties: by direct comparable evidence and by discounted cashflow analysis. Even so, it should be recognized that the first is a derivation of the residual method and the second an extension to it.

When employing comparable evidence, it is important to appreciate that the resultant figures are derived from prices achieved in the market and that the sum agreed by an individual vendor and a particular purchaser is likely to be unique, reflecting their personal predilections, tax liabilities and non-property interests. In this way, there is rarely such a thing as a true comparable, and it can be argued that the various adjustments to value or profit that might have to be made to take account of such matters as location, size, date of transaction and proposed use are every bit as contrived and prone to error as the manipulation that takes place in attuning the residual. Furthermore, many of the transactions selected for comparable analysis will, in all probability, have been based upon a residual approach in the first place, and it is surely more credible to construct an explicit and specially prepared residual for the property in question than to rely on the end results of other unknown computations. Markets are notoriously aberrant in both space and time.

Discounted cashflow analysis

The main criticism of the residual method of valuation is that it is not precise enough in the way it reflects the incidence of time and money payments during the period of development. In practice, expenditure upon construction is incurred at regular stages throughout the building contract period, with payments to the contractor usually being made on a monthly basis and assessed on the cumulative value of the work carried out and certified by the quantity surveyor. A typical pattern of payments on a commercial development project has been described as follows:

> During the first few weeks of the building period the valuation will be for relatively small amounts because the contractor is engaged in erecting site offices, taking levels, preparing the site and forming excavations. The rate of expenditure will then start to accelerate as the foundations are put in. If heavy plant, such as a tower crane, is necessary this may be brought in at a fairly early stage and the hire costs will start to be certified by the quantity surveyor after a month or two. Scaffolding costs and structure erection will follow, and the monthly payments will then build up to a fairly

consistent level until the first specialist subcontract work begins, such as the installation of lifts and boiler, when there will be a surge in expenditure. After these first large items of equipment have been paid for, there is sometimes a slight fall in the size of the monthly payments until the expensive finishing and fitting out work such as specialist joinery, light fittings, carpeting, panelling and marble work starts. After practical completion, some expenditure may still be outstanding on items such as landscape and planting. There will be an average time lag of approximately five weeks between the date on which the contractor carries out the work on site and the date on which the developer will pay him.

(Jolly 1979)

Other items such as professional fees and promotions budget will also display an irregular pattern of expenditure. As a consequence of this variable spending profile, the finance charges will accrue at a similarly fluctuating rate. Furthermore, in many development schemes, particularly those in the residential and industrial sectors, it will be possible to let or sell completed parts of the project as they become available. In this way, rental income or capital sums will be realized during the development period, which can be set-off against expenditure elsewhere.

Because the residual method only 'guesstimates' the time value of money, making some heroic assumptions about finance costs, it is at best really a rapid screening device employed in selecting among several alternative projects. What is needed is an approach that examines much more closely the cashflows of expenditure and income throughout the process of development, and apportions them to the appropriate time-periods, showing the real cost of finance.

Some advantages have been suggested in using a discounted cashflow analysis (Millington 2000).

- In phased, multi-use developments, the cashflow associated with each phase of the scheme can be spelt out and summed into a monthly or quarterly cashflow framework.
- The timing of both expenditures (notably building costs, which may be allocated manually or by use of built-in S-curves) and receipts can accurately be allocated to each month or quarter. This will increase the reliability of the interest rate calculation.
- Interest rates may be allowed to vary during the period of the project, allowing greater flexibility and accuracy.
- The developer obtains an accurate picture of potential cash exposure and will be able to identify points of greatest cashflow risk.
- Additional investment criteria including net present value (NPV) and internal rate of return (IRR) may be obtained as a supplement to the traditional 'return on cost' measure.

There are different methods by which cashflows during the development period can be valued. These include:

- The phased residual valuation
- The net present value discounted cashflow analysis
- The internal rate of return discounted cashflow analysis.

Phased residual valuation

The following example shows how the basic residual method can be modified to take account of phased development projects.

Example 3

Consider the freehold interest in a cleared site that has planning approval for the construction of ninety detached houses. It is thought probable that any prospective purchaser would develop the site in three phases, each of thirty houses. The total development period is estimated at three years, with separate contract periods of twelve months for each of the three phases. The sale price of the houses is set at £150,000 each. Construction costs are estimated at £85,000 per house plot. Finance is available at 1.5 per cent per month and a developer's profit of 10 per cent on gross development value is considered likely to be sought. A phased residual valuation can be conducted as in Table 13.3.

It can be seen that the value of each phase is in the order of £386,000 if development on all three phases started immediately. However, allowance has been made for the cost to the developer of holding Phase 2 for a further twelve months and Phase 3 for a further twenty-four months. Even if the three phases were sold separately to different developers, it is assumed that the local demand for new housing would not hold up sufficiently to permit consecutive development of all ninety houses within the first year. An alternative calculation with adjusted selling prices to reflect increased supply could with advantage be performed.

Although the method suggested above is an improvement to a global residual, it still gives only a broad indication of value. A detailed discounted cashflow analysis would provide a much better approximation of value.

Discounted cashflow analysis (NPV and IRR)

This next example compares the conventional residual method of valuation with a discounted cashflow analysis, using both net present value (NPV) and internal rate of return (IRR) approaches, in order to demonstrate the need to be more conscious of the effects of time and the incidence of costs and revenue in the valuation of development of properties.

Example 4

A local property development company has been offered a prime corner site on the high street of a prosperous provincial town for £1.5 million and is anxious to establish the probable viability for development with a view to disposing of

Table 13.3 Phased residual valuation

	£	£
Phase 1		
A. Sale price of house		150,000
B. Development cost		
Building costs	85,000	
Site works and services	8000	
Professional fees at 10%	9300	
Advertising, say	2000	
Finance on £104,300 at 1.5% for 12 months × ¹/₂	10,201	
Disposal fees at 3% of sale price	4500	
Developer's profit at 10% of sale price	15,000	
Total development costs		134,001
Balance per plot		15,999
C. Site value of Phase 1		
Number of plots		30
		479,970
Amount available in 12 months		
Let site value =	1.000x	
Acquisition costs =	0.040x	
Finance at 1.5% on 1.04x for 1 yr =	0.203x	
	1.243x	
1.243x = 479,970		
∴ x = 386,138		
Site value of phase 1 = Say		386,000
D. Site value of Phase 2		
Site value phase 1	386,000	
PV of £1 in 12 months at 1.5%	0.836	
		322,696
E. Site value of Phase 3		
Site value Phase 1	386,000	
PV of £1 in 24 months at 1.5%	.700	
		270,200
F. Value of entire site		978,896
Say		£980,000

it to an institution once fully completed and occupied. The site is currently used as a builder's yard with some vacant and near-derelict shops and has a high street frontage of 120 m and a depth of 45 m. It lies within an area allocated for shops and offices with an overall plot ratio of 1.5:1 and a general height restriction of three storeys. Preliminary discussions indicate that the usual parking standards of one space to every 200 m² of office floorspace and five spaces to every 100 m² retail floorspace could be relaxed if thirty spaces are provided on-site and a Section 106 obligation under the TCPA 1990 is entered into, whereby a further fifty spaces are funded by the developer in a nearby local authority car park to be constructed in one or two years' time. All ground-floor development must be retail and rear access to shops is considered essential. A small supermarket of approximately 100 m^2 is thought likely to attract support and, because the local planning authority are concerned that some form of suitable development takes place as soon as possible, negotiations should be relatively straightforward, with permission probably granted in three months.

The quantity surveyor retained by the company has supplied the following information:

- A 6 m grid to be used throughout with 5 m ceiling heights for retail space and 3 m ceiling height for offices.
- Building costs for shops to be taken at £400 per m^2, excluding fitting out and shop fronts, and equally phased over nine months. Standard shop units to be 6 m × 24 m.
- Building costs for offices to be taken at £800 per m^2 for letting, including lifts and central heating, and equally phased over fifteen months.
- Demolition and site preparation to be allowed for at £20 per m^2 across the entire site.
- External works, including landscaping, will cost £200,000.
- All payments to be made three months in arrears.

The property development company's knowledge of the area indicates rental levels of £150 per m^2 per annum for supermarket space, an average of £29,000 per annum or approximately £200 per m^2 per annum for a standard shop unit and £100 per m^2 per annum for offices. Given three months to obtain planning permission and prepare the site and nine months to construct the shops, it is envisaged that a further three months should be time enough to allow for a successful letting campaign and to complete the superstructure of the building, so that the shops could be let at the end of fifteen months. The letting climate of the offices is slightly more uncertain, and it is considered appropriate to allow a full six months following completion before they are fully let and disposition to an institution can be effected. Professional fees to the architect and quantity surveyor have been negotiated so that £60,000 is paid as a lump-sum following planning permission, and the remainder calculated subsequently at 10 per cent of building cost on a three-monthly basis. Short-term finance has been arranged with a merchant bank at 15 per cent (3.56 per cent per quarter).

It is well reported that institutions are interested in schemes of this nature, scale and location, but seek yields of between 7 and 8 per cent. It is therefore necessary to establish whether a yield can be accomplished that provides for this and also allows for the developer's risk. This is set out in Table 13.4.

Notes on Tables 13.4 to 13.7

- The present value of the profit indicated by the residual is £1,575,118. This may be compared with an appraisal by discounted cashflow. It is commonly thought that a discounted cashflow analysis produces a more accurate result

Table 13.4 Conventional residual valuation

Preliminaries			m^2
(a) *Site*			
Site area = 5400 m²			
Plot ratio = 1.5:1			
Therefore, gross permitted commercial floorspace		=	8100
(b) *Shops*			
Supermarket 30 × 36 m		=	1080
Standard units 90 × 24 m less 2 ground-floor offices entrances			
3 × 12 m		=	2088
Total gross retail floorspace		=	3168
(c) *Offices*			
(Gross permitted commercial floorspace – gross retail floorspace)			
8100 – 3168 m²		=	4932
Taking account of 6 m grid constraint: 2-storey above shops			
120 × 18 m		=	4320
Single-storey extension above supermarket 18 × 24 m		=	432
Add 2 ground-floor entrances 3 × 12 m		=	72
Total gross office floorspace		=	4824

(d) *Gross areas to net*			
Gross	Deduction		Net m²
Supermarket 1080 m²	10%		972
Standard units 2088 m²	15%		1775
Offices 4824 m²	20%		3859

(e) *Income*			£ pa
Supermarket: 972 m² at £150 per m² pa		=	145,800
Standard units: 1775 m² at £200 per m² pa		=	355,000
Offices: 3859 m² at £100 per m² pa		=	385,900
			£886,700

Conventional/residual	£	£
A. Gross development value		
(i) Estimated net rental income	886,700	
(ii) YP in perpetuity at 7.5 %	13.33	
(iii) Gross development value		11,819,711
B. Development costs		
(i) Building costs	1,267,200	
Shops – 3168 m² at £400 per m²	3,859,200	
Offices – 4824 m² at £800 per m²	108,000	
Site preparation	200,000	
Total	5,434,000	
(ii) Professional fees		
Architect and QS by negotiation	603,440	
(iii) Contingencies		
5% on (i)	271,720	

Table 13.4 (cont'd)

Conventional/residual	£	£
(iv) Finance on building		
3.56% pq for 7 quarters × ¹/₂ on (i)+(ii)+(iii)	875,297	
(v) Agents' fees		
Letting fees 15% on initial rent	13,3005	
Sale fees at 3% on GDV	354,591	
(iv) Land costs		
Land	1,500,000	
Acquisition	60,000	
Finance at 3.56% for 8 quarters	503,768	
(vii) Total development costs		9,736,221
C. Residual capital value		
(i) Capital value in 24 months' time		2,083,490
(ii) PV of £1 in 2 yrs at 15%		0.756
(iii) Net present value (developer's profit)		**1,575,118**
D. Profit		

$$\text{(i) Profit on GDV}\quad \frac{1{,}575{,}118}{11{,}819{,}711} \times 100 = 13.33\%$$

$$\text{(ii) Profit on cost}\quad \frac{1{,}575{,}118}{9{,}736{,}221} \times 100 = 16.18\%$$

$$\text{(iii) Development yield}\quad \frac{886{,}700}{9{,}736{,}221} \times 100 = 9.11\%$$

(in this case £1,572,170, virtually the same as the profit produced by the residual method).

- The principal advantage of using cashflows is that there is considerably more flexibility in the timing of payments and receipts. Generally, the same information (costs and values) is used initially in residuals and cashflows such that inaccuracies in these inputs will lead to errors whichever method is adopted. For investment and development appraisal, two discounted cashflow approaches are used commonly.
- The net present value approach involves the discounting of all inflows and outflows. The sum of the discounted inflows and outflows produces the net present value of the developer's profit. Individual developers have their own 'target' discount rates, but for initial appraisals it is logical to use the short-term finance rate. A positive NPV indicates that, potentially, the scheme is profitable, and a negative NPV that a loss is likely.
- Table 13.5 shows how the present value of developer's profit may be calculated. All the costs used are as in the residual, but an attempt has been made to indicate how these costs might be spread throughout the scheme.

Table 13.5 Discounted cashflow analysis (NPV)

Item/quarter:	0	1	2	3	4	5	6	7	8
Land cost	(1,500,000)								
Acquisition costs	(60,000)								
Site preparation		(108,000)							
Building costs:									
shops		(422,400)	(422,400)	(422,400)					
offices			(771,840)	(771,840)	(771,840)	(771,840)	(771,840)		
other					(25,000)	(25,000)	(150,000)		
Architecture[1]		(190,224)	(119,424)	(121,924)	(79,684)	(92,184)			
Contingency		(65,112)	(59,712)	(60,962)	(39,842)	(46,092)			
Agency[2]						(75,120)			(412,476)
Shop income[3]						125,200	125,200	125,200	11,819,711
Cashflow	(1,560,000)	(1,557,576)	(1,373,376)	(1,402,126)	(916,366)	(1,010,036)	125,200	125,200	11,407,235
PV of £1 at 3.56%	1.000	0.966	0.932	0.900	0.869	0.840	0.811	0.783	0.756
NPV	(1,560,000)	(1,504,618)	(1,279,986)	(1,261,913)	(796,322)	(848,430)	101,537	98,032	862,870
Cumulative NPV	(1,560,000)	(3,064,618)	(4,344,604)	(5,606,517)	(6,402,839)	(7,251,269)	(7,149,732)	(7,051,700)	1,572,170

Notes
[1] Includes Quantity Survey Fees
[2] Includes Legal Fees
[3] Includes Sale Proceeds

Table 13.6 Internal rate of return

Quarter	0	1	2	3	4	5	6	7	8
Cashflow	(1,560,000)	(1,557,576)	(1,373,376)	(1,402,126)	(916,366)	(1,010,036)	125,200	125,200	1,1407,235
PV at 6% per qtr	1.000	0.943	0.890	0.840	0.792	0.747	0.705	0.665	0.627
NPV	(1,560,000)	(1,468,794)	(1,222,305)	(1,177,786)	0.792	(754,497)	88,266	83,258	7,152,336
Total NPV									**414,716**

Quarter	0	1	2	3	4	5	6	7	8
Cashflow	(1,560,000)	(1,557,576)	(1,373,376)	(1,402,126)	(916,366)	(1,010,036)	125,200	125,200	11,407,235
PV at 8% per qtr	1.000	0.926	0.857	0.794	0.735	0.681	0.630	0.583	0.540
NPV	(1,560,000)	(1,442,315)	(1,176,983)	(1,113,288)	(673,529)	(687,835)	78,876	72,992	6,159,907
Total NPV									**(342,175)**

Table 13.7 Cashflow analysis. The cashflow is taken from Table 13.5

Item/quarter	0	1	2	3	4	5	6	7	8
Cashflow	(1,560,000)	(1,557,576)	(1,373,376)	(1,402,126)	(916,366)	(1,010,036)	125,200	125,200	1,1407,235
Cumulative costs	(1,560,000)	(3,117,576)	(4,546,488)	(6,061,577)	(7,143,819)	(8,375,552)	(8,512,564)	(8,694,868)	2,398,373
Quarterly interest		(55,536)	(112,963)	(165,876)	(221,697)	(262,212)	(307,504)	(313,994)	(320,715)
Cumulative cost at end each quarter	(1,560,000)	(3,173,112)	(4,659,451)	(6,227,453)	(7,365,516)	(8,637,764)	(8,820,068)	(9,008,862)	2,077,658

- If the finance rate is used for discounting, the difference between the discounted residual profit and the NPV derived from the discounted cashflow results entirely from the treatment of construction finance in the residual and the inclusion of income in the discounted cashflow before the scheme is sold. An alternative discounted cashflow approach enables the calculation of the internal rate of return (IRR) of the scheme. The IRR may be defined as the discount rate that when applied to inflows and outflows, produces a net present value of £0.
- The necessary calculations are shown in Table 13.6, which involve discounting the net cashflows at two trial rates, hopefully producing one negative and one positive NPV.
- The IRR is then found by interpolation, in this case 31.6 per cent per annum, (see Fig. 13.1 below) confirming that the return exceeds the finance rate of 15 per cent per annum (3.56 per cent per quarter). A full discussion of discounted cashflow theory is beyond the scope of this chapter, but it is felt necessary to repeat that measures of returns produced are not automatically more accurate than those given by the residual.
- Table 13.7 shows a cashflow analysis. With this method an accounting process is undertaken – that is, interest is added to expenditure on a period-by-period basis. The interest in each period is calculated at 3.56 per cent on the cumulative cost in the previous period. This analysis produces a developer's profit of £2,077,658 comparable approximately with the residual profit of £2,083,490. (Once again, the difference between these figures is attributable to finance charges and inflows of rent before the development is completed.)

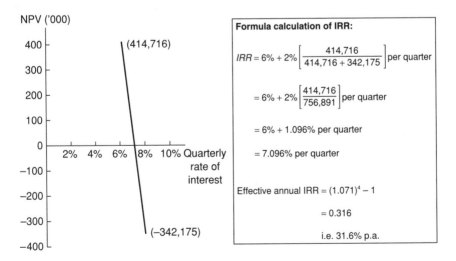

Figure 13.1 Graphical estimation of internal rate of return (see Table 13.6)

- Cashflows are useful in that they enable a developer (or the provider of finance) to assess the likely financial commitment throughout the scheme (i.e. in quarter 4, total spending amounts to £7,365,516). This facility is not available with residual or discounted cashflow methods. As a check, the discounted cashflow method should produce the present value of the cashflow profit (subject to rounding).

NPV or IRR?

One of the main advantages of IRR is that it avoids the arbitrary or subjective selection of a discount rate. It is said that the IRR method produces a true yield that obviates the need to anticipate alternative costs of funding. Otherwise, where a net present value approach is adopted, finance charges must be estimated as part of the calculation. Thus, where a project already comprises a mass of complex information regarding cost, rent and time, and the cost of capital is uncertain, it allows the developer to make, accept or reject decisions apart from, or against, the opportunity cost of capital.

On the other hand, it is possible to show that the IRR method is not always reliable in ranking alternative projects in order of their attractiveness. Using a discount rate of 10 per cent to ascertain the net present value of the two projects in Table 13.8, it can be seen that conflicting answers can result.

Similarly, the method poses problems where projects have unconventional cashflows, such as large negative payments following a series of positive payments. Moreover, it sometimes produces multiple yields – for example, the cashflow series –2000, +5000, –3150 has no internal rate of return at all. The technique is further affected by the volume of capital expended and the time-period for investment, and is also said to present certain reinvestment problems regarding positive cashflows.

Most of the criticisms levelled at the IRR method, however, apply to cashflows unfamiliar in property development. Comparisons are frequently made between the internal rate of return and the net present value methods of appraisal, and conclusions are drawn as to which approach is better. However,

Table 13.8 Ascertaining net present values using discount rate of 10 per cent

	Project A (£)	Project B (£)
Outlay	–90,000	–90,000
Proceeds		
Year 1	+30,000	+60,000
Year 2	+50,000	+40,000
Year 3	+60,000	+30,000
Net present value	+23,670	+20,140
Internal rate of return	22.5%	24%

such comparisons are largely invidious, as the two methods can be used to serve quite separate functions.

Currently, the IRR method remains principally a tool of analysis for comparing one project with another or for judging the viability of a project against the opportunity cost of capital where future cashflows are either known or can be anticipated. It is used mainly by development companies, owned by life insurance companies, and by some of the larger and more sophisticated developers. The conventional NPV method is a market-based tool of valuation relying upon a given discount rate, which can be used to determine the capital value of a project as well as explore its feasibility. However, it is fair to say that most appraisals conducted in the development field employ an NPV approach and thereby the market is conditioned by the resultant values and yields.

Risk and uncertainty

So far, all the valuations of development properties used as examples have assumed constant factors in terms of such components as rent, yield, cost, finance and time. In practice, of course, all these are a matter of judgement and are subject to change during the development period.

Risk is the very business of property development, and uncertainty the prevailing climate within which development takes place. Over the two or three years gestation period that sees many a development project progress from conception to completion, large and small changes to the variables used in an appraisal may change. For example:

- Anticipated rental income at the outset may be adjusted several times in response to changing conditions in the demand for and supply of the kind of premises in question.
- Initial yields in the property investment market may fluctuate according to the general state of the economy or the special circumstances of that particular sector.
- Building costs could increase, either as the result of an overall rise of prices across the construction industry, or because of localized difficulties in the provision of labour or materials.
- The time taken to execute the building works and let or sell the finished development may be longer than originally expected, because of any one of several reasons relating to planning, design, construction or marketing programmes.
- Finance charges on borrowed money will be affected by any changes in costs or time, and any agreed alterations to the rate of interest that occur during the development period as a result of external forces.

In any event, inflation can wreak havoc upon the best-laid of development plans. Therefore, whereas in more stable times the view could be taken that any changes in development costs would be roughly offset by similar changes in development revenues, that sanguine attitude has been shown to be both misleading and dangerous in what has been a volatile market over the last thirty-five years.

The traditional method for accommodating the risk of uncertainty in the assessment of the feasibility of projects has been to select a required level of developer's profit that would cover any likely adverse movements in rental income of investment yield, building cost, finance charges or completion time. Typically, high-risk projects would require higher profit levels. Another way of allowing for risk in the construction process is to include an allowance for 'contingencies' expressed as a percentage of building cost.

Over recent years a family of techniques drawn largely from the general field of investment analysis has been adopted and adapted for property development appraisal. The main techniques are sensitivity analysis and probability distribution, but there are a variety of related techniques that explore risk and uncertainty and assist in decision-making in development. Moreover, as a result of the increased use of computers and the greater availability of relevant software packages, the use of these techniques is gaining in popularity.

Sensitivity analysis

It is seldom that a development project can be evaluated adequately on the basis of a single set of figures reflecting but a single set of assumptions. For most projects there are degrees of risk and uncertainty surrounding such assumptions as rent, yield, cost and time. Small changes in any one of these prime variables can often exert a disproportionate effect on the residual solution. This uncertainty as to accurate estimation and sensitivity to change is compounded by the fact that the evaluation or feasibility study must take account of likely changes during the development period.

A widely used method of dealing with the inherent risk from such uncertainty is sensitivity analysis. The concept is a simple yet effective one, whereby each of the key variables (rent, yield, cost, time) is altered in turn in an informal and realistic way, so that the developer can test how sensitive the profitability of his project or proposed land bid is to possible changes in those variables. The developer is thereby able to identify the critical variables and take suitable action. For example:

- For rent – a pre-let might be sought
- For cost – paying close attention to the design brief and building contract
- For yield – searching through the investment market for a more competitive buy-out arrangement
- For time – a 'fast track' programme might be devised.

In any event, the management capability of the developer is enhanced.

Table 13.9 Minimum–maximum evaluation

I. Median *or* realistic valuation	£	£
A. Gross development value		
Rental income at £85 per m² on 4000 m²	340,000	
YP *in perpetuity at 8.5%*	11.76	
Gross development value		3,998,401
B. Development costs		
Building costs:		
4000 m² gross floor area at £500 per m²	2,000,000	
Professional fees:		
10% on building costs	200,000	
Finance costs:		
1.2% pm for 18 months × 0.5	263,458	
Agents' letting fee at 10% of rental income	34,000	
Land cost	500,000	
Acquisition cost		
4% of land cost	20,000	
Finance on land and acquisition		
1.4% pm for 21 months	124,544	
Total development costs		3,142,002
C. Development profit		
(iii) Sum available in 18 months		856,398
(iv) PV *of £1 in 18 months at 1.2% pm*		0.807
Profit now		691,113

$$\text{Profit on cost now } \frac{691,113}{3,142,002} \times 100 = 22\%$$

$$\text{Return on cost } \frac{340,000}{3,142,002} \times 100 = 10.8\%$$

II. Maximum *or* optimistic valuation	£	£
Rents predicted at £100 per m2		
Initial yield taken at 8%		
Building costs estimated at £450 per m2		
Finance at 1% per month		
Development period & letting 15 months		
A. Gross development value		
Rental income at £100 per m² on 4000 m²	440,000	
YP in perpetuity at 8%	12.5	
Gross development value		5,000,000
B. Development costs		
Building costs:		
4000 m² gross floor area at £450 per m²	1,800,000	
Professional fees:		
10% on building costs	180,000	
Finance costs:		
1.0% pm for 15 months × 0.5	159,359	

Table 13.9 (cont'd)

II. *Maximum or optimistic valuation*	£	£
Agents' letting fee at 10% of rental income	40,000	
Land cost	500,000	
Acquisition cost		
4% of land cost	20,000	
Finance on land & acquisition		
1.0% pm for 15 months	83,704	
Total development costs		2,783,063

C. Development profit
(v) Sum available in 15 months — 2,216,937
(vi) PV of £1 in 15 months at 1.0% pm — 0.861
Profit now — 1,908,783

Profit on cost now $\dfrac{1,908,783}{2,783,063} \times 100 = 22\%$

Return on cost $\dfrac{400,000}{2,783,063} \times 100 = 14.4\%$

III. *Minimum or pessimistic valuation*	£	£

Rents predicted at £70 per m^2
Initial yield taken at 9%
Building costs estimated at £550 per m^2
Finance at 1.4% per month
Development period and letting 21 months

A. Gross development value		
Rental income at £70 per m^2 on 4000 m^2	280,000	
YP *in perpetuity* at 9%	11.11	
Gross development value		3,110,800
B. Development costs		
Building costs:		
4000 m^2 gross floor area at £550 per m^2	2,200,000	
Professional fees:		
10% on building costs	220,000	
Finance costs:		
1.4% pm for 21 months × 0.5	410,251	
Agents' letting fee at 10% of rental income	28,000	
Land cost	500,000	
Acquisition cost		
4% of land cost	20,000	
Finance on land and acquisition		
1.4% pm for 21 months	176,306	
Total development costs		3,554,557
C. Development profit		
A loss of		(443,757)

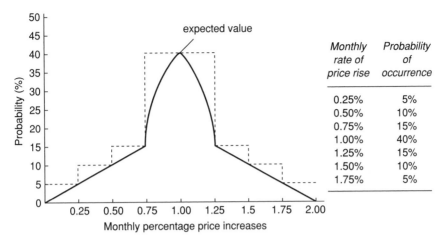

Figure 13.2 Probability distribution

are situated in a desirable part of north London and similar flats to those planned are selling for around £100,000 each, but demand is such that prices are confidently expected to rise by about 1 per cent per month over the next year (12.68 per cent per annum). Building costs to effect the conversion are estimated at £25,000 a flat but are considered likely to increase by 1.25 per cent per month for the next year (16.08 per cent per annum). Building costs are to be evenly spread over a twelve-month development period. It is intended that six flats will be sold in months nine to twelve inclusive. Professional fees are assessed at 10 per cent of building costs, and will be paid by equal instalments of 2.5 per cent a quarter. Agents' and solicitors' fees will be charged at 2 per cent of the sale price of each flat. A development profit of 25 per cent of the sale price is sought and bridging finance is available at 1 per cent a month (12.68 per cent per annum).

A prospective developer wishes to know how much he might have to pay for the eight houses now. It is assumed that surpluses in the later few months will be reinvested at the same rate of interest. The resulting residual represents an absolute maximum bid. The developer might offer £1 million for the eight houses, as per Table 13.10.

Simulation

Simulation is a development of the probability distribution using a computer to pick up the variables at random, but within a range according to the probability ascribed to them, and carry out a valuation any number of times (100, 1000, 10,000 ...). The result is normally a graphical probability distribution.

Table 13.10 Residual cashflow valuation based on probability analysis

---

Preliminaries

Receipts six flats sold per month at £100,000 each (+ 1% per month inflation) in:
  Month 9: × 1.0937 + £656,220
  Month 10: × 1.1046 + £662,760
  Month 11: × 1.1157 + £669,420
  Month 12: × 1.1268 + £676,080

Costs
  Total costs are 24 flats at £25,000=£600,000
  Average of £50,000 a month
  Increase by 1.25% per month

Month	£	
1	50,625	
2	51,258	
3	51,899	+ fees @ 10% of costs in months 1 to 3
4	52,548	
5	53,205	
6	53,870	+ fees @ 10% of costs in months 4 to 6
7	54,543	
8	55,225	
9	55,915	+ 10% fees + 2% fees + 25% profit
10	56,614	+ 2% fees + 25% profit
11	57,322	+ 2% fees + 25% profit
12	58,038	+ 10% fees + 2% fees + 25% profit

Residual

Month	Receipts	Costs	Net cashflow	Capital outstanding	Interest
1		(50,625)	(50,625)	(50,625)	(506)
2		(51,258)	(51,258)	(102,389)	(1024)
3		(67,277)	(67,277)	(170,690)	(1707)
4		(52,548)	(52,548)	(224,945)	(2249)
5		(53,205)	(53,205)	(280,399)	(2804)
6		(69,832)	(69,832)	(353,035)	(3530)
7		(54,543)	(54,543)	(411,108)	(4111)
8		(55,225)	(55,221)	(470,444)	(4704)
9	656,220	(249,662)	406,558	(68,509)	(686)
10	662,760	(235,559)	427,201	357,925	3579
11	669,420	(238,065)	431,355	792,859	7929
12	676,080	(257,777)	418,303	1,219,091	

Sum available in 12 months = £1,219,091
Let the value of the houses = 1.0000x
Acquisition costs at 4%   = 0.0400x
Finance at 12.68% on 1.04x = 0.1319x
$\therefore$ 1.1719x = 1,219.091
$\therefore$ x = **1,040,269**

Summary

Although traditional evaluations of development projects have proved effective and simple to use at the initial stages of appraisal, the vagaries of the market and the availability of useful and inexpensive computer software packages have combined to encourage the widespread adoption of cashflow models of one kind or another. It has been found that this wider use of cashflow techniques has prompted greater examination of not only cost but also the likelihood of incurring liabilities on ancillary costs such as planning fees, party-wall awards, rights of light and other elements that might previously have been ignored or included in a general fee or contingency. It is also more generally accepted that property is not an isolated investment, but one that has to be compared constantly and closely with other investments, resulting in cashflow techniques and risk and uncertainty analyses being more commonly used for evaluating alternative investment opportunities, including property. However, developers still regard some of the more theoretical probability and decision theory techniques as being too 'academic', potentially to their peril. It is hoped that as new generations of practitioners are informed about these issues and as property development is increasingly scrutinized as one of a list of potential investment opportunities, that a more mature approach to development appraisal will continue to evolve, but more quickly than to date.

14 Property development finance

It is a truism to state that finance is a critical resource in the process of property development. Nevertheless, when compared to the other resources that combine to produce a development scheme, there often appears to be a disturbing lack of proper understanding about the sources and types of finance for construction and property development, and the arrangements and procedures that accompany them. This is of growing importance, for not only are the margins between revenue and expenditure finer than ever before, but those responsible for providing the bulk of finance to the industry are much more closely concerned, and a great deal better informed, about the management of construction and development projects than they have been in the past. Consequently, they expect and demand development agencies, and those involved in managing their projects for them, to be equally well versed in the evaluation and control of the financial structure and progress of a scheme of development. This is as important as never before. The credit crunch which began in 2007 caused lenders to make much more rigorous demands of borrowers than they had in the preceding few decades.

A variety of ways exist in which finance for property development can be obtained from a wide array of agencies. The choice normally rests upon the status of the developer and the degree of risk attached to the proposed project. It can almost be stated that every deal dictates its own terms, but for convenience, and to facilitate description, several general areas have been identified below in order to consider the more conventional relationships established between borrowing developers and lending financiers.

In order to explore the increasingly complex subject of property development finance, the chapter is organized as follows:

- Sources of development finance
- Types of finance
- Criteria of funding
- Choice of fund
- The financial agreement
- Trends and prospects.

Sources of development finance

Most developers will have access to existing sources of finance. Larger companies will usually have multiple funding arrangements with a variety of financial agencies. Nevertheless, the field is becoming so complex and competitive that effective project management is increasingly concerned with the way in which control over a particular scheme will be influenced by the origin and nature of the development finance.

The following selection of possible sources of development finance has no pretensions to be exclusive or exhaustive. However, it does provide an indication of the principal sources that are currently available to the aspiring developer.

Insurance companies and pension funds

Insurance companies and pension funds enjoy a relatively high degree of stability in the availability of funds for investment in development projects, but take a longer-term and more cautious view than most other lenders.

The most popular form of finance provided by the insurance companies and pension funds is the 'forward sale', often coupled with short-term bridging finance at preferential rates. Some funds are also prepared to enter into 'sale and leaseback' arrangements, mortgage advances or an overall borrowing facility.

The lending policies of those financial institutions are characterized by their 'project-based' nature. This means that they tend to exercise extremely tight control over the entire project, including the land acquisition, design, construction and sale or letting programmes. Financial arrangements themselves are almost pre-ordained in terms of yield, interim fixed-rate loans, pre-letting and forward sale. Because of these constraints, a developer might experience problems in maintaining authority, especially once a purchaser or tenant has been found. This situation is further exacerbated where the fund appoints a consultant to monitor development, as happens increasingly.

Another feature is that, because institutions are such big investors in new development, they will usually look for fairly substantial schemes in which to invest. And, not surprisingly, the larger the fund, the larger the average size of scheme financed. But, by far the greatest hurdle a proposed development project must clear before it attracts institutional finance from either an insurance company or a pension fund is that it must be competitive when compared to other forms of investment such as equities, gilts and other forms of property.

Banks

Traditionally, banks are more concerned with the 'asset' base of those to whom they lend rather than the project in hand. The emphasis, therefore, will be more upon monitoring the balance sheet and security cover offered by the borrower.

For a developer, this provides a more open and flexible climate in which to work, where such factors as time, cost and quality can be traded off against the client's ability to generate funds or produce additional collateral. Bank finance, therefore, must be carefully tailored to fit the purpose to which it is applied, and a well designed package must be prepared to meet overdraft, term or equity financial requirements. Sometimes the additional flexibility afforded by more expensive arrangements is worthwhile.

Some clearing or retail banks became over-committed to the property development industry during the boom years of the 1980s, 1990s and early 2000s and found themselves embarrassed by the experience – none more so than those who lent to sub-prime borrowers in the early to mid-2000s, especially those in the USA. This encouraged them to step aside in the 1980s and 1990s and to retrench somewhat in 2007 and 2008 as a rapid reduction in liquidity in lending markets caused a reduction in the availability of development finance, as well as a hardening of the terms upon which any available finance was offered. Nevertheless, they show a propensity to return quite quickly to the market once a resurgence is evident, and a similar trait to retreat at the first signs of a slump. Although their policies vary widely, not merely between different houses, but within individual banks, they are generally a great deal more flexible and adventurous than the insurance companies and pension funds, being willing to consider, for example, the refurbishment and redevelopment of older buildings and the development of less conventional commercial properties. One principal reason for this is that a clearing bank is as interested in the business as it is in the property, if not more so. This applies whether the business is the intending occupier or a property development company.

Merchant banks have a reputation for having an even more enterprising approach towards development finance. Being concerned primarily with supplying short- and medium-term money to the development industry, they have evolved packages for linking their short-term lending with other investors' longer-term aspirations. Most leading merchant banks have established their own specialist property investment departments capable of tailoring bespoke financial arrangements to suit the individual needs of a particular developer. In this way, it is by far the most sophisticated sector of the institutional finance market. The more refined yet venturesome stance of the merchant banks is reflected in the high cost of borrowing from them, and their relative opportunism in respect of equity participation. Because of the risks which they are prepared to adopt and the international nature of their activities, the credit crunch which began in the USA and spread elsewhere rapidly thereafter in 2007 hit them harder than other lenders and caused development finance from this source to diminish significantly.

One of the more lucrative activities recently undertaken by merchant banks is arranging funding packages or syndications, which are then dissipated to other banks. Indeed, it has been reported that in this way some banks can make up to half their income from fees.

Trusts and bonds

Within the category of trusts and bonds can be included real estate investment trusts, investment unit trusts, property unit trusts and property bonds. The structure and purposes of these different media for investment are not explained in detail here, because from the standpoint of the developer their policies and practices are much the same and largely resemble those of the insurance companies and pension funds. However, their performance has been extremely variable, and their role in the development field is as yet not great.

Internal finance

Even though it is often alleged that the first rule of the developer is 'never use your own money', quite commonly property development agencies either deploy their own surpluses and reserves to support current projects or seek an expansion of their capital base.

Almost by definition, virtually all development undertaken by the major financial institutions, directly or by way of joint venture, can be categorized as internally financed. Similarly, many construction firms acting as developers use their own financial resources to fund projects, as do certain leading business and retail organizations. Funding by prospective owner-occupiers in all sectors of the commercial property market is quite popular. For as long as the capital is available, the risk acceptable and the opportunity cost satisfactory, internal finance has the great attraction of ensuring full recoupment of future rental growth.

A property development company can extend its capital base by increasing its share capital or its loan capital. In simple terms, the holders of the share capital (equity) own the company itself, and the holders of loan capital are creditors of the company. Thus, the holders of share capital are not creditors and have no security, and the holders of loan capital have no rights in the company beyond the receipt of interest and the repayment of the loan in accordance with the terms on which they were issued. The amount a company may borrow by way of loan capital is laid down in the articles of association of the company. There are two principal types of loan capital: debenture and loan stocks. Debentures and debenture stocks are roughly similar to mortgages and are secured either on certain specific assets of the company or as a floating charge over all the company's assets. Secured debts of this kind rank for repayment before unsecured debt in the event of the company being wound up. Unsecured loan stocks, the other form of loan capital, are debts, as their name implies, which are not charged on the company's assets. If the company falls into liquidation, they rank after secured loans along with other general creditors but before the holders of share capital. One kind of unsecured loan stock carries with it the right to convert into share capital on pre-arranged terms and within a limited period: this is known as convertible unsecured loan stock and it comes with a variety of conversion rights. A final form of fixed income company finance is preference shares, which do not form part of the loan capital, and on a winding-up do not rank for repayment until all creditors have been paid in full. Again, there are various types of preference shares, such as 'cumulative', where the right to a dividend can be carried forward from one year to another; 'non-cumulative', where once a dividend is passed for one year the right to receive it is lost; and 'participating' preference shares, where there are rights to share in profits above the fixed dividend.

The share capital held as ordinary shares is usually referred to as the equity. Equity in this sense means that which remains after rights of creditors and mortgagees are cleared and, although different forms of share capital exist, most public property companies do not have very complex share capital structures. The risk-bearing nature of equities is reflected in the 'gearing' of a company, that is the ratio of loan or fixed income capital to share or equity capital. In a period of growth and profitability, in a highly geared company, where loan capital is proportionately greater than share capital, holders of ordinary shares gain commensurately. In bad times, the reverse is true, and profits can easily be wiped out.

A detailed examination of how capital can be raised on the stock market is beyond the scope of this text. Suffice it to say that there are two types of new issue by which this can be achieved. First, the bringing to the market of companies that have not previously been quoted. Second, the raising of additional capital by companies already quoted. The former will normally be effected by an 'offer for sale', whereby an institution such as a merchant bank buys a block of shares from the existing shareholders and offers them to the general public at a fixed price; by a 'placing', where an institution may buy the stock or shares and arrange for the placing of the issue with various funds or companies known to be interested; an 'introduction' when a company already has many individual shareholdings and Stock Exchange quotation simply provides a public market for shares that previously could only be dealt in privately; or a 'tender', which is exactly the same as an offer for sale except that the price of the shares is not fixed in advance. One way in which companies already quoted can raise additional internal funds without increasing their debt charge is the issue of further equity capital. This is normally done by way of a 'rights issue', that is, the issue of shares to existing shareholders at a concession.

The performance of the stock market in the early years of the twenty-first century has prompted some property companies to 'de-list', i.e. buy back their shares and withdraw from the stock market, because their view is that the value of their property assets is not effectively reflected in the value of the company's shares.

As with most financial matters, the question of timing is important, not merely in respect of the general climate for borrowing but also the class of capital to be selected. In times of depressed equity prices, a rights issue is normally to be avoided and, if interest rates are at a reasonable level, a prior charge to increase loan capital is usually preferable. Conversely, when equity prices are high, leading property companies might be best advised to make a rights issue rather than increase their loan capital. However, it must be remembered that, although substantial sums can be raised from the market, the costs involved may be considerable, comprising not only the legal and valuation fees but also the costs of underwriting the issue, producing a prospectus, advertising and stockbrokers' charges.

It is in the field of internal or corporate finance that most innovation has been shown by property development companies over recent years. The range of devices, instruments and techniques has appeared endless, with many American mainstream corporate financing practices being adapted and adopted in global financial markets. The amount of 'commercial paper' issued by property development companies since the late 1980s has been enormous, largely because of its low cost, high flexibility and simplicity to the borrower, and its competitive yield, liquidity and range of maturities to the lender. However, the inherent dangers of such promissory activity were apparent in a period of worldwide recession during the first half of the 1990s.

The construction industry

Development finance is commonly supplied by the major building firms, either directly from their own cash reserves or through sources with whom they have a funding facility. From a pure funding point of view, this form of finance can be very attractive, because the loan-to-value ratio will often be very high, to include the cost of land acquisitions, building costs and fees. Speculative work will also be considered, and the debt rolled up at a small mark-up on the cost of finance to the construction company. From the stance of the developer, however, it is very important to be assured that the right contractor, on the right building contract, is appointed to work to the right price. There is always the danger that the authority of the developer and his project manager is diminished where the contractor is also the funder.

Conversely, this familiarity with the property development industry can often be an advantage and help limit risk. Such collaboration is often the result of a limited loan, say 70 per cent of cost, on the part of a bank, and the need by the developer to fund the shortfall through the good offices of an established construction company. Increasingly, this form of finance takes the form of a joint venture between the two parties. On the other hand, the degree of accountability on the part of the contractor during the construction stage and upon completion is likely to be heightened, and the extent of financial control throughout the building period much tighter than normally experienced. A construction company, however, will normally need to see a clearly identifiable exit in the form of a long-term take-out by a financial institution.

Property companies

A less familiar means of obtaining short-term finance is through one of the larger property investment and development companies. This can be by direct loan or by guarantee, and the principal motive is usually a desire to participate in the equity of the project. Apart from an erosion of profit, another disadvantage is that, as far as the developer is concerned, his funds are coming from a source thoroughly conversant with all aspects of the development process, who is likely to exercise an unusual degree of scrutiny.

Government

In a period of continuing worldwide public sector spending constraint, governments find themselves with little enough money for their own national and municipal development projects, let alone to be in a position to fund the private sector. Nevertheless, grants and loans are made available in certain circumstances, and projects are supported in other ways.

The Private Finance Initiative (PFI) is a long-term concession used by the UK government to capture private capital to fund public projects. Instead of following the usual practice of borrowing money, the government commissions services, not buildings or other works, and the contractor (usually a consortium) carries on providing that service for a pre-defined period of time (frequently more than twenty years). Thus public projects are paid for out of annual revenue rather than capital budgets.

Most straightforward is the direct provision of total development finance, which is usually undertaken to promote ventures that would not otherwise attract commercial funds. Government can also provide financial assistance to new or established businesses through loans for land and buildings. A method employed in many industrial development projects has been the 'headleasing' arrangement, whereby a government agency takes a lease from the developer to guarantee rental income and then sublets the floorspace to occupiers.

It may be that a government agency acts as a conduit to other funds. Many cities in various countries now offer incentives to encourage firms to invest in designated areas to promote economic and physical regeneration. This includes guaranteeing long-term loans for the conversion, improvement, modification or extension of existing buildings. Some local government authorities have also set up their own enterprise boards to stimulate economic activity. This often includes an extensive programme of property development and refurbishment projects, either independently or more usually in partnership with the private sector.

Another way in which a local government authority can participate in the overall funding of a scheme, without committing actual cash resources, is by providing land already in their ownership. Similarly, although there is a cost to the authority, the supply of certain kinds of directly associated site infrastructure may often be seen as a financial contribution to a development scheme, and treated accordingly in any negotiations surrounding the apportionment of profit.

There is really no limit to the potential sources available to borrow money for property development. Trading companies, financial services firms, charities, churches and wealthy individuals, either alone or in consortia with others, are but a few. Given sufficient time, therefore, a developer could unearth many sources of finance. Indeed, considerable time and effort can often be wasted by directing attention towards inappropriate sources, and it is surprising what an imperfect market the development industry is in respect of a central pool and comprehensive understanding of sources of finance.

Types of finance

Traditionally, the different types of development finance have been examined within the classification of short-term, medium-term and long-term. Although this remains a perfectly acceptable approach, it tends to oversimplify what has become a more sophisticated and complex market. Indeed, so refined are some funding arrangements that it is increasingly difficult to place them in any particular category, except their own. However, the following description attempts to outline the main methods currently employed in the financing of development.

Development finance

Development finance is also known as building, bridging or construction finance and is used to describe the short-term interest-bearing loans made for periods of anything up to about three to four years, covering all or part of the costs of development. These costs will include land, acquisition, building works, professional fees, marketing, finance itself and any contingencies involved in the development process. Customarily, there have been two main sources for such funds, the commercial banks and the merchant banks, but over recent years other sources have been tapped and other methods of funding employed.

The banks, however, have two basic requirements. First, that the developer must show that they will be able to meet the interest charges, which will usually be 'rolled-up' or 'warehoused' until the development is completed. Second, they must show that they will be able to repay, on time, the principal sum borrowed. This latter requirement implies in most cases the availability of long-term investment funds, out of which the short-term finance may be repaid. The linking of short- and long-term finance must normally be firmly established to the satisfaction of the lender before the development finance is approved. In some circumstances, it is possible that the lending bank might be prepared to assume that long-term financing will be forthcoming before the development is completed, or that the scheme will be sold outright on completion for investment or occupation, and advance the construction finance unencumbered by a forward sale commitment.

As previously intimated, the commercial and merchant banks tend to have slightly different attitudes towards development financing though both participate in securing their own borrowing from similar sources, which caused them to shift from their traditional approaches to setting lending rates during and subsequent to the credit crunch which began in 2007. The commercial banks frequently require security over and above that derived from the project in question and traditionally have sought to exact a rate of interest based upon prevailing swap rates equivalent to about 2–4 per cent above base lending rate, depending upon the standing of the borrower. They do not usually demand an equity share and they provide a procedure that is a relatively simple and stand-ard format, so that the loan is issued quite quickly and with comparative ease. The merchant banks, in most instances, only require the development presented to them as security, but traditionally charged a higher rate of interest at an equi-valent of about 4–6 per cent above base rate or, more usually, sought to share in the equity of the scheme. In return for the additional cost of the finance, however, the developer will probably find a merchant bank more enterprising than a commercial bank in bearing risk and structuring a loan. As discussed above, the credit crunch, however, resulted in both clearing and merchant banks pulling their lending margins in 1.25–1.5 per cent above LIBOR rather than basing margins on swap rates because the climate of the liquidity crisis meant that using LIBOR gave banks a decent margin from which to exact their own profits. By 2008, sources of finance to developers was all but dried up: debt was dead and cash was king.

Short-term development finance in the institutional market is often being provided as part of a complete funding package. A fund will normally acquire a site once planning permission has been obtained and will advance development costs throughout the construction period against architects' certificates and other relevant invoices. Interim finance, as it is known, is rolled up on the various advances and is payable at an agreed rate that invariably lies mid-way between the prevailing short-term borrowing rate and the ultimate investment yield. Both parties can be seen to gain from such an arrangement. The developer enjoys cheaper finance and the purchaser is afforded more control over the design and progress of development.

Mortgages

For many years up until the early 1960s, the fixed interest mortgage was the predominant form of long-term development finance. Rapid and prolonged inflation then drove lenders away from mortgages towards methods of invest-ment that allowed them some level of inflation-proofing through participation in rental growth. From the early 1970s onwards, high interest rates discouraged borrowers from pressing for long-term mortgage advances on fixed rates. The late 1980s and early 1990s witnessed the return of long-term fixed interest mortgage finance to the property development market. Since then, with inflation continuing to run at relatively low levels and interest rates at forty-year lows, fixed inter-est mortgage finance is still available. The willingness of lenders to provide fixed interest loans depends upon market conditions and can rapidly diminish during periods of interest rate volatility.

When it is available, the loan term will vary, usually running between ten and twenty-five years, depending upon the needs of the borrower and the nature of the development project, and the maximum level of advance invariably will be limited to approximately three-quarters of the agreed value of the project acting as security. For other than prime schemes it will often be less, and here lies the biggest drawback in mortgage finance, for a developer will often have to find substantial funds from his own resources if the project in question does not meet certain standard criteria in respect of design and letting.

Unless there are immediate and reliable prospects of an uplift in rents, say within a year of the draw-down of the mortgage facility, then the lending institution will wish to be assured that the initial income produced by the development is sufficient to cover the loan servicing costs. The rate of interest attaching to a loan is usually determined at the date of release of funds by reference to a margin of 1.75–2.25 per cent over the prevailing gross redemption yield on a comparable gilt-edged security on completion. Interest is mostly payable quarterly or half-yearly in arrears.

With most mortgages there will be a choice between interest-only and interest plus capital repayments. Generally, it is only the shorter mortgages of around ten years that are on an interest-only basis; the longer-term loans of fifteen to twenty-five years normally require at least 25 or 50 per cent of the capital to be repaid during the term, although they may often begin with a five-year moratorium to allow for rental growth to take place, thereby making the debt easier to service. It is commonly accepted that the annuity-certain method of repaying or reducing a mortgage is probably the fairest and least expensive, both in real terms and as far as cashflow is concerned, as it involves an effective sinking fund under which the benefit of a compound interest rate equal to the mortgage rate is received. Moreover, some companies operate a variable rate system. Although this might seemingly be a more volatile and potentially expensive way to pay off a loan, it will usually be operated on an 'even spread' basis, whereby the capital repayments are calculated at a median that, if market interest rates are lower for most of the term, means the loan will be repaid early, and vice versa.

Although mortgages are commonly considered to be medium- to long-term funding arrangements, it is sometimes possible to obtain interim finance against a limited number of architects' certificates as building works progress, in which case adjustments might have to be made to allow for fluctuating interest rates during construction. In any event, this kind of facility would only be countenanced with a pre-let to a good covenant on acceptable terms.

On the question of whether or not a developer should take up long-term fixed interest moneys, one leading specialist in arranging property finance has summarized the situation as follows:

> Our advice to borrowers has always been never to rely on one particular type of finance or one particular lender. A mix of different types of finance is essential to the well-balanced portfolio and a combination of part variable-rate and part fixed-rate mortgage monies will enable the borrower to take advantage of any further fall in interest rates while protecting against an increase. What can be said with reasonable confidence is that the present interest scenario presents an excellent opportunity for borrowers to switch a significant part of their present funding to, or to organize new acquisitions on, a fixed interest rate basis.

> (Burgess 1982)

As with all other forms of funding, however, mortgage finance has become increasingly sophisticated. For example, repayment patterns can be straight-term, amortized, partially amortized, graduated, renegotiable, shared appreciation or reverse annuity. Interest rate provisions can be straight rate, straight rate with escalator, or variable rate. And the types of security given might relate to what are known as deeds of trust, purchase money mortgages, open-end mortgages, participating mortgages, junior mortgages, and package or blanket mortgages. It has also been reported that financial institutions have started to provide funding in the form of debenture issues as opposed to straight mortgages. A mortgage debenture issue is a method of raising corporate finance whereby the institution makes a loan as a debenture secured against the developer's entire property portfolio. The return from the debenture may be fixed, or yield a 'stepped coupon' linked to the rental value of the property. At the end of the loan period the capital is repayable as a lump sum. This type of loan is known in banking circles as a 'bullet' loan. A variation upon this theme is the 'balloon' mortgage, where the coupon, incorporating both capital and interest repayments, increases and then decreases throughout the duration of the loan.

Two popular hybrid varieties of mortgage designed to match the requirements of lenders to the needs of borrowers are the 'convertible' mortgage and the 'participating' mortgage. These are employed where a borrowing developer is seeking to improve the conditions relating to the loan to value ratio, or the rate of interest, by surrendering a portion of equity or profit. Both the convertible and the participating mortgages are debts secured by way of a full charge over the property concerned and a share in the equity of the scheme at some predetermined point in the future. The convertible mortgage will continue to have an interest in the equity of the development following repayment of the principal and any interest secured under the mortgage. This interest will continue to exist until the agreed profit share is received by the lender at some future time. The participating mortgage is similar, in that the lender has an interest in the equity, but the sharing must be made by a certain point in time. The value of the 'equity charge' is usually predetermined, either by amount or by formula, and, whether or not the profits have been realized, the lender's share becomes due. These two instruments are said to be particularly useful in a development scenario where the lender can share in the profits for a higher level of risk (Shayle 1992).

Sale and leaseback

Over the years, the sale and leaseback has been a familiar form of long-term financing in the prime development market. Particularly popular in the 1960s and early 1970s, it returned to favour in the late 1980s and early 1990s. In essence, it involves a developer selling the freehold interest in the completed development to an investor while taking back a long lease at a rent that equates to the initial yield reflected in the selling price. The developer then aims to sublet the property, preferably at a rent in excess of that paid to the investor, thereby creating an immediate profit rent. Sometimes the freehold is owned by a third party, often a local authority, in which case a similar transaction known as a 'lease and leaseback' can be conducted, with the investor buying a long lease of, say, 125 years and the developer taking back a sublease of a slightly shorter term.

An alternative approach frequently adopted when the developer is hoping to trade the scheme (that is, to complete, let and sell it), is the 'leaseback guarantee'. By this arrangement, if the development is not let within, say, six months of practical completion, the developer receives a balancing payment from the fund, representing his profit in return for providing a leaseback guarantee at an agreed base rent. This base rent is usually the same as the rental income estimated at the outset of the scheme, and provision is made for the guarantee to be extinguished once a letting to an occupational tenant has been achieved. If a rent in excess of the base rent is eventually obtained, the agreement will normally provide for that extra rent, often known as 'overage', to be capitalized at a more favourable yield to the fund, usually at half the year's purchase applied to the base rent. In this way, the fund is able to share in the growth of rents between commencement and ultimate letting.

Returning to the conventional sale and leaseback, in which the developer is retaining an interest in the project, the most important part of the negotiation between the developer and the fund is the apportionment of rental growth at review. Few funding agreements are now concluded on the basis that the developer receives only an exposed 'top slice' income once the fund has taken a guaranteed 'bottom slice' return. Most arrangements these days involve some kind of 'side-by-side' or 'vertical' leaseback, whereby the two parties share the equity in predetermined proportions at, say, three- or five-year review. They also usually include a device in the contract known as a 'participation clause', which, like the overage adjustment mentioned above, allows the parties to share in any increase in rental income that is achieved at letting over and above the original estimate of likely rents. The possible permutations by which the returns from property development may be divided between the developer and the fund are many and varied. Different slices of income can be treated in different ways at different times. Inevitably, the eventual contract will be the result of negotiation and compromise, with the outcome depending upon the financial leverage and bargaining powers of the respective parties to the transaction. Who needs whom most is the real key.

One disadvantage of the straightforward sale and leaseback is that the developer is often left with an interest that is difficult to dispose of or refinance except at a value determined by a low capitalization factor. One way of overcoming this disability is to enter into a 'reverse leaseback', in which the developer retains a freehold interest at a peppercorn rent and grants a long lease to the fund under which a reviewable ground rent eventually becomes payable on full letting, but one that is subject to a prior charge in favour of the fund in respect of their share. The legal interest held by the developer is thereby made more marketable.

The principal advantages usually claimed for the lessee or vendor is that: it frees up capital at a lower cost and for a longer period than would otherwise be available; it can provide 100 per cent financing for a project; the funds released can be used to better advantage or at a higher return; problems of refinancing can be avoided; there can be an appreciation of the leasehold value; it might be possible to pass on certain management responsibilities; retention of use or occupancy can be achieved; and there might be certain tax advantages. In the same way, the main advantages to the lessor or purchaser are said to be that: the term of investment is long and thereby early repayment exposure is reduced; it provides an opportunity to invest in large amounts, which reduces management costs; most arrangements, by definition, provide a good covenant; the rate of return after amortization of the principal of the investment is normally relatively high; control over the management of the asset is much higher than with a conventional mortgage; and there may be a substantial remainder of value after the expiry of the lease. There may also be tax advantages to one or both parties.

Forward sale

As mentioned above, most short-term financiers will look for a guarantee that there is an arrangement with a long-term investor or a prospective owner-occupier to 'take out' their interest when the project is completed and often occupied. Contractual details regarding the precise sale date, effect of delays in building work, void lettings and rental growth during development will naturally be the subject of negotiation between the various parties. An outright forward sale along these lines takes place, of course, where a developer is trading and not investing. In such circumstances, the main concern of the long-term investor is to secure a guarantee of rent upon completion, and two principal methods are commonly adopted – the 'profit erosion' method and the 'priority yield' method.

Profit erosion

Also known as the 'profit dissipation' method of funding, profit erosion is a form of rental guarantee arrangement whereby the developer wishes to trade-on a scheme. Instead of taking up a leaseback or entering into a lease-back guarantee if the building is not let within, say, six months of practical completion, the developer stakes his profit, no more, against rent and other outgoings. The developer's profit as a balancing payment is placed on a joint deposit account, with interest accruing to the developer, and the fund draws down the base rent and other outgoings at quarterly intervals.

Once this balancing payment has run out, the developer ceases to have an interest and the fund assumes responsibility for letting the scheme. However, if letting takes place at more than the agreed base rent, the overage provision mentioned before generally applies for a limited period as an incentive to the developer.

Profit erosion schemes are held to be particularly useful where a scheme is large and the developer is either of insufficient strength to offer a satisfactory rental guarantee or, more likely, is of sufficient strength but unwilling to enter into a full leaseback agreement. The objectives of both the fund and the developer can be met in this way so long as sufficient rental cover is provided. Two years is generally thought to be an absolute minimum, and in a difficult letting market four might be more appropriate. In any event, given the greater risk borne by the fund, a slightly higher yield of, say, 0.25 per cent for prime properties is frequently required.

Priority yield

Priority yield is another variant on the financial sharing theme in trading situations where a fund is looking for a given yield on a development of, say, 6 per cent and is not prepared to share in anything below that level. If the developer produces a completed development showing an initial return of 7 per cent, then the fund will capitalize this extra point as an additional profit to the developer. Over 7 per cent, and some form of participation would be agreed, usually on an equal share basis.

Priority yield fundings are especially popular when a project of development is difficult to plan in respect of time and cost for one reason or another. It brings the developer and the fund into a close partnership where each party accepts a degree of risk against the potential profit inherent in a speculative development. There is also a considerable incentive for the developer to keep costs down and to complete and let the project as quickly as possible.

Project management fee

Another form of funding relationship is based on the 'project management fee'. This is used primarily as a method of funding for major development schemes where the size, impact on the market and time taken to complete and let the premises are such that neither party would wish for anything less than that the funding institution bear the full risk. In most circumstances the developer would have identified the potential for development and investigated the planning and market conditions. They may even have taken out options on the land and obtained outline planning permission. Upon successful introduction to a fund, a separate fee will usually be agreed. Subsequently, the developer simply receives a fee for project managing the development, which can either be calculated as a fixed percentage of construction cost or geared to the eventual profit of the scheme. Most project management fee arrangements tend to combine both elements, so that a basic minimum fee is agreed as a fixed sum and a proportion of profit over a certain level is offered as a kind of performance incentive.

General funding facility

'General funding facility' refers to an arrangement whereby an overall financial facility is provided to a development company and is not specifically related to any one project. It is secured across the company assets and it enables the developer to carry out a series of projects working within a pre-set lending limit. The loan may be repayable over a period of decades, thereby keeping repayments during the early years, when yields may be very low, to a minimum. A comparatively new kind of development finance is the 'drop lock loan', which is also a form of general funding facility. In general it allows a developer to have access to predetermined amounts of money over a given period of time. The loans may be for terms of anything between ten and thirty-five years, and the period during which a developer may exercise his option to use them between three and seven years. The special feature of a drop lock loan is that, if prevailing interest rates fall below a predetermined base rate during the option period, then the option can be exercised in reverse against the developer who is obliged to take up an agreed tranche or all of the loan at that rate, which is then 'locked' for the entire term. If the developer chooses to take up the loan before the predetermined interest rate is reached, he will pay a variable rate linked to that base rate until it falls to the predetermined level, when it is converted into a fixed rate for the rest of the term.

Another option is the unsecured multiple option financing facility, whereby large loans are made available to property development companies on a broad basis for fixed, but usually extendable, periods of time. One bank will normally act as arranger and facility agent, with anything from between six and thirty other institutions supplying or guaranteeing the loan as managers or co-managers. Multi-option financing facilities encompass a variety of alternative financing methods within one package. Short-, medium- and long-term lending can be related in a versatile manner. Syndicated loans, multi-currency arrangements, commercial paper loans and bankers' guaranteed loans can all be selected and mixed, together with choices of swaps, fixed or floating interest rates, bonds with warrants and the like (Pugh 1992). In this way the borrower can choose the best financing package to meet his individual requirements.

Term loans

Term loans provide a development company with the facility to borrow a certain amount from a bank or syndicate of banks, which may be drawn upon immediately or in stated amounts throughout the life of the loan. The loans are always made at rates of interest in line with prevailing market rates during the period of the loan. Such loans will specify the date or dates and manner by which the amount advanced by the banks is to be repaid.

Term loans can also carry the option to convert into a limited recourse loan, where the funds are for a project that will produce income soon after completion. In some cases, the interest rates charged on the loan will fall to a pre-specified level when the property under development has been pre-let. Term loans cannot be called in for repayment before the agreed date, which gives them a distinct advantage over overdrafts. Within the property development sector, most term loans are for amounts of less than £100 million, although loans of up to £350 million are not uncommon.

Overdrafts

In familiar terms, an overdraft occurs when a customer of a bank draws on an account to the extent that he falls into a negative balance. Company overdrafts may be for any size, provided the bank is satisfied by the asset backing and credit standing of the company concerned. Interest on overdrafts is charged at a pre-agreed rate or at the bank's currently published lending rate. Pre-arrangements regarding the interest rate are normally possible only for large corporate customers.

The main disadvantage of overdraft facilities is that repayment may be called for at any time and without notice, and could, therefore, come at a bad time when the company's liquid resources are low. Conversely, the principal advantage of an overdraft facility is that the borrower can repay the whole or part of the debit balance on his account at any time, also without giving notice. This contrasts with a term loan of a fixed amount, where the bank is not obliged to accept repayment before the agreed date, or may charge a penalty for so doing.

In the property development field, overdraft facilities are normally used only as supplementary funds to a principal loan, for exploratory work at the appraisal stage, for financing options to purchase land or for contingency payments.

Standby commitments

Standby commitments arise where a developer needs a temporary loan while seeking a permanent commitment for development finance from another lender. Unlike a take-out commitment in the form of a forward sale, neither the borrower nor lender expects the standby facility to become binding. The developer generally hopes in due course to borrow on more favourable terms elsewhere, but wants to begin development as soon as possible. Often, standby commitments are never concluded and funds never deployed – rather, the facility is used to enhance the confidence of a potential permanent lender in a proposed project. Few permanent lenders of development finance are willing to make loans against a standby commitment alone, unless there are very special circumstances.

Syndicated loans

The early 1990s witnessed the emergence of the 'syndicated' loan, sometimes known as 'project' or 'consortia' funding. Often arranged by way of tender panels and normally only appropriate for very large schemes, the essential requirement will usually be a blue chip covenant of considerable means, reflected in a substantial asset base, profitability and turnover. This may not be found in the developer client, but with prospective occupiers prepared to lend their covenant to the scheme. The number of parties involved, with their separate interests, can therefore pose problems of authority and control for the developer, as well as time and expense.

Nevertheless, the concept of the syndicated loan has come into prominence because it offers greater flexibility with regard to currencies and interest rates. Other advantages have been said to include flexible maturity, amortization schedules and credit structures, with less rigid documentation requirements than for a securities issue.

Securitization and unitization

Loan syndication has been supplemented by the securitization of debt, whereby the more conventional loans made by financial institutions are replaced by smaller monetary instruments that can be traded in the investment market. At the time of writing there have been several years of debate about the potential for 'unitization', which is very much the same thing as securitization. The idea is to provide a financial vehicle that facilitates the funding of large single development projects, increases liquidity in the market, enables the smaller investor to participate in the market, increases the flow of capital to the property industry, achieves homogeneity of the market by divisibility, permits wider ownership of property, and increases market information and public awareness. Various issues emerge from the debate concerning such matters as valuation, the size and membership of the market, potential conflicts of interest, and the management of the property, liquidity, marketability and taxation. Only time will tell how successful will be the notion of unitization.

One of the principal problems with securitized (and unitized) property vehicles has been that of double taxation – the management company pays tax on the rental income from the property and then the shareholder also pays tax on the dividend income from their investment. This means that if dividends are paid out of rental income it is effectively taxed twice. Real Estate Investment Trusts (REITS) are tax-efficient investment vehicles – there is limited tax payable if the majority of the income and gains are distributed. Such trusts have recently become available on the UK investment market.

Non-recourse and limited recourse loans

Non-recourse and limited recourse loans seek to restrict the lending institution to recovering any unpaid debt from the property in question rather than the borrowing developer. From the developer's point of view it obviously limits the risk, minimizing exposure while maximizing profit, and allows him to structure the transaction so that it is 'off balance sheet' through a joint venture company. From the lender's viewpoint he can expect higher fees and wider margins. Nevertheless, in reality, no loans are truly non-recourse as such, for the bank will impose conditions relating to the front-end injection of equity finance into the project by the developer as well as seeking guarantees against cost overruns and completion date. These facilities are only made to property companies with a proven track record in the management of development projects.

Joint ventures and partnership

Property companies without an adequate financial base to enable them to fund and carry out their own developments often have recourse to joint venture or partnership schemes. Likewise, public and private landowners lacking construction finance and development expertise have frequently entered into similar arrangements.

The advantages of joint ventures are generally obvious and do not need much explanation. However, they can be summarized as follows:

- to spread risk among participating parties
- to enable the development of large projects
- to attract market knowledge and development expertise
- to secure sufficient development finance.

In like manner, the main disadvantages are:

- control over the development project is dissipated
- disposal of a particular interest in a partnership scheme is more difficult
- the value of a part interest is invariably less than the proportionate share in the whole
- there may be double taxation.

Before embarking on a joint venture, the participants will need to identify the most appropriate form of structure to be used. This will normally depend upon the following:

- the number of participants
- the nature of the proposed scheme and the relative risks inherent in development
- the timescale involved, and the policy towards disposal or retention
- how the venture is to be financed, and the desired mix of debt and equity
- responsibility for losses and limitation on liability
- the tax position of the respective parties
- the way in which profits are to be distributed
- any relevant statutory legislation
- the ability and ease of disposing of interests by the parties involved
- any special balance sheet requirements.

There are various legal vehicles by which a joint venture can be effected. These include a trust for sale, a partnership agreement, a limited partnership, a joint venture company and a property unit trust. There are also potential investors looking to collaborate with reputable property development companies. These include: local government authorities with land and planning powers but no money; statutory undertakers with surplus land; trading companies and business enterprises looking to participate in the development of property, either for their own occupation or as an investment with shared risk; overseas investors on a learning curve for a particular market or location; life companies and pension funds with money but little expertise; and high net worth individuals. It has been stated that all of the above tend to be looking for the 'perfect development property', well let, high yielding and with potential growth. Most of them wish to enter into a 50:50 deal as equal partners, with each party putting up approximately 15 per cent of the equity and the joint venture vehicle borrowing the rest over a five-year term.

Venture or private capital

A phenomenon that has emerged since the mid-1980s is that of 'venture capital'. In the 2000s, private capital providers achieved a degree of notoriety because of the profits they achieved on a number of high-profile corporate ventures. This phenomenon can mean different things to different people, but is usually employed to describe those sources of finance willing to invest in higher-risk proposals in return for equity participation and a say in project control. The venture capitalist delves much more deeply into a proposition than does a lending banker, and will often seek a close involvement in the management of a project. Venture capital is also expensive, both in arrangement and through profit sharing. The 'hands-on' approach can constrain a developer, and it is preferable to try to obtain a 'layered' financial package commencing with bank finance, followed by any other loans or grants available and topped off with the venture capital tranche.

Mezzanine finance

With mezzanine finance, a developer seeks the assistance of a second, 'mezzanine', financier. Some prime debt lenders may consider providing a limited facility in excess of 70 per cent of value in consideration of a higher interest rate, or a single fee being taken out of the sale proceeds. It is more likely, however, that the top slice of funds will come from a separate specialist lender. These mezzanine financiers have in the past lent up to 100 per cent of the balance of funds required, but now they more usually look for an input from the borrower, in the form of either cash or collateral security. Nonetheless, they are still able to achieve effective gearing of around 85–90 per cent. There are also occasions when the prime debt financier is not prepared to provide as much as 70 per cent of value and the mezzanine financier may again top up the hardcore facility. This form of arrangement is also sometimes known as 'wrap-around', 'junior' or 'subordinate' financing.

Because there are obviously greater risks involved in providing this top slice loan, the mezzanine financier will seek a return that reflects a share in the anticipated profit from the development. Some lenders will insist on taking shares in the development company, whereas others prefer to take a second charge on the project, although the collateral security will rank behind the prime debt financier. The amount of profit share required will naturally depend upon the individual circumstances of the project concerned. The mezzanine financier tends to become more involved with both the developer and the project, often employing a team of property professionals, which can give considerable comfort to the prime debt financier, because in looking after its own interests it will also protect theirs (Berkley 1991).

Deep discount and zero coupon bonds

A deep discount bond (DDB) is a debt instrument issued at significantly less than its par value and which is repayable in full on its redemption. It may also carry a low rate of interest, with the lender being compensated by the high capital repayment at the maturity date. A zero coupon bond (ZCB) is similar, but no interest is ever paid during the loan period. The discount is, therefore, like the rolling-up of interest at a full rate until the redemption date. There is also the stepped coupon bond (SCB) whereby the coupon, or interest rate, rises at fixed intervals over the period of the loan by specified amounts. These different versions of the bond may be combined to form variations on the same theme.

The general terms for the issue of such bonds can be summarized as follows:

- maturity between five and ten years
- an interest rate margin of 2–4 per cent over base lending rate for development projects
- fees for arrangement, underwriting and participation totalling around 2 per cent of the loan
- security normally in the range of 70–75 per cent of loan to value, using the full redemption value of the bond
- income cover of at least one times, and preferably one and a half
- a good covenant
- borrower responsible for all associated costs
- early redemption penalties.

Although comparatively rare instruments in the property development finance fields, DDBs, ZCBs and SCBs offer attractive rewards in terms of cashflow, running yield and redemption value, as well as certain tax advantages.

Hedging techniques

Hedging techniques are used by a borrower to 'insure' against adverse interest rate and currency trends. There are a variety of such techniques, the most common of which are:

- 'Swaps', where a borrower is allowed to raise capital in one market, and can swap either one interest rate structure for another, or swap the liability for the maturity value and interest from one currency to another. In other words, the simultaneous exchange between two parties of one security or currency for another where there is mutual benefit to both.

- 'Caps' and 'floors', which are derived from the options and futures market, and guarantee that during the loan period the interest rate paid by the borrower will not rise above (cap) or fall below (floor) a set limit.
- 'Collars', where an agreement is reached combining a cap and a floor, putting both a maximum and a minimum level on the interest rate paid by the borrower. A premium is normally paid by the borrower for a cap and by the lender for a floor.
- 'Droplocks', as already mentioned, this facility enables the borrower to change the loan from a variable to a fixed rate of interest for the remainder of the loan period once long-term interest rates reach a predetermined level.
- 'Forward rate agreements', where a borrower can sell the currency in which he has obtained a loan forward by, say, twelve months in order to lock into a more favourable exchange rate.

Criteria for funding

In most circumstances developers will have well-established relationships with the funds from whom they seek development finance. Where it is the first time that a developer approaches a particular source of finance, understandably close scrutiny will be given to the property company as well as the proposal. For new developers setting out to undertake a first project, it is virtually an impossible task to attract financial support from conventional sources, unless on an individual basis they have successfully managed similar schemes for someone else.

In examining the criteria by which development propositions are judged, the following section is based on an established developer making the first approach to a fresh source of funds from a major financial institution.

Past performance

The starting point is bound to be the track record of the developer who is making an application for funding. However subjective the appraisal may be, the financier will probably form a fairly immediate opinion about the developers. In particular, if they were active during the downturn of a previous property cycle, it will reveal quite a lot about their judgement. Increasingly, it is expected that developers should themselves exhibit an expertise in the actual process of development, and the demonstration of true project management skills within the development company is now almost a prerequisite. Moreover, it is not sufficient for those skills merely to exist within the company. It must clearly be shown that they will be fully applied to the scheme in question, for even the most able of project managers can be expected to be responsible for only three or at most four major projects at any one time.

The necessary skills sought are not confined to the physical production of the property. A thoroughgoing competence in all aspects relating to the financial performance of the scheme is of paramount importance, because, when all is said and done, every facet of the development programme has a pecuniary effect. For this reason, it may occasionally be the case that proven financial expertise in another field of business aside from property could be considered as relevant in assessing a request for development funds.

Consideration will also be given to the supporting professional team selected by the developer. Some architects are best suited to particular types of development and certain projects demand the injection of specialist building, engineering, service, surveying and agency skills. The previous record of all the contributing disciplines and their likely corporate chemistry will, therefore, be taken into account.

It should almost go without saying that, even at first blush, the selection of the project by the developer should appear sound and attractive to the fund, for it is well accepted that where a developer sees opportunity a financier sees risk.

Company accounts

The accounts of a property company should tell their own story and will always constitute an essential part of an initial application for development finance. In appraising the assets of the company, the fund will look to see properties of a good physical quality occupied by tenants of repute on beneficial terms with regular upward reviews of rent. They will take note of the portfolio mix of properties owned, with special regard to geographic and sectoral spread. The development programme currently in hand should not appear to be too large for the financial and management resources of the company, and not all the assets of the company should be pledged.

On the other side of the coin, in examining the accounts of the company, an intending financier will be reassured to find a healthy proportion of equity to balance the liabilities. The total term debt borne by the company should ideally have a good balance of fixed rate loans with any variable loans they have taken on. In addition, it is important to ensure that in their financial planning the property company have managed to avoid the bunching of repayments on existing loans and not placed undue reliance on short-term borrowing, both of which could lead to unfortunate pressure to refinance in a manner that might have repercussions upon the security sought by the fund. Where a property company have an overseas position, it is also necessary to establish that their foreign currency liabilities are generally matched by their overseas assets and sources of income.

Overall, therefore, the profit and loss account should demonstrate that the quality and amount of present income should not only be adequate to meet current outgoings, but should also be sufficient to meet any future rises in interest rates and cover any unforeseen exigencies that might occur. In this respect, cash-flow is difficult to fudge, but some company accounts are otherwise less than revealing. This is especially true when it comes to the policy adopted towards the revaluation of existing property assets, and most funds pay close attention to how often the property portfolio is revalued, on what basis, and by whom. A careful watch will also be kept for the possibility of any off-balance sheet items, such as guarantees, being in existence and affecting the financial credibility of the company.

The project

From the fund's standpoint, the proposed project must not only meet the portfolio objectives of the developer – more importantly, it must meet their own. Broadly speaking, the project should be of a suitable size in terms of value, with no single investment property forming more than about 5–10 per cent total portfolio. It should be in accord with the sectoral balance of the property portfolio, which might be distributed along the lines of 35 per cent to 40 per cent offices, 35 per cent to 40 per cent shops, 10 per cent to 15 per cent industrial and 5 per cent to 10 per cent other forms of land and property investment. Locationally, it should meet the geographical spread adopted by the fund and critically it must be within easy reach of the developer to make certain of proper project management control.

More specifically, the fund will probably wish to assure itself of detailed property considerations, particularly if the developer is not a previous borrower. This might include conducting its own investigations relating to such matters as precise siting, local demand for space, flexibility of use, and market comparables. Design factors and performance standards loom large in meeting the criteria set up for funding approval by financial institutions, and are dealt with elsewhere according to their special requirements, sector by sector. Furthermore, virtually all funding agreements will reserve to the fund the right to approve tenants for the scheme and, although in practice this condition rarely proves a stumbling block, it is viewed as being a vital power of control over the project and the developer.

Amount to be borrowed

Most financiers will lend only a proportion of the total amount required to fund a development, normally on the strength of a first legal charge over the development, but although with mortgage finance this is usually limited to 70–75 per cent of cost, banks will usually advance anything up to 80–85 per cent for a quality development with a top-class covenant already agreed, and long-term leaseback or forward sale loans from the institutions covering the interim funding during development can often provide 90 per cent or more of total development cost. However, above 70–75 per cent, borrowings will often be considered as equity and deserving of a higher pricing. Almost as a matter of principle, it is felt right that the developer should make a contribution, however small, towards the financing of the project. As a rule of thumb, however, 25–30 per cent is frequently sought.

Sometimes developers will seek a loan geared to the value of the completed development as opposed to the cost. This may be countenanced by the lender, but usually a lower level of advance is made to compensate and ensure security of the loan. Obviously, different lenders in different markets will view funding applications in different lights and adopt differing criteria in relation to acceptable percentages of cost or value accordingly.

Loan periods

Few banks currently wish to consider commitments of longer than five years, but in exceptional circumstances will consider up to ten years. The insurance companies and pension funds will consider periods of up to thirty years, and often set ten years as a minimum term.

Interest rates

How rates are set has been explained above. As also already explained, some funding agreements adopt a fixed rate throughout the term, some a floating rate linked to the base rate, and some adopt a mechanism that combines fixed and floating rates. Increasingly, however, the rate of interest applied to a loan is traded against equity participation.

The timing of interest payments is also important, and methods of calculation vary from lender to lender. For example, a few lenders still calculate interest on the balance outstanding at the beginning of each year. If a loan of say £50 million is fully amortized over a period of twenty years at a fixed rate of 12 per cent, it can be shown that this could result in an additional payment of £8 million compared with a calculation on a day-to-day balance.

Yield

The factor by which income, anticipated or actual, derived from a development is capitalized will depend upon the relative degree of risk involved, and the relevant investment yield will be adjusted accordingly.

Where a fund was providing long-term finance for a scheme already completed and let, the appropriate yield might be, say, 5 per cent. If the finance was agreed on a forward commitment only once the scheme was completed and let, with no interim funding, then the yield might be 5.5 per cent. Where a forward commitment also provided interim development finance but a pre-let was concluded on full and acceptable rental guarantees supplied, then the yield could move to 5.75 per cent. If there was no pre-let and rents were only guaranteed for a limited period of, say, two years following practical completion, then a forward commitment with interim funding would require a yield of around 6 per cent. In the highest risk situation, where the fund was working on a priority yield, project management or profit erosion basis, then it would almost certainly look for a yield of about 6.5 per cent.

Rental cover

Very much as a rule of thumb, both fund and developer will be seeking sufficient rental cover in the margin allowed for developer's profit, and held as a balancing payment, to allow the completed building to stand empty for a period of around two-and-a-half to three years. Exactly how long the contingency period should be will rest on the strength of the market at the time. The stronger the market, the less the cover necessary, and vice versa.

Another way in which rental cover is used as a measure of ascertaining the degree of security is the ratio of initial estimated rental income against interest repayments. A ratio of 1.1 or 1.2 to 1 is normally sought.

General funding facility

As already indicated, where a developer has generated a high degree of confidence with a fund, it may often prove beneficial to both parties to agree that a general funding facility should be made available to the property company. These are usually provided by the merchant banking sector. The terms and conditions upon which such loans are made will vary, but they will commonly refer to such matters as the total amount available, the take-up rate, the level and compounding of interest charges, proportion of facility devoted to any individual project, maximum percentage of development cost allowed for any particular scheme, restrictions as to planning consent and land assembly position, right to approve individual projects, obligation to offer certain other development projects over a given period, revaluation rights, buy-out provisions for schemes slow in starting, equity-sharing arrangements, institutional long-term take-out requirements upon completion, repayment, and reporting and review procedures. Funding facilities of this kind can either be of a fixed term for, say, five or seven years, or 'revolving', subject to review at pre-ordained intervals. Security for the loan may also be attributable to particular assets of the company or arranged as a floating charge across all the company's assets.

More open-ended arrangements

The greater the degree of flexibility and discretion sought by a developer in a funding arrangement, the more a lending institution will look for further security to cover their risk. If the proposed project is anything less than conventional in respect of size, location, design, occupancy or letting terms, then a fund might be persuaded to relax its standard criteria on one or more of the following grounds: the land might already be owned by the developer; the company might be providing a substantial equity injection into the development; cast-iron collateral providing complete cover might be offered from elsewhere within the company's holdings; another financially strong partner such as a major construction firm might put up security alongside the developer; or bank guarantees may be supplied. Although they might not mean much in financial respects, personal guarantees undertaken by principals within the property company are thought to concentrate the mind wonderfully upon the successful outcome of development projects.

Sensitivity

It would be unusual for a lending institution not to conduct its own analysis of the sensitivity of a development scheme to changes in such component parts as rental income, initial yield, construction cost, finance charges and period to complete and let the development. Indeed, they would normally expect to see such an exercise performed for them by the prospective borrower in presenting the development for approval.

Tax

Although tax considerations are rarely the most significant issues in determining whether or not a scheme should be funded, they can affect the way in which a financial package is arranged. For example, because in some countries certain financial institutions are either wholly or partially exempt from tax, it is important to structure the funding agreement so that any concessions such as industrial building allowances or capital allowances relating to plant and machinery pass to the developer so that he can write them off against construction costs and improve his net profits position after tax. Further, it is sometimes the case that, whereas capital repayments do not attract tax relief, interest payments do, and in such circumstances borrowers are well advised to ensure that so far as is possible all fees and charges associated with funding the development are expressed in the formal finance agreement, so that they too become eligible for relief.

Costs

Apart from the obvious cost of interest on the loan and any equity share forgone, it should be recognized that the financing of a development can be an expensive business. There are arrangement fees of between 0. 25 and 1 per cent, payable to the fund or to intermediaries for effecting an introduction and putting a funding package together; commitment fees, which are usually about 1 per cent of the loan amount upon acceptance of a formal offer, and are repayable on completion of the advance but forfeitable if the borrower does not proceed; legal costs, which on the loan can amount to about 1.0 per cent of the advance, although it might be lower if it is a very large loan and higher if the deal is especially complex; valuation fees, which on average can cost up to a further 0.5 per cent of the advance; revaluation fees, during the currency of the loan; penalty fees, if by any chance the developer seeks early repayment of a mortgage advance; tail-end or exit fees; and the costs incurred in making the presentation itself.

Choice of fund

So far, attention has been focused upon the necessary attributes of the developer in the eyes of the fund. However, it is just as important that developers should carefully select their source of borrowing.

General considerations

In the same way that developers' underlying resources would be examined, it is for them to be assured about the financial strength of the fund, although this requirement is not as imperative as it was when regulatory control of financial systems was more lax. Of greater concern to the developer these days is the speed of response made by funds to a request for finance. Associated with this is the extent to which delegated authority is conferred upon the fund manager or executive director. The very location of the finance house can be a consideration in selecting a likely lender, for some funds can have a special regard for, or relationship with, certain towns or regions. It usually helps if the fund has developed an interest and expertise in property matters, particularly at the development end of the market. If so, it will often pay to make a few inquiries of other borrowers as to their experience of dealing with that fund.

The general attitude of the fund towards an approach for development finance will usually give a fair indication of what kind of business relationship is possible and how it is likely to evolve. As with most transactions, the level of success depends upon mutual trust and confidence, and even within the largest of organizations this often comes down to individual personalities on both sides. In this context, stability of management within both the property development company and the financial institution can only assist in forging close and effective links between the two agencies, but large organizations are notorious for moving people about. With this in mind, therefore, and for several other reasons, it is not always a good idea for a developer to rely too heavily upon a single source of money for funding their development programme. People and policies can change.

Given that most major development schemes in the prime part of the property market are funded either by insurance companies and pension funds in the 'institutional' sector, or by clearing, merchant or overseas banks in the 'banking' sector, it is worth considering the different characteristics of these alternative sources from the developer's viewpoint.

Institutional lending

By and large, the lending policies of the major insurance companies and pension funds are characterized by their project-based nature. This means that they tend to exercise extremely tight control over the entire project, including the design, construction and letting programmes. But although institutions are very risk-averse and maintain strict standards of building design and performance, some will lend up to 100 per cent of development finance to favoured borrowers.

What is required of the developer is a good knowledge of the institutional funding market. This includes an understanding of the locational and sectoral preferences of different funds, their recent transactions, investment objectives, portfolio balance and the amount of money currently available for particular projects. Some will tend to specialize in certain forms of financial arrangement – short-term bridging loan, medium-term mortgage, long-term leaseback or forward sale. Some will not consider a project costing less than £5 million to them, others concentrate on smaller schemes of, say, £1–3 million, and will have a ceiling figure beyond which they cannot lend. Particular funds will also either favour certain types of development – small industrial workshops, provincial shops or city offices, for instance – or be seeking to acquire them in order to balance their portfolios. A shrewd developer will always shop around. Consequently, contact has to be maintained with a range of fund managers and the agents who act on their behalf, so that by knowing who acts for whom, and which funds prefer a direct approach, careful targeting to selected institutions, rather than a shot-gun blast across the market, can be accomplished.

In the same way, the basis of agreement for obtaining finance can vary among funds and between projects. Some funds, for example, are less keen upon sale and leaseback arrangements than others. Similarly, with regard to the desire for a degree of partnership with a developer, some funds prefer the borrower to bear a reasonable proportion of risk, whereas others are less favourably inclined towards side-by-side arrangements, taking the view that too large a share to the developer gives him a disproportionate involvement in overall responsibility. The reverse can also be the case. It may be that the developer in question has no choice and, having to trade on, must opt for a forward sale. The manner in which such matters as bridging finance, rental projection and additional tranches of loans are agreed also varies across the market, and is often a question of careful negotiation.

A critical factor is the need to establish the extent to which potential profits are placed at risk. In this context, some form of equity-sharing leaseback arrangement tends to be less contentious than a straight taking of a capital profit through a forward sale, because both parties share a common interest. Nevertheless, whether the arrangement provides for rental guarantee, profit erosion or priority yield commitments from the developer, he must be aware of the respective consequences from each kind of agreement. In particular, attention should be paid to the length of the agreed letting period, and thus the amount of rental cover provided.

Pre-letting will also frequently be an important consideration. In fact, it will often be a condition of funding. However, despite what might be seen as the security and certainty afforded by a pre-let, for the developer there can be drawbacks that affect time, cost and quality. Not only might the demands of the tenant be in contradiction to the stipulations of the fund, but the added involvement of the tenant and his professional advisers in the construction process and upon completion can cause extra problems. Furthermore, it can affect the overall planning and phasing of the development programme, especially in respect of common parts and facilities. Nevertheless, the securing of a pre-let can attract a premium and avoid contingency payments, void rental periods and heavy marketing costs.

One area of increasing sophistication is that of funding documentation. In the thrill of the moment of approval, or during the cut and thrust of negotiations, certain matters can be overlooked or onerous undertakings entered into too lightly. Thus, the aim of the developer should be for an agreement that is not too tight and not too loose, but, above all, that the offer letter is binding and operable. Care must be taken about conditions relating to every aspect of the project – design, construction, funding and letting – and the result is usually a compromise between strict compliance with institutional criteria and cost minimization to optimize profit. It is more and more common for an institution to appoint their own consultant firm to monitor development, an arrangement that if not properly formulated can be very irksome to the developer and his project manager. Another important aspect of this kind of funding agreement is to ensure that the client's potential liabilities to the fund are matched by those of the contractor to him, and likewise between the developer, the project manager and the other members of the professional team.

Bank lending

Banks are traditionally more concerned with the 'asset' base of those to whom they lend rather than upon the particular project in hand. The emphasis, therefore, will be more upon monitoring and controlling the balance sheet and security cover offered by the borrower. For the developer this can provide a more open and flexible climate in which to work, where such factors as time, cost and quality can be traded off against the client's ability to generate funds or produce additional collateral. However, bank finance is founded on profitable lending rather than by direct investment in a scheme, and, because banks normally neither provide risk capital under conventional arrangements nor seek to participate in equity profits, it is common for only a proportion of development finance (typically around 70 per cent) to be loaned. It is, therefore, imperative for the developer responsible for securing finance to have an understanding of the policies, practices and procedures that determine bank lending. This is of greater moment here, for although institutional negotiations are invariably conducted between surveyors, bank lending is more usually transacted with a banker. Furthermore, the lending market is far from homogeneous. The banking sector broadly comprises major stock banks, the merchant banks, finance houses and overseas banks. All are different, and all are competitive, so bank finance must be carefully tailored to fit the purpose for which it is applied, and a well-designed package prepared to meet overdraft, term or equity financial requirements. And, as interest rates in the market tend to move closely together, so the aim of the developer is to seek the best deal in respect of such matters as quality of service, fees, costs and repayments. Indeed, sometimes the additional flexibility afforded by more expensive arrangements can be worthwhile. For example, the objectives with a smaller project might be for a quick decision, flexibility in execution and an ability to revise arrangements without excessive penalties. With a larger scheme, detailed arrangements regarding the term of the loan, interest rate options and adjustable repayment schedules might be of more concern.

Term loans, which impose a contractual obligation on the bank to provide finance for an agreed period, have become a popular way of funding development projects. Banks are increasingly experienced in tailoring proposals that give flexibility of approach on the one hand but are matched by covenants on the other, which can have considerable effect on the running of the borrower's business in the future. For instance, financial ratios are a valuable tool of control, the breach of which puts the lender in a strong position to call for initial or added security or for changes in the terms of the loan, with such options as accelerating the loan or cancelling any unused part of the facility. There are other alternatives of varying efficacy – the negative pledge, sharing-round clauses and contractual right of set-off. Additionally, where the loan is unsecured, which now is sometimes the case, the bank might also consider various forms of direct involvement in the borrower's company, ranging from the appointment of a nominee director, to a working capital maintenance agreement, with shareholders undertaking to ensure the maintenance of the borrower's capital to satisfy covenanted ratios. Thus, in general, term-lending can afford a flexibility that, depending upon the circumstances, can be preferable to long-term mortgages, sale and leaseback arrangements or debenture borrowing.

A feature of bank lending is that there has been a tendency for the borrower to rely upon the lender to propose the basis and structure of the lending facility. This occurs often through ignorance, and sometimes through a misplaced desire to please. Such a lack of initiative or awareness in negotiations on the part of the developer can all too easily lead to a costly and mismatched facility being accepted.

Customer relationships are a critical factor in bank lending policy. The early training of young bankers used to dwell on the 'canons of lending' – character, ability, means, purpose, amount, repayment and income (for which the acronym CAMPARI serves as a handy reminder). It is perhaps significant that there was not an 'S' for security, for banking theory held that a perfect loan arrangement should be unsecured. Modern practice, however, dictates otherwise. In many cases the prospective borrower will have developed a relationship with his bank through ordinary business and overdraft lending, and it is a golden rule in the clearing banks that the current account forms the basis of mutual confidence between banker and developer. Where there is no previous relationship, then it will be necessary to establish the financial status of the borrower and the viability of the proposed scheme with great care.

Several other factors warrant attention on the part of the developer when negotiating bank lending. These are:

- The extent to which standby facilities might be required, and the terms that might be attached to them.
- The type of charge secured over the assets of the borrower – making sure that they are neither overcharged, which can reduce the ability to obtain further loans, nor unduly restricted, so that, for example, disposal is limited.
- Ensuring that a proper presentation is made of the man, the market, the margins, the management information systems and the money requirement concerned with a particular project.
- Confirming the 'facility letter' from the bank to the borrower setting out the terms on which the loan has been agreed. Apart from specifying the amount, rate of interest, repayment terms and brief details of the security, if any, it will also normally include specific terms and conditions in the form of negative or positive covenants relating to such matters as default, other borrowings, supply of information and provision of warranties.

Whatever detailed arrangements are finally made, the project management objective must be to seek elasticity. Full allowance for the possible effects of inflation, time and cost overruns should be built in. Even the location of the bank and its officials, together with their speed of response, can be of importance. And these days, the very stability of the financial source is equally significant.

Problems in funding

Apart from the basic thesis that lack of knowledge and understanding of the principal sources of finance for property development and their respective policies, practices and procedures presents a major problem for aspiring developers, there are other issues that condition the climate for lending. A few of these are described, in brief, below.

Location

Within and among funding institutions a preferential treatment exists towards certain situations in, around and between selected cities and facilities. Some of this has the smack of hindsight about it, but much has to do with perceptions regarding environment, accessibility and communications. From the point of view of a developer approaching a potential source of funds, therefore, it is helpful to know the attitude and commitment of individual fund managers to particular towns, areas and regions.

Presentation

It is astonishing how little attention is paid to the professional presentation of proposed development schemes. Although not always the declared reason for turning a proposition down, poor presentation probably accounts for many funding refusals. At the very least, the following are required – a detailed appraisal of planning and market conditions, a cashflow analysis and a reasonable set of drawings, together with an explicit statement of the financial position of the intending borrower, contained in a well-illustrated, succinct and coherent document.

Personality can also play a part. Character assessment is always a matter of personal judgement, but it is nonetheless important to ensure that any presentation is made in an open, confident, informed and enthusiastic manner.

Speculation

It is almost a cliché to say that one man's profit is another man's risk. Nevertheless, it is probably true to say that developers as a breed are eternally optimistic, whereas bankers, and those of their ilk, are notoriously cautious in their approach towards new developments. Moreover, it is often harder for the small developer to borrow money than for the large established property company, for if one project goes wrong for the former, it will have a more profound effect upon overall security and performance than for the latter.

From the standpoint of the developer or project manager, it is always worth considering the way in which potential profits are placed at risk by the manner whereby funds adjust their yield parameters according to the financial arrangements agreed. For example, depending upon market conditions, an office scheme might variously be finely tuned as follows:

5%   completed and let
5.25%   pre-let, interim finance and forward commitment
5.5%   leaseback or lease guarantee
5.75%   profit erosion basis
6%   priority yield basis.

Collateral

A frequent explanation for funding agencies turning down applications to support proposed development projects is the inadequacy of existing collateral guarantees and proffered future equity participation. In fact, research indicates that this is probably the single most common reason for rejection.

Valuation

Lenders will invariably seek their own valuation of a proposed development project. This may often be at odds with the value perceived by the prospective borrower. In stagnant or recessionary markets, for example, the emphasis by the lender and his valuation advisers will normally be placed upon secure cashflow rather than anticipated capital value allowing for potential growth, which can lead to a wide divergence in estimating current open market value.

Thus, although regard is still paid to the loan to value ratio, the ability of the transaction to service the debt becomes of paramount importance. Pre-letting to a high-quality covenant on beneficial terms is, therefore, a vital factor in obtaining full financing in a falling or static market. In such markets it is always advisable to check that the lender's chosen valuer is prepared to confirm an approximate value, albeit verbal, prior to paying commitment fees, solicitors' costs and, of course, the valuer's full fees for a written report (Berkley 1991). Nevertheless, there are always the twin dangers of initial valuation or appraisal of a proposed development scheme being either too conservative or overoptimistic. Great care must be taken to explore the constituent components of rent, yield, building cost, finance, land cost, profit and time.

Currency

Given the global nature of property development finance, foreign currency loans have become increasingly popular. Interest rates can be lower, capital sums higher and terms easier. Foreign currency markets, however, are prone to constant fluctuations, and, in order to take advantage of such borrowing arrangements, developers should ensure access to any one of a number of different currencies, and be able to switch with ease. There are now versatile 'multi-currency' banking facilities available from leading international banks.

Refinancing

In many markets the issue of refinancing is extremely topical. Proper handling of this can often mean the difference between a property company's survival and its insolvency. Refinancing development property presents a particularly formidable challenge in depressed markets, as uncompleted and unlet projects lack the two basic attributes required to reassure a financier – cashflow and marketability.

Developments are most likely to be refinanced as part of an overall corporate refinancing exercise. Alternatively, where the scheme is in an area of strong demand or very prime, a development may be refinanced by the injection of fresh capital by a new equity investor, either as a joint venture partner or as a long-term investor. The unpredictability of development projects is not often compatible with the fine tuning of debt-oriented refinancing packages. A new financier's willingness to provide additional finance will primarily depend upon the quality of the security offered, although the company's past record will also play an important role. An existing financier will look especially at the feasibility of the company's corporate plan in comparison with other realization options, although it has been pointed out that the ultimate decision will invariably turn on the strength of the relationship between the parties involved (Clark 1991).

Loan workouts

In a period of widespread overbuilding, sluggish leasing activity and other demand-side problems, many development projects are faced with a situation where schemes seem unlikely to service their debt charges upon completion. In these circumstances a lender may agree to what is known as a 'loan workout', which provides the developer with sufficient time and support to achieve a turn round in their project.

Essentially, a workout is the debt restructuring for a single project or many projects or properties normally requiring assiduous management, new money and additional collateral.

A developer should seek a workout as soon as a problem is identified and should try to persuade the lender to participate (not always an easy task). At a minimum, a financial workout will allow the developer to make the best of his current position. Ideally, it will enable him to satisfy his obligations while maintaining equity in the property. Thus, a workout provides better odds that the developer will emerge from the crisis with his business intact.

What a developer basically wants from a workout is: temporary relief from all or part of the required debt service payment; an extension of a maturing loan without large extra fees; minimal additional encumbrances on the property or further dissipation of equity; personal liability relief; debt reduction, or even forgiveness; minimization of potential tax consequences; and cooperation to sell existing holdings. The incentives to the lender are: a belief that with temporary concessions the problem can be solved; minimization of the risk of foreclosure; reduction or elimination of negative media attention; lessening of the impact on the lender's loan portfolio and income recognition; and the avoidance of protracted litigation. It has been stated that the keys to a successful loan workout are the development and implementation of a financial plan that addresses the maximization of return to creditors, and the long-term survival of the debtor as a going concern, together with the smooth interaction of various functions, including legal, accounting, information systems, asset marketing and management, and business operation. A workout can be a very sobering process to even the most sanguine of developers.

From the above, it can be appreciated that it is essential to establish the correct financial base for the project, and for the developer to balance their aims with the aspirations of the lending agency, whose risk/reward criteria will determine the scope for negotiation between the parties. It can, therefore, be suggested that three basic elements of funding have to be assessed in any scheme:

- Availability – in terms of knowing the range of possible sources of finance, methods of approaching them and their current position
- Economy – in respect of interest rates and how they might fluctuate, as well as equity participation, incentives and penalties, and any hidden costs of borrowing
- Practicality – which integrates the elements of availability and economy into a feasible arrangement that might otherwise detract from the viability of the project or invalidate it completely.

Financial adaptability on the part of the developer at a time when the investment character of property is changing is now a must.

The financial agreement

Inevitably, perhaps, the aims of the funder and the developer will often conflict. It is increasingly important, therefore, that the respective responsibilities for control during the development period are clearly apportioned and understood, and that the financial agreement is properly documented. Although a developer or project manager will doubtless have recourse to competent legal advice, the cut and thrust of negotiation is often such that certain matters may be misinterpreted or overlooked in the false hope that, once building has begun, the financial agreement will be forgotten or set aside. However, the opposite is more often the case, for it is at those moments of crisis during development that the parties are more likely to spring to the small print and come to realize the true consequences of their earlier bargaining. A better understanding of the objectives and procedures of financial control and documentation on the part of the developer will normally enable him to negotiate with greater confidence and to deploy his professional team more effectively.

The funder's objectives

In structuring the financial arrangement, the funder will aim to control certain aspects of the proposed scheme, including the:

- criteria by which tenants are selected and leasehold terms agreed
- negotiations conducted and agreements concluded with third parties
- entry by the developer into any special legal agreements with the local government, authority, and the consequent liability if the developer defaults
- nature and level of indemnity policies and collateral warranties held or offered by the developer, his professional team, the contractor and the subcontractors, so that in the event of failure the developer can be dismissed and the fund can assume full authority for the completion of development
- taxation implications of the project
- the purchase price of the completed project, so that unnecessary premiums and over-renting are avoided.

The developer's objectives

In contrast, the developer, whilst wishing to retain long-term goodwill with an interested fund, will seek to ensure that the terms ultimately accepted in the finance agreement provide:

- a smooth flow of funds
- speedy responses by the funder
- minimum interference by the funder's professional consultants
- smooth letting arrangements without undue constraint by the funder.

The 'offer' letter

One of the most important stages of the documentation relating to the finance of development arises well before the formal issue of arrangements. This is the initial 'offer letter' by the funding agency or its professional representatives. In effect, it will set out the basic terms of the deal and outline the intentions and expectations of the funder. Such a letter will have particular significance if the developer has to commit himself to the purchase of land prior to the full finance agreement being formalized. Any condition precedent in the correspondence must, therefore, be carefully appraised as to its implications.

There is no such thing as a standard offer letter, but the following list represents the more usual draft proposed heads of agreement:

- description of the parties concerned
- intention to purchase and basis of acquisition
- type and amount of loan
- rate of interest and method of repayment
- identification of site and ownerships
- description of the proposed development
- planning position and local authority interests
- estimate of construction costs
- prospective letting agreements
- initial yield and resultant purchase price
- staged payments of costs and fees
- sharing of surplus rental income
- rental guarantees by developer
- approval building contract
- insurances and warranties.

The contractual agreement

The financial agreement will put into final contractual form the exact degree of control over the scheme the funder will expect to have. It is important for the developer, therefore, to ensure that the conditions imposed are not so onerous as to prejudice the proper management of the project or jeopardize the profitability through no fault of their own.

Apart from confirming the contents of the original offer letter, renegotiated or otherwise, the financial agreement, which is made under seal, will normally start by defining all the terms, procedures, parties and dates involved in the transaction. Of special concern to the funder will be the terms and conditions relating to any actual or proposed building agreements, or agreements for a lease. If the developer defaults, or if some other specified event takes place, the funder will wish to protect its position in respect of the determination of those agreements. The three main remedies normally incorporated into the financial agreement are:

- The power for the funder to assign the benefits under the agreement to another developer
- The power by the funder to complete the development and sell the created investment without any continuing liability
- An agreement whereby if a third-party freeholder exercises their right to re-enter for any reason under another contract, then the funder receives a payment relating to the improved value of the property achieved by the works to date undertaken by the developer.

Practical problems

It is impossible to cover all the matters that may be included in a financial agreement, and ultimately it is up to the developer whether or not the various terms and conditions are acceptable. Nevertheless, there are issues that recur, and they merit close attention on the part of the developer. In no particular order, these are:

- Design documentation attached to the agreement should clearly set out the objectives of the scheme and, as a general rule, the more details provided by the developer the better, so that subsequently the funder's surveyor cannot alter the initial specification.
- A developer is well advised to attempt to restrict the number of outside consultants the funder may appoint to act on their behalf in relation to the project. A single firm of surveyors should suffice.
- The necessity to obtain written approval for the appointment of subcontractors should be avoided by agreeing a list of nominated subcontractors, although difficulties might arise in the case of a management contract involving many subcontracts, all of which may not initially be known.
- A clear understanding of the definition of the date of practical completion should be established and, wherever possible, the views and visits of the developer's architect and the fund's surveyor should be harmonized.
- The date on which capitalization and transfer of purchase price takes place should be explicit, and not dependent upon the actions of third parties.
- Access to the site by the funder's surveyors and facilities to inspect and test materials and workmanship should be kept within reasonable bounds. Notice of any defects should also be notified at the time of discovery.
- A procedure for arbitration should be agreed.
- It may be necessary for the developer to consider the inclusion of a 'walk-about' clause, so that he can approach other sources of finance if a top-up of funds over and above the funder's maximum commitment is required.
- There should be some mitigation in respect of those delays that push the completion date beyond the agreed date, especially where such delays are outside the control of the developer.

Little has been published in the professional press about funding agreements, although a specialist breed of solicitors have grown up who seem to be developing ever more complex documentation, usually for funding-clients. The aspiring developer, therefore, must be increasingly aware of the many pitfalls ahead.

Trends and prospects

This chapter concludes where it started, by stating that finance is a vital dimension of property development, and a principal concern of project management for the real estate industry.

- The globalization of property finance markets will continue.
- Developers and financiers alike will have to become even more aware of occupational demands by property users, and willing to accept greater innovation in the design, construction and management of commercial premises.
- Construction companies are already an attractive source of short-term development finance, not only providing interim funds but also acting as security for a long-term take-out, and entering into a fixed-price contract in return for an equal share of the eventual profit, and it is probable that the number of joint venture schemes between contractors and developers will grow or, indeed, that 'contractors' will increasingly become 'developers'.
- Specialized markets in high-risk development schemes will continue to develop, depending upon more sophisticated market research, superior management skills and the spreading of risk over a well-balanced mix of investments and among enterprising investors. Active risk management through various methods of syndication has been successful in America.
- Joint venture and partnership agreements between public and private sector agencies will gain in popularity, as public sector finances dwindle.
- The consortia approach towards investment in all forms of property development will become increasingly common – small private, as well as public, investors being grouped together to finance relatively small schemes, and large institutional investors collaborating in funding the major development projects.
- Refined funding techniques, which can reduce dependence upon cashflow in the early years after the completion of a development project, will be introduced on a wider scale than hitherto, as will funding schemes that allow for the future consolidation of debt charges into equity interest, such as convertible mortgages, which permit the translation of fixed interest loans into equity shares once an agreed rate of inflation is reached.
- Among new arrangements structured specifically to attract additional funds for property development will be ever more complex multi-layered agreements in which each tranche of investment funding is designed to meet the tax needs and positions of the various parties to the deal, so as to take maximum advantage of tax allowances and relief.
- A new funding ethic needs to be formulated towards the regeneration of older building stock in inner-city areas.

- Environmental aspects of property development will play a larger part in the appraisal equation, progressing from mere checking of potential environmental liabilities in due diligence activities to more sophisticated consideration of the future-proofing of assets.
- Higher standards of professionalism will be demanded at every level.
- Worldwide, there is likely to be a contagious reappraisal of the concept of value.

Over the last few years more innovative approaches have, again, started to appear in the UK property market. Debt and asset-backed securitization have become more common, the traditional long UK institutional lease has shrunk in length of term and, with the expansion of the serviced office sector, new rent arrangements have emerged. All was well and good until the credit crunch which began in the late summer of 2007. It will take some time for normality to return to lending markets.

The search is always on for liquid, tax-efficient funding vehicles. Changes in the US, much influenced by tax changes, state intervention and the growth of the REIT market may have in turn influenced the introduction of REITS in the UK in 2007/08. The impact of these on development finance will be interesting to see.

The changing UK environment and innovations in the US are calling into question conventional attitudes to low-risk property development opportunities. Times they are a-changing!

15 Marketing for development

The days of certain markets, easy lettings and malleable tenants have gone, and, for the foreseeable future they are unlikely to return. Property as a product has become more difficult to sell, and those responsible for selling it perforce required to bring a higher degree of professionalism to the market. Users' needs have to be more closely identified and more carefully matched with product design. As with other property services, the agency function to date has been performed against a background that has rested heavily upon the historic monopoly enjoyed by established firms and a traditionally constant attitude towards transactions in land and property by owners and occupiers. This is changing.

This chapter is organized as follows:

- The marketing role
- Marketing functions
- Market segmentation
- Selling techniques
- The developer's viewpoint.

The marketing role

A useful definition of marketing is one provided by the Institute of Marketing, which runs:

> Marketing is the management function which organizes and directs all those business activities involved in assessing and converting customer purchasing power into effective demand for a specific production or service to the final customer or user so as to achieve the profit target or other objective set by the company.

More simply perhaps, marketing is the skill of matching the needs of a buyer with the product of a seller, for a profit. It is probably true to say that development property used to be a soft-sell product. An estate agent would erect a board, place an advertisement and wait. Nowadays, however, those marketing property developments are faced increasingly with a highly competitive and discerning market, and one that demands better information and more active attention to the selling process.

The agency function

The appointment of an estate agent is the usual means by which the commercial sector of the property development industry disposes of completed projects, whereas in the residential sector most major developers perform their own agency functions with or without the help of agents. There has also been a slight tendency on the part of some developers and local authorities to undertake agency on their own behalf. Nevertheless, despite criticism over recent years about the quality of their work, it should nearly always be possible to gain a wider access to the market by retaining an agent. Depending upon the nature of the development and the circumstances prevailing in the market at the time, an agent might be called upon to perform some or all of the following tasks:

- Find suitable sites or properties for development, redevelopment or refurbishment on behalf of clients
- Receive instructions and liaise with the developer at an early stage in the project to consider the overall concept of the proposed scheme and, in particular, to advise on those features of design and layout that could add to or detract from the marketability of the completed property
- Provide general economic advice and investigate rental levels and capital values in respect of the viability of the project
- Comment on the planning implications and assist in discussions with local authority officers
- Advise on potential occupiers and tenant mix
- Advise on the possible need for special building and occupiers' services, as well as considering the general operation of future management services
- Advise regularly throughout the period of development on prevailing market conditions
- Advise, arrange and implement a marketing strategy
- Monitor responses and handle prospective occupiers' inquiries
- Conduct negotiations with interested parties and investigate the credentials of potential purchasers or tenants
- Advise on and assist with the provision of development finance
- Negotiate and conclude the final sales or lettings.

With regard to payment for the various activities described above, it is usual for an agent to negotiate a separate fee for professional services rendered in connection with acquisition, development appraisal, funding, development consultancy, project management, letting and management. An interesting change that has taken place over recent years in respect of offering estate agency services and attracting instructions, is the increasingly liberal attitudes taken by professional institutions towards advertising. RICS members, for example, are actually encouraged to give interviews to the press and media, and the rules are stated to be designed to give the profession 'maximum freedom in accordance with current thinking'. This has allowed commercial agents quite a broad scope in marketing their own services as well as their clients' property.

There are said to be certain fundamental prerequisites to effective agency, based on the adage 'if you have no information, you have no product to sell' (Development Systems Corporation 1983). More specifically, the necessary market intelligence can be broken down into the following areas:

- *Knowing the owners*. Thorough market knowledge involves knowing who owns the buildings and the land in the locality. Ideally, a good agent should generate ownership data on every potential development or redevelopment site, for sale or not for sale, within his bailiwick.
- *Knowing the tenants*. An able agent will gather as much information as possible on tenants, large and small, operating within the market area, particular attention being paid to existing major tenants or high potential tenants. Tenant intelligence should go beyond knowing names to knowing why a tenant is there. Why did a tenant sign a lease on one building and not on another? What is the critical location and site criterion for the tenant? Does the tenant rely heavily on street patterns, demographics, signage, and skilled labour?
- *Knowing the deals*. The astute agent will know about all important deals transacted in their territory. Such deals define the economic character of the market, determining the level and pattern of leasing and selling values. The information on current and recent deals is not always easy to uncover, being a matter of confidentiality between the parties involved, but a good relationship is imperative between fellow agents and existing or prospective tenants and purchasers.
- *Knowing the property*. Understanding the physical land and property inventory of an area is the cornerstone of an agent's practice. Knowledge of the types of property in a given area, the amount of each type, the special features of particular properties and the plans for new projects is essential.
- *Knowing the competition*. From the viewpoint of the agent, as well as the client developer, it is important that he is aware of who else is in the market, and what size share of that market they are likely to absorb. Besides market share, it is always wise to know how the competition is operating, its strengths, its weaknesses and its marketing strategies (Development Systems Corporation 1983).

Types of agency

There are four essential bases upon which an estate agent may be instructed to sell a development. These are:

- *Sole agency*. A sole agency arrangement is one in which a single firm is instructed to dispose of a property. Preferred by agents because, if they are successful in selling the development scheme, then they receive the full measure of commission. A normal fee would be 10 per cent of full annual rental value for a letting, and between 1.5 and 3 per cent of agreed price for a sale.

- *Joint agency.* Where two agents are instructed by a developer to collaborate in the letting or disposal of a property, a joint agency is established. This arrangement is most commonly used in the sale of provincial property where national and local coverage is required, or in a scheme of mixed development where specialist marketing of particular components is thought desirable. It is also adopted where a property is considered especially difficult to sell and an element of competition is felt advisable, or where one agent has introduced a development to a client on the understanding that they will at least share in the agency, but the developer requires the marketing skills of another firm. Although fees are negotiable, it is probable that the developer will have to pay up to around one and a half times the normal fee, divided by the two agents by agreement.

- *Sub-agency.* It is always open for an agent, unless instructed otherwise, to appoint another firm as sub-agent to assist in the marketing of a particular property. The main difference between sub-agency and joint agency is that the responsibility to the client rests with the principal firm in the former case and commissions tend to be higher in the latter.

- *Multiple agency.* When several agents are individually instructed to dispose of a property and commission is only payable to the agent who achieves the sale, a multiple agency is formed. Resort to such form of agency is not normally taken in the marketing of a development project, because it invariably leads to a confused marketing campaign, abortive costs and a suspicion on the part of potential purchasers that for some reason the property is difficult to sell.

As already mentioned, some development organizations sometimes opt to perform the agency function themselves. In such circumstances, an 'in-house' team will assume responsibility for the promotion and disposal of a scheme. However, it should be recognized that established firms of estate agents are bound to be more informed about, and have wider access to, both property and business requirements and opportunities. Only very rarely does it benefit an individual developer to market a project entirely on their own.

The role of the provincial agent has also taken on a greater importance over the past few years in the field of development. Although the major national firms of estate agents based in London can offer unrivalled services in respect of the potential national and international occupancy market, and can also supply certain specialized support services such as research, planning and funding, local firms situated in major regional centres also supply invaluable expertise. The provincial agent tends to have a deeper knowledge of local markets, better information regarding the availability of suitable sites, a heightened awareness of the true state of prevailing planning policy and practice, and a favoured insight into the performance and intentions of local businesses and landowners. Furthermore, they will often have a superior understanding of local values and returns, being privileged with the precise details underlying local sales conducted by private treaty. At the letting stage they will also benefit from the accumulated experience of enquiries received across a whole range of properties over time, giving them a good idea of the vagaries of the market. Their ready availability to react to enquiries and respond informatively to questions regarding local services and conditions is an obvious advantage.

Rules and responsibilities

The year 1991 to 1992 proved something of a watershed for estate agency practice. After a decade or more of threats and promises the profession witnessed the introduction of The Estate Agents (Undesirable Practices) Order 1991, The Estate Agents (Provision of Information) Regulations 1991, both introduced under powers conferred by the Estate Agents Act 1979, and the Property Misdescriptions Act 1991.

The procedures dictated by the first two statutory instruments are wide-ranging. But in so far as they touch on agents dealing with clients, they essentially fall into two areas – the course of action to take as soon as a client–agent association begins, and the conduct required as that relationship progresses. The regulations, for example, are explicit about the information that must be furnished to the client and, importantly, the moment at which those details must be provided. A client–agent agreement must be established 'before the client is committed to any liability towards the estate agent'. An agreement will cover all aspects of agency – the length of instruction, fees and when they become payable, marketing budgets, circumstances in which other payments are due and definitions of 'sole agency', 'joint sole agency' and the like. Few problems, hopefully, face the experienced developer and worthy agent.

The Property Misdescriptions Act 1991, which became operable from April 1993, presents estate agents, and developers who market their properties directly, with a new form of criminal liability for misstatements. The kernel of the Act lies in Section 1(1) which provides:

> Where a false or misleading statement about a prescribed matter is made in the course of an estate agency business or a property development business, otherwise than in providing conveyancing services, the person by whom the business is carried on shall be guilty of an offence under this section.

As one leading authority in the field explains, agents and developers now face a criminal offence of strict liability (i.e. one in which the prosecution need prove neither intent to deceive nor even negligence), subject only to the possibility of avoiding conviction where the defendant can prove that all reasonable steps and due diligence have been taken (Murdoch 1993). Nevertheless, the Act does not require any particular information to be given about property that is being marketed. What it does require is that any information given should be accurate, or at least not false or misleading. The detailed degree of care that must be taken over such marketing tools as photographs, models, artists' impressions or demonstration units is clear following some legal decisions, such as in *Lewin* v. *Barratt Homes Ltd* (2000) (EGLR 77) where discrepancies between photographs of houses and show homes and purchased houses led to the conviction of the developer. Considerable caution thus needs to be exercised with sales aids of this kind and regular updating undertaken. The measurement of floor areas and rooms, whether relating to commercial or residential properties, requires particular care, and resort will inevitably be made to the ubiquitous caveat 'approximately'. With regard to disclaimers, however, the Department of Trade and Industry advises that they must be applied in as bold, precise and compelling a way as the statement to which they relate. Again, developers and agents of good standing will have nothing to fear from the legislation, but the more responsible representatives of the property industry for some years called for the implementation of Section 22 of the 1979 Estate Agents Act laying down minimum standards of competence and experience, with many preferring a full system of licensing or registration. The Consumers, Estate Agents and Redress Act 2007 updated the 1979 Act after an Office of Fair Trading report suggested that agents' clients needed a formal system of redress in the event of dispute. The principal elements of the act affecting agents are those which ensure that the OFT has the ability to investigate agents' files in particular cases and their fitness to practise generally.

Above all else, successful marketing in the property world depends upon confidence and credibility. It is distressing to record the lasting gratitude that both journalists and politicians afford to estate agents for keeping them from occupying the lowest position in repeated professional popularity polls. Nevertheless, in the commercial real estate marketing field, the winning and retaining of trust and confidence by client organizations, whether vendors or purchasers, is critical.

Marketing functions

Current pressures on estate agents to let or sell their clients' buildings is leading to a much higher degree of sophistication in the way development properties are marketed. In addition, as more and more commercial floor-space comes on stream and disposal becomes ever harder to effect, so the realization that getting the product right in the first place grows even stronger. Consequently, however faddish it might seem, the property world must gain a better understanding of the procedures and functions of marketing, and at the same time learn from the array of marketing principles and practices that have been developed in other sales markets. In stating this, however, it should be appreciated that the marketing of planned new developments ahead of construction breaks many basic marketing rules, in that a potential customer cannot test and experience the qualities of a product prior to purchase. The reputation of the developer and the climate of goodwill created between those involved in a potential sale or letting becomes a crucial factor in the marketing campaign.

Marketing tools

A useful classification of the four key tools of the marketing man has been provided as follows:

- *Market research and information.* It is suggested that for the purpose of the estates profession these two functions should be distinguished, because the term 'research' is used by most major firms of estate agents simply to describe the collection of largely retrospective statistics that show trends and can be used for producing forecasts, whereas market research in the true sense is described as an 'action-oriented procedure' aimed at informing the developer of a marketing or advertising plan.
- *Advertising.* This is the process of spreading information by preparing and placing paid-for material such as space in newspapers and journals or time in the broadcasting media. Advertisements are always identifiable with their sponsor or originator, which is not always the case with other forms of promotion or publicity.
- *Promotion.* Covers those marketing activities, other than personal selling, advertising and publicity, that stimulate consumers' purchasing and agents' effectiveness, such as displays, shows, exhibitions, and various non-recurrent selling efforts not in the ordinary routine.
- *Public relations.* The role of public relations is to establish and maintain understanding and goodwill for the development organization's product and services, activities and operating policies. In this, it is not only concerned with communicating for marketing purposes, but also for the broader purpose of creating a favourable atmosphere within which the organization may operate successfully.

Marketing research

The whole process of development essentially starts with market research, the goal of which is to project the rate of absorption for a particular property product based on the supply and demand for similar properties in a specified market area. Conducted at the outset of the development process, the developer seeks to identify an unfulfilled market need that might feasibly be met on a specific site. If the signs are promising, a formal market study might be commissioned and a marketing plan of campaign prepared.

The starting point of any marketing plan of campaign is the identification of the target groups of possible purchasers. Research is, therefore, essential, and it is really only in recent years that some of the leading firms of estate agents and a few of the major property development companies have committed themselves to the serious analysis of the markets in which they operate and consideration of the buildings they produce and sell.

It must be said, however, that certain pieces of published research are in fact just so much 'window dressing'. The compilation of crude vacancy rates for particular sectors, for example, says very little about market performance or prospects except at the most superficial level. Broad indications of rental value across wide geographical areas might be useful promotional material for the firms concerned, but cannot be held to contribute greatly to a better understanding of the property market. Effective marketing increasingly will depend upon more rigorous research into the underlying conditions and determinants of demand and supply in the property market.

In practice, marketing research is usually concentrated on a few recurrent problems, often on a continuous basis, which may be grouped as follows:

Up-to-date market knowledge

- The size of the regional and local markets for particular kinds of property, normally measured in floorspace for commercial sectors and dwelling units or habitable rooms for housing.
- Past patterns of demand and underlying economic, social, political, legal and technological factors that are likely to affect future levels of demand, together with an indication of the timescale involved and any cyclical variations.
- Buying or renting habits of consumers, along with an appraisal of the possible changes in attitude and behaviour by both customers and funding institutions that might take place.
- Actual and potential market share commanded by the development organization, and a breakdown of the market shares of major competitors.
- General appreciation of past and possible future trends in broad socio-economic terms covering such matters as population change, national income and expenditure, sales and output, availability of finance, construction industry performance and legislative or political change.

Overall policy and tactics

- An examination of competitive pricing structures and practices, looking at where, how and at what cost competitors promote and advertise their properties.
- A consideration of how marketing costs compare with other costs and with competitive costs, and what effect any change or differential in policy would make.
- An assessment of how sales and lettings differ by dint of location or type of use, and why.
- An evaluation of the probable effects of any radical change in the pricing structure of the developer's or competitors' property.
- An appraisal of the effect of promotional activity, looking at the effectiveness of advertising copy and placement and the result of incentive schemes to both agents and purchasers.

The product

- What is the company reputation or image for producing quality buildings and providing a good service to purchasers?
- How are previous developments thought of and used, and what features are found to be most important by occupiers?
- Should any changes be made to current or proposed development projects in respect of design, layout, materials or services?
- What property management, legal or planning restrictions might inhibit the ready sales or letting of a development?
- What are the strengths and weaknesses of previous development schemes constructed by the company and its competitors?

Primary and secondary data

- The data collection phase of marketing research draws on two main sources of information, which are distinguished as primary and secondary sources, or alternatively field and desk research.
- Secondary sources are those that already exist, but consist of data collected for purposes peripheral to the main line of research inquiry in hand, so care must be taken to ensure that the information is relevant, can be adjusted to the present problem and is reliable.
- There are internal and external secondary sources. Internally, agents and developers will have a mass of marketing information available from their own records, and although it is not always collected systematically or in the most appropriate form, modern computerized data-processing systems are making the access to and extrapolation of suitable information easier and faster. Externally, there is a growing wealth of published information from other agents, consultants, professional bodies, trade associations, research organizations and government departments. Secondary sources should be consulted before primary or original research is undertaken.
- Primary or field research will usually cover the potential market demand, occupiers' preferences, the precise characteristics of the actual or proposed development, the terms of sale or letting, and the methods of advertising. Original data of this sort may be collected by observation, experimentation or survey. Observation depends heavily upon the skill and objectivity of the observer. Experimentation is rarely appropriate to the property market. And survey can be time-consuming and expensive.

Marketing research process

Although research projects in the property development market are not susceptible to a single and inflexible sequence of steps, the following procedure is a useful guide (Giles 1978):

- Definition of the problems, a step of the greatest importance, and one treated in a cursory way too often.

- Specification of the information required.
- Design of the research project, taking into account the means of obtaining the information, the availability and skills of staff, the methods to be used and the time and cost involved.
- Construction and testing of any surveys, questionnaires or interviews.
- Execution of the project, with arrangements for a check on the reliability of data collected.
- Analysis of data.
- Preparation of report and formulation of recommendations.

However, it should be recognized that marketing research neither provides a panacea nor guarantees success, but it does assist in improving the quality and confidence of decision-making.

Marketing strategy

Over the past few years there has been a significant shift towards the devising of more formally structured and deeply considered marketing plans for proposed development projects. The advantages of a more rigorous planning process are that diverse marketing activities can be better coordinated, crisis management can either be avoided or reduced to a minimum, measurements of performance are easier to conduct against known standards, corrective measures can be applied in sufficient time when required, and participation by all those involved can be encouraged with improved commitment and motivation (Giles 1978).

It has been stated that a marketing plan for property should be much the same as for any other kind of product, in that it needs to:

> strive to create the tangible from the intangible and present a concept that will stimulate the imagination of the potential client. . . . This simple need becomes more and more difficult to achieve as the weight of communication channels and the material sent to them increases each year.
>
> (Watts 1982)

Accepting that the alliteration is a gross over-simplification, a favourite way of remembering the key variables that form the basis of marketing strategy and mix is known as 'the four Ps' – product, price, place, promotion. A preferred means of describing the most important steps in preparing a marketing plan to take account of the key variables involved in marketing operations can be more fully stated as follows.

Select the right team

In identifying, anticipating and satisfying customer requirements, to maximize profitability – the very nub of marketing – it is essential that all those involved in the entire process of development, from inception to completion and through to management afterwards, are selected with a view to optimizing the collective effort of the professional team. The chemistry between those directly concerned with design and construction and those specifically responsible for the actual marketing campaign must be right. It is not productive, for example, to have an architect who is either oblivious or unsympathetic to the advice of the agent, or to have an agent who is uncomprehending or hostile to those designing and building the project. In the past, the formulation of a marketing strategy has all too often been left to the agent acting alone, and invariably too late in the development process.

Identify the target groups

Properly conducted marketing research as outlined in previous sections should have identified the general categories of occupier that might be interested in the scheme in question, and hopefully the actual manufacturing, trading or business organizations who are either actively looking for new or additional accommodation or who might conceivably be enticed into taking or moving premises. Often the most difficult task is to identify and reach the person within the organization responsible for taking the decision.

Agree the message strategy

This involves deciding on how best to present the special sales characteristics of the building, its situation and wider environs. In the rather 'whiz-word' riddled world of marketing, this is known as creating the 'unique selling proposition' (USP) , and is concerned with striving to convey a concept that will stimulate the imagination of the potential occupier or purchaser. The overriding aim in designing general and specific USPs should be to see the whole strategy in terms of how it might benefit the eventual client. This might seem a trifle obvious, but somehow agency practice in the UK has been extremely slow in breaking away from a fairly standard and somewhat impersonal property-oriented approach towards a more original and individually directed user-based approach.

Write a communication plan

Having established the broad 'message' about the property that needs to be conveyed, the next step is to plan how best it is communicated. Any communications plan will usually combine a variety of direct and indirect selling techniques, called the 'marketing mix', all of which require careful orchestration. Direct methods such as the use of brochure, personalized mail shots, targeted circulation lists, exhibitions and agents' receptions will need to be synchronized with indirect methods involving national and local media, side advertising and contact networks within the property industry. Again, these techniques may seem patent and familiar, but the early and coordinated planning is often missing. There is also a positive wealth of face-to-face selling expertise accumulated in other fields of marketing that has lain largely untapped by the property profession, and might with advantage be explored and exploited.

Ensure follow-up activity

There are two distinct aspects to following through on the communication plan. First, there are those endeavours that have to be made to stimulate only very mild expressions of interest. And second, there are those efforts to make in converting strong interest into an actual sale and subsequently keep the purchaser content. With the former, an agent marketing a development should be aware that there are several kinds of barriers that may block their ability to communicate and must be overcome, or at least lowered. These are: personal barriers, arising from the fact that individuals differ, and that different people have to be approached in different ways: organizational barriers, thrown up by administrative structures and hierarchies, so that finding the right person and presenting the case in a corporately acceptable manner becomes even more vital; and mechanical barriers, which exist because some organizations lack the proper points of contact and channels of communication. When translating a positive response into a trouble-free transaction, it should simply be a matter of competence and professionalism, keeping the customer informed about progress and handling all inquiries and negotiations promptly, efficiently and pleasantly.

Agree a budget

Ascertaining an accurate figure for the total cost of marketing for development is an extremely difficult task. In the first place, however, there is need for a plan in order to determine a budget. From this plan can be extracted the various marketing activities that are proposed. It has been suggested that the following process be adopted (Miles *et al.* 1991):

- A plan is formulated to promote the product to the target market by the developers and their agents as early as possible in the development process.
- The plan typically begins with a description of the product and the target market, based on earlier market research, including statements about how the product will be attractive to the target market and how those responsible for marketing will reach that market.
- As more detail emerges, an extensive checklist of possible activities within each category of the marketing plan is prepared, excluding no reasonable ideas.
- A realistic cost estimate for each marketing activity on the checklist is compiled, sparing no expense at this stage.
- The initial total cost estimate is then scrutinized and pared down by examining closely and squeezing tightly every item. Each activity must justify itself, deleting rigorously those that do not, so that, although the net is cast widely, only the best of what is caught is kept.

- Some of the items in this process might be one-time investments, such as fitting out a show unit, and might last the life of the marketing campaign, whereas others, such as brochures, might have to be replaced periodically. Still others will recur continually, such as media charges, which could keep mounting as the campaign intensifies.
- The grand total is estimated, having predicted how long a presence is required in the market and taking account of likely absorption rates.

Another approach, which can be used as a check on the above, is to pose the question of how many new contacts will have to be made and cultivated in order to generate sufficient positive responses to achieve the predicted absorption rate. The cost of making these contacts can then be gauged. Commercial property marketing relies heavily on this 'prospecting' approach, whereas residential sales rely more upon general advertising (Miles *et al.* 1991).

Yet a further budgeting procedure has been described, termed the 'task method' and based upon a four-stage process:

- Market (What is it? Where is it?)
- Message (for that market)
- Media (most effect and most direct)
- Measurement (cost-effectiveness and results)

(Cleavely 1984)

This task method requires objectives to be set as part of the marketing strategy, which can be monitored and plans adjusted according to the degree of success achieved.

In practice, however, it has to be stated that marketing budgets for property development proposals are generally based upon the experience and judgement of the developer and marketing consultants involved. Moreover, it is important that a high degree of flexibility is afforded to allow for the unexpected in the market.

Methods of selling

An agent's prime objective is to sell or let property for the highest price or rent available in the market, not to pursue his own subjective assessment of value. To achieve this, the property must be freely exposed to the market in an orderly manner. The most appropriate method of selling a particular property largely depends upon the nature of the premises concerned and the prevailing market conditions. Four basic methods of property disposal can be distinguished.

Private treaty

Straightaway, it should be stated that the vast majority of all sales and lettings in the overall property market are normally conducted by private treaty. There have been periods when extreme conditions in the market have encouraged such practices as rental tendering, and formal and informal tenders and public auctions are always popular for certain sectors of the market. It has also been known for various kinds of informal tender to be used in order to resolve difficult and competing negotiations, but such recourse is rare. Private treaty is, therefore, the most prevalent method of selling property across all sectors of the development market. It simply involves the setting of an asking price or rent and negotiating to achieve it. As floorspace in most conventional development schemes, either proposed or completed, is bought and sold between property professionals, the basis of assessing a reasonable level of capital or rental value is likely to be very broadly the same. Therefore, so long as the developer and his agent have set the asking price properly, not so high as to stifle offers and not so low as to cause embarrassment and bad feeling by continued negotiation well above that opening price, all should be well. However, there are two main exceptions in the development world where sale by private treaty is not normally the best means of disposal – first, with the sale of land or buildings possessing development potential, but prior to development taking place, where offers will be determined by many variable and unpredictable factors and, second, where the market is especially uncertain or volatile. One renowned residential development on the riverside in London was quickly taken off the market when, much to everyone's surprise, offers massively exceeded the asking prices.

Public auction

In theory, this method should ensure an orderly market because, if the property has been properly advertised, it should attract everyone with a serious interest and force them to reach a decision in a competitive atmosphere and with no opportunity to withdraw. The preparation of particulars is critically important with this method of sale, for they must be detailed and accurate, yet enticing. The overwhelming drawback in selling agreed or completed developments at auction is that the major financial institutions are rarely interested in buying at auction. Moreover, they are normally unwilling to provide a firm commitment to a developer wishing to buy potential development properties at auction, unless perhaps the value of the site or the existing buildings is less than, say, £1 million, and only then if most of the uncertainties about the proposed scheme, particularly in respect of planning permission, have already been resolved.

Formal tender

The formal tender, whereby prospective purchasers are invited to submit sealed bids on or by a particular date, is similar to the auction in that all the bids constitute contractual offers that, if accepted, are binding. As with the auction, it is essential to reduce uncertainties to a minimum, and preferably to obtain planning consent beforehand. This not only takes time, but however assiduous the vendor and his agent, there can be no guarantee that the consent obtained is the most valuable possible, and prospective purchasers will bid for what has been approved and not what they think they get. The great advantage of the formal tender is that the highest possible bid for the property should be attracted, whereas at auction even an especially keen or special purchaser only has to exceed the second highest offer. As has been stated:

> Formal tenders are particularly attractive for undeveloped land where the planning situation is quite straightforward. Most housebuilders have adequate finance and are well geared up to acquire residential building land at tender, but bidders for industrial and commercial sites normally require funding from institutions and, quite reasonably, institutions are reluctant to enter into funding commitments until the site is secure.
>
> (Armon-Jones 1984)

Informal tenders

The informal tender method involves the selling agent inviting single and highest bids, subject to contract, from prospective purchasers attracted by an initial marketing campaign. Because there is an interval between the acceptance of an offer and exchange of contracts, the method is said to be vulnerable to the successful bidder trying to renegotiate the offer once other tenders have been disappointed and possibly withdrawn. Nevertheless, it is argued that in spite of this weakness the informal tender is often the best form of sale for the disposal of development sites. So long as the procedures are clearly established and abided by, full and consistent information given to all potential purchasers, confidentiality maintained between the parties regarding the various schemes proposed prior to tender, satisfactory financial assurances obtained and a package of relevant legal documents circulated to all serious bidders shortly before the closing date, most of the problems can be reduced or eliminated (Armon-Jones 1984). However, the method does depend upon a high degree of trust and respect on both sides.

Market segmentation

It should almost go without saying that the property market is highly diverse. Not only does this apply to the rich variety of occupational markets it seeks to supply, but also to the varying requirements within those markets, the different sales techniques appropriate to different sectors, the inconsistent attitude of differing client bodies and the divergent approaches towards marketing adopted by individual estate agency practices. A brief mention of some of the most notable characteristics of the main sectors of the market, therefore, is appropriate.

Shops

In the context of property development, the marketing of shops normally involves the letting of retail space to tenants and often the sale of the entire scheme to a funding institution. Thus, when an agent is selling shops, he is selling to:

- the investing institutions
- the retail industry
- the shopping public.

Inevitably, any financial institution contemplating the funding of a shopping development will want to be assured about the quality of income and the prospects of rental growth in the future. In large planned shopping centres, it will be necessary to show the actual or probable pre-letting of the major anchor units to one of the leading larger national multiples such as Tesco, Boots or Gap. Smaller schemes would need to be presented to an institution, with commensurate letting agreements involving national multiples and regional superstore chains. A clear indication of the likely overall market penetration for the scheme based upon an assessment of the population catchment area, the accessibility to the development and the existing and possible future competition for trade would have to be shown. And a fund would also be interested in the proposed tenant mix, the leasing structure and the proposals for continuing management services. Pre-letting of a significant proportion of space is often a prerequisite.

In marketing shop premises to retailers, regard should obviously be paid to the general design and layout of the scheme, with special emphasis upon such considerations as access, pedestrian flow, transport and parking facilities, and individual traders' market share. They will also want to know who else might be taking space in the scheme, so that they can evaluate the attraction factor of any anchor tenants and assess the probable degrees of competition and complementarity generated by surrounding units. Naturally, an acceptable level of rent and a lease without excessively onerous conditions will carry most weight in persuading a retailer to take space in a scheme. In addition, they will wish to be convinced by the developer's commitment and ability to promote and market the entire development so as to enhance public awareness of it and to provide reliable and effective management to it.

As far as the public are concerned, a shopping development must show itself to be conveniently accessible, offer a wide range and alternative choice of goods and services, and provide or be close to car parking if possible. With larger planned shopping centres it is also important to create a pleasant atmosphere, make available certain facilities such as restaurants and toilets, and increasingly guarantee a safe, clean and secure environment. It also helps if all or most of the space can be let before opening, and vacant units avoided, or at least attractively maintained.

Offices

In the present competitive climate it is becoming ever more incumbent upon the estate agency profession to possess a thoroughgoing knowledge and understanding of office users' requirements. Both in terms of crude locational space requirements and the required level of functional performance. An agent seeking to market an office development will, therefore, seek to ascertain if he can identify firms within international, national, regional or local markets who:

- might find advantages from 'hiving-off' certain activities or departments to a new location
- would benefit from consolidating already dispersed operations under a single roof or by bringing them in closer proximity to one another
- could effect substantial savings by moving their entire operation to a new location or new building
- are contemplating expansion
- have already made a decision to search for new or additional premises.

These days, it is essential for an agent marketing an office property to know in a fair amount of detail its relative suitability in respect of different kinds of business operation, including such factors as: face-to-face contact within and outside an organization; technological communication, like facilities for satellite, telephone, facsimile, intranet and Internet connectivity; internal environment, including temperature range and control, natural light and outside views and type and quality of working space; and corporate image, covering such matters as aspect, setting, entrances, reception area, services and other facilities. A prospective occupier will then primarily be interested in cost. Increasingly, office accommodation is considered by commercial organizations in relation to its 'all-in cost'. An agent must, therefore, be prepared to quote figures for rates, service charges, cleaning, security, heating, lighting, insurance and other maintenance and repair obligations, in addition to rent.

Industrial property

In addition to many of the considerations described above in respect of the shop and office sectors relating to questions of rent, lease conditions, design, layout and management, there are a few aspects of industrial property marketing that merit special mention. Generally, a potential occupier of industrial premises is more concerned about the performance factors of a building, such as quality of construction, eaves-heights, floor loadings, column spacing, loading and delivery facilities, and access and egress to and from the site and building.

Location is of course paramount, and an agent must have an intimate knowledge of the special labour, market, materials and component needs in terms of accessibility that are demanded by different trades and industries. In the same way, an understanding of the distributional hinterlands and networks commanded by various commodity markets is essential in the sale or letting of warehouse developments.

As with other forms of commercial property development, flexibility is a keynote of successful letting. The particular problem encountered in the industrial sector, however, is that flexibility not only applies to the ease with which it is possible to effect physical or functional changes within a building, but also to the freedom allowed an occupier to change the proportion of space given over to a particular use. This is often a matter of planning consent, and too constrained a permission can inhibit the marketability of a scheme. It must be recognized, in addition, that pre-lets are harder to achieve in the industrial sector.

Two other factors are beginning to characterize successful industrial sales and lettings. First, environmental quality both inside and outside factory premises is becoming more important to prospective occupiers. And, second, the availability of certain specialist services, whether on an industrial estate, or in close proximity to a particular development, plays a significant part in the decisions taken by industrial space users.

Residential property

At the outset it should be appreciated that residential development of any scale differs in one major respect from commercial property development in that almost all volume housebuilders tend to employ their own sales teams, and have recourse to estate agents as a second line of support, if at all. Because of this, advertising assumes an even more important role in the marketing of housing estates, for there is no network of agents as with the commercial sector, and not the same degree of high street representation as with the second-hand house market.

Prior to development, whoever is responsible for marketing, having established the basic demand for accommodation in the locality, the suitability of the locality, the amenities of the area and the extent of likely competition, is well advised to study former residential sales records in an attempt to find out why any cancellations took place. Non-buying attitudes are critical in the residential sector. Advertising studies, conversely, can show what features and what kind of presentation is most effective in generating interest in a particular development.

The usual method of marketing employed nowadays by the major housebuilders is to fit out and furnish one of the completed properties in a scheme as a show house. This will then be staffed up to six-and-a-half or even seven days a week, remembering that the majority of sales are introduced over the weekend. The advantage to the housebuilder is that the rest of the development can be monitored by their own agent, any damage can be made good immediately, access and response to inquirers is almost instant, all the energies of the sales force can be devoted to the one scheme and, in the case of phased development projects, information on reactions and probable market trends can be fed back to the design team. With show houses, it is always worthwhile laying out the garden to a high standard and making sure that the water and heating systems work efficiently.

In the residential sector, the role of aggressive promotion and marketing is probably most telling at either end of the market. Luxury housing is a volatile and predictable product. Well targeted, skilfully presented and extensively placed advertising can reap enormous dividends, for it is really a matter of reaching and attracting individual purchasers to whom marginal amounts of money at or around the asking price are of little consequence once they have decided that they want the house or flat in question. High-quality design and finishes, combined with an elegantly furnished and fitted show unit, are also an essential ingredient in successful luxury developments.

At the other end of the market, competition rages to attract the first-time buyer. A key element of marketing strategy for the first-time buyer of housing is the availability of mortgages. Virtually all the major housebuilders have agreements with one or more of the main building societies, giving ready access for potential purchasers to mortgage finance. These block allocations are a particularly valuable marketing tool when high demand causes mortgage queues and lending restrictions make it especially hard for first-time buyers. Other inducements offered as part of a marketing package often include one or more of the following:

- Payment by the developer of legal fees, survey fees and stamp duty
- Payment of a mortgage protection policy for, say, two to three years to ease the burden of worry; this has been extended by at least one volume housebuilder to the taking out, on behalf of the purchaser, of a personal protection policy against possible redundancy
- Provision of items of household furniture and equipment such as cooker, washing machine, refrigerator, fully fitted units and carpets; in some small starter units this can even reach to chairs, tables and beds
- Removal expenses
- Subsidized mortgage repayments for up to one year
- Repurchase at guaranteed levels of value
- Purchase of buyer's existing property
- Payment of the mortgage deposit.

All these concessions both help the developer's cashflow and give momentum to the sales drive. In a mixed development, moreover, the early sale of the smaller units may prove a useful catalyst in stimulating interest in the remainder of higher-priced units in the scheme.

Selling techniques

It has been stated that there are no new methods of marketing property; all that exists are refinements of long-established techniques (Butler 1982). As with any business venture, management skills count every bit as much as the product, perhaps even more so with the marketing of property developments, for given similar buildings, in roughly the same location and identical promotion budgets, apart from the unexplained foibles of the market, it can only be the personal qualities of those managing the marketing campaign that make the difference. Nevertheless, a basic understanding of the techniques brought to bear by estate agents in selling floorspace is an essential part of the overall management of development projects.

Public relations

Public relations is a form of untargeted promotion aimed at the public at large. The best generator of good public relations is ultimately the quality of the development itself. Nevertheless, it is important to recognize that property development is rarely a popular activity to those in proximity of a proposed project. They often view development schemes as being physically intrusive, socially damaging and a threat to property values. Therefore, the sensitivity with which property development proposals are handled can greatly affect the acceptability and hence the feasibility of a project.

The very way in which the developers present themselves, the company and the retained consultants to the political representatives, professional officers, the press, interested parties and the general public can all contribute to fostering a favourable impression. Supplying full information and readily responding to criticism in a sympathetic and constructive manner further assists in creating an open and positive climate of opinion. Some developers establish an information office on the site or near the project, hold exhibitions, make presentations, conduct their own consultation exercises and produce a regular newsletter regarding project progress. In fact, every aspect of the selling process described below should be seen as part of a broad public relations campaign aimed at merchandising the development group.

Brochures and particulars

Naturally, both brochures and more simplified forms of property particulars must describe the intended or completed development and convey all the details that a potential occupier might require. Normally this will include some or all of the following:

- A geographical description of the general area, which identifies the precise location of the site or building
- Communications facilities such as road, rail, air and water transport to and around the scheme
- For some kinds of development, a brief social and economic profile of the area is advisable, covering such matters as shopping, housing, education and recreational facilities, as well as the presence in the vicinity of leading commercial organizations
- Property particulars describing the accommodation, giving areas, heights and specification
- A description of the services supplied to the building, such as gas, water, cabling and electricity
- The nature of the interest being marketed, together with a broad explanation of the lease terms and a declaration about the existence of any restrictions to tenure
- An indication of the price or rent being sought

- Who to contact, how and where for more information, assistance or appointment to view
- A saving clause to protect the agent and developer, which might be along the following lines:

> The agents, for themselves and for the vendors or lessors of this property whose agents they are, give notice that plans and drawings are for identification purposes only and do not form part of any contract. Measurements and areas are approximate and although believed to be accurate, an intending lessee or purchaser must satisfy himself as to their accuracy. No responsibility is taken for any error, omission or misstatement in this brochure which does not constitute or form any part of an offer or contract. No representation or warranty whatever is made or given in this brochure or during any negotiations consequent thereon.

Vogues and styles in brochures have changed over the years, from the crude letting brochures of the 1960s, through to some of the extravagant productions of the 1970s and 1980s, to the full colour, expertly designed and professionally laid-out publications of today – sometimes supplemented by DVDs. Nevertheless, the brochure is likely to remain an important marketing aid, and great care is now given to the presentation of information, so that prospective purchasers or tenants can assimilate the relevant facts quickly. There has also been an increasing emphasis over recent years on the use of good graphic designers, artists' impressions for new development, and computer-generated images.

As with direct mailing (discussed below) it is vital that the brochure falls into the right hands. It may be necessary to produce more than one brochure during the course of marketing a development scheme. It also pays to attach a reply-paid card simply requiring interested parties to tick a box if they would like to receive further details.

Press advertising

Press advertising is obviously arranged at reaching the potential occupier or his professional advisers. They will, however, usually have different reading habits. The property professional is fairly predictable, and weekly scrutiny of the *Estates Gazette* and *Property Week* is something of a time-honoured ritual for the commercial agent. The potential occupier is more difficult to divine, and the agent must attempt to gauge which professions, businesses or trades might be interested in a particular property or unit. Thus, if the space is clearly located and signed to be attractive to architects, then an advertisement in the *RIBA Journal* or in *Building* might evoke a positive response. Similarly, for computing firms, *Computing* or *IT Today* would be appropriate publications and, for advertising agencies, *Campaign* or *Marketing Week*. National press coverage may also catch the attention of the managing director or decision-taker, and do so in a captive situation or reflective mood, as might more specialist publications such as airline club magazines. Again, agents often prefer to design their press advertising to facilitate a direct response by incorporating a reply form to be filled out and returned.

Commonly, agents have recourse to specialist advertising agencies, although some of the very largest firms have established their own in-house advertising departments. A director of one of the country's leading advertising agencies has commented on the best and worst of the output of property advertising copy where internally or externally prepared (Stewart Hunter 1983). The better advertisements were said to: stand out from the crowd and break through the 'noise' of competing claims on the readers' attention; be characterized by beautiful photography or illustration; have striking or unexpected headlines; and feature the building attractively or, in advertising language, make the product the 'hero' of the advertisement. The worst press advertisements were characterized, almost by definition, by having nothing striking about them, and likely to put off readers by virtue of the clutter, poorly laid out detail and unimaginative headlines and illustrations. Generally, moreover, property advertising was criticized as featuring the identity of the agents too prominently and yet also lacking a consistency in establishing a corporate identity.

It is generally recognized that the market has become increasingly sophisticated and developers far more aware of the power of the advertisement, in particular that potential tenants and targeted agents are different markets requiring different techniques. Some further comments by leading advertising agencies make telling, and sometimes contradictory, points about the advertising culture:

- Good design and clever ideas are not enough to sell a product – you've got to understand what is important to the audience.
- The biggest mistake is to go for too complex an image. It needs to be simple to survive what is a very noisy environment.
- You must not be afraid to be bold. The property press has been flooded with run-of-the-mill building adverts with square footages, agents' logos and piles of shopping bags. Your advert has got to be different.
- Any advertisement should be jazzy to look at, but it should be full of information.
- Humour has proved a particularly rich source of inspiration for corporate communication via advertising.
- A good picture highlights both the building itself and its chief asset, its location.
- Because we are always overestimating the importance of product, accepting that the product can take second place to concept allows us to talk about something other than the air-conditioning or lighting.

(Hall 1993)

One of the frustrations facing the advertising industry, however, is that the relative success of different approaches is difficult to quantify and largely remains a matter of speculation.

Alongside press advertising is editorial coverage. It often pays to keep journalists informed of market developments, especially for major or unusual schemes. This is best done in the form of a press release accompanied by a good photograph with a caption and forwarded personally to the appropriate journalist.

Direct mailing

The use of carefully targeted mail shots has become an extremely popular form of marketing communication. The main advantages are that: it enables direct contact to be made with individuals in the target occupational group; it is highly selective and it avoids unnecessary circulation; it does not compete at the same time with other advertising messages; it is flexible in terms of geographical area, frequency and design; and it is relatively quick and cheap to produce and distribute.

Mail shots are normally used to support a wider marketing campaign, and should be released to coincide with other advertising ploys, but they may sometimes be the sole method of promotion. It must be remembered, however, that the bulk of direct mail letters end up in the waste-paper basket. They must, therefore, be simply but compellingly written, preferably well-illustrated and addressed to a named managing director or finance director, marked 'personal' to circumvent over-protective secretaries. It is quite common practice for a local mailshot to precede a more widely directed regional or national mailing, using one of the better direct mail houses, properly briefed.

Despite the introduction of email and web-based dissemination of marketing material, the use of a posted 'mail shot' is still popular, due to the benefit of an assured receipt.

The Institute of Direct Marketing offers the following checklist for direct marketing planning:

- Set your objectives
- Set your budget
- Outline your campaign activity
- Check on the competition
- Identify your target audience
- Access your target audience
- Develop your creative approach
- Design your mailing package
- Draw up your production schedule
- Brief internal personnel and external agencies
- Analyse and evaluate your results.

Despite the increased facility to 'personalize' letters, however, it is quite possible that the effectiveness of the traditional direct mailshot will diminish. Nevertheless, good clear and precise covering letters accompanying other mailed particulars will always be an important marketing tool.

Siteboards and hoardings

Perhaps the most familiar marketing aid is the agent's board, providing on-the-spot advertising of the availability of property. There is a tendency, however, for development sites during the construction period to be weighed down with a welter of different boards – architects, building contractors, engineers and quantity surveyors, as well as developers and agents. In marketing terms they achieve little or nothing, even when sensibly grouped as a single display, unless considerable thought is given to their function and treatment. Moreover, there is often the lingering suspicion in the mind of the client developer that the board on a completed building does more to promote the image of the agent than it does the identity of the development.

However, the contribution made by sale or letting boards to the overall marketing campaign should not be underrated. On a new development such boards can be used not only to state the details of a proposed building or buildings under construction, but be employed as a linking display describing the programme of work and the progress to date. Casual visitors to the site may well be potential occupiers, and be converted into actual tenants by the continuing advertisement.

Over the past few years it is obvious that much greater care has been expended upon the design and location of siteboards by some leading property development companies. Dignified artists' impressions and stylishly presented wording can only help to enhance both the perceived quality of the building and the corporate image of the developer. Nevertheless, it is important to ensure that boards are regularly inspected and maintained, otherwise the opposite reactions might be engendered.

The development in photographic imaging offers much more scope for creativity and impact in the use of siteboards, letting boards and posters. Large pictorial boards can be produced at relatively little cost and can have a physical outdoor life of up to eighteen months.

Siteboards and hoardings are now popular vehicles for developers who have become increasingly enterprising in their use of the medium. A first-class hoarding can be commissioned for a relatively large development fairly cheaply. At the same time, a site can be made safer and the incidence of graffiti and vandalism reduced. The local community and emerging young artists can also be involved in the content and design of such hoardings. There is now even an annual competition held by the *Estates Gazette* for the best hoarding of the year.

It should be remembered that very large boards require advertising consent under town planning controls. Some local authorities apply even stricter controls in what are considered to be sensitive environmental areas.

Demonstration

The residential sector has long relied upon the tangible demonstration of its wares to sell property. No estate development of any size is complete and properly ready for marketing until a furnished and fitted show house or flat is made available for inspection. Over recent years this approach has spread to the office and industrial sectors. Show suites of offices, fully furnished and equipped, are now a common feature of marketing. Some shrewd consultants have even been able to persuade office furniture and equipment suppliers to fit out such show space at no cost. Reception areas are also invariably completed, decorated and 'landscaped' to high standards well before final building works are finished. Good housekeeping is important, with windows washed, rubbish cleared and common parts cleaned.

Many major commercial property developers have adopted the principle set by the volume housebuilders and have put their own people on site so that a constant and knowledgeable marketing presence is maintained. This is the kind of service that prospective tenants are coming to expect in the current letting market.

A modern surrogate for on-site demonstration is, of course, the virtual tour. In producing these, as well as with actual tours of inspection, it is worth recognizing that there is a best way to show someone over the property. Preferred routes should, therefore, be mapped out in advance, and so arranged as to make the first and last impressions of the development the most favourable (Butler 1982).

For major schemes, or ones of an especially sensitive nature, an exhibition might be necessary. Apart from displays put on as part of the process of obtaining a planning consent, the majority of exhibits of development projects are prepared as part of corporate promotions in both the public and private sector. It should be appreciated, however, that the mounting of exhibitions or, for that matter, the participation in exhibitions organized by others, is a costly and time-consuming affair.

Television and radio

The use of commercial television to advertise property is still the exception rather than the rule. The principal reason for this is cost, in terms of both preparation and presentation of material. Despite the expense, television is said to offer wide coverage, to be an intrusive medium that is well suited to demonstrating a building to its best advantage, and to be capable of targeting regional audiences with some precision.

Local radio is increasingly used for the advertising of property. Opinions vary as to how effective it is. On the one hand, it is reasonably cheap, offers relatively wide coverage and can lend itself to the creative and striking communication of information. On the other, although it might do wonders for the agent's image, it can be argued that the transitory nature of the message is unlikely to sell property. The right people rarely listen, except at the wrong time.

The Internet

A survey carried out by the *Estates Gazette* in October 2001 found that people had by then become more aware of the power of marketing, particularly using the massive power of the Internet. There are no limits to the amount of information, including multiple plans, pictures and spreadsheets that can be provided at a fraction of the cost of traditional printing and brochure distribution (*Estates Gazette* 2001).

These days, most development schemes of any significant size have a bespoke website and URL, providing all the usual particulars plus virtual walk-through, detailed floor plans, etc. There are also a number of property listing services – www.rightmove.co.uk offers residential property listings, for example, and www.propertymall.com provides searchable commercial property listings. These 'portal' sites are becoming the first port of call for clients wishing to browse a wide variety of properties offered by a range of agents. Many brochure sites fail on two counts – poor user interaction, and a failure to encourage visitors to stay longer and return. Web-based marketing is best suited to certain types of property when marketing is more interactive. 'Hyper targeted' advertising is almost a holy grail amongst online marketers and one wonders whether social networking sites will be used for property marketing purposes in the near future.

Monitoring the effectiveness of a firm's website is crucial to further development. Without strong statistics on the results of web marketing, more investment is impossible to justify.

Many of the techniques to web marketing are equally applicable to other areas. They include:

- Know your objectives
- Know your target audiences
- Integrate your web strategy with the main marketing plan
- Ensure the content is high quality, up-to-date and will promote interaction and repeat visits
- Develop online communities for targeted email campaigns
- Consider how an extranet could be used to reduce costs and enhance service delivery
- Consider how you could do things differently, rather than just put existing material online
- Ensure you can measure the effectiveness, revenue and savings from the site
- Ensure that live contact with people remains on the agenda.

Incentives

Apart from the traditional agents' lunch, and more recently agents' breakfasts and coffee mornings, more and more incentives seem to be on offer in the market. Luxury cars, holidays abroad and additional cash bonuses are all dangled before those who can introduce a successful letting. At the same time, in a difficult market, there is a continuing pressure to offer ever more attractive inducements to prospective occupiers. Rent-free periods, low starting rentals, fitting-out subsidies, reverse premiums and options to break are all employed at the moment, as incentives during negotiations to secure a letting. They should, however, be introduced with care. For it has been pointed out that if a property has been correctly marketed and stands in rental terms on an equal footing with competition, then to use these factors prematurely can often erode the base for negotiation. In addition, it is argued that very seldom is a businessman lured into the market-place purely by marginal short-term financial inducements. If the property is right, and the terms comparatively competitive, the deal should be struck notwithstanding the trappings. Conversely, because they are known to exist in the market, they become expected. In any event they should be properly costed at the outset of the scheme, as should the reception held on completion to launch the building on to the market, whether it has been pre-let or not. This has now become an important part of the promotion campaign, for the agent and funder as well as the developer, and it deserves careful attention. If, for example, it is a pure letting reception, the individual public relations of those concerned with the development should not be allowed to detract from the essential marketing thrust.

Other approaches

More and more firms of estate agents as well as developers and financial institutions are using the service of public relations advisers. With their consumer-based approach, the range and variety of promotional activities are bound to increase. Marketing plans will be more professionally drawn up and more persistently pursued. Special events and novel programmes will become a more common feature of property promotion and marketing.

Well-tried selling techniques include: the use of display models of a development; special naming of a building or the grant of naming rights; the design of a compelling logo and graphics for a project; ground-breaking, topping-out and opening ceremonies with attendant publicity; the use of holograms in demonstration units; special treatment of entrances and common parts; cold calling of possible purchasers; and the despatch or presentation of novelties. More recently the possibility of using 'interactive' or 'virtual reality' techniques has been explored by some property developers to market their buildings, so that at the press of a button you can move around the premises and experience different forms of finish, enclosure and fitting out – but it is costly.

Again, whatever combination of selling techniques is employed, the importance of effective follow-up activity cannot be stressed enough. Few sales are closed quickly, and patience and perseverance are invariably required. Follow-up should not stop once an agreement has been made or a deal struck. It should continue between signing and moving in, and beyond into occupancy. The good name of the developer and the reputation of the agent are themselves integral aspects of present and future promotion, marketing and sales.

The developers' viewpoint

It should be the overriding objective of all developers operating in the private sector to ensure that the buildings they produce are marketable. They must, therefore, concentrate the minds of all the members of the professional team, whether they are architects, engineers, quantity surveyors, builders or whatever, upon the marketing aspects of the project. Thus, from the developers' viewpoint there are several general factors that should be taken into account in planning the marketing campaign for almost any scheme of development.

The choice of agent

The question of marketing and the selection of those who will be responsible for the choice of agent should be made at the earliest possible stage in the development process. It may well be that a potential development site has been introduced by a particular agent. Alternatively, a firm might have been instructed by the developer, or by a prospective occupier, to find a suitable development site because of their special knowledge of the land market in a given locality. In both circumstances the agent concerned might wish to remain associated with the project and undertake the sale or letting. Indeed, it would be surprising if they did not, and in the case of an introduction to a site it is difficult to arrange otherwise. However, they may not be the best firm for the job. In selecting the right agent, several questions can be posed:

- *National or local?* A national firm of estate agents will have a broad coverage of markets and a wide range of business and property contacts, but on smaller or more difficult developments they may not be quite so hungry for success. A local firm might be eager to perform, conveniently available and familiar with the local market, but they may lack the necessary knowledge and network of commercial contacts and be unable to supply certain support services. Often a combination of the two is the best solution.
- *Large or small?* Much the same arguments as above apply to the size of estate agency firm retained. It is remarkable, however, how many major developers are increasingly willing to entrust the marketing of very large schemes to very small practices. Again, the answer is often a joint instruction.
- *Firm or individual?* It is important to select and instruct agents with care to ensure that it is not just the right firm, but also the right person within that firm who is fully responsible for selling the property.
- *Regular or infrequent?* Although there are often compelling reasons for sticking with an agent who has performed well in the past and has become accustomed to the individual ways of a given developer, it can sometimes be beneficial to try out someone different. Even in professional circles, familiarity occasionally can breed contempt, and it is always interesting to compare alternative approaches.
- *Generalist or specialist?* Certain estate agents gain a particular reputation for marketing expertise in special fields, either by sector or by geographical area. Even within such broad categories as shops, offices or industrial premises, performance can vary. With very special types of property, such as leisure

or hotel projects, it is a brave developer, or perhaps a foolish one, who does not avail himself of special marketing advice.

To get the best out of an agent it is not only necessary to appoint them at the inception of a project, but equally essential to make sure that they are involved at every stage of the development process. In this way, marketing factors are built into the original design and the agent gains a deeper understanding of the nature of the property. Although this close collaboration throughout the period of development is bound to be to the benefit of all concerned, it is nonetheless imperative that there should be clearly defined terms of reference and established levels of responsibility for marketing. This is especially true where two or more agents are instructed.

The marketing campaign

It is a cardinal priority for both the developer and the agent to satisfy themselves that the marketing campaign is properly planned and evenly spaced. As has been contended:

> One of the worst offences is the momentous first push, heavy over-exposure and comparative inactivity thereafter. Plan it so that you have a series of nudges rather than one forgettable blast.
>
> (Butler 1982)

Another common failing among development companies is the parsimonious allowance made for marketing at appraisal and project planning stages. It is astonishing, with the enormous capital sums involved and the difficult market conditions that prevail, how little money is made available for marketing. The developer and agent should, therefore, agree on a reasonable budget for promotion and marketing, remembering that smaller, less prominent buildings will often require a proportionately higher sum spent on selling them than do their larger, more splendid, counterparts.

As already mentioned, the contribution of the public relations firm to the promotion and marketing of property development schemes has grown over the past decade or so. Although the cost of retaining the services of a good firm of public relations consultants is additional to the usual agency commissions incurred, it is worth the developer of any special kind of development, particularly those dependent upon public custom, considering the use of such expertise. However, experience shows that it is advisable to negotiate a fixed fee rather than work to their preferred quantum merit basis. It is also important to make sure that a good working relationship and clearly defined terms of reference are established between the estate agent and the public relations firm, otherwise an element of suspicion can erode the effectiveness of both.

Naturally, a developer will also wish to approve the proposed selling techniques. Without re-examining the relative merits or otherwise of such methods of selling as brochures, DVDs, press advertising, direct mailing, siteboards, demonstration units, television or radio, a developer should have a basic understanding of the techniques used by estate agents in selling commercial floorspace. At the very least it is necessary to select the right agent in the first place. At best, it promotes a healthy climate of confidence between the agent and developer.

In any event, it is worth restating that there are really no new methods of marketing property, merely refinements of long-established techniques. With potential occupiers becoming increasingly aware of their space requirements, it is important not to present marketing material in too naïve, or even insulting, a manner. Moreover, if sufficient thought is given early enough in the development programme as to what exactly is involved, and where time and money are best expended, it may transpire that some of the traditional avenues of marketing are not necessary.

Monitoring marketing

Once an agent has been instructed and a marketing campaign agreed, it is essential that the developer retains continuing contact with the agent to monitor progress. Regular meetings, at say, monthly intervals, should be held, preferably on site. Moreover, the client developer should always insist that a written report on the previous month's activity is submitted to him at least two days before the meeting. This would itemize all the inquiries that had been made about the property, the names and positions of those inquiring and whether or not any visit to view had been arranged or taken place, and with what result.

Where appropriate, an explanation of why enquirers had not pursued their interest should be included, together with a reasoned argument examining how lettings have taken place in what are seen as directly competing properties. This discipline is not popular with agents, and there might indeed be occasions when excessive adherence to the routine becomes a contrivance. However, formality is easy to relax, but difficult to reassert. The reporting process must, therefore, be seen as a genuine evaluation of progress and not a mere ritual.

The developer will also normally wish to be consulted regarding the presentation and placement of advertising. Although the agent will be more familiar with the various vehicles for promoting the property to best advantage, it is as well to check that it is the development that has pride of place in an advert, and not the agent's corporate image. Another avenue worth exploring with the agent is the possibility of trailing editorial comment throughout the course of the campaign. It is hard to assess the true value of editorial exposure, but it is free.

There are several other matters worth mentioning regarding the relationship of the developer and the agent during the marketing process. These can be summarized as follows:

- Resist the natural urge to tinker with such matters as the design and format of the brochure or the structure and content of any covering letter. If dissatisfied, reject them – do not compromise.

- Do not be tempted to cut out the agent if an approach is made direct by a potential purchaser/lessee. Always refer such offers to the agent, for there is little purpose served in retaining an agent and conducting negotiations personally. In this way, a secondary negotiating position is reserved.

- Do not change agents midway through marketing unless there are very good reasons for so doing. Continuity is one of the more important ingredients of a marketing campaign. If the service from the agent is thought to be unsatisfactory, it is often better to give them two months' notice to quit or ask them to re-tender for the instructions against a major competitor. It is remarkable how rejuvenating this particular process can be. If, however, the dissatisfaction is deep-seated, then it is better to cut losses and change agents forthwith.

- Decide the degree to which the property will be finished, and what help might be made available to any incoming tenants for fitting out. There is a growing tendency in the office and industrial development sectors, as there always has been in retailing, to complete buildings only to a shell stage. Tenants are then encouraged to select wall, floor and ceiling materials and finishes, with the developer covering the cost up to a predetermined amount. Some developers are even providing free space-planning advice.

- Consider what kind and level of continuing services could be provided by the client and on what basis. It can be argued that, both to generate initial profitability and maintain income flow, the management of commercial property generally needs to be much more aggressive. To some extent, therefore, development does not end once a building is physically completed, but includes the establishment of a property management system.

- Furthermore, in terms of marketing and management, more flexible leases as well as more flexible buildings are being demanded by tenants, particularly by those in the new technology industries and specialized professional services. Tenants are increasingly looking for shorter leases with one-sided break clauses and a range of supporting business and personal services. Thus, good marketing, which has regard to good management, will play an ever more important part in assuring the success of development projects.

- Pay fees promptly, and once agreed do not attempt to renegotiate. There is almost a paradox in the property world whereby an agent achieving a good quick sale or letting is somehow not felt to have earned their fee, whereas the long and costly campaign is in a strange way thought to have shown value for money.

- Consider within the overall context of marketing the corporate image of the client. In these days of greater accountability and ever-growing public awareness, the image a property development company portrays to the public at large is fast becoming one of its more valuable assets. 'Public' in this sense refers to the whole professional and commercial milieu in which the company operates. Thus, it includes clients, competitors, local authorities, the news media, financial institutions, construction firms, professional practitioners and prospective purchasers.

In a business that, rightly or wrongly, is not exactly renowned for its high ethical or aesthetic standards, there is good reason for property development companies to ask themselves a few telling questions regarding their corporate image. It has been suggested that these should include the following:

> How do we think we are perceived by the public?
> How are we actually viewed by them?
> How would we wish to be thought of?
> What image is most likely to assist us in achieving our objectives?
> (Charlesworth-Jones 1983)

Unless all the answers to these questions coincide – which is unlikely – the next proposition should be, 'How do we go about designing and implementing a desirable corporate image?' This may involve a change in attitude by members of the company, an advertising campaign, public relations exercises, or even a change of name. In any event, the very act of self-assessment can be both salutary and rewarding.

Conclusion

Innovation in the process of promotion and marketing is bound to happen. What confronts the agency business is the extent to which property professionals can retain command over the sales team. Already we see leading firms of public relations consultants, with their skilful manipulation of the media and their flair for promotional activities, evident in the agency field. Changing systems of communication and information technology with wider and cheaper accessibility, together with new methods of conducting business, all point to changes in the way we buy and sell development and other properties. Education for marketing, both for existing members in practice and for new entrants to the estates profession, will become ever more essential.

Nevertheless, there are no magic formulas to the art of marketing. It is simply a logical stage-by-stage approach that employs a range of techniques and disciplines, and it is the firm that uses all the appropriate techniques and skills that will create the synergy that sells.

Part Five

Real estate development sectors

16 Retail development

For the thirty-odd years following the end of the Second World War, retailing was repeatedly heralded as the most innovative and changeable sector of the property market. New types of shop development emerged, one after another – department stores, variety shops, supermarkets, covered shopping precincts, hypermarkets, superstores, district centres, discount warehouses, and city-centre 'metro' stores. Preferred locations shifted away from the high street, to adjacent central-area sites, out of town to greenfield sites, back to town-centre and edge-of-town locations and even 'sideways' on to industrial estates. Modern forms of merchandising have altered the shape, size and layout of shops of all kinds, and advances in the methods of distribution have affected the design and position of retail outlets. Nevertheless, there remains considerable volatility in the shop market and a continuing dynamic in the field of retail development, fostered not least by developments in e-tailing.

This chapter is divided into five sections, as follows:

- The context for retail development
- Types of retail development
- Planning and retailing
- Design and layout
- Shopping centre management.

The context for retail development

As consumers have become increasingly discerning, affluent and mobile, so retailers have had to respond to changing market conditions and opportunities. In forecasting future trends in shopping and shop development it is worth recording briefly some of the more significant factors that have brought about the process of change in retailing over recent years. These can be summarized as follows:

- Food retailing on any scale has almost disappeared from many traditional town centres as superstore operators have relocated to locations on the edge of or out of town, where they can find sites capable of providing 50,000–60,000 ft^2 (4645–5574 m^2) or more of space with extensive car parking facilities.
- The fashion industry has extended its market to embrace every sector of society, whereas only a generation or so ago it was the preserve of the better-off.

- Likewise, eating-out was something of an occasional treat for most people, but over the past few decades a revolution has taken place in the catering industry, with a consequent impact upon all forms of retail property development.
- The majority of the population have more money to spend, fuelled by debt, than at any time in the past. They are also more likely to own a car and gain from greater mobility.
- Retailers have become more inventive and competitive in their promotional, marketing and merchandising policies.
- Low inflation and rising shop rents created a favourable climate for a boom in retail development in both in-town and out-of-town locations during the late 1980s.
- The government adopted a much more laissez-faire attitude to out-of-town retailing during this time than had previously been the case. Although current planning attitudes now favour town centres, the edge-of-town and out-of-town retail locations and sites are still expected to grow.
- For most of the past twenty years, the growth of capital investment in UK retailing has been enormous. The FT Index of leading UK retailers increased by 169 per cent in the two decades up to 2006 (British Council for Shopping Centres 2007a). Investment in shop development has, therefore, enjoyed continued and expanding support from financial institutions and retail operators alike.
- During the last thirty years retailers and developers increasingly detected a consumer need to provide 'one-stop shopping' combining comparison shopping, and leisure and catering facilities within an easily accessible, traffic-free and preferably enclosed environment.
- Speciality trading emerged during the 1980s as a powerful force in the retail sector, usually at the expense of the department store.
- As a result of re-targeting and redesigning by retailers, floorspace requirements have constantly been changing. Moreover, unit sizes have been affected by new ways of distributing and storing stock.

Decentralization of shopping, in its many forms, has, and continues to be, the central issue in the planning and development of retail space. The tide of trade flowing away from the high street can neatly be described as occurring in three waves. The first outward wave was that by the food-based superstores to edge- or out-of-town sites. The second wave, now well established, gained momentum towards the end of the 1970s, and included retailers selling bulk items such as DIY, furniture and electrical goods. The third wave is represented by the creation of regional and sub-regional shopping centres, and also includes the drift out of town of groups of major durable goods traders. There has been for some time a determined attempt to reverse this trend back towards the town centre so as to create a fourth wave, but the British Council for Shopping Centres (BCSC), for example, expects the next ten years to see 60 per cent of total new retail floorspace to be developed outside of town centres (British Council for Shopping Centres 2007b).

Forecasting and trends

In the context of retailing it has been said that forecasting is much easier than is generally realized, because what the rich do today creates the appetites of the masses in the future (McCollum 1985). Moreover, the USA acts as a kind of window into how people will want to work, live and shop in times ahead. There are, however, a few basic ingredients that help determine the likely future nature and mix of retailing, which are described below.

Population changes

Changes in the size, and the social and age structure of the population have a considerable influence upon property markets. The birth rate, which has been running at less than replacement level since the early 1970s, seems set to remain at a low level. Life expectancy, on the other hand, has increased by two years over the past decade and is steadily rising. Household size appears likely to reduce even further, so that by the year 2010 almost 60 per cent of all house-holds will consist of only one or two people. This all probably means that, with an ageing population and more households, more people will have more time to spend shopping. Indeed, forecasts suggest that the number of people over the age of 55 years will increase by 1.5 million by 2015 which could equate to a retail spend for this sector of the population with much leisure time of £120 bil-lion. At the other end of the spectrum, those in the 25–34 years of age bracket will potentially demonstrate an 18 per cent retail expenditure growth in the period to 2015 (British Council for Shopping Centres 2007a). Developers and retailers alike will need to consider the implications of such demographic changes and how to cater on one hand to a wealthy, older population and, on the other, to young families who are more heavily influenced by fashions and who require shops that are easy and quick to reach, are safe, are rich in services and facilities and provide family activities.

Spatial distribution

Although the overall size of the UK population has changed little over the past thirty years and looks fairly stable, if ageing, for the next ten or so, the spatial distribution is much more variable. Broadly speaking, the only parts of the country where more than 20 per cent population growth is forecast in the next twenty years are nine counties in an east–west split between Bedfordshire, Cambridgeshire, Suffolk, Norfolk, Lincolnshire and Northamptonshire and Cornwall, Devon and Somerset These are the areas where more retail floorspace will be required.

Consumer expenditure

After years of sustained economic growth, the shopping public in general is becoming more affluent. With interest rates at low levels, historically low levels of inflation and rising residential property values, growth in retail expenditure over the last two decades has been significant. Between 1986 and 2006, retail spending increased by 94 per cent in real terms to a value of £236 billion in 2006 (creating an added 668,000 jobs in the sector at the same time) (British Council for Shopping Centres 2007a). Much of this spending has been funded by debt finance. Personal debt in the UK by 2007 stood at over £1.4 trillion (Credit Action 2008). Greater polarization in the wealth of the UK's citizens has occurred over the last twenty years and this trend is almost certain to continue. Again, retailers and hence developers need to be able to respond to these trends.

Mobility and accessibility

Car ownership and its effect upon shopping behaviour are probably even more important than is commonly supposed. The number of cars on British roads is increasing by 2–3 per cent annually. Car ownership doubled between 1960 and 1980, and between 1980 and 2005 the number of households with two cars more than doubled (Department for Transport 2007). It has been estimated that around 60 per cent of all shopping trips are made by car.

Work and leisure

The average working week in all industries has fallen from around 42 hours in 1973 to about 40 hours in 1985 and is thought (although conflicting figures are produced) to have decreased to less than 37 hours today. In the salaried business sector this is probably lower. These estimates are difficult to produce because of the increasing informality and part-time nature of many people's working hours. It is interesting to note that figures adjusted to reflect the lives of full-time workers, including 'informal' working hours, suggest that a 45-hour working week is more accurate (Federation of European Employers 2008). We have seen changes in the last decade, with more women working and more people having more than one job. It is commonly expected that in future, not only will people have more time to go shopping, and more money to do it with, but shopping will increasingly style itself as a leisure activity.

Information technology

Improvements in information and communication technology have threatened to revolutionize the comparison, selection and ordering of certain goods. E-retailing in the UK grew from less than 1 per cent of UK shopping in 1999 to 3 per cent in 2003, with further increases year-on-year to 2007, when it amounted to around 5% of the total retail market. With growth of about 35% annually within the sector (compared to 3% annual increase for high street retail), leading retail opinion suggests that by 2010 the e-retail share could be as high as 10%, accepting that this will vary between retail categories – for example, higher for clothes than, say, electrical good or groceries. It is forecast to rise to 10.7 per cent by 2015 (British Council for Shopping Centres 2007a). Business to business (B2B) and 'just-in-time' systems have radically changed the stocking, distribution and control of merchandise. Some shopping centre owners even use information systems to record the turnover for each unit in the centre to establish the level of turnover rents that should be charged (where the rent paid by the retailer represents a proportion of sales turnover of their unit) but, as one might expect, retailers are jealously protective of this commercially sensitive information.

Consumer demands

Perhaps above all there has been the realization among retailers and developers that it is the customer who calls the tune. The shopping public constantly have to be wooed. They increasingly demand accessible, convenient, secure and enjoyable shopping environments with adequate parking, a wide and comparative range of goods at reasonable prices and the availability of attractive and useful facilities such as food, child care and leisure.

Basic research procedures

As the retail industry has matured, so shopping centre developers have become more and more aware of the need for reliable market research and analysis. Indeed, such retail studies are of benefit to all concerned. To the developers they confirm the degree of potential opportunity, provide a basis for planning application, set design and site layout constraints, furnish basic data for marketing and funding, and provide information vital to the future sale of the property. To the local community they contribute to the development planning and control processes – identifying existing and future shopping needs, allocating land for retail development, examining and catering for infrastructure consequences, assessing the impact of development proposals upon existing shopping facilities, and determining the outcome of applications for shopping schemes. And to prospective retailers they measure the opportunity for new units, sales potential and floor space, as well as assessing the competitive situation (McCollum 1985).

It should be appreciated that market research is not an exact science, for the analyst is essentially presenting a subjective evaluation of a project's potential, based upon available data and drawing upon personal experience and judgement. In fact, one leading consultant has gone so far as to state that 'traditional catchment analysis is a thing of the past' (Maynard 1990). Nevertheless, the basic procedure for conducting a retail market analysis is typically an economic area analysis, a trade area analysis and an appraisal of optimum size and mix for the proposed project (McCollum 1985).

Economic area analysis

Economic area analysis is conducted to determine whether a particular market can support additional retail development, and it includes an investigation of:

- *Employment trends*. These are critical as the form and level of employment naturally determine the overall purchasing power of the market area.
- *Population forecasts*. Such analyses would lean heavily upon information compiled and used by the planning authority for the area.
- *Income levels*. Extracting per capita and family income levels and estimating likely increases is a vital preliminary step in estimating retail expenditures for the area in question.
- *Retail sales data*. This study depicts which retail categories have achieved rapid sales growth, which are declining, and how they relate to population and income growth. They are usually divided into comparison or durable goods sales and convenience goods sales.

The prime objective of the economic area analysis, therefore, is to reveal the strength and nature of the employment base, the geographical centres of population and potential for population growth, the strongest retail categories, and the sales potential projected for the area. The analysts will then use these data when delineating a trade area and assessing sales potential for a proposed centre.

Assuming the economic base study has shown potential growth for the area, a market analysis of the trade area is undertaken to assess the potential of a given site for a shopping centre development. A trade area is the geographic sector for which the sustaining patronage for steady support of a shopping centre is obtained. Also known as the catchment area or hinterland, the boundaries are determined by various factors, including:

- the size and nature of the site itself, as well as character of the surrounding locality
- present and proposed accessibility to the site
- any physical or artificial barriers limiting the site
- the location of competing facilities
- the limitations of travel time and distance.

The total trade area is normally divided into three or more zones as a means to illustrate and assess variations in the impact of the proposed centre by use of established capture or penetration rates. By reference to population, income and capture estimates, total expenditure can be gauged.

Shopping centre sales potential

The principal aim of the market research is to assess the proposed centre's retail sales potential. This demonstrates ultimate profitability and optimum size and mix. There are two basic approaches to estimating sales potential:

- *Share of the market*. This approach essentially assumes that the shopping centre will gain a certain percentage of the total trade area sales potential. Experience, and the analysis of comparable developments in similar situations elsewhere, will indicate the probable proportion of the population falling within the trade area who will be prepared to travel to the proposed centre. An evaluation of the population employment and income data will show how much they might spend, and on what.

- *Residual analysis.* The potential trade for a new centre can also be calculated by employing what is variously described as the 'vacuum', 'residual', or 'remainder' method, whereby the total consumer expenditure going to other centres in the vicinity is assessed at first instance. The procedure briefly includes determining the prospective catchment area, gauging the total population by census district, calculating retail expenditure by goods and socio-economic groups, allocating expenditure to more accessible and convenient centres, allowing for local traders' share and then estimating the potential trade remaining. Where this remainder is positive, the turnover will be available to the new centre. Where negative, the area is already overshopped.

Project size and mix

Once total sales potential has been predicted, the need arises to translate this demand into a physical context, in terms of how much floorspace, in how many shops or what type, to determine the size and mix of the centre. This is achieved by use of conversion factors, which simply express turnover per square metre of gross floorspace. These factors display a variation according to broad region and specific locality. Other changing aspects of shopping also play a part in the steady rise of conversion factors – longer shopping hours, the reduction of non-productive space, and improved merchandising.

In the context of retail market research and analysis, it should be stated that over the years there has been a rapid advance in the development of sophisticated techniques that aim to assist in the assessment of the retail hinterland and the measurement of market penetration, and provide some explanation for retail land-use location. These techniques are grouped together as shopping models. They seek to represent a real-world situation in terms simple enough to permit examination of past and present shopping patterns and the prediction of future trends.

These models tend to be employed more by planning authorities and major retail organizations than they do by shopping centre developers. Some members of the property profession remain sceptical about the use of advanced techniques of analysis. But more than ever, given the increasingly complex nature of the retail market, the sector needs to be served by good research, not just in the form of quantitative studies, but in respect of customer behaviour and personnel requirements.

Types of retail development

A useful, but less than traditional, classification of shopping centres has been advanced by planning authorities and the retail sector, along the following lines:

- Those centres that are free-standing and suburban in location, providing for the general-purpose shopping needs of households. They may be neighbourhood, community or regional in terms of catchment, so that the small strip centre and the large super-regional centre are really subtypes of the same category.
- General-purpose centres located in shopping districts, sometimes known as renewal or redevelopment centres. Again there are several subtypes according to size and location, as well as their relationship to the shopping district in which they are positioned.
- Multi-use centres, where shopping is only one of several uses within the overall development. Once more, there are several kinds of centre within this category. They are a concept developed in the US that has gained popularity in the UK in recent years.
- Those centres where retailing is ancillary to other commercial activities, and is provided to complement the dominant function of the building complex. The subtypes here would be differentiated according to the dominant activity, whether it be hotel, office or transport interchange.
- Speciality centres (such as those specializing in high-class fashion) and focused centres (for example designer outlet villages) that concentrate upon a particular theme or tenant mix, sometimes purpose-built and sometimes housed in a renovated building.

No classification completely satisfies the market, but at least the one outlined above helps distinguish between the different processes of development, methods of funding and styles of operation, as well as forms of retailing. It has also been pointed out that different types of centre will succeed in different ways and must, therefore, be assessed accordingly.

In considering the shopping opportunities that have been taken across the various types of retail operation over the past few years, and exploring those that exist to be exploited in the immediate future, attention is paid primarily to the development side of the market rather than to the investment or business prospects of retailing.

The high street

As planning policy seeks to curb out-of-town development, large retailers and leisure operators are beginning to refocus on the town centre. The food retailers in particular have sought to exploit the growing 'metro' market by providing convenience stores in town centres, petrol stations, etc., often to the detriment of small shops occupied by local traders. The growth in cafés and bars is another facet of this urban renaissance. Some of the leading multiples in certain durable goods markets are also looking more closely at good secondary positions rather than their previous prime pitches, bringing with them a new injection of consumer interest and possible redevelopment potential. Moreover, while there appears to be an inevitable decline in the total number of standard units, it is sometimes surprising to discover the high turnover achieved by individual traders in specialized fields. Locally based development companies are also showing more interest in purchasing, refurbishing and re-letting single smaller units. Such developers are inclined to be more sensitive to occupiers' needs. Thus, leases are showing some signs of becoming shorter, review periods more regular and user conditions less onerous. In this way, the rate at which the trading mix of high streets changes is likely to quicken.

Other avenues for possible development in the high street can be summarized as follows:

- The acquisition and exploitation of land to the rear of high street shops to allow for the creation of stores with large floorspace and high street access, but where wide high street frontage for display is not a principal requirement.
- The assembly of several deep standard units, with or without additional rear land, in order to create small malls or precincts branching off the high street.
- The refurbishment of existing units to provide more suitable retail space for the changing needs of multiple traders.
- The incremental upgrading of side streets to the high street to establish a kind of 'Latin Quarter' atmosphere, with a grouping of complementary service trades.
- Capitalizing upon the pedestrianization of high streets or adjoining thoroughfares to refurbish or redevelop otherwise redundant or deteriorating premises.
- The renovation and conversion of historic buildings, or buildings of special architectural merit, to produce a type of speciality centre, probably incorporating some form of catering and leisure facility.
- Some braver developers have contemplated the creation of multi-level trading through the conversion of existing high street stores, normally in absolutely prime positions.

Uncertainty engendered by recession heightened the debate on the future of the high street, one element of which is the role that the major retailers play. The increased concentration of ownership and occupation of the high streets in the UK has been said to have brought both benefits and drawbacks (Bernard Thorpe and OIRM 1990). On the plus side, it has seen an immeasurable improvement in the internal and external appearance of shops, the product ranges on offer and the general ambience of shopping. On the minus side, the further decline of independent shops and a wider assortment of multiple retailers has led to a loss of variety and the 'higgledy-piggledy' character of older, traditional high streets. In the last decade we have seen significant improvements in town centre management addressing issues such as environment, security, investment, accessibility, marketing, and promotion. There is also the increased presence of pan-European and international multiples on the high street, particularly in the fashion sector. A wider variety of multiple trading names have appeared, encouraging high standards of shop design and quality of merchandise. In the larger cities the renaissance in urban living and enhanced leisure provision has breathed new life into some inner urban areas and this trend is expected to continue.

It cannot be denied, however, that the town centre in general and the high street in particular continue to face a challenge from accessible, convenient and secure out-of-town centres. Nevertheless, as has been maintained, the disappearance of food retailing from the town centre has been more than compensated for by the opportunity for extra retail floorspace for those traders specializing in comparison and durable goods. Moreover, major retailers and investors have enormous capital values and commitments locked into town centres and thereby have a strong vested interest in protecting and preserving their assets for the future. This challenge can be met, but it requires more local authorities to address the problems of their town centres on a comprehensive basis. The lessons learned and experience gained from the private sector management of planned shopping centres can usefully be applied to existing traditional town centres.

Speciality centres

Perhaps one of the most interesting areas of retail development that has engaged the property industry over the last decade has been the growth of speciality centres. These centres characteristically are close to prime locations, have no particular anchor tenant, tend to concentrate upon providing a carefully selected mix of retailers, have a high proportion of small units, and place the accent upon high-class merchandise. In addition, great attention is paid to layout, design and finishes in order to give a more friendly and comfortable atmosphere than that experienced in most forms of planned centre.

Most speciality centres aim to attract the better-off shopper willing to spend their income on goods they believe they 'want' to buy rather than 'need' to buy. Much of floorspace is normally given over to various forms of catering, often around 40 per cent, and the design and environment of the centre usually directed towards a particular theme intended to generate a 'shopping experience'. The tenant mix tends to favour the small independent retailer, often holding on short-term leases or even inclusive licences. New and expanding traders can, therefore, secure representation in or near town centres away from the competition of the high street and the multiple traders.

Intensive management is essential to the success of a speciality centre. It must be imaginative, flexible and highly involved in the trader's business. One of the problems in this respect is that service charges in speciality centres are inclined to be high, and developers state that they can sometimes experience difficulties in demonstrating to tenants the validity of these costs. Such centres also need to be promoted continuously by both advertising campaigns and the staging of live entertainment.

The need for strong and committed management combined with a relative lack of comparable schemes to analyse and appraise has led to a certain degree of institutional caution in terms of investment, and funding is not always easy to obtain. Nevertheless, there is evidence that as the market becomes more familiar with them as investment propositions and witnesses a pattern of good rental growth, comparative yields are falling. It is probable, therefore, that the speciality centre will play a leading part in helping to retain shopper loyalty to traditional town centres.

One form of speciality shopping is 'festival' shopping. This is described as a different type of shopping, because people do not go to festival schemes exclusively for shopping, but for the pleasure of visiting. At least 60 per cent of visitors to such projects give the major reason for their trips as 'browsing', and only 10–15 per cent go primarily to shop. Familiar in the USA since the beginning of the 1970s, and with Covent Garden an early example in the UK, other schemes such as the Albert Dock, Ocean Village, Cutlers Wharf and Quayside have followed. These schemes are said to accept not only the challenges of a new form of retailing and of a flagship role in urban regeneration, but also of an entirely new approach to retail property development and management (Brown 1990).

Another form of specialized retail development which spread across the USA and appeared in the UK is what is known as the 'category killer' 20,000–30,000 ft^2 (1858 to 2787 m^2) stores, concentrating on such single-product areas as sports, office products and books.

Planned central area schemes

The glamorous end of retail development is unquestionably the planned central area scheme, and it is here that opinions as to future opportunities vary widely. On the one hand, there are those who point to the long and uncertain gestation period, front-heavy infrastructure and holding costs, complicated site assembly, political sensitivity and high operating costs attached to such projects. On the other, it estimated that few towns up and down the country remain to be 'done'. Moreover, many towns that built centres in the 1960s and early 1970s will soon embark upon further phases, and many of these centres are already in the course of refurbishment.

What does seem certain is that, where planned shopping centres are developed, they will be smaller, more sensitively handled and afford greater energy-efficiency. Many will incorporate elements of renewal and conservation in their basic design. Others may concentrate upon the complete redevelopment and upgrading of existing older but outdated planned centres.

A few trends can be discerned. There will be less food shopping, apart from catering, which will increase, and the accent will be placed more upon creating a shopping 'experience' with a greater selection and better quality of goods. Centres will depend less and less upon department or variety stores as anchors in the way that they have previously done. More attention will be paid to good management and a satisfactory tenant mix. Turnover rents will become more popular and local traders made more welcome. Leisure and recreation facilities will also figure more prominently.

Since the early 1990s we have witnessed a tremendous improvement in the general ambience of shopping centres, with vastly better detailed design and good use of natural and artificial lighting. They are friendlier, safer and more security-conscious places for the shopper. Great advances have been made in improving the external appearances of the buildings. The difficulty is that the main planned town centre schemes form possibly the largest buildings that will ever be constructed in many towns and are prone to appear monolithic.

In assessing the potential performance of a planned shopping centre, there are factors that have been called the 'seven secrets of success' (Ringer 1989). Most of these are dealt with a little later in the chapter, but can usefully be listed here:

- *Location*. Shoppers must be able to get in and out of shopping centres with ease, and therefore access for both car and public transport is vital.
- *Planning*. This relates to the movement of people around the shopping centre, optimizing the flow of pedestrians and maximizing the total potential of all units.
- *Design*. The shopping centre must understand its target audience and then address them through design solutions that create a unique image and communicate the identity of the centre to the public.
- *Amenities*. This really includes everything from well-lit and safe car parks, through to toilets, crèche, and facilities for disabled persons, so that customers feel good about being within the centre, stay longer and spend more.
- *Mix*. The tenant mix should be focused on the target audience, with the developer thinking like a retailer and planning the centre layout as one big department store.
- *Programming*. Shopping centre owners, in conjunction with the tenants, should ensure a promotion events programme throughout the year.
- *Management*. The centre must be kept clean and safe, with a sense of common purpose shared by the management and the tenants.

The coming years will undoubtedly reveal increasingly discriminating consumer tastes, which will need to be assessed by research into community needs and implemented by centre management teams ready to run shopping centres as dynamic businesses. Developers and landlords who ignore this approach do so as their peril.

District centres

Perhaps the least contentious retail development is the district centre, apparently popular with planners, developers, shoppers, traders and financiers alike. Serving a catchment area of anything between 20,000 and 120,000 population, but usually around 50,000, it normally provides about 100,000 to 200,000 ft^2 (9290 to 18,580 m^2) of retail floorspace comprising anything from twenty to forty standard units built around a superstore and invariably a few civic facilities such as a library, health centre or sports hall. Occasionally, the term 'district centre' is something of a euphemism, being coined by a superstore operator to gain a more favourable response from a planning authority. But despite their seeming acceptance by planning authorities, it could be argued that they pose a greater threat to the traditional high street than do single free-standing superstores.

Increasing restrictions on out-of-town and edge-of-town developments have encouraged developers to focus on the development of district centres in declining inner-city areas, which are then used as a catalyst to help regenerate the local economy. The idea is that the land is made available by the local authority and a consortium of retail operators underwrite the scheme via their covenants, with the smaller traders anchored and supported by a major superstore.

Superstores

Once anathema to planners, the superstore or hypermarket became firmly established in the 1980s and 1990s. However, tightening of planning controls of PPG6 and then PPS6 took effect from the mid- to late 1990s, leading to a decline in the rate of superstore development in the new millennium, although that is not to say that new schemes are rare. A change has occurred, however, in terms of the formats of 'supermarkets'. The big food retailers, like Tesco, Sainsbury, Morrison, Asda and Marks & Spencer, all now have small town centre convenience formats, usually of 3000 ft^2 or smaller. Mid-sized formats, such as Sainsbury Local, at 3000–150,00 ft^2, locate in busy town centres where people will buy small quantities at lunchtimes and early evenings. As well as traditional supermarket formats, we have also seen the advent of big, hypermarketsized store formats, such as Tesco Extra, at 60,000+ ft^2.

Food retailers will obviously have different criteria for determining the feasibility of locations for these different formats. In general terms, retailers will keep a strategy database for their different formats with their desired store sizes. Their general strategy is often to go into a town as the largest store with best accessibility. If available sites only permit the development of a store which is smaller than the competition's but in a prominent location with excellent access, they will often proceed with the scheme on this basis, taking the risk that the larger competitor store may improve access and parking in the hope that they could extend their new store in the future.

The key determinants for supermarkets and larger formats are:

- 'Drive time', with the size of the population within fifteen minutes being considered key
- Location, which should preferably be stand-alone on arterial roads
- Car parking minimum of one space per 10 m^2 gross floor area
- Access will ideally be from a roundabout or traffic-light controlled junction and be clearly signed and visible
- Separate and secure servicing, capable of easy access and manoeuvring and able to accommodate an appropriate number of articulated vehicles
- A petrol filling station located on the main exit.

The superstore has become more and more accepted as a part of everyday life, and arguably many of the initial fears voiced by planning authorities about the effect of such stores on existing town centres have not really materialized. Indeed, some positive advantages have been experienced in terms of taking the pressure of excessive traffic off many older town centres. Car-borne customers also demand the convenience, quality and service they provide.

The pace of expansion of superstores has been considerable over the last decade, and rental growth and institutional investment interest, where available, has remained buoyant. One reason for this high level of activity is that leading super-store operators frequently act as their own developers, and are not dependent on the vagaries of the financial markets, raising substantial sums through internal cashflow. It has been pointed out, however, that the continuing proliferation of new stores is not just being undertaken for the fun of it. The retailers are not only planning to satisfy what they still see as an expanding market, but there is also an element of 'spoiling', whereby they seek to deny rivals access to promising new market areas, to secure sites that are not immediately profitable, and to push up market share by invading territory occupied by competitors (Cole 1993). Whilst many bemoan the alleged practice of land banking by superstore operators, hard evidence of this as a widespread activity is hard to come by. If it is occurring, operators would probably argue that this is a legitimate means of protecting their market share.

Concerns were expressed in the 1990s that the spread of the discount retail warehouse and the warehouse club could challenge the pre-eminence of the superstore in the shopping hierarchy. These concerns have so far proved wholly unfounded and are likely remain to do so.

Retail warehouses

To some extent, superstores have been replaced as the *bêtes-noires* of planning authorities by retail warehouses. These can best be defined as single-level self-contained retail stores, selling non-food goods, often specializing in a particular trade, with at least 10,000 ft^2 (929 m^2) of floorspace occupying a warehouse or industrial-type building and supported by a car park. Usually they are around 25,000 to 50,000 ft^2 (2322–4645 m^2) in size, and demand a large catchment area of about 100,000 population within a thirty-minute drive time. Because they concentrate on bulky goods, such as furniture and electrical appliances, out-of-centre locations are required.

The original concept of retail warehousing has seen significant change during its short evolution. Initially, such developments consisted of scattered units, often trading with planning battles unresolved, tucked away on industrial estates, invariably with inadequate parking. They have quickly developed to such an extent that they can now be found on new out-of-town retail parks, which provide purpose-built units allowing the warehouse retailers to congregate together. They also permit enough space for retailers to shop-fit the frontage to their own design and fit-out the interiors, which are now used predominantly for retailing as opposed to storage. The whole development is normally surrounded by numbers of car parking spaces undreamed of in the early 1970s. As experience of warehouse development grows, so characteristic features emerge in terms of their specification and design. These can be summarized as follows:

- Location is the single most important factor, with an optimum balance between accessibility, hinterland and visibility. A catchment population of 70,000 within a drive time of twenty minutes is seen as a minimum.
- Some traders prefer a cluster of complementary retail outlets, and others are perfectly happy with a single free-standing unit.
- Many retailers avoid high-standard specifications and adhere to a 'keep-it-simple' approach towards their stores' interiors. However, corporate image is considered important by all.
- As a general rule, pitched roofs tend to be unpopular, because they are difficult to 'sign'.
- Direct access and exposure to surface car parking is essential, and an ideal ratio is one space to 10 m² (200 ft²), which can be lower in a large retail park where parking facilities can be shared.
- Attention to the internal layout, configuration and subdivision of buildings at design stage is critical. In a park scheme, the design must be flexible enough to allow for a range of unit sizes from, say, 5000 to 50,000 ft² (464 to 4645 m²) with a frontage to depth ratio of at least 1:2.
- An increasing number of retailers are incorporating some kind of catering facilities.
- Service vehicles should be separated from customer car parking.
- Pedestrian movement must be facilitated.
- Retail warehouse park layouts have progressed from the initial simple 'parade' of units, to a more efficient use of site area by utilizing shared parking between the different units forming two parallel blocks or occasionally an 'L' or 'U' shaped plan form.
- With regard to tenant mix, an ideal size for a retail warehouse park has been suggested at around 125000 ft² (11,613 m²) typically comprising (Fletcher King 1989):

DIY and garden centre	3250 m²+ (35,000 ft²)
Carpets	930–2300 m² (10,000–25,000 ft²)
Furniture	2800–3700 m² (30,000–40,000 ft²)
Auto	1400 m² (15,000 ft²)
Electrical	650–930 m² (7000–10,000 ft²)

This produces a well balanced park with a variety of users and building size.
- The environment (in terms of landscaping) around retail warehouse parks is beginning to be improved and some older parks are now being upgraded. As the trend for integrating leisure and retail facilities continues, however, the environmental factor will become increasingly important.
- Building specification has advanced and corporate image has become increasingly significant to retailers who have developed readily identifiable

logos, colours and house styles. This is due to both mature traders entering the market and institutional investors setting high standards of building design.

- Proactive management, earlier neglected in the sector's rapid expansion, is now more and more common.
- Specialist themed retail warehouse parks around a particular use might be the next phase of development.
- The discount food sector seems set to expand, with additional retailers operating simple shop fit, low capital, low storage cost, high-intensity and minimal staff expense outlets.
- The discount warehouse and warehouse club sector, a concept imported from the US and not legally within the strict definition of retailing, was expected to grow significantly in the late 1990s and concern was expressed that these stores would take trade away from traditional retail outlets. However, they did not.

Department stores

The difficulties facing department stores are generally well known, and virtually all major operators have experienced serious trading problems since the mid-1980s, mainly as a result of the costly nature of this type of retailing operation. However, these retailing difficulties give rise to some unusual and exciting redevelopment opportunities. The growth in the use of concessions and franchising, promoting the concept of a store within a store, is not a development activity in the true property sense, but business reorganization along these lines often forms part of a larger redevelopment programme. It also provides more flexibility for achieving an optimum tenant mix within a single large store than within a planned shopping centre comprising many separate shop units. Management services are also easier to coordinate.

Many stores came on to the market as a result of the rationalization of the major chains of department store operators. This released development potential, and some interesting schemes have been undertaken. One of the main problems in effecting a redevelopment of department stores is the preponderance of upper floorspace, but a mixed development of offices above retail space on the ground floor is the conventional solution, although the office space so created is often less than ideal.

In the cyclical way of things, the department store enjoyed something of a revival in the early 1990s. The major reasons for this were identified by Hall (1993):

- A long-standing appeal remains based upon familiarity and confidence.
- Many specialist traders have performed poorly by comparison.
- They did not embark on highly expansionist programmes prior to the recession of the mid-1990s.
- Many held property on a freehold basis in good locations.
- Their targeted customer base tends to be older and less financially affected by the recession.

- The massive expansion in shopping centre development during the 1980s benefited many stores, with developers eager to lure them into projects at concessionary rates to secure funding and specialist traders.
- Most stores reorganized themselves, often along North American lines, with the removal of certain product lines, including food, once considered fundamental to the traditional department store, and replacing them with a wider range of clothing, footwear, accessories and home ware. Reliance upon concessions was greatly reduced. Thus, many have become large-space speciality retailers, appealing to the mass market for mid-price family and home fashions.
- They offer good staffing levels, delivery and after sales service, and also provide such amenities as toilets.

Generally, the changing demographic pattern of an increasingly ageing population is favourable to the future of the revamped department store.

Arcades

The shopping arcade, built originally on narrow strips of land (usually connecting two main streets) by developers anxious to optimize the use of land or by owners seeking to prevent incursion or misuse of their property, often now occupy prime positions and command high pedestrian flows. Probably the best known of all is the Burlington Arcade connecting Piccadilly with Burlington Gardens, but other notable ones that have been refurbished include the nearby Royal Arcade, the Great Western Shopping Arcade in Birmingham, and the Barton Arcade in Manchester. Units tend to be small, with as little as 125 ft^2 (11.6 m^2) on the ground floor, and frequently have a basement and two upper floors. However, rents can be high.

Leases are frequently shorter than usual, at around fifteen years, and landlords have come to accept that, as they attract specialist traders and not multiples, there can be more problems, and greater understanding must be afforded. Arcades also need very careful and positive management, but where this has been provided there are definite signs of it paying off.

Regional shopping centres

In many countries the decentralization of comparison shopping has been accommodated in regional shopping centres. Until the mid-1980s, with the notable exception of Brent Cross in north London, attempts to develop regional shopping centres were thwarted, largely on planning grounds due to their presumed impact upon established town centres. However, the outlook for such centres changed dramatically from about 1985.

New regional shopping centres, strategically located close to the national motorway network and intended to serve an extensive catchment population, became an important feature of retailing in the early 1990s. Such centres comprise 100,000 m^2 (1 million ft^2 or above) or more of purpose-built retail floor area on a site of 40–60 ha (100 to 150 acres) with a minimum of 5000, and more usually 10,000 to 13,000 car parking spaces at surface level. It has been argued, moreover, that regional shopping centres must be worthy contenders and alternatives to existing town and city centres. Brent Cross (London), the Metro Centre (Gateshead), Cribbs Causeway (Bristol) and the Trafford Centre (Manchester) have all shown that tradition can eventually be created where none previously existed. The tenant mix, therefore, must be a response to consumer requirements and not just a reflection of the development team's aspirations. It should blend the results of research and experience, from which there has been a welcome and understandable desire to break away from look-alike centres occupied almost exclusively by well-known multiples that are controlled by a handful of companies (Hammond 1989).

Leisure has also figured large in the design of regional shopping centres. A good example of this can be seen in the Lakeside scheme at Thurrock in Essex, developed by Capital Shopping Centres. Here, a landscaped area with a water feature forms the focal emphasis of the central mall. There is also a water sports and diving centre, a multi-screen cinema and a range of theme restaurants and small cafés. Because leisure and catering facilities encourage customers to stay longer, there are as many as 13,000 parking spaces. Great care is also taken to locate car parking, model the slope of the land, and design entrances and walk-ways so as to maximize pedestrian flow equally around the two levels of the centre. The developers recognize that shopping is a leisure activity, and the potential uniformity of shopping malls underlines the need for each of them to be presented as a stylish and individual package.

Although an examination of the potential for regional shopping centre development has suggested that there is capacity for considerably more schemes than exist in Great Britain, with many of these in London and the outer Metropolitan area, the number of new regional centres opening is likely to be severely limited because of continuing government planning guidelines towards such out-of-town shopping becoming extremely restrictive.

Planning and retailing

Straightaway, it is tempting to suggest that planners should be more broad-minded in their attitudes towards shopping, less afraid of innovation and change, and more prepared to accept the positive part that retail development can play in sustaining the urban economy. Developers, conversely, should be more sympathetic to the environmental impact of their projects and sensitive to the needs of the less mobile members of the community. All too often there has been a lack of understanding between local planning authorities and retail developers. The former are seen as principally focused upon protecting and reinforcing the existing shopping hierarchy, whereas the latter are viewed as being narrowly occupied with exploiting a particular trading position for their own gain. There are, of course, merits in both cases, and it is probably fair to say that, of late, much more common ground between the parties has been found.

Development frameworks

Shopping, as a sector, is prone to sudden and dramatic changes in location, layout, design and operation. Planning authorities, therefore, need to display a fast response towards shifts in retail fashion, facilitating desirable new modes of shopping in line with consumer preference, and controlling the worst excesses of an unfettered competitive market. Some of the major problem areas where planning and development agencies collide can be summarized as follows:

- The development of superstores, retail warehouse parks and regional shopping centres
- The location of retail outlets outside established shopping districts
- The development of large non-food stores
- The loss of local shops and rural shops
- Maintenance of a hierarchy of shopping districts
- Regeneration of inner-city areas
- Urban conservation and heritage-led regeneration
- Traffic management within established shopping districts
- Maintenance of viable shopping districts
- Shopping provision on industrial estates.

From the viewpoint of the development industry, those development plans that reflect a traditional shopping hierarchy based upon selective and tightly controlled strategic centres should be re-examined in the face of changing consumer mobility and fluctuations in the economics of shopping development and retail trading. Specialist advice of a kind rarely sought – operational not merely analytical – should be incorporated at plan preparation stage and referred to at regular intervals during implementation. One of the sorrier aspects of retailing in development planning is said to be the conflict that occurs between strategic and local planning authorities. Dissonance of this kind is said not only to produce market uncertainty but also to discredit the machinery of planning and lower the credibility of the authorities involved. Since the advent of regional planning bodies (currently the Regional Assemblies), there has been some progress to change this situation.

Needs testing

From a planning perspective, the government has produced guidance reflecting a plan-led approach towards development and reaffirming its belief that town centres should remain the anchor of the retailing system. This guidance was originally set down in a revised PPG6, which was published in June 1996 and in PPS6 which was published in 2005. The main objectives of the policy were:

- To sustain and enhance the vitality and viability of town centres
- To focus development, especially retail development, in locations where the proximity of business facilitates competition from which all consumers are

able to benefit and maximizes the opportunity to use means of transport other than the car
- To maintain an efficient, competitive and innovative retail sector
- To ensure the availability of a wide range of shops, employment, services and facilities to which people have access by a choice of means of transport.

This guidance was consistent with PPG13 (originally published in 1994 and updated in 2001), which focused on the inter-relationship between transport and land use and sought to 'reduce growth in the length and number of motorized journeys, to encourage alternative means of transport which have less environmental impact and hence reduce reliance on the private car' (Jones and Hillier 1999).

PPG6 introduced a new 'sequential' approach to site selection for retail development, which required planning authorities and developers to look first at town centre sites where buildings are available for redevelopment and conversion, then at edge-of-town sites and only then, if these are not available and suitable, at out-of-town sites that are accessible by a variety of means of transport. Probably the most uncertain and potentially contentious issues related to the interpretation of the terms 'vitality' and 'viability' and assessing the impact of large-scale development proposals on existing town centres. A strictly quantitative approach to impact assessment can lead to problems where even small variations in assumptions about trends in turnover, population, expenditure and the efficiency of use of existing floorspace can lead to a wide range of forecasts. Impact assessment is an inexact science coloured by the subjectivity of its users, a better practice being to afford greater weight to a qualitative analysis, centre-based survey approach that is simple, robust and pragmatic. This is explained elsewhere and involves the construction of an 'index of vitality' based upon a comparative study of certain main indicators, such as:

- Relative rental levels in centres
- Vacancy and occupancy rates
- Relative branch performance of major retailers
- Level of retailer representation and retail mix
- Presence of covered malls, speciality centres and new shopping centre proposals
- Presence of pedestrianization schemes
- Relative access to the centres for both public and private transport
- Level of car parking in the centres relative to their net retail floorspace
- Health of secondary shopping areas
- Presence of town centre management and promotion schemes
- Presence of other unique attractions such as tourism, conference venues, cinemas, theatres
- The size of the local town or town centre employment base.

(Norris and Jones 1993, URBED 1994)

This is argued to provide a more detailed insight into the local property market, which should make a significant contribution to the decision-making process at appeal.

Effects of the 'town centre first' policy

The new regime instituted by PPG6 and then carried forward by PPS6 has caused major changes in the development of retail space. Chief amongst these were:

- An end to out-of-town regional shopping centres and limited expansion of them
- Slower development of retail warehouse parks
- Changes in investment patterns to major shopping centres in regional centres like Birmingham, Manchester, Liverpool, Bristol, Nottingham, Sheffield and Leicester, and away from medium-sized towns and secondary shopping areas
- Increased confidence to invest in major city centre schemes
- Retailers having to put up with less preferable new development sites
- Extensions and mezzanine floors developed in existing out-of-town sites.

(British Council for Shopping Centres 2006)

The increase in in-town retail development can be seen in the Figure 16.1, which demonstrates that with the advent of the revised PPG6 in 1996, the tide has turned in favour of town centre schemes. It is interesting to note, however, that since the all-time low of 1995, the proportion of new retail floorspace built in town centres and their buffer zones has only increased to 35 per cent.

Despite this change in the amount of new store development, the effects of PPG6/PPS6 have not been felt in the same way, as is evident from Figure 16.2, which suggests that annual change in terms of the number of stores out of town and in town centres and neighbourhoods involves steady (if declining) growth out of town and steady falls elsewhere.

Future planning policy for shopping locations

Despite publishing PPS6 in 2005, the government-instituted review of the planning system led by Kate Barker which reported in 2006 (HM Treasury 2006a) cast doubt upon elements of the 'town centres first' policy, and this uncertainty has been compounded by the publication of a subsequent Planning White Paper and then Planning Bill which supports Barker's challenge of the policy. On the one hand, one might expect the property industry to have welcomed the challenge to the policy as it might lead to a reversion to the pre-1996 planning policy which supported profitable out-of-town development. However, as noted above, there has been considerable investment in town centre retail schemes and these are often high-cost, complex and only marginally profitable schemes which require long-term revenue streams from which to derive sufficient returns. If a

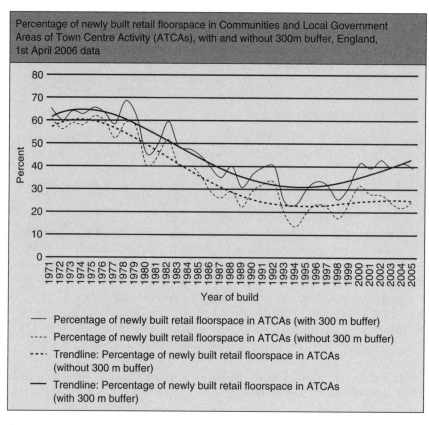

Figure 16.1 Percentage of newly built retail floorspace in local government ATCAs

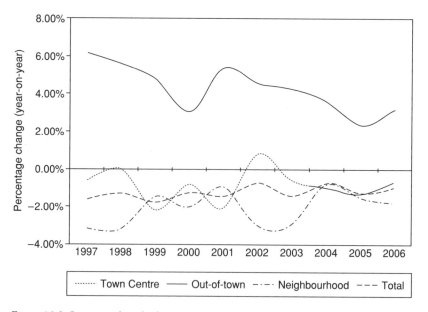

Figure 16.2 Store numbers by location (Verdict 2007)

new wave of out-of-town schemes were to be developed, in-town regeneration schemes led or even partly funded by retail components will be potentially fatally threatened.

Other planning considerations

An important, although at times forgotten, feature of retail development relates to the level of employment generated by new shopping centres. Even a small superstore of around 40,000 ft^2 (3787 m^2) can provide up to 150 full-time equivalent jobs and a hypermarket of 50,000 ft^2 (4645 m^2) as many as 220. Larger superstores can create work for anything from 300 to 700 people and even most of the new DIY stores employ about 20 to 30 people for every 10,000 ft^2 (929 m^2). Even more attractive in employment terms is the fact that these jobs are largely aimed at the young, the unskilled and those seeking part-time work. Furthermore, the development of an individual shopping project will usually have multiplier effects in the locality, generating demand for local goods and services and attracting other employers and business to the area. Case studies (Collens 1980) of two of the earliest hypermarket developments in the UK tend to support this view, although it is pointed out that any losses in employment are often geographically dispersed and therefore not so noticeable.

Not only is the retail sector of the commercial property development market the one in which local planning authorities have become most involved – it is also the one where most opportunity now exists for the extraction of planning gain (and is potentially ripe for the community infrastructure levy) from individual private development projects or the provision of community benefits in partnership schemes. Leisure and recreation facilities have been a popular addition to many new town centre schemes, and superstore operators have probably shown themselves to be among the most generous and flexible providers of planning gains. Such negotiations need to be carefully prepared and conducted.

Shopping patterns are particularly sensitive to significant changes in road networks and parking provisions. The requirement to refer planning applications for shop developments bordering major roads to highway authorities has often proved to be a rich source of frustrating and expensive delay. Major superstore operators are especially wary about traffic problems when prospecting for sites, and will usually be willing to make the necessary contributions to upgrade a local road network and create a good access. Nevertheless, some local planning authorities tend to overreact to such retail development proposals with regard to traffic generation, for superstore traffic has an uncanny propensity to adjust to peak hour flows.

Most planning authorities operate some form of retail frontage policy for shopping parades. Within primary parades the policy is normally to seek to maintain a level of around 70 per cent of those retail uses falling within Class A1 of the Use Classes Order (which is discussed in more detail in Chapter 3), but secondary parades are usually treated much more flexibly. Some strictly non-retail uses can prove an attractive draw and sometimes generate a greater pedestrian flow than conventional retail uses.

On a more positive note, it is clear that town centres are facing a challenge from out-of-town centres – a challenge of increased accessibility, convenience, environment and security. The argument runs that this challenge can be met, provided local authorities look at the problems of their centres on a comprehensive basis. Many planned shopping centres exhibit high-quality management, so there is no reason why local authorities should not examine ways of managing a whole town centre to ensure that it provides the best possible facilities and convenience to the shopping public.

Design and layout

It has been said that demographic changes, urban congestion and growing concern for the environment will precipitate a radical reappraisal of the purpose of shopping centres, their appeal, how they function and how their returns can be optimized (Walker 1990). An ageing population placing an emphasis on quality, convenience, high standards of service, leisure and lifestyle will dictate a different pattern of consumer behaviour. The design and layout of shopping centres will play an important part in providing a suitable environment to meet these changing expectations.

Whereas inflation fuelled the surge in retailers' sales volumes during the 1970s and 1980s, they are now having to find real sales growth in a highly competitive market, and are turning to design to achieve it. Retailers increasingly see design as more than a mere extension of architecture or shelf engineering, and rather a mainspring of the marketing drive, so that developers in the UK now continually monitor what is happening to the shops and shopping malls in the USA in order to review their approach here. This accent upon good design is underlined by the statement made by one leading retail designer:

> At its best shopping is an important experience that triggers off all the senses – visual, tactile, oral, audible and smell.

Planned shopping centres

The practical requirements in shopping are space, servicing, parking and accessibility, but increasingly these have to be matched with creative design, visual interest, character and feel. Thus, enormous opportunities exist for both the developer and the architect, and, although there can be no magic formula for success, a few basic principles underlying shopping centre design can be described as follows.

Size and shape

Generally speaking, new centres are becoming smaller and better integrated into the towns they serve. Even within the centres, many major retailers are themselves looking for somewhat smaller premises than they did a few years ago. Elevations are also being designed to a smaller scale. However, there is a recognition that the traditional strict rectangular shape is not essential to successful performance. Knowing retailers' requirements and being flexible enough to accommodate them is the important factor. At the Ashley Centre, Epsom, for example, where Bredero developed a 26,000 m² (280,000 ft²) centre, Marks & Spencer increased in size by 25 per cent, Waitrose reduced planned space by 10 per cent and the House of Fraser store was cut by 30 per cent to 4200 m² (45,000 ft²). With regard to the size of standard units within a centre, the favoured size of the majority of retailers is around 280 m² (3000 ft²) with a frontage of 7.5 m (24 ft) and adequate storage and ancillary space either at basement or first-floor level. The choice of size of structural grid is important to efficiency and flexibility, and, although there is no recognized norm, a grid of 11 m (35 ft) allows for a wide variety of unit sizes (Source: Northen 1977).

Enclosure

Opinions vary as to the future of the fully enclosed, environmentally controlled shopping centre. Suffice it to say that reports of its imminent demise a few years ago proved to be greatly exaggerated. In fact, many previously open centres have been enclosed. Nevertheless, that fast tempo of centre development during the late 1980s and early 1990s has slackened in recent years. However, where it takes place one major keynote of enclosure is buildability, because problems of cracking, movement, inadequate drainage and water leaks have been relatively common with older shopping centres. Roofs, for example, are frequently a cause for concern, especially with the fashion towards the introduction of atria, and the advice of a specialist roofing contractor early in the design process is imperative.

Cladding

The perimeter of a shopping centre is a massive area, and while light-coloured tiles might be attractive, they can be costly to clean. For this, and for other reasons of taste, there has been a marked return to the use of brick cladding. Whatever material is selected, the important thing is to pay careful attention to the finer detailing, so as to avoid costly difficulties if there is a component failure in the panels of brickwork.

Climate

Where a fully controlled environmental system is provided, the optimum climate is said to be somewhere between an office temperature and the outside temperature. Energy conservation is extremely important, and space heating, lighting and air-conditioning facilities must all be appraised for cost-effectiveness in terms of running costs as well as installation. Nevertheless, architects have become much more skilful at designing centres with a high proportion of natural lighting, but avoiding excessive heat loss or gain.

Environment

Experience drawn from the USA shows that it is crucial for a shopping centre to establish a distinct identity and create a pleasing environment. For too long the temptation has been to mimic successful schemes elsewhere, and, in a sense, one Arndale centre tended to look very much like another. The pressure now is for creativity and innovation, or as one leading American shopping centre developer has described it, 'a touch of the ethnic', arguing further that what people want is a return to the feeling of the Middle East bazaar or the market town of the middle ages, not the faceless could-be-anywhere shopping centre that has dominated the scene for so long. Greater use of domestic architecture and materials could be made, and much more tasteful use of colour and texture introduced. Extensive planting along the malls, with more trees, and not just low level shrubs, together with a wider variety of water features such as fountains, waterfalls and streams, should be encouraged, despite cries of high management costs. The use of carpets on stairs and ramps has also proved popular. Generally, therefore, the movement should be more towards the 'street scene' approach as opposed to the 'grand manner' of so many 1970s centres. As part of this approach, the design of signposting and facades should be sympathetic to the overall theme running through the architecture and landscaping of the centre.

Security

Apart from electrical surveillance equipment and management staff on patrol, the security aspects of a centre should be taken into account during the design stage of the development process. As regards safety, sprinkler systems and fire shutters can sometimes be a headache, and specialist advice is essential. In respect of vandalism and hooliganism, the number and siting of entrances, the clear run of malls, the location of security doors and the existence of blank spots and corners must all be considered.

Mixed use

Large mixed-use development schemes located in central city areas seem to be the order of the day in North America. It has been suggested that the pace of retailing activity fell in shopping centres during the 1970s and 1980s except where such projects were combined with hotels and entertainment facilities. Today, almost every centre across Europe is being reinvented as a leisure 'destination'. Cinemas, food courts, amusement arcades, and fitness centres are common, as shopping has itself become a leisure activity. Lawson (2003) identifies the following advantages of the incorporation of leisure activities in a shopping development:

- Leisure can draw in extra visitors
- It can give an edge over competing centres by creating excitement
- It can provide massive extra turnover for hybrid leisure/retail operators such as fast-food operators, which feeds through in higher rents
- It may future-proof a shopping centre against changes in shopping patterns.

Amenities

Most successful shopping centres provide, so far as possible, a wide range of amenities to cater for customers' needs. The most common of these are catering, toilets, crèches, telephones and play sculptures. The provision of catering is a controversial area, and solutions range from somewhere to sit down for a drink and a light meal to a full-blown food court. It has been found that, although food courts generally increase pedestrian flow into shopping centres, they do not necessarily increase retail sales, because well over half of the food court users do not visit other shops. Food courts are also expensive to furnish, maintain and refurbish. However, the food court concept has proved extremely successful in many centres, with location, circulation, visibility, light, height overhead, good service and variety being important factors. Toilets are now almost essential, sometimes together with a baby-care room, and should be away from major shopping frontages, but clearly signed. A crèche tends to be an expensive luxury, but some developers have partially solved the problem of cost by having properly supervised paying playgroups in their centres.

Parking

It is normally uneconomic to provide surface parking for town centre development schemes, but usually essential to provide such a facility in a suburban or edge-of-town location. Car parking, whether it be multi-storey or surface, can be provided specifically for the centre or as part of a wider community facility. Some retail developers, wherever possible, insist upon control over their own parking areas. The ideal provision is about four to six spaces for every 1000 ft^2 (93 m^2) of retail floorspace, and in town centres this can fall to under three, but the total amount of land for car parking works out to around 350 ft^2 (32.5 m^2) per space to allow for access and manoeuvring room. In respect of car parking provision there are design issues to be addressed, including:

- The attractiveness of the interface of the car park and the shopping centre
- Visible access and egress points, with adequate queuing areas
- The suitability of external screening and the sufficiency of cross-ventilation
- Effective control systems and efficient operation
- Well-placed pick-up points and trolley parks
- Good standard finishes and services
- A reasonable standard of lighting.

Servicing

A great deal of space is often wasted in over-providing for servicing, resulting in vast open areas. It is now recognized that only about 25 per cent of lorries using service yards are 15 m long (49 ft) or more and not every unit in the centre is visited. Most modern town centre schemes now have centralized unloading and servicing bays with localized trolley distribution. Among the questions that arise in the design and layout of service areas are: the degree of security afforded; the extent of separation of service and customer traffic; hours of access; level of ground, bays and ramps (not exceeding 1:10); adequate drainage; provision for waste disposal; sufficient turning room; and proper access for fire-fighting vehicles.

Malls

Shopping centre malls are becoming more varied in all respects – length, width, roof height, layout, frontage and decoration. There is really no such thing as an ideal length to a mall – interest and convenience to shoppers are by far the most important factors. Likewise, with mall widths – though there has been a tendency to design narrower double-fronted malls of between 5 m and 8 m (16– 26 ft) width to encourage shoppers to cross over and shop both sides of the mall. Increasingly, moreover, malls are broken up by squares and courts of varying sizes to create a more attractive environment. With regard to the shopping frontage, popular treatments over recent years have been the cranked line of shop fronts and the repeated bay-window style along a splayed frontage to a court. Apart from visually breaking up a flat surface, cranked or splayed frontages also give tenants two-sided representation. A further refinement is to distinguish separate malls by differing tenant mix. Mall heights are another design consideration. A low ceiling breaks up the perspective of a long mall, reduces building costs and minimizes energy consumption. A high ceiling can allow for unusual architectural treatments, and may be unavoidable in multi-level centres. Some interesting effects can also be achieved by combining a high roof with low eaves heights. Wherever possible, however, the tendency is for lower ceilings, on cost rather than aesthetic grounds. Other considerations to be taken into account in mall design include: the sympathetic use of natural light; attractive entrances; rest areas with seating and plants; focal points for displays and promotions; fixed and free-standing litter bins; special features, such as water, sculpture or lighting effects; and public information points.

Levels

Traditionally it has been thought daring for a developer in the UK to provide shopping on two levels, let alone more, and always provident to encourage horizontal rather than vertical movement around a centre. However, eight-storey shopping centres in Singapore and Hong Kong manage to break all the rules and succeed. American shopping developments seem to be able to make two-, three- and even four-storey shopping work well. Underground servicing avoids pedestrian and vehicular conflict and permits efficient exploitation of constrained town centre sites. However, it is relatively costly to construct and sometimes it creates difficulties in access.

Maintenance

It is important to design for low maintenance costs. Maintenance-free and vandal-proof materials and finishes should be selected wherever possible. Structural components should be designed for ease of cleaning, and services installed to facilitate access for inspection and repair. Circulation areas should be laid out with the need to use cleaning machines on a daily basis in mind.

Sustainable store developments

Chapter 10 discussed the motivations and actions of retailers in terms of their approach to sustainability, as well as tools such as BREEAM and the Green Guide to Specification which assist developers in providing retail premises that meet retailers' sustainability criteria. Examples, from an increasing number available, of how one retailer developed premises which demonstrated its sustainability aspirations are provided by Tesco at its Wick (Scotland) and Shrewsbury (England) store developments. These stores have 50 per cent and 40 per cent smaller carbon footprints than conventional supermarkets of comparable size. The designers of these stores managed this achievement by using technologies which include (Keeping 2008):

- Wooden frame and plywood external walls
- Boreholes to aid heating and cooling
- Five micro wind turbines powering the checkouts
- Rainwater harvesting
- Roof lights supporting photovoltaic cells
- Cold air retrieval which moves cold air from refrigerated areas to warm areas of the stores.

It is expected that attending to increasing demands for sustainable practices by retailers will become critical for developments that wish to attract major retailers in future.

Pedestrian flow

Shopping centres are all about pedestrian flow – the total amount drawn to the centre and the maximizing of circulation around it. The location of magnet stores, careful siting of entrances, skilful arrangement of malls and subtle manipulation of circulation space to create areas of interest all conventionally contribute to an optimum flow and high trading volume. Some simple guidelines can be laid down from the experience of pedestrian behaviour in various centres developed over the years.

Entrances

The first function of a centre is to attract customers to it. Two basic approaches can be identified to the location and design of shopping centre entrances. First, the strikingly obvious entrance that heralds access to the centre and does not depend overly upon the surrounding area. Featured entrances of this kind are of particular importance to free-standing and wholly enclosed shopping centres as a relief to the otherwise monolithic appearance and as an environmental control barrier. The second approach uses the psychologically more subtle entrance that entices shoppers into the centre. All entrances should be inviting and should not present the shopper with a choice. The use of tenants having interesting displays at the entrance is effective, and striking signing on the exterior of the shopping centre is critical. For out-of-town centres, the customer will already have decided to visit the centre, but helpful signage for parking and shopping must be provided. In major centres it is essential to indicate clearly the various entrances to different sectors.

Magnets and anchors

There are certain tenants and retail uses whose presence in a shopping centre is held to be critical to the success of a scheme of development. Known as the 'magnet' or 'anchor' tenants, they traditionally comprise department stores, variety stores, superstores and certain other major multiple traders. A magnet not only draws shoppers into a centre, or from one end to another, but as a pre-letting for a new development it is also the bait with which to catch acceptable tenants for other individual shop units. Variations in layout to generate pedestrian flow by the different siting of magnets have been tried over the years. Sometimes a magnet has been placed at each end of a single mall. Sometimes several magnet traders have been placed at extreme ends or at intersections of malls and, with smaller centres where there is only one obvious major space for an anchor, it will be placed as far away from the entrance as can be arranged. It is also common practice with stores to try to keep them away from the prime frontage positions along the mall, because they are able to trade from what might be thought inferior pitches because of the immense consumer loyalty they command, whereas the standard unit type of tenant depends upon a high degree of comparison and impulse buying, triggered by prominent window displays. However, times are changing with regard to magnets. Department stores are still opening new outlets, but they are also closing down others, and no longer can a developer rely upon attracting such tenants as John Lewis, Debenhams or Selfridges to a scheme. The superstores are an obvious alternative, and the likes of Waitrose, Tesco and Sainsbury are all prepared to consider town centre locations, but prefer predominantly single-storey space and look for generous parking provision. Supermarkets are only effective as true magnets in conjunction with leading non-food stores in schemes of any significance, and, on their own, they tend to give the centre a convenience-good flavour. More recently, the concept of the food court as an anchor to a planned shopping centre has been adopted from North America. One example of this focus on food is the Trafford Centre in Manchester where a substantial two-storey section of the centre is given over to dining. A large range of fast-food outlets are available on the ground floor and more traditional restaurants and bars are situated on the first floor. The variety of outlets concentrated in a themed environment, together with access to a multi-screen cinema, keeps the centre buzzing long after the shops have closed.

Vertical circulation

Many planned centres include two, and sometimes more, levels of shopping with varying access. Sloping sites have helped some, such as Brent Cross and the St George's Centre in Preston, where it has been possible to avoid making either level especially dominant. Elsewhere, by skilful design, shoppers must be persuaded to ascend (or preferably to descend, which they are more inclined to do) to secondary floors. This requires the inclusion of strong visual links between floors, usually by means of open balconies, prominent staircases or alluring escalators, assisted by good signposting and seductive advertising. Themed floors are another possibility, for, in one way or another, a prime objective in the design and management of future shopping centres will be to get shoppers to use more than just the ground floor. However, it must be appreciated that multi-level centres create problems of fire control and smoke as well as heavy reliance on artificial lighting and ventilation.

Refurbishment

Most of the major planned shopping centres built in the 1970s and 1980s are now obsolescent and in need of substantial refurbishment. Many of them have problems with open malls or central areas, poor natural light, inadequate services and facilities, and outdated circulation patterns. In addition, many existing centres do not fully comply with stricter fire regulations and they possess certain other inherent design faults. Whereas high streets experience a constant rejuvenation, and leading department stores and superstores under a single ownership have been revitalized in response to economic pressure, shopping centres often have not. With diminishing market share and growing competition, refurbishment is now the name of the game.

Any decision to refurbish on a large scale must obviously be preceded by a careful study to ensure that the expenditure is justified. In this process, several common problems can be identified:

- The multiplicity of ownership, where there is often a financial institution, a developer, a local authority and sometimes a multiple store holding long-term interests in the property, and it is often necessary to renegotiate the lease structure or buy-in the freehold.

- Retailers are keen to improve their trading prospects, but less willing to pay for the improvements, or suffer the disruption while building works are carried out.
- The formula for viability is extremely difficult to calculate, depending as it does upon renegotiated rents at review related to comparative turnover and profitability.

In the context of the above problems, it has been pointed out that the financial sharing formulae provided in development agreements were often generously loaded in favour of the ground landlord, both in terms of initial rent and sharing provisions. Few imagined that such profound changes at such a high cost would have to be undertaken so soon to sustain the market share and investment worth of centres. The problem is frequently compounded by what is known as 'adverse' gearing, which has been described succinctly as follows:

> Take a centre which originally cost £10 million to build, with the developer achieving a notional return of 7.5 per cent on this amount. The fixed element of the ground rent was, say, £275,000 and the original occupational rents amounted to, say, £1.3 million, with the provision to review the rents to 50 per cent of the occupational rents after allowance for the developer's notional return on his investment. If the occupation rents have now increased to say £4.2 million on such a formula, the local authority's share of the income will have increased from 21 per cent of occupational rents at the outset to 42 per cent within a 15 year time-span. The curve is exponential and the situation continuously gets worse at the expense of the management owners.
>
> (Clifford 1994)

Thus, the cost versus income equation to the party responsible for necessary comprehensive refurbishment is often a difficult one to balance, with different areas performing differently in different years. A report produced by the British Council of Shopping Centres in 1994 concluded that most refurbishments, stemming from a 'defensive' justification, take place at a later point in the economic cycle of the shopping centre than the optimum period, and that by tracking more closely the shopping centre lifecycle investment decisions can be made earlier to reduce time-lag between the deterioration of a centre's performance and the completion of the refurbishment. The report further suggests various evaluation techniques that can be applied to ensure that the timing of refurbishment is undertaken in such a way as to maximize cashflow, taking into account risk, project running costs and the consequence of not refurbishing.

In general, however, if major retail investments are to be protected they must at least hold on to, and preferably increase, their market share. However, the extent to which reconstruction and reorganization takes place will vary according to individual circumstances. But, inevitably, opportunities will be presented to buy-out leases and re-let premises; to create extra letting space in useless voids or by extending the building or narrowing the malls; to enclose open areas; to install new plant and building servicing facilities; to adjust the tenant-mix and add missing traders; and to generally upgrade the environment and decor of the centre. If the work is successful, turnover will increase and higher rents will be achieved on review to produce an acceptable return to the investor.

This was the approach adopted by retailer Marks & Spencer at one of its high street stores, in Bournemouth. This shop was identified by the retailer as atypical and thus one which would present challenges for the design team who were charged with designing a 'green refurbishment' of the 51,000 ft^2 premises. It is interesting to note the lack of obvious 'green' features at this store – it does not include wind turbines for example and although its roof does accommodate plants which help prevent water runoff, they cannot be seen from the street. Also, 80 per cent of the waste from the refurbishment scheme was sent to recycling rather than landfill. Technologies used in the refurbishment include (Keeping, 2008):

- Insulated entrances
- Light sensors in fitting rooms and efficient lighting generally
- Efficient air conditioning which is targeted at head level rather than for general circulation
- Shelving made from recycled wood fibre board
- Dual-flush, water saving toilet cisterns.

Shopping centre management

Of all the commercial sectors of the property market, shop developments have traditionally depended upon good management, and arguably have much to teach the office, leisure and industrial sectors.

Much also remains constantly to be learned from good practice at home and abroad, especially from North America. Shopping centre developers and owners are acutely aware of the continuing set of challenges that face them. It is well recognized that the shift to out-of-town locations, the emergence of new retail concepts, a squeeze on retailers' profit margins and low expectation of growth in consumer spending make it even more important to ensure that a centre has the ability to gain market share from its competitors, for the benefit of its retailers, and ultimately the developer and owner. Location, accessibility, local dominance and tenant mix all play a part in this, but it has been stated that of equal importance is the style in which the centre is managed (Saggess 1993).

Tenant mix

The aim of any shopping development should be to attract tenants who will maximize turnover and profitability, so that rental income can also be negotiated to the highest possible level.

For a long time, developers in the UK, having conceived a retail scheme, would place the units on the market and allow market forces to determine the ultimate shopping mix. In some instances this remains true, especially in difficult letting markets where any tenant willing to pay a reasonable rent is likely to be welcome. However, creating and maintaining a productive tenant mix is essential to the economic performance of any centre, although implementation sometimes calls for a steady nerve. In achieving this there are several criteria to be examined:

- *Cumulative attraction:* produced by the clustering of different but related shops together, in a manner that generates the same magnet effect as that of a major user.
- *Competition and comparison:* where several similar shops offering the same kinds of goods are grouped together so that shoppers are attracted to a centre knowing that they will be able to compare and contrast goods and prices.
- *Compatibility:* some shops are positively prejudicial to one another in respect of lighting, noise, marketing, smell and crowding, so special care must be taken in both the selection of certain trades and their positioning in a centre.

A useful definition of tenant mix can be provided as follows:

> Tenant mix is a continuous policy of maximizing public patronage of a shopping centre by optimizing the number of traders, the size of their premises, their styles and goods sold or services rendered.

The objective is to secure a range of retailers who will appeal to the largest possible proportion of the catchment population commanded by the centre. The right mix will, therefore, be determined by the size, composition and quality of the catchment area. Large but low-income group hinterlands would justify an emphasis upon a variety rather than a department store and might encourage a developer to include a market in the centre. A smaller, but more affluent local population would suggest a greater concentration upon high fashion and jewellery shops and fewer accents upon general convenience shopping. The younger the population, the more fashion, children's wear and electrical goods shops, and an extensive and varied catchment area could support a specialist retailer such as a book shop or healthfood shop. Some of the other considerations to be taken into account regarding tenant mix can be summarized as below:

- What proportions of convenience and durable goods shops to include?
- How many, if any, service shops, such as banks, betting shops, launderettes and public houses to permit?
- Whether to try to attract small local traders as well as national multiples?

- Is a 'themed' floor approach, focusing on such topics as 'the home' or 'women' or 'leisure', worth developing?
- What steps must be taken to avoid or overcome the creation of 'dead spots'?
- Are fast food outlets to be encouraged, and is a gourmet food hall a potential component?
- What is the appropriate ratio between floorspace given over to major 'anchors' and to other units (usually about 40:60)?

A survey of retailers showed that tenant mix is the single most important factor in selecting a suitable trading location, and also a major source of occupier dissatisfaction. The same survey also revealed: that the role of anchor stores should be considered both in terms of the type of store involved and the amount of space allocated (a little less, and more accent on convenience goods); that the independent retail sector should be allocated significant amounts of space; but that the argument for incorporating considerable leisure facilities within shopping centres has not yet been made (Watt and Valente 1991). It concludes by stressing that a successful tenant mix does not occur naturally, but requires careful consideration of both consumer needs and those of retailers themselves. However, above all it calls for a positive approach to be adopted, that treats the scheme in its entirety and places due emphasis on both primary and secondary space.

Initial research must be coupled with continuous monitoring of the catchment area in order to change the balance of traders, as both supply and demand evolve in a particular location. It can still be argued that this presupposes a degree of management flexibility, which does not sit entirely comfortably alongside the current landlord–tenant relationship (Watt and Valente 1991).

Leases

For some time there has been considerable debate about the legal relationship between shopping centre owners and retail tenants. The combination of over-supply, recession and national economic policy during the early 1990s has allowed many occupiers to rewrite lease terms, but major issues still persist. These include:

- *Privity of contract.* Many retail tenants have found to their cost that if an assignee goes bust, then the responsibility for lease and the payment of rent returns to the original leaseholder. Some landlords refuse a re-let, or accept a lower rent, looking to the head leaseholder for the difference, because of the covenant position. However, the Landlord and Tenant (Covenants) Act 1995 has changed the ground rules, so that: for new tenancies the tenant will cease to be liable on assignment; a tenant may be required to guarantee his immediate successor; a landlord can apply to be released from liability after assignment; the landlord can pre-define terms upon which the tenant will be allowed to assign commercial leases; and all covenants are enforceable by and against assignees. For new and existing leases, a former tenant cannot be liable for variations to the lease and has the right to an overriding lease upon paying the arrears.

- *Length of lease*. Pension funds and insurance companies, the major owners of shopping centres in the UK, traditionally demanded a multiplicity of blue chip tenants contracted on twenty-five year leases before property investments became acceptable. Turnover rents and short leases, which arguably are needed if a centre is to be run as a business, are still treated at valuation as insecure income. There is now a tendency towards shorter leases, however, prompted by economic circumstance, but also in recognition of the need to concentrate upon quality of income rather than length. Ten or fifteen year leases are far more commonplace these days.

- *Upwards-only rent reviews*. Another chief target of retail tenants is the upwards-only rent review, and support for this view is found from those close to government who see such a practice as profoundly inflationary. However, institutional investors funding retail development argue that the whole basis of their equity financing of property requires a relatively low return on the basis that rent will grow. Anything less would represent an unfair balance between returns and risk.

Further changes towards a more flexible structure in the leasehold relationship between landlords and tenants in the retail sector seem possible. However, it has to be recorded that it all depends on the state of the economy, and on where you stand, as to the benefits or otherwise of particular terms and conditions at any given time.

Turnover rents

Turnover rents first originated in the USA during the 1930s, and now few units in shopping centres there are ever let on any other terms. However, they remain the exception rather than the norm in the UK. Nevertheless, having been pioneered by Capital & Counties in the early 1970s, the use of turnover rents is now more familiar among shopping centres.

Typically, a turnover rent in the UK comprises two elements. First, a base rent, which is usually expressed as a proportion of agreed open market rental, and commonly set at about 75–80 per cent. Second, a percentage of the annual sales turnover of the tenant, which can be as low as 1.5 per cent and as high as 15 per cent, but normally ranges from around 7 to 12 per cent, according to trade. The basic formula is subject to any number of refinements. The basic rent may refer to an average of past years' rents; turnover provisions may be delayed until, say, the third year of opening; large stores may claim an exempt first slice of turnover; it may be calculated gross or net of tax; or the percentage figure may change according to different levels of sales. Table 16.1, however, shows a typical example of turnover rate percentages.

The advantages of employing turnover rents are that:

Table 16.1 Turnover rent percentages

Trade	%
Jeweller	10–11
Women's fashion	8–10
Men's fashion	8–9
Radio & electrical	7
Catering	7
Shoes (fashion)	9–10
Shoes (family)	8–9
Records	9
Sports goods	9
Greengrocer	6
Butcher	4–5
Baker	5

- Landlord and tenant share an objective to maximize income.
- The landlord has an incentive to promote the centre and provide a high standard of management.
- The landlord receives an annual share of rental growth.
- Rent review problems and negotiations are minimized.
- It can be a useful device in an inflationary period as far as the landlord is concerned.
- It can be helpful in circumstances where the trading potential of a new development is uncertain.
- More attention is paid by the landlord to establishing the correct tenant mix.

On the other hand, there are various difficulties associated with turnover rents. These include:

- Some trades, such as television hire, building societies and banks, are not suitable for turnover rents.
- New traders might not have a track record and cannot easily be assessed
- The system really works best when traders can quickly and simply be moved around the centre, or poorly performing traders substituted by potential high-turnover ones, as occurs in the USA.
- Landlord and tenant legislation in the UK is not designed for turnover rents, for apart from the security of tenure provisions there are some doubts about the status of such arrangements.
- Problems may arise in controlling assignments, and landlords must take care not to disturb the tenant mix.
- Some traders are reluctant to disclose turnover figures, and the monitoring of accounts can be difficult and costly, but externally audited certificates are normally provided.

- Unknown levels of rental income are said to deter financial institutions from funding developments let on a turnover basis, but this criticism is probably exaggerated.
- Similarly, it is suggested that valuation is a problematic exercise, but again growing familiarity is showing such fears to be groundless.

In managed centres, overall, the use of turnover rents should forge the relationship between all the parties ever closer and contribute towards mutual success.

Promotion and public relations

A shopping centre will need active promotion before, during and after development, the aim being to increase public awareness and thereby increase pedestrian flow and turnover. To foster or retain goodwill on the part of both shoppers and retailers, there is also a need to ensure a high and constant level of public relations.

The promotion of shopping centres has become almost an industry in itself. Extensive promotional campaigns will normally be mounted at the launch of a new centre, where there are still a substantial number of units vacant, or when sales are static, declining or threatened. It is not possible to detail all the techniques of promotion or aspects of public relations that have evolved or emerged over recent years, but some of the most effective policies can be summarized as follows:

- The centre should have a clear identity, reinforced by a memorable name and a striking logo.
- Likewise, a friendly and cooperative stance should be adopted towards local community groupings, such as Chambers of Trade and Commerce, Rotary, Lions Club, Round Table, schools, clubs, women's organizations and the local council.
- Special events of a community nature such as a Christmas carol service, a wine festival or a gymnastics display could be held to draw attention to the centre and make shopping interesting.
- A programme of tenant-oriented promotions should be prepared in collaboration with the retailers and might include events such as fashion shows, craft displays or exhibitions.
- Regular press releases should be prepared and carefully placed.
- A survey of shoppers' views about the centre, its competition, travel and parking behaviour, the shopping mix, facilities provided, spending habits and desired changes or additional trades or service should be conducted from time to time.
- Many larger centres now have their own websites providing details of retailers in the centre, facilities, location, forthcoming events, and employment opportunities.

Most important of all, however, is to ensure that all public relations and promotional activities take place against a deliberate and agreed overall policy, otherwise the image portrayed will be at best commonplace, and at worst counterproductive.

Centre management

The primary functions of a shopping centre management have succinctly been described as (Martin 1982):

- *Paperwork:* the administration of head leases and leases, accounting for rent and service costs and secretarial, insurance and legal services.
- *People:* human relations, comprising public relations, publicity, promotion and security.
- *Premises:* maintenance, primarily of common areas in respect of both buildings and plant.

In a shopping centre of any size there will be a shopping centre manager, representing the interests of the developer or owner. Since the late 1980s there has been a tremendous elevation in the status of the shopping centre manager and a consequent rise in the skills and standards of performance expected of them. A good manager can make the difference between a successful centre and mediocre one. Among the many duties falling upon the centre manager will be the following.

Maintenance of common area

This includes: routine housekeeping, such as cleaning, polishing, rubbish and litter collection, plant watering and changing of light bulbs and air filters; regular maintenance, such as repainting, turning of carpets and overhaul of plant and machinery; repairs, such as cracked floors, chipped walls and broken elements; and occasional replacement of such components as escalators, lights, carpets, toilets, boilers, mall seating and entrance doors.

Security

Different levels of security will have to be provided, depending upon the size and nature of the centre, its location and setting, the kind of traders represented and the availability of regular fire, police and other services. Aspects of security to be considered will include hooliganism, vandalism, shoplifting, lost children, health and safety at work, protection during building work, fire precaution, emergency lighting, illness or accident procedures and employment of suitable staff. Good security has been defined as:

> A state of benevolent vigilance at all times towards the public, tenants, staff and contractors by way of well thought-out and constantly reassessed routines and resources.

> (Martin 1982)

Service charge

The service charge is the levy by the landlord upon the tenant for all the operational, maintenance, repair and security services provided at the centre. Although such charges used to be based upon an agreed sum, the common practice now is for full recovery of all the costs of specified services to take place. Although there are a variety of ways of apportioning charges, in a large enclosed centre this can work out at about £54 per m^2 (£5.00 per ft^2) a year. A proportion of the service charge should also be set aside as a sinking fund for the replacement of major items of plant.

Insurance

The main aspects of insurance with which a shopping centre manager will be concerned are the preservation of income, the reinstatement of property, those liabilities incurred under the terms of the head lease, and any legal liabilities arising out of statute or common law. Rightly, however, it has been stated that insurance is not a substitute for vigilance and good management (Martin 1982).

Traders' associations

There appears to be a notable lack of interest by both landlords and tenants in the formation and running of traders' or merchants' associations in the UK. This is beginning to change as each party recognizes the benefits to be gained. Indeed, most modern leases insist that tenants join an association if one exists. It is really then for the centre manager to ensure that there is an appreciation of the role of the association as being to promote the interests of the centre as a whole.

Town centre management

Many of the principles and practices relating to the effective management of planned shopping centres can equally be applied to town centres themselves. Over recent years the high street has become a fashionable policy focus, which has been formalized with the emergence of Town Centre Management (TCM) initiatives aimed at addressing the issue of enhancing the vitality and viability of town centres. Town centre management has generally been defined by the Association of Town Centre Management as follows:

> Town Centre Management is the effective coordination of the private and public sectors, including local authority professionals, to create, in partnership, a successful town centre – building on full consultation.

In particular, TCM is said to provide (Parker 1994):

- a means to co-ordinate the more effective use of public resources
- a new policy/resource priority and focus
- a conduit for establishing private and public sector partnerships
- a lever to secure further private sector investment in the high street
- a cooperative vehicle for community participation and mobilization
- a riposte to out-of-town competitive retail pressures.

Since its inception in 1986, TCM has been adopted by many towns. It has been widely endorsed and actively promoted by government, leading retailers, local community ventures and property-owning institutions, but remains largely a local authority initiative. The origin of TCM lies in the threat posed by out-of-town retail facilities and a growing concern over the health of the high street. It is founded on the property management practices employed by the leading shopping centre owners, but without the legal powers available to them through tenure.

A key element in successful TCM is the appointment of an effective town centre manager whose main functions have been described as follows (Court and Southwell 1994):

- to promote an area rather than a function-based focus to the management of town centres
- to represent the opinions and priorities of all interested public and private sector groups
- to coordinate private and public sector roles and policies to achieve a common aim (i.e. the improvement of the town centre)
- to manage effectively town centre initiatives/developments
- to liaise between local authority functions and private sector requirements
- to promote the town-centre and TCM concept.

Research and experience shows that the application of TCM, to date, varies very substantially in organization, finance, power and purpose. Being primarily local authority based, it is also largely dependent upon public funding, with notable but limited private sector contributions.

A report produced in 1994 found little to suggest that TCM was not considered to be an effective approach to an urgent and obvious problem. Nevertheless, it suggested that private–public sector cooperation was an integral part of successful TCM, which could be encouraged by:

- real participation
- a town centre manager
- aims beyond the janitorial
- an absence of 'political' debate
- effective decision-making
- rational 'business' planning projects rather than politically oriented TCMs
- initiatives backed by authority.

Conversely, it has been argued that it is important to acknowledge that the high street is a market place and not a homogeneous community of common interests. The application of public resources to one priority over another is also seen as a conflict faced by many elected members, requiring political as opposed to 'technical' resolution. Likewise, the argument runs that, for the private sector, whereas the high street is the traditional economic focus of the commercial activities that sustain the urban fabric, it must at the same time be recognized that the high street is also the social and cultural stage for the wider urban community (Parker 1994).

One approach to town centre regeneration that has been used to great effect in urban regeneration in North America and now to some degree in the UK is Business Improvement Districts (BIDs). In essence, BIDs are a technique that property owners and businesses can use to organize and finance improvements to retail, commercial and industrial areas. Tax is usually collected by the relevant government agency and then returned to the BID from which they were collected to be used for such items as:

- Improving the appearance, convenience, and day- and night-time appeal of the district for employees, residents, shoppers, and visitors
- Enhancing commercial property values
- Increasing business profitability.

Conclusion

The face of shopping continues to change. Large stores, having gained a place out-of-town, are now to be subject to much more selective planning control. There is an increasing awareness of the vital need to improve and promote traditional town centres, and a conscious attempt by many councils to adopt a management approach towards the issue. Category killers in such areas as electronics, office goods, household linens and sporting goods are a significant force, as are factory outlets. Conventional leasehold terms and conditions will surely change to produce a much more flexible system. Considerable imagination is also being brought to bear upon the retail sector as witnessed by the refurbishment of many old inner-city buildings to form new shopping centres and arcades. Similarly, dated existing planned shopping centres are being revitalized. Nevertheless, in respect of shopping centre management, we still have much to learn from the active and intensive management practices of US centres.

Online shopping is growing in the UK, with sales having grown from 1 per cent of retail sales in 1999 to 5 per cent in 2007. Forecasts suggest that it might rise to 10.7 per cent by 2015 and will probably continue to focus on those areas of retailing which are today most popular with online shoppers – books, music and DVD, groceries, software, hardware, clothing, footwear and gifts.

This will have consequences for retailers and developers of their properties, not least in how turnover rents will be judged if sales have occurred online but goods are collected from a store.

The bigger issue, however, for developers to consider over the next decade will be the evolution of planning policy on town centres and the focus, or not, on 'town centres first'. If policy reverts away from this, the viability of many recent town centre schemes, including those which have been responsible for enabling regeneration schemes, will be severely tested.

17 Office development

The pace of change within the world economy over the last decade, fostered by rapid globalization of business, geo-political factors and developments in communications and information technology, has arguably been the most rapid ever. A technological revolution has occurred which has affected the nature of urban areas more significantly than anything since the original industrialization of modern economies. The old economies of Western Europe and North America are competing with the new economies of Asia, the Pacific Rim, South America and Eastern and Central Europe.

The rapidity of development in countries such as China and India, as well as others like Brazil and Russia easily outstrips that of the 'old guard' economies like the USA, UK, Germany and Japan. Amongst the reasons for this are the relatively cheap availability of abundant natural and human resources. These new economies are servicing the West's needs for manufactured goods by providing cheaper and increasingly better quality products to a far greater degree than was previously the case. Furthermore, a more recent phenomenon has been the provision of more and different types of services by the new economies to the older ones – the 'off-shoring' of back-office functions, such as call or contact centres, IT support (including software design, helpdesk functions and data centres and accounting) to locations such as India and South Africa is commonplace and driven by cost-focused decision-making. These circumstances have led to incredibly rapid urbanization within these countries, not only to provide the accommodation for manufacturers and service providers, but also to satisfy the residential and retailing needs of local populations as they have become more affluent and urbanized.

Meanwhile, in Europe, the ongoing evolution of management systems and the corporate drive for cost effectiveness have been stated (Chapman 1995) to affect the nature of cities in at least four ways:

1. The historic migration of high-volume, low-value-added ('back office') activity out of the city
2. The subsequent, and sometimes simultaneous migration of this type of activity to other lower-cost countries ('off-shoring')

3. The higher-value-added, lower-volume activity remaining within the urban area, but now dispersing from the centre
4. The reverse of these dispersal trends in the new magnetism of the concentration of specialist, relatively low-volume, but high-value-added activity into the core of the city, especially for those activities that require a great deal of cooperation among people.

The continuing search for increased business efficiency within the global economy has led to a desire for the optimization of real estate assets in terms of location, quantity, specification and tenure. Cities themselves need to compete as businesses, with: an awareness of their inherent strengths and weaknesses; an evaluation of the necessary management, skill, resource and marketing abilities required to maintain and enhance the city economy; and the desirability and direction of specialization, excellence and expertise. In this context, it has been argued that effective, properly resourced partnerships of central and local government and the business community, with coherent reliable strategies to underpin the existing economies in order to attract more firms, will be essential for the long-run demand for offices (Chapman 1995).

It was the advent and application of communication and information technology that brought about the need for changing office design and location, even more rapidly than most professional observers anticipated. An awareness and understanding of the requirements of information technology can rightly be said to have been the keynotes of successful space management since the 1980s. Office activities and structures need to adjust so quickly and so often in response to new business demands and services that, however much of a cliché it has become, the watchword in office development has always been flexibility.

In addition, it has been argued that the workplace has changed for several other reasons (Steelcase Strafor 1990). Information technology has altered the social composition of the office, producing a more equal, demanding and discriminating workforce who expect to enjoy choice at work. There is greater freedom, moreover, in the use of time and the location of the office. And the economics of office-space use has changed so that far more money is now spent on relatively short-life interiors and proportionately less on the shell and exterior elements of office buildings.

Many of the great issues concerning office development that have emerged in Europe over the last two decades were originally identified by Dr Frank Duffy as:

- Harmonization of environmental and product standards throughout the European Community
- Increasing awareness of what can be learned from the best international initiatives – North American, Japanese, Scandinavian, German
- The increasing importance of 'green' issues in the workplace – avoiding deleterious products, energy used in component manufacturing and building use, sustainability in materials usage

- Rethinking the costs of commuter transportation, given the potential of information technology
- The increasing power of better educated, more scientific facilities managers
- The opening up of the design process to end users
- Much more inventive use of the increasingly expensive resources of time and space.

(Steelcasef Strafor 1990)

Perhaps not even Frank Duffy, as visionary as he is, could have foreseen what will arguably be the most significant force for change to the location and design of office buildings in the twenty-first century – environmental sustainability. Now, at the beginning of the century, we are witnessing significant and rapid change in terms of the development of environmental policy and regulation as it affects the built environment. Developers are becoming better advised and are demonstrating clearer thinking about how to respond to this agenda. Regulations are certainly prompting this change of approach but so too are corporate attitudes to sustainable development. This is arguably a more potent driving force, as it is those seeking office space as occupiers and those providing development finance for new office buildings who are demanding a more sustainable approach by developers. The provision of so-called 'green buildings' (however their definition might evolve) will increasingly influence the market for new and existing property.

The new order created by this change in priorities and environmentally based decision-making will also have consequences for how we build offices as well as where we build them. This latter issue is now being influenced by the evolution in the workplace which began in the 1980s and was fostered by the communications and information technology revolution. Managerial concepts are different from those of the last century – systems are more fluid, hierarchies are less prevalent, organizations are leaner, and 'value-added' activities are prized ever more highly than systematic ones. The consequences of these and the increasing value placed on individuals' time mean that workplaces and their design and locations must also evolve. Organizations now require less space than previously, and they want it in different places.

Over the last twenty years we have witnessed profound changes in the office function that have required developers to have a greater appreciation of not only the prospective tenants' operational needs but also those of their staff. Nothing can be taken for granted for very long in the world of office work.

In examining trends and prospects for the planning and development of offices, this chapter is divided into the following sections:

- Location and provision
- Planning and office development
- Design and layout
- Services and facilities
- Business and office parks
- Facilities management.

Location and provision

Hunch and intuition are no longer sufficient attributes in the analysis of office markets to determine planning policies and development opportunities. Office forecasting has become a more specialized task. For example, trend extrapolation might be a useful starting point in examining market conditions, but as an accurate indicator of future demand it is a poor device. Likewise, vacancy rates give a very broad guide to the imbalance between demand and supply in the market, but conceal the effect of a multitude of determining factors.

What seems clear from a succession of major surveys is that location remains the single most important factor to occupiers, out of the four major determinants of location, building design, cost of occupation and lease terms. One commentator has summarized the pressures on office location as follows:

> Although some demand has been diverted away from city centres to business parks and the communication revolution has allowed such activities as home working and hot-desking, the prospects for the city-centre office are still good. First, the concept of the office is remarkably durable. People do not need to work in offices but they choose to do so because of the human need for social interaction. Second, governments and pressure groups throughout the world are pressing for a sustainable use of resources. This implies a long-term reduction in car use, the regeneration and repopulation of city centres, and the development of improved and more modern public transport systems. All of this suggests yet more use for and demand for city-centre offices.
>
> (Havard 2002)

Moreover, the traditional notions of office and business location in respect of towns and cities and town and city centres are being transformed. Advanced tools of communication such as video-conferencing, PC video-phone, telepresence and remote diagnostics enable business people to be in contact with customers, colleagues, collaborators and support services from almost anywhere to anywhere (Chapman 1995).

In terms of provision, the pre-eminence of London is striking. For the purposes of investment decision-making in the development process, a hierarchical classification of UK office markets is obvious:

1. Central London
2. London suburbs and M25 locations
3. Metropolitan regional centres, such as Birmingham, Bristol, Manchester, Leeds, Edinburgh, Glasgow and the Thames Valley
4. Major second-tier centres such as Nottingham, Newcastle, Sheffield and Cardiff
5. Minor second-tier centres such as Brighton, Peterborough and Oxford.

Demand

Demand for office accommodation can be said to arise from one of three causes – growth, replacement or relocation. Growth can be the emergence of new businesses or the expansion of existing ones, resulting from general growth within the economy or specific growth within individual sectors. Replacement implies the need for more modern premises, and demand for this can often be gauged from a physical analysis of the existing stock. It sometimes leads to the older properties being re-let and the stemming of rental growth. Relocation can be provoked by reorganization, rationalization, or again by growth.

There are several basic sources from which the demand for office accommodation can stem – central government, local government, quasi-government agencies, private sector service industry and private business firms and corporations. Private-sector commercial organizations are the principal catalyst for office development, with Financial and Business Services occupiers taking the lion's share. The influence of the public sector is not insubstantial and attempts to reduce the overall amount of public sector floorspace have not been significantly effective, despite the Lyons Review of 2004. Generally speaking, the total amount of new floorspace requirements emanating from these various sources has risen significantly over time but this will slow as the organizational changes discussed above take effect. What will change more radically are the average size, location and type of office accommodation demanded. The demand by major commercial organizations, for instance, is not usually for more space, but for better space. In the same way, national and multinational takeovers frequently lead to a fall in the overall demand for office accommodation, but can produce a fresh requirement for new space more appropriately designed and positioned. Nevertheless, in such circumstances it is common to find that the headquarters function is significantly reduced and the requirement for decentralized office space enhanced. Although there might be less aggregate demand for accommodation from some of the very largest corporations already established in the UK, there is a constant call for space from other multinational organizations moving into the UK, and a healthy demand from successful small and medium-size companies looking for new offices to accommodate their growth.

Analysing the market demand for office development is perhaps the most difficult and least accurate of all land uses. Statistics on business use of office space are difficult to come by and are frequently outdated. There is considerable flexibility in terms of the intensity of office occupation. A firm can effectively delay the need to move premises by increasing the concentration of workstations in the existing space. This suggests demand elasticity not evident in other sectors. Wide swings in overbuilding and underbuilding distort market perceptions. The 'image' of particular locations or individual buildings or the quality of continuing property management can all conspire to make it hard to forecast market demand. Moreover, office buildings do not have a catchment or trade area in the same way as shopping centres or even housing projects. Nevertheless, there are any number of factors that affect the demand for office space. These can be summarized as follows:

- national, regional and local economic performance
- service sector employment growth
- trends within different categories
- communications
- local planning and amenity
- floor space to worker ratios
- level of rents and values
- costs of occupation
- lease terms
- building services and facilities
- complementarity of neighbouring occupiers.

In stressing that the modern occupier of office accommodation is becoming much more selective than his predecessor, it is clear that:

- Conventional concepts of location in the office market are rendered redundant by improvements to communications, and although activities such as insurance, shipping and commodities are likely to remain grouped in traditional areas, other kinds of business are now much freer in their approach and inclined to be more supply-oriented.
- In recent years, tenants have been seeking shorter leases compared to the old standard institutional lease of twenty-five years. Leases of ten years are now more common, with one-sided break options, or a series of renewal options, and downward as well as upward rent review clauses. This has meant that landlords now look more closely at the flexibility of their buildings and are happier to accept multi-occupation. The consequence for tenants has been that rents have risen in compensation for the diminished certainty of income.
- Facilities managers now play a large part in determining the suitability of premises, and the critical factors are floor sizes and loading, air conditioning, power supply facilities, self-adjustable working environment, underfloor and vertical communication space, servicing costs, and cost-effective divisibility.
- Security is a prime consideration, not only in terms of the physical access to and from buildings, but also access to data and external communications systems.
- Environmental concerns – predominantly energy use and waste management but surely increasingly water conservation as well – are a major factor. Furthermore, the location of premises and proximity to public transport nodes is also considered important.

Lowe (1995) suggested that there have been 'repeated forecasts that we are "on the verge" of a profound technological revolution, whereby there will be less commuting and a great deal more working from home using computers, faxes and modems which will transform the way that we live, work and move around'. Yet only a tiny proportion of the workforce is currently employed as home-based tele-workers and these tend to be highly skilled, self-employed or freelance workers.

In assessing the broad measures of demand for offices, it should not be forgotten that, as with other sectors of the property development industry, there is an element of 'fashion' to take into account. Certain towns and cities can suddenly be in vogue. In the 1970s around London and the West, for example, Reading, Bristol, Swindon, Watford and Luton were enormously popular. The 1980s saw the likes of Aylesbury, Chelmsford and Newbury come to the fore and since the 1990s we have witnessed a re-emergence of regional centres such as Birmingham, Glasgow, Manchester, Leeds and the Thames Valley. Moreover, given that 95 per cent of all office-based organizations employ fewer than fifty people, the creation of smaller office buildings, and the construction of buildings capable of multiple occupation, is a noteworthy area of development. The success of serviced office providers, such as Regus, acts as evidence of this fact.

Corporate image will even override marginal financial considerations. Many so-called 'blue chip' companies either relocating from Central London or moving into the UK from Europe and America are looking for buildings in well-landscaped settings in a pleasant locality. The increasingly sophisticated nature of the work undertaken by such companies, and the higher executive status of the staff accommodated there, means that developers can no longer be content with providing standard-specification buildings. Special space and performance requirements, coupled with a desire to avoid excessive increases in rent at review, are pushing many potential occupiers towards building their own offices.

The changing nature of work itself will obviously exercise a considerable effect upon the demand for office space. As will be discussed below, the information explosion and the increased need for support services by decision-makers will continue to dictate different space requirements. For a variety of reasons, including more room to accommodate the paraphernalia of information technology and the aspirations of employees to work in a more conducive environment, floorspace to worker ratios will inevitably rise. In this context, the following trends and factors have been recorded:

- Evidence suggests that floorspace to worker ratios have already been increasing since the 1970s. This is explained by the increase in administrative and professional over clerical occupations, the predominance of larger office organizations, which tend to be more generous with space provision, and the scale of office mechanization brought about largely through major advances in information and communications technology.
- Wide variations in individual floorspace to worker ratios can occur, often as a result of different gross to net usable floor area ratios between buildings, but also because of differing sizes and types of office activity between businesses, and their stage of commercial development.

- Typical London office workers occupy only about two-thirds of the space occupied by their counterparts in mainland Europe. This is hardly surprising, given the relative expense of space in these locations.

Therefore, although it seems possible that worker densities will fall, the extent to which this happens will vary according to the design and age of the building concerned and the business activity, workforce, structure, equipment employed and life-cycle stage. Other factors, such as the extension of flexi-time and job-sharing, the continuous use of certain office premises, the sharing of space between firms, the increasing use of serviced offices, hot-desking and flexible working practices and the movement towards a shorter working week, will all combine to influence demand in respect of office location and design decisions.

Supply

It is important to remember that the office sector of the property development industry suffers from a strong counter-cyclical pattern of performance. In other words, responses to increased demand tend to take so long to put into effect that, by the time supply is increased to meet it, the market has changed so that supply greatly exceeds demand. Likewise, as supply is curtailed, so the market recovers and demand picks up again, overtaking declining supply. This counter-cyclical effect in the late 1970s and again in the late 1980s and early 2000s saw a shortage of office property, a rise in rental levels and a fall in investment yields – all of which combined to produce higher capital values in the office market. Not unnaturally, these symptoms encouraged developers to institute new projects. On both of the earlier occasions, the country moved into severe recession, just as these projects began to come on stream. An extreme example of this phenomenon was seen in the City of London office development market when in the year August 1989 to August 1990 more office space was constructed, 47,806 m^2 (514,600 ft^2), than had been built over the previous decade, 47,639 m^2 (512,800 ft^2). Similarly, after the boom years of the 2000s, the credit crunch saw many proposed tower developments being put on ice.

As with most other sectors of the property market, supply is much easier to assess than demand. The principal factors underlying the supply of office accommodation are:

- government and local authority policy
- existing approvals (as a proportion of stock)
- projects under construction (likewise)
- projects proposed but not yet approved (likewise)
- vacancy rates (likewise)
- rental and yield trends
- availability of utilities and services
- construction cost trends
- availability and terms of finance.

Local and regional authorities collect data on the amount of office space within their jurisdictions, as do national governments in the UK. For example, in England and Wales, it is estimated that there were 100,528,000 m² (approximately the same amount as retail space and about two thirds of the amount of ware-housing) at the end of 2007 (DCLG 2008b). It must be remembered that these are estimated amounts and good local market intelligence is always worth investing in.

Once data on demand and supply have been assembled, an analysis can take place to assess the relationship between the two, for the developer is not so much concerned with demand and supply as such, but rather the difference between them, which is known as the 'absorption rate'. Since it can take two to three years to bring an office building on to the market, the developer is principally concerned with the likely future absorption rate for office space in a given locality, rather than present rate. Simple quantitative market models have been proposed but are rarely employed in practice (Detoy and Rabin 1985).

Decentralization and relocation

Perhaps the most hotly debated issue in respect of office location is that of decentralization and relocation, and, linked with it, the future of the main office centres, especially London. However, conflicting views are advanced regarding the pace, degree and direction of decentralized office development.

During the 1980s one of the most powerful engines of the property boom was the growing number of companies that decided to relocate their business premises. The number of jobs that relocated from Central London, for example, doubled from an annual total of 5675 in 1986 to 11,380 in 1990 (Rawson-Gardiner 1993). With the erosion of the property cost differential between London and the regions, one key incentive for companies to relocate office employment to provincial cities became much more reduced. While rapid rental inflation in Central London in the late 1980s helped trigger a record volume of decentralization in the years 1990–1992, this tailed off very sharply in 1993–1994.

As the property cost differential returned in the 1990s and again particularly in the mid-2000s, decentralization returned. The phenomenal rental growth rates experienced in the mid-2000s in the West End of London, for example, sparked a certain amount of movement out towards 'Midtown' (Holborn), the outer London boroughs and beyond (such as into the Thames Valley), amongst corporate occupiers and professional advisers.

Looking at the future of London as a main office centre, it is clear that the process of decentralization has been taking place over a long period of time, and is not a sudden phenomenon. In fact, it is unlikely that the scale and type of decentralization that has happened since the mid-1960s will recur. Nevertheless, it is possible to advance the case that in forthcoming years only those activities that absolutely have to be centred in London will remain. Increasingly, operations that depend upon a high level of close business contact, such as finance, property, advertising and the law, will predominate, together with a concentration of top management in the headquarters offices of major national and international companies. Moreover, the influx of foreign business, especially banks, continues apace and, initially at least, London is viewed as being the only acceptable location. As a consequence of this constant drift towards the provision or retention of higher-level jobs, the overwhelming demand will be for offices supplying superior space standards.

However, major increases in house prices in recent years have brought recruitment challenges as workers for key public-sector positions (such as teachers and nurses) find themselves unable to afford housing in the capital. There is already a tendency on the part of large business organizations to situate their corporate headquarters in locations well away from major centres. Even some international banking corporations have opted for decentralized locations and many other traditional central area operations are looking very seriously at the balance of advantages that might lead them to decant a significant part of their business, or to decamp altogether, to more provincial or Home County locations. What could well happen is that office functions and structures might be polarized between very high-order activities occupying top-quality expensive office premises in central-area positions, and all other operations being conducted in low-rise, low-density and relatively inexpensive locations out of town. In this way, it appears almost certain that the South East region outside London is bound to expand. Already considerable pressure has been placed upon towns (sometimes referred to as growth 'hubs') around motorway corridors, resulting in considerable knock-on effects requiring investment in new transport infrastructure in areas like the M4 western corridor (Slough–Reading) and M25 London fringe (Guildford–Woking) areas.

One of the consequences of the desire to decentralize, the increase in personal transport and improvements in communication technology, is the demand for accommodation situated in office parks. These campus-style developments are characteristically located on the edge of towns and comprise a mix of low-rise, low-density buildings with extensive car parking, a wide range of business and sometimes leisure facilities, set in an attractive environment close to motorways, good schools and high-grade housing. Frequently, they are not restricted purely to office buildings but are composed of various business activities, including research and light engineering as well as conventional clerical and administrative functions. (Business and office park developments are discussed more fully below.)

Planning and office development

Many of the basic aspects of planning policy and practice affecting office development are beyond the scope of this text. Nevertheless, some comment on specific planning considerations is called for because office development proposals are so frequently singled out for special treatment by local authorities, especially in London and the South East. There has often, in fact, been a heavy bias against office development in certain areas, sometimes politically inspired and sometimes resulting from pressures exerted by vested interest. Somehow, offices attract a degree of vituperation not directed towards other forms of development such as industry and housing. The fact that office-based activities provide a major source of employment is seemingly overlooked by some councils and the lobbies that influence them. Strangely, vacant new industrial estates attract sympathy, whereas vacant recently completed office premises attract opprobrium. A certain underlying rationale can be divined, in that office developers are typically cast in the mould of persons who display a general indifference to the social ramifications of their proposed schemes and have a particular tendency to ignore the public costs of private development.

The general principles that govern the framing of most planning policies as they relate to office development can usefully be summarized as follows:

- to control the scale, standards of design and layout of individual buildings according to established planning objectives
- to control the location of office development, in accordance with the objectives of land-use or spatial planning
- to control the overall level of office development activity with respect to the objectives of economic development policy.

These policies are abstracted from the late Greater London Council's published approach towards office development control and they epitomize the somewhat negative approach often taken towards offices. There has always appeared to be a basic ambivalence by planning authorities at a strategic level regarding a decision as to whether support should be given towards central area development along with better housing and public transport facilities, or whether suburban decentralization with improved road and traffic management schemes should be encouraged. In any event, policies towards offices have proved difficult to formulate, because of what appears to be an inherent inability to examine and interpret true office needs, which is made worse by the lack of a proper database relating to business occupation.

Strategic planning for office development

As discussed above, the Planning and Compulsory Purchase Act 2004 enabled regional spatial strategies (RSSs) in each English region. These replaced existing regional planning guidance and provide a strategic planning context for property development.

The London Plan (approved in 2004 and further revised in 2007), as an example of strategic planning guidance, sets out a strategy for accommodating major growth in London in a sustainable way. The plan envisages a 30 per cent increase in the total office floorspace in London by 2016 and a pronounced eastward shift in the pattern of office development to serve regeneration objectives. Within the Plan, the Mayor acknowledges that office development policies will work only if the transport infrastructure (especially Thameslink 2000, the East London Line extension and the Crossrail link) is in place.

Furthermore, the Plan also imposes substantial obligations on office developers, in particular in respect of contributions to infrastructure costs, which would be necessary to enable the required level of development. It is estimated that growth in financial and business services (FBS) will generate an additional 463,000 jobs by 2016, creating a demand for 87 million square feet (8.1 million square metres) of office floorspace, assuming some vacancy.

It has been argued that reshaping the geography of office development in London is essential to achieving the objectives of regeneration. However, many areas of East London are likely to be relatively low-value locations in commercial property terms, and this suggests difficulties in maximizing developer contributions through planning obligations and by means of the future implementation of a community infrastructure levy. This is the challenging environment in which office developers in Central London will have to operate in the coming decade.

In the rest of the South East the strategic context is provided by the South East Plan, produced in 2006 and subsequently the subject of governmental and public scrutiny, with Secretary of State approval in 2009. The South East Plan includes a general objective of sustaining the attractions of the region for inward investment and the location of corporate headquarters, and facilitating new developments for industry and commerce, but bearing in mind that environmental constraints will limit scope for further growth west and south of London. It acknowledges the extent of vacant space and the very substantial scale of existing planning permissions in all parts of the region. A number of key regional 'hubs' are proposed as key locations of office growth. Additionally, the South East Plan places emphasis on the concept of 'smart growth' whereby such developments will be encouraged without damaging the region's ecological footprint. One key component and one ripe for exploitation by office development, is the use of ICT in new development, to reduce the need to travel or commute unnecessarily.

At the local level, many local authorities traditionally opposed to significant office development proposals now recognize the importance of the office sector in securing overall employment objectives. In this, the attraction of major corporations moving to the country or relocating from Central London has been seen to play an important role. However, it has been pointed out that at the current time there are probably more towns seeking large single-space users than there are potential occupiers for this type of accommodation. Planners and developers alike, it is argued, would do well to pay attention to the regional and sub-regional role played by a town, which might in future have a greater effect on the office absorption rate, than continued attempts to entice outsiders from the fast-shrinking pool of large mobile companies. There is also a tendency for many towns to resist office development on the edge of the urban area, and in a few less restrictive towns a dual market has emerged between greenfield and town-centre locations.

Planning policy can be highly successful in battening down office development, but it is much less effective in encouraging it. Nevertheless, several principal factors outlined below exercise a considerable effect upon the outcome of office development proposals.

Floorspace

The popular way by which the total amount of planned floorspace for a local authority is calculated is to establish a relationship between predicted population levels, proportion of office employees and consequent office space used. Each of these factors is highly susceptible to error, and this is compounded when they are combined. Employment generation assessed by worker density standards, therefore, is extremely difficult to compute and virtually impossible to enforce. From this it can be argued that floorspace as an indicator or regulator of office development is a very crude instrument. A more discretionary approach is adopted by many planning authorities, although some are peculiarly reluctant to release additional approvals in order to reduce obvious scarcities and deflate excessively high levels of rent, which discourage business activity and employment. A certain amount of discrimination is also required to ensure the sensitive release of sufficient land and planning consents in the right locations, so as to capture internationally footloose companies. One further aspect of floorspace is the means of controlling the intensity of development on individual sites. The nature and operation of plot ratio and floorspace index controls is explained elsewhere, but it is important to recognize that different authorities attach varying degrees of adherence to the precise designation of particular areas and density levels. Some are open to negotiation around an established figure, some are not. In general, however, it is fair to say that most authorities are less rigid and less definitive than previously.

Transport and parking

Problems of communication and traffic beset all forms of property development, but despite planning arguments to the contrary, it is possible to put forward the case that in many ways offices cause the least amount of disruption to the transportation system. To a great extent, most office developments are creatures of communications networks, and have a strong capacity to adjust to them. The real question that confronts planning authorities is how, in the aggregate, to preserve a balance between, on the one hand, ensuring that there is a sufficient minimum level of service provision to permit proper access to a proposed development and, on the other, preventing an overload of the existing system. Because of this, sites immediately adjacent to transport termini or interchanges are often favoured. In appraising a potential development, or in making an application for planning permission in respect of offices, there are various factors that should be taken into account. These can be summarized as follows:

- the number of employees who will be working within the building
- the likely number of visitors attracted to the development, and their probable mode of travel
- the amount of delivery and service traffic generated by the prospective users

- the extent to which loading and unloading operations might take place, the noise that could be created, and the time when the building will be used and the various operations occur
- where access is to be provided.

Parking is an important consideration. Standards and regulations vary enormously throughout the country, depending normally upon the proximity to the town or city centre and the degree of congestion enjoyed at the place in question. It is common nowadays for some local authorities to preclude parking facilities altogether except for those reserved for disabled drivers and an absolute bare minimum of other spaces, with ratios at levels of up to 1 space per 10,000 ft^2 (929 m^2). Others insist upon levels as high as one space for every 350 ft^2 (32.5 m^2) of floorspace. Outside Central London, however, a commonly sought level of provision for in-town sites separates operational and non-operational requirements, setting standards for the former at around a maximum of one space for every 750 ft^2 (80 m^2) of gross floorspace. For out-of-town office parks the standard is around one space to every 300 ft^2 (23 m^2), and sometimes lower.

With non-operational parking provision it is not unusual for local planning authorities to try to insist that the car parking spaces should be made available for public use, and also sometimes to look for a commutation of the cost of provision towards the construction of general public car parks. In certain circumstances, where no such commutation takes place, councils will seek to enter into agreements with developers for the transfer of private off-street parks to public use at weekends.

No office development scheme of any considerable size is these days granted planning permission without a 'green travel' plan having been submitted and approved by the local planning authority. The purpose of these plans is to ensure that occupiers abide by strategies for reducing dependency on car-borne travel. Carefully made plans are 'live' documents which are regularly reviewed and updated, and commonly provide for:

- encouraging staff to travel to work via bicycle, by providing shower facilities and secure bike storage
- websites emphasizing public transport routes for staff and visitors
- subsidizing the public transport costs of staff
- devising a car-sharing scheme for staff.

Restricted user

As part of a policy of restraint, some local planning authorities traditionally attempted to limit or control the use or occupancy of office buildings by means of:

- *Local user conditions*, restricting occupancy to businesses already established and operating in the area

- *Named user conditions*, where specified firms alone are allowed to occupy the premises
- *Small suite provision*, where all or part of the development must be let in small office units of, say, not more than 5000 ft^2 (464 m^2).

These policies are very much less prevalent than previously, partly because of many successful appeals against their imposition.

A radical change in the restriction of use was introduced by the original Town and Country Planning (Use Classes) Order 1987, which listed sixteen classes, placed in four general use categories:

A – Shopping area
B – Other business and industrial
C – Residential
D – Social and community uses.

The Order was subsequently amended in 2005 and now includes fourteen distinct classes within four categories. With regard to office development, the Class B1 (Business) brings together offices, so long as they do not provide a service for visiting members of the public, and light industry. For certain projects, therefore, developers might seek a wider range of uses than hitherto had been possible. Nevertheless, local planning authorities still retain their power of development control and can look to restrict the freedom to change uses to a narrower range than the order permits. However, Statutory Instrument 03/2005 'Changes of Use of Buildings and Land' makes it plain that the Secretary of State will regard the imposition of such restrictions as unreasonable unless there is clear evidence that the uses excluded would have a serious impact on the environment or on amenity, not susceptible to other control. In practice, the business use class has provided considerable opportunities for the owners of multi-storey industrial buildings to refurbish their properties to meet the demands of a growing studio market.

Urban design

Although beauty is said to lie in the eye of the beholder, it is true to say that over recent years the design and siting of offices has become a very much more critical consideration than hitherto. Many local authorities are willing to extend a greater degree of sympathy towards well-designed, sensitively proportioned office buildings, or countenance higher levels of density than would otherwise be the norm if a proposed scheme is attractive and harmonizes with its surroundings. In 1994, for example, the City of London abandoned a strict adherence to the use of plot ratio as an instrument of development control in favour of a more discretionary approach towards building design.

The relative popularity of renovation as opposed to redevelopment is becoming general across all sectors of the commercial property market, but the preference towards refurbishment on the part of planning authorities is particularly marked in the case of office development projects. More than this, there appears to be a growing awareness and understanding of the economics of conservation, so that there is no longer quite the antipathy in some quarters towards the change of use of buildings of architectural or historic interest to offices, where otherwise they might have continued to deteriorate. In most instances, conversion to offices is infinitely preferable to redevelopment or radical refurbishment for shops. Work by the Commission for Architecture and the Built Environment (CABE) and others on the promotion of public realm in office developments (such as at Brindleyplace) can be found in Chapter 7.

Regeneration

Although this section on planning and office development opened on a negative note as to how office projects are seen by planning authorities, it ends with a more positive theme – the role that planned office schemes can play in the regeneration of local economies. Increasingly, it is recognized that many older cities with serious problems of social deprivation, high unemployment, environmental degradation and general decline have large sites, which are otherwise well located, that have potential for the development of business parks or office campuses. An excellent example of this was the Newcastle Business Park, one of the Tyne and Wear Development Corporation's flagship developments. Here a vacant, derelict and contaminated 24 ha (60 acre) site was transformed through the expenditure of around £140 million, in partnership with the private sector, on a major business park, providing around 4000 jobs when fully let. Although such initiatives do not always directly benefit the local population with long-term employment, they do generate short-term job opportunities and act as a general catalyst for economic growth within the urban area.

The same is true of some rural regeneration schemes as well. Regional authorities in England, the Scottish Parliament, the Welsh Assembly Government and the Northern Ireland Assembly often look to small-scale office schemes to provide for much needed rural employment. PPS7 on sustainable development in rural areas supports the principle of such schemes, provided that they would protect the special character of the countryside and not harm it.

Design and layout

For almost thirty years following the end of the Second World War, the design of office buildings was uniformly dull and unimaginative. Architects were all too frequently nervous about the mystical design and performance standards laid down by the major financial institutions and their professional advisers, and as a result tended to allow the control of design to pass out of their hands. In matters of new office development it almost appeared as if the accountant had gained ascendancy over the architect, and the approach to commercial development seemed to be the provision of functionally clad and serviced floorspace. The 1980s can be said to have witnessed a constant improvement in the standard of design of office developments. Nevertheless, the trend in low-rise blocks back to brick as a facing material, prompted by demands from property and planning interests alike, gave rise to a certain amount of fresh criticism. This resulted from the rash of three- and four-storey brick-built developments, topped with lead or copper mansard roofs and adorned by dinky dormer windows, some of which were reasonably well done, some decidedly not.

Broad principles

More recent office design, through the 1990s and 2000s, has continued to improve and is much more influenced by occupier demand, although sound principles by which office design and layout might be judged had already been set down in the 1980s (Marber 1985) as follows:

- Relationship of the building to its surroundings in terms of appearance, height and size, and response to outside factors such as railway lines and noisy streets
- Pedestrian and traffic access, and the position of entrances and service points
- Structural grid and facility in meeting subdivision requirements
- Natural light penetration
- Floor to floor heights
- Size and shape of floors in relation to likely tenant demand and flexibility in dividing floors or letting separate floors singly
- Position and design of service cores
- Efficiency of building, i.e. relationship between gross area and net lettable accommodation
- Car parking content and location
- Extent and suitability of any landscaped or other amenity areas.

The importance of getting design and layout right from an occupier's perspective has been stated by the British Council for Offices (BCO 2003):

> Poorly located and designed places of work are not only bad for the wider environment, they are also bad for business. Evidence collected for and on behalf of CABE shows that poor workplaces are:
>
> - bad for business productivity and efficiency
> - bad for recruitment, retention and employee satisfaction
> - bad for the balance sheet – costing more over the lifetime of the building.

In terms of the shell, scenery and settings, it has been pointed out that buildings take a long time to build, are difficult to change, and once built are there to last (Worthington and Kenya 1988). Firms, on the other hand, are continuously in a state of flux, as the economy, technology and market changes around them. Because of this, building design decisions reflect different timescales, where:

- Building shells have a lifespan of around seventy-five years and may have many owners.
- Services have a lifespan of around fifteen years and adjust one shell to specific functions.
- Furnishings and fittings may change every five to seven years as organizations grow and change.
- On a daily, weekly or monthly basis, furnishings and fittings may be moved to reflect specific activities.

With regard to office building specification, the British Council for Offices (BCO) has produced a document, *BCO Guide 2005: Best Practice in the Specification for Offices*, which supplies a reference source for those needing, providing or investing in offices (British Council for Offices 2005). This document aims to achieve consensus towards the approach to office building specification, reviewed as necessary in the light of new technology. It also aims to standardize, wherever possible, the design approach, the choice of materials and of components as they relate to the issues of specification, so that the practice of 'reinventing the wheel' is eliminated. The key criteria that the Guide sets out are shown in Table 17.1.

On the subject of specification, the era of decision-making based upon landlords' preconceived ideas has passed – to a trend of occupier-driven developments as landlords more frequently respond to a tenant-driven agenda. Many occupiers are now calling for less elaborately specified space that still meets their needs. Huge power and heat-removal capabilities, structural loading provisions (twice the British Standard with no credible justification), overestimation of electrical loadings and associated air-conditioning capacity, fitting-out tenant space rather than letting a basic shell, and costly bespoke design of the components – all have led to waste and expense, which with the diminishing popularity of air conditioning because of its environmental and economic costs, dropping power consumption needs for information technology, and better building-services control mechanisms, means that the new generation of office buildings should be substantially cheaper than those built during the late 1980s.

Sustainable offices

As is discussed above, the recognition that environmental sustainability is important in the design and specification of office premises has led to a change in thinking about how offices are designed and specified, for which purposes the development of the Building Research Establishment Environmental Assessment Model (BREEAM) has been very helpful. Reference to the BCO 2005 Guide should therefore be made in conjunction with the latest thinking on how best to achieve suitably environment-conscious design and specifications, the

Table 17.1 BCO 2005 Best practice in office specification quick guide to key criteria (British Council for Offices 2005)

Occupancy	
Net area/person diversified occupancy	12 m^2–17 m^2
Net area/person escape	6 m^2
Plan Efficiency NIA:GIA	80–85%
Urban buildings	75%
Plan depth & ceiling height	
Window to window (not core)	13.5 m–21 m
Finished floor to underside of ceiling	2600 mm–3300 mm
Grids	
Column grid	7.5 m–9 m
Planning grid	1.5 m
Toilets	One person per 14 m^2 NIA
Lifts	
Standards	80% loading 30 sec. interval
	One person per 14 m^2 NIA
Raised floors	150 mm
	300/500 mm (subfloor A/C)
Structural loading	
Live	General: 2.5 kN/m^2
	High: 7.5 kN/m^2
Dead	Partitions: 1.0 kN/m^2
	Raised floors: 0.85 kN/m^2
Small power	
Loading diversified	15 W/m^2
Risers/busbars on floor distribution boards	25 W/m^2
Lighting standard	
Office minimum average maintained illuminance	
VDT use	300–500 lux
Paper-based tasks	500 lux
Task uniformity	0.7
Comfort	
Standard summer air conditioned space	22 °C +/– 2 °C
Winter	20 °C +/– 2 °C
Fresh air standard	12–16 l/s
Noise criteria	
open-plan offices	NR 38 (Leq)
cellular offices	NR 35 (Leq)

principal benefits of which are very much occupier-oriented. For office development schemes, these benefits have been described thus:

> Sustainable office design can deliver higher performance in energy and other resource use, and higher productivity in human terms. People simply work, see and think better in offices that have more natural lighting, fresher and cleaner air, and where they have more control over their immediate lighting or temperature levels. At a practical level, it simultaneously minimises the number, amount, volume, weight, toxicity and use of materials, energy and water, while maximising the use of materials, energy and other components that are clean and safe, renewable, easy to repair, reuse, recycle or refurbish and benign towards the environment.
>
> (Morgan Lovell n.d.)

Chapter 10 included discussion about the growing need for developers to provide sustainable space to meet their clients' growing demand for it. In addition to anecdotal indications, research evidence suggests that this is the case. Gensler (2006), for example, undertook a study of Directors of property occupier companies, which found that:

- 59 per cent of the Directors believe that spiralling energy costs over the next decade will increase their organization's operating costs significantly.
- 57 per cent consider energy-efficiency and emissions when planning their property portfolio for the next twenty-five years.
- 72 per cent believe that business is 'picking up the bill' for badly designed, inefficient buildings.
- 26 per cent believe that the state of the UK's office stock is damaging UK productivity.

Furthermore, the Gensler survey also assessed developers' opinions. Of interest particularly are the findings that:

- 73 per cent believe that spiralling energy costs over the next decade will make operating costs a much more important factor in tenants' choice of property.
- 69 per cent believe that this will force developers to commission more energy-efficient buildings.
- Whilst 75 per cent agree that the operating cost of a building in use is a primary consideration for tenants when procuring commercial property, just 33 per cent believe that future operating costs are a primary consideration for developers when developing commercial property.

    This last point is worrying for the industry, because it represents a mismatch between developers' and occupiers' thinking on this important issue.

Good design should also address how upgrading can be achieved economically, for it is more economic in the long term to adapt regular office space than it is to custom-design specialist areas in the base building. The growing trend for 'flexible space' being required is likely to encourage better design in this regard.

It is now possible to suggest, therefore, that we stand at something of a threshold in respect of office design, where all concerned with development are being asked to match space utilization to occupiers' requirements, building cost, premises layout and awareness of the environmental impact of the property occupation. In exploring new dimensions in design it can be stated that two key themes increasingly will dominate the creation of good office space:

- Low energy design
- Adaptability of space for occupier satisfaction.

Size and shape

Naturally there will be a continuing demand for new office developments of all sizes from 2500 ft^2 (232 m^2) to 250,000 ft^2 (23,225 m^2). All that it is possible to do is to point to several trends that are likely to be most apparent in the market. Two particular features that will probably typify the sector in respect of the size of offices are worthy of mention. First, it seems almost certain that smaller individual units of office accommodation will be in demand, with the accent being on the provision of buildings in the 10,000–20,000 ft^2 (929–1858 m^2) range for single occupancy. Second, and related, will be the shift to multiple occupation among business users, and the development of office buildings that have the facility to be divided conveniently into discrete units of anything from 1000 ft^2 (93 m^2) upwards. As a direct corollary of these trends, it would seem reasonable to conclude that the number of large speculative buildings in excess of 100,000 ft^2 (9290 m^2) will decline significantly.

It is equally difficult to generalize about the likely future shape of office buildings, except again to identify the principal direction in which the market is moving. The probable polarization of the office market between central city area and suburban or greenfield site locations has already been promulgated. Suffice it to say that the former will be inclined to retain a concentration upon multi-storey development, whereas the latter will focus more upon two- and three-storey construction. However, the most significant feature in respect of building shape is the optimum width of offices. The era of the shallow rectangular block is over, and so too for that matter is the very deep-plan office design. Few offices in future will be constructed to a width of much less than 12–14 m (40–45 ft), and much more than 15–17 m (50–55 ft). On large sites and for bigger buildings, therefore, a popular form of development shape will be a roughly square building surrounding a central atrium or courtyard. This trend will be reinforced by the increasing desire on the part of the occupiers to have cellular offices with outside views, which, on average, take up about 60 per cent of usable space. Within sensible limits, however, atria should be designed so that a proportion, if not all, can be infilled at a later date.

Structural arrangement

It has been argued that the importance of structural design is seldom fully recognized, let alone properly appreciated, for it carries with it the genetic code for a building, comprising (Anderson 1985):

- the method of construction
- the speed of construction
- the cost of the structure and related elements
- the internal planning of the building
- fire resistance
- acoustic performance
- structural stability
- lifespan of the building
- elevations of the building
- the articulation of mechanical and electrical services
- the response of the heating and cooling systems
- the ability to change.

All structural design elements are to some extent significant, but several deserve special mention from the developer's standpoint: the structural frame, the service core and the floor arrangements.

Structural frame

At the outset of the design process, careful consideration should be given to the position, size and number of columns constituting the vertical dimension of the structural frame, the basic rule being that a building should be as column-free as possible and the main constraint being one of cost. Ideally, columns should form a structural grid more than 8 m apart and preferably situated on a floor edge in order to allow the provision of unobstructed office space. However, structural grids of less than this are quite common. Where columns are placed within the internal area, account must be taken of future division, if desired, and possible corridor construction, if adopted. In the same way, perimeter wall details will need to be able to accept partitioning at many different points. In addition to the structural grid, which dictates the frequency of columns, and both determines, and is determined by, the distance between external walls, there is also the planning grid and the construction grid. The planning grid, of interest to the space planner, is defined by the same items as those of the structural grid, but is further affected by the distances between windows and the frequency of the mullions. The construction, or product grid is the module to which standard building products are made. The successful design is the one in which all these grids are integrated into a harmonious whole (Salata 1990).

The BCO Guide 2005 recommends a 1.5 metre planning grid and a column grid of 7.5–9 metres although requirements for longer spans are common. The

1.5 metre grid is considered ideal for sizing rooms and the provision of corridors. Clearly, the structural or column grids chosen must be a multiple of the planning grid. It is not considered advantageous to try to create column-free space in excess of 9 m width, however, because of the effect on structural depths and therefore building height, and also because buildings are rarely fitted out in a way that column space would gain any visual or space-planning advantage. In choosing the column grid it is necessary to avoid excessive column size, and perimeter and core columns should be integral with or about the perimeter or internal walls. With creative thought, the base can be put to various uses such as circulation, café or exhibition space, but requires additional life safety systems if it is to be used for general office area. In the life of the larger buildings it may well be an advantage to be able to create a large area of deep-plan space on at least one floor.

In terms of the materials to be used for the structural frame, steel or reinforced concrete are equally acceptable. Concrete solutions incorporating pre-stressing, post-tensioning or pre-stressed concrete floor slabs are less flexible and inhibit the user in altering the building to suit varying needs. However, where these design solutions could confer real benefits, they should be considered.

Service core

The service core of an office building consists of lifts, stairs, toilets, service ducts and ancillary accommodation, such as special storage, cleaners' cupboards and machine bays. An optimum placement is a balance between space maximization and construction cost, taking into account such factors as entrances, circulation routes within the building, vertical interdepartmental communications, natural lighting and means of escape. There are advantages and disadvantages to central, peripheral and offset or external core provision, depending upon individual circumstances. The internal finishes to core spaces should generally be simple, hard-wearing, maintenance-free and attractive.

Floor arrangements

It is usually advisable to avoid the use of power-floated *in situ* slabs as a floor finish. If they are employed, it is important to consider the problems that arise in the eventual distribution of electricity and other services to central areas, particularly if no partitions are planned. With regard to live floor loading for the general area, which normally accounts for about 95 per cent of the total space, the BCO Guide 2005 has a minimum threshold of $2.5 kN/m^2$ over approximately 5 per cent of the total area. Where there is a dead load, an extra allowance of $1 kN/m^2$ should be made for such items as demountable partitions, raised floors, ceilings and building-service equipment.

Another factor in the structural design of some modern office developments, principally those located on out-of-town business parks, is that provision should be made for the creation of several potential entrance points, as opposed to a single front door and reception area.

Internal layout

The strictly cellular office blocks of the 1940s, 1950s and early 1960s gave over to the deep open-plan offices of the late 1960s and 1970s. Open-plan offices with liberal indoor landscaping, pioneered in Germany as the *burolandschaft*, claimed savings of 20 per cent in space and in cost, but overall increases in business efficiency have been seriously contested. In short, what we have arrived at is a combination of space uses, comprising a mix of cellular, group and open-plan office space, together with suitable integrated space provision for support services. The physical design and layout of buildings responds to the demands of effective business organization and preferred commercial practice. Thus, there has been a breakdown in the rigid compartmentalization of activities throughout commerce and industry, be they industrial, research, distributive, storage, administration, executive, clerical or marketing, etc.

With a modern office building, it is likely that up to 50 per cent of space will be given over to what conventionally have always been considered to be ancillary uses, such as meetings, conferences, presentations, training, libraries, relaxation and machine rooms. The advent of advanced technology has obviously quickened the pace of change, but this has been put into proper perspective as follows:

> Face to face meetings are likely to remain crucial, with formal technology-based communication channels highlighting rather than detracting from the importance of informal, unofficial and non-routine communication.
>
> (DEGW 1983)

An overriding criterion in the layout of offices is an ability to change the physical environment. Divisibility, therefore, is important, both in terms of facilitating different working arrangements within a single organization as well as allowing for simple subletting of parts of the premises. It is also necessary to create convivial space for small teams working within large organizations. As has already been stated, most people desire their individual work spaces to have an external view if at all possible, and, to this end, nearly all ancillary operations can be situated towards the central core of the building.

Less uniformity throughout an office complex along the lines described requires that the keynote must again be flexibility. This used to mean the basic ability to alter internal partitioning. It now means a facility to change the proportion of cellular offices, open-plan offices, support space and service equipment, together with an ability to respond to changing occupancy and methods of work. Much of this flexibility can be achieved by differentiating the building shell from the re-locatable elements in the office scenery. Moreover, the use of certain space-defining components, such as fin walls, can give some backbone to office planning and layout, and can even assist in office management.

From the developer's point of view it is essential to optimize the amount of lettable floorspace, and, as has been mentioned, a net to gross relationship of about 80 per cent is the normal target in new buildings. It is sometimes possible to accomplish slightly more, and occasionally acceptable to supply a little less, all depending upon the individual circumstances of the scheme. Small suite provision, for example, will normally be lower than single occupancy design. In this context, entrance halls should be as spacious as possible, with a very high standard of finish and separation from certain service functions.

On the subject of space utilization, a note about worker space or occupational density is pertinent. It is commonly accepted at the design stage that an overall figure of one worker to every 9 m^2 (100 ft^2) of net floor space may be assumed as a minimum requirement. The legal minimum is expressed as one worker to every 11 m^3 (388 ft^3) on the basis of, say, 5 m^2 (50 ft^2) floorspace and 2.5 m (8 ft) ceiling height, but this is extremely low. The BCO Guide 2005 suggests a range of between 12 and 17m^2 per person. Combination layouts are also very economic because they concentrate upon function rather than a crude average. People do not occupy their workstations continuously, for example, and conference space can achieve high worker to space ratios. This having been stated, it should be appreciated that the nature of many people's work is changing. Skills are increasing. There is less clerical activity and more managerial, executive and professional work. Consequently, there is a growing demand for better quality of space – and this usually means more.

One interior designer observed that: 'Unfortunately, the determining factor in 75 per cent of today's design and planning work is not increasing productivity or enhancing interaction, but saving real-estate costs and, ideally, creating more flexibility in the work environment and reducing the cost of churn and change' (Battle 2003).

Glazing

With regard to the provision and design of windows in new office developments, it is becoming increasingly critical to pay attention to insulation and energy-saving standards. Many of the extensively glazed buildings of the late 1960s and 1970s proved costly to run and uncomfortable to work in. More recent developments, therefore, either employ a much more advanced system of glazing or have reverted to a lower proportion of external fenestration, set within opaque cladding, or even more commonly, traditional brickwork. However, unless they are well designed, many buildings with restricted window areas can look extremely austere.

Problems of solar glare can often be overcome by the use of tinted glass or blinds, with or without the complement of air-conditioning. Some of the specially coated glasses can greatly increase the thermal value of the building envelope. With many, if not most, major new office development schemes, the incorporation of an atrium in the basic design enhances the provision of natural lighting.

Although every individual office design must be judged on its merits, it can generally be said that the necessary balance of daylight and energy consumption usually results in a proportion of 25–30 per cent glazing of the external surface.

Reference to Parts L and N of the Building Regulations will ensure adequate thermal efficiency in this regard. Turning again to design, it has been found that tall thin windows extending from floor to ceiling give the best daylight penetration. Experience has also shown that a certain proportion of a building's windows should be capable of opening, even if only by way of a caretaker's key, not merely as a fire precaution but in case the air-conditioning system fails. One other problem that can arise is the nuisance caused to neighbouring buildings by strong solar reflections from extensively glazed buildings.

Office refurbishment

Very simply, in examining the market for office refurbishment a simple division can be made between the renovation of period buildings and the upgrading of post-war offices.

With period office buildings, the cost of refurbishment can be very difficult to assess, for the main structure can suffer from extensive dry rot to timbers or severe rust to steel frames, which might be uncovered only after work has begun. Planning requirements or aesthetic considerations may dictate or favour the restoration of a period building's existing facade, rather than re-cladding and the opportunity to create additional office space by constructing extra mezzanine or gallery floors, or by bringing basement space into more effective use. Local authorities are also now empowered to relax certain statutory regulations where refurbishment would enable an historic building or group of buildings to be given a new lease of life.

Many, if not most, post-war office buildings constructed before the early 1970s are now outdated and are in desperate need of refurbishment. The popular 16.5 m width, with a 1.5 m wide central corridor, and 6 m deep cellular offices leading off it, is normally too inflexible to cater for modern office users' demands. An owner or developer will, therefore, need to ascertain if there are design possibilities of rearranging the internal layout of such a building to remove the rigidly determined central corridor and utilize the space provided, possibly by introducing a mixture of cellular and open-plan areas. The removal of non-loadbearing walls might also provide opportunities to utilize 'dead' areas in the building. Although it will normally prove to be too costly, it can sometimes be worth replacing the central service core with an external core, which creates considerable extra lettable space. In any event, some reduction in the size of the existing core will usually be feasible. A typical refurbishment will also include re-cladding the building, renewing all the heating and plumbing systems, providing false ceilings and/or raised floors to accommodate new service ducts, as well as upgrading all common parts and renewing windows and window frames.

Services and facilities

The most important change to have taken place in the design and development of offices over recent years concerns building services and facilities. Providing an acceptable level of modern business services within a high-quality working environment has become much more important to the creation of successful office premises than the mere production of a serviced concrete and brick shell it once was. As a consequence, those involved in the process of commercial property development have had to become better acquainted with the range of services available and the level of provision required by occupiers.

Provision and distribution

To begin with, the modern office building demands an integrated approach towards building fabric and building services. The previous tendency was for services to be planned following the basic design of the building fabric. Unfortunately, with notable exceptions, current designs still attempt to adjust traditional building types to new service demands.

Design should provide for the possible and easy incorporation of additional facilities at a later date. This may involve the trimming of floor slabs in such a way that shafts can readily be added in the future. Some schemes have been drawn up so as to allow extra lift shafts to be inserted if they become necessary. Surplus vertical ducts are also fast being considered as essential in preserving the economic life of a building. One modern office complex, for example, has elevations that include a series of turrets that not only give a pleasing visual effect but also supply internal voids that could accommodate a variety of additional services, if and when required. The space needed for vertical ducting is roughly 2 per cent of the gross floor area and should be distributed among several risers rather than be concentrated at a single core.

The prime difficulties that arise in the provision and distribution of services usually relate to machine rooms, cabling and localized heat concentrations. The first and last are essentially questions of heating and ventilation, dealt with below. With regard to cabling, however, it is not everyone who likes cable drops from a suspended ceiling, and although it is possible to employ wall-mounted cabling systems if there is no alternative, the best solution is commonly considered to be the construction of a raised floor, usually of about 150 mm. This is because it is accessible and it lends itself to workstation cabling and local environmental control. Another method is to provide three-channel floor ducts at, say, about 1.5 m centres, but this approach can actually prove to be less flexible and more expensive. In considering the provision of power, it is worth noting that if a standby generator is not installed at the outset then provision should be made for connecting one to the power supply at a suitable point.

As already mentioned, however, the 1980s witnessed something of an over-specification in the provision services of office buildings, largely as a result of the advances in information technology. Flexibility considerations seemed to dictate that it was necessary for every part of a building to be able to carry any load. With the advent of smaller, portable and distributed computer systems this notion is now seriously in question.

Core and shell

The differing space and facility requirements of different office users have led to a 'core and shell' approach on the part of many developers. It was becoming absurd for a tenant to move into a newly completed building only to have to set about changing and removing many of the finishes and fittings so recently installed. Tailoring floorspace areas to the special needs of a particular tenant often involves a great deal of modification in terms of partitioning, lighting and mechanical and electrical distribution.

Core and shell, therefore, aims to provide a development where all common areas are fully furnished and the lettable areas are left for tenants to fit out themselves, or for the tenants' particular requirements to be incorporated before fitting-out work is finalized. Cost and time savings accrue to both parties, and the tenant has 'customized' accommodation.

Opinions vary as to how much fitting-out work is done by the developer. Generally, all vertical distribution of services would be installed, with the duct work, for instance, blanked off where it enters the shell. Fire protection requirements will apply to the whole building and will usually mean the installation of a full sprinkler system. For finishes to shell areas, some developers do not install any floor, wall or ceiling finishes. Others may install a false floor because it improves the appearance and permits immediate partitioning. The entrance hall, staircases, common parts, toilets and core would be fully finished. The key as far as the developer is concerned is being able to predict which elements tenants are likely to remove, adapt or change when they take up occupancy and therefore leave them out. Flexibility again enhances lettability. The developer naturally retains the right to approve any deviation from a standard specification, and differences in cost may either be borne by the tenant as a lump sum, or charged for within the rental agreement.

Internal environmental control

The nature, form and degree of internal environmental control provided within modern office developments depends primarily upon the design, location and use of the buildings, together with the economics of the market and the requirements of the occupier. From the point of view of both developer and occupier, however, the reduction of fuel costs, allied with the maintenance of a comfortable environment, is a principal objective. Broadly speaking, this is best attained by providing a daylight building of energy-efficient design. Put very simply, a highly glazed day-lit all-electric and fully air-conditioned building is roughly twice as expensive as a deep-planned air-conditioned building with gas heating, and three times the cost to run as an energy-efficient day-lit and naturally ventilated building.

In April 2002, Part L of the Building Regulations came into force, requiring building services and offices to be designed to minimize energy consumption and contribute to the UK's stated aim of reducing carbon emissions by 60 per cent over the next fifty years. This was updated in April 2006 and will be further updated every five years, with energy use in buildings being driven down with each revision. Some Local Planning policy (for example, in the London Borough of Merton) requires 10 per cent renewable energy supply in new commercial schemes.

Air conditioning is a problematic issue in a country where the climate does not really justify the expenditure of installing sophisticated systems nor, perhaps, the energy required to operate it. Again, to a great extent it all depends upon the location of the proposed office development and the state of the property market whether or not it is necessary to install artificial air-conditioning equipment. Although it is often, if decreasingly, seen as a sign of a 'prestige' building for marketing purposes, tenants are not always impressed by the existence of the service, and are often concerned at the costs of running and maintaining it. Sometimes, therefore, it is installed quite unnecessarily, with external noise rather than excessive heat being a more popular reason for having such a facility. Nevertheless, where it has not been incorporated initially, provision for future installation should be allowed by ensuring that the basic building design has sufficient floor-to-ceiling heights and that the roof, walls and floors have knock-out panels to permit ready ducting. It has, however, been suggested that, where a developer wishes to include facilities for air conditioning, they should be installed in combination with heating radiators, together with variable volume units, so that the tenant may control the environment in separate parts of the building (Salata 1990). Moreover, it is increasingly advisable to consider the provision of separate floor systems and, even further, to make individual controls available in positions that allow sensible partitioning and maintain the proper balance of the system. Although the installation of an overall system is initially very costly, it is often best to design for the full potential and then add or subtract as required.

Several other factors regarding the provision of heating and ventilation systems are worthy of mention:

- Information technology has posed certain environmental problems, because desk-mounted equipment produces local hot spots and requires the introduction of local cooling facilities in selected 20–30 m² zones (215–323 ft²).
- Appropriate systems include variable air volume, fan coils, displacement ventilation and chilled ceiling or beams according to circumstances.
- Space should be provided at the busy interconnecting junctions of vertical and horizontal ducts.
- Where the structure is massive, it may not cool down too much overnight, otherwise if economically possible it is normally best to maintain some background heating at all times.
- Most users prefer to have some proportion of natural ventilation, and a minimum of about 15 per cent of windows should be capable of opening.
- Packaged ventilating or heating units can often be placed on roofs and terraces to give greater flexibility.

- Water is usually preferred as a heating or cooling transfer medium rather than air, because of its compactness.
- Heat recovery systems are becoming very attractive propositions.
- One very useful and efficient development in the field of heating and ventilation is the heat pump, which is basically a refrigeration machine that generates heat in its cooling.

Lighting

Good lighting is extremely important in modern offices. Between the 1960s and 1970s there was a general increase in the levels of lighting, but this was found to be both wasteful and uncomfortable. It was not only the level of illumination that caused discomfort and distraction but also the glare caused by the form of lighting employed. Since then the tendency has been to lower internal lighting levels from around 1000 lux to 750 lux and even to 300–500 lux in many instances. Some areas of an office building might be dimmer still, and it is more and more common to install adjustable lighting so that tenants can arrange their own requirements as needs change. With the advent of new office technology, lighting systems have to be capable of special adjustment in order to cope with different levels of light emission from visual display units. Providing lighting that is suitable for the mix of different office tasks in a modern business organization is a much more demanding design exercise than it has been in the past. The trend is towards the combination of background and 'task' lighting, with the developer providing the background fixtures and a sufficiently flexible network of power points for occupiers to install task lighting of their own choosing and at their own expense. Over the past few years there has been greater use of 'uplighters' with sodium lamps. These are usually free-standing, which gives a high degree of flexibility and a clean finish to walls and ceilings. They also make the reorganization of partitioned offices much easier, reduce the costs of electricity for lighting by about half, and lower the developers' initial costs of construction. Moreover, soft uplighters are best for users of screen equipment.

Communications

The adoption of ever more sophisticated office machinery and the increasing reliance in business operations of all kinds upon advanced information systems means that modern office buildings must be designed to house a variety of communications equipment and facilitate flexible usage of it. The need to intercommunicate a range of devices within a building requires a local area communications network and/or wireless routers to be installed.

The guiding principle for making decisions should be the three Rs – rooms (for the installation of telecoms equipment both centrally and locally), routes (for cable trays or trunking, giving easy access for addition and movement of cables) and risers (making sure that these are accessible from common areas that are not another tenant's domain).

Cabling for both data and voice connections is relatively straightforward as each service provider no longer requires a bespoke cabling system. Many building occupiers now 'flood wire' their buildings – cables that can be used for almost any IT purpose are run throughout the occupied parts of the building on a regular grid for maximum flexibility.

Office machinery

Office machinery includes the possible provision of telephones, faxes, printing, photocopying, scanning, email, Internet access, document management, and mobile computing through wireless networks. Many modern offices still require a local equipment room to house communications equipment and servers, but these are much smaller than even ten years ago. The accent here is on flexibility and data security rather than a controlled environment.

One of the consequences of introducing new forms of office machinery is the need to provide more power sources and accommodate heavy-duty cables in the office environment. Humidity levels also have to be regulated, and something within the range of 30–50 per cent is desirable, whereas 20–60 per cent might just be acceptable for most machines.

The creation of workstations is probably the most distinctive feature of the modern office compared to, say, fifteen or twenty years ago. Workstations combine a degree of personal privacy with varying levels of information technology. There is now a wide range of proprietary packages available on the market. In many, worktops, filing drawers, cupboards and the like are hung from tracks fitted to modular partitions or walls. This permits many variations to be introduced and ensures that there is little waste to floorspace. In this way, workstation systems liberate space, make more efficient use of internal areas, and improve occupancy rates.

Lifts

The planning and development of any substantial office building is inextricably bound up with the matter of lift production. In the past it was a common failure in design to neglect proper consideration of the size, number, type, speed and location of lifts until too late in the process. It is not too much of an exaggeration to state, as has one leading manufacturer, that a successful office scheme of any size and quality has, to a very large extent, to be built around its lifts from the beginning. It is not possible merely to insert them at a later stage in standard-size holes, which have been left in the concrete. The lift manufacturer should, therefore, be brought in at the earliest possible stage of design, preferably in the capacity of a nominated subcontractor.

One of the main considerations in the provision of lifts is the future nature of occupancy that is envisaged. Single-tenant or owner occupation usually calls for a different lift layout – and produces a different pattern of lift traffic – to multiple occupancy. On the other hand, it is normally advisable to ensure that the flexible letting potential of the building is not circumscribed by an inappropriate lift provision. Lift installation must therefore be capable of satisfying the needs of different users as well as a single occupant. Modern microtechnology now enables lift services to be reprogrammed in accordance with changing occupiers' needs. As a guideline, lift provision of one person per 14 m² of net lettable area is considered to be good practice within the BCO Guide 2005.

In order to maximize the amount of lettable floorspace and facilitate the internal organization of business activity, a popular recourse has been to design the lift and stairwell services as a separate external unit adjacent to the office building shell. Alternatively, 'wall climber' lifts are beginning to be fashionable for large office as well as shopping developments.

With regard to lift lobbies, up to three lifts may conveniently be planned in a row, and a row of four is an absolute limit for efficient use, with two facing two preferred. Where the number of lifts exceeds four, three in a row should be the limit in cul-de-sac lobbies. For tall buildings up to sixty levels, conventional lifts can be used, with some form of interchange at, say, every twenty-five to thirty floors (Battle 2003) which will usually mesh with mechanical/plant zones.

A local authority may insist that one or more of the lifts in a building is designated for manual operation by visiting firefighters, usually at the principal exit floor. Moreover, large office buildings will normally be provided with a goods lift whose main function is the distribution of heavy items of furniture, stationery, equipment, food and other stores. Escalators are still not common in office buildings, but their ability to handle continuous inter-floor traffic makes them attractive in owner-occupied buildings (Case 1985).

Problems with lifts are frequently the major cause of complaint from tenants, and lifts need constant care. Therefore, the treatment of lifts as an important part of the overall design is attracting more attention as developers become increasingly aware of the need to create a more attractive and harmonious environment.

Other services and facilities

Among the other services and facilities that might have to be considered in the design and development of a modern office block are the following:

- *Fire protection system*. With attention paid to hose and reel location, dry and wet risers, alarms, sprinklers, gas suppression systems and external access and areas for fire appliances.
- *Emergency lighting*. This should be installed in staircases, toilets and other common parts.
- *Escape routes*. Designed in consultation with the fire brigade and with the cost-effectiveness of office layout firmly in mind.
- *Toilets*. For both sexes on each floor, with the potential for additional facilities and finishes and fittings to a high quality, as well as good ventilation.

- *Ventilated cleaners' cupboards.* On each floor, with power, water supply and drainage.
- *Drinking water.* Supply on each floor.
- *Tea-making facilities.* On each floor, depending upon the size of the building.
- *Waste disposal.* Areas should be provided for the storage of waste material as well as the usual waste disposal facilities.
- *Security.* It is increasingly important to provide a full and integrated manned and electronic intrusion system, which can range all the way from access control through to closed-circuit television and movement monitors detecting body heat.
- *Healthy building control.* More and more attention needs to be paid to designing buildings and providing monitoring systems to counteract the 'sick building syndrome'.
- The Disability Discrimination Act 1995 imposes important obligations on building owners and occupiers with respect to accessibility that require careful consideration at both the design and fitting-out stages.

Serviced offices

There is demand for the provision of serviced offices in the UK, by development, refurbishment and reorganization. Serviced offices have been defined as small office units between 15 m^2 (161 ft^2) and 50 m^2 (538 ft^2) available to let on short lease or licence terms for periods of one month upwards, but outside the security of the tenure provisions of the 1954 Landlord and Tenant Act. They normally provide a combination of secretarial support, photocopying facilities and post handling, telecommunications facilities, catering and dining room facilities, boardroom facilities, interview rooms, staffed reception area and electricity, lighting and heating. Payment of rent is on an inclusive basis and covers rents, rates, property insurance, a service charge, and include the use of many of the facilities described.

Serviced offices is a sector that is much in vogue, offering flexibility in occupation and the ability to set up an office without the usual infrastructure costs. Surveys identify this need for flexibility as the primary reason for using serviced offices, with cost, security and image seen as less important. The most likely period for occupation is less than two years. Banking, business services, electronics and the media have been some of the major serviced office users.

Business and office parks

The late 1980s witnessed the emergence of the business park as a major new force in the UK property market. Without doubt, the growth in development of business parks was fuelled by the introduction of the B1 Use Class in 1987, but the more perceptive developers had already recognized the need for flexible 'office look-alike' space out of town, and had closely researched the American experience (Healey and Nabarro 1988, *Estates Gazette* 1990). Business parks have experienced mixed fortunes over the last two decades. Declining popularity in the early 1990s was succeeded by revival in the late 1990s, with enormous growth in 2000 and 2001, during the 'dot.com bubble', only to slip back in 2002 and 2003 before regaining small momentum thereafter. The principal difference between the downturn in the early 1990s and that of the early 2000s was the shift in the market from speculative to pre-let (*Property Week* 2002), which resulted in a softer landing.

The term 'business park' tends to mean different things to different people, usually according to the particular circumstances pertaining and the position in which they stand. To some, the concept lies somewhere between high-tech and traditional industrial sheds, with elements of both in many schemes. To others the mix is much richer, to include not only business and office users but also retail, leisure and even residential developments. Moreover, a more recent arrival on the scene has been the corporate office park, which is predominantly office-based, with selected support facilities and normally aimed at substantial organizations – often within the financial services or marketing sectors of the economy – looking for international, national or regional headquarters buildings located in a parkland setting. The Royal Bank of Scotland's Gogarburn site, to the west of Edinburgh, is a leading example of this model.

Definitions of business parks vary, but they generally exclude research, science and technology uses (which tend to be branded as 'science parks'). A useful set of descriptors is provided by Holden (1986):

- A good business location, including easy access to road, rail and air transport
- High-quality, low-density development, well landscaped and with good car parking provision
- An actively managed, well-serviced development, including power, security and communications facilities, as well as recreational and business community provision.

Looking more closely at the corporate office or commerce park, the following common characteristics are revealed:

- Most buildings are on two, or possibly three, storeys in order to limit the amount of vertical movements.
- Entrances and reception areas should be impressive and spacious, so as to allow tenants to promote a strong corporate image.
- Tenants seem to prefer relatively conventional layout and design specifications, such as an office width of around 14 m (45 ft), at least 40 per cent of partitionable space to create individual rooms and an occupation density of about one employee to 14 m^2 (150 ft^2).
- Car parking is around one space per 20 m^2 (215 ft^2) gross (no more than one per 25 m^2 and sometimes as low as one per 15 m^2) all at ground level, appropriately divided, easy to manoeuvre round, well lit and suitably screened.

- A good image for the park as a whole, as well as for particular buildings, necessitating an attractive approach providing a sense of arrival, clear signposting, carefully selected tenant mix and the setting and grouping of individual buildings to create a feeling of dignity and importance.
- A low density of development with a site coverage or 'footprint' of around 15 per cent producing about 10,000–12,500 ft² (929–1161 m²) of lettable floorspace per acre with a two- to three-storey development.
- High standards of landscape to include such features as streams, sculpture and seating.
- A significant element of brick and tile as opposed to curtain walling seems most popular with tenants, together with tiled sloping roofs on timber trusses and rafters allowing the elimination of internal columns.
- The facility in terms of design for tenants to install their own air-conditioning.
- A raised floor to accommodate complex cabling.
- High quality of management.

Although it was already generally accepted that a true business or office park should stand on at least 40 ha (100 acres), the second generation of business parks across Europe have included larger park developments of 160–200 ha (400–500 acres) and more resembling mini new towns. These will be based on a master-plan, which would provide a planned and controlled environment within which companies can retain and express their individual and corporate image, give a clear and functional infrastructure of roads and attractive landscapes, provide a variety of flexible plot sizes that enable occupants to expand and adapt their space to accommodate their own growth, develop a phasing policy to ensure that the development appears complete at each stage, while minimizing disruption to existing occupants during construction, and sustain the quality of the original concept through design development guidelines for each plot (Michalik 1990). The attitude of some ambitious developers and their consultants is to create:

> an alternative town centre with a wide range of facilities and amenities provided or close by including shopping, leisure, recreation, childcare and catering with high-quality design building and services standards served by good public as well as private transport facilities so as to recruit and retain key staff. One major obstacle to this is government policy aimed at preserving the status of the town centre and creating a climate of sustainable development. The future of business park development, therefore, has succinctly been stated to be about 'the integration of flexible buildings with a quality landscape – within the community'.
>
> (Auckett, quoted in MacRae 1993)

Trends in sustainability, regeneration of town centres and reduction in use of the private car have for some time suggested that the days of development of the larger business park were numbered, and this has been borne out. Few such schemes have been developed since the late 1990s.

Facilities management

No examination of office development would be complete without some mention of the emergence of the discipline of facilities management. Until relatively recently the property industry regarded management as very much the unglamorous end of the business – a mixture of rent collection and caretaking. However, property or premises management is changing from being the industry's Cinderella to playing a central role in all sectors of commercial development. Shopping centre management led the way, back in the late 1970s and throughout the 1980s. Facilities management for offices is more a creature born in the late 1980s and 1990s.

According to the British Institute for Facilities Management:

> Facilities management is the integration of processes within an organisation to maintain and develop the agreed services which support and improve the effectiveness of its primary activities.
>
> Facilities management encompasses multi-disciplinary activities within the built environment and the management of their impact upon people and the workplace.
>
> Effective facilities management, combining resources and activities, is vital to the success of any organisation. At a corporate level, it contributes to the delivery of strategic and operational objectives. On a day-to-day level, effective facilities management provides a safe and efficient working environment, which is essential to the performance of any business – whatever its size and scope.
>
> (BIFM 2008)

In both private business and public service sectors of society, the profound changes which took place in the 1980s and 1990s, with an emphasis upon the twin forces of enterprise and quality, were reliant on the rapid spread of new ideas, technologies and practices resulting from advanced international communications and a much more highly competitive global economy. A major consequence has been the recognition by all kinds of organizations of the importance of property – its location, design and use – as a prime asset in the operational effectiveness of commercial and civic undertakings, as well as a principal factor in the equation of capital worth. Simple premises management has, thereby, evolved into the somewhat more complex and sophisticated discipline of facilities management. This is especially true of large corporations and utilities.

It is not surprising, therefore, that facilities management is a sector of property asset appraisal that has evoked increasing interest worldwide from both the design and the real estate professions over the past decade. It is still viewed with uncertainty, however, and remains an ill-defined field. Nevertheless, as organizations strive to cope with constantly changing economic conditions, they are obliged to seek increasingly efficient and productive work environments.

Information technology

As already intimated, the workplace has swiftly transformed, largely because of the introduction of an unprecedented scale of new information technologies in organizations. Work processes, physical environments and the social milieu of organizations have been redefined. There is now a body of knowledge and experience enabling design and management problems of high-technology workplaces to be solved in an integrated way. Indeed, the progress of work automation has been so fast over the past decade that the pace has often outstripped the capacity of organizations to absorb new technology and to reap their potential benefits effectively. High technology, moreover, is seen to be affecting the workplace in two different and complementary ways. Directly, it is being invaded by a whole new range of equipment, with new, and frequently conflicting environmental needs. Indirectly, it must change to adapt to the transformations of work processes and organizations that result from automation.

The advent of the 'intelligent building' was a striking feature of the 1980s. Stimulated by the globalization of the financial services industry, with the accompanying cascade of terminals, cables, atria and dealing rooms, it coincided with a radical reassessment of building procurement, construction and management processes (Duffy 1991). Buildings must obviously be capable of accommodating new demands and be developed accordingly. They must also be managed as business assets showing an acceptable return.

The nature, form and effectiveness of the intelligent building have been the subject of much study, definition and debate since the mid-1980s. What is often required is adaptable and cost-effective space capable of delivering high levels of operationally networked performance providing an integrated environment for those involved. Put another way:

> The intelligent building straddles two vastly different, but essential demands made by the modern firm. Buildings must respond to changing demands effectively and quickly, and must support a high level of interworking by workers.
>
> (Robathan 1993)

Developers and their designers need also to understand that intelligent buildings should be in the control of users themselves, rather than providing technological solutions to occupational problems which have been perceived before the occupiers have had a chance to use the building itself. Developers therefore need to ensure:

- a better understanding of occupant requirements and behaviour
- more effective transformation of design intentions into built reality
- a commissioning process which recognizes the need for support beyond practical completion with programmed involvement of management and the design team

- better understanding of designs by management and management by designers
- better provision, functionality and usability of control interfaces: frequently items that are desirable are either absent, inappropriate, or out of reach.

(Cohen *et al.* 1998)

The facilities manager

Opinions differ about the nature and scope of facilities management, and thus the role of the facilities manager. From a management perspective, it is suggested that facilities managers may be said to look after five key aspects of an organization:

- *Shareholders:* by maintaining the asset value – regular checks of fabric, etc.
- *Employees:* by creating efficient working environments conducive to high morale and productivity
- *Customers:* by maintaining and reinforcing the good image of the organization
- *Community:* the impact of the organization on the environment and the local community
- *Suppliers:* by ensuring the quality of suppliers and services.

(Powell 1990)

Barret and Baldry (2000) identify typical facilities management activities as follows:

Facility planning
- Strategic space planning
- Set corporate planning standards and guidelines
- Identify user needs
- Furniture layouts
- Monitor space use
- Select and control use of furniture
- Define performance measures
- Computer-aided facility management (CAFM).

Building operations and maintenance
- Run and maintain plant
- Maintain building fabric
- Manage and undertake adaptation
- Energy management
- Security
- Voice and data communication
- Control operating budget
- Monitor performance
- Supervise cleaning and decoration
- Waste management and recycling.

Real estate and building construction
- New building design and construction management
- Acquisition and disposal of sites and buildings
- Negotiation and management of leases
- Advice on property investment
- Control of capital budgets.

General/office services
- Provide and manage support services
- Office purchasing (stationery and equipment)
- Non-building contract services (catering, travel, etc.)
- Reprographic services
- Housekeeping standards
- Relocation
- Health and safety.

From the above, it can be seen that the responsibilities of the facilities manager are remarkably wide-ranging.

Facilities management and property development

The need to provide premises in the right place, at the right time, with the right services, offering the right level of management and at the right price is paramount. Current user markets have done much to alter the attitude of building owners and developers.

Much lip-service is paid to landlords focusing on the needs of the end user, but because most property is built speculatively, the ultimate occupiers generally have to compromise their requirements or deal with severe restrictions imposed at the design stage. It is suggested that these restrictions fall into two categories – those imposed by the building shell and its plant and equipments, and those dictated by real estate procedures, that frustrate the efficiency of the occupier (Prodgers 1992). Tenants are becoming less and less willing to live with inadequacies in the original design of a building, and more demanding of a flexible and service-oriented approach by the landlord towards tenure than hitherto.

The message is perhaps a simple one – the future management of properties facilities, in the very widest sense, should be incorporated as part of development planning at the very earliest stage of the development process. It has been argued that the management of an organization's facilities, its built environment and its infrastructure must take into account the nature of the activities that take place within the building and which the facilities are serving. Moreover, it must be fitted not only to the formal goals of the organization, but also to the way that the organization is structured – its pattern of work and its pattern of decision-making. Therefore, an approach to facilities management that looks beyond current best practice and is aware of predicted trends and changes, is to be recommended (Barret and Baldry 2000).

Conclusion

We have seen many changes in office development in the last few decades, none more so because of the workplace revolution that has occurred since the 1980s. The key drivers of this change have been:

- The increase in the globalization and decentralization of services
- The revolution in the capabilities of communication and information technologies
- Having more 'footloose' enterprises in the economy
- Demand for a more sustainable approach to doing business.

Looking forwards, it is likely that these drivers will have a variety of consequences for office development. The total outsourcing of property and facilities management is likely to increase in popularity and the capacity of the serviced offices sectors to absorb short-term requirements for office space will also probably have to increase.

New ways of working, sustainability and productivity are the watchwords for the future. Office owners and developers will have to manage their developments and buildings they create and provide after-sales care. Occupiers are – and should increasingly be seen as – customers, rather than subjugated tenants. The real challenge faced by developers is to deliver guaranteed buildings tailored to the company's business plan priorities and reach the level of service attained by other suppliers. Gone are the days of the 'let and forget' philosophy prevalent for so many years. Developers will increasingly have to compete on this playing field. To do so they will need suitably qualified teams to manage the entire development process, challenge previously accepted norms and preconceptions, transfer experience, knowledge and innovation, enhance the value of advisers and reduce potential conflicts of interest to deliver commercially valuable cost-effective buildings.

18 Industrial development

Low unemployment and interest rates, changing industrial processes, new technology and new ways of working have all combined to require a reconsideration by both public and private sector agencies involved in the production of industrial and business development properties in respect of what they build, where and for whom. The 1980s witnessed a transformation in both the location and property requirements of modern industries because of the decline in traditional manufacturing and the growth in the service sector. The 1990s saw globalization and radical changes in information and communication technology. In the new millennium we are seeing a continued contraction of the manufacturing sector, the increasing dominance of the service sector, and major advances in the integration of information and communication technology in the manufacture, assembly, storage, sale and delivery of goods and services. Table 18.1 illustrates these changes in terms of employment in each industry sector between 1997 and 2007, and Table 18.2 demonstrates the dominance of the services sector in terms of contribution to UK GDP in the first seven years of the 2000s.

In this way, it has been projected that by 2014 the manufacturing workforce will have fallen to 3.17 million, from 3.55 million in 2004 (Wilson *et al.* 2006) and from an estimated 8 million in 1971. The industrial real estate market has therefore had to contend with revolutionary change – and continues to do so. The efficiency of traditional distribution centre sizes, locations and designs has changed to reflect a market where new logistics processes are allowing shorter product cycles, lower inventory levels and faster turnaround.

In terms of the broad characteristics of modern industry, research (DEGW 1985) has concluded that:

- The shift in economic activity from manufacturing industry to the information and service sectors has changed the types of sites and buildings required for modern industry.
- These sectors are concerned with mental skills – the applications of specialist knowledge – rather than manual skills. This loosens traditional ties and generates new demands – in particular to provide a 'people environment' rather than a 'machine environment', resulting in a specification more akin to an office than a factory.

Table 18.1 Changes in workforce by industry sector 1997–2007

	Q4 1997 (%)	Q4 2007 (%)
All in employment (000s)	26,698	29,471
Public sector	22.8	23.9
Private sector	77.2	76.1
Agriculture & Fishing	1.7	1.4
Energy & Water	1.1	1.2
Manufacturing	18.6	12.6
Construction	7.2	8.1
Distribution, Hotels and Restaurants	20.3	19.2
Transport & Communications	6.5	6.6
Banking, Finance & Insurance, etc.	14.4	16.6
Public admin, Education & Health	24.3	28.3
Other services	5.9	6.2
All services	*71.4*	*76.8*

Source: Office for National Statistics 2008a

Table 18.2 Annual contributions to GDP by industry sector 2001–2007

Growth, year-on-year, for the output components of GDP

Component	2001	2002	2003	2004	2005	2006	2007
Agriculture	−9.4	12.3	−2.1	−1.0	4.4	2.8	0.9
Total production	*−1.5*	*−1.9*	*−0.3*	*0.8*	*−2.0*	*0.3*	*0.3*
Manufacturing	−1.3	−2.6	0.2	2.0	−1.2	1.5	0.6
Extraction	−5.5	0.4	−5.1	−7.9	−9.2	−8.0	−1.7
Utilities	3.2	0.4	1.6	1.1	−0.4	−2.0	0.1
Construction	2.3	3.6	4.7	4.0	1.5	1.1	2.4
Total services	*3.5*	*2.6*	*3.2*	*3.9*	*2.9*	*3.7*	*3.7*
Distn, hotels & catering	3.4	4.6	3.8	5.2	1.2	3.5	3.9
Transport, storage & comms	4.5	1.2	1.9	2.5	4.3	3.9	4.3
Business services & finance	4.1	2.0	3.9	5.1	4.4	5.3	4.8
Government & other	2.3	2.5	2.4	2.0	1.8	1.8	1.9

Source: Office for National Statistics 2008b

- To meet market demands and keep abreast of the latest technology these sectors are also concerned with producing limited product runs of specific customized products. This requires the centralization under one roof of research and design, product assembly and customization, and marketing and consumer services. The building must have flexibility to vary the mix of uses within any part of the building as the organization and its products grow and adapt.

Thus, good property developers appreciate the general implications that these changes have for businesses, workers and local authorities, as well as for buildings, and the kind of responses that will be needed.

This chapter explores the nature of industrial and business property development by examining the following issues:

- Location for industry
- Warehousing and distribution
- High-technology development
- Planning policy
- Design and layout
- Estate management.

Location for industry

Conventional industrial location theory has assumed that firms behave in a rational and logical manner and are able to achieve their optimum locations. Rational behaviour in location decision-making was felt to be determined by the aim of profit maximization. However, it has been pointed out that more recent theories of industrial location have abandoned the pretence of the optimal location and have acknowledged that locational decisions are often surrounded by uncertainty and personal preference. Land may be prevented from passing to the highest possible bidder by factors such as owners' expectations and behaviour, the cost of redevelopment and upheaval, or the existence of planning controls. As with other property sectors, because of substantial imperfections, land markets operate only at partial equilibrium. Supply and demand do not automatically equate, supply being determined primarily through the planning system, whereas demand depends upon private sector actions. This is said to make it extremely difficult to apply competitive market analysis to the industrial land market (Adams *et al.* 1993).

Basic factors of location

Although it remains broadly true that the combination of correct location and good design sells space everywhere, it is also true that the industrial development market is highly segmented, and different categories of user possess different locational requirements. Likewise, certain parts of the country enjoy strong competitive advantages over others. However, there are several basic factors that exercise a growing influence over the location and demand for industrial and business property. These can be summarized as follows:

- *Communications.* The need to have quick and ready access to clients, markets, suppliers, labour, services and complementary parts of the business is an absolute prerequisite to modern industry. Thus, transport linkage and high car parking standards are crucial.
- *Flexibility.* A healthy firm has to be able to adapt quickly to changing requirements in respect of both the amount and the use of available space. Room to expand, and the capacity to reorganize methods of production and alter

the nature of activities taking place within a building, are becoming more and more critical. Open flexible space, an easily extendable and convertible structure and low site coverage are, therefore, necessary ingredients.

- *Environment.* The image portrayed by the site and building chosen by a firm are increasingly important. So too is the internal working environment, and desired conditions in many industrial premises are fast approaching those demanded in offices. Semi-rural positions on the outskirts of town are most popular.
- *Design.* From the above it can be seen that modern industrial design must be not only stylish, creating an individual identity through character and quality, but also capable of conversion into offices, research, training and production space. Moreover, it must create a building that can accept electronic communications systems and be constructed to minimize running costs.

Many modern cities have an abundant stock of disused factory and warehouse buildings, which tend to occupy land in strategic urban locations with excellent accessibility to major transport routes and waterfronts.

Manufacturing was usually the initial magnet for urban growth, drawing in capital, labour and expertise from the surrounding regions and stimulating new economic activities in business and services. However, when urban economies develop to a more advanced stage, economic restructuring inevitably leads to a shift from industrial into higher-value activities in finance, business and services. High urban land prices and space demands of manufacturers resulted in a massive exodus of industrial activities from urban areas (Tang and Tang 1999). An acceleration of this trend has been experienced since the mid-1980s.

With the decline of rail transport and the growth of car ownership, residential and working populations have become more dispersed. This is reflected in the decline of major cities, a process often called 'counter-urbanization'. The 1980s and 1990s saw a decline in the population of large urban areas (such as inner and outer London, Birmingham, Manchester, and Liverpool), which can be compared with the growth of a selected number of smaller towns over the same period (such as Bracknell, Milton Keynes, Guildford, Solihull, and Bromsgrove).

As with office developments, there is what has been described as a 'push-me, pull-you' interplay of factors encouraging companies to locate either in or out of town. The push away from town centres involves increased congestion, rising costs and longer commuting times. Conversely, the out-of-town location may be able to offer cost savings, an attractive working environment, better car parking provision and generally greater accessibility. Against this, however, out-of-town sites often show certain disadvantages, such as inadequate amenities and facilities. The town centre might also have certain advantages in terms of accessibility to the public transport network and benefits from a variety of shopping and recreational activities. A survey of companies showed the relative importance of various locational factors. Proximity to motorways and environmental quality were stressed as of most importance, followed by access to markets, airports, the rest of the company, and staff availability, attraction and skills, all well ahead of the availability of public transport, leisure and housing (Debenham Tewson Research 1990).

Regional trends

The deep structural changes that have been taking place within the economy since the mid-1980s – whereby emerging industries are based upon information and communications more than raw materials and productive processes, with a workforce more dependent upon management and innovation than on handling and manufacturing – have meant that such knowledge-based companies are increasingly mobile. As a result, the concentration of new industrial development upon the South East of England has accelerated throughout the 1980s and 1990s and into this century.

The much vaunted 'Golden Triangle', formed within the area marked by Hammersmith, Swindon and Guildford, has grown and changed shape to create a kind of 'Golden Trapezium' bounded by lines joining Bristol to the west and Southampton to the south, as well as those connecting Guildford and Hammersmith. Within this area, demand to occupy industrial floorspace and pressure to release land have become especially focused along the Western Corridor created by the M4 leading from Hammersmith to Heathrow (the latter having the most expensive industrial premises in the world), Reading, Swindon and Bristol. A premium can be discerned on sites within a thirty-minute drive time of Central London and Heathrow, and to a lesser extent along the M1, M3 and M40 motorways, up to a distance of 75 to 100 miles. The existence of the M25 orbital route around London has a dramatic effect upon commercial and industrial location decisions.

Demand for new industrial space in the South East is generated from a variety of sources. There are large multinational and national companies decentralizing from Central London. Then there are major fast-growth companies already located in the South East but in need of new and larger premises. Smaller fast-growth companies, both home-grown and from overseas, are also actively seeking and occupying space. Probably the greatest demand for new industrial development since the mid-1980s has, in fact, come from abroad.

Globalization has meant that British labour has had to compete with less economically developed countries where labour is a fraction of the cost. This has led major retailers to reduce the proportion of clothing they buy from the British textile industry significantly. With the decline of heavy industry and the coming of globalization, manufacturing has declined in the northern half of the country and the population has declined too in favour of the thriving south (Schiller 2001).

Relative economic success within the South East during the 1980s brought with it certain disadvantages that began to impinge upon the ability of existing firms to expand. Problems in the supply of suitably skilled and affordable labour, together with increased congestion and a slowdown in economic growth, resulted in oversupply of exclusively business-use accommodation in certain parts of the South East. This raised questions concerning the nature and location of new development. It encouraged, in part, a shift towards the provision of more traditional industrial premises and, in part, a shift in attention towards other regions within the UK. With regard to the business park type of development, the South West, East Anglia, North West, Yorkshire and Humberside regions all experienced significant increases in floorspace provision in the 1990s and 2000s. This shift in development activity towards other regions should be seen as a long-term trend that is unlikely to challenge the predominance of the South East. Indeed the South East Plan examination-in-public (2007) heard evidence to the effect that currently its regional economy enjoyed a surplus of around 100,000 jobs in excess of the existing workforce. While this was expected to narrow over the plan period of some ten years, it was not expected to fall below a surplus of some 67,000.

Major transportation infrastructure projects are natural catalysts for industrial and business developments. Another generative factor influencing development growth in the sector is the decision of a single substantial investor or producer to locate in a particular town, city or region. A prime example is in the Tyne and Wear region, where Nissan, the Japanese car manufacturer, has chosen to locate its 140,000 m^2 plant in Washington, near Sunderland. Known as the 'Nissan effect', the massive investment has brought significant spin-off benefits, not only in terms of the immediate 3500 jobs directly created but also by generating renewed business confidence in the region (Mills 1992).

No examination of regional trends would be complete without some mention of the European dimension. Here it has been found, in a survey from the University of Cambridge, that the quality and size of the labour force is a key factor affecting company location decisions in Europe (Moore *et al.* 1991). As might be expected, the availability of regional development assistance was identified as being important for production companies and for companies relocating from abroad. However, the level of wage costs was generally less important than the quality and size of the labour supply. It is interesting that the quality of infrastructure did not rate highly, and neither did the level of rents, nor the attractiveness of the environment. On the evidence of the survey, preferred regions are those offering minimal costs, but also quality and supply of labour and good access to markets. This would suggest the run-down industrial areas of northern France, Belgium, the Netherlands and the Ruhr. In Britain it would point to the Midlands and the North.

Types of industrial development

The industrial property market comprises both facilities for the production of goods, i.e. space for manufacturers, and those for the storage and distribution of goods, i.e. warehouses and distribution units – 'sheds'. As far as 'pure' property developers are concerned, it is the latter market which is of more interest to them because it is open to speculative development and attracts far more interest from investors than that for manufacturing facilities. The chief reason for this is that manufacturers, on the whole, require factory facilities which are very often bespoke or tailored to their needs. It is also unlikely that manufacturers will frequently move, making the market for their property less liquid. Sheds, on the other hand, can usually be occupied by many different occupiers, seldom having been made bespoke for a single occupier.

The occupier group in the sheds markets is populated by:

- Manufacturers of everything from plush toys to aeroplanes, who are storing raw materials and finished products.
- Wholesalers and retailers of all products, who are storing and packaging goods for resale.
- Logistics operators, who service the needs of those manufacturing and selling goods.

As can be surmised from the above list, the industrial development sector is highly segmented. An understanding of the different types of industrial development is important, because they invariably involve different user requirements, development agencies, sources of finance, design requirements, and management policies. A useful classification was devised some time ago (Worthington 1982) but is still worthwhile considering today. It identifies categories of traditional, new growth and innovation industries, as below.

Traditional industry

- *Community workshop:* small workshops aimed at encouraging embryo enterprises by developing skills and providing equipment and administrative support. Located close to residential areas in old buildings.
- *Flatted factory:* multi-storey industrial buildings, with goods lift and corridor access to some small independent tenancies.
- *Industrial estate:* mixture of manufacturing and service uses. Industrial character where delivery areas predominate.
- *Trading estate:* warehouse uses with some office content. May attract retail warehousing and trade outlets.

New growth industries

- *Working community:* a group of independent small firms cooperating in sharing a building and joint services. The objective is to enjoy a scale of premises and facilities normally available only to larger companies. The group will normally have a policy of selecting compatible or complementary firms.
- *Commercial/business park:* having a high-quality low-density environment. Aimed at firms requiring prestige or high-calibre workforce. Mixtures of manufacturing, office and sales functions.

- *Trade mart:* a multiple tenanted building with office showrooms and centrally provided exhibition, conference areas, reception and support services. Normally developed around a theme.

Research/innovation

- *Innovation centre:* an individual building, immediately adjacent to a university campus, providing small units 30–150 m^2 (323–1615 ft^2) for starter firms growing out of research projects within the university and drawing upon its facilities and support services.
- *Research park:* sites or advanced units for young or established firms in the field of research or development. Often close to a university and associated with university research laboratories and amenities. Such schemes are often joint ventures.
- *Science/technology park:* with universities and research institutions within a 30-mile catchment area. Attractive lifestyle, low-density development aimed at scientific or technology-oriented companies.
- *Industrial park:* aimed at clean manufacturing organizations with a landscaped setting and leisure amenities for staff.

Warehousing and distribution

A key feature of the property scene in the UK since the mid-1980s has been the phenomenal growth of the distribution industry and its consequent land-use and property requirements. The traditional concept of the warehouse as a crudely converted simple storage building situated in a run-down industrial area has undergone a fundamental change. There is now a widespread demand among distributors of goods for purpose-built, fully automated storage premises designed to satisfy their operational requirements, located on strategically identified sites within, and adjacent to, urban regions and throughout the country generally (Taylor 1993).

Research undertaken by DTZ Debenham Thorpe pointed to a period of sustained activity in the warehouse property sector throughout the 1990s, as major operators responded to the emergence of new markets. Distribution networks that were previously viewed as effective and efficient were becoming less so as a result of the combined effect of lower rates of economic growth, the employment of 'just-in-time' methods (JIT) and automation in the warehouse, as well as the effect of existing and proposed legislation. Together, these elements brought about a major shift in the location and property requirements of many companies, a shift with implications for both developers and investors. The Internet has raised consumer expectations about choice and efficiency and has created an assumption that immediacy of the virtual order can be matched by the speed of the actual delivery. This will continue to have implications for supply chain management, with fluid vision needed for the design, style, location, size, and connectivity of distribution property in the years to come.

The distribution sector underpins all economic activity. It provides the link between suppliers, manufacturers and retailers in a complex network that is increasingly taking on a pan-European dimension. The warehouse lies at the heart of the supply chain, providing a buffer between fluctuations in supply and demand. Warehouses are increasingly viewed not simply as a place to store goods but as an integral element of the logistics network capable of making a positive contribution to corporate well-being or, negatively, acting as a major constraint on operational efficiency. The incredible growth demonstrated by Tesco, for example, in the 1990s and 2000s was in no small part due to the way it transformed logistics thinking and practice.

The increasingly widespread use of JIT means that warehouses perform a set of functions different from those undertaken in the past. Much greater emphasis is placed on stock rotation, trans-shipment activities and break-bulk, as well as a range of ancillary activities including repackaging and some light assembly. This range of emerging needs requires a comprehensive reassessment of the location and specification of premises deemed suitable in the late 1990s.

Major issues in warehouse and distribution development

Some major issues affecting the development of warehousing and distribution property over the next decade or so can be identified, as described briefly below.

Europe

Manufacturers, retailers and other companies throughout Europe are considering their distribution needs on a pan-European basis, with the phenomenon of a single distribution site with a super-warehouse servicing all of Europe. However, several sites are a more popular solution. Although northwest mainland Europe has distribution facilities similar to the UK, including traditional estates and free-standing distribution centres, the region has seen developments rarely witnessed in the UK. They include groups of road-haulage depots on a single site and loose groupings of depots and warehouses offering a range of logistical services at one site, including modal interchange. Strong competition, standardization and sophistication are destined to become the themes of European distribution development. Legislation regarding environmental taxes, working time and operational constraints and exchange rates, will all have an effect on location.

UK regional distribution centres (RDCs)

An RDC is difficult to define according to size or function, but will require a location part way between the point of manufacture or import and the point of sale (i.e. the location of the markets). As a consequence, the West and East Midlands of England provide the best area, and counties like Northamptonshire and Leicestershire contain many such distribution centres. Most major retailers prefer no more than 2–2.5 hours between distribution depots. In recent years, the number of RDCs has reduced and they have grown in size as the restructuring of both logistical and distribution activities has occurred. A number of factors has enabled this, including the growth in the size of the lorries which carry the vast majority of goods around the country, improvements to racking systems and other warehouse management operations which enable more goods to be stored in individual sheds and more efficient management of logistics operations through the use of information technology.

Although some logistics operators have flirted with the use of rail and even canal routes for the distribution of freight, often for 'greenwashing' purposes, the road will continue to dominate as the route of first choice for regional distributors. Generally owner-occupied or pre-let, the RDC market is for units over 250,000 ft² square feet with some 'mega sheds', at 1,000,000 ft², now being provided.

Classification and specification

In an attempt to understand the various levels of warehouse requirement, a useful classification of operations into simple, medium and sophisticated storage can be made. Simple storage operations are those where the goods in question can be block-stacked to a limited height, using ordinary counter-balanced fork-lift trucks and need a clear height of up to 5.5–6.0 m (18–20 ft). Some of the traditional standard units, therefore, are suitable. Medium storage operations take place where goods are stored in racked pallets with wider aisles and handled by the use of reach or turret trucks. Clear heights of up to 8.0–8.5 m (26–28 ft) are required. Sophisticated storage operations imply the existence of an automated warehouse and thus a high commitment to mechanical handling equipment. Wire guidance systems, automatic stacker cranes and computer-assisted stock control are all features of such operations, and buildings with clear heights of up to 36 m (118 ft) have been constructed to accommodate demand. In fact there is a burgeoning growth in the development of high-bay warehouses. There are plenty of examples of such developments these days because their large storage capacity is created for little more cost than that of a smaller, traditional warehouse, largely because of the smaller footprint and subsequent land cost.

The basic object of modern warehouse design, therefore, is to maximize the amount of usable storage volume out of the gross volume of a building. Although costs of construction increase with height, the rate of increase falls, and produces what has been described as a lower cost of pallet aperture. Unlike manufacturing premises, it is important that offices should actually oversee the loading bays. A single-sided approach for cars and trucks is thereby created and consequently back-to-back development is possible. Another difference is that insulation to the skin may or may not be necessary, depending upon what is to be stored. Level access doors are a necessity for modern logistics operators, as are the option of refrigerated loading bays and sealed door systems.

Distribution parks

The lack of large suitable sites for low-density development, the need for good motorway access and the trend towards 24-hour operations, coupled with the availability of both public transport and ancillary services and facilities are all factors likely to enhance the apparent attractiveness of dedicated distribution parks.

At 200 acres, one of Europe's largest fully integrated national distribution centres has been developed at Magna Park in Leicestershire. Started in 1988, 715,000 m² (7,700,000 ft²) was completed by 1998. Situated in the 'golden triangle' of the country's road network, from this site nearly 92 per cent of the population of Great Britain can be reached with the return journey being undertaken on the same day. The scheme features high-quality designed structures with a distinct architectural style, steel portal-frame warehouses with eaves heights of 15 m or more, leases of 999 years allowing the use of positive covenants to control estate maintenance and management, superior landscaping provision, and a cost-effective centralized sewerage system. Since its inception, Magna Park has secured an impressive range of tenants and investment deals and the aspiration of its developers, Gazeley and Land Securities, is for it to be the most sustainable distribution park in Europe – a fact which helped to lure John Lewis plc as a key tenant in 2007.

Freight villages

These are massive distribution centres located at strategic points around the country, providing integrated multimodal high-bay facilities based on rail as well as road networks, the rail link being used for long haul and the road service for collection and delivery. The EU and British government both promote multimodal transport in an attempt to reduce the amount of freight being carried on the road network with a preference for long-haul, large-load freight movements by trains that carry the equivalent of fifty lorry loads. Strategic Rail Freight Interchanges present the key to the success of these schemes. Table 18.3 shows the hierarchy of the interchanges.

Severn Trent Properties' Strategic Rail Freight Interchange, Daventry International Rail Freight Terminal (DIRFT) is located on the west coast mainline near the M6, M1 and A14 interchange and was opened in 1997. It was one of the first new-generation multi-modal hubs to be developed in the post-Channel Tunnel era as a core intermodal handling area, acting as a receipt and dispatch point of trunk rail flows from both the Channel Tunnel and the port of Felixstowe. It serves rail and non rail-connected warehousing on the freight village, acting as a strategic access point to the rail network for traffic in the wider region, including regular flows from companies based on the nearby Lutterworth distribution park. Businesses attracted to DIRFT for the development of warehousing have been a combination of logistics service providers, servicing retail customers, and end retail customers on their own account,

Table 18.3 Rail Freight Interchange hierarchy

Type of RFI	Function	Likely size	Indicative transport requirements
Strategic	Major interchange with significant intermodal and warehousing, located at nationally strategic sites proximate to major conurbations	100–400 ha	Requires high-quality links to motorway and trunk road network. Rail links need high capacity and good loading gauge.
Non-strategic sub-regional	Large interchange with significant intermodal warehousing, located at important sites within regions	20–250 ha	Requires high-quality links to motorway and trunk road network. Rail links need sufficient capacity and good loading gauge
Intermodal only	Interchange handling only intermodal traffic, often located at key points in urban locations	10–30 ha	Requires good links to urban road and trunk road network. Rail link requires sufficient loading gauge.
Rail-linked warehouse	Single warehouse unit providing rail services	10–30 ha	Requires good links to urban road and trunk road network
Bulk terminal	Bespoke terminal for single bulk product types such as aggregates and minerals, often linked to a manufacturing or processing facility. Also includes car, automotive and waste terminals.	5–10 ha	Road and rail links need to be appropriate for bulk commodity – often heavy loads. Aggregates and minerals terminals often require urban location to serve construction industries and road maintenance.

including investment by the Royal Mail to create a hub as part of their network rationalization.

High-technology development

The term 'high-tech' became the buzzword of the 1980s, but there seemed to be little or no common understanding as to the way it was used in the property world. It would often appear to have had as much to do with industrial marketing and architectural fancy as with the true needs of occupiers. The labelling of estates with colourful claddings, tinted glass and expensive landscaping as being high-tech led one leading agent to observe, 'It is not entirely unreasonable to regard the high-tech chapter in industrial marketing as something of an elaborate self-deception by a number of architects and agents'.

The growth of high-technology estate development has its roots in the USA where, although many early American business parks were actually poorly located, a more risk-conscious and responsive property industry led the way in the design and development of accommodation to suit high-technology based companies. The explosive growth that took place in Santa Clara County ('Silicon Valley') during the 1970s is now familiar. However, there were lessons for the UK to be learned because the rapid establishment of well over a thousand major companies across an area of 70 square miles eventually led to a state of over-development, with a fall in environmental design standards, increasingly inadequate infrastructure services that became seriously overtaxed, and a massive rise in domestic house prices. Nevertheless, the strong trading links between US and UK companies means that high and selective standards of location and design are increasingly sought.

The definition of high-technology development

Perhaps too much time and effort has been expended upon worrying away at what is high-tech and what is not. Everyone seems to become very excited about categories and definitions, but it is possible to wonder just how relevant is such sophism. For straightaway, one important distinction to make is that between high-tech buildings and high-tech users. Many high-tech users can happily operate in low-tech accommodation. Many high-tech buildings house very low-tech operations. What has really happened, is that there has been a response to the demand by a variety of industrial and commercial users for adaptable, high-quality, comfortable and attractive buildings set in pleasant surroundings, which are well-located and available on acceptable terms to potential occupiers. Nevertheless, for the purposes of this text, the term 'high-technology property' includes:

- Buildings in an architectural style of design that has come to be known as 'high-tech'
- Buildings occupied or intended for occupation by high-technology companies
- Modern buildings in which mixed and flexible uses of space (including administrative use, laboratory, business, assembly and storage) occur.

(Fletcher King 1990)

Since the introduction of the 1987 Use Classes Order (now the 2005 Order), the term B1 has been rapidly adopted to imply the multi-use space that was previously described as high-tech, despite the fact that pure office buildings also fall under the B1 heading in planning terms. The high-tech definitions can now be seen as forming two distinct groups. The first is where there is academic involvement or where research and development is an important part of the occupiers' activities. The main group here is science parks, together with research parks, technology parks and innovation centres. The second cluster contains the main group of business parks and also the office parks group, which because of the misuse of the B1 (Business) Class description within the Use Classes Order can be seen almost as a specialized form of business park. These are dealt with elsewhere (Chapter 17).

The high-technology developments identified in the first group above have been defined (Fletcher King 1990) as below.

Science Park

A science park is a collection of high-technology companies or research institutes, situated in attractive surroundings developed to a low density, engaged in product research and prototype development, close to a tertiary education establishment with which there are significant opportunities for interaction and cross-fertilization of ideas. The term has suffered from imprecise use, but an attempt has been made to insist on a link with a tertiary education or research establishment in order to constitute a true science park.

Research park

Also known as a research science park and discovery park, a research park is very similar to a science park, but with the specific exclusion of conventional production and office activities.

Technology park

A technology park is a collection of high-technology industrial companies situated in attractive surroundings developed to a low density, engaged in research and manufacturing, probably within a reasonable distance of a tertiary education establishment, but not dependent upon it.

Innovation centre

Also known as science nursery, seed-bed centre and enterprise centre, an innovation centre is a collection of newly formed companies, usually housed in an existing building or buildings, converted to form small units, engaged in developing commercial applications of academic research projects and situated within or alongside a tertiary education establishment.

Upgraded industrial estate

Also known as an industrial park, industrial mall and industrial area, an upgraded industrial estate is a development of industrial buildings with certain characteristics of high-technology property, which, although distinguishing it from other more traditional industrial estates, does not change its nature from being an industrial estate. These estates may be designed in a high-tech style or have more extensive landscaping than the previous generation of industrial estates, but despite marketing attempts they do not legitimately fall into any of the previous groups.

Another concept developed in the USA puts occupiers with a common business on one park. Thus, a 'medi-park' contains medical research and development tenants with private hospitals, rehabilitation centres and sports clinics. It would seem that a medi-park is a technology park with medicine common to the tenants. Similarly, tenants with other industries as the common denominator would attract a generic title; for example, a park based upon the food industry would constitute a 'food park'.

The features of high-technology development

Although a great deal has been researched and written about high-technology developments, there would seem to be three basic ingredients common to all successful schemes, not always in accord with the definitions given above. These can briefly be described as follows:

Location

Location is critical, and certain locational factors can be categorized as essential, important and relevant. Those deemed essential are proximity to an international airport, a good road network with motorway access, pleasant residential and working environments, and the availability of a specialist skilled workforce. Those considered important are proximity to markets, proximity to the capital city, good rail links to the capital city, and the availability of support from a university or leading research establishment. Those thought relevant are proximity to suppliers, proximity to a domestic airport, good cultural and recreational amenities, and the existence of selective financial assistance (Williams 1982). Put another way, it has been stated that five factors have a significant influence on the location decisions of high-technology companies (Taylor 1985):

- The market for their product and the proximity of purchasers
- The availability of suitable premises and their cost
- A high-quality environment
- The accessibility of the motorway network
- The residence of directors and key personnel.

Flexibility

With regard to the type of buildings suitable for high-technology users, perhaps the most important factor is flexibility. There are several aspects to this:

- *Flexibility of use within the structure.* So that the various functions of research and development, production and offices can mix and match, change emphasis and grow or contract according to the needs of the company, a suitable layout might permit any of the three elements to be changed, with only the removal or fitting of carpets for certain types of space or thermoplastic tiles for others. Some true high-tech companies are working to state-of-the-art specifications and do not know, almost from one month to another, exactly how they need to organize their space.

- *Flexibility for growth.* Studies usually identify that many companies active in this sector are expanding at a rapid rate, with many planning to expand in the forthcoming five years and envisaging that their corporate expansion would involve occupying more accommodation. Thus, on the one hand, there is a need to allow for physical flexibility for expansion *in situ* and, on the other, for a flexibility of leasehold terms so that firms can move to altern-ative accommodation without undue constraint. A twenty-five-year lease is a very long time for a company that can scarcely predict its own market for more than a year or two at a time, hence the reduction in lease lengths.
- *Flexibility of covenant strength.* Many firms will be relatively new and explor-ing fresh markets, often without a track record, and sometimes without the necessary three years acceptable sets of accounts.

Design

Some of the interior and exterior designs for high-technology developments rival many prime office headquarters buildings, and probably one of the most powerful motivations behind many moves to new technology parks is the desire for a strong and attractive corporate image. Nevertheless, there is a danger of building to specifications unrelated to consumer demand, as it is often the case that occupiers are perfectly happy to accept traditional exteriors – preferring to spend their money on better interior facilities. The likely truth is that the mar-ket comprises a wide range of potential occupiers with varying requirements and perceptions. However, there are a few special points of design worth noting:

- Extensive car parking facilities are essential.
- Adequate underfloor space for cabling must be provided.
- Roofing must sometimes have to take loads of up to 1.5n/m^2.
- Reinforcement for dish aerials will normally be wanted.
- Cleanliness is occasionally a problem.
- Energy-efficient buildings are increasingly sought.
- The facility to introduce air-conditioning should be allowed.
- Very high standards of landscaping must be provided.
- A high level of security is often required.
- A range of finishes should be on offer rather than the typical tenants' norm.
- The preference for two-storey development could well extend to three storeys.
- With larger schemes, a village centre with small retail and service outlets could be beneficial.
- Excellent voice and data communication infrastructure will be needed.

In the property context of high-technology developments, it should be appre-ciated that, because of the rapid changes that are taking place in the field and the relatively slow gestation period of development projects, a site being developed in phases over several years can start out in one form and then alter its nature in response to demand. For example, phase I of an upgraded industrial estate may be succeeded by phase II units of multi-use space, more specialist high-technology space or even office or business space, so that taken as a whole the character of the estate may change through time. Telecommunications companies have been eager occupiers of high-technology developments.

Planning policy

Industrial development is now perceived as a major area of government responsibility in much the same way that public housing was some years ago. At central government level, a report by the Trade and Industry Select Committee in April 1994 told government to shrug off the vestiges of its *laissez faire* approach to industry. The report, in examining competitiveness, urged the government to enshrine the importance of manufacturing in economic policy, reflecting a widespread belief that the decline of Britain's manufacturing industry since the 1960s poses a serious threat to the country's ability to sustain economic growth. However it is now recognized that, although the industrial sector is important, warehousing and distribution activities to support the ever-growing service sector are now a vital focus of activity. At local level, many planning authorities are very progressive in their approach towards development proposals and supportive of initiatives. The effect of local authority planning can most conveniently be discussed by reference, on the one hand, to the exercise of their negative powers under development control and, on the other, the more positive attitudes that some of them adopt, which are demonstrated through an array of employment-generation policies.

The national context

Given the situation discussed at the beginning of this chapter concerning the decline of the manufacturing sector in the UK, one problem that has to be faced is that of what to do with redundant and obsolescent industrial space. It is clear both that there will be much less demand for manufacturing floorspace than now and that much existing space will have reached the end of its physical and economic life. We have seen this for many years now – as space is redeveloped, it is the best located, least polluted sites that are creamed off for redevelopment for alternative uses, leaving a rump of contaminated, derelict land with little or no chance of change.

To date, the attitude of planning authorities towards storage and distribution-related development has been relatively low key, with very few specific expressions of interest having been published at either national or local level. There is little to find on the subject in most LDFs, despite the importance to local as well as regional and national economies. Purely in design terms, warehousing is unlikely to present any real issues or major conflicts with local planning authorities, whose prime concern in this respect should be satisfaction that environmental and amenity considerations are met. Despite the fact that the purpose-built warehouse is higher and larger than its single-storey predecessor, there is no reason why warehouses should not be designed to look pleasant. Locational factors are the ones most likely to concern planners. Traditional locations in urban areas are no longer attractive to distributors. They need a great deal of space, which cannot normally be found in built-up areas. Rural areas, preferably near to motorway interchanges, are their preferred locations. However, it is at these locations, where planners are anxious not to allow development, that sustainability, environmental and countryside policies take preference. Taking the situation on an ad hoc basis, therefore, it is realistic to assume there would be planning opposition to developments of this nature on these sites, unless sites were identified by planners in advance within the context of a clear policy framework. Such a framework would certainly need to indicate sites for major distribution parks. This property form is seen in some distribution industry quarters as the answer to their property requirements, where planning objections can be overcome through well-designed, well-landscaped layouts (Taylor 1993).

One aspect of planning policy, if just one is to be chosen, that frustrates and bemuses developers and others is that too often the planning system is used to present entrenched opposition to changes in use where land has formerly been in 'employment use'. The perception is that, by retaining land for industrial development, this will in itself attract industrial employers. However, the planning system simply cannot hold out against the pressures for change caused by a shrinking manufacturing workforce.

Another sector of the industrial property market deserving of government attention and guidance is that of storage and distribution. It can be argued that the planning system has not yet come properly to terms with the explosive nature of the distribution industry. The interests of the national economy might well be served if the government were to issue more specific guidance to local planning authorities on the matter, distinguishing the sector from retail activities. Otherwise an unproductive disarray might take place, similar to that which took place in the 1980s in respect of major out-of-town shopping centres. Revised guidance in the form of the PPS4 (Planning for Sustainable Economic Development) was updated in 2008 and now seeks to promote economic development without negative environmental consequences. The foreword in this PPS, by the Secretary of State, sets the planning system the key task of 'achieving a proper balance between economic opportunity and environmental and social issues'.

Because of their economic importance, for example, it could be argued that certain strategic gaps and rural sites adjacent to the motorway interchanges should not be squandered unless there are compelling environmental objections. As has been pointed out, through the years of the B1 (Business) office boom, most such key locations allocated for development have been mopped up for business campus uses, and warehousing has frequently been diverted to low-value sites remote from the communications network. As a result, heavy lorry traffic is often sucked through residential areas, with adverse environmental effects.

On the question of traffic, a popular sentiment echoes around the property development industry that government lacks a coherent policy towards transport. PPG13 and other government edicts seek to limit car journeys and promote modal shift. The distribution of goods throughout the country depends primarily upon heavy goods vehicles and, although many believe it is lorries that clog up the system, surveys have showed that such carriers typically account for no more than 15–20 per cent of traffic flows. Indeed the vast majority of the estimated 84 per cent increase in road traffic volumes from 1980 to 2006 comprises private cars and not commercial lorries. Persuading passenger traffic to switch to public transport would greatly ease the movement of freight but dealing with the nation's congested roads has always been a political minefield. However, it is now widely accepted that toll roads and private intervention in motorway construction are the way forward. The first toll route in Britain – the M6 Toll – opened in 2003 and the Mayor of London has introduced congestion charging (for private vehicles) within sections of the capital, and emissions charging (for commercial vehicles) for the whole city.

Local planning practice

The more detailed application of development control regulations as they apply to industrial property, especially the operation of the Use Classes Order 2005, is dealt with elsewhere (Chapters 2 and 3). Suffice it to say that in a post-industrial society, such as that in the UK, a distinction between factory-based employment and office-based employment is an artificial and largely unhelpful one. Increasingly this is recognized, but the fact remains that, for whatever reason, many local authorities fear creeping office use in what they ostensibly approved as industrial buildings. The B1 (Business) use class has greatly reduced this problem by accepting light industry and office floorspace as having the same external impact on issues like car parking and general activity.

However, another circumstance where difficulties of mixed use used to emerge is the combination of residential accommodation with workspace. Not only were planning authorities reluctant or unprepared to consider such proposals, but building regulations, in particular those relating to fire, rendered mixed-use developments complex and expensive to design and build. Nevertheless, it is an interesting field of possible future invention. These and other factors led investors to shun mixed-use development but changes to planning policy and better returns being achieved has led to a reversal of this situation. Further, the notion of 'live–work' units in central city areas has promoted the notion of mixed-use living, albeit that the market has not taken up such initiatives as rapidly as many planning authorities had anticipated.

A distinctive feature of local authority policy since the mid-1980s has been the concentration of effort upon the generation of employment, by both the encouragement of existing local industries and the attraction of more mobile ones from elsewhere. Among the initiatives that have been taken by councils to support the level of employment in their area and assist the development of industrial property are the following:

- *Development plans revision.* Amendments to RSSs and LDFs, releasing additional land for industry or rolling forwards planned future allocations, have been made by many authorities. Similarly, site-specific planning and development briefs identifying potential industrial estates or where existing ones could benefit from renewal have become a popular means of attempting to stimulate private sector development.
- *Economic development units.* Under a variety of titles many regional and local authorities have special departments and appointed economic or industrial development officers responsible for employment generation. These offer a wide range of schemes covering both business advice and financial assistance.
- *Serviced sites and development.* In order to induce potential firms to come to their area, local authorities have frequently laid out the principal roads and services on selected sites, and sometimes have erected speculative units in advance of demand. Many councils and other public bodies (e.g. the Welsh Assembly Government and the Welsh Development Agency before it) have gone further and acted as developer.
- *Head-leasing.* Where market uncertainty exists and, because of either doubts about the location of the site or the size and nature of the units, private sector developers are wary about taking all the risks of letting and management entailed in a proposed scheme, it has become quite common for public authorities to take the head-lease of the property and subsequently to sublet the units to occupying firms. A variation to this agreement is typified by the agreement entered into by various councils, whereby they have undertaken to take a head-lease from a developer if the particular project is still unlet after a certain period of unsuccessful marketing.
- *Key worker and affordable housing.* In an attempt to overcome some of the problems experienced by firms in relocation to new premises, a few local authorities have provided subsidized housing or cheap building land for key workers. The conversion of high-rise flats into hostels for single people or young couples is another way of retaining or attracting desired workers. Partnership with Registered Social Landlords (RSLs) is important in this regard.
- *Other initiatives.* It has been suggested, at one time or another, that local authorities might:

  - Introduce special long-term incentives on rates. These remain one of the greatest worries among the business community, which does not always benefit from the services provided.
  - Offer rental guarantees to developers and investors, possibly linked to some form of indexing. In this way, dubious investments let to relatively young companies or firms that are recovering from a recession, will immediately acquire a 'blue chip' quality.

- Concentrate on improving the physical environment in existing and proposed new business areas through better roads, landscaping (hard and soft), refuse collection, lighting and the like.

Design and layout

Historically, the design of industrial buildings has been poor, often being more the preserve of the engineer than the architect. The adherence to strict zoning regulations tended until recently to constrain any serious consideration of the need for good design. It is really only since the late 1970s that employers and management have become concerned about the working environment of their labour force, realizing that pleasant and effective buildings are synonymous with high productivity and satisfactory returns. Moreover, with the relaxation of rigid industrial zoning policies and a movement away from the separation of industrial processes into large estates, it became obvious that many small industrial developments would have to be sympathetically moulded into existing urban areas, and other large industrial developments would have to be sited in exposed and sensitive rural locations, often close to motorways where they would be most apparent. The general quality of design for industrial development has improved enormously with such leaders in the architectural field as Terry Farrell, Nick Grimshaw and Norman Foster bringing a kind of respectability to what was previously a largely drab utilitarian approach. Nevertheless, a strong conservative influence survives among occupiers, and a degree of tenant reluctance to accept some of the more exciting modern design concepts is exemplified by the initial slow letting of certain notable quality estates.

Changing character

As never before, developers need to market their product largely through excellence of design and specification. Architects, therefore, are having to respond with flair and imagination, for they are being asked to devise new buildings that are economic to construct, suitable for new industries and trades, acceptable to institutions that still have half an eye to long-term flexibility, and are in themselves positive marketing and promotional statements. Not only must the buildings conform to newly established criteria, however, but the settings in which they are placed must generate an attractive and compelling business climate. Developers now demand estates that demonstrate upon entry an excellent working environment with genuine landscaping and full amenities. The main reason for this changing character can be summarized as follows:

- The industrial sector, as such, has given way to a business sector comprising retail, high-technology and office use as well as production and distribution.
- During times of recession or excess supply, the negotiating balance between landlord and tenant tilts sharply towards the tenant.

- Businesses are much more mobile than in the past, and tend increasingly to seek a consolidation of their administrative activities with their productive operations.
- Employees are also mobile, with higher levels of car ownership and different perceptions of work opportunities.
- With changing business functions and different forms of productive process, the single-storey rule is disappearing.

Density and layout

Traditionally, an overall site cover of 45–50 per cent was always considered to be an appropriate density for modern industrial estate development. The trend over recent years has been for a lower site coverage, and it is likely that an acceptable average for the foreseeable future will be closer to 30–35 per cent. With certain special developments, such as science parks and office campuses, the average density can fall even lower – to between 20 and 25 per cent and below. However, it must be remembered that a lower site coverage by no means implies a lower density, for many forms of modern industry it is perfectly acceptable to operate on two or more storeys. In fact, with some processes in both the light electronics and pharmaceutical fields, a 'layer cake' concept of factory design is most suitable, whereby the production area is laid out on the ground floor, and one or more levels of service or handling space are built above. Not multi-storey in the true sense, developments of this kind rarely suit a portal frame structure, for it is generally not sufficient to carry the loads involved. Nevertheless, the footprints of buildings across a site so developed can be quite scattered. Mezzanine floors are sometimes introduced to increase floor-space and they will require planning consent.

With regard to the overall layout of estate roads and parking facilities, changes in both the use of the private car, and in the size and nature of delivery vehicles, have dictated changes in the assessment of siting, road circulation, address and services. Not only is the general level of car ownership much higher these days, but the nature of many new industries creates a greater need for car parking facilities, because of the higher income group of employees, the increased level of office-type activity and the additional amount of visiting traffic from clients and other members of the company. A higher level of provision is necessary if there is any retail warehouse element within the estate, whereas pure warehousing operations demand very much less. The advent of the juggernaut has meant that all industrial estates now need to cater for 15 m (49 ft) plus lorries. Access and forecourt roads need to be wider, longer and more substantial than hitherto, to allow for manoeuvrability. An incidental gain from this is that it produces large open areas for landscaping. Forecourt layouts and delivery parking facilities are critical if an estate is to be successful, and certain industrial activities and freight operators will require plenty of parking space for vehicles and trailers. Special trailer parking areas are also sometimes needed. Common open areas of concrete or tarmac can be laid out and marked for individual units, or segregated spaces with a physical barrier to prevent encroachment can be provided. Although it is important to supply loading and parking facilities to a high standard, it is also important these days to separate them from the office areas on an estate. The roads themselves can be of either a concrete or a tarmac finish. Concrete costs more initially, but tarmac is more expensive to maintain, leading to complaints from tenants and high service charges.

Design principles

Although the concept of dual capacity – whereby buildings on industrial estates are designed so that they can be adapted for both warehouse and production uses – in order that institutional investors and developers can cast their letting net as wide as possible, is now regarded as redundant, the keynote of good design remains that of flexibility. The guidelines below represent an attempt to describe good design practice that will retain flexibility of use without sacrificing the individual quality of buildings.

- *Floor slab.* This should be designed to ensure that an adequate loading capacity, say 50 KN/m^2, can be offered through time to a wide range of uses. Once constructed there is very little that can be done to rectify any deficiency.
- *Eaves height.* Reference is often made to the institutional requirement for a 5.5 m (18 ft) eaves height, but in many ways this standard is too high for most modern factory buildings, too low for current warehousing needs and insufficient to allow for horizontal conversion. A clear height of 6.7 m to 7.3 m (21–24 ft) permits the inclusion of a mezzanine floor or the conversion into two-storey offices, and retains the possibility of warehouse use. For purpose-built single-storey light industrial buildings, however, a clear height of 3.7 m to 4.6 m (12–15 ft) is much more popular than the traditional 5.5 m to 6. 1 m (18–20 ft). Special high-bay warehouses require at the very least 10 m (33 ft) eaves height for a minimum 10,000 m^2 (108,000 ft^2) floorspace at 45 per cent site cover.
- *Column spacing.* As a general rule, columns hinder flexibility. Where the structure, span and loads are such that they have to be provided, it is essential that correct column spacing is planned to allow for the possible need to provide extra support for mezzanine floors, subdivide into self-contained smaller units or facilitate pallet racking.
- *Cladding materials.* Once again the aim should be to achieve a reasonable degree of flexibility, not merely in the selection and design of cladding but also in respect of the provision of glazing, doors and bays. In attaining this, architects have benefited from the development of profiled metal sheeting with factory-bonded insulation. External finishes on profiled metal are virtually maintenance free. Advances have also been made in the use of glass-reinforced concrete and glass-reinforced plastic, which in sheet cladding form are said to offer a whole new range of design possibilities in both aesthetic and practical terms. All these insulated flexible skins can be produced in

a variety of modular panel systems incorporating interchangeable door, window and service-bay openings so as to provide a range of sophisticated and highly adaptable façades. However, some doubts have been expressed regarding the extensive and exclusive use of demountable and interchangeable cladding panels. For example, great care is required in their selection, because the testing of new materials is not all it should be. The exclusive use of either glazing or cladding is not always popular with tenants and, although the notion of interchangeability is fine in theory, it is less likely to be adopted in practice, for some developers would say that it is often better to provide for internal flexibility within the building rather than in the structure itself.

- *Roofs.* Until recently it has probably been fair to say that absolutely flat roofs were not acceptable because of performance and maintenance problems, but nearly flat roofs could normally be achieved successfully. Now, however, it is feasible to produce a leak-proof flat roof by using a plastics-based membrane material. The object of obtaining as flat a roof as possible is to optimize the internal volume of the building. Nevertheless, it is commonly accepted that a slightly pitched steel trussed roof, which permits the ready attachment of tenants' equipment, is best, so long as the truss is constructed deep enough for the installation and maintenance of services to be easily effected. False ceilings are often installed to facilitate the introduction of additional services, as well as to create a better working environment and reduce energy consumption. In both walls and roofs it should always be recognized at the basic design stage that windows and rooflights might have to be added or subtracted at some future date. Likewise, both environmental and process services may have to come through either roofs or walls. Indeed, the very structure should be designed to carry these services, on top of any mechanical handling equipment a tenant may wish to install.

- *Building services.* Although an increasing emphasis is placed upon the provision of adequate internal services, there are a growing number of developers who prefer to construct a simple shell capable of accommodating a wide range of building services, but await an actual letting before the specified services are installed. One of the most effective means of supplying electrical services is by way of a ring main around the perimeter of the building. In respect of distribution across a building, building regulations in the UK insist upon the boxed trunking of electrical transmission, unlike the USA where taped carpet tiles can be employed, giving ultimate flexibility. With regard to lighting, good-quality daylighting factors are often required, and natural lighting to office standards is sometimes sought. Otherwise, artificial lighting to around 500 watts is normally sufficient, often to be found hung from a suspended ceiling. Air-conditioning is a sought-after facility in many modern industrial estate developments, and is obligatory in some of the more sophisticated high-technology schemes. In any event, consideration in design should be given to ensure that the basic structure and skin are suitable for power, heat and ventilation systems to be added later if required. Similarly, the fundamental design should aim at high standards of insulation, with an airtight skin, because good insulation can literally halve the heating costs of small units and substantially reduce those of larger ones.

- *Office content.* The traditional proportion of ancillary office space, at 10–15 per cent of total floorspace, still adopted as a standard by some local planning authorities, is no longer a reliable guide to real need. In fact, most occupiers of modern industrial premises are rarely satisfied with less than 20 per cent, and with certain high-technology operations as much as 50 per cent or more is required. At planning approval stage, a prospective developer would definitely be well advised to gain consent for around 30–40 per cent office use in any proposed estate development, or alternatively avoid any condition as to a fixed percentage. With regard to design, there is a growing desire on the part of potential occupiers, particularly in the South East of England, to create a headquarters building on an estate alongside their distribution operations. This creates a need for an individual or corporate identity for the firm to be created. At the very least, therefore, it is sensible for a developer to reserve land accordingly, or to make sure that certain buildings could be converted if need be. In the context of office space industrial buildings, it is now a common convention that buildings on industrial estates should not have a rear elevation as such, but rather that there should be a double-sided design, with a separate approach for office staff and visitors, preferably on the south side of the building, on the opposite side to the properly planned loading bays and goods handling facilities. It is also the case that a greater area of glazing to permit views and afford natural light for the workforce, or the ability to create it, is required nowadays.

- *Fire.* It is often argued that in the UK the cost of fire prevention and control is excessive. Nevertheless, such requirements remain an important consideration in all forms of development. Regulations provide that, in order to avoid the need in larger units for complete compartmentalization, they must be served with sprinkler installations. Although some developers still do not supply such facilities, the extra cost and effort on the part of the potential tenant could easily tilt the balance against a letting if two or three possible premises have been short-listed. As a small point, it might be worth noting that the fire-proofing of steel structures has become more economical over recent years with the use of appropriate paints and coatings, which also have the added advantage that they are a more attractive finish than the normal concrete or dry lining.

- *Loading bays.* Not only should consideration be given to how many doors there should be, where they might be located and how vehicles will get to and from them, but some thought should be given to the provision of weather-protected, tailboard-height bays reached over carefully planned approach areas. For speculative developments it is advisable to provide floodlit unloading areas and adjustable levellers, and to ensure some kind of shelter from the bay to the inside of the building.

- *Office and amenity areas.* Provision should normally be made for such facilities as: an attractive entrance hall and reception area; well-finished and insulated curtain walling systems with double-glazed tinted window units; fully fitted carpets and good quality wallpaper; easy subdivision of open-space office area; suspended ceiling and recessed light fittings; perimeter skirting trunking for power, telephone and VDU installations; double-socket power outlets positioned in the ceiling voids; fully tiled spacious male and female toilets, possibly with shower units and dressing areas; central heating system; and drinking fountain, tea bar and cleaners' cupboards.
- *Energy conservation.* Some developers are beginning to give consideration to the incorporation of sophisticated energy-saving systems. One such approach is known as 'condition-based maintenance' that uses advanced technologies such as remote temperature sensors, electronic flue gas analysers and current injection test sets. The savings in running costs and reduction of down-time can be a good selling point, as has been experienced at Magna Park in Milton Keynes, Gazeley's 'Sustainable Logistics Park', as is discussed below.
- *Others.* Special drainage facilities cannot always be added, particularly in heavy load-bearing floors, and it is often worthwhile providing a flexible facility, either by having a soft floor finish or by incorporating floor trenches at convenient intervals. Good toilet and showering facilities should not be forgotten by developers, although movable prefabricated bathroom modules have been found to be a positive advantage in some industrial estate development schemes. Toxic waste disposal services might be demanded by prospective tenants, not merely those from more traditional noxious industries, but also from some of the newer high-technology firms. Likewise, advanced fume-extraction facilities might have to be incorporated.

Sustainable design

As is discussed in Chapter 10, operators of logistics warehouses, whether they be retailers or logistics providers, are increasingly being offered opportunities to occupy sustainable sheds. The John Lewis Partnership is one such occupier at Gazeley's Magna Park. Gazeley has gone a few stages further with designs for a scheme in Chatterley Valley in Staffordshire which will be carbon positive – i.e. it will use less energy than it generates from renewable technologies. The site's biofuel micro power station (fuelled by oilseed rape) will heat the on-site buildings and the surplus energy will be used by up to 650 local homes. Other features of the designs are:

- Thermally efficient buildings which have 25 per cent better airtightness and thermal insulation than current building regulations
- Cutting-edge lighting
- Maximum use of natural light
- Underfloor heating

- Solar-cell technology in rooflights which will eliminate night-time light pollution
- Kinetic plates to capture energy when vehicles enter the site.
- Over half of the site will be open space with public footpaths, links to canal towpaths and preservation of habitats
- £9 million has been spent on remediation of contaminated land.

(Carter 2008)

Regulations are constantly tightening as far as carbon emissions are concerned, and developers of distribution warehousing would be well advised to consider how their designers can use tools like BREEAM and the *Green Guide to Specification* (discussed in Chapter 10) to deliver real cost savings to occupiers as well as other sustainability benefits.

Refurbishment

A great deal has been said and written about the need to reuse old redundant buildings, and since the mid-1980s a growing number of successful refurbishment projects undertaken by a variety of development agencies have been implemented. Many of these fall outside the mainstream of conventional property development but, equally, many opportunities exist for profitable commercial development to be tackled by entrepreneurs who understand the special factors that underlie the market.

All that is possible in this section is to list some of the more critical factors that determine whether or not a viable refurbishment or conversion can be effected. These can conveniently be summarized as follows:

- *Initial outlay*. This must be kept to a minimum, not merely in respect of the capital sum, carrying a debt charge, expended on the purchase of the building, or the head rent that has to be paid, but also with regard to the cost of works that have to be undertaken before all or part of the building can be let. Wherever possible, it is advisable to try to plan a gradual programme of upgrading, so that some of the costs can be funded from income.
- *Overheads*. In the same vein, most successful conversions of old industrial buildings take place where overheads have been reduced as far as possible. This invariably means that professional fees are minimized or avoided, with developers performing most of the professional tasks themselves. Similarly, contractors' and developers' profits are often absorbed in the same way, so that developer, contractor and project manager, and even agent at times, are all rolled into one, and a single slice of fees and profits is sought by that party.
- *Location*. Experience shows that buildings best suited to conversion are convenient for both staff and customers, say five minutes at most from the nearest public transport, are situated in an area of some existing and

potential business demand and have good access off a main road on to a two-way street wide enough for parking.

- *Site coverage.* It is desirable to have 60 per cent or less site coverage and to possess good site access with off-street parking and delivery facilities.
- *Building configuration.* Evidence suggests that deep buildings with poor aspects should be avoided. Under 14–16 m (46–52 ft) depth is preferable, and in no circumstances should buildings over 18m (59 ft) be considered if natural lighting and ventilation are to be exploited. Likewise, a three- or, better still, four-way aspect is best.
- *Structure and condition.* Obviously, a building possessing a superior initial construction, and where there is little need for major structural repair, is most attractive. At least the structure should be fairly sound and the building capable of being made windproof and watertight without too much trouble. Ideally, the building should be of fireproofed frame construction and either brick or concrete. More than three storeys become problematical, and the ground floor should have a floor height of 2.5–4 m (8–13 ft) at most. It is also important that there are wide stairways and the facility for incorporating a goods lift if required.
- *Statutory requirements.* It must not be too difficult or costly to have to comply with such statutory requirements as fire or public health, and it often helps if there is no need to apply for planning permission for a change of use. Above all, perhaps, the single common factor that seems to characterize all successful conversions of old industrial buildings is the presence of a strong personality responsible for the development, who is thoroughly committed to the scheme.

Much professional attention is paid to the new, relatively simple, clean, large estates designed for established national and international organizations but, as a last word on the subject of the refurbishment of old industrial buildings, it is worth noting the role that has still to be played by the small business sector of the economy. There is a shortage of very small premises of around 10–50 m^2 (108–538 ft^2) in multiple-tenanted accommodation, with shared access on flexible occupancy agreements and offering varying amounts of central support services. Therefore, enormous opportunities exist for the small developer with sufficient initiative and sympathetic funding.

Estate management

For many years, a large proportion of industrial estate development in Britain lacked even the most basic level of management services, which accounts for their general unsightly appearance. Apart from the New Town Development Corporations and a few notable private development companies such as Segro and Brixton, the management function was largely eschewed, and the burden of responsibility passed on to tenants. However, over more recent years a realization of the importance of good industrial estate management has dawned upon the property development industry. Most of the fundamental principles relating to the planning and design of estates have already been discussed, but other points are worthy of mention:

- *Image*. Not merely for initial marketing, but also for subsequent letting and rent review negotiations, it pays to establish and maintain an appealing corporate image for an industrial estate. The naming of an estate, the creation of a special logo, well-designed name boards at access points, the construction of an attractive gateway building, and the publication of professionally presented marketing material all make for a sense of community and a successful letting record.
- *Tenant mix*. In the same way that there has been an appreciation of the importance of selecting the right mix of tenants in the management of planned shopping centres over the years, so a similar awareness is beginning to grow in the management of industrial estates. The correct identification of likely occupiers will help in planning estate layout and services, because freight operators, distribution centres, retail warehouses, light industry, office and research-based users all dictate different buildings, service and traffic management solutions. Complementarity of use, which generates business between tenants, is also a consideration in small unit estates.
- *Signposting*. Although it may not seem to be a major aspect of industrial estate development and management, the careful selection and siting of directional signposts around an estate can greatly enhance the general appearance. The careful incorporation of tenants' logos with a corporate framework, both at the entrances to an estate and on the individual buildings, can also add to the overall impression of the development.
- *Landscaping*. What used to be regarded as an unnecessary and expensive luxury, often imposed as a condition of planning approval, is now usually seen as an essential attribute of any successful industrial development by investors, developers and occupiers alike. In fact, it is becoming quite fashionable to retain large striking natural features within an estate plan, or even to create artefacts such as an artificial lake or a folly type of building as a focal point to an estate. However, it should be remembered that even the selection and care of trees and shrubs is a relatively specialist affair. Effective landscaping will also attempt to avoid the fencing-in of industrial plots. As a corollary to this, it has been found that the imposition of positive covenants in the lease upon the tenant is rarely the best way of looking after the common landscaped areas of an estate. It is normally much better for a developer to arrange for the management of the estate as a whole at the outset, and recover the cost by way of a properly accounted service charge.
- *Security*. Even on the smallest estates, security is a matter of considerable concern to tenants. Control at gate houses, the entrances to the estate, is often required, and they should be sited for maximum visibility around the estate roads. On larger estates, or where there are special tenants'

requirements, it is these days necessary to install cameras around the estate, or even to provide 24-hour security. How much security is provided, of what kind and who pays, is obviously a matter of negotiation between landlord and tenant.

- *Power.* Some estate developers undertake the bulk purchase of oil and gas, which they make available on a metered supply. Segro's Slough Trading Estate is perhaps exceptional in that Scottish and Southern Energy generates 270 GWh of renewable electricity for the 400 tenants on the estate. It also supplies water and steam to the 700,000 m^2 estate per year, while also supplying useful renewable heat (in the form of hot water and steam). Central sprinkler installations are another facility commonly provided.
- *Refuse disposal.* Although on most estates this is normally looked upon as a tenant's responsibility, some developers have installed central compactors, where demand for such service is thought likely to be high. Otherwise, one of the main problems encountered in day-to-day industrial estate management is the monitoring and enforcement of conditions relating to the storage of rubbish and the placing of skips.
- *Personal services.* Increasingly, developers are conscious of the need to consider the possible provision of shopping, catering, health, banking, bus services, leisure and recreation facilities. Many of these services can now be accessed online – for example, major supermarkets have experimented with delivery of groceries ordered over the Internet to a number of high-profile business locations.
- *Tenants associations.* Although such organizations are comparatively rare on industrial estates, some landlords and tenants recognize the mutual benefits that can be gained from the formation of a tenants association.

Conclusion

The industrial property market in the early to mid-2000s experienced a dramatic increase in the amount of speculative development and procurement of 'bigger and better' distribution centres by the major retailers. Future expectations of demand for distribution property are much brighter than those for manufacturing properties, but one hopes that the boom in speculative development was not too much for the market in the second decade of the tewnty-first century. In 2007, for example, new available floorspace in the West Midlands increased by 80,000 m^2 (861,000 ft^2) – a rise of almost half over the course of a year – and the amount of available industrial floorspace in the UK was at its highest in over twenty years (King Sturge 2007).

The future for shed development will almost certainly be affected by a continued drive by:

- Logisticians, particularly those working for the major retailers, trying to drive down costs and the time it takes to fetch and carry goods around the country.

- Attention being paid to the fact that the road network is ever more congested. As already noted, this is a political minefield and one suspects that it will be up to the private sector to find solutions to this problem rather than waiting for a regulatory solution.
- It is possible that tolls will become more commonplace on busy road networks, adding to the cost burden of existing delays and increasing the necessity to determine a solution to reducing the costs of transporting goods.
- Larger lorries will also probably come to visit the UK's roads, which will help retailers and logistics companies, at least, to decrease the number of trips required. Development schemes will need to accommodate these.
- Reverse logistics will also probably increase in importance in order to reduce the number of empty lorry trips being made, but a concerted effort by different elements of the logistics sector will need to be made to effect this.
- Planning policy is unlikely to stay still as far as storage and distribution property development is concerned and is likely to continue to attend to the environmental problems associated with road freight.

19 Residential development

> Today the demands on planning have never been greater as we seek to deal with household growth and climate change.
>
> (TCPA and DCLG 2007)

Any examination of the many issues surrounding residential development will require knowledge of the detailed nature of design and layout in new-build housing or conversion of existing stock, as well as knowledge of the wider debate surrounding the allocation of new housing land via regional policy (the regional spatial strategy) and locally (in core strategies and site allocation development plan documents). This chapter will consider both issues. This subject area is heavily influenced by the debate surrounding regeneration, building on previously developed or brown land and the desire to make new housing more energy-efficient in its use, even carbon neutral, in an attempt to mitigate the impact of climate change. National planning policy (in PPS1) and the work of agencies like the Commission for Architecture and the Built Environment (CABE), has in recent years raised the profile of design within residential development. Yet, much remains to be achieved when seeking to promote locally distinctive design and a real sense of local identity. Paragraph 36 of PPS1 requires that developments 'must respond to their local context and create or reinforce local distinctiveness', while paragraph 13 of PPS3 goes on to say that 'design which is inappropriate in its context, or which fails to take the opportunities available for improving the character and quality of an area and the way it functions, should not be accepted'.

This chapter is divided into four sections as follows:

- Submitting planning applications for residential development
- Housing land availability
- The Sustainable Communities Plan, Housing Pathfinder and beyond
- Urban villages.

The starting point for any examination of residential development is to be found in government guidance, as set out in PPS3, which was comprehensively revised in November 2006. This document deals with both design and layout issues and the allocation of housing land on both existing open countryside or previously developed land.

Strategic objectives are set out in paragraph 9 of PPS3, in which the government establish the key aims for UK housebuilding as:

- To achieve a wide choice of high-quality homes, both affordable and market housing (i.e. privately owned), to address the requirements of the community.
- To widen opportunities for home ownership and ensure high-quality housing for those who cannot afford market housing, in particular those who are vulnerable or in need.
- To improve affordability across the housing market, mostly by increasing the supply of allocated land for housing.
- To create sustainable, inclusive, mixed-use communities in all areas, both urban and rural.

The thrust of this national planning policy is that new housing must use land both flexibly (i.e. that it is allocated quickly in response to market demands) and efficiently (i.e. raising density) but must, just as importantly, have a minimal environmental impact and high design quality.

Government policy is committed to allowing appropriate housing development, i.e. development that protects both the urban and the rural environment. This would, theoretically, restrict the erosion of agricultural and green belt land from development or the 'cramming' of new buildings within the urban area. However, with ever-increasing demands for new housing, some new land must be allocated, and although a debate rages about whether greater use should be made of existing derelict or vacant land (estimated to be around 35,000 hectares at 2006) or the green belt relaxed (about 1 per cent of green belt is lost annually to greenfield housing development), it appears inevitable that the strategic objectives of PPS3 will be compromised in an attempt to meet housing demands. At two different ends of this spectrum fall the Sustainable Development Commission Report (2007) into the government's housing policy and the findings of Kate Barker on housing supply (in HM Treasury 2006a). The Sustainable Development Commission arrived at the tentative conclusion that government policy was more about building new homes, compared to the creation of balanced and integrated communities, deeming the original (2003) plan for housing growth to be 'focused very heavily on housing growth without due consideration for the environment, for what is sometimes called "liveability" or for social needs' (Sustainable Development Commission 2007). Kate Barker was more concerned with increasing housing supply, in an attempt to improve its affordability. Barker reported that over the last thirty years the number of households had increased by 30 per cent while the level of housebuilding had correspondingly fallen by 50 per cent and concluded that 'if we build at current rates, by 2026 less than one-third of 30 year old couples will be able to afford their homes on the basis of their earnings' (HM Treasury 2006a). Barker's central conclusion that housing supply was not sufficiently responsive, led to a number of key new policies and reinvigorated some existing ones. When the Barker review reported in 2005, annual house building in England amounted to around 150,000 dwellings.

The principal impact on government policy was to increase supply, increase affordable provision, make the planning system more responsive, improve design and sustainability and deliver new infrastructure. A cross-cutting approach was thus deemed necessary in which, by way of example, the planning system would be vested with responsibility to release more land for housing while ensuring that those homes were much more energy-efficient, than previously, by means of tougher building regulations and a mandatory code for sustainable homes (applied from 2008). The government's target was that by 2016 annual rates of house-building would be substantially increased. The July 2007 Housing Green Paper, in which future housing policy options were set out, put this annual target at 240,000 dwellings per year (up 40,000 on the 2005 response to the Barker review). Research commissioned by the Department for Communities and Local Government, when seeking to verify some of Barker's conclusions and arrive at a measured response (DCLG 2006c), concluded that such an approach would halt a move to 'worsening affordability' in which house prices would continue to outstrip earnings. In other words, the gap between earnings and affordability would slow or cease growing as opposed to a narrowing. Barker herself had reported that the UK as a whole had experienced a long-term upward increase in real house prices over the last thirty years, with a 2.4 per cent annual increase, year-on-year. The comparable figure for the European Union (EU) over this period was a 1.1 per cent annual increase. Barker postulated that to reduce the UK figure to the EU average would require an additional 120,000 new homes per year (i.e. at 2005 figures, 150,000 current rates plus 120,000 increase, amounting to 270,000 homes annually in England).

Self-evidently, the housing sector faces considerable challenges over the next twenty years or so, as government housing policy pushes for a step-change in the delivery of new homes, including the percentage of affordable units, while also creating communities and contemporaneously reducing environmental impact. The delivery of growth in southern England is significant at 3.4 million new homes by 2026 as well as the renewal of areas of housing market failure (the so called housing Pathfinders) in parts of Liverpool, Manchester and North Staffordshire. Further, new growth points (outside the south) are to be identified for increased housing provision and a series of 'Eco-Towns' created as exemplars of low-energy living and zero carbon production. The demands on the planning system and development sector to deliver sufficient allocated sites, necessary infrastructure and the right mix of policies is, therefore, considerable. Infrastructure to facilitate this growth (mostly consumed by expenditure on new roads, affordable housing subsidy and green infrastructure) has been estimated at more than £1.6 billion per annum. Such an eye-watering sum has focused government thinking on the thorny question of who will pay for such works. The Barker Review preference for a Planning Gain Supplement (PGS) to capture some of the development gains that landowners benefit from following the grant of residential consent was dismissed as an option in 2007. A significant portion of this burden will, inevitably, fall on the developer. The currently unresolved question is just how it will be calculated and indeed implemented. By 2008 the government had opted for the Community Infrastructure Levy, to capture an element of planning gain in the funding of such infrastructure.

Submitting planning applications for residential development

It is important to recall that planning consent will be required for both operational development, including new buildings and structural alteration, rebuilding, additions to buildings and other operations normally undertaken by a person carrying on business as a builder (such as demolition) and conversion of one dwelling into two or more dwellings.

Outline or full?

It has been common practice for developers to submit outline applications when seeking planning permission for major residential development (ten or more dwellings). This establishes whether or not the *principle* of residential development is acceptable. An outline planning permission provides the developer with an element of certainty before drawing up detailed plans and may therefore enhance the valuation of the land prior to its potential sale. The outline application can be made with all 'reserved matters'[1] to be considered at a later stage, but it is usually the practice to submit details of siting of the dwellings and means of access on to the highway.

This allows the local planning authority to consider the safety of the access and relationship of the proposed dwellings to adjoining ones at the outline stage. Such issues may be vital in the consideration of whether or not to grant outline consent. Although nothing prevents the developer from submitting a full application, it is most commonly employed in preference to outline/reserved matters, when dealing with minor residential development (less than ten dwellings) or applications within conservation areas or affecting the setting of a listed building. The smaller the site, the greater the potential for concern regarding the impact of the development on adjoining occupiers – for example, by reasons of 'loss of light' to habitable rooms in neighbouring properties or by appearing 'cramped' and out of character with the surrounding development because the plot is too small. Such smaller plots are mostly found within existing urban areas, where the need for new housing makes the development of small plots economically viable. Such town infilling (i.e. adding built development within the existing urban fabric) has been referred to as 'town cramming' by critics who argue that it results in an erosion of character and, despite control exercised by local planning authorities, results in a loss of amenity to adjoining occupiers. During the 1980s and again after the millennium, the dramatic rise in the value of residential property resulted in a significant increase in such 'windfalls', especially within the South East Region and London suburbs (Case study 19.1). Many local planning policies will (rightly) continue to stipulate that development must be broadly in character with its surroundings. Yet, over time it is difficult to prevent the incremental erosion of this character as house plots give way to sub-division or flatted development. It appears inevitable in light of the pressures to make efficient use of land and to meet housing targets without massive and politically unacceptable expansion on to greenfield sites. The low-density London suburbs of the 1930s and urban fringes generally are vulnerable to such pressures, resulting in concerns expressed by English Heritage (2007c) about the future character of such areas and some research work which argues in favour of greater policy to protect and reinvigorate suburbs by new and appropriate development (2007b). This 'densification' of development has implications for both the character of a place, as single or semi-detached housing gives way to flats, but also the mix, as smaller units replace family homes. Concern has been expressed that this pressure falls unevenly and badly affects urban areas, especially London (Greater London Assembly 2006).

Examples of residential development

Houses to flats

Since the late 1960s, housebuilding has taken place at higher densities as a direct reflection of the increased cost of land with residential planning permission. Between the late 1960s and late 1980s the price of building land increased sevenfold (Cheshire 1993) and by 2007 the notion of living at 'super-density' became widely accepted (URBED 2004).

Consider the following scenario (see Figure 19.4). Developers purchase several houses, usually with spacious gardens, and apply to demolish and build a series of two- and three-storey flats (with the second-floor accommodation contained within the roof void). The relative size of the overall plot permits separation

---

Case study 19.1 Housing layout and backland development

Arcadian Developments acquire a house with a large rear garden located within outer London. They propose to demolish the existing house, run a road into the backland and build a block of ten flats. The site is large enough to satisfy all local development framework policies regarding amenity space, car parking and separation between developments. The new road width satisfies highway considerations in *Manual for Streets* (Department for Transport 2007) and incorporates a sufficient 'buffer' width on either side to allow for screen planting, so that the residents on either side are not affected by the movement of vehicles to and from the new development.

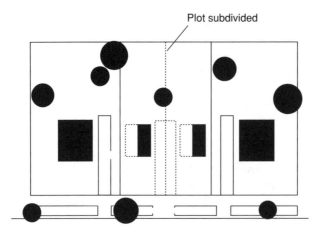

Figure 19.1 An example of infill development. (Infill – to build one or two dwellings within the gap between existing dwellings and facing on to the same road.)

Figure 19.2 An example of backland development. (Backland – to develop existing large back gardens.)

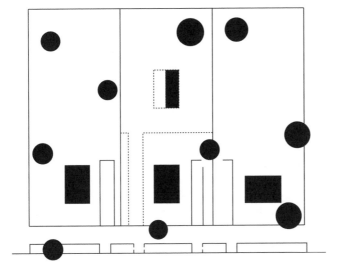

Figure 19.3 An example of tandem development. (Tandem – one house immediately behind another and sharing the same access. This is generally considered to be unacceptable, as the vehicular use of the access would result in a loss of amenity to the occupier of the frontage dwelling.)

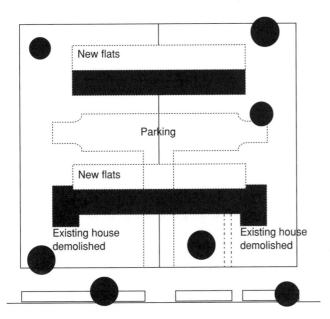

Figure 19.4 An example of flatted development on land previously occupied by houses

from neighbouring property, car parking, sizeable garden/amenity space to satisfy council provision and similar scale of development by maintaining predominantly a two-storey bulk. Permission is granted as the proposal satisfies many of the detailed development control criteria found in local plan policy, as well as meeting the demand for lower-cost one- and two-bedroom residential units. During the next five years many other such applications are submitted and granted. The overall result is that the character of an area has been changed incrementally from a low-density residential area to a medium- or high-density one.

This creeping and piecemeal change has become increasingly difficult to resist as national planning policy increasingly pushes for more and more housing on previously developed land, rising from 56 per cent of all housing in 1997, to 77 per cent in 2005 (DCLG 2007a). Considering that current estimates of brown-field land put the total supply at around 27,000 hectares suitable for housing and another 35,000 vacant or derelict land with potential, a crude arithmetic calculation tells us that (at current policy of 40 dwellings per hectare) this will yield 2.48 million homes. Thus, and ignoring the geographical spread of this current brown-field land (which is predominantly outside southern England), we cannot reasonably infer that all new future housing demands up to 2026 will fit on existing brown-fields. Such a mismatch of supply and demand, which is more acute in southern England outside London, will inevitably push up density as some local authorities seek to increase land efficiency. It is inevitable that housing will have to be allocated on greenfields at the urban fringe or elsewhere.

Design and layout

In considering residential design and layout certain specific issues must be considered, as below (see Table 19.1).

Design

The ability of a planning authority to engage meaningfully in detailed design control has, in past years, been highly constrained by national planning policy. This has progressively changed as a consequence of the growing desire to enhance urban environments. Influential think-tanks like the Urban Task Force (reporting in 1999 and 2005) and the creation of agencies like the Commission for Architecture and the Built Environment (CABE) have pushed for more control to engender better 'townscapes' and promote design that creates a strong sense of identity and place. While government guidance has consistently emphasized that such decisions must avoid arbitrary personal judgements as to the appropriateness of aesthetic treatment, PPS1 (2005) and PPS3 (2006) have clearly promoted various principles of good design to promote residential environments that are attractive, safe, accessible, functional, inclusive and have a distinct identity. In this context, key design features involve much more than the look of a development and include matters like local connections (to public transport, community facilities and green infrastructure), integration with

Table 19.1 Examples of residential town planning standards

Topic	Standard	Source
Overlooking	21 m minimum window to window	Supplementary Planning Documents/Design Guides
Car parking	Varies, but usually no greater than one and a half spaces per dwelling	National Planning Policy (PPS3)
Roads	4.8–5.5 m width (will vary)	*Manual for Streets* (2007)
Amenity space	Standards generally discouraged but as a 'rule of thumb' of 10 m² per habitable room (flats) and 40 per house	Standards discouraged
Density	40 dwellings per hectare minimum, except in exceptional cases	National Planning Policy (PPS3)
Conversions	To ensure some parking and/or amenity space	Development Plan Document
Separation of development	Varies between 20 and 30 m	Development Plan Document
Rear garden depths	Standards generally discouraged but as a 'rule of thumb' at between 10 and 15 m depth in new development	Standards discouraged

surroundings (scale, density, layout and access), adaptation to climate change issues, promotion of local pride or civic identity, the retention or re-establishment of bio-diversity and the creation of high-quality public realm. At long last it appears that a real consensus is emerging to raise the standards of residential design (Carmona and Dann 2007).

Within conservation areas, areas of outstanding natural beauty (AONBs) or in proximity to listed buildings, design control faces a much more precise task. In such areas and in compliance with duties set out in the Countryside and Rights of Way Act 2000 (for AONBs) or Planning (Listed Buildings and Conservation Areas) Act 1990, a detailed appraisal will be required of 'context', that is to say the way in which history and landscape have shaped a place and how new development will integrate acceptably into this pattern (Brown 2008). The developers' design and access statement, accompanying any application, will need to fully address such issues. For example, this context may be made up of a consistent layout and design of fine period-housing layouts such as the Georgian properties in Bath or historic New Town of Edinburgh; others may not be so impressive, yet it is important to maintain examples of twentieth-century development, for example, 'Metroland' – 1930s suburban design and layouts as found in north west London, (Case study 19.2)[2] or a particular palette of distinctive building materials, such as the predominance of local flint and brick as found in the Chilterns AONB and promoted in the supplementary design guidance as produced by the Chilterns Conservation Board. In all such examples the respective planning authority will pay close scrutiny to very detailed matters of building form and materials used. This is not a manifesto for merely replication of historic design or indeed pastiche housing (where historic copies are mixed up in inappropriate detail) but simply to establish that in such locations the design of new housing must go the extra mile in enhancing townscape or landscape. Outside such areas new housing must respond to context and create or reinforce local distinctiveness and provide other benefits such as better public space and the creation of pedestrian- and cycle-friendly layouts.

Scale, mass and bulk

The terms 'scale', 'mass' and 'bulk' are widely and often colloquially used by planning and property professionals. To ensure some precision of language they are defined (South West Planning Aid 2007) as below.

- Scale refers to the overall size of development and its impression within the context of its surroundings, especially when viewed against the scale or proportion of an individual (human scale).

Case study 19.2   Housing development within a conservation area

Arcadia Developments seek outline planning permission to develop a pair of detached dwellings in the Sylvan Park Conservation Area.

The Sylvan Park area was developed between 1890 and 1910 for workers' homes by a local industrialist who was influenced by the writings of Ebenezer Howard. The local planning authority designated the conservation area to protect the town planning layout, incorporating deep rear gardens, cul-de-sac road layout and considerable tree planting on both the street frontages and in rear gardens.

The proposal satisfies Council residential standards for existing dwellings and car parking. However, it is considered to result in an erosion of the character of the conservation area. The 'form' of development is alien to the original layout, and planning permission is refused because:

'The proposal introduced a form of development which is not compatible with the layout of Sylvan Park and therefore harms the character of the Conservation Area.'

If the site was not within a conservation area, the proposal would be considered as an acceptable form of development.

- Bulk refers to the volume of development combined with its height and shape. It often refers to the overall impression of a building or group of buildings.
- Mass refers to the height and width of elevations but is often used interchangeably with bulk to ensure that a building will 'fit' within its context and would not dominate (detrimentally) the buildings or open spaces that surround it.

With reference to the earlier discussion of context, an examination of such criteria is important in any such evaluation. The planning system does not exist to ensure that all new development simply replicates the scale, mass and bulk of existing or surrounding development. In some cases this is indeed important, to ensure that new development fits harmoniously with the existing development. Yet, more fundamentally, the key challenge for the designer or architect is to ensure the careful application of context, in other words the way that the proposal draws upon the surrounding layout, vernacular design and landscape, so that it is harnessed to shape and inform the new design. Thus mere replication of historic styles in new development (sometimes called pastiche) misses the point, which is to ensure that new development draws inspiration, as appropriate, from the nature of its surroundings. This may appear a nebulous objective. Yet, many past failures in residential design have been a consequence of layouts and patterns that exhibit no relationship to or pedigree with historic street patterns, plot dimensions or relationships between the plots (urban grain).

Overlooking

If a planning authority were to refuse planning permission on grounds of overlooking, this overlooking would need to be material, that is to say result in a *demonstrable* loss of amenity. This is usually taken to be direct overlooking between habitable rooms. A distance of 21 m window to window is a commonly applied 'rule of thumb' in such cases and is often contained in local development document or supplementary planning documents.

Highways and car parking

Highway planning criteria have perhaps exercised the greatest impact over residential housing layouts in recent years. The configuration of a road layout effectively dictates the layout of plots and overall urban design of the scheme. Until recently the principal source of guidance on this was Design Bulletin 32 (DB32) of 1992, which details standards for road widths, pavement widths and most significantly visibility requirements at access points and junctions. For example, the Design Bulletin requires a 5.5 m road width to allow all vehicle types to pass each other, a 4.8 m to allow a car to pass a service vehicle and 4 m for only single-file traffic (Figure 19.5).

Policy-makers and especially urban designers became increasingly aware of the implications of such technical guidance, which prescribed a whole set of

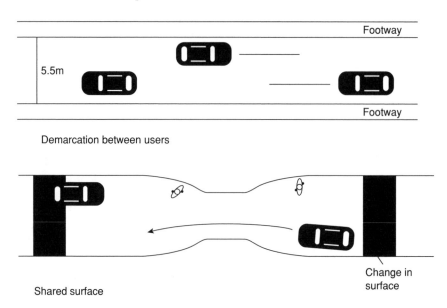

Demarcation between users

Shared surface

Change in surface

Figure 19.5 Road layouts following criteria as stated in Design Bulletin 32

criteria dealing with traffic and pedestrian safety. It was widely transposed into practice at the local level by highway engineers, who advised planning officers on highway issues within individual residential applications. This resulted in little real discretion at the local level, as issues of highway safety dominated, in an attempt to accommodate the car (and the forward visibility of the driver) within residential layouts. Therefore, the majority of layouts contain roads of 4–5.5 m width, some with a separate footway and others with no footway (where a shared surface serves both pedestrians and vehicles). Any implementation of a 'home zone', based on a mainland European notion of slowing traffic movements by virtue of urban design layout, was thwarted by the almost rigid adherence to these standards. The resulting urban layout was dictated by the highway engineering because the road configuration will shape the plot relationships and ultimately the form of the entire scheme (Biddulph *et al.* 2006). Concern that adherence to this 'roads first, houses later' approach was producing a poor quality of urban design in residential environments led to the government issuing *Places, Streets and Movement: A Companion Guide to Design Bulletin 32* (DoE 1998d) and *By Design* (DETR 2000d). This promoted a more imaginative approach to matters of radii and visibility to improve the layouts produced by residential developers. Yet, this promotion of good practice was not widely adopted, and in 2007 both DB32 and the Companion Guide were replaced by *Manual for Streets* (Department for Transport 2007) which advocated various strategies to create places and not merely traffic corridors when designing 'lightly trafficked' residential layouts. *By Design* remains in force. A summary of the relevant policy recommendations from both documents is set out below.

Manual for Streets (2007)		By Design (2000)	
Context	• That 'streets' are distinct from 'roads' • A street should be an attractive space, which is well-connected, and permeable, promoting security and a sense of ownership • Design code and master-plans should be used to create a 'place' with a distinctive character and design of public spaces, and after that the road network should fit those requirements	Objectives of urban design	• Character – promote townscape • Enclosure – continuity of street frontage • Quality urban realm – accessible public space • Ease of movement – promotes pedestrian movement • Legibility – recognizable landmarks and easy to understand environment • Adaptability – can respond to changing social, technological and economic conditions
Overall emphasis	• Emphasis on the creation of a place • Promote walking and cycling • Look for local context, e.g. density, layout of buildings and spaces, scale, mass and local materials • Use designs to reduce crime and anti-social behaviour	Applied to planning system	• Diversity – mixed uses and diversity of environment • Development briefs • Urban design frameworks • Development plan policy • Master-plans • Design codes

Dwelling mix/internal standards

Although internal alterations fall outside the definition of development and therefore planning control, the size of individual rooms in new developments or resulting from conversion is a material planning consideration. The most complete set of minimum internal space standards were the Parker Morris Standards, which were employed in council house building during the 1960s and 1970s (Parker Morris Committee 1961). For example, a two-storey family dwelling should incorporate 72–92 m^2 (770–900 ft^2) floor space. Today, no such standards exist for public or private sector, although compliance with Parker Morris was always voluntary. As with design issues, the government position is that such matters should be left to the judgement of the developer and not the planning authority. The mixture of dwelling types is also of importance, and some planning authorities, most notably in inner London, will seek to control such dwelling types to meet sectoral needs so as to maintain family housing when faced with increasing pressure to convert existing stock into one- and two-bedroom flats. The increased pressure to deliver housing on previously developed land has inevitably resulted in a push for greater provision of smaller units (flats, apartments) at the expense of family housing. While the notion of 'densification' (i.e. combining density and intensification) can deliver the efficient use of land, considerable attention must be paid to the delivery of a quality place. English Partnerships (in 2007) proposed the reintroduction of minimum internal space standards in developments that it sponsored on its own land. Research work commissioned by both English Partnerships and the Housing Corporation (English Partnerships *et al.* 2007) produced a compendium of good urban design examples, including the Greenwich Millennium Village scheme in south east London which provided an exemplar of a well-designed yet high density brown-field redevelopment of former gas works land into 1300 homes and public space.

Landscaping/amenity space/green space

In similar tone to internal space standards, government guidance on garden sizes is again deemed to be a matter for the developer. Many planning authorities will produce amenity space standards for new residential development or conversion, setting out minimum garden depths, or require communal space provision per bedroom or habitable room. In most major residential proposals the planning authority will expect some form of landscaping proposal detailing new tree and shrub planting as well as existing trees/shrubs to be retained. In some schemes the developer may propose a communal play area. The ownership and maintenance may be passed on to the council by means of a planning obligation agreement. As a generally applied rule, such space must be useable and therefore of sufficient size to allow for recreation and play. Many authorities still apply standards prescribed by the National Playing Fields Association (the six-acre standard). Provision of natural green space (i.e. with a predominant biodiversity content) is increasingly being promoted in regional spatial strategies. This involves the creation of sites in excess of two hectares, providing the opportunity for both habitat creation and quiet recreation or even a feeling of relative tranquillity. Natural England has been at the forefront of such policy development.

Affordable housing

PPS3 of 2006 offered a single and widely accepted definition of what constitutes affordable housing. Generally, the term refers to low-cost homes to either rent or buy. PPS3 clearly established that the notion of affordable housing refers to a specific housing product, covering either socially rented housing (owned and managed by housing associations and local authorities) or intermediate housing. Intermediate usually involves private housing with values set below normal market rates but above the social rented sector or involves what are most commonly referred to as shared equity products. These involve shared ownership schemes whereby the homeowner buys a portion of the value so as to reduce mortgage payment levels. The need for affordable housing provision (as compared to affordability, which is a measure of cost), is a consequence of market failure. In such circumstances the private housing sector is unable to provide housing to meet needs at a price that everyone can afford. This is a consequence of many external factors but in most part has been blamed on the planning system, for restricting supply. Rightly or wrongly, the 2004 review of housing supply, by Kate Barker, focused heavily on the need to add a measure of flexibility to the housing system through the allocation of housing land in local development frameworks, together with the release of additional land supply when triggered by market signals. While the Barker review on housing also called for additional investment in social housing (up to £1.6 billion per year) and the creation of a community infrastructure fund to unlock some of the barriers to development, inevitably the fall-out of the report concentrated on land supply.

Socially rented housing is provided by registered social landlords (RSLs), mostly housing associations, who both own and rent the property, at a subsidy. The RSL is registered with the Housing Corporation, an agency of government who regulate and fund this sector. Intermediate housing predominantly involves some element of discount when compared to private (open) market housing. This usually involves shared equity (for example, the government's 'HomeBuy' scheme) in which part of the value is purchased by traditional mortgage borrowing while the remainder is discounted. This discounting may involve government subsidy to set the rate below current rates of borrowing and/or to offer a holiday scheme in which payment is not required for a set period. The intermediate sector is not the sole preserve of housing associations, with a number of private developers (such as Redrow-Debut housing) increasingly engaging in such projects. However, the majority of shared equity schemes do involve housing associations as many of the discounts are linked to government funding and are regulated by the Housing Corporation. Affordable provision should not be confused with key worker or low cost housing. Key worker housing deals with accommodation specifically identified for public sector and service employees, unable to afford housing locally on the open market. Low cost housing is specifically excluded from the affordable definition in PPS3 and refers to housing made available at a cost significantly below normal market values by virtue of simple construction or subsidy. Such low cost provision can be either to purchase or rent. Prior to 2006 such a housing type *was* included in the definition and rather unhelpfully will still be found in some (mostly) local planning documents that predate this revision. Councils are now expected to account for low cost and also key worker housing within their overall housing mix and not within data dealing with affordability.

National government policy, following recommendations in the Barker report, expects that all new housing will include a proportion of affordable provision. The exact amount of affordable housing in the development pipeline is a consequence of demand (measured in the Strategic Housing Market Assessment), the amount of public subsidy available (channelled via the Housing Corporation) and the targets set in planning policy (now contained in the regional spatial strategy produced by the regional assembly). The London Plan (adopted 2004), the 'Regional Spatial Strategy for the Capital' led the way in creating a 50 per cent provision (itself split 70/30 socially rented to intermediate) for all housing on sites above a threshold of 15 or fewer dwellings. The South East Plan has a target of 35 per cent. The borough/district/city councils vested with responsibility for producing a local development framework will then apply this target locally, with an assessment of the likely economic viability of so doing. This will be a consequence of available public subsidy and the level of developer contributions that can be secured. They can discriminate between the amount of socially rented and intermediate affordable housing required and set minimum thresholds for provision (usually set by site area) and the amount of developer contribution required to facilitate this. PPS3 establishes a presumption in favour of affordable housing provision within a site, to ensure the creation of a mixed community. Off-site provision (paid in-lieu of provision within the development site) is only acceptable if it can be supported by a robust justification and would contribute to the creation of a mixed use within the wider local authority area. Most housing associations would prefer provision within a certain defined part of the site, compared to a 'pepper-potting' across the entire development, because this is easier to manage and maintain. In rural areas, where site availability for affordable housing tends to be more limited, allocations can include a 'rural exceptions site policy', where the needs of a rural community are served by developing a typically small parcel of land that would otherwise be constrained by other policies of restraint. This may also apply in rural locations that are also green belt.

Density and sustainability

Density is a measure of the amount of housing occupation on a site. Today, this quantum is commonly measured in the number of dwellings on a site. It is calculated in a very exact way as follows:

$$\frac{\text{Habitable room}}{\text{Site area in hectares}} = \text{density, expressed as habitable rooms per hectare}$$

A habitable room is a bedroom, living room, dining room or kitchen (taken to be greater than 13 m^2). The now replaced PPG3 (2000) heralded the beginning of an attempt to substantially raise density standards to between thirty and fifty dwellings per hectare net. Current policy in PPS3 (2006) maintains this position and establishes that planning permission will only be permitted below the bottom of this range in exceptional cases. At its most elementary, density standards have been applied to increase land efficiency. As this policy has been rolled out nationally across the development industry, so other benefits have been attributed, including the creation of a balanced community and neighbourhood (Derbyshire 2007). Further, work by Lord Rogers and the Urban Task Force suggests that by raising density, local shops and services are supported and public transport networks justified. It remains to be seen if close proximity to such facilities will increase walking or physical activity more generally, and a research study in 2007 suggested that little real evidence exists to support this claim or to establish a clear cause and effect relationship between higher-density living and a propensity to walk or cycle (Forsyth 2007). This would indeed be worrying when measured against both a sustainability and health agenda, with the Department for Health issuing a national target in January 2008 to tackle future adult and child obesity levels. The need to roll out more housing land while protecting the countryside and urban fringe remains a powerful incentive to maintain this policy or even raise the density thresholds for residential (to fifty dwellings per hectare as suggested by the Urban Task Force and Sustainable Development Commission). To some extent, population growth and change is driving this policy forward (Derbyshire 2007) and presenting many opportunities to build at these new 'super densities' in the creation of new neighbourhoods and communities and the increasing identification and delivery of new housing on previously developed land (Llewellyn-Davies Yeang *et al.* 2007).

Raising residential density appears to be motivated by a combination of both planning and political factors. First, planning or land-use factors in that development land is finite and brown-field, vacant or derelict land readily available. Secondly, political factors in that, by avoiding development on green fields on the urban fringe or within the open countryside, local and national politicians avoid courting controversy by being allied with the more locally contentious end of the development spectrum.

Yet, the extent to which raising density of itself makes land more sustainable remains open to some interpretation. For example, are residents more likely to avoid car use because they live in higher-density environments (close to services and public transport) or is such modal shift (i.e. changing transport modes to move away from the car), a factor of other issues such as fuel price or demand management (for instance as congestion charging)? Arguably, the real cutting-edge rationale for raising density must be to secure climate change objectives and energy-efficiency savings. With around one third of the UK's carbon emissions produced by domestic heating and energy use, this is a clear policy priority (Royal Institute of British Architects 2007). A number of exemplary low carbon housing schemes have been built, for example at BedZED (Beddington Zero Energy Development), which derives all its energy needs (in use) from a combination of wind cowls, wind turbines, sedum turf roofs, photovoltaic solar cells, wood pellet boilers and thermal panels. This is combined with the additional benefit of employing reclaimed materials (in construction) and the most novel component – the pooled resource of an electric car. Individual components as well as the totality of the architect, Bill Dunster's, vision are being implemented across other examples of UK housing. Yet, and as identified by the Sustainable Development Commission (in 2007) it is baffling as to why this is not much more commonplace. Other examples at Andover, Hampshire (the Zed factory), Altringham, Cheshire (Stamford Brook) and Cliveden Village, South Buckinghamshire (Countryside Developments and the National Trust) apply many of the BedZED principles in both harvesting renewable (i.e. non-fossil fuel) energy and in adopting high insulation technologies to reduce energy use. It is clearly acknowledged that sustainable architecture will play a major role in dealing with both the adaptation to and mitigation of climate change (Turrent 2007 and Royal Institute of British Architects 2007) but a greater policy push is required to make this the norm and not the exception. Two initiatives point the way here, combining planning and building specification. First, in 2007 the government launched the 'Eco-towns' initiative in which they set out a vision of new housing growth fused with zero carbon development (mostly housing). Some ten such projects would be set up to deliver a mix of objectives combining environmental, social and economic sustainability with a real test-bed for delivering carbon neutrality. Secondly, the Code for Sustainable Homes (formerly Eco-homes) would become mandatory for all new housing from 2008, combined with more rigorous energy-efficiency measures in revised building regulations (Part L). A discussion paper on the future of energy-efficiency requirements in the building regulations, in 2007 (DCLG 2007b) considered ways of raising standards of insulation and air leakage. The government committed to improve energy efficiency in new housing by 25 per cent to 2010 and 44 per cent to 2014 (against a baseline of the 2006 Part L building regulations).

As a consequence, new housing would yield a better environmental performance by dint of greatly reduced energy use, based principally upon renewable and not fossil fuel-dependent sources (such as oil and gas). Most policy-makers would support this but consumers would benefit greatly as the projected cost increase on fossil fuel energy supplies will greatly outstrip inflation (as supplies diminish) over the next twenty-five years.

Housing land availability

Notwithstanding the considerable emphasis on developing brown-field land at ever increasing densities, greenfield land will continue to be developed, and for two fundamental reasons. First, demand and supply of brown-field/previously developed land (PDL) land is not evenly matched, when viewed nationally. Secondly, the areas identified for growth in southern England tend to have a very limited supply of PDL and much market demand exists for homes on the fringe of or outside urban areas. Yet, the allocation of new housing land on greenfield sites continues to expose many political tensions that underlie the current planning system. During the 1980s various private sector housing consortiums sponsored large-scale new settlements (such as the unsuccessful Foxley Wood in Hampshire), to accommodate the growing demand for new housing while reducing the pressure on existing urban areas. In the 1990s the problem did not go away, with other major schemes at Micheldever New Town (also Hampshire – and also unsuccessful) sponsored by major developers and landowners. By the millennium completions of new houses were at their lowest level since 1946 (under 150,000). Since then little real improvement in numbers has been in evidence while demand for homes has increased and the affordability gap between earnings and prices widened.

The housing pressures experienced in southern England have resulted in the creation of two new acronyms NIMBYISM[3] (not in my back yard) and BANANA (build absolutely nothing anywhere near anyone), reflecting the political impact on the planning system following the local backlash against increasing amounts of greenfield residential development. To understand this pressure we must examine the process of housing land allocation. Following enactment of the Planning and Compulsory Purchase Act 2004, regional planning and thus inter-regional housing allocations became reality, after many years of 'informal' regional conferences and the issuing of guidance by national government on the broad direction of regional growth (in the now defunct regional planning guidance notes). Housing allocations for each district/city/borough council are set out in the regional spatial strategy (the Regional Plan) and agreed following publication, public and other stakeholder consultation and the review of an independent panel of planning inspectors at an examination-in-public. The regional spatial strategy is produced by the regional assembly and will have an important implementation element, in which necessary infrastructure needs are identified and funding addressed. The panel will also need to have regard to an independent sustainability appraisal of the policies.

Individual district/city/borough councils must conform to these *targets* when producing their local development frameworks. PPS3 (2006) requires that they maintain a five-year supply pipeline of allocated sites. The maxim here is that of 'plan, monitor and manage' in which each planning authority plans for an overall annual rate of housing delivery, monitors provision against set targets and releases additional land for housing if targets are amended or are not met. Each council must identify broad locations and specific sites that will enable continuous delivery of housing for at least fifteen years from the date of adoption. The identification of sites begins with the completion of a Strategic Housing Land Availability Assessment, which examines local and sub-regional evidence of need and demand. Councils will also have regard to advice from the National Housing and Planning Advice Unit on the impact of affordability issues in the

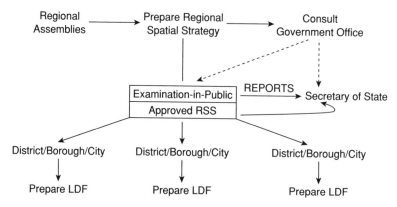

Figure 19.6 Bodies responsible for housing allocations

locality, national projections on household formations and data on vacant, derelict and brown-field land in the National Land Use Database. After gathering all this evidence, the council will apply it to local circumstances and assess options against various location-based criteria (mostly the environmental, social and economic impacts of development). As these options feed into a draft development plan document, the key mantra of national planning policy is that such sites are both developable and deliverable. This tends to mean that such land is both suitable for housing development and a reasonable prospect exists that it will come forward for development either when the plan is adopted or at the point envisaged during the fifteen-year programme of its implementation. This will be a matter for scrutiny by the independent planning inspector who presides over the examination of the plan and who will want to consider matters of sustainability (in location and development criteria) and delivery (in looking at functional features such as ready access). This process is shown in Figure 19.6.

During the production of the local development framework (in particular the development plan document with responsibility for site allocations) a good deal of argument occurs as to whether or not an adequate supply of land exists and the extent to which the sites identified by the planning authority are economically capable of being developed and are free from any planning, physical or ownership constraints that would otherwise prevent implementation of a housing scheme, for example the existence of a restrictive covenant (a civil contract limiting what can be built regardless of any planning consent). To avoid protracted disputes, the planning authority is encouraged to discuss the provision of such sites with landowners or developers in advance. This is common practice.

The notion of 'plan, monitor and manage' was designed to give greater encouragement to the absorption of new housing allocations within the existing urban fabric. PPS3 (2006) establishes that an effective use must be made of previously developed land. Councils would be required to include in their plans a target for the proportion of housing development to be built on such land and the creation of a 'trajectory' which looks to bringing forward vacant and derelict sites in the future. The current system of land allocation involves an element of consultation but is largely a top-down process, as the Secretary of State issues target guidelines to the regional assemblies, who in turn allocate to the district/city/borough councils via the regional spatial strategy and then local development document.

Case study 19.3   Housing land availability in the South East Plan

The draft South East Plan, as produced by the South East of England Regional Assembly (SEERA), proposed a regional level of 578,080 dwellings over the plan period of twenty years from 2006. This amounted to an average annual delivery of 28,900 dwellings. Research undertaken by the regional assembly estimated that about 70 per cent of this was required to meet natural change (in other words, local rates of household formation), 10 per cent to deal with the backlog of housing need and the remaining 20 per cent to address net inward migration into the area. Evidence and argument put to the public examination of the plan, dealt with the supply-side relationship between housing supply and affordability, the need to maximize urban capacity and the infrastructure challenges that would be a prerequisite for growth. The independent panel of planning inspectors in their report to the Secretary of State, were firmly of the view that the 'regional housing level should be increased' and to a raised annual target of 32,000. This increase was seen at the lower end of the scale, when looking at factors like affordability. Some developers had called for a much higher target increase (as high as 41,000 per annum) to tackle the high house prices in the region. Ultimately the independent panel were persuaded by argument based on existing employment patterns and demographic trends and were perhaps nervous to dramatically raise the apportionment of housing numbers per district/city/borough. Instead they dished out a rather more modest increase but were clear in their conclusions that 'new land will have to be found', to accommodate housing needs for the next twenty years. While old style solutions such as the new town at Micheldever were comprehensively ruled out, the South East Plan would still require a significant amount of development on green fields around existing towns and in new major urban extensions, such as proposed between Portsmouth and Southampton. Conversely, in the capital, the London Plan accommodates a comparable annual target (at 30,500) with the population projected to increase by in excess of one million by 2026. This would all be accommodated on brown-field land, accepting that in some parts of London (mostly the Thames Gateway corridor) large areas of vacant and derelict land is available for and actively seeking to be developed.

Table 19.2 Production of Housing Allocations

Stage	Development Plan Document (core strategy and Site Allocations and Area Action Plans and Development Control Policies)	Supplementary Planning Documents (these do not have formal status of a Development Plan)
1 **Pre-production stage**	Evidence gathering: Survey and collection of evidence to justify a plan or policy	Evidence gathering
2 **Production stage**	Preferred options → Preparation of document → Submission of document →	Consultation on Draft and review after representations
3 **Examintion stage**	Any amendments after consultation → pre-examination meeting → examination by an independent inspector → issues report → (sound or unsound)	
4 **Adoption**	Sound → Adoption *and* monitoring Unsound → returned for additional work	Adoption and monitoring

The Sustainable Communities Plan, Housing Pathfinder and beyond

In 2003 the government published its vision for urban development in the form of the Sustainable Communities Plan. It combined planned growth (four, and later five key growth areas in the South East Region at Ashford, Milton Keynes–Aylesbury, Stansted–Cambridge, Portsmouth–Southampton and the Thames Gateway), a £5 billion commitment to delivery of affordable housing and a commitment to protect existing green belt and other special landscapes. The planning system would need to accommodate around one million extra homes in the South East region by 2026 but additionally would need to address 'market failure' in certain parts of the Midlands, North West, Yorkshire and North East regions where a lack of demand had created decay and dereliction. These 'Pathfinder' projects would spend money to refurbish, demolish and rebuild housing stock with the central aim of eradicating the blight imposed upon these districts. Thus, the housing market in England was split between the old industrial heartlands with a declining manufacturing base and loss of demand and that of the South East region (including London) where increasing economic buoyancy created a demand for housing that was 'boiling over' and causing severe problems of affordability and acute environmental pressures (Power and Houghton 2007). The overall strategy would be floated on a combination of government funding to address market failures (in the North) and government funding to provide some (but not all) infrastructure to facilitate growth (in the South) and to 'lever in' much needed private sector investment. The Thames Gateway, stretching from East London to the North Sea, presented the only location that crossed this spatial divide, with its many areas of poor housing, contaminated land and creaking infrastructure, yet located within the South East economic powerhouse and incorporating the 2012 Olympic site. The 2003 Sustainable Communities Plan would present an immense challenge to government in its attempt to regenerate on one hand and plan for major growth with limited environmental impact on the other. In southern England these new growth strategies would need to be approved within the new regional spatial strategies for the East of England and the South East. A new planning lexicon was to emerge, such as the concept of 'water-neutral' development (in the Sustainability Appraisal for the East of England Plan) and 'sustainable urban extensions' for the growth in South Hampshire around Southampton and Portsmouth. Problems were to be encountered along the way, including the shelving of a major urban extension to the post-war new town of Harlow in north Essex (due to the unsustainable nature of the development) and the lack of funding to put in place the rail infrastructure to link the many 'pockets' of development that would form the Thames Gateway. Yet, the Sustainable Communities Plan would greatly shape the nature of future development over the next twenty years and probably beyond. One major component would be the delivery of affordable housing and the creation of communities. The Campaign for the Protection of Rural England (CPRE 2007) identified ten key statistical indicators to gauge and/or assess the environmental, economic or social trends in the Thames Gateway area. These included (i) levels of unemployment and, (ii) educational attainment, (iii) proportion of land allocated to housing or (iv) to commerce and industry, (v) access to local amenities and services, (vi) residential density, (vii) design quality of the urban environment, (viii) town centre renewal, (ix) environment of designated areas, and (x) green space management.

Two previously established models are advanced for the future delivery of such housing within the delivery of the Sustainable Communities Plan, in the form of urban villages and sustainable urban extensions. Work by the Town and Country Planning Association (TCPA) promoted best practice in urban extensions and new settlements (TCPA 2007). This report drew lessons from six case studies involving development at Dickens Heath (Birmingham), Upton (Northampton), Great Park (Newcastle), Hampton (Peterborough), Caterham Barracks (Surrey) and South Woodham Ferrers (Essex) in which a variety of both brownfield and greenfield sites were redeveloped for new homes and a mix of community, employment and transport links to nearby settlements. The principal argument put forward here was that such new towns (seen as a more politically acceptable term in recent years) could be built in clusters around existing settlements, with a finite development limit (set at around 5000 population), linked by public transport, with a good range of community infrastructure and constructed to high environmental (low carbon) standards. While the case study locations varied in size, from Caterham with only 292 dwellings to Hampton or South Woodham Ferrers with around 5000 each, the basic theory was that the pendulum had swung back in favour of grander solutions to housing need. Albeit, that the extent of that swing had not completely embraced large-scale out-of-town new settlements. The independent panel's report on the South East Plan neatly illustrated this when they concluded that a new settlement (or town) at Micheldever was now considered unacceptable, whereas their predecessors who had vetted the old (and now redundant) Hampshire County Council Structure Plan had deemed the scheme a suitable means of accommodating growth.

Yet, while the TCPA sought to reinvigorate the idea of new towns, an option perhaps stigmatized by the soulless post-war environments created to accommodate housing shortages of the 1950s and 1960s, the report was also careful to advocate a clustering of town extensions or major development areas so that they were linked and integrated into existing services and indeed the social and commercial fabric. A significant problem of past planning was the construction of large-scale developments that both matured at the same rate and often needed repairing or regenerating at the same time. A more thought-out approach would involve linking new development with existing development. This could be achieved by public transport links. Thus urban expansion need not always be physically adjoined to existing towns. Taking the example at Caterham Barracks (as a microcosm) these issues can be illustrated. A modest amount of housing was created but with much community support and a development that worked respectfully within existing conservation limits, supported a new retail store and a bus link to the nearby town. A small-scale scheme served to point to the fact that working with the context of a place was the best means of implementing a quality design and a good way of harnessing support amongst the local population.

Urban extensions and new settlements and urban villages should not be seen as somehow mutually exclusive but indeed quite the reverse. They tend to overlap, most commonly, where towns and cities are extended into the surrounding countryside. The urban village clearly has its principal focus within the existing urban envelope but many of its key features are just as applicable within urban extensions on greenfield sites. Poundbury is often much vaunted as a good example of both. The development of this 180-hectare western urban extension of Dorchester in Dorset has created far-reaching ripples of interest across the planning and property profession. The original master-plan promoted by the landowners, the Duchy of Cornwall, set out a vision of a pedestrian-friendly and traditional street layout which would incorporate terraced housing, courtyards, alleys and squares to foster a traditional urban feel or 'grain'. The urban designer, behind this vision, Leon Krier was keen to avoid the suburban layouts of the post-war years in which housing was spread out and of a low density. The community-based focus previously advocated by Prince Charles was to be achieved by a mixture of tenure (The Guinness Trust Housing Association/ private owner-occupier) and house type.

The urban design master-plan gave rise to an 'urban style' using local materials and with vernacular detail, combined with a series of public spaces and community uses. Poundbury presents a model of housing development that accentuates the aesthetic. Its construction has resulted in much comment and debate amongst planning professionals. While it displays Prince Charles's personal vision, it has influenced considerations of the design and layout of many other residential environments. In this respect the development of only a small parcel of land in West Dorset has been highly instrumental in creating an appraisal of how planners and developers may improve the aesthetics of domestic dwellings. Density at forty dwellings per hectare and parking at 110 per cent (i.e. 1.1 spaces per dwelling, the 0.1 being allocated to visitor parking within courtyards) combines to deliver an efficient use of land. Poundbury is strongly influenced by Dorset vernacular design, which delivers a strong sense of place. Yet, the broader design in respect of garden size, parking layout, proximity of dwellings and pedestrian permeability, provides the real key to its success.

In 2000 the Prince's Foundation published a report entitled 'Sustainable Urban Extensions: Planned through Design' which promoted an alternative model of community involvement, in preference to past public participation whereby local people merely commented on a completed scheme instead of getting involved with its formulation. The Foundation's own mission was to promote 'a return of human values to architecture, urban design and regeneration'. The report took a critical view of much in the design of past residential environments, railing against the piecemeal low-density outward expansion of towns and cities. It went on to argue that a consensus is emerging amongst planners and the public that far greater priority needs to be given to urban design, environmental sustainability and public involvement. New greenfield development will continue to exist (up to 40 per cent is accepted by government in its housing projections) so a new approach is needed. The Foundation promoted the 'Enquiry by Design' technique comprising community workshops and design review techniques. Landowners, council officials and the public or other interested groups would assemble to devise new-build residential layouts against the background of an anti-sprawl and sustainability agenda. Workshop facilitators help the stakeholders to debate, discuss, enquire and design collaboratively, usually focused on the key criterion that housing is organized into walkable neighbourhoods of a five-minute/400 metre radius from public transport or community facilities. A key factor and objective of these design sessions is that density quality must be raised without harming amenity. A lot of these ideas were incorporated into the most recent policy pronouncement, entitled 'Manual for Streets' (Department for Transport 2007).

Urban villages

> I am hoping we can encourage the development of urban villages in order to reintroduce human scale, intimacy and a vibrant street life. These factors can help to restore people to their sense of belonging and pride in their own particular surroundings.

> (HRH the Prince of Wales 1989)

In 1989 Prince Charles expressed his desire for both investigation and promotion into the concept of planned mixed-use and mixed-tenure developments that would enhance the quality of life for those people who lived and worked in them as well as creating a form of sustainable development. Later that same year, the Urban Villages Forum was formed to promote the idea. 'The Urban Villages Forum' was an amalgamation of various property-related professions who believed that a new approach was required when building urban areas. This new approach constituted a reaction against many forms of post-war urban planning in which planners zoned separate areas for separate uses and developers built mass-volume housing estates on the edge of towns and offices in the centre. The housing lacked any sense of community or urban design and at night the town centres were 'dead', devoid of any life or activity. The commuting between the two resulted in a waste of resources. What was needed was a revitalized form of housing and employment to bring life – or to be precise vitality – back to the cities. That message has, almost year-on-year, grown in importance and culminated in the need for mixed-use/mixed-neighbourhood planning as a fundamental and mainstream component of sustainable planning. By 2000 the work of the Urban Villages Forum was taken on board by the Prince's Foundation for Architecture and the Built Environment. Subsequent pronouncements from bodies like CABE and the Academy for Urbanism have developed an evidence base in favour of this approach and expanded on how to implement such schemes. Yet, the key foundations, even the turning point can be traced to the work of the Urban Villages Forum/ Princes Foundation.

The key features of the urban village are:

- Mixed-use buildings and areas comprising housing, small businesses, shops and social amenities. Although one of the key objectives is to provide housing, it is considered important that an urban village maintains a degree of 'community' in which people may live and work in the same area.
- Mixed ownership (or tenure) with rented and owner-occupied housing.
- A high standard of urban design to enhance the public spaces and quality of development.
- A total finite development limit or population of between 3000 and 5000 residents.
- A form of development suitable for previously developed or vacant or derelict land within existing urban areas, but also possible for new-build schemes on greenfield sites. There is considerable overlap with sustainable

urban extensions because such projects could incorporate these urban village features.

A considerable obstacle to this initiative was originally cost, and the initial reluctance of financial institutions to lend money on buildings that involve a mix of uses on different floors, as this increases the cost of managing the investment and may reduce the future value of the building. For example, a building split into general office and residential units results in separate tenants with exclusive tenancy terms and conditions. Flats above may adversely affect the letting of the office, as occupiers perceive the flats will create a problem of security. This in turn may suppress the value of the offices and therefore the investment potential resulting from the scheme. As the roll-out of such schemes has been increasing and planning policy more insistent on its inclusion as a guiding principle of development, so this hurdle has been overcome by careful design and layout considerations. Many urban planning authorities (for example in the London Borough of Camden Unitary Development Plan) have specific policies to promote mixed-use schemes, while urban fringe planning authorities confronted with town extensions (such as in Milton Keynes and Aylesbury Vale) are keen to adopt these principles to promote efficient and effective future land-use patterns.

The theory behind the urban village would dictate that such development areas should be finite at 40–80 ha (100–200 acres) total area, with a combined resident and working population of 3000–5000. Suitable locations would include brown-land (mostly vacant inner-city land), suburban or edge-of-town sites or satellite greenfield sites. To engender social and economic integration, the urban village promoter (housebuilder or developer/investor) will be encouraged to provide not just a balance of uses but also a variety of housing tenures and commercial freehold and leasehold tenures (Urban Villages Forum 1992, Savills and Prince's Foundation 2007).

The urban village concept has, during the last fifteen years or so, pushed the planning system towards a greater consideration of mixed-use development, whether it is within component buildings or entire neighbourhoods. This has required, at times, a rethink of some planning policy standards that prescribe requirements for parking and amenity space. It has also required the development of a particular language of design as it applies to growth and regeneration. As a consequence, the new-style development plan documents (responsible for allocations of land) contain an ever-growing lexicon of design terms, whereby planning details are laid down for physical features like high-quality public realm, local distinctiveness and sense of place and a mix of appropriate uses at efficient urban densities.

Some early examples of urban villages provided an encouraging vision for the further employment of this idea to provide housing and deliver environmental quality. At Crown Street, Glasgow the redevelopment of a 16-ha (40-acre) site formerly occupied by a 1960s high-rise housing estate, promoted a high-quality public realm that was overlooked by the new residential developments. A masterplan was devised, which established layout mix of unit types, including family accommodation and with a split of 75 per cent owner-occupation and 25 per cent rented, elevation treatment and creation of a community trust to manage the development. The form of development recreates traditional Scottish tenement living with four storeys incorporating residential accommodation and shops, workshops and studios on the ground floor. Private amenity space would be created within each block and a different architect appointed for each development, creating an 'organic' feel in which the overall master-plan would not be perceived as one development. In this case the urban village promoter was a combination of housing developers – city council, Glasgow Development Agency and a housing association. The results include a high-quality sequence of public spaces with vehicles clearly separated from pedestrians, without any harm to the sense of urban design or identity. Public art abounds and the soft and hard landscaping elements are impressive.

At Hulme in Manchester, the redevelopment of one square kilometre of 1960s eight-storey deck-accessed concrete housing blocks allowed new opportunities, not just to redevelop a run-down place but to reconnect it to the nearby city core. Since construction in the early 1970s it had become notorious for its social, economic and health problems, irrespective of (but not helped by) the inhuman architecture and planning of the estate. The isolation of the place was compounded by breathtakingly bad planning in which links to central Manchester were blocked by the new axis of tower block developments. Redevelopment work began in 1992, involving the demolition of the housing blocks and the rebuilding of the area employing the principles of mixed-use high-density urban form of redevelopment with a strong element of urban design. The master-plan for redevelopment was a product of public consultation. It emphasizes the fact that merely rebuilding the physical form of an estate such as Hulme is not sufficient – attention is required to create a feeling of community. The Hulme regeneration involves a mix of uses within buildings and areas, as well as a mix of housing tenure and a projected population sufficient to sustain a local school, businesses and community facilities into the longer term. New corridor links were established to the wider area. The promoter incorporated Manchester City Council, private housebuilders/developers and housing associations.

At Brindleyplace, central Birmingham, a much lauded mixed-use scheme comprising 6.88 ha of offices, retail, leisure and residential uses has proved a great commercial success and popular new city centre venue. The scheme incorporates a strong urban design element with creation of public spaces linking the development to existing city and canal-side waterfront locations. The success (both commercial and physical) of Brindleyplace has spurred on other mixed-use projects in the city, most notably the nearby Birmingham Mailbox – the redevelopment of a former Royal Mail sorting office into hotel, retail, leisure and residential use. A new pedestrian street was carved through the centre of the development, and permeability further enhanced by linking the development to a new canal pedestrian footbridge and under an inner urban flyover, to connect with central Birmingham and public transport.

At Gallions Reach, Woolwich the redevelopment of a former vacant (and before that contaminated) site was completed with the deployment of a land-reclamation project, funded by English Partnership between 1997 and 2001. Remediation of contaminated soil was completed on-site by means of a newly developed soil washing technology. A spatial master-plan was developed on the lines of mixed uses and urban densities linked by new connections and corridors. The project was implemented in stages from 2001 and now comprises 700 homes, light industrial workshops, a commercial leisure centre, refurbished listed building (the former Royal Artillery Building), an ecological corridor of open space and an 'eco-park' of energy-efficient homes. The whole project epitomizes the 'retrofit' approach of the Urban Task Force (1999 and 2005) by linking to existing areas and adding around 3500 new residents to support existing services and enhance new ones. The site is close to central London but has been historically isolated by poor public transport linkages. This scheme brought the necessary economic power to justify better transport networks, including a station on the Docklands Light Railway and so benefits the wider area in which it is located.

Other notable success stories include the Greenwich Millennium Village and the wholesale urban renaissance of Liverpool city centre, promoted by Liverpool Vision. The Greenwich Millennium Village was a project secured following a 'high-profile international competition' (Urban Task Force 1999 and English Partnerships *et al.* 2007) to create a mixed-tenure community, integrated with a variety of public spaces (streets, square, open spaces and communal gardens) and today it is critically acclaimed in its strong delivery of this brief. The nature of the resulting development was commended by the Urban Task Force as a model of design-led regeneration that harnessed a competitive process to produce innovations in design and sustainability (energy-efficiency). This scheme did command a good deal of public investment and it has been subsequently questioned that in the absence of such a financial commitment a more 'run of the mill' regeneration project compared to a 'flagship' one would have resulted. Yet, as it is it provides a beacon of good practice to be followed.

Liverpool Vision, one of the foremost Urban Regeneration Companies (a hybrid public–private body responsible for promoting renewal through design) set in train a series of action plans (in the form of supplementary planning documents), dealing with urban design strategies and coordinating them with cultural projects, notably the European City of Culture 2008. The City Council and the Grosvenor Estate were also implementing a major retail and city centre redevelopment around Paradise Street, with vastly improved retail offer and a significant new public space (at Chavasse Park). Liverpool Vision developed their principal objective of city centre renewal around the principles of an urban village. At Ropewalks (also within the city core) Liverpool Vision developed a renewal strategy (of a very historic but largely neglected city centre neighbourhood, abutting Paradise Street), based on residential, employment and night-time leisure economy. The historic grid of tightly drawn streets (the layout itself dictated by the original production of maritime rope), was harnessed to create a few pockets of public realm with a variety of refurbished heritage buildings and contemporary residential, cultural, educational and leisure buildings. Initially the residential market was slow here, discouraged by the previously poor quality environment. Liverpool Vision was able to draw in public realm improvements and as this took hold, so new development activity created a new momentum and a catalyst of change was created. Such initiatives are not confined to areas traditionally associated with regeneration, and a similar strategy was developed for the Smithfield–Farringdon area of London in 2007, commissioned by English Heritage and undertaken by Terry Farrell Architects. This strategy again employed the development of a master-plan to appraise existing historic context and to plot future areas of development and uses, including the further development of creative industries (such as design- and media-related employment) which had increasingly become established in the area over the previous few years.

Urban extensions and new settlements

The concept of building new communities away from or close to existing urban areas is not a new phenomenon. The very origins of the British town planning movement and profession can be traced back to 1898, when Ebenezer Howard first published his ideas on the 'Garden City'. Letchworth and Welwyn Garden City were constructed on this model. The New Towns Act of 1946 introduced a wave of post-war new towns to accommodate overspill housing from Britain's major conurbations. Between 1946 and 1950 a first wave of fourteen such new towns were designated in England and Wales, there was one further designation between 1951 and 1961, and then in a second wave an additional fourteen between 1961 and 1970. The final designations in the late 1960s included Milton Keynes (1967), Warrington (1968) and Central Lancashire (Leyland) in 1970. The post-war new town policy was combined with a planned expansion of existing country towns around London during the 1950s and 1960s. Such a development model was grounded in the idea of a strong state or national government role in facilitating the project. Principally, a key public sector vesting body would be established to acquire land, grant the necessary consents for development and then dispose of it. Social, community and other infrastructure (including roads) would be funded by the vesting body (usually called a development corporation), who would capture a proportion of the considerable uplift in value achieved by taking land at agricultural value and selling it at residential and commercial value. In Milton Keynes, often viewed (inaccurately) as the last post-war new town, this uplift funded some of the finest landscaping and parkland ever created in any new urban environment. When the Milton Keynes Development Corporation was wound up in 1992, following completion of a twenty-five-year project timescale, such immensely important social and environmental assets were transferred to the Milton Keynes Parks Trust, with the creation of an endowment sufficient to fund future maintenance and management, in perpetuity.

By the mid-1980s a new model was to emerge, with a general retreat from the creation of development corporations (created by national government) to a more incremental approach in which major housebuilders promoted their own new towns, albeit on a much smaller scale than the numbers delivered in the post-war new towns. In 1985 a group of major house builders[4] formed Consortium Developments Limited (CDL) to submit planning applications for private sector sponsored new communities or new settlements on several sites. The idea was seen by its promoters as preferable to the town extensions or infilling of existing settlements. This approach permitted a fresh start, with a planned integration of residential, industry/employment, retail and educational uses. New settlements would accommodate housing growth and reduce the pressure for new housing, which had been directed to town cramming within existing urban areas. The concept was in size many ways closer to the Garden City ideas of Ebenezer Howard than the post-war new towns, because it was sponsored by the private and not the public sector. The proposed size of settlement would be much smaller than Howard's population of 30,000 in each Garden City or 250,000 in the polycentric social city. CDL proposed a population of around 10,000 in each new settlement. The idea received favourable, if qualified support, among the planning community, notably the Town and Country Planning Association, an organization itself founded by Ebenezer Howard.[5] This support expressed a desire that such new settlements must be used to provide a form of balanced development in a good environment, taking pressure away from existing towns and villages and protecting existing countryside. Sites should be carefully chosen to be away from high-grade land while being integrated with existing transport infrastructure (Hall 1989).

The three most prominent examples were at Tillingham Hall, Essex (5000 homes and refused planning permission and dismissed on appeal 1988), Stone Bassett, Oxford (6000 homes and refused planning permission and dismissed on appeal, 1990) and Foxley Wood, Hampshire (4800 homes and refused planning permission and dismissed on appeal in 1989). In both Foxley Wood and Stone Bassett, the appointed government inspectors who dismissed the appeals, acknowledged the harm caused to the character of existing urban areas by past policies of peripheral expansion and infilling. However, these were considered against and outweighed by ecological and environmental harm caused by such large-scale development proposals. The planning system appeared unready to accept major new development within the open countryside, in an attempt to address the growing need for housing as a consequence of population change and social need.

At the Foxley Wood inquiry, Hart District Council, the local planning authority made submissions to the effect that ad hoc appeals do not provide the best process within which to deal with issues of such strategic importance. Government planning policy has in the past and continues today to support such a stance. The promotion of such major growth is now a matter for both regional and local planning policy. Yet, during this period a number of notable successes were floated by means of the adoption of new planning policy to accommodate new communities at Chafford Hundred, Grays (Essex), New Ash Green (Kent), Chelmer Village, Chelmsford (Essex), Church Langley, Chelmsford (Essex), Great Notley Garden Village, Braintree (Essex), Dickens Heath, Solihull (West Midlands) and Peterborough Southern Township (Cambridgeshire).

The new PPS3 of 2006 promoted the concept of the urban extension and new settlement in appropriate locations and broke the previously established policy prerequisite that an urban extension would only be allowed in the event that all other options had been exhausted. The new 2006 incarnation of PPS3 threw out a previously established and informal policy test in which all urban land would need to be exhausted of opportunity before any extensions or other outward growth could be countenanced.

The policy pedigree of the sustainable urban extension is really traced to a report published by the Prince's Foundation in 2000 and entitled 'Sustainable Urban Extensions: Planned through Design'. This document promoted both the policy value behind such a planned approach and, importantly, an alternative model of community involvement. The Foundation's own stated mission was to promote a return of human values to architecture, urban design and regeneration. The report took a critical view of much in the design of past residential environments, railing against the piecemeal low-density outward expansion of towns and cities. Private sector housing estates offer little choice of house type and predominate in creating 'placeless' low-density suburbs. As previously dealt with in this chapter, the need to break the mantra of 'roads first and houses later' was strongly endorsed. This involved residential layouts in which highway radii and driver-visibility issues dominated urban design considerations. The report argued that a consensus was emerging amongst planners and the public that much greater priority needed to be given to urban design, environmental sustainability and public involvement in decision-making. The idea of developing major greenfield housing allocations with greater public engagement was pioneered in two English pilot studies at Basildon and the south western expansion of Northampton (both during 1999). Two urban extensions into greenfield sites were redesigned from a traditional low-density volume housebuilder model to create significantly greater housing yields and more sustainable layouts. In Basildon a 35 ha site would yield 1120 homes (preserving 7 ha open space) at forty dwellings per hectare, compared to 875 units of traditional low-density detached equivalent. In Northampton 6400 dwellings were devised for a site of some 250 hectares, compared to 3700 by the traditional method. This 70 per cent increase in units was achieved not by compromising the amenities enjoyed by future occupiers but by the very reverse in which a quality urban design (based on urban and not suburban principles) allowed for increased residential density with integration into public space and transport. Such an 'Enquiry by Design' approach creates, it is argued, more sustainable environments. It is unsurprising, therefore, that such an approach should be strongly endorsed by the Urban Task Force when the direction of government policy (in PPS3) accepts that urban extension will occur in the future. Taking this on board, such an approach will need to be brought to bear on the future development of the many green fields that will need to be ploughed up for housing by 2026 in pursuit of the government's Sustainable Communities Plan.

Conclusions

The planning and delivery of urban extensions/new settlements and urban villages should not be viewed as mutually exclusive development options. It is conceivable that a new settlement could be developed on the principles of an urban village as originally promoted by the Urban Villages Forum and now by the Prince's Foundation. Both initiatives have predecessors in planning history, notably the works of Ebenezer Howard and the Garden City movement. The problem of housing demand exceeding supply will clearly exacerbate the growth in house prices. The HM Treasury-commissioned review of housing supply (undertaken by Kate Barker) in 2004 considered a zero trend in house price growth to be both 'undesirable and unachievable' (HM Treasury 2004). Market volatility aside, the past thirty years witnessed average annual house price growth at 2.4% (the EU average being 1.1%) and this trend was anticipated to continue over the longer term. To tackle supply, the government would set out to raise housing targets across many English regions (in the Regional Spatial Strategies) and in some areas promote a relaxation of restraint policies (for example in the green belts around Oxford and Luton). Such policies would improve the general affordability of housing but the change would not be dramatic and notwithstanding the economic slowdown of the late 2000s the overall longer-term trend in house prices would remain on an upward path. Even with implementation of a step-change in the delivery of new housing, as called for by Kate Barker in her 2004 review of housing land supply, the best estimates predict that the gap between house prices and earnings (i.e. affordability) will be narrowed but not eliminated. All that said, the government's urgent desire to increase supply is also necessary to address demographic changes and social trends in which people seek their own housing at a younger age than their parents, while at the same time people live for longer. National planning policy concentrates the principal supply towards southern England, with a limited extra source of new homes allocated to a number of growth towns and the so called eco-towns, as drawn from a pool of fifteen candidate locations announced in spring 2008. Beyond these areas, the Housing Pathfinder provides an attempt to rebuild communities where poor urban quality and other features of deprivation have blighted communities.

A matter of fundamental importance is that new housing developments contribute to the creation of communities and not just homes. Planners and developers have become increasingly aware that new-build housing must form part of a wider mixed-use/mixed-ownership strategy to create a high-quality environment with a social and economic power that fosters a sense of place or community among its inhabitants. Changes to the Building Regulations, combined with the mandatory introduction of the Code for Sustainable Homes tackle the other great issues of energy-efficiency. Government aspirations to make all new housing zero carbon (in use) by 2016, point in the right direction. Yet, with domestic energy use responsible for about one-third of all UK carbon emissions, more needs to be achieved in respect of refurbishment and upgrade of existing stock.

The challenges for the future rest, therefore, with a combination of both low/zero carbon heating and power as well as housing layouts that make efficient use of land and create environments that people want to live in. Such challenges apply across both greenfield and brownfield land. Planning authorities are vested with responsibility for ensuring that land is used efficiently and allocated appropriately with reference to both environmental considerations and market needs. Developers are vested with responsibility to seek innovations in design and layout to deliver these low carbon solutions – and at an affordable price. Only a harmonious integration of these two responsibilities will deliver efficient and sustainable housing communities over the next twenty years.

Notes

Legal citations

The following citations are referred to in the text when citing sources of relevant case law:

AC   Appeal Cases
All ER   All England Reports
EGCS   Estates Gazette case summaries
JPL   Journal of Planning and Environment Law
P & CR   Property Planning and Compensation Reports
PLR   Planning Law Reports
WLR   Weekly Law Reports

1 Urban planning and real estate development: the context

1 Report on the Sanitary Condition of the Labouring Population of Great Britain (1842).
2 Published as *Tomorrow: A Peaceful Path to Real Reform* and re-issued in 1902 as *Garden Cities of To-morrow*.
3 Strictly, this was the first planning legislation applied nationally with the very first such legislation dealing with 'town planning' being the Hampstead Garden Suburb Planning Act, passed in 1906.
4 A concept defined further in Chapter 6 Planning gain, planning obligations and the community infrastructure levy.

2 Policy and implementation of urban planning

1 Established in May 2002 and taking responsibility for policy areas from both the former Department for Transport, Local Government and the Regions and the Cabinet Office. A new and separate Department for Transport was also created. After 2006 the Office of the Deputy Prime Minister was replaced by the Department for Communities and Local Government.
2 'Shaping the nation', editorial opinion in *Estates Gazette*, 14 November 1992.
3 For example, Woking Borough Council in 1992 published a series of targets dealing with such matters as responding to letters and dealing with pre-application advice. Many authorities now have a 'fast-track' system for the speedy delivery of decisions on more straightforward applications.
4 So that targets are separated for major commercial/industrial applications, minor commercial/industrial applications and all other applications.

5 Similar to Simplified Planning Zones of the 1980s, where specific types of development related to business use are exempt from planning permission.

6 See the section beginning the 'definition of development' in the next chapter.

7 To avoid any uncertainty regarding whether permission is required, an application
can be made for a Certificate of Lawfulness of Existing or Proposed Use or Development. See section on enforcement in the next chapter.

8 Guidelines on planning conditions can be found in DoE Circular 11/95: The use of
conditions in planning permissions, or in Scottish Office Circular 18/86 or Welsh
Office 35/95.

9 See DoE Circular 15/92, Publicity for planning applications.

10 Introduced by the Planning and Compensation Act 1991, in which responsibility for
publishing all planning applications was imposed on LPAs.

11 The LPA may impose conditions on a planning permission 'as they think fit'. Such
planning conditions will need to be related to land-use planning as well as the development being permitted. In all cases they must be reasonable. Government guidance
on the use of such conditions is contained in Department for Communities circular
advice, which states that all conditions must be necessary, relevant to planning,
relevant to 'the development', enforceable, precise and reasonable. Further guidance
on planning conditions can be found in Circular 11/95, The use of conditions in
planning permissions.

12 DoE Circular 8/93, Award of costs incurred in planning and other proceedings
(para. 9 of Annex 3) EGCS 9 and *Regina* v. *Selby District Council, ex parte Oxton
Farm* (1997), ECGS 60.

13 Section 220 of the Town and Country Planning Act 1990 and Town and Country
Planning (Control of Advertisements) Regulations 2007.

14 Section 336 of the Town and Country Planning Act 1990.

15 Ombudsman powers are found in the Local Government Act (1974: Part III).

16 Annual statistics published by the Ombudsman reveal that housing issues constitute
the largest number of complaints at 35–40 per cent, with planning second, at 20–25
per cent of all complaints.

17 In the remaining cases the Ombudsman found no maladministration had occurred,
or that there was maladministration with no injustice, or that the investigation had
been discontinued.

18 See Chapter 9, Urban renaissance and regeneration.

19 For example, officers who are members of the Royal Town Planning Institute are bound
by a code of professional conduct that requires members to 'impartially exercise their
independent professional judgement'.

20 Each council, since May 2002, must publish its own code of conduct covering the
behaviour of elected members and officers and the creation of a Standards Committee
for each authority.

21 Part III of the Local Government Act 2000.

22 Report of an Independent Inquiry into Certain Planning Related Issues in Bassetlaw
to the Bassetlaw District Council (1996).

23 Commentary on Nolan Third Report in 'Current Topics', *Journal of Planning and
Environment Law* (1997), September, p. 795.

3 Town planning law and regulation

1 Agriculture is defined by Section 336(1) of the TCPA 1990 as including horticulture,
fruit and seed growing, dairy farming, market gardening, grazing land, meadow land
and nursery land.

2 Definition provided in Section 290, Town and Country Planning (Minerals)
Regulations 1971. Also see Minerals Planning Guidance Notes (MPGs), Town and

Country Planning (Minerals) Act 1981 and Schedule 14 of the Environment Act 1995.
3 *Cambridge City Council* v. *Secretary of State for the Environment and Another* (1991), JPL 428. Demolition control is described by Sir Desmond Heap (1991) as 'a ghost which haunted planning law. The time has now come for the ghost to be laid to rest' (p. 114).
4 Please refer to sections on listed buildings and conservation areas in Chapter 7.
5 For more guidance, see the Town and country planning (demolition—description of buildings) Direction 1995 and DoE Circular Guidance on planning controls over demolition.
6 *Burdle* v. *Secretary of State for the Environment* (1972), 1 WLR 1207.
7 Served under Article 4(1) of the Town and Country Planning (General Permitted Development) Order 1995.
8 Such breaches of planning control are established by Section 171A of the TCPA 1990.
9 Interest in land means a legal or equitable interest such as ownership or the grant of a tenancy or lease. A PCN may also be served on an occupier who is carrying out operations or uses such as a builder. Refer to subsections 171C and D of the TCPA 1990.
10 Served under Section 187A of the TCPA 1990.
11 Refer to subsections 191 and 192 of the TCPA 1990.
12 That is, the four-year immunity does not start to run until the operational development has been largely finished.
13 Similar powers were previously available under the Local Government Act 1972 but were introduced specifically to town planning by this section. Section 3 of the Planning and Compensation Act 1991 introduced a new section, 187B, into the TCPA 1990.

4 Planning appeals

1 See the Planning Inspectorate Annual Report and Accounts for a yearly update. This document is published towards the end of each year.
2 Refer to the judgement of David Widdicombe QC in *Pound Stretcher Ltd* v. *Secretary of State for the Environment* (1988), 3 PLR 69.
3 Sir Frank Layfield in *Barnet Meeting Room Trust* v. *Secretary of State for the Environment*, 3 PLR 21.
4 Legal reference 65 P&CR (1992) 137–147.
5 Usually contained in Statutory Instruments, e.g. the Town and Country Planning (Appeals) (Written Representations Procedure) Regulations 2000 (SI 1628), the Town and Country Planning (Hearings Procedure) (England) Rules 2000 (SI 1626), the Town and Country Planning (Inquiries Procedure) (England) Rules 2000 (SI 1624), and the Town and Country Planning Appeals (Determination by Inspectors) (Inquiries Procedure) (England) Rules 2000 (SI 1625).
6 See *Ricketts & Fletcher* v. *Secretary of State for the Environment and Salisbury District Council* (1988), JPL 768, on how the Inquiry method may be considered as a direct, effective and efficient means by which evidence can be tested.
7 Every year the Planning Inspectorate publishes its Annual report, which includes statistical analysis of appeals allowed for each appeal method. (See www.planninginspectorate. gov.uk.)
8 Town and Country Planning (Appeals) (Written Representations Procedure) Regulations 1987 (SI 701). Also see DoE Circular 11/87 Written representation procedure.
9 See Planning Inspectorate (1993a).
10 Legal reference (1998) JPL 778.

11 See Annex 2(i) and Annex 2(ii) to DETR Circular 5/00.
12 For guidance on the detailed content of proofs of evidence and statements of common ground, see (DETR) Circular 5/00 Planning Appeals: Procedures (DETR 2001e).
13 Refer to Royal Institution of Chartered Surveyors, Surveyors Acting as Expert Witnesses, Practice Statement and Guidance Notes.
14 Royal Town Planning Institute, Chartered Town Planners at Inquiries, Practice Advice Note (Number 4).
15 This legislation is applied to town planning appeals by virtue of section 320 of the Town and Country Planning Act 1990. The modern system governing such awards was established by an influential report in the 1960s, Report of the Council on Tribunals on the Award of Costs at Statutory Inquiries (1964), Cmnd 2471, 1964.
16 Section 320(2) and Schedule 6 of the TCPA 1990. Similar provisions are to be found in Section 89 of the Planning (Listed Buildings and Conservation Areas) Act 1990 and Section 37 of the Planning (Hazardous Substances) Act 1990.
17 Discussion of this threshold is contained in the judgement of Justice Auld in *R v. Secretary of State for the Environment ex parte North Norfolk District Council* (1994), 2 PLR 78.
18 The Advisory Panel on Standards for the Planning Inspectorate publish an annual report of their work. That of 2002 was the eighth such report.
19 Although the government stated that it would make the award of costs available in Written Representations, as soon as resources allow. While this reform was promised for the mid-1990s it never materialized due to the additional burden of work it would have imposed upon the Planning Inspectorate.
20 *Estates Gazette*, editorial, 2 July 1994, p. 43.
21 *Financial Times*, 18 December 2000.

5 The future for dispute resolution in planning

1 Paper published as C. Shepley (1997) Mediation in the Planning System, *Planning Inspectorate Journal*, Spring, no. 7, pp. 9–15.
2 This flyer stated that in a mediation, 'A solution . . . is produced by the parties themselves with the help of the mediator'. It established that mediation is 'confidential, voluntary' and that the mediator is a neutral party 'who helps the parties find an acceptable solution'.
3 Government planning policy guidance (PPG2) accepts the principle of replacement dwellings in green belt locations where the new dwelling is comparable in size and site coverage to the one that it is replacing.
4 DETR news release 385/30 May 2000.
5 Mediations were employed in the Examination in Public of the East Midlands Regional Planning Guidance (2000) and Barnet Unitary Development Plan (2001–02).
6 Providing such a challenge was deemed admissible by the European Commission in Strasbourg.
7 See *Human Rights Act 1998: Home Office Core Guidance for Public Authorities: A New Era of Rights and Responsibilities*, London: Home Office.
8 Article 1 of the UN Economic Commission for Europe Convention on Access to Information, Public Participation in Decision Making and Access to Justice on Environmental Matters, agreed at Aarhus, Denmark, June 1998.
9 Public Authority as defined by Section 6 of HRA covers (in planning) Government Minister and Department (e.g. DETR), Local Authorities (e.g. LPAs), Courts, Tribunals (e.g. Public Inquiry) and any organization that carries out some function of a public nature (e.g. Planning Inspectorate, National Rivers Authority, English Heritage).

10 Challenge is made in High Court by way of judicial review of public law (which includes planning) and by civil action.
11 Section 174(f) of Town and Country Planning Act 1990.
12 For details of such an approach refer to *Sparkes* v. *SETR* in *Journal of Planning and Environment Law* (2000), pp. 1090–91 and see Purchas and Clayton (2001), p. 137.
13 Referred to as the 'Alconbury' case. Legal reference (2001) 1 PLR 58 and see *The Times*, 24 January 2001.

6 Planning gain and planning obligations

1 Planning gain, community gain, community benefit, planning advantage, planning requirements, planning obligations, planning agreements, developer's contribution, legal arrangements, improvements and additional facilities, community impacts, environmental impacts.
2 Housing, Town Planning Etc. Act 1909 followed by Section 34 of the TCPA 1932.
3 Advisory group composed of property professionals, independent of government.
4 Although a little confusing, the 1991 Act amended the 1990 Act. Therefore, the reforms came into force in 1991 on the basis of a statute of 1990.
5 By injunction against failure to comply.
6 Provides power to do anything that will facilitate the discharge of their functions.
7 See Department for Communities Circular 11/95, The use of conditions in planning permission.
8 Introduced by Section 12 of the Planning and Compensation Act 1991.
9 Section 106A and 106B of 1990 Act.
10 Relying on a separate research report commissioned by the Task Force, see Punter (1999).
11 (1988) AC 578.
12 (1993) EGCS 113.
13 (1995) 1 WLR 759, (1995) AUER 636.
14 The practice of impact fees in the United States, unpublished paper presented to Royal Institution of Chartered Surveyors Conference 'Impact Fees: Could They Work Here?', March 1999.

7 Specialist town planning controls

1 A fourth grade of 'local interest' identified by the LPA but not the Secretary of State is now obsolete and carries no statutory significance.
2 The six are The Ancient Monuments Society, The Council for British Archaeology, The Georgian Group, The Victorian Society, The Society for the Protection of Ancient Buildings, and The Royal Commission on Historical Monuments (England).
3 Such an appeal may be lodged on the grounds that the building is not of special interest and should be removed from the list. In deciding upon such an appeal, the Secretary of State or Inspector may find that it should remain on or be removed from the list.
4 Served under Section 38 of the Planning (Listed Buildings and Conservation Areas) Act 1990.
5 For a discussion of the merits of such post-war listing, see English Heritage (1992b).
6 This is the dictionary definition. The relevant Act provides no definition of 'special' in the context of Conservation Areas.
7 Section 72 of the Planning (Listed Building and Conservation Areas) Act 1990. In Scotland reference should be made to the Town and Country Planning (Scotland) Act 1972.

 8 (1992) 1 All ER 573 and (1992) 2 WLR 204.
 9 (1989) JPL 259.
10 By Town and Country Amenities Act 1974.
11 PPG15, Planning and the historic environment (1994: para. 4.27).
12 From 30 March 1994, LPAs were given additional powers to withdraw selective permitted development rights without the need for an Article 4 Direction. No authority would be required from the Secretary of State. These 'selective' works would include insertion of new doors, windows and roofing materials.
13 Section 211 of the TCPA 1990. Also refer to DoE Circular 36/78.
14 PPG2, Green belts (issued 1995 and revised 2000). In Scotland similar guidance can be found in Scottish Office Circular 24/85, Development in the countryside and green belts.
15 Surveys of derelict land in England, Wales and Scotland.
16 Extract from PPG2, Green belts (1995: para. 2.10).
17 The Cambridge Green Belt makes for an interesting study in itself, as the local planning authority themselves countenanced an enlargement of the city by sustainable urban extensions within the proximity of the inner green belt boundary. Such 'erosion' of the inner boundary coupled with extension of the outer boundary is arguably a more sustainable option than 'leapfrog' development. This illustrates the tensions between green belts and sustainable development (Cambridge City Council 1999).
18 See PPG7, The Countryside: Environmental Quality and Economic and Social Development (para. 4.2) and para. 61 of Part III, Environment Act 1995.
19 Under powers in Section 28 of the Wildlife and Countryside Act 1981.
20 Designation under provision within the Wildlife Countryside Act 1981.
21 Under Section 1 of the Ancient Monuments and Archaeological Areas Act 1979.
22 Those bodies comprising English Nature, East Midlands Biodiversity Forum, RSPB, The Countryside Agency, English Heritage, The National Trust, Bedfordshire County Council, Environment Agency, Luton Borough Council and The Chilterns (AONB) Conservation Board.
23 Milton Keynes and South Midlands Sub-Regional Strategy (2005). Nottingham, Government Office for the East Midlands.

8 Sustainable development

 1 By the UK Climate Change Impacts Review Group.
 2 Referred to as the 'Earth Summit'.
 3 The Earth Summit: Press Summary on Agenda 21. United Nations Conference on Environment and Development, Rio de Janeiro, 3–14 June 1992.
 4 *Sustainable Development – The UK Strategy* 1994 (Cmnd 2426) London: HMSO.
 5 *Climate Change: The UK Programme* 1994 (Cmnd 2424) London: HMSO.
 6 *Biodiversity: The UK Action Plan* 1994 (Cmnd 2428) London: HMSO.
 7 *Sustainable Forestry: The UK Programme* 1994 (Cmnd 2429) London: HMSO.
 8 Agenda 21 strategies comprise local action plans for sustainable development, prepared with the broad involvement of the local community.
 9 In part by reducing VAT for listed buildings that are places of worship.
10 Via tax relief for the costs of converting redundant space over shops into residential accommodation.
11 Via reducing the level of VAT charged on conversion and renovation of residential property.
12 In 1988 Department of Environment statistics estimated that some 60,000 ha of vacant or derelict land existed in England, Scotland and Wales. Other estimates by environmental campaigners have been far higher. Stephen Joseph puts the figure at 110,000 ha for England and Wales (Joseph 1987).

13 For more details on this debate refer to DoE (1994c) ch. 11, and to Urban Task Force findings (DETR 1999a), Part Three.

14 A political agreement on the 1998 Kyoto Protocol was eventually reached in Bonn in July 2001. A total of 180 countries agreed both to cut various emissions and to provide funds to developing countries for climate change related activities.

15 Other ozone-depleting chemicals include carbon tetrachloride 1.1.1, hydrobromo-fluorocarbons (HBFCs) and hydrochlorofluorocarbons (HCFCs).

16 Montreal Protocol on substances that deplete the ozone layer, held in 1987.

17 Extract of a speech by the Secretary of State for the Environment, John Gummer, to the Town and Country Planning Association, January 1994.

18 The government published fifteen 'headline' indicators by which objectives of sustainable development could be measured. The government department vested with responsibility for their appraisal (DEFRA) publishes an annual report every Spring, with appraisal of delivery measured against each target.

19 More detailed consideration of the impact of parking on urban design is considered in Chapter 9.

20 See *Gateshead District Council* v. *Secretary of State for the Environment and Northumbrian Water* (1994), JPL B8.

21 Refer to PPG23, 1994, Planning and pollution control and the comments of Lord Justice Glidewell in *Gateshead MBC* v. *Secretary of State for the Environment and Northumbrian Water Group PLC* (1994), EGCS 92, where it was accepted that pollution was a material planning consideration.

22 *Bolton MDC* v. *Secretary of State for the Environment* (1994), JPL B37. While this decision was later overturned, these comments remain valid.

23 Section 54A of the TCPA 1990, introduced by the Planning and Compensation Act 1991and now replaced by Section 38(6) of the Planning and Compulsory Purchase Act 2004. See Chapter 2.

9 Urban renaissance and regeneration

1 Contained in Design Bulletin 32 (DoE 1992).

2 City Challenge involved the competitive bidding by cities for regeneration funding. A total of thirty-one equally funded partnerships were implemented for a five-year period.

3 The SRBs were established to allocated funding towards a mix of economic, social and physical regeneration for any period up to a maximum of seven years. By the late 1990s, 600 SRBs were established, replacing the City Challenge, which terminated in 1998. In 2001, government announced that no further funding rounds would be pursued, with future responsibility for funding such locally based employment and skills training passing to the Regional Development Agencies.

4 DETR response to House of Commons (1999–2000) Environment, Transport and Regional Affairs Select Committee Report on the Proposed Urban White Paper.

5 In other words, to avoid setting long-term housing targets to be met by councils, in favour of a more flexible system of shorter-term targets, adjusted in the light of continuous review.

6 Development plans should follow a sequence of site identification for housing, starting with reuse of previously developed land, then urban extension and finally around nodes in public transport corridors.

13 Development valuation

1 The examples used in this chapter, and some of the associated text, are taken from the chapter on development valuation by John Ratcliffe and Nigel Rapley in W.A. Rees (ed.) *Valuation: Principles into Practice*, London: Estates Gazette, 4th edn, 1993.

19 Residential development

1 Refer to the section in the 1990 Act.
2 Some outer London boroughs have designated certain inter-war suburban roads as conservation areas.
3 First used by the late Nicholas Ridley to describe forceful local opposition to the building boom of the late 1980s.
4 Barratt, Beazer, Bovis, Ideal, Laing, Lovell, McCarthy & Stone, Tarmac, Wilcon and Wimpey.
5 It was suggested by the former Director of the Town and Country Planning Association, David Hall, that about one dozen substantially new towns of 7500–100000 are required in the South East and the southwest Midlands regions of England.

Bibliography

Abel, R. 1982. The Contradictions of Informal Justice. In R. Abel (ed.) *The Politics of Informal Justice*. New York: Academic Press.

Academy for Sustainable Communities 2007. The Academy for Sustainable Communities Business Plan. Leeds: ASC.

Acland, A. 1990. *A Sudden Outbreak of Common Sense*. London: Hutchinson Business Books.

—— 1995a. Mediation Goes Green. *Family Mediation* 5(3), 11–12.

—— 1995b. Simple Negotiations. *Legal Action*, November, 8–9.

—— 1995c. *Resolving Disputes Without Going to Court*. London: Century Business Books.

Acton, J. 1998. Planning Gain Risks our Reputations, *Planning*, 9 January, 11.

Adams, C.D., L. Russell and C.S. Taylor-Russell 1993. Development Constraints: Market Processes and the Supply of Industrial Land. *Journal of Property Research* 19(1), 49–61.

ADR Group 1993. *Making the Most of Mediation*. Bristol: ADR Group.

AIREA 1979. *What to Look for in an Appraisal*. Chicago: American Institute of Real Estate Appraisers.

Anderson, F. 1985. Structural Engineering. In P. Marber and P. Marber (eds) *Office Development*, 177–203. London: Estates Gazette.

Anderson, J. and D. Shiers 2008. *The Green Guide to Specification*. Oxford: Blackwell.

Armon-Jones, C. 1984. Revealing the Art of Estate Agency. *Estates Times* (March).

Ashworth, W. 1954. *The Genesis of Modern British Town Planning*. London: Routledge.

Association of Metropolitan Authorities 1990. *Costs Awards at Planning Appeals*. London: Association of Metropolitan Authorities.

Astor, H. and C. Chinkin 1992. *Dispute Resolution in Australia*. Sydney: Butterworths.

Atkinson, R. and G. Moon 1994. *Urban Policy in Britain*. London: Macmillan.

Audit Commission 1992. *Building in Quality: A Study of Development Control*. London: HMSO.

—— 1999. *Local Authority Performance Indicators in England*. London: Audit Commission.

Auerbach, J. 1983. *Justice Without Law*. Oxford: Oxford University Press.

Avis, M., V. Gibson and J. Watts 1989. *Managing Operational Property Assets*. Department of Land Management and Development, University of Reading.

Bailey, N., with A. Barker and K. MacDonald 1995. *Partnership Agencies in British Urban Policy*. London: UCL Press.

Baldry, C. and D. Pitt 1993. Building for the New Organisation. In K. Alexander (ed.) *Facilities Management 1993*, 78–91. London: Haston Hilton.

Bannock, G. & Partners 1994. *Property in the Boardroom – A New Perspective*. London: Hillier-Parker.

Barnard, L. 1993. The Concept of Sustainable Development and its Impact on the Planning Process. *Property Review* 2(9), 394–7.

Barret, P. and D. Baldry 2003. *Facilities Management: Towards Best Practice*, 2nd edn. London: Blackwell.

Barrett, V. and J. Blair 1982. *How to Conduct and Analyze Real Estate Market and Feasibility Studies*. New York: Van Nostrand Reinhold.

Barton, H., M. Grant and G. Guise 2003. *Shaping Neighbourhoods: A Guide for Health, Sustainability and Vitality*. London: Spon Press.

Battle, T. (ed.) 2003. *The Commercial Office Handbook*. London: RIBA Enterprises.

Baum, A. 2001. *Freeman's Guide to Property Finance*. London: Freeman Publishing.

Baum, A. and D. Mackmin 1989. *The Income Approach to Property Valuation*, 3rd edn. London: Routledge.

Beckwith, D. 1987. ADR in Australia. *Arbitration* 53(3), 213–14.

Benjamin, A. 2007. Beyond the Grave. *Guardian* special supplement, 21 March 2007, 1.

Bentley, I., S. McGlynn, G. Smith and A. Alcock 1985. *Responsive Environments – A Manual for Designers*. Oxford: Architectural Press.

Berkley, R. 1991. Raising Commercial Property Finance in a Difficult Market. *Journal of Property Finance* 1(4), 523–9.

—— 1992. Funding Review. *Journal of Property Finance* 2(4), 517–19.

Bernard Thorpe and Oxford Institute of Retail Management 1990. *Who Runs Britain's High Streets?* London: Bernard Thorpe (chartered surveyors).

BERR (Department for Business Enterprise and Regulatory Reform) 2007. Draft Strategy for Sustainable Construction A consultation paper. London: BERR.

Bevan, A. 1992. *Alternative Dispute Resolution: A Lawyer's Guide to Mediation and Other Forms of Dispute Resolution*. London: Sweet & Maxwell.

—— 2000. Mediation: Lifting the Veil – the Concepts of Privilege and 'Without Prejudice' in Mediation. *Solicitors' Journal*, 948.

Biddulph, M., A. Hooper and J. Punter 2006. Awards, Patronage and Design Preference: An Analysis of English Awards for Housing Design. *Urban Design International* 11(1).

BIFM 2008. Facilities Management Introduction (http://www.bifm.org.uk/bifm/about/facilities, accessed 25 March 2008).

Blackhall, J.C. 1990. *The Award of Costs at Public Inquiries*. Newcastle: Nuffield Foundation and University of Newcastle upon Tyne.

—— 1993. *The Performance of Simplified Planning Zones*. Working Paper 30, Department of Town and Country Planning, University of Newcastle upon Tyne.

Blackie, N. 2004. The Significant Part of a Listed Building. *Journal of Planning and Environment Law*, 268–72.

Blake, J. 1995. Energy Policies and Planning. Paper presented at the Town and Country Planning Association Annual Conference, London, April.

Blowers, A. 1993. Planning for a Sustainable Environment: A Report by the Town and Country Planning Association. London: Earthscan.

Bourne, F. 1992. *Enforcement of Planning Control*, 2nd edn. London: Sweet & Maxwell.

Box, J. and C. Harrison 1994. Natural Spaces in Urban Places: Minimum Targets for Accessible Natural Green Space in Urban Areas, *Nature's Place* 5, 14–16.

Boys, K. 1983. Bridging the Communication Gap. *Chartered Surveyor Weekly*, 15 September.

Bramson, D. 1992. Joint Ventures and Partnership Funds Today: The Art and Practice of Financing Property. Paper presented at Henry Stewart Conference, London.

Brindley, T., Y. Rydin and G. Stoker 1989. *Remaking Planning*. London: Unwin Hyman.

Briner, R. 1997. The Role of Lawyers in ADR. In J. Ross-Harper (ed.) *Global Law in Practice*. The Hague: Kluwer Law International.

British Council for Offices 2003. *Social Engagement – Profiting from the Community*. London: BCO.

—— 2005. *BCO Guide: Best Practice in the Specification for Offices*. London: British Council for Offices.

British Council for Shopping Centres 2006. *Future of Retail Property Report 6 – In Town or Out of Town?* London: BCSC.

—— 2007a. *Future of Retail Property Report 10 – Shopping Places for People*. London: BCSC.

—— 2007b. *Future of Retail Property Report 9 – Future Shopping Places*. London: BCSC.

British Government Panel 2000. *Sixth Report of Panel on Sustainable Development to the Prime Minister*. London: DETR.

Brown, C. 1990. Retail Property: Development in the 1990s. *Estates Gazette* (9004), 20–4.

Brown, H. and A. Marriot 1993. *ADR Principles and Practice*. London: Sweet & Maxwell.

Brown, T. 2008. The Compact City (Sustainable Urban Form). *Planning in London* 66, July/September.

Brownhill, D. and S. Rao 2002. A Sustainability Checklist for Developments – BR436: A Common Framework for Developers and Local Authorities. Watford: Building Research Establishment.

Brownhill, S. 1990. *Developing London's Docklands: Another Great Planning Disaster?* London: Paul Chapman.

Bruton, M.J. and D.J. Nicholson 1987. *Local Planning in Practice*. London: Hutchinson.

Building Research Establishment and Cyril Sweett 2005. *Putting a Price on Sustainability*. Watford: BRE.

Bullock, H. 1993. *Commercial Viability in Planning*. Occasional Paper 21, *Journal of Planning and Environment Law*.

Burgess, J., C. Harrison and M. Limb 1998. People, Parks and the Urban Green: A Study of Popular Meaning and Value for Open Spaces in the City. *Urban Studies* 25(6), 455–73.

Burgess, K. 1982. Long-term Mortgages are Back in Favour. *Chartered Surveyor Weekly*, 9 December.

Burns, A. 1992. A Break from Tradition Helps Settle Disputes. *Chartered Surveyor Weekly* 41(3), 54.

Burton, J. 1988. *Conflict Resolution and Prevention*. London: Macmillan.

Butler, J. 1982. Making the Most of your Marketing. *Estates Times Review*, October.

Butt, R. 2006. Last Chance for Betterment Taxation? (Planning Gain supplement). *Town and Country Planning* 75(1), 20–2.

—— 2007. Steady Progress, Must Try Harder (Planning Gain supplement). *Town and Country Planning* 76(1), 22–3.

Byrne, S. 1989. *Planning Gain: An Overview – A Discussion Paper*. London: Royal Town Planning Institute.

CABE (Commission for Architecture and the Built Environment) 2001. *By Design: Better Places to Live: A Companion Guide to PPG3*. London: Thomas Telford.

—— 2004a. *CABE and the Historic Environment*. London: CABE.

—— 2004b. *The Councillor's Guide to Urban Design*. London: CABE.

—— 2005a. *Design Coding: Testing its use in England*. London: CABE

—— 2005b. *The Use of Urban Design Codes: Building Sustainable Communities*. London: CABE.

—— 2006. *Building for Life*. Corporate Strategy. London: CABE.

—— 2008. *Annual Report 2007/08*. London: The Stationery Office.

CABE and DCLG 2006. *Preparing Design Codes: A Practice Manual*. London: RIBA Publishing.

CABE, University College London and DETR 2001. *The Value of Urban Design: A Research Project Commissioned by CABE and DETR to Examine the Value Added by Good Urban Design*. London: Thomas Telford.

Cadman, D. and L. Austin Crowe 1983. *Property Development*, 2nd edn. London: Spon.

Cadman, D. and R. Topping 1995. *Property Development*, 4th edn. London: Spon.

CALUS 1974. The Property Development Process. *The Future of the Office Market*. Derby: College of Estate Management.

Cambridge City Council 1999. *Cambridge Green Belt: Towards 2016*. Cambridge: Cambridge City Council.

Campaign to Protect Rural England 2007. *Green Belts Shrink despite Prescott Pledge*. London: CPRE Press release 5 February 2007.

Campbell, H. 2001. *Planning Obligations and the Mediation of Mediation*. London: RICS.

Carmona, M. 2003. *Public Places, Urban Spaces: The Dimensions of Urban Design*. Oxford: Architectural Press.

Carmona, M. and J. Dann 2007. Design Codes in England – Where to Now? *Urban Design* 101.

Carnwath Report 1989. *Enforcing Planning Control*. London: HMSO.

Carter, H. 2008. North-east to Pioneer Building of Eco-friendly Warehouses. *Guardian*, 14 January 200. http://www.guardian.co.uk/environment/2008/jan/14/carbonemissions.renewableenergy, accessed 1 April 2008.

Case, J. 1985. Building Services. In *Office Development*, P. Marber and P. Marber (eds), 283–315. London: Estates Gazette.

CB Hillier Parker 2000. *The Sequential Approach to Retail Development: Report on a National Research Project for the National Retail Planning Forum, British Council of Shopping Centres, Department of the Environment, Transport and the Regions*. London: CB Hillier Parker.

CBI/RICS 1992. *Shaping the Nation: Report of Planning Task Force*. London: Royal Institution of Chartered Surveyors.

CEC 1990. *Green Paper on the Urban Environment*. London: HMSO.

CEC Directorate General for Environment, Nuclear Safety and Civil Protection 1992a. *A Community Programme of Policy and Action in Relation to the Environment and Sustainable Development*, Vol. II: *Towards Sustainability*. Brussels: Commission.

—— 1992b. *The Impact of Transport on Environment – a Community Strategy for Sustainable Mobility*. Brussels: Commission.

CEC Directorate General for Regional Policy 1991. *Europe 2000: Outlook for the Development of the Community's Territory*. Luxembourg: Office for Official Publications of the European Communities.

Centre for Dispute Resolution 1977. *Mediator Training Course Handbook*, London: CEDR.

Chapman, H. 1995. Tomorrow and Beyond: Office Occupiers. *Property Review* 5(2), 34–6.

Charlesworth-Jones, S. 1983. Promoting the Corporate Image. *Estates Gazette* 265, 942–4.

Cheshire, P. 1993. Why NIMBYism has gone BANANAs. *Estates Gazette* (9321), 104–5.

Choreneki, G. 1997. Mediating Commercial Disputes. In *Rethinking Disputes: The Mediation Alternative*, J. MacFarlane (ed.). London: Cavendish.

CIoB 1992. *The Code of Practice for Project Management for Construction and Development*. Ascot: Chartered Institute of Building.

Clark, R. 1991. Refinancing. *Journal of Property Finance* 1(3), 435–9.

Cleavely, E. 1984. The Marketing of Industrial and Commercial Property. *Estates Gazette* 217, 1172.

Clifford, C. 1994. *The Retail Development Process*. London: Routledge.

Cohen, R., P. Ruyssevelt, M. Standeven, W. Bordass and A. Leaman 1998. Building Intelligence in Use: Lessons from the Probe Project, a paper presented at the 'BRE Intelligent Buildings: Realising the Benefits' conference, Watford, October. Watford: Building Research Establishment.

Cole, H. 1993. The Irresistible Rise of the Superstore. *Estates Gazette* (9301), 73.

Collens, G. 1980. Planning for Shopping, *Landscape Design*, March.

Commission for Local Administration in England 1994. *Annual Report for the Local Government Ombudsman 1993–94*. London: The Commissioner.

Committee on Standards in Public Life 1995. *Standards of Conduct in Parliament, the Executive and Non-departmental Public Bodies*. London: HMSO.

—— 1997. *Standards of Conduct in Local Government in England, Scotland and Wales. Vol I: Report*. London: HMSO.

—— 1997. *Standards of Conduct in Local Government in England, Scotland and Wales Third Report*. *London*: HMSO.

Council for National Parks 1997. *National Parks for Life: An Agenda for Action*. London: Council for National Parks.

—— 2007. Focus on Thames Gateway 2: 10 Key statistics highlighting environmental, social and economic performance in the Thames Gateway Growth Area. Second report. London: CPRE London Branch.

Countryside Commission 1991. *Green Capital: Planning for London's Green Space*. Cheltenham: Countryside Commission.

Countryside Recreation Network 2005. A Countryside for Health and Wellbeing: The Physical and Mental Health Benefits of Green Exercise. Sheffield: Countryside Recreation Network/Sheffield Hallam University.

Coupland, A. 1992. Docklands: Dream or Disaster? in A. Thornley (ed.) The Crisis of London, 149–62. London: Routledge.

—— (ed.) 1997. Reclaiming the City – Mixed Use Development. London: E. & F.N. Spon.

Court, Y. and Z. Southwell 1994. Town Centre Management: Are the Initiatives Effective? *Estates Gazette* (9436), 138–9.

CPRE (Campaign for the Protection of Rural England) 1992. *Where Motor Car is Master*. London: CPRE.

—— 1994. *Green Belts – A Response by the CPRE to the Department of the Environment's Draft Revised Planning Policy Guidance Note 2*. London: CPRE.

—— 2006. Protected Landscapes Threatened as Never Before. CPRE News Release, number 2006/48. London: CPRE.

Credit Action (2008) Total UK Personal Debt. http://www.creditaction.org.uk/feb.html, accessed 2 April 2008.

Crow, S. 1997. Planning Gain: A Time for Change. *Planning*, 31 October, 10.

Cullen, G. 1961. *Townscape*. London: Architectural Press.

Curle, A. 1990. *Tools for Transformation*. Stroud: Hawthorn Press.

Damesick, P. 1994. The Major Provincial Office Centres: Offices Opportunities, Values and Trends. Paper presented at 'Offices' (Henry Stewart Conference, London).

—— 2003. A Growth Platform on Shifting Sands. *Estates Gazette*, 15 February.

Dana, D. 1990. *Talk it Out*. London: Kogan Page.

Davies, H.W.E. and D. Edwards 1989. *Planning Control in Western Europe*. London: HMSO.

Davies, H.W.E., J.A. Gosling and M.T. Hsia 1993. *The Impact of the European Community on Land-use Planning in the United Kingdom*. London: Royal Town Planning Institute.

Davis Langdon 2005. City of London Offices, Part L – Cost Model. *Building*, August, Issue 31.

Dawson, M. 2002. Countryside Change: A View from the Frontline. *Landscape Design* 312, 210–24.

DCLG (Department for Communities and Local Government) 2005. Circular 05/05 Planning Obligations. London: DCLG.

—— 2006a. *Planning for Mixed Communities: A Consultation Paper*. London: DCLG.

—— 2006b. *Planning Policy Statement: Planning and Climate Change* – Supplement to PPS1. London: DCLG.

—— 2006c. *Planning Policy Statement 3: Housing*. London: DCLG.

—— 2006d. *Planning for the Protection of European Sites: Appropriate Assessment under the Conservation (Natural Habitats) (Amendment) England and Wales Regulations*. London: DCLG.

—— 2006e. *Valuing Planning Obligations in England: Final Report*. Research report by University of Sheffield and Halcrow. London: DCLG.

—— 2006f. *Green Space and Public Space Research: Mapping Exercise, Full Report*. London: DCLG/Edinburgh College of Art.

—— 2007a. *Autumn Performance Report*. London: DCLG.

—— 2007b. *Building Regulations: Energy Efficiency Requirements for New Dwellings: A Forward Look at what Standards May Be in 2010 and 2013*. London: DCLG.

—— 2007c. Code for Sustainable Homes Technical Guide, September, Wetherby: DCLG.

—— 2007d. Housing Green Paper: Homes for the Future – More Affordable, More Sustainable. London: DCLG.

—— 2007e. *Land Use Change in England: Residential Development in 2005*. London: DCLG.

—— 2007f. *Revisions to Principles of Selection for Listed Buildings*. London DCLG and DCMS.

—— 2007g. *Thames Gateway: Interim Plan Development Prospectus*. Wetherby: DCLG.

—— 2007h. *Improving the Appeal Process in the Planning System: Government Responses to Consultation*. London: DCLG.

—— 2008a. *The Community Infrastructure Levy*. London: DCLG.

—— 2008b. *Live Tables on Commercial and Industrial Floorspace and Rateable Value Statistics 2007*. London: DCLG.

DCMS (Department for Culture, Media and Sport) 2001. *The Historic Environment – A Resource for our Future*. London: DCMS.

—— 2004. *Review of Heritage Protection: The Way Forward*. London: DCMS.

—— 2007. *Heritage Protection for the 21st Century*. London/Cardiff: DCMS and Welsh Assembly Government.

Debenham, Tewson & Chinnocks 1988. *Planning Gain: Community Benefit or Commercial Bribe?* London: Debenham, Tewson & Chinnocks.

—— 1991. *Business Parks*. London: Debenham Tewson.

Debenham Tewson Research 1990. *Development Trends*. London: Debenham Tewson.

DEFRA (Department of Environment, Food and Rural Affairs) 2003. *Local Sites: Guidance on their Identification, Selection and Management*. London: DEFRA.

—— 2003a. *The Impact of Climate Change: Implications for DEFRA*. London: DEFRA.

—— 2003b. *UK Air Emission Estimates and Climate Change*. London: DEFRA statistical news release.

—— 2005. *The UK Government Sustainable Development Strategy – Securing the Future*. London: HMSO.

—— 2006. *Sites of Special Scientific Interest: Encouraging Positive Partnerships*. London: DEFRA.

—— 2007. *Survey of Public Attitudes and Behaviours toward the Environment: 2007 Full Report*. London: DEFRA.

DEGW 1983. *Office Research on Buildings and Information Technology*. London: DEGW.

DEGW 1985. *ORBIT: Office Research on Buildings and Information Technology*. London: DEGW.

Department of National Heritage 1996. *Protecting Our Heritage – A Consultation Document on the Built Heritage of England and Wales*. London: Department of National Heritage.

Department for Transport 2006. *The Eddington Transport Study: The Case for Action*. London: HMSO.

—— 2007. *Manual for Streets*. London: DoT.

Department for Transport, DCLG and Welsh Assembly Government (2007) *Manual for Streets*. London: Thomas Telford.

Derbyshire, B. 2007. Recommendations for Living at Super Density. Design for Homes: London.

Detoy, C. and S. Rabin 1985. Office Space: Calculating the Demand. In *Readings in Market Research for Real Estate*, J. Vernor (ed.), 243–57. Chicago: American Institute of Real Estate Appraisers.

DETR (Department of Environment, Transport and Regions) 2000a. *Planning Policy Guidance Note 3*. London: DETR.

—— 2000b. *Our Towns and Cities. The Future – Delivering an Urban Renaissance* (Urban White Paper). London: DETR.

—— 2000c. *The State of English Cities*. London: DETR.

—— 2000d. *By Design – Urban Designing the Planning Process: Towards Better Practice*. London: DETR and CABE.

—— 2000e. *Mediation in the Planning System*, Michael Welbank in Association with Nick Davies and Ian Haywood. London: DETR.

—— 2000f. *Environmental Court Project – Final Report*. London: DETR.

—— 2000g. *Sustainable Development: Local Quality of Life Counts*. London: HMSO.

—— 2000h. *Housing* (PPG3). London, HMSO.

—— 2000i. *Circular 5/2000 Planning Appeals; Procedures*. London: HMSO.

—— 2001a. *Reforming Planning Obligations: A Consultation Paper*. London: DETR.

—— 2001b. *Strategic Gap and Green Wedge Policies in Structure Plans – Final Report*. London: DETR

—— 2001c. *Transport* (PPG13). London: HMSO.

—— 2001d. *Land Use Change in England Bulletin No.16*. London: DETR

—— 2001e. *Planning: Delivering Fundamental Change*. London: DETR

DETR and CABE 2000. *By Design – Urban Design in the Planning System*. London: DETR.

Development Systems Corporation 1983. *Successful Leasing and Selling of Property*. Chicago: Real Estate Education Company.

Dixon, T. 2003. Buy into Better Cities. *Estates Gazette*, 22 March 2003.

—— 2005. *The Role of UK Development Industry in Brownfield Regeneration: Stage 2 Report.* Reading: College of Estate Management.

—— 2007. *Sustainable Brownfield Regeneration: Liveable Places from Problem Spaces.* Oxford: Blackwell.

Dobry, G. 1975. Review of the Development Control System. London: HMSO.

DoE (Department of the Environment) 1988. *Town and Country Planning Assessment of Environment Effects: Regulations.* London: HMSO.

—— 1990a. *This Common Inheritance: Britain's Environmental Strategy* (Cm 1299). London: HMSO.

—— 1990b. *The Urban Programme Management Initiative: A Consultation on Proposal Changes.* London: HMSO.

—— 1991. *Circular 16/91. Planning and Compensation Act 1991. Planning Obligations.* London: HMSO.

—— 1992. *Design Bulletin 32. Residential Roads and Footpaths*, 2nd edn. London: HMSO.

—— 1992a. *The Use of Planning Agreements.* London: HMSO.

—— 1992b. *Development Plans and Regional Guidance* (PPG12). London: HMSO.

—— 1993. *Enquiry into the Planning System in North Cornwall District.* London: HMSO.

—— 1993a. *Town Centres and Retail Developments* (PPG6). London: HMSO.

—— 1993b. *Alternative Development Patterns: New Settlements.* London: HMSO.

—— 1993c. *Reducing Emissions through Planning.* London: HMSO.

—— 1994a. *Transport* (PPG13). London: HMSO.

—— 1994b. *Roads to Prosperity.* London: HMSO.

—— 1994c. *Sustainable Development – The UK Strategy.* London: HMSO.

—— 1994d. *Planning and Pollution Control* (PPG23). London: HMSO.

—— 1995. *A Guide to Better Practice* (PPG13). London: HMSO.

—— 1995. *Urbanization in England. Projections 1991–2016.* London: HMSO.

—— 1996a. *Indicators of Sustainable Development for the United Kingdom.* London: HMSO.

—— 1996b. *Household Growth. Where Shall We Live?* London: HMSO.

—— 1997. *The Use of Density in Land Use Planning. A Practice Manual.* London: HMSO.

—— 1998a. *Land Use Change Statistics.* London: HMSO.

—— 1998b. *Parking Standards in the South East.* London: HMSO.

—— 1998c. *Planning for Sustainable Development: Towards Better Practice.* London: HMSO.

—— 1998d. *Places, Streets and Movement. A Companion Guide to Design Bulletin 32: Residential Roads and Footpaths.* London: HMSO.

—— 1998e. *Planning for the Communities of the Future.* London: HMSO.

—— 1999a. *A Better Quality of Life. A Strategy for Sustainable Development for the United Kingdom.* London: HMSO.

—— 1999b. *Development Plans* (PPG12). London: HMSO.

Dower, M. 1995. What Change for the Countryside? Town and Country Planning Association Annual Conference. London, April.

DTZ Debenham Thorpe 1995. Special Report on Shopping Centre Refurbishment (June).

Duffy, F. 1991. *The Changing Workplace.* London: Architecture Design and Technology Press.

—— 1994. The Future of Work: Renaissance of the City. *Property Review* 4(1), 7–10.

Dukes, E. 1996. *Resolving Public Conflict.* Manchester: Manchester University Press.

Dyker, D.A. 1992. *Restructuring the Soviet Economy*. London: Routledge.

Eames, R. 1993. *The Enabling Council: Planning for Recovery*. London: Sweet & Maxwell.

Early, J. 1994. Urban Regeneration: A Developer's Perspective. *Property Review* 4(5), 158–60.

Edwards, M. and J. Martin 1993. Planning Notes. *Estates Gazette* (9313), 106–7.

—— 2003. Get to Grips with the Bill. *Estates Gazette*, Planning Notes, 11 January 2003.

Edwards, R. 1991. *Fit for the Future*. Cheltenham: Countryside Commission.

Egan, J. 1998. *Rethinking Construction: The Report of the Construction Task Force to the Deputy Prime Minister, on the Scope for Improving the Quality and Efficiency of UK Construction*, London: DETR.

—— 2002. *Accelerating Change: A Report by the Strategic Forum for Construction, Rethinking Construction*. London: Strategic Forum for Construction.

Eldred, G. and R. Zerbst 1985. A Critique of Real Estate Market and Investment Analysis. In J. Vernor (ed.), *Readings in Market Research for Real Estate*, 133–42. Chicago: American Institute of Real Estate Appraisers.

Elliott, D. 1996. Med:Arb – Fraught with Danger or Ripe with Opportunity? *Arbitration* 62(3), 175–83.

Elson, M. 1986. *Green Belts: Conflict Mediation in the Urban Fringe*. London: Heinemann.

—— 1990. *Negotiation for the Future: Planning Gain in the 1990s*. Gloucester: ARC.

Elson, M. and A. Ford 1994. Green Belts and Very Special Circumstances. *Journal of Planning and Environmental Law*, 594–601.

Elson, M., C. Steenberg and N. Mendham 1996. *Green Belts and Affordable Housing – Can We Have Both?* Bristol: Policy Press.

Elson, M., C. Steenberg, and L. Nichol 2000. *Strategic Gap and Green Wedge Policies in Structure Plans*. Oxford: Oxford Brookes University School of Planning.

Elson, M., S. Walker, R. MacDonald, and J. Edge 1993. *The Effectiveness of Green Belts*. London: HMSO.

Elvin, D. and J. Maurici 2001. The Alconbury Litigation: Principle and Pragmatism. *Journal of Planning and Environment Law*, August, 883–902.

English Heritage 1990. *The Conservation Areas of England*. London: English Heritage.

—— 1992a. *Buildings at Risk: A Sample Survey*. London: English Heritage.

—— 1992b. *A Change of Heart*. London: English Heritage.

—— 1995a. *Monitor Report*. London: English Heritage.

—— 1995b. *Developing Guidelines for the Management of Listed Buildings*. London: English Heritage.

—— 1995c. *English Heritage Grants for Buildings at Risk*. London: English Heritage.

—— 1998. *Conservation-led Regeneration*. London: English Heritage.

—— 1999. *The Heritage Dividend – Measuring the Results of English Heritage Regeneration*. London: English Heritage.

—— 2000. *The Power of Place: The Future of the Historic Environment*. London: English Heritage.

—— 2001. *Annual Report and Accounts*. London: English Heritage.

—— 2003. *Guidance on Tall Buildings*. London: English Heritage and CABE.

—— 2005. *Regeneration and the Historic Environment: Heritage as a Catalyst for Better Social and Economic Regeneration*. London: English Heritage.

—— 2006a. *Buildings at Risk. The Register 2006*. London: English Heritage.

—— 2006b. *Heritage Counts: The state of England's Historic Environment 2006*. London: English Heritage.

—— 2006c. *Valuing our Heritage: The Case for Future Investment in the Historic Environment*. Swindon: English Heritage.

—— 2007a. *Conservation Principles: Policies and Guidance for the Sustainable Management of the Historic Environment*. Swindon: English Heritage.

—— 2007b. *The Heritage of Historic Suburbs*. Swindon: English Heritage.

—— 2007c. *Suburbs and the Historic Environment*. Swindon: English Heritage.

English Partnerships, The Housing Corporation and Roger Evans Associates 2007. *Delivering Quality Places: Urban Design Compendium 2*. London: English Partnerships.

English Partnerships, The Housing Corporation and Urban Design Alliance 2000. *Urban Design Compendium*. London: English Partnerships.

EPI 1994. *Why Manufacturing Still Matters*. London: Employment Policy Institute.

Essex County Council 1973. *Design Guide for Residential Areas*. Chelmsford: Essex County Council.

Estates Gazette 1990. Focus on Business Parks. *Estates Gazette* (9026), 65–157.

—— 1999. Industry Slams Planning Consents. *Estates Gazette*, 1 May.

—— 2001. 'E'-briefing. *Estates Gazette*, 3 November.

—— 2002a. The Big Gamble, Focus. *Estates Gazette*, 26 October.

—— 2002b. Northern Exposure, Focus. *Estates Gazette*, 19 October.

—— 2002c. How to Improve your Aim. 29 June.

—— 2002d. Stock up the Lockup. *Estates Gazette*, 12 January.

Evans, A.W. 1988. *No Room! No Room! The Costs of the British Town and Country Planning System*. London: Institute of Economic Affairs.

Evans, D. 1997. *A History of Nature Conservation in Britain*, 2nd edn. London: Routledge.

Faludi, A. (ed.) 1973b. *A Reader in Planning Theory*. Oxford: Pergamon.

Federation of European Employers 2008. *Untangling the Myths of Working Time*. London: FEE.

Fisher, R. and W. Urry 1997. *Getting to Yes. Negotiating an Agreement without Giving In*. London: Arrow Business Books.

Flannery, T. 2005. *The Weather Makers*. London: Penguin.

—— 2006. *The Weather Makers: The History and Future Impact of Climate Change*. London: Allen Lane.

Fletcher King 1989. *Retail Warehousing*. London: Fletcher King.

—— 1990. *Business Parks*. London: Fletcher King.

Foley, D. 1960. British Town Planning: One Ideology or Three? *British Journal of Sociology* 11(2), 211–31.

Folger, J. and T. Jones (eds) 1994. *New Directions in Mediation*. London: Sage.

Forsyth, A. 2007. Does Residential Density Increase Walking and Other Physical Activity? *Urban Studies* 44(4).

Fowler, R. 1992. Environmental Dispute Resolution Techniques – What Role in Australia? *Environment and Planning Law Journal* 9, 122–6.

Franks, D. 1957. *Report on the Committee on Administrative Tribunals and Inquiries*. London: HMSO.

French, R.A. and F.E. Hamilton 1979. *The Socialist City: Spatial Structure and Urban Policy*. Chichester: John Wiley.

Fryer, D. 1994. Viewpoint – European Council of Town Planners. *Town Planning Review* 65(2), iii–iv.

Garner, J. and B. Jones 1997. *Countryside Law*, 3rd edn. Crayford, Kent: Shaw & Sons.

Genn, H. 1998. *The Central London County Court Pilot Mediation Scheme: Evaluation Report No. 5/98*. London: The Lord Chancellor's Department Research Secretariat.

Gensler 2006. *Faulty Towers: Is The British Office Sustainable?* London: Gensler.

Gerald Eve Research 1995. *Whither the High Street?* London: Gerald Eve.

Gibson, V. 1995a. Is Property on the Strategic Agenda? *Chartered Surveyor Monthly* 4(3), 34–5.

—— 1995b. Is Property on the Strategic Agenda? *Property Review* 5(1), 104–9.

Giles, G. 1978. *Marketing*, 3rd edn. Plymouth: MacDonald & Evans.

Gilman, S. 2006. Levy Creates Cash Concerns. *Planning* 29 September.

Glasson, J., R. Therivel and A. Chadwick 1994. *An Introduction to Environmental Impact Assessment*. London: UCL Press.

Government Office for London, Association of London Boroughs and London First 2008. *Connecting Councillors with Strategic Planning Applications: A Good Practice Guide for London*. London: Government Office for London.

Graaskamp, J. 1981. *Fundamentals of Real Estate Development*. Washington DC: Urban Land Institute.

Grant, M. 1989. *Permitted Development: the Use Classes Order 1987 and General Development Order 1988*. London: Sweet & Maxwell.

—— 1992. Planning Law and the British Planning System. *Town Planning Review* 63, 3–12.

—— 1993. Planning Gain: the Legal Question. *Housebuilder* 52(3), 26–7.

—— (ed.) 1995a. *Encyclopaedia of Planning Law and Practice* (6 vols). London: Sweet & Maxwell.

—— 1995b. Planning Obligations: What's Going On? *Property Review* 5(2), 50–2.

—— 2000. Human Rights and Due Process in Planning. *Journal of Planning and Environment Law*, December, 1215–25.

—— 2001. Alconbury: Human Rights or Planning? *Encyclopaedia of Planning Law and Practice*, Monthly Bulletin, May, 1–6. London: Sweet & Maxwell.

—— 2003. *Encyclopaedia of Planning Law and Practice*. London: Sweet & Maxwell.

Greater London Authority 2001. *Green Spaces Investigation Committee: Scrutiny of Green Spaces in London*. London: Greater London Assembly.

—— 2006. *Tomorrow's Suburbs: Tools for Making London more Sustainable*. London: Greater London Assembly

Gregory, T. 1989. So We've Found Another Roman Palace. *Estates Gazette* (8922), 20–2, 62–4.

Grime, K. and V. Duke 1993. A Czech on Privatisation. *Regional Studies* 27(8), 751–7.

Hall, D. 1989. The Case for New Settlements. *Town and Country Planning* 58(4), 111–14.

Hall, P. 1975. *Urban and Regional Planning*. London: David & Charles.

—— 1988. The Industrial Revolution in Reverse? *The Planner*, 74,.

—— 1992. *Urban and Regional Planning*, 3rd edn. London: Routledge.

—— 1993. Forces Shaping Urban Europe. *Urban Studies* 30(6), 883–98.

—— 1995. Planning Strategies for Our Cities and Regions. *Property Review* 5(10), 302–5.

Hammond, B. 1989. Keys to Success. *Estates Gazette* (8945), 95–9.

Harding-Roots, S. 1998. Finding Fault with Listing Process. *Planning*, 29 May.

Harris, J. 1980. *Legal Philosophies*. London: Butterworths.

Harrison, C., K. Burgess, J. Millward and G. Dame 1995. *Accessible Natural Green Space in Towns and Cities: A Review of Appropriate Size and Distance Criteria*. Peterborough: English Nature.

Harrison, J. 1997. Environmental Mediation: The Ethical and Constitutional Dimension. *Journal of Environmental Law* 9(1), 81–102.

Hart, D. 2000. The Impact of the European Convention on Human Rights on Planning and Environmental Law. *Journal of Planning and Environment Law*, February, 117–33.

Harvey, D. 1973. *Social Justice and the City*. London: Edward Arnold.

Harwood, E. 2000. *England: A Guide to Post-War Listed Buildings*. London: Ellipsis.

—— 2001. This is Tomorrow: The History of Post-War Architecture in England. In Macdonald, S. (ed.) *Preserving Post-War Heritage: The Care and Conservation of Mid-Twentieth Century Architecture*. Bath: Donhead Publishing.

Havard, T. 2002. *Contemporary Property Development*. London: RIBA Enterprises.

Hawking, H. 1992. Checkout Superstores. *Estates Gazette* (9205), 146, 170.

Hayward, R. and S. McGlynn 1993. *Making Better Places: Urban Design Now*. Oxford: Butterworth.

Healey, P. 1983. *Local Plans in British Land-use Planning*. Oxford: Pergamon Press.

—— 1991. Models of the Development Process. *Journal of Property Research* 8(3), 219–38.

Healey, P. and A. Baker 1986. *National Office Design Survey*. London: Healey and Baker.

Healey, P., P. McNamara, M. Elson and A. Doak 1988. *Land-use Planning and the Mediation of Change*. Cambridge: Cambridge University Press.

Healey, P. and R. Nabarro (eds) 1988. *Applied Property Research UK 2000: An Overview of Business Parks*. London: Applied Property Research.

Healey, P., M. Purdue and F. Ennis 1993. *Gains from Planning? Dealing with the Implementation of Planning*. York: Joseph Rowntree Foundation.

Healey, P. and R. Williams 1993. European Urban Planning Systems: Diversity and Convergence. *Urban Studies* 30 (415), 701–20.

Heap, Sir Desmond 1991. *An Outline of Planning Law*, 10th edn. London: Sweet & Maxwell.

Heilbron, H. 1994. Civil Justice on Trial. *ADR Law Journal* 2(3), 83–90.

Henney, A. 1983. *Tomorrow's Office for the 1980s*. London: Town and City Properties.

Higgins, J. 1997. Mediation: The Training Component. In *Rethinking Disputes: The Mediation Alternative*, J. MacFarlane (ed.). London: Cavendish.

HM Revenue and Customs (2006) *Paying PGS: a Planning-gain Supplement Technical Consultation*. London: HM Revenue and Customs.

HM Treasury 2004. *Barker Review of Housing Supply: Delivering Stability – Securing our Future Housing Needs*. London: HM Treasury.

—— 2006a. *Barker Review of Land Use Planning. Final Report – Recommendations*. London: HM Treasury.

—— 2006b. *Stern Review on the Economics of Climate Change*. Cambridge: Cambridge University Press.

HM Treasury, HM Revenue & Customs and Office of the Deputy Prime Minister 2005. *Planning-gain Supplement: A Consultation*. London HM Treasury.

HMSO 1983. *Streamlining the Cities: Government's Proposals for Reorganising Local Government in Greater London and Metropolitan Counties* (Cm 9063). London: HMSO.

—— 1994a. *Climate Change: The UK Programme* (Cm 2424). London: HMSO.

—— 1994b. *Sustainable Forestry: The UK Programme* (Cm 2429). London: HMSO.

—— 1994c. *Biodiversity: The UK Action Plan* (Cm 2428). London: HMSO.

—— 1994d. *Sustainable Development – The UK Strategy* (Cm 2426). London: HMSO.

Holdaway, E. and G. Smart 2001. *Landscapes at Risk? The Future for Areas of Outstanding Natural Beauty*. London: Spon Press.

Holden, R. 1986. Business Parks and Science Parks. *Estates Gazette*, 278, 684–6.

Holgate, D. and I. Gilbey 2001. Business as Usual. *Estates Gazette*, 19 May 20.

Home, R. 1989. *Planning Use Classes: A Guide to the 1987 Order*, 2nd edn. Oxford: Blackwell Scientific.

Houghton, G. and E.C. Hunter 1994. *Sustainable Cities*. London: Regional Studies Association.

Houghton, J., B. Callender and S. Varney (eds) 1992. *Climate Change*. Cambridge: Cambridge University Press.

House of Commons 1999a. *Environment, Transport and Regional Affairs Select Committee Seventeenth Report, Housing: Planning Policy Guidance Note 3*. London: London Planning Advisory Committee.

—— 1999b. *Environment, Transport and Regional Affairs Select Committee Report, Human Well-Being, Natural Landscapes and Wildlife in Urban Areas*. Final Report. London: HMSO.

—— 1999–2000. *Environment, Transport and Regional Affairs Committee. Thirteenth Report. The Planning Inspectorate and Public Inquiries, Vol. 1, Report and Proceedings of the Committee*. London: HMSO.

Housing Corporation and Countryside Agency 2006. *The Provision of Affordable and Supportive Housing in England's National Parks*. Cheltenham: Commission for Rural Communities.

Howard, M. 1989. Planning Applications, Appeals and Development Plans, *Journal of Planning and Environment Law*. Proceedings of Oxford Law Planning Conference, Occasional Papers No. 16.

HRH The Prince of Wales 1989. *A Vision of Britain*. London: Doubleday.

Hughes, J., R. Therivel and J. Riley 2007. *Appropriate Assessment of the Draft South East Plan*. Basingstoke: Scott Wilson.

Hyde, T. and P. Midmore 2006. *Valuing our Environments: Economic impact of the National Parks of Wales*. Warrington: National Trust for Places of Historic Interest and Natural Beauty.

Investment Property Databank 2005. Royal Institution of Chartered Surveyors. *The Investment Performance of List Offices*. RICS Findings in Built and Rural Environments: London.

—— 2006. *The Investment Performance of Listed Buildings*. London: IPD, English Heritage and RICS Foundation.

Isaac, D. 1996. *Property Development: Appraisal and Finance*. Basingstoke: Macmillan.

Jacobs, J. 1961. *The Death and Life of Great American Cities*. New York: Random House.

Jansen, M. 2006. An Incalculable Burden (Planning Gain Supplement). *Property Week* 71(6) 10 February.

Jansen, M. and M. Pattinson 2007. One-Way Street (Unilateral Undertakings). *Property Week*, 19 January.

Jenks, C. 1988. *The Prince, the Architects and New Wave Monarchy*. London: Academy Editions.

Jenks, M. *et al.* 1996. *The Compact City: A Sustainable Urban Form*. London: E. & F.N. Spon.

Jennings, R. 1984. *The Role of the Developer*. London: Henry Stewart.

John Lewis Partnership 2007. *A Framework for Delivering Sustainable Construction in the Retail Sector*. London: John Lewis Partnership.

Jolly, B. 1979. *Development Properties and Techniques in Residual Valuation*. Property Valuation Handbook B1. Reading: College of Estate Management.

—— 1995. Retailing in the 1990s. *Property Review* 5(5), 148–50.

Jonas, C. 1994. Property in the European Economy. *Property Review* 4(1), 11–17.

Jones, P. and D. Hillier 1999. Changing the Balance: The 'Ins' and 'Outs' of Retail Development. *Property Management* 18(2).

Jones Lang LaSalle 2000a. *Bricks and Clicks II – Sheds in the New Economy: New Distribution Networks, New Sheds?* London: Jones Lang LaSalle.

—— 2000b. *Wired for Profit*. London: Jones Lang LaSalle UK Property Research.

Jones Lang Wootton 1990. *The City Office Review 1980–89*. London: Jones Lang Wootton.

Joseph, S. 1987. *Urban Wasteland Now*. London: Civic Trust.

Jowell, J. 1977. Bargaining in Development Control. *Journal of Planning and Environment Law*, 414–33.

Kee, D. 1990. *Europe's International Retailers – Shopping Centre Horizons No. 18*. Reading: College of Estate Management.

Keeble, L. 1969. *Principles and Practice of Town and Country Planning*. London: Estates Gazette.

—— 1985. *Fighting Planning Appeals*. London: Construction Press.

Keeping, M. 2000. What about demand: Do investors want sustainable buildings?, a paper presented at the RICS Cutting Edge conference. London: RICS.

—— 2008. Taking a Stand. *Journal of the RICS Building Surveying Faculty*, January/February.

Keeping, M. and D. Shiers 2004. *Sustainable Property Development*. Oxford: Blackwell Publishing.

Keeping, M. and S. West 2008. Needed: A Decent Environmental Policy Map. *Property Forecast* 11 (3).

Kendrick, R. 1995. Finding an Alternative Way. *Legal Executive*, January.

Key, T., T. Key, E. Zarkesh, B. MacGregor and N. Nanthkumaran 1994. Understanding the Property Cycle. *Property Review* 4(2), 61–3.

King Sturge 2002. *Industrial and Distribution Floorspace Today*. London: King Sturge Research.

—— 2007. *Industrial Floorspace Today*. London: King Sturge.

Kit Campbell 2001. *Rethinking Open Space*. Edinburgh: Scottish Executive Central Research Unit.

Knight Frank (2006) *Planning Gain Supplement Audit: Final Report*. London: British Property Federation.

Knutt, E. 2001. Fortress Under Fire. *Estates Gazette*, 14 July.

Kolb, D. 1983. *The Mediators*. Cambridge, MA: MIT Press.

Land Use Consultants 2004. *Making the Links: Green Spaces and Quality of Life: Scottish Natural Heritage Commissioned Report*. Edinburgh: Scottish Natural Heritage.

—— 2006a. *Evaluation of Local Nature Reserves*. Perth: Scottish Natural Heritage.

—— 2006b. *Thames Basins Heaths SPA: Audit and Assessment of Land to Mitigate Effects of Housing Development*. Guildford: SEERA.

Latham, M. 1994. *Constructing the Team: Final Report of the Government/Industry Review of Procurement and Contractual Arrangements in the UK Construction Industry*. London: The Stationery Office.

Lawless, P. 1989. *Britain's Inner Cities*. London: Paul Chapman.

Lawson, D. 2003. All the Fun of the Shopping Centre, *Estates Gazette*, 1 March.

Layfield, F. 1993. *A Retrospect: Planning Inquiries*. Occasional Paper 20, Journal of Planning and Environment Law.

Leahy, Sir T. 2007. Tesco, Carbon and the Consumer, speech at the Tesco, Carbon and the Consumer launch event 18 January. London: Tesco. (http://www.tesco.com/climatechange/speech.asp).

Lichfield, N. 1989. From Planning Gain to Community Benefit. *Journal of Planning and Environment Law*, 68–81.

—— 1995. Economics of Urban Villages. *Property Review* 5(2), 42–5.

Littlefair, P.J. 1991. *Site Layout Planning for Daylight and Sunlight – A Guide to Good Practice*. Watford: Building Research Establishment.

Lizieri, C., C. Ward, S. Palmer 2002. *Financial Innovations in Property Markets: Implications for the City of London*. Corporation of London and RICS Research Foundation.

Llewelyn-Davies and the Association for the Protection of Rural Scotland 1998. *Green Belts – Frames or Fragments? A Study of the Edinburgh Green Belt*. Edinburgh: Association for the Protection of Rural Scotland.

Llewellyn-Davies Yeang, English Partnerships and the Housing Corporation 2007. *The Urban Design Compendium*. London: English Partnerships.

London Wildlife Trust 2002. *Brownfield? Greenfield? The Threat to London's Unofficial Countryside: A Report by London Wildlife Trust on behalf of the London Brownfield Forum*. London: London Wildlife Trust.

Lowe, P. 1995. *National Trust Centenary Conference*. London: National Trust.

Lowes, V. 2000. See that Rights are Protected. *Estates Gazette*, 26 August, 80–1.

LPAC 1994. *Advice on the Revision of RPG3 1989*. London: London Planning Advisory Committee.

McCollum, W. 1985. Basic Research Procedures. In J. Vernon (ed.) *Readings in Market Research for Real Estate*, 183–206. Chicago: American Institute of Real Estate Appraisers.

McCoubry, H. 1990. *Effective Planning Appeals*. Oxford: Blackwell Scientific.

MacDonald, R. 1991. *The Use of Planning Agreements by District Councils: Report of Research Findings*. Oxford: School of Planning, Oxford Polytechnic and Association of District Councils.

MacEwen, A. and M. MacEwen 1987. *Greenprints for the Countryside – The Story of Britain's National Parks*. London: Allen & Unwin.

MacFarlane, J. (ed.) 1997. *Rethinking Disputes*. London: Cavendish.

McGlynn 1993, in R. Hayward and S. McGlynn, *Making Better Places: Urban Design Now*. Oxford: Butterworth.

McKee, W. 1994. The Image of the Property Market. *Property Review* 2(11), 466–9.

McKernan, P. and Grose M. 2007. *An Analysis of Accessible Natural Greenspace Provision in the South East*. London: South East AONBs Woodland Programme, Forestry Commission England and Natural England.

Mackie, K. 1991. *A Handbook of Dispute Resolution*. London: Routledge.

——— 1997. Mediation Futures. In J. MacFarlane (ed.) *Rethinking Disputes: The Mediation Alternative*. London: Cavendish.

Mackie, K., D. Miles and W. Marsh 1995. *Commercial Dispute Resolution: An ADR Practice Guide*. London: Butterworths.

McLoughlin, J.B. 1969. *Urban and Regional Planning: A Systems Approach*. London: Faber.

McNamara, P., A. Jackson and S. Mathrant 1985. *Appellants' Perceptions of the Planning Appeal System: Final Report to DoE*. Oxford: Oxford Polytechnic.

MacRae, J. 1993. Rail Freight. *Estates Gazette* (9346), 157–8.

Marber, P. 1985. Project Managing Office Development. In P. Marber and P. Marber (eds) *Office Development*, 177–201. London: Estates Gazette.

Marriott, O. 1989. *The Property Boom*. London: Abingdon Publishing.

Marshall, P. and C. Kennedy 1993. Development Valuation Techniques. *Journal of Property Valuation and Investment* 11(1), 57–64.

Martin, P. 1982. *Shopping Centre Management*. London: Spon.

——— 1993. Review of Planning Obligations. *Estates Gazette* (9306), 98–100.

Maynard, P. (Jones Lang Wootton) 1990. Contribution during International Council of Shopping Centres, Helsinki.

Meadows, H. 1972. *The Limits to Growth: A Report for the Club of Rome's Project on the Predicament of Mankind*. London: Earth Island.

Michalik, A. 1990. Breathing Life into B1. *Estates Gazette* (9026), 110–12.

Miles, M., E. Malizia, M. Weiss, G. Berens and G. Travis 1991. *Real Estate Development: Principles and Process*. Washington DC: Urban Land Institute.

Miller, M. 1989. *Letchworth: The First Garden City*. Chichester: Phillimore Press.

—— 1994. Planning: A Mixed Outlook. *Estates Gazette* (9446), 124–5.

Miller, M. and M. Gray 1992. *Raymond Unwin: Garden Cities and Town Planning*. Leicester: Leicester University Press.

Millington, A. 2000. *An Introduction to Property Valuation*, 5th edn. London: Estates Gazette.

Mills, L. 1992. Nissan Still Drives the Market. *Estates Gazette* (9242).

Ministry of Agriculture, Fisheries and Food 1997. *Agricultural Land Classification of England and Wales*. London: Ministry of Agriculture, Fisheries and Food.

Ministry for the Environment 2005. *A Guide to Sustainable Office Fit-outs*. Wellington, New Zealand: Ministry for the Environment (Manatū Mō Te Taiao) (available from: http://www.mfe.govt.nz/publications/sus-dev/office-fitouts-dec05/office-fitouts-dec05.pdf).

Ministry of Transport 1963. *Traffic in Towns: A Study of the Long-term Problems of Traffic in Urban Areas*. London: HMSO.

Moore, B., P. Tyler and D. Elliot 1991. The Influence of Regional Development Incentives and Infrastructure on the Location of Small and Medium-sized Companies in Europe. *Urban Studies* 28(6), 1001–26.

Moore, C. 1996. *The Mediation Process*. San Francisco: Jossey-Bass.

Moore, V. 2007. *A Practical Approach to Planning Law*, 10th edn. Oxford: Oxford University Press.

Morgan, P. and S. Nott 1988. *Development Control: Policy into Practice*. London: Butterworth.

Morgan Lovell undated. Sustainable Office Design: Unlocking Performance and Productivity. London: Morgan Lovell (available from: http://www.morganlovell.co.uk/downloads/ML-Sustainability.pdf).

Morphet, J. 1995. *The Planning System: Broken or Fixed?* Town and Country Planning Association Annual Conference, London.

Moss, N. and M. Fellows 1995. A Future for Town Centres. *Estates Gazette* (9506), 141–3.

Murdoch, J. 1993. Property Misdescription: Staying Afloat. *Estates Gazette* (9313), 85–8.

Murrain, P. 2002. *Understand Urbanism and Get Off its Back*. London: Town and Country Planning Association.

Mynors, C. 2006. *Listed Buildings, Conservation Areas and Monuments*, 4th edn. London: Sweet & Maxwell.

—— 2007. Working with the Heritage: the New Rules. Journal of Planning and Environment Law, occasional papers number 34.

Nairn, I. 1955. *Outrage*. London: Architectural Press.

National Audit Office 1990. *Regenerating the Inner Cities*. London: HMSO.

National Trust, CRPE and Heritage Link (2004) *Recharging the Power of Place*. London: The National Trust.

Naughton, T. 1992. Mediation in the Land and Environment Court of New South Wales. *Environmental and Planning Law Journal* 9(3), 219–24.

Neal, P. (2003) *Urban Villages and the Making of Communities*. London: Butterworth.

Needham, B. 2006. Planning, Law and Economics: An Investigation of the Rules We Make for Using Land. London: Routledge/RTPI.

New Economics Foundation and D. Nicholson 2003. *Green Cities and Why We Need Them*. London: New Economics Foundation.

Newman, P. 1996. ADR Class – Problems of Enforceability, *Construction Law* 7(1), 9–12.

Norris, S. and P. Jones 1993. Retail Impact Assessment. *Estates Gazette* (9304), 84–5.

Northen, I. 1977. *Shopping Centres: A Developer's Guide to Planning and Design*. Reading: College of Estate Management.

O'Connor, P. 1992. Alternative Dispute Resolution: Panacea or Placebo? *Arbitration*, 58(2), 107–15.

Office for National Statistics 2008a. *Labour Force Survey Historical Quarterly Supplement: All in Employment by Industry Sector*. London: ONS.

—— 2008b. *Quarterly National Accounts First Release Q4 2007*. London: ONS.

Office of the Deputy Prime Minister 1998. Circular 6/98 Planning and Affordable Housing. London ODPM.

—— 2002. *Guidance Note: Best Value Performance Plan and Reviews*. London: ODPM.

—— 2003. *Sustainable Communities: Building for the Future*. London: ODPM.

—— 2004. *Planning Policy Statement 7: Sustainable Development in Rural Areas*. London: ODPM.

—— 2005 *Value for Money of Delivering Affordable Housing Through Section 106. Planning Research Summary Number 5*. London: ODPM.

Office of the Deputy Prime Minister and DEFRA (2005). Circular 06/2005. Biodiversity and Geological Conservation: Statutory Obligations and their Impact within the Planning System. London: ODPM

Office of the Deputy Prime Minister and DEFRA and English Nature (2006). *Planning for Biodiversity and Geological Conservation: A Guide to Good Practice*. London: ODPM.

Oliver, P., I. Davis and I. Bentley 1981. *Dunroamin: The Suburban Semi and its Enemies*. London: Barrie & Jenkins.

Owen, A. and D. Alexander 2006. *Management Plans and Development Control within AONBs in England and Wales*. London: Town and Country Planning Association.

Parfect, M. and G. Power 1997. *Planning for Urban Quality*. London: Routledge.

Parker, A. 1994. Town Centre Management: A New Urban Panacea. *Property Review* 4(5), 161–3.

Parker, B. 1995. 'Planning and Transport – The Key Relationship'. Town and Country Planning Association Annual Conference, London.

Parker Morris Committee 1961. *Homes for Today and Tomorrow*. London: HMSO.

Parliament of New South Wales 1991. 57th Report of the Public Accounts Committee. *Hansard Report 57*. Sydney: New South Wales Government.

Parnell, L. 1991. *A Project Manager's Companion Guide*. Reading: College of Estate Management.

Paul Drury Partnership/English Heritage 2003. *Streamlining Listed Building Consent: Lessons for the Use of Management Agreements*. London: English Heritage/Office of the Deputy Prime Minister.

Pearce, B. 2000. Mediappeal: A New Kind of Appeal Procedure? *Journal of Planning and Environment Law*, December, 1240–5.

Pearce, D. 1994. *Blueprint 3: Measuring Sustainable Development*. London: Earthscan.

Pearlman, Chief Justice M. 1995. 'Where and Why Environmental Mediation Works', paper presented at Mediation Conference for Local Government. Sydney: Australian Commercial Dispute Centre.

Pearlman, J. 2005. National Park purposes as a material consideration. *Journal of Planning and Environment Law*, July, 890–3.

Pennington, M. 2002. *Liberating the Land*. London: Institute of Economic Affairs.

Pharoah, T. 1992. *Less Traffic, Better Towns*. London: Friends of the Earth.

Planning Inspectorate 1993a. *Customer Survey: Study of the Appellants' Experience of the Written Representation Appeal System*. Epsom: W.S. Atkins.

—— 1993b. *Customer Survey: Study of Appellants' and Local Authorities' Experience of the Hearings System*. Epsom: W.S. Atkins.

—— 2007. *Report to the Panel for the Draft South East Plan Examination-In-Public on the Thames Basins Heaths SPA and Natural England's Draft Delivery Plan*. Guildford: SE Plan Panel Secretariat.

Powell, C. 1990. *Facilities Management: Nature, Causes and Consequences*. Ascot: CIOB Technical Information Service.

Powell, J., P. Selman and A. Wragg 2002. Protected Areas: Reinforcing the Virtuous Circle. *Planning Practice and Research* 17(3), 279–95.

Power, A. and J. Houghton 2007. *Jigsaw Cities: Big Places, Small Spaces*. Bristol: Policy Press.

Prince's Foundation 2000. *Sustainable Urban Extensions: Planned Through Design*. London: The Prince's Foundation.

Prodgers, L. 1992. Facilities Management: Facing up to Responsibilities. *Estates Gazette* (9238).

Property Advisory Group 1980. *Planning Gain*. London: HMSO.

Property Week 2002. Pretty Vacant, Sector Profile: Business and Science Parks. *Property Week*, 3 May.

Pugh, C. 1992. The Globalisation of Finance Capital and the Changing Relationships Between Property and Finance – 2. *Journal of Property Finance* 2(3), 369–79.

Punter, J. 1993. *Development Design Skills for Development Controllers*. In R. Hayward and S. McGlynn (eds) *Making Better Places: Urban Design Now*. Oxford: Butterworth.

—— 2007. Developing Urban Design as Public Policy: Best Practice Principles for Design Review and Development Management. *Journal of Urban Design* 12(2), 167–203.

Punter, L. 1999. *The Future Role of Planning Agreements in Facilitating Urban Regeneration*. London: DETR.

Purchas, R. and J. Clayton 2001. A Field Day for Crackpots? The Human Rights Act Development Projects and Control. *Journal of Planning and Environment Law*, February, 134–49.

Purdue, M. 1991. *Planning Appeals: A Critique*. Buckingham: Open University Press.

PwC 2005. (http://www.pwc.co.uk/eng/aboutus/environmental_policy.html)

—— 2007. (http://www.pwc.co.uk/eng/aboutus/corporate_responsibility_environment.html)

Raggett, B. 1993. Implications of the New PPG6. *Estates Gazette* (9330), 78–9.

Rawson-Gardiner, C. 1993. Where Next for Relocation? *Estates Gazette* (9344), 106–7.

Redcliffe-Maud Report 1969. *Report of the Royal Commission on Local Government in England* (Cm 4040). London: HMSO.

Redman, M. 1991. Planning Gain and Obligations. *Journal of Planning and Environment Law*, 203–18.

—— 1993. European Community Planning Law. *Journal of Planning and Environment Law*, 999–1011.

Reeves 2001. Plain Speaking. *Estates Gazette*, 8 December.

Regional Studies Association 1990. *Beyond Green Belts: Managing Urban Growth in the 21st Century*. London: Regional Studies Association.

RICS 1999. Planning Policy Guidance 6: Town Centres and Retail Development. *Public Policy*, RICS, 12 March.

—— 2002. Report Into the Industrial Property Sector. *RICS News*, 20 June.

—— 2005. Green Value: Green Buildings Growing Assets, London: RICS (available from www.rics.org/greenvalue).

—— 2006. *RICS Appraisal and Valuation Manual*. London: RICS.

—— 2008. 'Investing in a Sustainable Built Environment' Conference Report, February, Brussels: RICS.

RICS, British Property Federation, English Heritage and Drivers Jonas (2006). *Heritage Works*. London: RICS.

RICS Foundation 2002. *Red Man, Green Man. Indicators for Urban Sustainability.* London: RICS Foundation.

—— 2006. *The Investment Performance of Listed Office Buildings: A Regular Survey Carried out by Investment Property Databank for English Heritage and the RICS Foundation.* London: RICS.

Ringer, M. 1989. Is the Shopper Really King? *Estates Gazette* (8945).

Robathan, P. 1993. The Intelligent Building. In K. Alexander (ed.) *Facilities Management*. London: Haston Hilton.

Roberts, S. 1995. Litigation and Settlement. In A. Zuckerman and R. Cranston (eds) *Reform of Civil Procedure*, Oxford: Oxford University Press.

Robertshaw, P. and J. Segal 1993. The Milking of ADR. *Civil Justice Quarterly*, 12, 23–38.

Rodgers, C. 2005. Protective Sites of Special Scientific Interest: The Human Rights Dimension. *Journal of Planning and Environment Law*, August, 997–1009.

Roger Tym & Partners 1984. *Monitoring Enterprise Zones Reports*. London: HMSO.

Roger Tym & Partners, Hewdon Consulting and South East of England Regional Assembly 2005. *Paying for Growth*. Guildford: South East of England Regional Assembly.

Rogers, A. 1990. *Alternative Dispute Resolution: Keynote Address to the Australian Dispute Resolution Association Conference, Dispute Resolution in the 1990s.* Sydney: ADRA.

Rogers, R. and Power, A. 2000. *Cities for a Small Country*. London: Faber.

Romm, J. 1999. *Cool Companies: How the Best Businesses Boost Profits and Productivity by Cutting Greenhouse Gas Emissions.* Washington, DC and Covelo, CA: Island Press.

Ross-Goobey, A. 1992. *Bricks and Mortals: The Dream of the 80s and the Nightmare of the 90s, the Inside Story of the Proper World.* London: Century Business.

Royal Commission on Environmental Pollution 1994. *Transport and the Environment.* Oxford: Oxford University Press.

Royal Institute of British Architects (RIBA) 2007 *Outline Plan of Work*, London: RIBA (http://www.ribabookshops.com/site/title_pdfs/08112007124207.pdf).

Royal Society for the Protection of Birds. 2004. *Natural Fit: Can Green Space and Biodiversity Increase Levels of Physical Activity? A Report by Dr William Bird for the RSPB.* London: Faculty of Public Heath, Royal College of Physicians.

Royal Town Planning Institute (RTPI) 1991. *Planning: Is it a Service, and How Can it be Effective?* London: RTPI.

—— 1993. *The Character of Conservation Areas.* London: RTPI.

—— 1997. *The Role of Elected Members in Plan Making and Development Control. A Summary of the Study Commissioned from the School of Planning, Oxford Brookes University.* London: RTPI.

—— 2007. *Chartered Town Planners at Inquiries. Practice Advice Note 4.* London: RTPI.

Rydin, Y. 1993. *The British Planning System: An Introduction.* London: Macmillan.

Saggess, J. 1993. *Shopping Centre Management: The Way Forward, Shopping Centre Progress 1993–94*. London: British Council of Shopping Centres.

Salata, A. 1990. The Starting Grid. *Estates Gazette* (9026), 122–3.

Samuels, A. 2000. Planning and Human Rights, *Solicitors Journal*, 972–5.

Sands, D. 1993. Service with Style. *Estates Gazette* (9341), 66.

Satterthwaite, D. 1999. *The Earthscan Reader in Sustainable Cities*. London: Earthscan.

Save Britain's Heritage 2007. *Buildings at Risk*. London: Save Britain's Heritage.

Savills 1990. *Financing Property*. London: Savills.

Savills Residential Research and the Prince's Foundation 2007. *Valuing Sustainable Urbanism*. London: The Prince's Foundation.

Scanlon, K., A. Edge and T. Willmott 1994. 'The Economics of Listed Buildings'. MS, Department of Land Economy, University of Cambridge.

Schiller, R. 1983. Shopping Trends as they Affect the Investor. *Estates Gazette* 267, 420.

—— 2001. *The Dynamics of Property Location*. London: Spon Press.

Scruton, R. 1996. Under Scrutiny. *Perspectives on Architecture*, February/March, 89.

Sharland, J. 2005. Listed Buildings and the Historic Environment: a critique of the government's review of heritage policy. *Journal of Planning and Environmental Law*, 1552–8.

Sharp, T. 1942. *Town Planning*. London: Penguin.

Shayle, A. 1992. 'Deep Discount Bonds, Convertible Mortgages, Participating Mortgages: The Art and Practice of Financing Property'. Paper presented at Henry Stewart Conference, London.

Sheail, J. 1998. *Nature Conservation in Britain: The Formative Years*. London: The Stationery Office.

Shelbourne, C. 2006. Preserving the Cherished Local Scene: A Comparison of Conservation Area Controls in England and Historic District Controls in the United States. *Journal of Planning and Environmental Law*, 1466–80.

Shilston, A. 1996. Why Not Arb-Med? *Arbitration* 63(3), 161–3.

Simmie, J. (ed.) 1994. *Planning London*. London: UCL Press.

Simmonds, M. 1994/5. Planning for Office Development: A Strategic Approach. *Property Review* 4(7), 213–16.

Sinclair, G. 1992. *The Lost Land: Land-use Change in England 1945–1990*. London: CPRE.

Smith, N. 1994. The End of Grants As We Know Them. *Property Review* 4(5), 152–5.

Smith-Morris, E. 1997. *British Town Planning and Urban Design: Principles and Policies*. Harlow: Longman.

Society for Advanced Legal Studies 1998. *Report on Planning Obligations*, London: The Advanced Legal Studies Planning and Environmental Law Reform Working Group.

Solesbury, W. 1974. *Policy in Urban Planning*. London: Pergamon Press.

Somers, B. 1984. 'The Role of the Contractor'. Paper presented at the Property Development Workshop. Henry Stewart Conference, London.

South East Climate Change Partnership and Sustainable Development Round Table for the East of England (2006). *Adapting to Climate Change Impacts: A Good Practice Guide for Sustainable Communities*.

South East of England Regional Assembly (2006). *The Administration of Planning Gain Supplement: Final Report*. Guildford: SEERA.

South West Planning Aid 2007. *Planning 'Jargon Buster': A Glossary of Technical Terms Used in Town and Country (or Spatial) Planning*. Bristol: South West Planning Aid.

Steelcase Strafor 1990. *The Responsive Office*. Streatley on Thames: Polymath Publishing.

Stewart Hunter, D. 1983. Property Marketing: The Impending Revolution. *Estates Gazette*, 265, 86.

Street, L. 1991. The Courts and Mediation: A Warning. *Judicial Officers' Bulletin* 3(1).

Stubbs, M. 1994. Planning Appeals by Informal Hearing: An Appraisal of the Views of Consultants. *Journal of Planning and Environment Law*, 710–14.

—— 1997. The New Panacea? An Evaluation of Mediation as an Effective Method of Dispute Resolution in Planning Appeals. *International Planning Studies*, 2, 347–64.

—— 1999. Informality and Fairness: Unlikely Partners in the Planning Appeal? Dyason Mediation and Informality, *Journal of Planning and Environment Law*, February, 106–12.

—— 2000. When Councillors Overturn the Chief Planning Officer – Do Costs Follow? *Journal of Planning and Environment Law*, November, 1102–4.

—— 2001. Councillors and Costs: The Vulnerability of Member-led Planning Refusals to an Award of Costs at Planning Appeal in England and Wales. *Planning Practice and Research* 16(2), 121–41.

—— 2004. Heritage-Sustainability: Developing a Methodology for the Sustainable Appraisal of the Historic Environment. *Planning Practice and Research*, 19(3), 285–305.

Stubbs, M. and J. Cripps 1993. Planning Obligations and Future Prospects. *Property Review* 2(3), 102–5.

Stubbs, M. and A. Lavers 1991. Steinberg and After. *Journal of Planning and Environment Law*, 9–19.

Suddards, R. and J. Hargreaves 1996. *Listed Buildings*, 3rd edn. London: Sweet & Maxwell.

Sustainable Development Commission 2007. *Building Houses or Creating Communities? A Review of Government Progress on Sustainable Communities*. London: Sustainable Development Commission.

Syms, P. 1997. *Contaminated Land: The Practice and Economics of Redevelopment*. Oxford: Blackwell Science.

Talbot, J. 1988. Have Enterprise Zones Encouraged Enterprise? Some Empirical Evidence from Tyneside. *Regional Studies* 22, 507–14.

Tang, B. and R. Tang 1999. Industrial Property, Market Initiative and Planning Policy: Restructuring Obsolete Industrial Properties in Hong Kong. *Journal of Property Management* 17(2), 157–68.

Tanner, J. 2001. More than an Ad Hoc Tool. In K. Tasso, *Estates Gazette*, Professional Articles, 13 October.

Tasso, K. 2001. More than an Ad Hoc Tool. *Estates Gazette*, Professional Articles, 13 October.

Taussik, J. 1992. Surveyors and Pre-application Inquiries. *Estates Gazette* (9221), 96–100.

Taylor, R. 1985. New High-technology Survey. *Estates Gazette*, 275, 20.

Taylor, T. 1993. Shedding Light on Storage. *The Valuer* 62(5), 23.

Thame, D. 1992. From the Past to the Future. *The Valuer* 61(6), 14–15.

Thorne, J. 1994. Green Belts and Institutions Standing in Extensive Grounds. *Journal of Planning and Environment Law*, 308–13.

Thornley, A. 1991. *Urban Planning Under Thatcherism: The Challenge of the Market*. London: Routledge.

—— 1993. *Urban Planning Under Thatcherism*, 2nd edn. London: Routledge.

Todd, E. 1993. Offices Head for Home. *Estates Gazette* (9318), 98.

Town and Country Planning Association and DCLG 2007. *Urban Extensions and New Settlements: Best Practice in Urban Extensions*. London: TCPA.

Tugnett, T. and M. Robertson 1987. *Making Townscape*. London: Mitchell Publishing.

Turner, T. 1991. *Towards a Green Strategy for London: Strategic Open Space and Green Chains*. Romford: London Planning Advisory Group.

Turrent, D. (ed.) 2007. *Sustainable Architecture*. London: RIBA.

Twining, W. 1993. Alternative to What? Theories of Litigation Procedure and Dispute Settlement. *Modern Law Review* 56(3), 380–92.

Tyndall Centre for Climate Change Research 2007. Assessment of World Climate Change Conference. Norwich: Tyndall Centre, University of East Anglia.

United Kingdom Government 2005. *UK Sustainable Development Strategy*. London: The Stationery Office.

United Kingdom Round Table 1999. *Fifth Annual Report*. London: HMSO.

United Nations 1980. *World Conservation Strategy: Living Resource*. New York: United Nations Environment Programme.

—— 2001. *World Urbanisation Prospects*. New York: United Nations Population Division Department of Economic and Social Affairs.

Urban Green Spaces Task Force 2002. *London Green Spaces Better Places: Good Practice for Improving Urban Green Spaces*. London: HMSO.

Urban Task Force 1999. *Towards an Urban Renaissance*. London: DETR and Thomas Telford.

—— 2005. *Towards a Strong Urban Renaissance: An Independent Report by Members of the Urban Task Force Chaired by Lord Rogers of Riverside*. London: Urban Task Force Review.

Urban Villages Forum 1992. *Urban Villages: A Concept for Creating Mixed-use Urban Development on a Sustainable Scale*. London: Urban Villages Forum.

—— 1994. *Economics of Urban Villages*. London: Urban Villages Forum.

URBED 1994. *Vital and Viable Town Centres: Meeting the Challenge*. London: URBED and Comedia Consultants.

—— 2004. *Attitudes to Higher Density Developments in the South East: Report on Survey and Workshops with Planning Committee Members from Local Authorities*. London: URBED.

Vail, J. 1994. The Ills of Over-intensive Development. *Estates Gazette* (9414), 118.

Verdict 2007. *UK Town Centre Retailing 2007: Tackling the Challenge of Slowing Demand*. London: Verdict.

Walker, B. 2006. Development Tax: the View from the Ground. *Regeneration and Renewal*. 17 March, 20–5.

Walker, J. 2006. The PGS – Questions and Options. *Town and Country Planning* 75(1), 22–4.

Walker, T. 1990. *Design Revolution in the 1990s*. London: Estates Gazette.

Ward, S. 1994. *Planning and Urban Change*. London: Paul Chapman.

Wates, N. 1999. *Action Planning*. London: Prince of Wales's Institute of Architecture.

Watson, J. 2006. *Understanding Planning Gain: What Works?* York: Joseph Rowntree Foundation.

Watt, D. and J. Valente 1991. Tenant Mix – Retailers' Views. *Estates Gazette* (9143), 82–3.

—— 1995. Invest at Leisure. *Property Review* 5(7), 220–5.

Watts, R. 1982. 'Marketing for a Pre-let'. Paper presented at Henry Stewart Conference, London.

Welbank, M. 1995. Planning and Uncertainty. *Property Review* 5(7), 204–7.

White, A. 1995. The Future of Offices. *Property Review* 5(5), 138–40.

The Wildlife Trusts 2007. *A Living Landscape for the South East: The Ecological Network Approach to Rebuilding Biodiversity for the 21st Century*. Maidstone: Kent Wildlife Trusts.

Wilks, D. and H. Brown 1980. Selling Techniques Have Become More Vital. *Estates Times Review* (October).

Williams, J. 1982. *A Review of Science Parks and High-technology Developments*. London: Drivers Jonas.

Williams, R. 1990. ADR: Salvation or Chimera? *Arbitration* 56–7(2), May, 101–9.

Wilson, R., K. Homenidou and A. Dickerson 2006. *Working Futures 2004–2014: National Report*. Coventry: Institute for Employment Research, University of Warwick.

Winter, R. and R. Vergine 2000. Planning and Human Rights. *Solicitors' Journal*, 972–5.

Wood, C. and G. McDonic 1989. Environmental Assessment: Challenge and Opportunity. *The Planner* 75(11), 12–18.

Woolf, L.J. 1996. *Access to Justice: Report to the Lord Chancellor on the Civil Justice System in England and Wales*, London: Lord Chancellor's Department.

World Commission on Environment and Development (Brundtland Report) 1987. *Our Common Future*. Oxford: Oxford University Press.

Worthington, J. 1982. Changing Industrial Environments. *Architects Journal* 175(16), 80.

Worthington, J. and A. Kenya 1988. *Fitting Out the Workplace*. London: The Architectural Press.

Index

Page numbers in *Italics* represent Tables. Page numbers in **Bold** represent Figures